DATE DUE

DEC 20 2005	
GAYLORD	PRINTED IN U.S.A.

St

SOCIOLOGY SERIES

John F. Cuber, *editor*

Alfred C. Clarke, *associate editor*

Paul B. Horton
WESTERN MICHIGAN UNIVERSITY

Gerald R. Leslie
UNIVERSITY OF FLORIDA

Studies in the Sociology of Social Problems

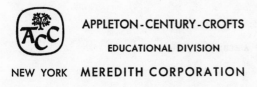

APPLETON-CENTURY-CROFTS

EDUCATIONAL DIVISION

NEW YORK   MEREDITH CORPORATION

Copyright © 1971 by
MEREDITH CORPORATION

780-1

Library of Congress Card Number: 78-132412

PRINTED IN THE UNITED STATES OF AMERICA

390-46030-3

Preface

With a market flooded with "readers," what possible excuse is there for another?

Readers generally fall into one of two categories: collections of scholarly essays and research studies or collections of popularized descriptions, analyses, and anecdotes. Each has value. Students need some easy access to significant research and theory in social problems. They also need the popularizations, life histories, case studies, and personal testaments which more formal academic sources rarely provide. Readers not only bring the student interesting material, but they also help the student see how sociology is the study of everyday life. Sociology belongs not just in the ivory tower, but also in the streets, playgrounds, battlefields, ghettos and Main Streets—everywhere that life is lived.

Our general formula in this reader has been to include in each chapter one formal academic source—a research study, theoretical contribution, or authoritative sociological analysis—and one or more (usually several) items of varying length from popular or semipopular sources. This introduces the student to both the academic and the popular brands of sociology. Once he leaves the campus, it is likely that popular sociology will be the only sociology he encounters. The use of this reader will give him some supervised practice in evaluating and interpreting the popular sociology which will probably be his only source of information about social problems for the rest of his life.

P. B. H.
G. R. L.

Contents

1 The Study of Social Problems

Sociology originated, in large part, in the humanitarian effort to "do something" about social problems. In the three-quarters of a century since sociology courses began appearing in colleges and universities, the definition and study of social problems has become increasingly sophisticated. Yet the following article, nearly fifty years old, sounds surprisingly current. The language of this article is highly value-laden; writing styles of sociologists have changed, but many of the problems discussed are those which concern us today.

WHAT IS A SOCIAL PROBLEM?

Hornell Hart

Former Professor of Sociology
Duke University

The subject of "social problems" has covered a somewhat vague and amorphous field. Believing that the best approach toward the conscious promotion of human progress is through research in this field, the writer has undertaken a preliminary inductive study with a view to a more accurate definition of the term and a clearer statement of the relationship of social problems as a general subject to sociology, to social work, and to special social problems.

The procedure in this study consisted in collecting a list of all of the problems discussed in all of the available books and articles published under the designation "social problems" or under more or less equivalent terms, and the attempt to classify these problems in as simple and logical a way as possible. The resulting outline is as follows:

From *The American Journal of Sociology*, 29 (November 1923) pp. 345–349.

AN OUTLINE LIST OF THE LEADING SOCIAL PROBLEMS

A. Economic Problems: How can poverty and excessive wealth be minimized?

1. How may earnings be maximized and the cost of living minimized?
2. How may the output of industry and the psychic income of the consumer, per unit produced, be maximized?
3. What forms of taxation tend to stimulate the largest production and to promote the most just distribution of wealth and incomes?
4. How may land and other natural resources be utilized with maximum service to the community?
5. How can the ratio between population and natural resources be adjusted at the most desirable point?
6. In what other ways than by increasing real income can standards of living be raised?
7. What effects has immigration upon standards of living?
8. What factors determine the standards of living of negroes and how can they be optimized?
9. What are the best methods of caring for dependents and defectives?
10. How can undeserved misfortunes, such as widowhood, non-support, desertion, unemployment, and invalidity, and the suffering therefrom, be minimized?
11. What influence upon standards of living may be expected from the various forms of such actual or proposed institutions as social insurance and pensions; birth control; profit sharing; government wage and price regulation; collective bargaining; immigration restriction; the protective tariff; trusts and other combinations; scientific management; co-operation in production and distribution; public ownership of public utilities; socialism; and communism?

B. Health Problems: How may the average span of life be lengthened, health be made more universal and more intense, and sickness be minimized?

12. How may the germ plasm from which future generations are developed be improved in quality?
13. How may feeblemindedness, insanity, epilepsy, and other psychopathic conditions, tuberculosis, venereal and other infectious diseases, alchoholism and other drug addictions, be minimized?
14. How may housing conditions, conditions of work, and recreational surroundings be made most healthful?

15. How may water, milk, and other elements in the food supply be kept free from poisons and infections?

16. What influence upon health can be expected from such proposed measures as health insurance; school, industrial, and other types of medical examinations; health centers; open air schools; the socialization of medicine; institutional care; birth control, sterilization or segregation of defectives; minimization of war; eugenics?

C. Political and Socio-psychological Problems: How can human relationships be made most conducive to the general welfare?

17. How may crime be minimized and respect for law be maximized?

18. How may happy marriages be promoted and unhappy marriages and divorce be minimized?

19. How may misery due to illegitimate births be minimized?

20. How may happy and wholesome home life for children be maximized?

21. How may loneliness, misunderstanding, quarreling, and conflict be minimized, and fellowship be maximized?

22. How may relations between employers and employees be so adjusted as to give each the opportunity for the fullest personal development, and still promote efficient production?

23. What are the most desirable relationships between government and capital and labor?

24. What relationship should exist between private initiative and governmental control?

25. How may the conflicting interests of such groups as agriculturalists and manufacturers, and producers and consumers, be adjusted for the best interests of all?

26. How may lynching, peonage, and other forms of racial injustice be minimized and racially and nationally conflicting elements be brought into harmonious co-operation?

27. What forms of government and what relationships between city, state, and national governments are most conducive to social welfare?

28. What types of suffrage and what electoral methods are socially most desirable under given conditions?

29. How may backward and undeveloped countries be brought to make their maximum contributions to world welfare, with a minimum of limitation of the freedom of the inhabitants?

30. How may war be minimized and international co-operation be maximized?

31. What effects upon social relationships may be expected from such measures and programs as adult and juvenile probation; indeterminate

sentence; juvenile courts; parole; self-government schemes among convicts and among students; Americanization; strict divorce laws; city manager government; anarchy; secret organizations like the Ku Klux Klan; guild socialism; the soviet type of government; city planning; the League of Nations; protectorates; universal military training; mandates; military "preparedness"; and the like?

D. Educational Problems: By what social means may individual personalities be most enriched and rendered most serviceable to society?

32. By what methods and to what extent should existing social traditions, conventions, and institutions be modified with a view to promoting progress?

33. What types of personalities are most useful to society and what types are most dangerous; how may these types be identified and measured; and what educational methods will maximize the desirable types and and minimize the undesirable?

34. What information and what methods are most important for children of various types to learn?

35. How may the educational advantages offered be adjusted to the individual needs of the children?

36. How may retarded children be dealt with to the best interests of themselves and of society?

37. How may maximum development and utilization of unusual abilities be achieved?

38. How may the learning process be made most efficient?

39. Through what agencies and by what methods should religious and moral training be given?

40. How may children best be given necessary information on sex problems?

41. What are the relative values of interest as compared with discipline, of information as compared with the acquisition of skill, of practical as compared with cultural education?

42. How may children be protected from such premature, excessive, or improper occupations as interfere with their maximum development?

43. How may young people entering industry best be guided into the occupations most fitted to their personalities?

44. How may gainful occupations be adjusted, with minimum loss in productivity, so as to have the maximum interest and cultural value to the persons occupied?

45. How may adults gainfully occupied be given the maximum opportunity for education?

46. How may parents best be prepared for their responsibilities toward their children?

47. How may the best opportunities be offered for the enrichment of personality in leisure time?

48. What degree and type of freedom of speech, freedom of the press, freedom of art, freedom of teaching, and freedom of preaching best promote social welfare?

49. How may the channels of publicity be kept free from obstruction or perversion by selfish interests?

50. How far should the functions of the home be transferred to the school and to other outside institutions, and what relationship between school and home is most conducive to child welfare?

51. What influence upon the success of educational ideals have such measures, methods or systems as the Gary plan; the Montessori plan; junior high schools; consolidation of rural schools; departmentalization; industrial education; visiting teachers; mental tests; achievement tests and measuring scales; the socialized recitation; the project method; interscholastic athletics; social centers and playgrounds; public parks and museums?

Such a list may readily be attacked as being so vastly comprehensive as to be valueless. Yet it is difficult if not impossible to pick out from the above list any problem which has not repeatedly been discussed in textbooks on social problems or in magazines devoted to social problems. The fact is that one cannot be an intelligent citizen without at least a casual acquaintance with almost all of these problems, and one cannot satisfactorily investigate any one of them without studying its interrelationships with a great number of the others. Some such list as this must be accepted as a basis for research and for citizenship.

A definition of social problems comprehending those in the above list emerges from a study of them. *"A social problem is a problem which actually or potentially affects large numbers of people in a common way so that it may best be solved by some measure or measures applied to the problem as a whole rather than by dealing with each individual as an isolated case, or which requires concerted or organized human action."* . . .

How many of these fifty-one problems listed by Professor Hart are no longer problems today? Have a few of these problems ceased to concern us because we have "solved" them or because social changes have made these particular problems less troublesome than some newer ones?

This next brief item is a sardonic illustration of how few of us are concerned about a problem until it unpleasantly affects *us*.

It may have been a local inconvenience, but the Montreal power failure which was attributed to air pollution could prove to be a most fortuitous occurrence.

Hitherto, only a handful of hydro engineers were aware of this curious phenomenon—the tendency of high-voltage electricity to flash across insulators which had accumulated heavy deposits of pollutants. Now a large number of Canadians have learned the dreadful truth: pollution can cut off not only their breathing but their television viewing.

Something must be done at once to deal with this threat to our way of life.

—From an editorial in the *Toronto Globe and Mail,* quoted in the *Wall Street Journal,* May 31, 1968, p. 4.

The following essay by Perrucci and Pilisuk shows how the revolutionary changes of contemporary society create social problems and how the *definitions* of a social problem contain implicit biases, values, and assumptions which largely predetermine the solutions which will be sought. For example, if the problem of poverty is stated, "How can poor people become productive enough to earn a larger income?", the implication is that there is nothing seriously wrong with our social structure; that the personal inadequacies of poor people are responsible for poverty. If the problem is stated, "What kind of society would eliminate poverty?" or "What structural arrangements in the society promote poverty?" the focus of the study and the probable solution is shifted from personal inadequacies to social institutions. Thus to be completely value free is impossible, for our definitions of social problems channel our research and prejudice our conclusions.

SOCIAL PROBLEMS AND THE TRIPLE REVOLUTION

Robert Perrucci

Professor of Sociology
Purdue University

Marc Pilisuk

Professor in Residence
School of Social Welfare
University of California, Berkeley

In March 1964 in Washington a meeting of 32 noted social critics produced a policy statement entitled "The Triple Revolution" (1964). The purpose of the statement was to call attention to changes in our society which were so revolutionary in magnitude that the society's current response to them was proving totally inadequate, and to point out that radical new measures were needed. The three revolutions—in warfare, cybernation, and human rights—were seen to reflect the theme of man's being increasingly compelled to play the servant rather than the master role in the technologies he has created. While most of the paper dealt with the cybernetic revolution and with policies appropriate to the resultant large-scale displacement of labor, the authors also presented the idea that the three problem areas were interrelated, and that the points of convergence among them exposed some of the critical foci of balance and stress in American society.

It seemed to us that the authors of the paper had hit upon a compelling theme and one that would be helpful in understanding the mass of seemingly separate and unrelated problems in our society. (An extremely negative press reaction to the proposals of that paper revealed that the analysis had cut into cherished values which were the underpinnings of the social fabric.) We felt this paper provided an excellent starting point from which to define and explore a pattern of illness which gave rise to many diverse symptoms of human distress on the American scene.

Before we can attempt to show the extent to which the umbrella of the triple revolution covers the field of contemporary problems, it is first necessary to give our own definition of a social problem and to explain the nature of the social scientist's concern with the world of problems.

SCIENCE AND SOCIAL PROBLEMS

All scientists rely on their value preferences, for these are ultimately their guides to selection of what is worthy of study. The study of social problems has provided social scientists with the particular advantage of permitting them to test the applicability of their knowledge to the resolution of human problems. There are, however, some apparent conflicts between the scholar's motivation to study people and societies and his motivation to study social problems. As an ideal (which is only approximated but, never-theless, important) the impulse of the social scientist stems from a desire to discover principles governing the operation of social systems. He brings to this task scientific methods involving strict attention to the standards of a value-free approach to his chosen subject matter. For example, when he asserts that certain procedures at meetings are dysfunctional to the achieve-ment of certain outcomes or that certain practices reduce the frequency of deviant actions, he is not passing judgment on whether efficiency in meet-ings, or deviant actions, should be reduced or encouraged. But as soon as that same "pure" social scientist selects a social problem as the starting point of his inquiry he is in effect saying, "Certain social conditions are 'bad' and others are 'good.' " His motivation here is to change the "bad," and extend the "good."

These two motives for the study of society have been able to flourish (without creating a major social problem in professional associations of social scientists) because of accommodations between scientific and amelio-rative interests. These accommodations:

1. assert the reality of the interplay between "pure" theory and ap-plied-practical work—theory can be advanced by practical work and much can be accomplished in problem solution by the use of established social theory;

2. maintain a commitment to the "machinery" of science such that investigations of social problems are carried out according to accepted standards of scientific research;

3. develop a definition of social problems that will isolate the subject of study without requiring individual social scientists to state their own value preferences.

An examination of many existing definitions of social problems re-veals several common properties: Social problems are conditions that (1) affect a large number of people, (2) in ways that negatively affect their own value preferences, and (3) about which they think some action can and should be taken. Most of the elements in this definition can be traced to the early work of Fuller (1938) and Fuller and Myers (1941a; 1941b).

The difficulties involved in maintaining the above view of social prob-

lems have become increasingly apparent. First of all, the extreme sub-
jectivism of this approach limits the social analyst to examining those conditions which have been found to be undesirable by consensus. Merton
(1966) has raised a similar criticism in his response to Fuller and Myers'
definition and has noted how considerations of power and authority enter
into the process of defining a condition as a social problem. Becker (1967)
has also raised questions about Fuller and Myers' conception of social
problems, but he, essentially, supports the view that a defining process by
certain persons or groups provides the important starting point for study.

In addition to the above-mentioned limitations there are several other
factors that we believe severely limit the usefulness of current social science
perspectives on social problems.

1. Different persons and groups in American society possess varying
amounts of social power and prestige. Relative advantage in this connection
allows some persons and groups to get items of interest placed on the
social agenda (i.e., to define social problems). The differential distribution
of opportunity to place items on the social agenda invalidates the free
competition of ideas notion implicit in current views, and itself represents
a social problem.

2. The idea of a collectivity of concerned citizens defining social problems is much like that of participatory democracy of the pluralist society,
and the pure competition of the free market. The view seems less well
suited in an age of professional social problem definers, and governmental
agencies whose mandate is uncovering and solving social problems. The
specialization inherent in the organization of professional problem-solvers
serves to fragment definitions of problems in accordance with departmental
or bureau interests, and encourages the avoidance of massive attacks on
social problems that cut across jurisdictional lines.

3. The dominant view of citizen as definer of social problems fails to
take into account the distinction between "personal problems of milieu"
and "public issues of social structure" (Mills, 1959). Definitions made in
terms of immediate problems of milieu are most likely to lead to solutions
that are ways of *handling* or *combating* social problems rather than eliminating the social structural conditions responsible for them. Thus, city riots
are handled with more portable swimming pools and anti-riot legislation;
neighborhood youth gang disturbances are handled with better police protection; unemployment is handled with welfare checks.

4. Related somewhat to Point 3 above is the tendency among current
social problems analysts to define in a restrictive and limiting fashion the
boundaries of the social system in which problems exist; the most extensive
boundaries are usually the nation state. The growing international involvement of most countries would seem to demand that domestic problems be
placed within an international perspective by examining relationships between institutions in the internal system and those in the external system.

5. Current views on social problems may be especially well suited to studying how people respond to social problems *after they have become problems* (in the objective sense that their presence necessarily intrudes on people's consciousness). This may be a part of the reason why social scientists are frequently embarrassed by their failure to anticipate significant national and international events such as the civil rights movement and frequent foreign entanglements involving shooting wars. We cannot satisfactorily anticipate events if we restrict our study to problems which have already emerged full blown.

The remainder of this introduction will consider the concept of social problems that has guided the editors in this book; the concept is related to the interrelated themes of *The Triple Revolution*.

DEFINING SOCIAL PROBLEMS

The definition of a social problem reflects the norms and values of the definer. Science helps us little, for in it there are, in a sense, no troubles, pathologies, or evils; there are only conditions and structures which are consequences of other conditions and structures. It is as scientific for a cancerous cell to undergo growth destructive to other parts of the organism as it is scientific for other cells to undergo their more common patterns of growth. The definition of health is a normative concept dependent upon the shared values of longevity, physical capability, and upon the specific preference for normal function as dictated by the theories of medicine about healthy organs.

Our own values and preferences follow from our assumptions about a healthy human being. First, we assume that a healthy individual must be recognized to have intrinsic worth. We believe that his worth is not dependent upon particular achievements but is implicit in the fact of his birth. From this it seems that permitting a child to starve amidst plenty or the loss of a soldier in battle, no less than the assassination of a president, are social problems. This concern with the preservation of life is thrown into the forefront of our attention by the three revolutions occurring in society; particularly by the revolution in the nature of warfare. It is augmented further by a population problem radically different from any which existed previously. During our lives the number of childhood deaths has grown greater than ever before in history and the number is increasing with every year of material progress. Soldiers continue to kill and be killed; deaths of civilians are gradually outweighing those of armies. These are prima facie evidence of problems. Likewise, the possibility of nuclear war represents a social problem of unprecedented magnitude.

Next in importance to the value of life itself is our belief that an individual's worth entitles him to minimum standards of respect from other people. When police with bullwhips, or insensitive hospital personnel, or unfair voting registrars or short-tempered parents abuse the dignity of other people, then social problems are present.

A healthy individual must have resources sufficient to meet his most basic physical and psychological needs and leave him free from anxieties over deprivation or resignation to a life of scarcity. The anguish and despair which follow poverty, discrimination, and illness are also social problems.

There are psychologists who claim further that the healthy individual must maintain a measure of freedom in his choices (Rogers, 1951) and a means to actualize his potentialities (Maslow, 1954). We modify these conceptions slightly to conform to the limitations imposed on man as a member of society. People must be free and able to participate in the formation of those policy decisions which will affect their daily existence. An individual left jobless by his company's decision to move or conscripted to serve in an overseas war of which he disapproves is not living in health if his reservations about the policy concerned were not a material part of the policy decision. By this measure apathy is itself a social problem because it represents an absence of power which makes participation impossible and creates resignation and despair.

Last, a healthy society must develop individuals who will contribute to the well-being of other members of the society. In a highly interdependent society, the consequences of one group's actions have widespread repercussions. The scientist who designs methods of chemical and bacteriological warfare, the investor in a new enterprise, the city planner, the ward nurse, and the voting citizen share responsibility for the consequences of their decisions upon the well-being of others. Conscience and existential guilt are needed in human communities. A social problem exists where people do not assume responsibility for the consequences of their own action or inaction. It should be clear that in our conception conflict, disorder, and value clashes are not by themselves social problems. Disorder could point up an underlying problem, but it could also be indicative of an adaptive attempt to improve upon bad conditions. The emphasis here is *not* upon social harmony but upon the well-being of the individual as we understand the conditions of such well-being. These are our values and the assumptions by which we define what is and what is not a social problem.

In addition to using our own values and assumptions about a healthy person and healthy society, we are also guided in our selection of problems by a notion of central and peripheral problems. When a man considers his own personality, he is prone to think of his achievements, his aspirations, and his ideals as the central and general characteristics of himself. He tends to see his more serious problems as accidents, as specific deficiencies, or as caused by someone else (if indeed he admits to seeing them at all). There is a tendency among social scientists and laymen alike to look upon their own society in much the same way. Its successes and its ideals are the permanent characterization. Its problems, when they are discovered, are accidents, specific casualties or unfortunate by-products of an otherwise healthy society. The net effect of such social perceptions is to introduce a bias into the analysis of what must be done to meet problems. Perceiving personal problems as superficial and specific permits the individual to carry on his daily activities much as usual without need for a radical and painful reappraisal of himself. Seeing social problems as separate misfortunes or as failures to achieve facile integration into the healthy mainstream of society precludes a search for the underlying pathology beneath such surface eruptions as delinquency, racial violence, bigotry, alienation, conformity, urban slums, and the high school dropout. But the affects by which we label problems are consequences rather than accidents of the social order. It is our desire to show that these and other problems can be understood as manifestations of larger difficulties which are central and even necessary features of American society as it is currently structured.

THE TRIPLE REVOLUTION

The 20th century has confronted American society with both unprecedented progress and unprecedented problems. Economic, scientific, and technological advances have brought material abundance, improved health standards, and a phenomenal ability to control nature and turn it to man's uses. Existing alongside all this wealth and mastery over nature are continuing states of international warfare and tension, persistent poverty and despair among millions of Americans, and a growing inability of the many to influence and control the social and political processes that so significantly affect their lives.

Efforts by many public and private groups to deal with these conditions have not yielded results that would encourage optimism. To be sure, in most approaches, war, poverty, and powerlessness are considered either as necessary evils (although not always evil, as wars are fought to preserve our freedoms) or as temporary dislocations which can be remedied. However, under the corrective responses which stem from current approaches, the conditions not only persist but they grow worse. Greater productivity and abundance for some leads to more poverty for the disadvantaged; technological advances that spark economic growth can also be measured in unemployment, worker insecurity, and alienation; and growing sophistication in military weaponry that promised supremacy and reduction of the likelihood of war seems not to have aided in keeping the United States from military involvements in the Middle East, Latin America, Africa, and Southeast Asia.

Conventional attempts to remedy these problems do not seriously question the viability of the American institutions dealing with them. Race relations, delinquency, alienation, and poverty are conceived as problems of specific sub-groups which have not yet achieved adequate integration into the larger society or into one of several interest groups providing individuals with a sense of identification and potency. Other current conceptions assume that a problem emerges when interest groups disagree on the existence of, or solution to, some social condition. People experiencing dissatisfaction with existing arrangements, it is argued, can come together and have their views tested in the free marketplace of ideas. When groups are not powerful enough to obtain a public hearing of their complaints, it is argued that larger, more powerful forces (e.g., government, business, unions) do balance each other's interests and power in a way that contributes to the general interest.

These traditional views on the emergence and solution of social problems fail to confront the current distribution of power in American society. Established views on interest group politics, pluralism, and countervailing power do seem quite appropriate for dealing with problems that are easily absorbed by American institutions; they seem inadequate for dealing with the revolutionary changes which challenge the very nature of these institutions.

A different conception of social problems and of ways of eliminating them is required by the impact of the three revolutions upon the contemporary scene. The solutions to problems may require a basic reexamination and remodeling of our existing values and institutions. It is our belief that the revolutions that have occurred in warfare, in cybernation, and in the mobilization of demands for human rights present the society with pressures that threaten the very bases of its stability. Moreover, these revolutions reflect the increasing difficulty experienced by existing institutions in giving full expression to the simple, yet profound, principles by which American society has chosen to be known: democratic processes and the dignity of man.

The technological militarism revolution is found in the elaborate nuclear and ballistic missile technology that is having far-reaching effects upon every phase of American life. The psychological impact of nuclear capabilities may lead to "dehumanization" of certain social relationships and of persons in certain social categories. This psychological defense mechanism is one way of handling anxiety in painful situations. A second consequence is a social defense mechanism, wherein new forms of social organization are devised to handle the threats posed by international tensions. Among these forms are the shelter-centered society with a regimented populace, and the weakening of such values as individual liberty, democratic values, and a community-based society. The final consequence of an existing nuclear technology is its role in maintaining a high level of international tension which permeates many aspects of American life, and gives the military a rationale for its own continuation.

These social and psychological conditions are more than just consequences of nuclear capabilities; they also have the potential for creating greater dependence on military technology to control the fears that the technology itself has created. This process reflects one of the persistent theoretical themes of this book: certain types of technically-oriented social patterns become, with time, autonomous and impervious to attempts designed to redirect activities toward new ends.

The cybernation revolution is reflected in the combined efforts of computers and automated machinery largely though not exclusively as they are applied to the processes of production. The result has been increased productive capacity and decreased dependence upon human labor. For some, cybernation brings great material benefits and the promise of release from the degrading and unchallenging aspects of work; others see in cybernation the problems associated with reduced employment, loss of economic security, and the meaning of a life without work.

The secondary effects of cybernation which extend beyond production and employment are those which threaten to reorganize the nature of economic and social life. The emergence of "conglomerates" in American industry and their relationship to governmental power are indicative of patterns of centralization that render a citizen's participation in the affairs of his nation increasingly difficult. Moreover, cybernation technology shapes the patterns of social life through greater planning of social systems and through increased use of the technology to shape and control the behavior and attitudes of citizens by government or other large organizations.

The human rights revolution is found in the growing demand for full economic, political, and social equality by millions of people in the United States and in many other countries around the globe. The demand for equality in all spheres of life reveals that established institutions have adapted to long-standing inequalities.

The three revolutions are interdependent and mutually reinforcing trends which present us with the progress-problem paradoxes described earlier. The health of a social system must be evaluated relative to the challenges which confront it. The very strengths of American institutions which provide cohesion under moderate challenges may introduce rigidities under conditions which call for a more drastic reorganization of the social order. It is our belief that American society is in serious trouble; that the revolutions wrought by the rapid changes in weaponry, in the utilization of information in cybernetic systems, and in the revolutionary demands of the impoverished around the globe cannot be met by the civilian and military institutions that have so far evolved in our society. Neither does a fair examination of these institutions reveal a capacity for adaptive changes capable of mitigating the emerging problems of centralization in decision-making, of inequitable distribution of opportunities, and of a third world war.

REFERENCES AND ADDITIONAL READING

Ad Hoc Committee, "The Triple Revolution," *Liberation* (April, 1964) 1–7.

Becker, Howard S., ed., *Social Problems: A Modern Approach* (New York: John Wiley, 1967).

Dahl, Robert, *Who Governs? Democracy and Power in an American City* (New Haven: Yale University Press, 1961).

Fuller, Richard C., "The Problem of Teaching Social Problems," *American Journal of Sociology* (*44*, November, 1938) 415–435.

Fuller, Richard C. and Richard R. Myers, "Some Aspects of a Theory of Social Problems," *American Sociological Review, 6* (February, 1941) 24–32.

Fuller, Richard C. and Richard R. Myers, "The Natural History of a Social Problem," *American Sociological Review, 6* (June, 1941), 320–328.

Maslow, A. H., *Motivation and Personality* (New York: Harper, 1954).

Merton, Robert K., "Social Problems and Sociological Theory," in R. K. Merton and R. A. Nisbet, eds., *Contemporary Social Problems*, 2nd ed. (New York: Harcourt, Brace and World, Inc., 1966).

Mills, C. Wright, "The Professional Ideology of Social Pathologists," *American Journal of Sociology, 49* (September 1943) 165–180.

Mills, C. Wright, *The Sociological Imagination* (New York: Oxford University Press, 1959).

Presthus, Robert, *Men at the Top: A Study in Community Power* (New York: Oxford University Press, 1964).

Rogers, Carl R., *Client-Centered Therapy* (Boston: Houghton Mifflin, 1951).

In the following editorial, an editor of *TRANS-action*, a semi-popular journal of the social sciences, claims that too little sociological research is policy-oriented. For example, a number of citizens are pressing for more legislation to suppress pornographic literature while others are demanding freedom from censorship. Sociologists cannot help them, for we have no research studies which show the effects of pornography upon people. The federal government has launched a massive effort to shut off the supply of marihuana entering the country, while marihuana threatens to become the relaxation norm of the young and the nation debates changing laws which can punish less severely for killing a man than for giving him "pot." Where are the definitive research studies upon the short-run and long-run effects of marihuana which would permit social policy to be based upon more than prejudice and guesswork? We simply do not have them.

Can research be both rigorously scientific and, at the same time, be directly useful to those who must frame social policy?

WHERE SOCIOLOGISTS HAVE FAILED

Herbert J. Gans

*Joint Center for Urban Studies of
Harvard University and the
Massachusetts Institute of Technology*

Social scientists are often accused of having no interest in the pressing problems of the day. I can speak only for my own discipline of sociology, but this accusation is disproved by the speed with which sociologists have climbed on the antipoverty bandwagon. In a few short years, poverty has become a legitimate field for sociological teaching, research, and publication.

Even so, sociology's role in the antipoverty effort strikes me as disappointing. Judging by all the anthologies on poverty that have been announced, sociologists seem to be mainly concerned with informing their students about the existence and causes of poverty. I see a much more urgent concern: research to help *eliminate* poverty. A particularly great need is policy-oriented research: for example, studies that evaluate current antipoverty efforts and propose or test alternative solutions. Sociology is particularly suited for such research—because it specializes in the study of ordinary people. Sociology can thus compensate for the policy-maker's inability, or unwillingness, to find out whether his programs are reaching his intended clients in the intended way.

But new research on poverty, basic or policy-oriented, is sparse. Few sociologists, in addition, have applied past findings to evaluate existing antipoverty programs. Evidence indicates, for example, that many lower-class people do not share the status aspirations of the middle class. Yet there has been too little sociological criticism of Federal antipoverty programs, many of which have proceeded on the assumption that lower-class people have precisely such aspirations.

Nor have sociologists proposed policies that would further the aspirations poor people do have. One of these aspirations is for more money.

From *TRANS-action*, 4 (October 1967) p. 2. Copyright © by *TRANS-action* Magazine, New Brunswick, N.J. Reprinted by permission.

Yet sociologists have not launched studies on the specific handicaps imposed by lack of money. Nor have they introduced sociological considerations into the current debate over the negative income tax. If data are lacking, why have sociologists not suggested giving a sample of poor people a negative income-tax grant, then studying whether the grant helped them solve some of their other problems? Economists and social workers—not sociologists—have taken the lead in formulating such experiments.

The fact is that sociologists have mounted too few policy-oriented studies on *any* topic.

Part of the fault lies with the discipline. Sociology has long limited itself to describing and explaining human behavior, using methods and concepts not easily adapted to the needs of policy. As a result, sociologists find it easier to catalogue the behavior (and misbehavior) of the poor than to suggest experiments that would test ways of eliminating poverty.

Part of the fault also lies with the agencies that fund sociological research. Not many have challenged sociologists to propose policy—or given them the grants needed to meet such challenges.

Another impediment is the university, which does not encourage full-time research. Few universities appoint research professors, and even fewer give tenure to those they appoint. These universities are willing to set up research institutes, but unwilling to staff them properly.

The academic organization of sociology does not help either. Despite newspaper articles that complain about teachers' deserting their classes for lucrative research grants and consulting fees, this is not true of most sociologists. Sociologists still see themselves primarily as teachers, doing research between lectures and on sabbatical leaves. So now, although many policy-making agencies are ready to use social-science research, the sociologists themselves are not ready. Too many of their studies are still small and narrow, often intended more for colleagues than for application to current social problems.

The end result is that sociology contributes precious little to policy-making. And, consequently, policy-makers often base their solutions to social problems on popular stereotypes about the causes of the problem and the characteristics of the affected population; or on outdated sociological findings they recall from their college days; or on scraps of sociological reporting they pick up at random. Such practices do not help either policy-making or sociology.

When the Federal government adopts social accounting and calls for studies to measure the social benefits and costs of governmental programs, the need for policy-oriented sociological research will become even greater than it is now. If universities cannot adapt to meet this need, perhaps we should turn to the independent policy-research institute. Such institutes might be modeled on the research and development laboratories of private industry, the defense establishment, and the Office of Education—and on existing policy-research agencies like the Brookings Institution and the Institute for Policy Studies. Their staffs should be drawn from all the social sciences. They must offer the working conditions, prestige, security, and freedom of research that professional appointments provide. In this way, perhaps, sociologists can be tempted to leave the campus, intellectually as well as physically, and transform at least a part of sociology into a policy-oriented discipline.

Most sociologists have long viewed themselves as political liberals, sympathizers with social reform, and friends of the poor and the oppressed. We have often been attacked by conservatives who believed that we were undermining the capitalistic system, promoting communism, etc. Today, however, we are under attack from the student left, who view us as craven intellectuals who have sold out to the establishment.

The following statement is one of the milder examples of handbills which appear at national and regional meetings of sociologists. This one was distributed at the 1968 annual meeting of the American Sociological Association by the Sociology Liberation Movement, a highly critical group of graduate and undergraduate students with a sprinkling of young instructors.

KNOWLEDGE FOR WHOM?

The values, beliefs, and formal affiliations of the field of sociology bind it too closely to the governing structures and the powerful interests in our society.

—Posing as disinterested scholars, we perform policy research for the powerful organizations in our society, providing them with the knowledge they need to influence or control their "problems." We have placed our expertise at the disposal of the establishment, letting the development of our field be guided by the needs of those who can pay for our time. In the name of value neutrality, we have failed to contribute equally to the efforts of the poor, the powerless or the disorganized to control or influence the powerholders.

—In our attempts to share the prestige of "science" we have pursued the development of "scientific" methodology at the expense of meaningful content and have developed "scientific" theories at the expense of a knowledge of society. We have willfully turned from the problems of our time, and he who interests himself in a confrontation with reality is dismissed as a "mere journalist."

—In our attempts to adopt the prestige of professionalism we have restricted entry to our field, isolated our discipline from others, and enforced conformity to the mainstream as the price of professional success. The interests of the professional hierarchy have worked against meaningful innovation in methods, theories, and areas of study.

—The liberal conservative bias of our "theory" exaggerates consensus, ignores conflict, and assumes that everything can be settled with a little communication, a little patience, and a lot of good will. This is more of a prayer than a theory, reflecting not reality but the hopes of our own social class.

—In the illusion that we can be responsible members of society and yet above its petty quarrels, we have abstained from our moral duty to speak out against the forces of repression in our society. The reactionary nature of our government becomes "beyond the scope of our field." But silence means consent, and by not speaking out we are speaking up for the status quo.

SOCIOLOGY WILL NOT CHANGE UNLESS SOCIOLOGISTS CHANGE IT

JOIN THE SOCIOLOGY LIBERATION MOVEMENT!

Come to our desk in the reception area to find out what you can do about it.

Come to the radical caucus of the New University Conference and to the action meeting of the SOCIOLOGY LIBERATION MOVEMENT directly following.

Sociology Liberation Movement handbill, 1968.

2 Approaches to the Study of Social Problems

Virtually all scholars agree that value conflicts are deeply involved in the creation and amelioration of social problems. The following brief portion of a newspaper item, which might have appeared in almost any city in the United States, illustrates a number of things about these conflicts: the formation of groups organized to promote opposing values; the inability of regulatory bodies to satisfy all factions; the use of emotionally laden terms (e.g., property rights, communism) to promote one's interest; and the flaring of tempers when people feel their interests being threatened.

MOBILE HOME ZONING ISSUE COOLS OFF, BUT NO ACTION

Eric Filson

Almost two hours of arguments mostly against a proposed change in mobile home zoning regulations were voiced before the county commission Tuesday during a crowded but orderly meeting.

The commission deferred any immediate decision until at least next week on the proposal to require a special use permit for mobile homes in agricultural districts five acres or larger.

County Commission Chairman Sidney Martin said, "We're not going to make a decision today."

"This needs some real study."

Martin said the Board of County Commissioners felt it should not make a hasty decision on the issue and complimented the crowd for its orderly behavior.

The session was in marked contrast to a county zoning board last Wednesday night when several hundred persons appeared to protest the proposed zoning change.

In the tulmultuous session that followed, County Attorney Wayne

Gainesville, Florida *Sun,* September, 1968.

Carlisle was jeered and insulted while he tried to explain the proposed changes in the law.

One woman last week labeled the proposed changes "communism" and Attorney James Quincey said it was "another restriction on the rights of property owners."

Quincey said Tuesday at the county commission meeting that he represented Capital Enterprises, Inc., and mobile home interests.

He presented petitions to the commission he said contained 827 signatures of persons who opposed the zoning regulation change.

Quincey also denied that he and his client Ernest Tew of Ernest Tew Realty, Inc., had any connection with trying "to stir this thing up (the Wednesday meeting)."

"I want to disclaim any interest that we had of stirring anything up before anybody in this county."

He said he and Tew had only sent out letters advising people of the zoning commission meeting along with advertisements and circulation of a petition against the zoning proposal.

"There was no pre-planned arrangement whereby anyone was instructed what to say or how to say it or how to conduct themselves," Quincey said.

"In fact, we were embarrassed by some of the things that were said and done."

"Now I do feel there are certain things that have come up such as the editorial appearing in last night's Gainesville Sun in which people were referred to as worms and the fact that they said that mobile home owners were permitted after the meeting to return to their cocoons—I don't think tends to salve the feelings of the people in our community nor does it do justice to the board of county commissioners," Quincey said.

Careful reading of the Monday Sun editorial will reveal no reference to "worms."

Quincey said he understood the reasons advanced for the zoning regulation changes were to prevent flooding, to protect the mobile home owner from unscrupulous land developers, to make first-class citizens out of second-class citizens, and that it was being pushed by land developers.

The attorney indicated he felt none of the reasons was valid or sufficient to cause a change in the present zoning procedures. . . .

    In many instances, value conflicts are rendered even more acrimonious by extremists who, either individually or in organized groups, foment hatred in the guise of seeking solutions. The item that follows, from *Harper's Magazine,* particularly attacks the radical right but also castigates such representatives of the left as Dr. Benjamin Spock, Black Power advocates, and opponents of the Vietnam war.

THE POLITICS OF FRUSTRATION

American politics has often been an arena for angry minds," historian Richard Hofstadter wrote in his article "The Paranoid Style in American Politics," which appeared in this magazine in November 1964. "Historical catastrophes or frustrations may be conducive . . . to situations in which they can more readily be built into mass movements or political parties."

We wondered whether such a situation was indeed at hand last fall as we heard Dr. Benjamin Spock name the President of the United States as "the enemy" while peace marchers cheered at the Pentagon. A few weeks earlier a New Politics convention in Chicago had surrendered to a militant Black Power minority. Subsequently Senators James Eastland and John McClellan launched subversion hunts reminiscent of Joseph McCarthy's finest hours. And at the University of Iowa, anti-Vietnam demonstrators soaked the steps of the Memorial Union with their own blood, carried to the scene in paper cups. "The land," Richard H. Rovere despairingly reflected in *The New Yorker*, "is filling up with cranks and zanies."

Because extremists of the Left have preempted the headlines, the Radical Right has seemed quiescent. In fact, it is very much alive, having regrouped its forces with remarkable speed after the 1964 Goldwater debacle. By 1966, Americans for Constitutional Action—a group which interlocks with the John Birch Society—could boast of victories for 180 out of 255 candidates it had endorsed for local and national office. In the same year the far-right New York State Conservative party nudged the Liberals out of third place on the ballot. In Idaho a movement to recall Senator Frank Church was financed by William Penn Patrick, a San Rafael, California, millionaire cosmetics manufacturer. The courts declared the petition illegal, but a second recall drive was launched late in 1967. Its backers are said to be affiliated with the Liberty Lobby, a Washington-based organization which has taken over the *American Mercury* magazine and installed editors even more conservative than their predecessors.

"The Rightists are using much more sophisticated tactics nowadays," we were told by Wesley McCune, director of Group Research, a nonprofit organization devoted to the study of extremism. By way of example, he cited their circumspection in avoiding a public embrace of their cherished rising star, Ronald Reagan. Meanwhile, the John Birch Society is making increasing use of front organizations. One is TACT (Truth About Civil

Turmoil) which sends out Negro speakers to preach that the civil-rights movement is a Communist plot.

Many of the right-wing fundamentalists were introduced to *Harper's* readers in 1961 in Willie Morris's article "Houston's Superpatriots." Since then, the Reverend Billy James Hargis has built himself a new cathedral and headquarters in Tulsa and is hard at work exposing the machinations of Walter Reuther and Martin Luther King. (He shares the latter task with a specialized group, INKO—Investigate Now King and Others.) TV and radio shows sponsored by H. L. Hunt and other ultraconservatives are on the air some 2,500 hours a week. And Dr. Fred Schwarz collects over half a million dollars a year for his Christian Anti-Communism Crusade.

Right-wing publications have a combined circulation of around a million. Among the newer ones is a Washington newsletter, *Ammunition,* edited by Martha Rountree, who will be remembered by TV viewers as the original moderator on "Meet the Press." Among ultraconservative books, a recent favorite is *Pass the Poverty.* Written by two housewives, it has a strong appeal for taxpayers angered by the well-publicized instances of waste and inefficiency in the Poverty Program.

"The people who buy books of this sort," Mr. McCune said emphatically, "are not 'little old ladies in tennis shoes.' They are respectable types, the folks next door. We should take them seriously." A sound admonition. But it would be easier to follow if the Rightists would curb their passion for peculiar acronyms. Our favorite is STENCH of Tennessee (Society to Exterminate Neo-Communist Harbingers).

Even scientists are not immune to becoming caught up in value conflicts. Traditionally, sociologists have sought to maintain their objectivity by giving explicit allegiance to the values of science, but treating all other values as data. By the end of World War II, when Gunnar Myrdal directed the monumental study of United States' race relations published as *An American Dilemma,* it was evident that such a posture was not wholly adequate. In the years that followed, sociologists became somewhat divided over what role, as professionals, they should play in the solution of social problems. One view, that sociologists inevitably take sides with one of the competing factions, is represented in the following article which was the 1966 presidential address to The Society for the Study of Social Problems.

WHOSE SIDE ARE WE ON?

Howard S. Becker

Professor of Sociology
Northwestern University

To have values or not to have values: the question is always with us. When sociologists undertake to study problems that have relevance to the world we live in, they find themselves caught in a crossfire. Some urge them not to take sides, to be neutral and do research that is technically correct and value free. Others tell them their work is shallow and useless if it does not express a deep commitment to a value position.

This dilemma, which seems so painful to so many, actually does not exist, for one of its horns is imaginary. For it to exist, one would have to assume, as some apparently do, that it is indeed possible to do research that is uncontaminated by personal and political sympathies. I propose to argue that it is not possible and, therefore, that the question is not whether we should take sides, since we inevitably will, but rather whose side we are on.

I will begin by considering the problem of taking sides as it arises in the study of deviance. An inspection of this case will soon reveal to us features that appear in sociological research of all kinds. In the greatest variety of subject matter areas and in work done by all the different methods at our disposal, we cannot avoid taking sides, for reasons firmly based in social structure.

We may sometimes feel that studies of deviance exhibit too great a sympathy with the people studied, a sympathy reflected in the research carried out. This feeling, I suspect, is entertained off and on both by those of us who do such research and by those of us who, our work lying in other areas, only read the results. Will the research, we wonder, be distorted by that sympathy? Will it be of use in the construction of scientific theory or in the application of scientific knowledge to the practical problems of society? Or will the bias introduced by taking sides spoil it for those uses?

We seldom make the feeling explicit. Instead, it appears as a lingering

From *Social Problems* 14(3) (Winter, 1967) pp. 239–247. Reprinted by permission of The Society for the Study of Social Problems, and the author. (Presidential address, delivered at the annual meeting of The Society for the Study of Social Problems, Miami Beach, August, 1966.)

worry for sociological readers, who would like to be sure they can trust what they read, and a troublesome area of self-doubt for those who do the research, who would like to be sure that whatever sympathies they feel are not professionally unseemly and will not, in any case, seriously flaw their work. That the worry affects both readers and researchers indicates that it lies deeper than the superficial differences that divide sociological schools of thought, and that its roots must be sought in characteristics of society that affect us all, whatever our methodological or theoretical persuasion.

If the feeling were made explicit, it would take the form of an accusation that the sympathies of the researcher have biased his work and distorted his findings. Before exploring its structural roots, let us consider what the manifest meaning of the charge might be.

It might mean that we have acquired some sympathy with the group we study sufficient to deter us from publishing those of our results which might prove damaging to them. One can imagine a liberal sociologist who set out to disprove some of the common stereotypes held about a minority group. To his dismay, his investigation reveals that some of the stereotypes are unfortunately true. In the interests of justice and liberalism, he might well be tempted, and might even succumb to the temptation, to suppress those findings, publishing with scientific candor the other results which confirmed his beliefs.

But this seems not really to be the heart of the charge, because sociologists who study deviance do not typically hide things about the people they study. They are mostly willing to grant that there is something going on that put the deviants in the position they are in, even if they are not willing to grant that it is what the people they studied were originally accused of.

A more likely meaning of the charge, I think, is this. In the course of our work and for who knows what private reasons, we fall into deep sympathy with the people we are studying, so that while the rest of the society views them as unfit in one or another respect for the deference ordinarily accorded a fellow citizen, we believe that they are at least as good as anyone else, more sinned against than sinning. Because of this, we do not give a balanced picture. We focus too much on questions whose answers show that the supposed deviant is morally in the right and the ordinary citizen morally in the wrong. We neglect to ask those questions whose answers would show that the deviant, after all, has done something pretty rotten and, indeed, pretty much deserves what he gets. In consequence, our overall assessment of the problem being studied is one-sided. What we produce is a whitewash of the deviant and a condemnation, if only by implication, of those respectable citizens who, we think, have made the deviant what he is.

It is to this version that I devote the rest of my remarks. I will look first, however, not at the truth or falsity of the charge, but rather at the circumstances in which it is typically made and felt. The sociology of knowledge cautions us to distinguish between the truth of a statement and an assessment of the circumstances under which that statement is made; though we trace an argument to its source in the interests of the person who made it, we have still not proved it false. Recognizing the point and promising to address it eventually, I shall turn to the typical situations in which the accusation of bias arises.

When do we accuse ourselves and our fellow sociologists of bias? I think an inspection of representative instances would show that the accusation arises, in one important class of cases, when the research gives credence, in any serious way, to the perspective of the subordinate group in some hierarchical relationship. In the case of deviance, the hierarchical relationship is a moral one. The superordinate parties in the relationship are those who represent the forces of approved and official morality; the subordinate parties are those who, it is alleged, have violated that morality.

Though deviance is a typical case, it is by no means the only one. Similar situations, and similar feelings that our work is biased, occur in the study of schools, hospitals, asylums and prisons, in the study of physical as well as mental illness, in the study of both "normal" and delinquent youth. In these situations, the superordinate parties are usually the official and professional authorities in charge of some important institution, while the subordinates are those who make use of the services of that institution. Thus, the police are the superordinates, drug addicts are the subordinates; professors and administrators, principals and teachers, are the superordinates, while students and pupils are the subordinates; physicians are the superordinates, their patients the subordinates.

All of these cases represent one of the typical situations in which researchers accuse themselves and are accused of bias. It is a situation in which, while conflict and tension exist in the hierarchy, the conflict has not become openly political. The conflicting segments or ranks are not organized for conflict; no one attempts to alter the shape of the hierarchy. While subordinates may complain about the treatment they receive from those above them, they do not propose to move to a position of equality with them, or to reverse positions in the hierarchy. Thus, no one proposes that addicts should make and enforce laws for policemen, that patients should prescribe for doctors, or that adolescents should give orders to adults. We can call this the *apolitical* case.

In the second case, the accusation of bias is made in a situation that is frankly political. The parties to the hierarchical relationship engage in organized conflict, attempting either to maintain or change existing relations of power and authority. Whereas in the first case subordinates are typically unorganized and thus have, as we shall see, little to fear from a researcher, subordinate parties in a political situation may have much to lose. When the situation is political, the researcher may accuse himself or be accused of bias by someone else when he gives credence to the perspective of either party to the political conflict. I leave the political for later and turn now to the problem of bias in apolitical situations.[1]

We provoke the suspicion that we are biased in favor of the subordinate parties in an apolitical arrangement when we tell the story from their point of view. We may, for instance, investigate their complaints, even though they are subordinates, about the way things are run just as though one ought to give their complaints as much credence as the statements of responsible officials. We provoke the charge when we assume, for the purposes of our research, that subordinates have as much right to be heard as superordinates, that they are as likely to be telling the truth as they see it as superordinates, that what they say about the institution has a right to be investigated and have its truth or falsity established, even though responsible officials assure us that it is unnecessary because the charges are false.

We can use the notion of a *hierarchy of credibility* to understand this phenomenon. In any system of ranked groups, participants take it as given that members of the highest group have the right to define the way things really are. In any organization, no matter what the rest of the organization chart shows, the arrows indicating the flow of information point up, thus demonstrating (at least formally) that those at the top have access to a more complete picture of what is going on than anyone else. Members of lower groups will have incomplete information, and their view of reality will be partial and distorted in consequence. Therefore, from the point of view of a well socialized participant in the system, any tale told by those at the top intrinsically deserves to be regarded as the most credible account obtainable of the organizations' workings. And since, as Sumner pointed out, matters of rank and status are contained in the mores,[2] this belief has a moral quality. We are, if we are proper members of the group, morally bound to accept the definition imposed on reality by a superordinate group in preference to the definitions espoused by subordinates. (By analogy, the same argument holds for the social classes of a community.) Thus, credibility and the right to be heard are differentially distributed through the ranks of the system.

As sociologists, we provoke the charge of bias, in ourselves and others, by refusing to give credence and deference to an established status order, in which knowledge of truth and the right to be heard are not equally dis-

---

[1] No situation is necessarily political or apolitical. An apolitical situation can be transformed into a political one by the open rebellion of subordinate ranks, and a political situation can subside into one in which an accommodation has been reached and a new hierarchy been accepted by the participants. The categories, while analytically useful, do not represent a fixed division existing in real life.

[2] William Graham Sumner, "Status in the Folkways," *Folkways* (New York: New American Library, 1960) pp. 72–73.

tributed. "Everyone knows" that responsible professionals know more about things than laymen, that police are more respectable and their words ought to be taken more seriously than those of the deviants and criminals with whom they deal. By refusing to accept the hierarchy of credibility, we express disrespect for the entire established order.

We compound our sin and further provoke charges of bias by not giving immediate attention and "equal time" to the apologies and explanations of official authority. If, for instance, we are concerned with studying the way of life inmates in a mental hospital built up for themselves, we will naturally be concerned with the constraints and conditions created by the actions of the administrators and physicians who run the hospital. But, unless we also make the administrators and physicians the object of our study (a possibility I will consider later), we will not inquire into why those conditions and constraints are present. We will not give responsible officials a chance to explain themselves and give their reasons for acting as they do, a chance to show why the complaints of inmates are not justified.

It is odd that, when we perceive bias, we usually see it in these circumstances. It is odd because it is easily ascertained that a great many more studies are biased in the direction of the interests of responsible officials than the other way around. We may accuse an occasional student of medical sociology of having given too much emphasis to the complaints of patients. But is it not obvious that most medical sociologists look at things from the point of view of the doctors? A few sociologists may be sufficiently biased in favor of youth to grant credibility to their account of how the adult world treats them. But why do we not accuse other sociologists who study youth of being biased in favor of adults? Most research on youth, after all, is clearly designed to find out why youth are so troublesome for adults, rather than asking the equally interesting sociological question: "Why do adults make so much trouble for youth?" Similarly, we accuse those who take the complaints of mental patients seriously of bias; what about those sociologists who only take seriously the complaints of physicians, families and others about mental patients?

Why this disproportion in the direction of accusations of bias? Why do we more often accuse those who are on the side of subordinates than those who are on the side of superordinates? Because, when we make the former accusation, we have, like the well socialized members of our society most of us are, accepted the hierarchy of credibility and taken over the accusation made by responsible officials.

The reason responsible officials make the accusation so frequently is precisely because they are responsible. They have been entrusted with the care and operation of one or another of our important institutions: schools, hospitals, law enforcement, or whatever. They are the ones who, by virtue of their official position and the authority that goes with it, are in a position to "do something" when things are not what they should be and, similarly, are the ones who will be held to account if they fail to "do something" or if what they do is, for whatever reason, inadequate.

Because they are responsible in this way, officials usually have to lie. That is a gross way of putting it, but not inaccurate. Officials must lie because things are seldom as they ought to be. For a great variety of reasons, well known to sociologists, institutions are refractory. They do not perform as society would like them to. Hospitals do not cure people; prisons do not rehabilitate prisoners; schools do not educate students. Since they are supposed to, officials develop ways both of denying the failure of the institution to perform as it should and explaining those failures which cannot be hidden. An account of an institution's operation from the point of view of subordinates therefore casts doubt on the official line and may possibly expose it as a lie.[3]

For reasons that are a mirror image of those of officials, subordinates in an apolitical hierarchical relationship have no reason to complain of the bias of sociological research oriented toward the interests of superordinates. Subordinates typically are not organized in such a fashion as to be responsible for the overall operation of an institution. What happens in a school is credited or debited to the faculty and administrators; they can be identified and held to account. Even though the failure of a school may be the fault of the pupils, they are not so organized that any one of them is responsible for any failure but his own. If he does well, while others all around him flounder, cheat and steal, that is none of his affair, despite the attempt of honor codes to make it so. As long as the sociological report on his school says that every student there but one is a liar and a cheat, all the students will feel complacent, knowing they are the one exception. More likely, they will never hear of the report at all or, if they do, will reason that they will be gone before long, so what difference does it make? The lack of organization among subordinate members of an institutionalized relationship means that, having no responsibility for the group's welfare, they likewise have no complaints if someone maligns it. The sociologist who favors officialdom will be spared the accusation of bias.

And thus we see why we accuse ourselves of bias only when we take the side of the subordinate. It is because, in a situation that is not openly political, with the major issues defined as arguable, we join responsible officials and the man in the street in an unthinking acceptance of the hierarchy of credibility. We assume with them that the man at the top knows best. We do not realize that there are sides to be taken and that we are taking one of them.

The same reasoning allows us to understand why the researcher has

---

[3] I have stated a portion of this argument more briefly in "Problems of Publication of Field Studies," in Arthur Vidich, Joseph Bensman, and Maurice Stein, eds., *Reflections on Community Studies* (New York: John Wiley, 1964) pp. 267–284.

the same worry about the effect of his sympathies on his work as his un-involved colleague. The hierarchy of credibility is a feature of society whose existence we cannot deny, even if we disagree with its injunction to believe the man at the top. When we acquire sufficient sympathy with subordinates to see things from their perspective, we know that we are fly-ing in the face of what "everyone knows." The knowledge gives us pause and causes us to share, however briefly, the doubt of our colleagues.

When a situation has been defined politically, the second type of case I want to discuss, matters are quite different. Subordinates have some degree of organization and, with that, spokesmen, their equivalent of re-sponsible officials. Spokesmen, while they cannot actually be held respon-sible for what members of their group do, make assertions on their behalf and are held responsible for the truth of those assertions. The group engages in political activity designed to change existing hierarchical re-lationships and the credibility of its spokesmen directly affects its political fortunes. Credibility is not the only influence, but the group can ill afford having the definition of reality proposed by its spokesmen discredited, for the immediate consequence will be some loss of political power.

Superordinate groups have their spokesmen too, and they are con-fronted with the same problem: to make statements about reality that are politically effective without being easily discredited. The political fortunes of the superordinate group—its ability to hold the status changes demanded by lower groups to a minimum—do not depend as much on credibility, for the group has other kinds of power available as well.

When we do research in a political situation we are in double jeopardy, for the spokesmen of both involved groups will be sensitive to the impli-cations of our work. Since they propose openly conflicting definitions of reality, our statement of our problem is in itself likely to call into question and make problematic, at least for the purposes of our research, one or the other definition. And our results will do the same.

The hierarchy of credibility operates in a different way in the political situation than it does in the apolitical one. In the political situation, it is precisely one of the things at issue. Since the political struggle calls into question the legitimacy of the existing rank system, it necessarily calls into question at the same time the legitimacy of the associated judgments of credibility. Judgments of who has a right to define the nature of reality that are taken for granted in an apolitical situation become matters of argument.

Oddly enough, we are, I think, less likely to accuse ourselves and one another of bias in a political than in an apolitical situation, for at least two reasons. First, because the hierarchy of credibility has been openly called into question, we are aware that there are at least two sides to the story and so do not think it unseemly to investigate the situation from one or another of the contending points of view. We know, for instance, that we must grasp the perspectives of both the resident of Watts and of the Los Angeles policeman if we are to understand what went on in that outbreak.

Second, it is no secret that most sociologists are politically liberal to one degree or another. Our political preferences dictate the side we will be on and, since those preferences are shared by most of our colleagues, few are ready to throw the first stone or are even aware that stone-throwing is a possibility. We usually take the side of the underdog; we are for Negroes and against Fascists. We do not think anyone biased who does research designed to prove that the former are not as bad as people think or that the latter are worse. In fact, in these circumstances we are quite willing to regard the question of bias as a matter to be dealt with by the use of technical safeguards.

We are thus apt to take sides with equal innocence and lack of thought, though for different reasons, in both apolitical and political situations. In the first, we adopt the commonsense view which awards unquestioned credibility to the responsible official. (This is not to deny that a few of us, because something in our experience has alerted us to the possibility, may question the conventional hierarchy of credibility in the special area of our expertise.) In the second case, we take our politics so for granted that it supplants convention in dictating whose side we will be on. (I do not deny, either, that some few sociologists may deviate politically from their liberal colleagues, either to the right or the left, and thus be more liable to question that convention.)

In any event, even if our colleagues do not accuse us of bias in research in a political situation, the interested parties will. Whether they are foreign politicians who object to studies of how the stability of their government may be maintained in the interest of the United States (as in the *Camelot* affair) [4] or domestic civil rights leaders who object to an analysis of race problems that centers on the alleged deficiencies of the Negro family (as in the reception given to the Moynihan Report),[5] interested parties are quick to make accusations of bias and distortion. They base the accusation not on failures of technique or method, but on conceptual defects. They accuse the sociologist not of getting false data but of not getting all the data relevant to the problem. They accuse him, in other words, of seeing things from the perspective of only one party to the conflict. But the accusation is likely to be made by interested parties and not by sociologists themselves.

What I have said so far is all sociology of knowledge, suggesting by whom, in what situations and for what reasons sociologists will be accused of bias and distortion. I have not yet addressed the question of the truth of the accusations, of whether our findings are distorted by our sympathy for

[4] See Irving Louis Horowitz, "The Life and Death of Project Camelot," *TRANS-action,* 3 (November/December 1965) pp. 3–7, 44–47.

[5] See Lee Rainwater and William L. Yancey, "Black Families and the White House," ibid., 3 (July/August, 1966) pp. 6–11, 48–53.

those we study. I have implied a partial answer, namely, that there is no position from which sociological research can be done that is not biased in one or another way.

We must always look at the matter from someone's point of view. The scientist who proposes to understand society must, as Mead long ago pointed out, get into the situation enough to have a perspective on it. And it is likely that his perspective will be greatly affected by whatever positions are taken by any or all of the other participants in that varied situation. Even if his participation is limited to reading in the field, he will necessarily read the arguments of partisans of one or another side to a relationship and will thus be affected, at least, by having suggested to him what the relevant arguments and issues are. A student of medical sociology may decide that he will take neither the perspective of the patient nor the perspective of the physician, but he will necessarily take a perspective that impinges on the many questions that arise between physicians and patients; no matter what perspective he takes, his work either will take into account the attitude of subordinates, or it will not. If he fails to consider the question they raise, he will be working on the side of the officials. If he does raise those questions seriously and does find, as he may, that there is some merit in them, he will then expose himself to the outrage of the officials and of all those sociologists who award them the top spot in the hierarchy of credibility. Almost all the topics that sociologists study, at least those that have some relation to the real world around us, are seen by society as morality plays and we shall find ourselves, willy-nilly, taking part in those plays on one side or the other.

There is another possibility. We may, in some cases, take the point of view of some third party not directly implicated in the hierarchy we are investigating. Thus, a Marxist might feel that it is not worth distinguishing between Democrats and Republicans, or between big business and big labor, in each case both groups being equally inimical to the interests of the workers. This would indeed make us neutral with respect to the two groups at hand, but would only mean that we had enlarged the scope of the political conflict to include a party not ordinarily brought in whose view the sociologist was taking.

We can never avoid taking sides. So we are left with the question of whether taking sides means that some distortion is introduced into our work so great as to make it useless. Or, less drastically, whether some distortion is introduced that must be taken into account before the results of our work can be used. I do not refer here to feeling that the picture given by the research is not "balanced," the indignation aroused by having a conventionally discredited definition of reality given priority or equality with what "everyone knows," for it is clear that we cannot avoid that. That is the problem of officials, spokesmen and interested parties, not ours. Our problem is to make sure that, whatever point of view we take, our research

meets the standards of good scientific work, that our unavoidable sympathies do not render our results invalid.

We might distort our findings, because of our sympathy with one of
the parties in the relationship we are studying, by misusing the tools and
techniques of our discipline. We might introduce loaded questions into a
questionnaire, or act in some way in a field situation such that people
would be constrained to tell us only the kind of thing we are already in
sympathy with. All of our research techniques are hedged about with pre-
cautionary measures designed to guard against these errors. Similarly,
though more abstractly, every one of our theories presumably contains a
set of directives which exhaustively covers the field we are to study, specifying all the things we are to look at and take into account in our research.
By using our theories and techniques impartially, we ought to be able to
study all the things that need to be studied in such a way as to get all the
facts we require, even though some of the questions that will be raised and
some of the facts that will be produced run counter to our biases.

But the question may be precisely this. Given all our techniques of
theoretical and technical control, how can we be sure that we will apply
them impartially and across the board as they need to be applied? Our textbooks in methodology are no help here. They tell us how to guard against
error, but they do not tell us how to make sure that we will use all the
safeguards available to us. We can, for a start, try to avoid sentimentality.
We are sentimental when we refuse, for whatever reason, to investigate
some matter that should properly be regarded as problematic. We are sentimental, especially, when our reason is that we would prefer not to know
what is going on, if to know would be to violate some sympathy whose
existence we may not even be aware of. Whatever side we are on, we must
use our techniques impartially enough that a belief to which we are especially sympathetic could be proved untrue. We must always inspect our
work carefully enough to know whether our techniques and theories are
open enough to allow that possibility.

Let us consider, finally, what might seem a simple solution to the
problems posed. If the difficulty is that we gain sympathy with underdogs
by studying them, is it not also true that the superordinates in a hierarchical relationship usually have their own superordinates with whom they
must contend? Is it not true that we might study those superordinates or
subordinates, presenting their point of view on their relations with their
superiors and thus gaining a deeper sympathy with them and avoiding the
bias of one-sided identification with those below them? This is appealing,
but deceptively so. For it only means that we will get into the same trouble
with a new set of officials.

It is true, for instance, that the administrators of a prison are not free
to do as they wish, not free to be responsive of the desires of inmates, for
instance. If one talks to such an official, he will commonly tell us, in private,

that of course the subordinates in the relationship have some right on their side, but that they fail to understand that his desire to do better is frustrated by his superiors or by the regulations they have established. Thus, if a prison administrator is angered because we take the complaints of his inmates seriously, we may feel that we can get around that and get a more balanced picture by interviewing him and his associates. If we do, we may then write a report which *his* superiors will respond to with cries of "bias." They, in their turn, will say that we have not presented a balanced picture, because we have not looked at *their* side of it. And we may worry that what they say is true.

The point is obvious. By pursuing this seemingly simple solution, we arrive at a problem of infinite regress. For everyone has someone standing above him who prevents him from doing things just as he likes. If we question the superiors of the prison administrator, a state department of corrections or prisons, they will complain of the governor and the legislature. And if we go to the governor and the legislature, they will complain of lobbyists, party machines, the public and the newspapers. There is no end to it and we can never have a "balanced picture" until we have studied all of society simultaneously. I do not propose to hold my breath until that happy day.

We can, I think, satisfy the demands of our science by always making clear the limits of what we have studied, marking the boundaries beyond which our findings cannot be safely applied. Not just the conventional disclaimer, in which we warn that we have only studied a prison in New York or California and the findings may not hold in the other forty-nine states— which is not a useful procedure anyway, since the findings may very well hold if the conditions are the same elsewhere. I refer to a more sociological disclaimer in which we say, for instance, that we have studied the prison through the eyes of the inmates and not through the eyes of the guards or other involved parties. We warn people, thus, that our study tells us only how things look from that vantage point—what kinds of objects guards are in the prisoners' world—and does not attempt to explain why guards do what they do or to absolve the guards of what may seem, from the prisoners' side, morally unacceptable behavior. This will not protect us from accusations of bias, however, for the guards will still be outraged by the unbalanced picture. If we implicitly accept the conventional hierarchy of credibility, we will feel the sting in that accusation.

It is something of a solution to say that over the years each "one-sided" study will provoke further studies that gradually enlarge our grasp of all the relevant facets of an institution's operation. But that is a long-term solution, and not much help to the individual researcher who has to contend with the anger of officials who feel he has done them wrong, the criticism of those of his colleagues who think he is presenting a one-sided view, and his own worries.

What do we do in the meantime? I suppose the answers are more or less obvious. We take sides as our personal and political commitments dictate, use our theoretical and technical resources to avoid the distortions that might introduce into our work, limit our conclusions carefully, recognize the hierarchy of credibility for what is is, and field as best we can the accusations and doubts that will surely be our fate.

> Becker struggles, of course, to maintain as much objectivity as possible in the face of the presumed inevitability of personal value commitments. That not all sociologists accept Becker's analysis of the situation is shown by the following article written by a former president of the Society for the Study of Social Problems in direct rebuttal of Becker's article. Gouldner maintains that the sociologist's allegiance must be, not to any competing factions, but either to a larger concept of the welfare of the total society or to certain basic values that are widely shared in the society.

THE SOCIOLOGIST AS PARTISAN:

Sociology and the welfare state

Alvin W. Gouldner
Professor of Sociology
Washington University

Sociology begins by disenchanting the world, and it proceeds by disenchanting itself. Having insisted upon the nonrationality of those whom it studies, sociology comes, at length, to confess its own captivity. But voluntary confessions should always be suspect. We should try to notice, when men complain about the bonds that enchain them, whether their tone is one of disappointed resentment or of comfortable accommodation.

In 1961, in an address to a learned society, I attacked what I took to be the dominant professional ideology of sociologists: that favoring the value-free doctrine of social science. Today, only six years later, I find myself in the uncomfortable position of drawing back from some who found

From *The American Sociologist* 3 (May, 1968) pp. 103–116. Reprinted by permission.

my argument against the value-free myth so persuasive. I now find myself caught between two contradictory impulses: I do not wish to seem ungrateful toward those who sympathized with my position, yet the issue is a serious one and I also do not want to encumber discussions of it with considerations of personal tact or professional courtesy.

In a nutshell: I fear that the myth of a value-free social science is about to be supplanted by still another myth, and that the once glib acceptance of the value-free doctrine is about to be superseded by a new but no less glib rejection of it. My uneasiness concerning this came to a head upon reading Howard S. Becker's paper which boldly raises the problem, "Whose Side Are We On?" Rather than presenting the storybook picture of the sociologist as a value-free scientist, Becker begins by stating that it is impossible for a social scientist to do research "uncontaminated by personal and political sympathies." We are told that, no matter what perspective a sociologist takes, his work must be written either from the standpoint of subordinates or superiors. Apparently one cannot do equal justice to both.

The most telling indication of just how large a change sociology has recently undergone, may be seen not so much from the position that Becker takes but from the way his position is presented. There is nothing defensive in the manner that Becker rejects the older, nonpartisan conception of the sociologist's role. Instead, Becker presents his rejection of this position as if it needed no explanation; as if it were completely obvious to everyone; and as if there were nothing to argue about. His posture is not that of the cocky challenger but of a blasé referee announcing the outcome of a finished fight, and whose verdict must be obvious. More than anything else, this suggests that there has been a substantial change in the occupational culture of sociologists in the last decade or so.

Becker's conception of the partisan sociologist would be unimportant were it simply an expression of his own idiosyncratic individuality. The fact is, however, that there is every reason to believe that he is voicing the sentiments of a substantial and probably growing number of sociologists, and, in particular, those whose interests focus upon the study of social problems, or the sociology of "deviant behavior." It is notable that the article in which Becker asks "Whose Side Are We On?" was delivered originally as his Presidential Address to the Society for the Study of Social Problems. This implies that Becker's constituency was at least enough to have elected him to this modestly notable position in the structure of American social science. In short, Becker does not speak for himself alone.

That Becker's is a representative voice is further indicated by his own writings on deviant behavior, especially his books The Outsiders and Social Problems, which are presently one of the two dominant standpoints in American sociology concerning the analysis of social problems. Becker, then, is a leading spokesman of a viable coterie of sociologists specializing in the study of social deviance, whose members include such able men as

Howard Brotz, Donald Cressey, John Kitsuse, Raymond Mack, David Matza, Sheldon Messinger, Ned Polsky, and Albert J. Reiss; and this coterie in turn overlaps with a larger network that essentially comprises the "Chicago School" of sociology. Becker's plea for a partisan sociology may be regarded as a weather-vane signaling that new winds are beginning to blow. Yet the direction from which they come is not altogether clear.

Since Becker forcefully entitles his discussion "Whose Side Are We On?," we might reasonably expect that he will, at some point, give a straightforward answer to his own straightforward question. Yet one reads it through and puts it down, only suddenly to notice that Becker gives no direct answer at all to his own question. Indeed, we pick it up once again to make sure that our first impression is correct and discover that this is indeed the case. If, in an effort to puzzle this through, we turn to Becker's earlier work, *The Outsiders,* we find that he does essentially the same thing there. In the culminating pages of that volume, he also asks: "Whose viewpoint shall we present?" And once again we find that no straightforward answer is given. If there is a difference between this volume and Becker's Presidential Address, it is that, in the earlier volume, he states explicitly that there is no basis in terms of which an answer to the question can be formulated. That is, he holds that neither strategic considerations, nor temperamental and moral considerations can tell us "to which viewpoint we should subscribe."

It seems equally clear, however, that, although Becker refuses explicitly to answer his explicit question, he does have an answer to it. If instead of looking at the explicit formulations advanced by Becker or other members of his group, we look, rather, at the specific researches that they have undertaken, we find that they unmistakably do adopt a specific standpoint, a kind of *underdog* identification. As I have said elsewhere, theirs is a school of thought that finds itself at home in the world of hip, drug addicts, jazz musicians, cab drivers, prostitutes, night people, drifters, grifters, and skidders: the "cool world." Their identifications are with deviant rather than respectable society. "For them, orientation to the underworld has become the equivalent of the proletarian identifications felt by some intellectuals during the 1930's. For not only do they study it, but in a way they speak on its behalf, affirming the authenticity of its style of life." Their specific researches plainly betray, for example, that they are concerned with and resent the legal straitjacket in which the drug addict is confined in the United States, or the degrading impact of the mental hospital on its inmates. In one part, this school of thought represents a metaphysics of the underdog and of the underworld: a metaphysics in which conventional society is viewed from the standpoint of a group outside of its own respectable social structures. At any rate, this is how it began; but it is not how it remains.

When Becker tells us that the world is divided into subordinate superordinates, and that sociologists must look at the world from one side or the other, his implication seems to be that they should look at it from the standpoint of the deviant, of the subordinate, of the underdog. For these people, Becker says in his Presidential Address, are "more sinned against than sinning." The question arises as to why it is that, although Becker's leanings are clear enough, he chooses not to express them explicitly. Why is it that Becker does not declare openly for the standpoint of the underdog, since he clearly feels this way? If partisanship is inevitable, why doesn't Becker clearly state whose side *he* is on, rather than simply goading others to take a stand? There are probably both intellectual and practical reasons for Becker's failure to give a definitive answer to his own question—whose side are we on? First, I want to explore briefly some of the intellectual and practical factors that lead to Becker's reticence.

THE THEORY AND PRACTICE OF COOL

In *The Outsiders,* Becker makes it plain that his own theoretical contribution leads to a focus, not merely on the rule breakers or deviants, but also to a study of those who make and enforce the rules, and most especially the latter. Although much of Becker's concrete research has been on deviants, his own theory, which came later, has largely focused on rule-makers and rule-enforcers. A crucial stage, in what Becker calls "the deviant career," occurs when someone declares that someone else's behavior has violated the rules of their game. The deviant, in short, is made by society in two senses: first, that society makes the rules which he has broken and, secondly, that society "enforces" them and makes a public declaration announcing that the rules have been broken. The making of the deviant, then, entails a process of social interaction. That being the case, the deviant-making process cannot be understood unless rule-making and rule-enforcing procedures or persons are studied.

The question then arises as to *whose* standpoint shall be adopted when rule-*makers* or rule-*enforcers* are themselves studied. Shall we describe their behavior from their own "overdog" standpoint or from that of the "underdog" deviants? One answer is given by Becker's more general theoretical position, the tradition of George Herbert Mead, which requires that men— even if they are "overdogs"—be studied from the standpoint of their *own* conceptions of reality. The point here, of course, is that men's definition of their situation shapes their behavior; hence to understand and predict their behavior we must see it as they do. Becker's own specific theory of deviance, then, constrains him to look at the behavior of rule-*enforcers,* while his Meadian tradition requires him to look at it from *their* standpoint, rather than that of the deviant-breakers.

But this, by itself, would still create no difficulties. For, if Becker were entirely comfortable with this position, he would simply recommend that studies be conducted from the standpoint of *whoever* is being studied, be they rule-enforcers, rule-makers, or deviant rule-breakers. If he were to be consistent, then, Becker would answer the question, whose side are we on?, simply by stating that we are on the side of whomever we are studying at a given time. In other words, he would advocate the devotional promiscuity of sacred prostitution.

The reason that Becker cannot adopt this fairly obvious conclusion, and why he cannot give any answer to his question, is a simple one: his *sentiments* are at variance with his theories. Becker is sentimentally disposed to view the entire ambience of deviance from the standpoint of the deviant persons themselves. It is this that makes him sit on a fence of his own construction. Caught in the divergence between his theories and his sentiments, he is unable to answer his own question, whose side are we on? His sentimental disposition to see the world of deviance from the standpoint of the deviant conflicts with his theoretical disposition to take the standpoint of whichever group he happens to be studying. Becker "solves" this problem by raising the question, whose side are we on?, with such blunt force that makes the very question seem like an answer; and he evidences his own sentiments so plainly that he need not assert them and, therefore, need never take responsibility for them.

In suggesting that Becker has refused to answer his own question because of this conflict between his theories and his sentiments, I do not mean that this is the only reason for his reticence. For there are other, more practical, costs that would have to be paid were Becker (or anyone else) to announce such a position in a direct manner. A straightforward affirmation of sympathy with the underdog would, for one thing, create practical difficulties for Becker as a researcher. For he might one day wish access to information held by rule-enforcers and rule-makers who, in turn, might be dismayed to hear that Becker was disposed to view them from the standpoint of those whom they feel to be threats to society. Again, a straightforward affirmation of sympathy with the underdog or deviant might create a certain uneasiness among those who, either directly or indirectly, provide the resources which Becker, like any other research entrepreneur, requires. An outright expression of concern for or sympathy with the underdog thus conflicts with the sociologist's practical and professional interests. In other words: even genuine attachments to the underdog must be compromised with a tacit but no less genuine attachment to self-interest. We are, in short, also on our own side.

There is, I believe, still another reason why Becker fails to say whose side he is on. It has to do with the fact that he is not only on his own side and that, for all its underdog sympathies, his work is also on the side of one of the currently conflicting elites in the welfare establishment. But I must hold this for development at a later point. Becker's reticence about answering his own question, then, derives in part from a conflict between his sentiments and his interests, in part from a conflict between his theories and his sentiments, and, in part also, from a conflict within his sentiments.

There is still another way that Becker copes with the conflict between his sympathetic concern for the underdog and his equally human concern for more practical interests. We can see this if we notice the implicit irony in Becker's position, an irony that contributes importantly to the persuasiveness of his argument. Becker's central thesis is the impossibility of being value free and the necessity of taking sides. In other words, he argues that real detachment is impossible. Yet one of the very things that makes Becker convincing is that he somehow manages to convey a sense of dispassionate detachment. This is largely accomplished through his *style*. Written in a nonpolemical and flaccid style, Becker's rhetoric conveys an image of himself as coolly detached, despite his own explicit argument that partisanship and involvement are inevitable. The limp sobriety of his style projects an image of him as someone who has no axe to grind. It is through his style, then, that Becker invites us to believe that it is possible for a work to be biased without paying intellectual costs.

In effect, Becker appears to hold that emotional blandness is somehow an effective antidote to partisanship. Indeed, at various points, one suspects that Becker believes that blandness is also an effective substitute for analytic probing and hard thought. As I shall later develop, Becker believes that the real enemy of good social science is not a one-sided value commitment, but, rather, something that he calls "sentimentality."

Thus, while Becker invites partisanship, he rejects passionate or erect partisanship. In the very process of opposing the conventional myth of the value-free social scientist, Becker thereby creates a new myth, the myth of the *sentiment*-free social scientist. He begins to formulate a new myth that tacitly claims there is such a thing as a purely cerebral partisanship, which is devoid of emotional commitment and "sentimentality." Underlying this is Becker's tacit assumption that these entail intellectual costs, and costs *alone*. It seems equally reasonable to believe, however, that passion and sentimentality serve not only to produce costs and intellectual blindness, but may just as likely serve to enlighten, and to sensitize us to certain aspects of the social world. Indeed, it may be suspected that it is precisely, in some part, because there are certain intellectual gains derived from emotionally tinged commitments that it is possible for social scientists to sustain such commitments. In short, sentimentality does not seem to be the heartless villain that Becker makes it out to be. It is Becker who is being "sentimental" when he fosters a myth that holds it possible to have a sentiment-free commitment.

To recommend that sociological researches be undertaken from the standpoint of subordinates or underdogs creates as many problems as it resolves. While such a standpoint expresses a sympathy that I share, I still feel obligated to ask: How do we know an underdog when we see one? Who and what are underdogs? What marks someone as an underdog? And we have to ask an even more difficult question: Why *should* we undertake our studies from the standpoint of the subordinate, underdog?

Becker may recognize the intellectual bind in which he has placed himself by inviting research from the standpoint of the underdog. But he has only begun to glimpse it. Although acknowledging that a superior may be a subordinate to someone else, he fails to recognize that this works both ways: everyone who is a subordinate, *vis-à-vis* his superior, is also a superior in relation to some third party. If we regard every man as both superior and subordinate, overdog and underdog, how then do we know and on what basis do we select the underdogs whose standpoint we shall take? Clearly, Becker presents no logical solution to this quandary; he can intend it to be resolved only by the impulses of the very sentimentality that he deplores. It is also likely that Becker never confronts this problem —with *which* underdog shall he sympathize?—because he tacitly assumes that good liberals will instinctively know, and always agree, who the true underdogs are.

Let me acknowledge, once for all, that I share Becker's underdog sympathies. Yet I also believe that sociological study from an underdog standpoint will be intellectually impaired without clarifying the *grounds* for the commitment. A commitment made on the basis of an unexamined ideology may allow us to feel a manly righteousness, but it leaves us blind.

SOCIOLOGY AND SUFFERING

The question then is: Are there any *good* reasons to conduct research from an underdog standpoint? One such reason may be that a feelingful commitment to the underdog's plight enables us to do a better job as *sociologists*. Specifically, when we study a social world from an underdog standpoint, we elevate into public view certain underprivileged aspects of reality. These are aspects of social reality that tend to be comparatively unknown or publicly neglected because they are dissonant with conceptions of reality held by the powerful and respectable. To take the standpoint of the underdog in our researches, then, does two things. First, it gives us new information concerning social worlds about which many members of our society, including ourselves, know little or nothing. Secondly, it may give us new perspectives on worlds that we had thought familiar and presumed that we already knew. To that extent, then, taking the underdog's standpoint does indeed contribute to the successful fulfillment of the intellectual obligations that we have as sociologists. It helps us do the distinctive job we have.

I have acknowledged a sympathy with the underdog and with impulses to conduct researches from his standpoint. Yet in searching for the justification of my sentiments I must also candidly confess that I see no special virtue in those who are lacking in power or authority, just as I see no special virtue that inheres in those who possess power and authority. It seems to me that neither weakness nor power as such are values that deserve to be prized.

The essential point about the underdog is that he suffers, and that his suffering is naked and visible. It is this that makes and should make a compelling demand upon us. What makes his standpoint deserving of special consideration, what makes him particularly worthy of sympathy, is that he suffers. Once we see this, however, the nature of our relationship to the underdog changes; correspondingly, the nature of the obligation that we experience as *sociologists* may also change.

First, we can recognize that there may be forms of human suffering that are unavoidable, that cannot be remedied in some particular society or at some particular time. Correspondingly, however, there are also forms of suffering that are needless at particular times and places. I think that it it the sociologist's job to give special attention to the latter, while recognizing that it is no easy task to distinguish between avoidable and unavoidable suffering, and while fearing that some will all too easily categorize certain kinds of suffering as unavoidable so that they may disregard them with comfort.

Moreover, I would also insist that even when men experience needless suffering, a suffering which is unavoidable, tragic, and truly a part of the eternal human condition, that they still deserve sympathy and loving consideration. It is vital for sociologists also to portray this unyielding part of the world. For this reason, I cannot imagine a humane sociology that would be callous to the suffering of "superiors." A sociology that ignored this would, so far as I am concerned, neither manifest a respect for truth nor a sense of common humanity.

But if all men suffer and to some extent unavoidably, is there any reason at all to feel a special sympathy for underdogs? Is there any reason to make a special effort to conduct research from their standpoint? I think that there is.

For one thing, the suffering of some is still simply and literally unknown to many in society. This is a special and important part of reality which, I think, is one of our important responsibilities to understand and communicate. The problem is not simply that there exists what Becker calls a "hierarchy of credibility"—in which men in power are presumably granted the right to declare what is real and true in the world around them. It is rather that these dominant conceptions of reality, sustained and fostered by the managers of society, have one common defect: they fail to grasp a very special type of reality, specifically the reality of the suffering of those beneath them. In failing to see this, what they must also fail to see is that those beneath them are indeed very much like themselves, in their suffering as in other ways.

This, in turn, implies that a sociology truly concerned with representing the standpoint of the underdog, would most especially seek to communicate the character of his suffering, its peculiar sources and special intensity, the ways and degrees in which it is avoidable, the forces that contribute to it, and his struggle against it. The underdog's standpoint therefore deserves to be heard in sociology not because he has any special virtue and not because he alone lives in a world of suffering. A sociology of the underdog is justified because, and to the extent, that his suffering is less likely to be known and because—by the very reason of his being underdog—the extent and character of his suffering are likely to contain much that is avoidable.

Although Becker leans toward a sympathy and special consideration for the underdog's standpoint, and although the underdog's suffering is particularly visible, it is still one further paradox in Becker's discussion that we find him displaying no such concern for suffering. Rather, what we do find is a fear of such a concern, a fear that this concern will make us lose our cool. I would guess that it is in some part because of this fear that Becker makes such a point of rejecting "sentimentality."

Yet if it is not the suffering of the subordinate or the deviant that involves Becker—and others of his school—with the underdog, then what is it? It is my impression, from many years of reading their researches and of talking with them, that their pull to the underdog is sometimes part of a titillated attraction to the underdog's exotic difference and easily takes the form of "essays on quaintness." The danger is, then, that such an identification with the underdog becomes the urban sociologist's equivalent of the anthropologist's (onetime) romantic appreciation of the noble savage.

The Becker School's view embodies an implicit critique of lower middle class ethnocentrism, of small town respectability, of the paradoxical superiority that one ethnic can feel toward another. Indeed, one might say that theirs is most especially a critique of the uneducated middle classes. Now this is no mean thing, for the piety of these strata is certainly pervasive in the United States. Becker's rejection of their smug narrowness is wholesome and valuable.

At the same time, however, Becker's school of deviance is redolent of Romanticism. It expresses the satisfaction of the Great White Hunter who has bravely risked the perils of the urban jungle to bring back an exotic specimen. It expresses the Romanticism of the zoo curator who preeningly displays his rare specimens. And like the zookeeper, he wishes to protect his collection; he does not want spectators to throw rocks at the animals behind the bars. But neither is he eager to tear down the bars and let the animals go. The attitude of these zookeepers of deviance is to create a comfortable and humane Indian Reservation, a protected social space, within which these colorful specimens may be exhibited, unmolested and unchanged. The very empirical sensitivity to fine detail, characterizing this school, is both born of and limited by the connoisseur's fascination with the rare object: its empirical richness is inspired by a collector's aesthetic.

It is in part for this reason that, despite its challenging conception of a partisan sociology and its sympathy with the underdog, Becker's discussion is paradoxically suffused with a surprising air of complacency. Indeed, what it expresses is something quite different from the older, traditional sympathy with the plight of the underdog. Basically, it conceives of the underdog as a *victim*. In some part, this is inherent in the very conception of the processes by means of which deviance is conceived of as being generated. For the emphasis in Becker's theory is on the deviant as the product of society rather than as the rebel against it. If this is a liberal conception of deviance that wins sympathy and tolerance for the deviant, it has the paradoxical consequence of inviting us to view the deviant as a passive nonentity who is responsible neither for his suffering nor its alleviation— who is more "sinned against than sinning." Consistent with this view of the underdog as victim, is the more modern conception of him as someone who has to be managed, and should be managed better, by a bureaucratic apparatus of official caretakers. In short, it conceives of the underdog as someone maltreated by a bureaucratic establishment whose remedial efforts are ineffectual, whose custodial efforts are brutal, and whose rule enforcement techniques are self-interested. While it sees deviance as generated by a process of social interaction, as emerging out of the matrix of an unanalyzed society, is does not see deviance as deriving from specified master institutions of this larger society, or as expressing an active opposition to them.

The underdog is largely seen from the standpoint of the difficulties that are encountered when the society's caretakers attempt to cope with the deviance that has been produced in him by the society. Becker's school of deviance thus views the underdog as someone who is being mismanaged, not as someone who suffers or fights back. Here the deviant is sly but not defiant; he is tricky but not courageous; he sneers but does not accuse; he "makes out" without making a scene. Insofar as this school of theory has a critical edge to it, this is directed at the caretaking institutions who do the mopping-up job, rather than at the master institutions that produce the deviant's suffering.

It is in some part for this reason that the kinds of researches that are undertaken from this standpoint tend to exclude a concern with *political* deviance, in which men do actively fight back on behalf of their values and interests. We thus find relatively few studies of people involved in the civil rights struggle or in the peace movement. For however much these deviant groups are made to suffer, no one could easily conceive of them as mere victims well under the control of bureaucratic officialdom. It is not man-fighting-back that wins Becker's sympathy, but rather, man-on-his-back that piques his curiosity.

What we have here, then, is essentially a rejection of unenlightened middle class bigotry. And in its place is a sympathetic view of the underdog seen increasingly from the standpoint of the relatively benign, the well educated, and the *highly* placed bureaucratic officialdom: of the American administrative class. What seems to be a rejection of the standpoint of the superior is, I shall argue, actually only a rejection of the *middle-level* superior.

We may see this more clearly if we return to the problem that gives Becker his greatest uneasiness, the observation that every superior has his own superior, and, correspondingly, Becker's failure to observe that every subordinate has his own subordinate. (Lower than the prostitute is the pimp; lower than the pimp is the errand boy; and lower than the errand boy is the kid on the fringe of the gang who would like his job.) Now, since everyone may have someone or something above or below him, this does not make it more but less possible to know *which* subordinate's standpoint we should adopt. But this does not deter Becker for a moment. As he gayly says, "I do not propose to hold my breath until this problem is solved."

I, for my part, however, continue to be preplexed about the manner in which a specific stratum of underdogs comes to be chosen as the focus for an orienting standpoint. There is a hidden anomaly in any recommendation to look upon the world from the standpoint of underdogs. The anomaly is this: to a surprising degree, underdogs see *themselves* from the standpoint of respectable society; Negroes, in fact, often call one another "niggers." Thus, if we did study underdogs from "their own" standpoint we would, inevitably, be adopting the standpoint of the dominant culture. It is precisely insofar as the deviant and subordinate do accept a role as passive victims rather than as rebels against circumstances, that they do view themselves from the standpoint of the dominant culture.

In the very act of viewing deviants and subordinates from *their own* standpoint, we are bound to see them from the standpoint of respectable society and its dominant institutions. We will also see deviants in terms of conventional categories not only when we look upon them as passive victims, but, also, to the extent that they are looked upon from the standpoint of the bureaucratic caretakers who are publicly chartered either to put them into custody or to correct their behavior. Paradoxically, then, although Becker invites us to adopt the standpoint of the subordinate, and thereby presumably braves giving offense to respectable values, I believe that he himself is still using some version of the outlook of respectable society.

OMBUDSMAN SOCIOLOGY: CRITIQUE OF THE MIDDLE MAN

Becker seems to be adopting the position of the outcast. In point of fact, I believe that he is also embracing the position of "enlightened" but no less respectable liberalism toward the outcast. Becker appears to be taking up arms against society on behalf of the underdog. Actually, he is taking up arms against the ineffectuality, callousness, or capriciousness of the care-takers that society has appointed to administer the mess it has created. Becker's argument is essentially a critique of the caretaking organizations, and in particular of the *low level* officialdom that manages them. It is not a critique of the social institutions that engender suffering or of the high level officialdom that shapes the character of caretaking establishments.

Much of deviant study today has become a component of the new style of social reform which is now engineered through caretaking public bureaucracies. The idiological standpoint implicit in Becker's School embodies a critique of the *conventional* welfare apparatus and of the *old* style welfare state, before it extricated itself from social movement reform. It is, as such, a critique of the ethnocentrism and the ineffectuality with which deviance is regarded and treated by certain of the local caretakers immediately responsible for it today. Becker's theoretical school is indeed taking sides; it is a party to the struggle between the old and the new elites in the caretaking establishments; between the welfare institutions inherited from the 1930's and those now promoted today; and between the "locals" working in the municipalities and the "cosmopolitans" operating from Washington, D.C. His ideology is, in each case, injurious to the former and supportive of the latter. If this is seen, it can be better understood how certain of the other difficulties in Becker's discussion are to be resolved. We therefore need a temporary detour to obtain a view of these difficulties.

Becker makes a distinction between the conduct of research in two settings: in political and nonpolitical situations. He is moved to make this distinction because he wants to hold that accusations of bias against sociologists, and reactions to them, differ, depending upon whether the situation studied is political or not.

Becker holds that in *non*political situations sociologists are more likely to accuse one another of bias when their studies adopt underdog perspectives, than when they look at things from the standpoint of superiors. The reason for this, he says, is that in these nonpolitical situations there exists an accepted "hierarchy of credibility" which credits superiors with the right to define social reality in their spheres; since most sociologists, like others, tend to accept the established hierarchies of credibility, they therefore tend to view studies conducted from underdog perspectives as biased.

Now this is very curious. For what Becker is arguing is that most sociologists, who he says are liberal, will, despite this ideology, nonetheless identify with the overdog in their studies of nonpolitical situations. In short, while most sociologists will presumably give free rein to their liberal ideologies when studying political situations, they will turn their backs on these same liberal ideologies, and act as if they were non-liberal, when studying non-political situations. If this is true, surely one must ask: How is this switch effected? What brings it about? Indeed, is it really a switch? We must consider the other side of the equation; that is, if we ask how some liberal sociologists come to identify with the underdog, we must also ask, how does it happen that others failed to do so?

Becker recognizes that *some* explanation is called for to account for sociologists' adoption of overdog viewpoints in their researches. He says that (in nonpolitical situations) most sociologists tend to accept the dominant hierarchy of credibility. In other words, in these situations, most sociologists conduct their studies from the standpoint of responsible officials, says Becker, because they accept the standpoint of responsible officials. Becker's invocation of this tautology at least acknowledges that an explanation is in order. Yet when it comes to explaining why a minority of sociologists adopt an *underdog* standpoint in the same nonpolitical situations, Becker does not even see that this, too, is a problem that needs explaining.

BLEAK HYPOTHESES

What, indeed, are the sources of these sociologists' identification with underdogs? Clearly we cannot simply hold that such an identification with the underdog stems predominantly from the sociologists' liberal ideology. For Becker is quite right in stating that most sociologists are politically liberal. It is clear therefore that many, if not most, who adopt the overdog standpoint must share this liberal ideology. Thus, while the liberal ideology may be a necessary condition for adopting an underdog standpoint, it cannot be a sufficient condition for doing so. The question here, the most important question we ever confront in understanding how moralities and ideologies work in the world, is: By what specific mechanisms are men kept honest? In other words, how is it that they are made to conform to their ideologies or values?

It may be surprising, but there are actually many things that keep men—including sociologists—honest. First, remember, as Becker acknowledges, that an underdog standpoint is adopted by only a minority of sociologists. Being infrequent, a minority perspective is more likely to be visible in the larger professional community from whom sociologists seek recognition. Of course, such notice may take the form of hostile criticism. But while an underdog standpoint thus has its risks, it may also bring higher and quicker returns than the adoption of an overdog standpoint which, being common, tends to glut the market and to depress the price paid per individual contribution.

An underdog perspective may, then, be thought of as a career strategy more appealing to high variance betters who, in turn, are more likely to be found among the ambitious young. Bear in mind, however, that the larger professional audience to whom their work is addressed will for the most part conceive themselves as "liberals"—and on whose sympathy an underdog standpoint has some claim. Those adopting an underdog standpoint are, therefore, probably not engaged in as risky an undertaking as their minority position might imply. We are, in summary, suggesting a bleak hypothesis: sociologists with liberal ideologies will more likely adopt underdog perspectives when they experience these as compatible with the pursuit of their own career interests.

Implicit in this bleak hypothesis is the assumption that there is probably some positive relationship between the youth and low professional status, on the one hand, and the adoption of an underdog perspective, on the other. In brief, I would expect that younger intellectuals would, other things constant, be readier to adopt this high variance bet than older intellectuals. It may also be that older intellectuals who feel that they have been bypassed, or whose rewards have somehow not been appropriate, would also be more likely to adopt an underdog standpoint.

Correspondingly, I would also expect that as sociologists get older, as they become increasingly successful, more likely to live next door to or associate with those who are also successful, or themselves become involved in the practical management of public (including university) affairs, they too will come increasingly to adopt overdog standpoints despite their continued public professions of liberalism. Moreover, as sociologists become better established, recognized, and successful, they are—as they begin to move toward the zenith of their careers—risking more should they make a high variance wager on underdogs. The additional net advantage still possible to them is in this way diminished. In short, for the rising sociologist, identification with the underdog may mean greater risk than it does for the younger or less successful sociologists.

I would, however, suggest one important qualification concerning this disposition of older men toward increasing overdog standpoints. As they achieve (rather than merely approach) the zenith of their careers, the rewards that older sociologists are given for conformity to conventional overdog positions, are especially subject to a diminishing marginal utility; in the result some of them may be less subject to professional controls that dispose them to the conventional standpoints of their contemporaries. Thus some senior sociologists, beginning to think about the judgment of "posterity" rather than the views of their contemporaries, may return to the underdog standpoints of their youth. Moreover, as their own age group thins out through death, they may receive more encouragement from the young with whom they are not in competition, than from the middle aged; and they may begin to feel that the future of their reputations will be more enduringly affected by the judgment of the relatively young. These, at any rate, are some of the ways in which the career and personal interests of some older sociologists may dispose them to defy the established hierarchy of credibility and to opt for the underdog. We might call it the "Bertrand Russell Syndrome."

But men are prompted to heed the voice of conscience and to abide by high principle by still other considerations. We can see some of these if we ask, how is it that the young, high-variance betters are not brought under control by their elders in the course of their education, apprenticeship, and common research undertakings, and are in this way constrained to adopt the respectable overdog standpoints more congenial to the older? Here, again, things are not simple. In some part, the young men's underdog impulses will be protected by the academic ideology of collegiality, which nominally governs relationships. Thus even when working under the supervision of older men, the young men can lay claim for the protection of their underdog standpoints.

Once more, however, we must call attention to the role of bleak factors in keeping men honest. These essentially have to do with the ramifying and powerful role of the new funding structures in social science today which, in turn, are linked to the growth of the new welfare state and its new conceptions of social reform.

Nothing is more obvious than that these are plush times for American social scientists, and there is never any reason to underestimate the power of the obvious. So far as the older and better known men are concerned, they are often so fully funded that they may have little time to supervise their researches personally, to administer them with the continuing closeness that could effectively imprint their overdog identifications on the research. Sometimes the older men are so loosely connected with the researches they have funded that even basic research decisions are made by younger men from their different standpoints. Older men today are often constrained to surrender wide discretionary power to their juniors, if they are to keep them in today's seller's market in social research. The irony of the matter, then, is that the more successful the older man is in funding his research, the less successful he may be in having it conducted according to his lights: the research is less likely to be "his."

With the new funding situation and the greater ease of access to research money, it is now also much simpler for younger men to procure funds for themselves, for their own researches, and at an earlier age. Being their own masters, they can now more readily express their own underdog standpoint, insofar as they have one.

But it would seem that there should be a fly in this ointment. For the question that now arises is whether the new funding situation may simply mean that the younger men have only exchanged one master for another; for even if they are no longer subjected to the direct pressure of senior professors, they may now be subjected to the direct pressure of the funding agencies. In my opinion, this is exactly what has happened.

With growing ease of funding, younger men gain independent access to research resources at a time when their liberal underdog ideologies are still relatively strong and can shape their research. At the same time, however, the career gratifications of these funding opportunities, as well as the personal gratifications of being close to men of power, become vested interests that constrain to a dependency on the new sources of funding. Thus the younger man's more salient, underdog identifications now need to be accommodated to his new-found "appreciation" of overdogs. This is in part accomplished by submerging this "appreciation" in a subsidiary awareness that is maintained by a collegial reciprocity: each tactfully agrees not to look the other's "gift horse in the mouth." (There are, alas, "deviant" cases: e.g., those who make a career of denouncing Project Camelot and then themselves apply for a half-million dollar grant from the State Department.)

This accommodation of underdog identification to overdog dependencies is, quite apart from skillful rationalizing, not too difficult today. For the new funding agencies now desperately need information about underdogs; and these are not unreceptive even to researches conducted from the latter's standpoint, for much the same reason that colonial governments supported similar researches in anthropology. Overdogs in the welfare state—in Washington bureaucracies and New York foundations—are buyers of underdog research for much the same political reasons that the Johnson regime initiated the "war on poverty." To explore a few of the implications of this, I must revert to some of the larger institutional changes that come to a head in the welfare state.

Perhaps the crux here is the manner in which social reform in the United States has changed in character. What is new is not the "plight of the cities," however increasing their deterioration, but rather that this becomes an object of a measured "concern" rather than of "shame." What is new, in a somewhat larger historical perspective, is that the locus of reform initiatives and resources is increasingly found on the level of national politics and foundations, rather than in the political vitality, the economic resources, or the zealous initiatives of elites with local roots.

The reform of American cities was once a process that involved small businessmen, muckraking journalists, and local political machines, all of whom had some vital involvement and interest in their communities. Today, however, with the changing structure, character, and ecology of the middle classes, many who might give leadership to urban reform live neither in the city itself nor in the still politically powerful rural areas, but live rather in suburbia and exurbia. The educated, bureaucratically employed, and highly mobile middle classes have a dwindling localistic attachment and a narrowing base of power on the *local* levels, which could provide them with the economic and political leverage to effectuate urban reform. They must, in consequence, seek a remedy not on the local but the national level.

As the locus of reform efforts moves upward from the local to the national level, the conception and meaning of social reform changes. The urban reforms being sought by this new middle class are now aimed at the reform of a community to which they are less tied by complex interests, urbane pleasures, or by a round of familiarizing daily activities. It is not "their" community that they now wish to reform—for their suburbs are decent enough as they view them. When they concern themselves with the plight of Negroes, it is not even "their" Negroes whom they seek to help, but Negroes viewed abstractly and impersonally.

Social reform now becomes an effort largely motivated by bland political appraisal, removed economic calculus, prudent forecasting, or a sense of pity and sympathy that becomes increasingly remote as it loses rooting in daily experience and encounter. The community to be reformed becomes an object, something apart from and outside the reformer. The nature of the reform becomes less a matter of moral zeal or even of immediate personal interest and more of a concern prompted by a long range appraisal and prudence. Social reform now becomes a kind of engineering job, a technological task to be subject to bland "cost-benefit" or "system-analysis." The rise of the welfare state then means the rise of the uninvolved reformer: It means the rise of reform-at-a-distance. Reform today is no longer primarily the part-time avocation of dedicated amateurs but is increasingly the full-time career of paid bureaucrats.

Today civil rights reforms and the war against poverty are pursued by many in a Bismarckian mood. Reform is no longer prompted by the twinge of conscience or the bite of immediate personal interest but, rather, by "reasons of state," and on behalf of the "national interest." Personal liberalism becomes state liberalism. Liberalism changes in character from a matter of conscience, which had a penetrating claim upon private and daily decision, to electoral loyalty to the Democratic Party and to marginal differentiations in career strategies. The operational meaning of liberalism for the sociologist now tends to become calibrated in terms of the government agency for which he will work, or whose money he will take. From some current standpoints, for example, a truly "liberal sociologist" is one who will reject money from the Defense Department but will seek and accept it from the State Department!

The funding agencies of social science today, whether government agencies or massive private foundations, are essentially the welfare state's purchasing agents for market research: they are the instrumentalities of this new reform movement. They express the "detached concern" of educated but bureaucratically dependent middle classes who no longer have effective bases in localities; whose cosmopolitan sympathies are not personally and deeply engaged by a daily encounter with urban suffering; and whose fears are not deeply aroused by a close dependence upon the deteriorating urban community. Prodded partly by mild discomforts, vague forboddings, prudent extrapolations, partly by concern to maintain a decent image of themselves, and, not least, by the growing rise of the militant politics of public demonstrations, they approach the task of modern urban reform with a thin-lipped, businesslike rationality. This is the social context in which we can better understand some of the ramifying meanings of Becker's bland program for an underdog sociology. It is the larger context which makes it possible for some sociologists today to stay honest: that is, to implement their liberal ideologies with an effort at underdog identification.

The superiors whose dominant "hierarchies of credibility" are resisted by this underdog sociology are essentially those whose powers remain rooted in, and hence limited by, the local level. The sociology of the underdog is a sociology that rejects the standpoint of only the *local* officials: the head of the medical school, the warden of the prison, the city director of the housing agency. In short, the respectables who are being resisted, and whose hierarchy of credibility is disputed, are those local officials who, for the most part, do not control access to large supplies of research funds.

TOWARD A NEW ESTABLISHMENT SOCIOLOGY

The new underdog sociology propounded by Becker is, then, a standpoint that possesses a remarkably convenient combination of properties: it enables the sociologist to befriend the very small underdogs in local settings, to reject the standpoint of the "middle dog" respectables and notables who manage local caretaking establishments, while, at the same time, to make and remain friends with the really top dogs in Washington agencies or New York foundations. While Becker adopts a posture as the intrepid preacher of a new underdog sociology, he has really given birth to something rather different: to the first version of new Establishment sociology, to a sociology compatible with the new character of social reform in the United States today. It is a sociology of and for the new welfare state. It is the sociology of young men with friends in Washington. It is a sociology that succeeds in solving the oldest problem in personal politics: how to maintain one's integrity without sacrificing one's career, or how to remain a liberal although well heeled.

The social utility of this new ideology is furthered by the fact that, for some while now, there has been a growing tension between the entrenched local welfare establishments and the newer and powerfully supported federally based agencies and programs of the "Great Society." These new federal agencies, headed by personnel with substantially greater education than the local elites, are presently attempting to implement their new programs against the resistance of the local notables. It is the ultimate function of the federally based programs to win or maintain the attachment of urban lower and working classes to the political symbols and machinery of the American state in general, and of the Democratic Party in particular. While the local caretaking elites usually share these political aims, they also feel that their own local prerogatives and position are threatened by the growth of programs over which they have less control, since they derive from national resources and initiatives. Becker's new underdog sociology functions to line up sectors of sociology against the "backward" resistance the officialdom on the municipal level, and in favor of the most powerful "enlightened" sectors on the national level.

Essentially Becker's type of research does this because, in adopting the standpoint of the underdogs, it simultaneously shows how ignorant local caretakers are of this standpoint and how badly local caretaking officials manage their establishments. It must not be thought for a moment that Becker's work performs this ideological function through any intention to further the ambitions of the upper officialdom or by any intention to conduct his research in any narrowly conceived applied manner. It achieves its ideological consequences primarily by taking and revealing the standpoint of those for whom local caretaking officials are responsible and by "unmaking" the ignorance of these officials. This is not an incidental or trivial byproduct; rather, this is exactly what carries the political payload. For it is this discrediting of local officials that legitimates the claims of the higher administrative classes in Washington and gives them an entering wedge on the local level.

Becker's readiness to sacrifice the middle dogs to the top dogs can be gleaned when he states that there is no point in attempting to adopt the standpoint of middle level officialdom. Looking at the situation from the standpoint of middle level officials—in other words, from the standpoint of the prison warden, the school principal, the hospital administrator—simply leads to an infinite regression, says Becker.

This has a seeming persuasiveness, but it is too glib by far. First, it is by no means certain that an "infinite regress" problem is involved. Is it really true that every superior has a superior who, in turn, limits and prevents him from doing as he really would like? Isn't there some point at which the buck-passing ends? This would seem to be part of what C. Wright Mills had in mind when he spoke of the "power elite." We can, of course, maintain that even the highest officers of state in turn always require the consent of the governed. But this brings us back full circle; and we would then have to acknowledge that the very underdogs, who Becker says are more sinned against than sinning, are at least in part responsible for the sins against them; and why, then, should sociologists conduct their studies primarily from their standpoint?

It would seem that there is one way out of this impasse for Becker. He could say that it is not a matter of superiors and subordinates as such, but, rather, of the *institutions* governing their relationship. He might maintain that the need is not to study social situations from the standpoint of subordinates as an end in itself, but of conducting studies with a view to understanding how some are crushed by certain institutions, and how all alike are subjected to institutions that do not permit them to live as they wish. As I say, this position would be one way for Becker. But he neither sees it nor takes it. For this undercuts his "infinite regress" gambit and leads research inevitably to the doorstep of power; it would force the research focus upward, fastening it on the national levels.

Parenthetically, but not irrelevantly, I think that *radical* sociologists differ from liberals in that, while they take the standpoint of the underdog, they apply it to the study of overdogs. Radical sociologists want to study "power elites," the leaders, or masters, of men; liberal sociologists focus their efforts upon underdogs and victims and their immediate bureaucratic caretakers.

For all its difficulties, Becker's position does provide a vantage point for a criticism of local managers of the Caretaking Establishment, of the vested interests and archaic methods of these middle dogs. This is all to the good. But this vantage point has been bought at a very high price. The price is an uncritical accommodation to the national elite and to the society's master institutions; and this is all to the bad.

There is, I think, one other way in which Becker's position is too glib. It is premised upon a conviction (or sentiment) to the effect that, as he says in *The Outsiders,* while it may be possible to see a situation from "both sides," this "cannot be done simultaneously." This means, explains Becker, that "we cannot construct a description . . . that in some way fuses perceptions and interpretations made by both parties involved in a process of deviance. . . . We cannot describe a 'higher reality' that makes sense of both sets of views." I assume this means that although the sociologist can, at some point, present the views of one group and then, at another point, present the views of a different group, that nonetheless, the sociologist's own standpoint—when he speaks in an omniscient voice—tends inevitably to favor one of these sides more than the other, to present one side more attractively than the other This frank confession of human fallibility is so appealing that it seems almost churlish to question it. But I do.

One reason that Becker sees no way out of this impasse is because he is committed to a kind of interpersonal social psychology which, with all its humanistic merits, fails to see that men—superiors as well as subordinates —may be powerfully constrained by institutions, by history, and indeed by biology. Becker's position is largely that of the undefeated, pragmatic, history-less and still optimistic American to whom "everything is possible" in man-to-man, and manly encounter. If, however, we acknowledge that superiors no less than subordinates live within these limits—which may not be impossible to penetrate, but only costly to do so—we do not, I think, degrade their humanity but rather sensitize ourselves to it. We may then see that the issue not only entails a conflict between superiors and subordinates but a larger kind of human struggle. Such a perspective does not require us to restrain our sympathy for the underdog or ignore his special plight, but gives us a broader comprehension of it. To have a sense of man's common humanity does not demand a superhuman capacity to transcend partisanship. But a partisanship that is set within the framework of a larger humanistic understanding is quite different from one devoid of it. This is one difference between the merely political partisanship of daily involvements, and the more reflective and tempered partisanship which may well be such objectivity of which we are capable.

There are works of art that manifest this objective partisanship. The dramas of the great classical tragedians are a magnificent case in point. What makes them great is their objectivity; and what makes them objective is their capacity to understand even the nobility of their Persian enemies, even the dignity of their "barbarian" slaves, even the bumbling of their own wise men. They do indeed express a viewpoint which in some sense does take the standpoint of both sides, and does so simultaneously. If great art can do this, why should this be forbidden to great social science? That it is not common is precisely what makes its accomplishment an expression of greatness.

Despite the inevitability of bias and the unavoidability of partisanship, the fact remains that two researchers may have the same bias but, nonetheless, may *not* be equally objective. How is this possible? Becker notes "that our unavoidable sympathies do not render our results invalid" and that, despite them, research must meet "the standards of good scientific work." This does not clarify the issue as much as we might wish, for there never was any suggestion that partisanship impaired the "validity" of research. There is also no doubt that partisanship does not necessarily impair the "reliability" of a research. The validity and reliability of researches are matters quite apart from their *objectivity*.

And it is primarily this last concern which is engaged when the problem of partisanship is raised. The question here is only whether partisanship necessarily vitiates objectivity, and, this in turn requires that at some point we clarify our conception of objectivity and of how it may be attained.

ONCE AGAIN: THE PROBLEM OF OBJECTIVITY

How, then, does Becker seek to enhance the objectivity of even partisan research? His views concerning this are sketchy in the extreme. Although he speaks of a need to maintain scientific standards, he quickly recognizes that there is no way in which we can be sure that sociologists will *apply* these standards "impartially across the board." He also expresses the qualified hope that, over the years, the accumulation of "one-sided" studies will gradually produce a more balanced picture of a social situation; but he also recognizes that this does not help the individual researcher in the here and now.

The remedies in which Becker apparently reposes greater confidence consist rather of two other things. First, he recommends that we honestly confess the partisan position we have adopted, openly acknowledging that we have studied the problem from the standpoint of only certain of the actors involved and not of all. Considering that Becker has himself refused openly to acknowledge his own underdog standpoint, this solution to the problem of objectivity is not entirely confidence inspiring. Secondly, Becker also recommends—and it is this that he seems to feel most strongly about —the avoidance of "sentimentality," whatever that may mean.

For my part, it seems to me that other things might be done.

For one, I would encourage a condemnation of complacency rather than of sentimentality. For it is complacency which allows us to think, *a la* Myrdal, that we have solved the problem of objectivity by good-naturedly confessing that, yes, we do indeed have a standpoint and by openly specifying what it is. Confession may be good for the soul, but it is no tonic to the mind. While the "heart may have reasons of its own," when it simply chooses to assert these without critical inspection, then reason must condemn this as complacency. Of course, it is a good thing for sociologists to know what they are doing; and it is a good thing for them to know and to say whose side they are on. But a bland confession of partisanship merely betrays smugness and naiveté. It is smug because it assumes that the values that we have are good enough; it is naive because it assumes that we know the values we have. Once we recognize that complacency is the mind's embalming fluid and once we move to overcome it, we are then forced to ask, what is it that is now making us so complacent?

The complacency of Becker and of his school of deviance derives in large measure from its own unexamined, comfortable commitment to political liberalism. It has wrapped itself in the protective covering of the liberal Establishment which dominates American sociology today, as well as American academic life in general. Becker blandly acknowledges, without making the least effort to explore its appreciable consequences, that "it is no secret that most sociologists are politically liberal . . ." But it is complacency to allow ourselves to be appeased by a confession of the commonplace. To confess that most sociologists are politically liberal is like "confessing" that men are conceived in sexual intercourse. The question is whether Becker sees any *consequences* in the thing confessed. Without considering these, confession becomes a meaningless ritual of frankness.

The important problem is the exploration of the ways in which the political liberalism of many sociologists today affects the worth, the scope, the bite, and the objectivity of their sociology. The very blandness of his confession implies that Becker fails to grasp that liberalism today is not simply the conscientious and liberating faith of isolated individuals. Political liberalism today instead verges on being an official ideology of wide sectors of the American university community as well as broader strata of American life. For many American academicians, liberalism has now become a token of respectability, a symbol of genteel open-mindedness, the fee for membership in the faculty club; in point of fact, liberalism is also an operating code that links academic life to the political machinery of the Democratic Party.

Far from being the conscientious code of isolated individuals, much of liberalism today is the well-financed ideology of a loosely organized but coherent Establishment. It is the dominant ideology of a powerful group that sprawls across the academic community; that is integrated with American politics. that has its opinion leaders in various publications; that has its heroes whose myths are recited. Liberalism, then, is the mythos of one of the dominating American establishments; it is not simply the hard-won faith of a happy few. As the ideology of an establishment, such official liberalism has things to protect. It has reasons to lie. It has all the social mechanisms available to any establishment by which it can reward those who tell the right lies, and punish and suppress those who tell the wrong truths. In its meaner moments, it is an intellectual Mafia. It is not only, therefore, as Becker says, that "officials must lie because things are seldom as they ought to be." Like any other member of an establishment, the sociologist who is a political liberal is expected to lie along with his fellow members of the Establishment, to feel the rightness of their cause and a responsibility for its success.

The bias of the sociologist, then, does not derive simply from the fact that it is inherent in the human condition or in sociological research. The sociologist also lies because he is a political person. It would seem, however, that sociologists have no right to be complacent about anything that they, more than others, should have good reason to know makes liars of them. They thus have no right to be complacent about the intellectual consequences of their own liberalism.

The complacency that oozes from Becker's discussion, the vapid frankness of its confessional style, rests upon a simple sociological condition:

upon the fact that it is allied with official liberalism, is embedded in the liberal Establishment, and is supported comfortably by the welfare state.

This still leaves the question as to whether there is any road toward objectivity, and what direction it might take. In my view, the objectivity of sociologists is enhanced to the extent that they critically examine all conventional "hierarchies of credibility," including their own liberal "hierarchy of credibility," which is today as respectable, conventional, and conformist as any. Becker acknowledges that it is sometimes possible to "take the point of view of some third party not directly implicated in the hierarchy we are investigating." This would, indeed, he agrees, make us neutral to the contending groups in the situation under study. But, he adds, this "would only mean we would enlarge the scope of the political conflict to include a party not ordinarily brought in whose view the sociologist has taken." But isn't this precisely one possible meaning of an avenue toward objectivity?

Isn't is good for a sociologist to take the standpoint of someone outside of those most immediately engaged in a specific conflict, or outside of the group being investigated? Isn't it precisely this outside standpoint, or our ability to adopt it, which is one source and one possible meaning of sociological objectivity? Granted, all standpoints are partisan; and, granted, no one escapes a partisan standpoint. But aren't some forms of partisanship more liberating than others? Isn't it the sociologists' job to look at human situations in ways enabling them to say things that are not ordinarily seen by the participants in them? This does not mean that the sociologist should ignore or be insensitive to the full force of the actors' standpoints. But it does mean that he himself must have a standpoint on their standpoint. Objectivity is indeed threatened when the actors' standpoints and the sociologists' fuse indistinguishably into one. The adoption of an "outside" standpoint, far from leading us to ignore the participants' standpoint, is probably the only way in which we can even recognize and identify the participants' standpoint. It is only when we have a standpoint somewhat different from the participants that it becomes possible to do justice to their standpoints.

There are, it seems to me, at least three other possible conceptions of sociological objectivity. One of these can be characterized as "personal authenticity" or "awareness," another can be termed "normative objectification," and the third may be called "transpersonal replicability."

To consider "normative objectification" first: when we talk about the bias or impartiality of a sociologist we are, in effect, talking about the sociologist as if he were a "judge." [1] Now, rendering a judgment premises the existence of conflicting or contending parties; but it does not imply an

---

[1] The next paragraph or so is indebted to the excellent discussion by Rostein Eckhoff, "The Mediator, the Judge and the Administrator in Conflict-Resolution," *Acta Sociologica*, 10, pp. 148–172.

intention to *mediate* the difficulties between them. The function of a judge is not to bring parties together but is, quite simply, to do justice. Doing justice does not mean, as does mediation or arbitration, that both the parties must each be given or denied a bit of what they sought. Justice does not mean logrolling or "splitting the difference." For the doing of justice may, indeed, give all the benefits to one party and impose all the costs upon another.

What makes a judgment possessed of justice is not the fact that it distributes costs and benefits equally between the parties but, rather, that the allocation of benefits and costs is made in conformity with some stated normative standard. Justice, in short, is that which is justified in terms of some value. The "impartiality" or objectivity of the judge is an imputation made when it is believed that he had made his decision primarily or solely in terms of some moral value. In one part, then, the objectivity of the judge requires his explication of the moral value in terms of which his judgment has been rendered. One reason why Becker's analysis founders on the problem of objectivity is precisely because it regards the sociologists' value commitment merely as an inescapable fact of nature, rather than viewing it as a necessary condition of his objectivity.

Insofar as the problem is seen as one of choosing up sides, rather than a working one's way through to a value commitment, I cannot see how it is ever possible for men to recognize that the side to which they are attached can be wrong. But men do not and need not always say, "my country right or wrong." Insofar as they are capable of distinguishing the side to which they are attached from the *grounds* on which they are attached to it, they are, to that extent, capable of a significant objectivity.

It should again be clear, then, that I do not regard partisanship as incompatible with objectivity. The physician, after all, is not necessarily less objective because he has made a partisan commitment to his patient and against the germ. The physician's objectivity is in some measure vouchsafed because he has committed himself to a specific value: health. It is this commitment that constrains him to see and to say things about the patient's condition that neither may want to know.

But in saying that the explication of the sociologist's value commitment is a necessary condition for his objectivity, we are saying little unless we recognize at the same time the grinding difficulties involved in this. For one, it is no easy thing to know what our own value commitments are. In an effort to seem frank and open, we all too easily pawn off a merely glib statement about our values without making any effort to be sure that these are the values to which we are actually committed. This is much of what happens when scientists conventionally assert that they believe only in "the truth." Secondly, a mere assertion of a value commitment is vainly ritualistic to the extent that the sociologist has no awareness of the way in which one of his commitments may conflict with or exclude another. For example, there is commonly some tension between a commitment to truth and a commitment to welfare. Third, we also have to recognize that the values in terms of which we may make our judgments may not necessarily be shared by the participants in the situations we have studied. Our objectivity, however, does not require us to share values with those we study, but only to apply the values that we claim are our own, however unpopular these may be. In other words, this form of objectivity requires that we be on guard against our own hypocrisy and our need to be loved. This creates a problem because the values we may actually hold may differ from those we feel that we must display in order to gain or maintain access to research sites.

To come to another meaning of sociological objectivity, "personal authenticity." If the previous conception of objectivity, "normative objectification," emphasizes that the sociologist must not deceive *others* concerning the value basis of his judgment, then personal authenticity stresses that the sociologist must not deceive *himself* concerning the basis of his judgment. By personal authenticity or awareness, I mean to call attention to the relationship between the sociologist's beliefs about the actual state of the social world, on the one hand, and his own personal wishes, hopes, and values for this social world, on the other hand. Personal authenticity or awareness exists when the sociologist is capable of admitting the factuality even of things that violate his own hopes and values. People do differ in this regard, some having a greater capacity and need for self-deception and others possessing less talent to attain the comforts born of such self-deception. Not all conservatives are equally blind to the fragility of the status quo; not all radicals are equally blind to its stability.

In this sense, then, one form of sociological objectivity involves the capacity to acknowledge "hostile information"—information that is discrepant with our purposes, hopes, wishes, or values. It is not the state of the world, then, that makes information hostile, but only the state of the world in relation to a man's wants and values. Here, then, objectivity consists in the capacity to know and to use—to seek out, or at least to accept it when it is otherwise provided—information inimical to our own desires and values, and to overcome our own fear of such information.

Both forms of objectivity imply a paradoxical condition: namely, that one cannot be objective about the world outside without, to some extent, being knowledgeable about (and in control of) ourselves. In normative objectification, one of the central problems is to *know* our values, and to see that such knowledge is problematic. In personal authenticity there is a need for a similar knowledge of the self, but for a knowledge that goes beyond values into the question of our brute impulses and of other desires or wants that we may not at all feel to be valuable. In both forms of objectivity, also, it would be foolhardy to expect that the requisite knowledge is acquirable through a simple process of friction-less "retrieval." Rather, we must expect that either form of objectivity entails some measure of *struggle* in and with the sociologist's self and, with this, a need for courage. It now should be clear why I have taken up the cudgels against complacency, for it is the very antithesis of the kind of moral struggle required for objectivity.

PROFESSIONALISM AND OBJECTIVITY

Insofar as the pursuit of objectivity rests upon what I must reluctantly call "moral character," we can also see another source from which sociological objectivity is deeply undermined today. It is undermined, from one direction, by a compulsive and exclusive cultivation of purely technical standards of research and of education, so that there is neither a regard nor a locus of responsibility for the cultivation of those very moral qualities on which objectivity rests. The truth is that to the extent that sociology and sociological education remain obsessed with a purely technical focus they have abdicated a concern with objectivity; it is merely hypocritical for those with such a standpoint to enter occasional accusations about others' lack of objectivity.

A second basic inner locus for our default with respect to the problem of objectivity is the growing transformation of sociology into a profession. This may seem paradoxical again, for surely professions profess value commitments, at least to client, if not public, welfare. Professions, however, do not tend to see value commitments as questions of personal commitment but tend, instead, simply to treat the values they transmit as nonproblematic givens. Most civic professions tend to take the larger culture and institutions in their society as given. But it is precisely the peculiar nature of the sociologist's task to be able to take them as problematic. The development of professionalization among sociologists deserves to be opposed because it undermines the sociologist's capacity for *objectivity* in any serious sense. In effect, the growth of professionalization means the substitution of a routine and banal code of ethics for a concern with the serious kind of morality on which alone objectivity might rest.

A third specific conception of objectivity common to many American sociologists—and so common, in fact, that even C. Wright Mills agreed with it—is what has been termed "transpersonal replicability." In this notion, objectivity simply means that a sociologist has described his procedures with such explicitness that others employing them on the same problem will come to the same conclusion. In effect, then, this is a notion of objectivity as technical routinization and rests, at bottom, on the codification and explication of the research procedures that were employed. At most, however, this is an *operational* definition of objectivity which presumably tells us what we must *do* in order to justify an assertion that some particular finding is objective. It does not, however, tell us very much about what objectivity *means* conceptually and connotatively. It says only that those findings which are replicated are to be considered to be objective.

It is quite possible, however, that any limited empirical generalization can, by this standard, be held to be objective, however narrow, partial, or biased and prejudiced its net impact is, by reason of its selectivity. Thus, for example, one might conduct research into the occupational-political distribution of Jews and come to the conclusion that a certain proportion of them are bankers and Communists. Given the replicability conception of objectivity, one might then simply claim that this (subsequently verified) finding is "objective," and this claim could be made legitimately even though one never compared the proportions of bankers and Communists among Jews with those among Protestants and Catholics. It might be said that, without such a comparison among the three religions, one would never know whether the proportion of bankers and Communists among Jews was higher or lower than that among Protestants and Catholics. But this objection would simply indicate the technical statistical condition that must be met in order to justify a statement concerning the Jewish *differential.* Insofar as one happens not to be interested in making or justifying a statement about this, the objectivity of the original statement remains defensible in terms of the technical conception of objectivity as replicability. Thus it would seem that the replicability criterion falls far short of what is commonly implied by objectivity.

This technical conception of objectivity is in part, but in part only, reminiscent of the manner in which Max Weber conceived of it. We might say that the current conception is a kind of mindless corruption of Weber's. Weber essentially thought of scientific objectivity as something left over. It was a residual sphere of the purely technical, a realm in which decisions should and could be made without thought of their ultimate value relevancies. Weber's approach to objectivity comes down to a strategy of segregation—the conscientious maintenance of a strict separation between the world of facts and the world of values. Weber's emphasis here, therefore, is not on the manner in which scientific objectivity depends upon value commitments; this tends tacitly to be assumed rather than deliberately insisted upon. Weber's stress is placed, rather, upon the separation and discontinuity of facts and values. As a result, one may come away believing that, to Weber, the objectivity of research need not be colored by the scientist's personal values or the manner in which these are arrived at and held. *En principe,* neither the sanity nor maturity of a scientist need affect his objectivity. The madman and the teenager can be as scientifically objective as anyone else in this view, so long as they adhere to purely technical standards of science, once having committed themselves to some problem. Weber's theory invites a fantasy that objectivity may, at some point, be surrendered entirely to the impersonal machinery of research.

The passionate artfulness with which Weber argues this case endows the world that he conjures in imagination to be mistaken for reality, and we may fail to notice just how *grotesque* this conjured world is. Actually, Weber's entire enterprise here is born of his attempt to overcome his conception of the world as grotesque by formulating a salvational myth of a value-free social science. Through this he strives to still his furious sense of uneasiness that the real world, in which science and morality do cohabit, is a world of mutually destructive incompatibles. Weber fantasies a solution in which facts and values will each be preserved in watertight compartments. The tensions and dangers of the conjunction of facts and values are to be overcome by a segregation of the sequential phases of research, so that: first, the scientist formulates his problem in terms of his value interests and, then, having done this, he puts his values behind him, presumably never again allowing them to intrude into the subsequent stage of technical analysis.

To overcome his experience of the world as grotesque, Weber formulates an incipient utopia in which the impure world is split into two pure worlds, science and morality. He then attempts to bridge the cleavage he has created by pasting these two purified worlds together, so that each is made sovereign in a different but adjacent period of time. The incongruity of the world has not so much been overcome as transcended in myth. The experienced unmanageability of the one world gives way to the promised manageability of the two worlds. The reality gives way to the myth, but the grotesqueness abides.

One central difference between Weber's and the current technical conception of objectivity is that Weber recognized that the technical sphere would have to be brought into some sort of alignment with the value sphere. The modern technical conception of objectivity, however, simply regards the value problem and its relation to the technical as either negligible or dull. It allows it to remain unclarified. The modern technical approach to objectivity also differs from the Weberian in a second way. The former takes it for granted that, somehow, social scientists will do the right thing. It asumes that, in some manner, there will be a mustering of motives sufficient to make social scientists conform with their technical standards and rules.

Commonly, the source of these motives is not explored. Sometimes, however, it is today held that the mutual inspection and the checks and balances of modern *professionalization* will suffice to keep social scientists honest. In short, it is assumed that the machinery of professionalism will make the machinery of science work.

This expectation underestimates the ease with which professionalism is corruptible as well as the power of the corrupting forces. Perhaps the most important example of this in the present generation was the work of the Warren Commission appointed by President Lyndon Johnson to investigate the assassination of President John Kennedy. Whatever one's conclusion concerning the substantive issues, namely, whether Lee Harvey Oswald was the assassin, and whether or not he alone or in conspiracy with others murdered President Kennedy, one miserable conclusion seems unavoidable: that there was scarcely a civic profession—the military, the medical, the police, the legal, the juridical—that was not involved in suppressing or distorting the truth, and which did not bow obsequiously to power. And I am far from sure that this was always motivated by a concern for the national welfare. The more that the respectable professions are transformed from independent vocations into bureaucratic and federally sponsored dependencies the more corruptible they will be in the future. Those who think that professional associations and universities will immunize the professions from the pressures and temptations of power have simply not understood the revelations about the CIA penetration into these very associations and universities. For these show that they were willing and eager parties to their own corruption in the name of a well-financed patriotic devotion.

For his part, however, Weber never assumed that the technical machinery of science would be self-winding and self-maintaining. For Weber, the maintenance of objectivity at least required a persisting moral effort to prevent one's personal values from intruding into purely technical decisions. The machinery was really never thought of as operating successfully apart from men's characters. Weber premises that, even in the purely technical stages of later research, work will be subject to an ongoing superintendence by the social scientist's moral commitment to "truth." Since the continued force of this personal value is conceived to be compatible with the maintenance of technical standards, its significance is left unexplicated. It is only implicitly, therefore, that Weber indicates that the objectivity of research depends continuingly and not only in the early problem-formulating stages, upon something more than the technical machinery of research.

The question arises, however, as to the meaning of this extratechnical, "transcendental" commitment to the truth. Does it entail anything more than a commitment to the segregation of facts and values? Either it has some meaning beyond this or it does not. If it does not, then we are still left wondering how and why social scientists may be relied upon to adhere to this very segregation of facts and values: What endows it with binding force? If it does, and if the "truth" that it demands is something more than the mere application of technical standards alone, then it must entail something more than a belief in reliability or validity. If "truth" is not merely a summarizing redundancy for these terms it must be embedded with some conception that embodies or resonates value commitments that call for something more than pure truth alone.

The pursuit of "truth for its own sake" is always a tacit quest for something more than truth, for other values that may have been obscured, denied, and perhaps even forbidden, and some of which are expressed in the quest for "objectivity." Objectivity expresses a lingering attachment to something more than the purely technical goods of science alone and for more than the valid-reliable bits of information it may produce. In this sense, "truth for its own sake" is a crypto-ethic, a concealment of certain other substantive values through a strategy that, leaving them entirely in the open, diverts attention from them to another dramatically accentuated valuable: truth. The old Druidic sacred place is not destroyed; it is merely housed in an imposing new cathedral. In affirming that he only seeks the truth for its own sake, the scientist is therefore not so much lying as pledging allegiance to the flag of truth, while saying nothing about the country for which it stands.

What are the other values that lie obscured in the long shadows cast by the light of pure truth? In Western culture, these often enough have been freedom—the truth will set you free—and power—to know, in order to control. Underlying the conception of truth as objectivity there is, however, still another value, a faint but enduring image of the possibility of wholeness. One obvious implication of objectivity has commonly been to tell the "whole" story. The longing here is to fit the partial and broken fragments together; to provide a picture that transcends the nagging sense of incompleteness; to overcome the multiplicity of shifting perspectives. Underlying the quest for objectivity, then, is the hope of dissolving the differences that divide and the distances that separate men by uniting them in a single, peace-bringing vision of the world.

In such a conception of objectivity there is, I suspect, the undertow of an illicit yearning that links science to religion. Perhaps this conclusion is an illusion. Worse still, perhaps it is "sentimental." Yet it will not seem so fanciful if it is remembered that the modern conception of an objective social science was born with early nineteenth century Positivism. This set itself the task of creating both an objective social science and a new religion of humanity, each informing the other and aimed at reuniting society. The objectivity of the new sociology was, from its very beginnings, not an end in itself; it was clearly aimed at the enhancement of human unity and it then had the most intimate connection with an openly religious impulse.

The conception of objectivity has commonly projected an image of the scientist as linked to a higher realm, as possessed of a godlike penetration into things, as serenely above human frailties and distorting passions, or as possessed of a priest-like impartiality. The realm of objectivity is the higher realm of *episteme,* of *wahrheit,* of *raison,* of Truth, which have always been something more than sheer information. In other words, the realm of objectivity is the realm of the *sacred* in social science. But why has the quest for this realm been encrusted under the defensive conception of truth for its own sake?

Essentially the fate of objectivity in sociology is linked with, and its fortunes vary with, the changing hopes for a peace-bringing human unity. Some power-tempted social scientists are simply no longer able to hear this music. Others may withdraw because their hope is so vital that they cannot risk endangering it by an open confrontation. For some, an open admission would be dissonant with their conception of themselves as tough-minded and hardheaded. Still others have a genuine humility and feel that the pursuit of this high value is beyond their powers. There are also some who doubt the very value of peace itself because, oddly enough, they want men to endure and to live, and they suspect that the successful quest for a peace-bringing unity spells death: they ask themselves, after unity and peace, what?

Perhaps what has been most discrediting to the quest for human unity is that, since its classical formulation, its most gifted spokesmen have often had totalitarian proclivities; they came to be viewed as enemies of the "open society," who denied the value and reality of human difference. In short, the plea for human unity has often, and quite justifiably, been inter-preted as a demand for a tension-free society that was overseen by a close superintendence of men from nursery to graveyard, and was blanketed with a remorseless demand for conformity and consensus. What has really been discredited, however, was this chilling version of the dream of human unity, although it remains extremely difficult to extricate the larger hope from the nightmare form that it was given.

Whether objectivity is thought possible comes down then to a question of whether some vision of human unity is believed workable and desirable. It comes down to the question, as C. Wright Mills once said, of whether there is still some vision of a larger "public" whose interests and needs transcend those of its component and contending factions. In this sense, one possible meaning of objectivity in social science is the contribution it might make to a human unity of mankind. But to make such a contribution the social sciences cannot and should not be impartial toward human suffering; they must not make their peace with any form of human unity that complacently accommodates itself to or imposes suffering.

At the same time, however, an empty-headed partisanship unable to transcend the immediacies of narrowly conceived political commitment is simply just one more form of market research. A blind or unexamined alliance between sociologists and the upper bureaucracy of the welfare state can only produce the market research of liberalism. It rests upon the tacit, mistaken, but common, liberal assumption that the policies of this bureaucracy equitably embody the diverse interests of the larger public, rather than seeing that the bureaucracy is one other interested and power-ful contending faction, and is more closely allied with some of the con-tenders rather than equally distant from all. It is to values, not to factions, that sociologists must give their most basic commitment.

3   Interpretation of Data

The interpretation of data involves, first, accurate perception of the data, and, second, sound analysis of the data preparatory to drawing conclusions. Both of these processes are fraught with pitfalls for the unwary.

People don't always see what they think they see. Even experienced observers, who are presumed to be expert in observing a particular class of data, may make mistakes.

THIS IS HOW THEY THOUGHT IT WAS

HOUSTON, Tex. (AP)—Police searched today for an elusive sniper who laid down an intermittent barrage of gunfire around an oyster shell crushing plant on the Houston ship channel.

"Whoever it is, he seems to get the urge to shoot about every 30 or 40 minutes," nightwatchman Leroy Jones reported near dawn today.

Policemen estimated 75 to 100 bullets had been fired since the shooting began about 8:30 p.m. Wednesday.

One slug clipped the right boot heel of Deputy Sheriff John Brite but he was not wounded. All the others went wild, many of them ricocheting off a big steel tank used to store cement at the Mayo Shell Co. plant.

Up to 75 city, county and state officers, including a Texas ranger with an armored car, joined in the hunt for the gunman.

There was concern for a time that a stray shot might set fire to one of the tanks in the area containing highly volatile fuel.

"It seems like one time he shoots from one direction and the next time another," said Jones, who was alone on duty at the Shell plant. "You can't tell if its one man moving around or more."

Most of the bullets apparently went too high and no windows were broken, the watchman said.

"The men we have out there seem to think the gun makes a little more noise than a .22 rifle but less than a carbine," related Frank Wingo, a sheriff's dispatcher.

Officers searched atop fuel tanks and in several buildings on both sides of the ship channel east of downtown Houston without finding a trace of the sniper.

AND THIS IS HOW IT REALLY WAS . . .

HOUSTON, Tex. (AP)—Sheriff's officers said today that shorted electrical wiring apparently created a false impression that shots were being fired around an oyster shell crushing plant on the Houston Ship Channel.

They had searched through the night for a phantom sniper blamed for firing an estimated 75 to 100 bullets in intermittent bursts.

"Our men on the scene radioed that the loud popping noises—they sound just like a .22 rifle—were coming from inside a big hopper used to load cement," deputy sheriff Steve Aaron said near dawn.

He said wiring inside the machinery carried 440 volts of electricity and sparks leaping across the shorted area presumably caused the sounds.

Up to 75 city, county and state officers began a search after night watchman Leroy Jones reported gunfire was peppering around the Mayo Shell Co. plant. It is beside the ship channel in an area east from downtown Houston.

Jones and sheriff's dispatcher Frank Wingo both told newsmen that shots were fired at intervals of 30 to 40 minutes.

Wingo said deputy sheriff John Brite even believed that a bullet struck his right boot heel but all the other supposed shots went wild.

It was not until the shell company's yard foreman, Ed Selke, arrived about 6 a.m. that the apparent source of the crackling sounds was suspected.

"A conveyor recently has been installed on the shell hopper," Selke said. "A wire must have shorted inside a conduit. I'm sure that's what it was but we're having an electrician check it out."

—Reported in many newspapers about May 23, 1968.

Not all examples of inaccurate perception are so amusing. During the 1967 riots in Detroit and elsewhere, there were numerous reports of sniper fire. Later it was learned there had been very little genuine sniper firing; much of the time when police and troops heard what they believed to be sniper fire, they were actually listening to one another. But a number of people were killed by police and troops "returning" the fire. Thus an inaccurate perception can have grave consequences.

After "What are the data?" has been answered, next is, "What do the data mean?" But data mean nothing until analyzed and interpreted. Among the most common types of social-problem data are statistical associations—observed phenomena appearing significantly more often, or significantly less often, than would normally be expected. In the table quoted below, if only the right column (accident repeater) were presented, could we know whether there is any association? Do you believe the data warrant the conclusion that bad driving is associated with irresponsible behavior in general?

DRIVING RISKS USUALLY ANTISOCIAL, ALCOHOLIC

Thomas A. Puschock

Managing Editor
Health Bulletin

Earlier this year, a man who had been fired from his job in a restaurant drove his car head-on into a bus and killed 20 people, including himself. That is just one example of how emotional instability can cause highway accidents. There are many, many others, according to a Michigan study by psychiatrists and police. The survey revealed that 50 percent of 72 drivers who were killers on the highway had serious drinking problems, and 30 percent had histories of severe emotional depression. And in still another study in the *American Journal of Psychiatry,* it was found that those drivers exhibiting high accident frequency tended to have a history of poor adjustment to life in general, alcoholism, and a high rate of contact with various social agencies.

On the basis of that study, the author reached the conclusion: "Truly it may be said that a man drives as he lives. If his personal life is marked by caution, tolerance, foresight and consideration for others, then he will drive in the same manner." The survey also indicated that a person without those characteristics will drive in an aggressive manner "and over a long period of time he will have a much higher accident rate than his more stable companion."

Statistics gathered by the Ontario Department of Highways indicating the social records of 96 accident repeaters and 100 accident-free drivers are given in Table 1.

From *Health Bulletin,* May 4, 1968, (Emmaus, Pa.) Thomas A. Puschock, Managing Editor. Reprinted by permission.

TABLE 1.   Social Records of Accident Repeaters and Accident-Free Drivers

	Accident-Free	Accident Repeater
Trouble with credit bureau	6%	34.3%
Contact with social service agencies	1%	17.7%
Contact with public health and V.D. clinic	0%	14.4%
Adult court (excluding traffic charges)	1%	34.3%
Juvenile court	1%	16.6%

The *American Journal of Psychiatry* also noted that personality traits and attitudes of high accident drivers are different from the rest of the population. Once again test scores proved that psychological-sociological testing could separate good drivers from bad ones. Unfortunately, personality tests are not widely used in granting driving licenses. If they were, countless thousands of lives could probably be saved by keeping emotionally unfit drivers from behind the wheel.

This brief exercise in interpreting data introduces a more exacting example. Two sociologists analyzed and interpreted data collected by Dr. Alfred Kinsey and associates, and reached conclusions opposite to Dr. Kinsey's. They seek to show that his data do not properly support his conclusions. What do you think? In order to make an informed opinion, would it be necessary to consult Dr. Kinsey's presentation to see how he arrived at his conclusions?

PREMARITAL EXPERIENCE AND THE WIFE'S SEXUAL ADJUSTMENT

Robert L. Hamblin   Robert O. Blood, Jr.
Professor of Sociology   *Professor of Sociology*
Washington University   *Pendle Hill*

The publishers of *Sexual Behavior in the Human Female* in an advertisement appearing in the November 1953 issue of the *American Journal of Sociology* announced that this book would be referred to "again

From *Social Problems,* 4(2), pp. 122–130. Reprinted by permission of the authors and The Society for the Study of Social Problems.

and again for factual information on such problems as . . . [the] relation of premarital sexual experience to the women's sexual adjustment in marriage." The chief pertinent finding reported in the 1953 volume is that there is "a marked, positive correlation between experience in orgasm obtained from premarital coitus and the capacity to reach orgasm after marriage." (4, p. 328) Otherwise stated, this finding means that a woman's orgasmic capacity in coitus before marriage is a good predictor of her orgasmic capacity in coitus after marriage. It would be surprising if this correlation were not found. (Ability to have orgasm in coitus ought to correlate highly with ability to have orgasm in coitus!)

Omitted from the Kinsey volume, however, is an analysis of the relationship of premarital coital experience per se and the sexual adjustment of the female in marriage. It seems appropriate that this relationship should be explored with the Kinsey data since prior research on this socially important question has yielded contradictory results. (2, 3, 5, 8)

Fortunately there are relevant data in the Kinsey volume (as the advertisement suggests) which can clarify the relationship between premarital coital experience and sexual adjustment of the female in marriage. Harriet Mowrer has published the results of an analysis of some of these data. (6) She used indices other than orgasm rates as measures of sexual adjustment. Our purpose is to complement her analysis of the relevant Kinsey data by using orgasm rate as a measure of sexual adjustment.

ANALYSIS

For a *preliminary* answer to this problem, a record of the marital orgasm rates of women with and without experience in premarital coitus is needed. Such materials are available in Kinsey's Table 109 (4, p. 406), which is entitled "Premarital Coital Experience vs. Percentage of Marital Coitus Leading to Orgasm." Because the Kinsey table separates those with and without premarital orgasm from various sources, it is necessary to combine together all those who had, and all those who did not have, premarital coital experience. The results of this combination are shown in Table 1.

The data indicate that there is, in general, a small association between experience in premarital coitus and marital orgasm rate. During the first year of marriage the association is reliable at the .01 level of confidence. During the fifth year of marriage, however, the association is reduced so as to be unreliable (*P* is approximately .14). Our first conclusion, then, is that experience per se in premarital coitus is associated with the female's sexual responsiveness during the first year of marriage. However, further analysis is indicated before it can be determined whether or not this observed association is causal in nature.

Why should females who engage in premarital coitus have a higher

TABLE 1.   First- and Fifth-Year Marital Orgasm Rates of Women With and Without Premarital Coital Experience

% of Marital Coitus with Orgasm	First Year of Marriage [a]		Fifth Year of Marriage [b]	
	No Pre-marital Coitus	With Pre-marital Coitus	No Pre-marital Coitus	With Pre-marital Coitus
None	27%	23%	17%	14%
1–29%	11	11	12	15
30–59	12.5	13	16	14
60–89	12.5	12	15	15
90–100	37	41	40	42
Total	100%	100%	100%	100%
Number of cases	1129	1082	784	646

Source: Adapted from Table 109 (4, p. 406).
[a] First Year of Marriage: Marshall's $C = 2.34$; P is less than .01.
[b] Fifth Year of Marriage: Marshall's $C = 1.08$; P is approx. .14 (7).

It should be noted that the published Kinsey data seldom make possible rigorous comparison between homogeneous groups of subjects. For instance, we infer that the discrepancy between orgasm rates of those with and without experience in premarital coitus is reduced between the first and the fifth year of marriage. However, the former group is larger because many subjects were interviewed prior to the fifth year of marriage. Throughout this paper we have selected groups which are as nearly comparable as possible and hope that our analysis will stimulate the future publication of controlled analyses by Kinsey and his associates. Presumably the comparisons we have made are the best available basis for predicting the findings of such controlled analyses.

orgasm rate during the first year of marriage? If a reliable answer can be found for this question, we can infer whether or not the observed relationship is causal.

What theories are available which would, if substantiated, account for the observed association between premarital coital experience and the sexual adjustment of females in marriage? Kinsey gives two suggestions and we add an obvious third. The theories themselves will be explained below as each is tested. However, since it is important to control the variables not being tested in a given test, it is appropriate to indicate in advance the crucial variables in each of these theories. These are: (1) the age at which the female begins her coital experience, (2) the amount of coital experience she has, and (3) the strength of her inhibitions about engaging in premarital coitus.

AGE AND SEXUAL RESPONSIVENESS

The first theory is taken from the Kinsey volume. If supported, this theory would account for the observed association and establish causality:

At least theoretically, premarital socio-sexual experience . . . in coitus should contribute to this development of emotional capacities. In this as in other areas, learning at an early age may be more effective than learning at any later age after marriage. (4, p. 328) When there are long years of abstinence and restraint, and an avoidance of physical contacts and emotional responses before marriage, acquired inhibitions may do such damage to the capacity to respond that it may take some years to get rid of them after marriage, if indeed they are ever dissipated. (4, p. 330)

Here it is hypothesized that *the sooner after puberty a female begins her coital experiences the more she will respond since it will be easier to overcome inhibitions.**

In order to test this hypothesis it would be useful to compare the marital orgasm rates of two groups of women which have the following characteristics: (*a*) They ought to have the same amount of coital experience at the time of the test to control the experience variable. (*b*) The proportions of each group who engaged in premarital coitus ought to be the same. This would control the premarital inhibitions variable. (*c*) The two groups ought to differ with respect to the test variable—the average age at which coitus was first experienced.

Kinsey's data for groups of women who marry early or late may be used for this purpose. Kinsey's Table 79 (4, p. 337) shows that women married between the ages of sixteen and twenty (the "early" group) and those married between twenty-one and twenty-five (the "later" group) have similar amounts of premarital coital experience. By interpolation it is possible to estimate that the median "early" bride married at age nineteen whereas the median "later" bride married at twenty-three. At these two ages, the interpolated proportions who have ever engaged in premarital coitus are almost identical (39 percent and 40 percent respectively). Moreover, the accumulative incidences of the premarital coital experience at varying ages indicate that the later-marrying women consistently tend to lag behind the early-marrying women in the age at which their first premarital coitus occurs. This implies that the two groups are essentially comparable in terms both of the proportion who have ever had premarital coitus and in the length of time they had engaged in coitus before marriage. Therefore, the later-marrying group on the average experienced their first coitus (whether premarital or marital) several years later than the early marrying group.

If sexual inhibitions allowed to go undisturbed for several years longer are harder to overcome, we would expect the later-marrying group to have a less satisfactory sexual adjustment after marriage than those who marry early. The figures from Table 2—which are reproduced directly from

* For an independent examination of this hypothesis against the same data see (1).

TABLE 2.   First-Year Marital Orgasm Rates by Age at First Marriage

% of Marital Coitus with Orgasm	Age at First Marriage	
	Under 21	21–25
None	34%	22%
1–29%	9	11
30–59	10	13
60–89	12	13
90–100	35	41
Total	100%	100%
Number of cases	575	1118

Source: Table 107 (4, p. 405).
Marshall's $C = 4.14$; P less than .001.

Kinsey's Table 107 (4, p. 405), show that the reverse is true, that is that during the first year of marriage it is the later-marrying women who experience the higher orgasm rate.

We may tentatively conclude from the reversal in these data that the first theory about a causal relation between premarital coital experience and marital orgasm rate has been disproved. With proper controls, a reversal is the best possible evidence that a hypothesis is untrue. In this case, however, the adequacy of the controls is limited. This is apparent from asking, "Why should orgasm rates be negatively associated with the age at first experience?" An obvious answer is that another factor, maturation, could be responsible for the reversal since it was uncontrolled. Hence, the early conclusion is questionable. But this much is certain, if maturation is the factor responsible, early experience is not appreciably effective in overcoming inhibitions since its presumed effects are masked so completely by another variable. This test of the theory, then, is less than adequate for giving a reliable explanation for the original observation that premarital coital experience and marital orgasm rates are associated during the first year of marriage.

PREVIOUS EXPERIENCE AND SEXUAL RESPONSIVENESS

Perhaps *response to orgasm depends upon the development of coital skills which the female learns through experience.* Presumably these skills increase with the amount of experience, so that the observed association between female orgasm rate during the first year of marriage and premarital coital experience may result from greater experience. If verified, this theory would establish causality.

A comparison of the same early- and later-marrying females when age is held constant (both groups averaging twenty-four years of age) allows us to test this theory. At age twenty-four, the early-marrying group averages four years' more coital experience than the later-marrying groups. Hence, the groups differ with respect to the test variable—amount of experience. As indicated above, the two groups are comparable in terms of the number experiencing premarital coitus and, presumably, premarital inhibitions. Also, since the averages and ranges of the ages of the two groups are the same, maturation is controlled. The other variable, age of first experience, is uncontrolled, however. It also becomes a test variable whose predicted effects are in the same direction as those of the other test variable—amount of experience. If there is no difference between the two groups with respect to marital orgasm rates, both theories may be rejected. If there is the predicted difference between the two groups with respect to marital orgasm rates, then it is impossible to tell which of the two variables is responsible. But if the predicted relationship does obtain, we shall have an indication that the observed association between premarital coital experience and orgasm rates during the first year of marriage is causal in nature.

If the amount-of-experience and/or the early-experience theories are true, then, the early-marrying group should have a higher orgasm rate. The data in Table 3 indicate, however, that the later-marrying group has

TABLE 3. Marital Orgasm Rates at Median Age 24 for Early and Later Marrying Women

% of Marital Coitus with Orgasm	Early Marrying Group Married under 21 (Md. 19) (Fifth Year of Marriage)	Later Marrying Group Married 21–25 (Md. 23) (First Year of Marriage)
None	21%	22%
1–29%	14	11
30–59	13	13
60–89	16	13
90–100	36	41
Total	100%	100%
Number of cases	333	1118

Source: Table 107 (4, p. 405).
Marshall's $C = .82$; P approximately .20.

a slightly higher orgasm rate. The difference is unreliable, however. (P is approximately .20.) The proper inference is that there is no difference between the two groups with respect to orgasm rates. Hence, both theories considered thus far may be rejected with some confidence. An explanation of the observed association must be found in another theory.

INHIBITIONS AND SEXUAL RESPONSIVENESS

Kinsey provides the third theory that would account for the difference in marital orgasm rates of females who did and did not engage in coitus before marriage. It involves the generalization of inhibitions.

As children grow . . . it is customary in our culture to teach them that they must no longer make physical contacts, and must inhibit their emotional responses to persons outside of the immediate family. Many persons believe that this restraint should be maintained until the time of marriage. Then, after marriage, the husband and wife are supposed to break down all of their inhibitions and make physical and emotional adjustments which will contribute to the solidarity of the marital relationship. Unfortunately, there is no magic in a marriage ceremony which can accomplish this. The record indicates that a very high proportion of the females . . . find it difficult after marriage to redevelop the sort of freedom with which they made contacts as children, and to learn again how to respond without inhibition to physical and emotional contacts with other persons. (4, p. 328)

Interpreted loosely, the above quotation may be condensed into the following theory: *moral scruples which inhibit females from engaging in premarital coitus tend to become generalized, thereby interfering with orgasmic response in marital coitus.* In order to test this theory directly, it is necessary to find marital orgasm data for two groups of women, one of which was more inhibited about premarital coitus than the other.

Since premarital coitus is tabooed in Judeo-Christian teachings, devoutly religious women ought to be more inhibited about engaging in premarital coitus than those who are less devout. In the Kinsey volume, relevant data are available for married samples of religiously active and inactive Protestant and Catholic females and moderately active and inactive Jewish females. Of the three possible combinations, Protestant and Catholic samples were chosen. The available data support the inference that devout Protestant and Catholic women are more inhibited about premarital coitus than the respective inactive groups. (See Table 4.)

The data in Table 4 show that devout Protestant and Catholic women are somewhat more inhibited before marriage, in the sense that (*a*) they are more apt to refrain from premarital intercourse, (*b*) they are more apt to fail to achieve orgasm if they do engage in premarital coitus, and (*c*) they are more apt to regret coital experience if they have it. Hence, it seems safe to conclude that the two groups differ with respect to the test variable—premarital inhibitions.

Are these two sets of groups matched with respect to other relevant variables? They are not controlled with respect to age at first experience

TABLE 4. Experiences of Devout and Inactive Protestant and Catholic Women in Premarital Coitus

| | Protestants | | Catholics | |
	Devout	Inactive	Devout	Inactive
Female experience in pre-marital coitus up to age 20				
Premarital coitus	14%	25%	12%	41%
No premarital coitus	86	75	88	59
Total	100%	100%	100%	100%
Number of cases	860	887	261	122
Female experience in orgasm from premarital coitus up to age 20				
Coitus with orgasm	43%	48%	25%	63%
Coitus without orgasm	57	52	75	37
Total	100%	100%	100%	100%
Number of cases	121	222	31	50
Female expression of regret regarding experience in pre-marital coitus, all ages				
Regret	38%	20%	50%	16%
No regret	62	80	50	84
Total	100%	100%	100%	100%
Number of cases	295	490	86	90

Sources: Adapted from Table 89 (4, p. 342) and Table 92 (4, p. 345). The percentage of women experiencing orgasm from premarital coitus is derived by dividing the published percentage of the total sample who had experienced orgasm from this source by the percentage of the total sample who had engaged in premarital intercourse.

and amount of experience. However, since these variables have been shown to be unrelated to orgasm rates, controlling them is unnecessary. Maturation of the two sets of groups is an unknown factor, but we have no reason to believe that such groups would differ with respect to maturation. Our above analysis indicates the proportion of females engaging in premarital experience is not related to age at marriage (at least for those who marry before twenty-five). Of course each set is controlled with respect to religious affiliation.

If sexual inhibitions are actually generalized from premarital to marital coitus, the orgasm rate of the "devout" women would be lower than the orgasm rates of the "inactives" after marriage. The data in Table 5 give mixed results, however. There is an unreliable difference between the orgasm rates of the devout and inactive Protestant females. (P approximates .40) The difference between the orgasm rates of the devout and inactive Catholics is reliable (P is less than .01) and in the predicted direction.

TABLE 5.   First-Year Marital Orgasm Rates of Devout and Inactive Protestants and Catholics

% of Marital Coitus with Orgasm	Protestants		Catholics	
	Devout	Inactive	Devout	Inactive
None	27%	26%	32%	22%
1–29%	10	12	18	7
30–59	13	10	13	11
60–89	10	13	5	14
90–100	40	39	32	46
Total	100%	100%	100%	100%
Number of cases	430	564	112	88

Source: Table 106 (4, p. 404).
Devout vs. Inactive Protestants: Marshall's $C = .23$; P greater than .40.
Devout vs. Inactive Catholics: Marshall's $C = 2.89$; P less than .005.

What do these differential results mean? In our judgment, they may mean two things. (*a*) Protestant inhibitions may differ in kind from Catholic inhibitions. In Catholic doctrine, sexual pleasure is not a legitimate end in itself. Rather, such pleasure is justified only if there is a possibility of conception. Hence, the Catholic position on contraceptive procedures, homosexuality, masturbation, and celibacy. It is possible that the more devout Catholic females tend to acquire scruples against sex per se. On the contrary, devout Protestant females apparently develop scruples against premarital coitus per se but feel that sexual pleasure in marriage is not only legitimate but desirable. Hence, the observed discrepancy in Table 5.

(*b*) The Catholic Church discourages the use of contraceptive procedures in general and forbids the use of contraceptive devices in particular. Protestant churches are more permissive in this respect. This taboo against the use of contraceptive devices may produce a conflict for many devout Catholic females which her Protestant counterpart may escape. If she adopts reliable contraceptive practices, she is likely to suffer guilt feelings. If she refrains from using contraceptives, she is likely to be anxious about excessively frequent pregnancies. The permissible Catholic method (rhythm) was found in the Indianapolis study to be less than one-tenth as effective as the diaphragm and jelly method. (9) Insofar as anxiety or guilt is present, it would presumably distract most individuals during coitus and decrease their orgasm rates. Hence, the differential beliefs of the devout Protestant and Catholic females might also account for the pattern observed in Table 5.

If either of the above explanations is valid (and both are consistent with the data in Table 5), then the third theory which would account for the association between premarital coitus and marital orgasm rates is likewise unsupported. Scruples about engaging in premarital coitus per se evidently do not generalize to marital coitus and, hence, do not depress the female's marital orgasm capacity.

Also, if either of the above explanations is valid, the association between premarital coital experience per se and marital orgasm rates would be predicted. Either could be a spurious factor which would account for the relationship. It is probable that more females who refrain from premarital coitus have generalized scruples against all sexual pleasure than is the case with those who engage in premarital coitus. It is also likely that more females who believe the use of reliable contraceptives is morally wrong refrain from premarital coitus than do females who believe the use of reliable contraceptives is permissible. It is impossible at present to test directly either of these theories since the data are unavailable.

SUMMARY AND CONCLUSION

The purpose of this paper has been to test hypotheses about the relationship of premarital coital experience per se and the wife's sexual adjustment as measured by marital orgasm rates. Data from the Kinsey report were recombined and interpreted for this analysis.

A reliable association was found between premarital coital experience and wives' orgasm rates during the first year of marriage. Three hypotheses, any one of which would give direct causal significance to this association, were then tested with Kinsey data. These are:

(a) The earlier after puberty a female begins her coital experience, the more she will respond (since it will be easier to overcome inhibitions).

(b) Response to orgasm depends upon the development of coital skills which the female learns through experience.

(c) Moral scruples which inhibit the female from engaging in premarital coitus tend to become generalized and, thereby, to interfere with orgasmic response in marital coitus.

None of these hypotheses found empirical support. Two spurious factors (generalized scruples against all sexual pleasure and internalized taboos against the use of reliable contraceptives) are consistent with and presumably account for the observed relationships. In combination, the results cast doubt on the validity of the hypothesis that premarital coital experience per se facilitates the wife's sexual adjustment as measured by orgasm rates. It should also be pointed out that the notion that premarital coital experience per se hinders the wife's sexual adjustment is also doubtful if orgasm rates are used as the measure. Rather, experience or inexperience in premarital intercourse seems to bear no consistent causal relationship to the wife's sexual adjustment.

Further research is needed. The three explanatory hypotheses ought to be retested in controlled *ex post facto* experiments. The relationship of generalized moral scruples to marital orgasm rates ought to be investigated more directly. The relationship of internalized taboos against the use of reliable contraceptives to marital orgasm rates should also be investigated directly. It is hoped that this paper will constitute a stimulus to such further investigations of these important questions.

REFERENCES

1. Clausen, John A., "Biological Bias and Methodological Limitations in the Kinsey Studies" in Jerome Himelhoch and Sylvia Fleis Fava, eds., *Sexual Behavior in American Society* (New York: W. W. Norton, 1955), p. 48.
2. Davis, Katherine B., *Factors in the Sex Life of Twenty-two Hundred Women* (New York: Harper, 1929), p. 59.
3. Hamilton, G. V., *A Research in Marriage* (New York: Boni, 1929), p. 388.
4. Kinsey, Alfred C., Wardwell B. Pomeroy, Clyde E. Martin, and Paul H. Gebhard, *Sexual Behavior in the Human Female* (Philadelphia: W. B. Saunders, 1953).
5. Landis, C., *et al.*, *Sex in Development* (New York: Paul B. Hoeber, 1940), pp. 97, 315.
6. Mowrer, Harriet R., "Sex and Marital Adjustment," in Jerome Himelhoch and Sylvia Fleis Fava, eds., *Sexual Behavior in American Society* (New York: W. W. Norton, 1955), pp. 147–149.
7. Smith, Keith, "Distribution-free Statistical Methods and the Concept of Power Efficiency," in Leon Festinger and Daniel Katz, *Research Methods in the Behavioral Sciences* (New York: Dryden, 1955), pp. 553–555.
8. Terman, Lewis M., *Psychological Factors in Marital Happiness* (New York: McGraw-Hill, 1938), pp. 383, 387.
9. Westoff, Charles F., Lee F. Herrera, and P. K. Whelpton, *The Use Effectiveness, and Acceptability of Methods of Fertility Control* (New York: Milbank Memorial Fund, 1953), pp. 900, 927.

One frequently faces the decision of whether a book is of sufficient scholarly value to buy or read. In making such decisions, the discriminating reader will note the scholarly stature and professional connections of the author, and whether the advertisement or book jacket description is written in a manner which suggests a work of responsible, authoritative scholarship. After reading the following advertisement, what conclusions would you reach?

PSYCHOLOGICAL REVOLUTION!

Nathaniel Branden has written a book that will make history—a book that will change the future of the science of psychology. More important, it can change lives, and may change yours. It is called *The Psychology of Self-Esteem*.

Once in a generation a book appears that blazes new intellectual trails and overturns the stale, ineffectual bromides in which we are accustomed to think. Such a book is Nathaniel Branden's *The Psychology of Self-Esteem*.

For decades, psychologists have fought over the merits of two competing schools of psychology: the rat-and-earthworm school of behaviorism, which claims that man is a robot controlled by his environment—and the Id-and-Oedipus school of Freudian psychoanalysis, which claims that he is the passive plaything of his instincts and heredity.

To look at the world around us—at the profound agony of so many people beset by anxiety, self-doubts and depression—is to know that *both schools have failed*. Neither has provided man with the self-understanding he so desperately needs. Neither has provided an intelligible and valid account of human nature, or explained what motivates man or generates his emotional responses.

Now, in *The Psychology of Self-Esteem*, there *is* an alternative—a fundamental new approach to the understanding of man's psychological nature. Challenging the profoundly anti-intellectual bias of contemporary psychology, this book presents a view of man based on his distinctive nature as a *rational being*. Its author sees man as a being capable of achieving an integrated harmony between his mind and emotions, and of attaining a rational, productive, fulfilling existence, free of guilt and fear—a being eagerly responsive to the challenges of life.

Its originator, Nathaniel Branden, has long been recognized as one of the most original and controversial thinkers of our time. Thousands have attended his lectures on psychology and philosophy; millions have seen him on television; hundreds have had the benefit of his personal counselling, or received training in his theories and therapeutic methods under the auspices of the newly-formed Institute of Biocentric Psychology, which he heads.

Advertisement by the Nash Publishing Corp., Los Angeles, Calif., in *The New York Times Book Review*, October 19, 1969. Reprinted by permission.

The central theme of Nathaniel Branden's book is the role of self-esteem in man's life: the need of self-esteem, the nature of that need, the conditions of its fulfillment, the consequences of its frustration—and the crucial impact of a man's self-esteem (or lack of it) on his values and goals.

The Psychology of Self-Esteem explores the cause-and-effect relationship between the degree of a man's rationality and the degree of his self-esteem. It analyzes the relationship between self-esteem and mental health. It shows the relationship between the nature and degree of a man's self-esteem and his behavior in the spheres of work, love and human relationships. And it presents the radical and fascinating new view of man on which these theories rest.

Only by studying man as a biological entity, holds Nathaniel Branden —only by recognizing that man's nature and needs as a living organism are the source both of his unique achievements and his potential problems— only by understanding the meaning and implications of the fact that man is the organism uniquely characterized by the power of conceptual thought and self-awareness—can the science of psychology achieve an accurate portrait of man.

It is such a portrait that is provided in *The Psychology of Self-Esteem*. Comprehensive in scope, this major psychological work explores and illuminates every basic aspect of man's existence. Illustrating theory by means of examples and case histories, Nathaniel Branden discusses such issues as:

· The nature of psychological freedom and self-responsibility
· The relationship of reason and emotion
· The psychological destructiveness of religion and mysticism
· Romantic love and sexual choice
· The psychological importance of productive work
· The meaning of mental health and illness
· The problem of emotional repression
· The nature of man's mind as contrasted with the consciousness of lower animals
· The effect of a man's thinking processes on his self-esteem or lack of it
· The attempt to fake self-esteem . . . and the disastrous consequences.

Professional psychologist and laymen alike will recognize the overwhelming relevance and importance of this masterful and revolutionary work. Some will attack it, misrepresent it, attempt to dismiss it. But it cannot be ignored. For the science of psychology, it is a new beginning.

Here are only a few of the many subjects discussed in *The Psychology of Self-Esteem:*

Psychology as a science—Critique of the robot view of man—What accounts for differences in character and personality?—Why are rats in mazes not the proper source of knowledge about man?—The nature and source of emotions—The causes of mental illness—The definition of mental health—Thinking as a volitional act—Are we products of our environment?—Critique of Freud—The forming of values—The need of self-esteem—The achievement of self-esteem—The betrayal of self-esteem—Pseudo self-esteem—The cause of psychological dependence—The nature of neurotic anxiety and depression—Psychological maturity—The nature of romantic-sexual love—The roots of romantic affinity—The ethics of Objectivism—Psychotherapy.

4 Vested Interest and Pressure Groups

Perhaps nothing is more ubiquitous in modern society than the phenomenon of interest and pressure groups. Close to the center of American society, however, stand the notions of private property, profits, and business enterprise. If pressure group activity is not more typical of business activity than of other organizations, it is at least larger and better organized.

Liberal scholars in the United States, along with some members of government and much of the labor movement, have long feared the effects of separation of ownership and control that have accompanied the development of a managerial elite in modern corporations. In 1932, separation of ownership from control was the thesis of *The Modern Corporation and Private Property*. A study conducted in 1963 which traced developments in this area from 1929 to 1963 shows that management control has increased over the past thirty-five years. There is no evidence, however, that managers perceive their interests to differ from those of their stockholders.

OWNERSHIP AND CONTROL

Robert J. Larner

Assistant Professor of Economics
Brandeis University

"Ownership of wealth without appreciable control and control of wealth without appreciable ownership appear to be the logical outcome of corporate development." This was a central proposition of the Berle and Means classic, *The Modern Corporation and Private Property,* published in 1932 and based on data from 1929. In the September 1966 *American Economic Review,* Robert J. Larner, a graduate student at the University of Wisconsin, brings Berle and Means up to date by analyzing the relation

"Ownership and Control in the 200 Largest Non-Financial Corporations, 1929 and 1963," *American Economic Review* 66 (September 1966), pp. 777–787. Reprinted by permission.

between ownership and control in the 200 largest nonfinancial corporations in 1963.

Each of these large corporations (the smallest had book assets of $423 million) was classified into one of five categories: (1) privately owned if an individual, family, or other group associates holds 80% or more of its voting stock, (2) majority owned if such a group holds 50 to 80% of the voting stock, (3) minority controlled if such a group holds 10 to 50% of its voting stock, (4) controlled by a legal device, for example a voting trust, (5) management controlled otherwise. Berle and Means required at least 20% ownership for minority control, but this is much too stringent.

There are always difficult cases in such a classification scheme, but they are too few to affect the broad tendency shown in Table 1.

TABLE 1.   Control of U.S. Corporations

Type of Control	1929 Number of Corporations		1963 Number of Corporations	
	Total	Industrials	Total	Industrials
Private	12	8	0	0
Majority	10	6	5	3
Minority	46½	34½	18	18
Legal device	41	14½	8	5
Management	88½	43	169	91
Receivership	2	0	0	0
Total	200	106	200	117

Evidently, the private ownership of giant corporations has disappeared. In 1929, some 45% of the 200 largest nonfinancial corporations were management-controlled, and only a slightly smaller percentage of the industrial corporations (i.e., nonpublic-utility, nontransportation) among them. By 1963, almost 85% of the 200 largest were management-controlled, and 78% of the industrial companies among them.

Larner classified as management controlled in 1963 five companies evidently controlled by a single family. They were IBM (Watson), Inland Steel (Block), Weyerhaeuser (Weyerhaeuser), Federated Department Stores (Lazarus), and J. P. Stevens (Stevens). In each case the dominant family had a strategic and long-standing position in management, and owned only a very small fraction of the voting stock.

The extent of management control has certainly increased in the past 35 years. One important reason is that the absolute size (not the concentration) of the 200 largest corporations has simply become too large to admit substantial ownership interests. In 1929, 27 of the 40 largest firms were classified as management controlled, and the number fell fairly smoothly down to 9½ of the 40 smallest among the 200 giants. In 1963, there was no such relation; the incidence of management control was about the same among the first 40 and the last 40 on the list, and in between.

If these facts are clear, their meaning is not. It is not at all certain that management controlled firms *behave* very differently from those with a substantial ownership interest. From the economic point of view, one might expect the corporate manager to have an interest in the survival and growth of "his" enterprise, even when the profits of the stockholders might better be served by a shift of their capital elsewhere. But no such bias has been demonstrated. What seems to be the case is that managers and stock-holders have a common interest in large, growing, and secure profits, and that this central shared interest is likely to outweigh a divergence of interest at the fringes.

> If corporations have changed over the past thirty-five years, their chief apparent adversaries, labor unions, appear to have changed even more. The selection below indicates that labor, by and large, has joined the establishment.

UNION LABOR:

Less militant, more affluent

Editors of *Time*

In Los Angeles' splendid new Music Center, 1,500 members of the Retail Clerks Union sat in red-plush comfort beneath crystal chandeliers. Before getting down to the business of a union meeting, they heard a concert climaxed by a specialized composition called *The Shopping Center Blues*. They chuckled appreciatively when Local Leader Joe De Silva explained that his hoarseness was caused by "executive flu." De Silva noted that a minority of the Music Center's board had protested that a union meeting was not the sort of "cultural" activity for which the $32.2 million center (including $25,000 contributed by the Retail Clerks) had been created. Said De Silva: "I looked up 'cultural' in the dictionary, and it covers a lot more than just music. If a union isn't part of American culture today, I don't know what is."

De Silva's point was unarguable. Unionism is woven throughout the fabric of present American life, both social and economic. "The labor movement," says Chicago's Sidney Lens, longtime labor leader and writer, "is really a carbon copy of capitalism." It is more than that: it *is* capitalism. Its relations with management remain adverse to a degree; but the action is that of cogwheels moving in opposite directions to operate the whole free-enterprise machine.

The threat of breakdowns in the machine can never be discounted; there is no guarantee that the old wage-price spiral, with excessive labor demands resulting in inflationary prices, will not reappear. But the steel settlement just concluded is a typical example of labor's present condition and its relation with industry. A strike, while the threat was real enough, did not materialize; increasingly, labor gets its results not through strikes but through other pressures, including the psychological. Steel negotiations were relatively relaxed; the big issue was not pay but fringe benefits. Labor has won the wage battles and is increasingly concerned with vacations, pensions, job security. Finally, a reasonably satisfactory settlement came about through the intervention of the President. This dilutes free collective bargaining, but nobody is very indignant because no one doubts that management's and labor's business are in fact the nation's business. Says AFL-CIO President George Meany, without apologies to industry's late "Engine Charlie" Wilson: "What is good for America is good for the AFL-CIO."

Turning that coin, what's bad about organized labor is bad for the U.S. And organized labor today is afflicted by a multitude of problems, some blaring, some subtle, and virtually all springing from failures to keep pace with change. For one thing, the labor movement is middle-aged and increasingly middle class, powerful and sometimes arrogant, but without the lean, hungry and imaginative leaders of the past. For another, unions are faced with a new industrial revolution in automation, which promises to alter the very role and function of human labor.

LEADERSHIP LAG

Since 1957, U.S. employment has risen from 65 million to 75 million —while union membership has actually dropped a bit from the 1957 mark of 18,430,000. Such statistics are slightly deceptive. They do not include members of the growing professional and semiprofessional organizations like the National Education Association; these look like unions, act like unions and often sound more militant than unions, but call themselves "associations" to avoid the union label that their membership considers a bit demeaning.

Many unions have been content to consolidate their gains and have neglected organization drives, failing to go after workers in those areas that are growing fastest, such as the service industries. Others have demonstrated that aggressive (and often expensive) organizing can still win members. Since being kicked out of the AFL-CIO in 1957 for Jimmy Hoffa's happy hooliganism, the Teamsters have actually grown from 1,600,000 to 1,760,000. Hoffa's creed is simple: if it breathes, organize it. The Teamsters include hairdressers in Newark, employees at an animal cemetery in Illinois, stewardesses for the Flying Tiger airline and attendants at the San Diego Zoo.

"Have you looked at the AFL-CIO executive committee?" says Hoffa. "If you cut all the decay out of that committee, there'd be no one left standing up. They're a bunch of tired old men. They couldn't plan nothing." Jimmy may not be the most respectable witness, but he has a point. At 71, George Meany grows more curmudgeonly by the day. The average age of Meany's eight-member executive committee is 66, against 62 for the U.S. Supreme Court.

SPIRITUAL SAG

Union bosses wield personal power far beyond most politicians and businessmen. Huge national headquarters staffs are answerable only to the national leader, and until fairly recently, it was as rare for a major union chief to be voted out of office as it is for a baseball player to thumb an umpire from the ballpark. The effects of the Landrum-Griffin Act of 1959 are changing some of that. Among other things, the law required that unions overhaul their constitutions so as to give rank-and-file members more protection against fraud and coercion in voting on their leadership. Thanks in part to more democratic procedures, six major national union heads have been voted out within the last year. Most notable were the International Union of Electrical Workers' James B. Carey, 54, whose nasty disposition finally caught up with him, and the Steelworkers' David J. McDonald, 62, whose image in the locals was that of the soft-living "labor statesman" negotiating at the 19th hole in management's country clubs. Their successors, Paul Jennings, 47; and I. W. Abel, 57, are men of ability, but not likely to furnish imaginative new leadership.

Organized labor lacks a new generation of prospective leaders; in the vast majority of major unions, the heir apparent to the incumbent is of the same generation. Examples: International Machinists' President Al Hayes, 65, was succeeded by Vice President Roy Siemiller, 60; the Brotherhood of Electrical Workers' Gordon Freeman, 68, is likely to be followed by

Joe Keenan, also 68; waiting in line behind the United Mine Workers' Tony Boyle, 60, is old John L.'s youngest brother, Ray Lewis, 64.

It is a measure of labor's past success that the cause no longer seems to cry out for crusaders. Says Harry Van Arsdale, president of the New York City Central Labor Council: "How far can a young college graduate go in a union? Compare his opportunities there with those at General Motors. We all know that a young man's future in organized labor is limited." For those motivated by idealism, the real excitement is elsewhere, as in civil rights, on which organized labor's attitude is ambiguous. While the national leadership has constantly backed Negro rights, many locals are tightly and nastily exclusive.

Says New York Printers' boss Bert Powers: "Somebody has convinced the membership that a union is like a tollgate and that all it does is collect dues. There isn't the feeling there used to be for the whole labor movement. Our own printers aren't interested in how the cab drivers are being organized. A picket line is an annoyance."

There is agreement from Carroll R. Daugherty, professor of labor economics at Northwestern University and a nationally known labor-management arbitrator: "We've ceased having a labor movement as the term 'movement' used to be known. The people in a movement act with an almost religious fervor. A movement has martyrs, priests, hymns, slogans, symbols. That's not what we have today." The International Ladies' Garment Workers' elderly president Dave Dubinsky reluctantly admits that the old pizazz is missing, but points out that in places where the going gets tough, the "spirit of 1900 comes back to us. In the South and in Puerto Rico, we have good militant strikes, just like old times."

Up to a point, the unions try to observe the old fraternal forms. Members still call one another "brother" and "sister"—but mostly in formal correspondence, not in face-to-face conversation. The interior walls of many a meeting hall in many a fancy local headquarters are of unadorned cinder blocks to recall unionism's hard-knocks days; chances are that more money has been put into the locals' recreation rooms, with air conditioning, paneled walls, billiard and ping-pong tables and bars (the staple still is beer).

"Lord," says an AFL-CIO official in Washington, "I haven't heard *Joe Hill* sung at a meeting in 15 years—or anything else, for that matter." The typical local meeting is deadly dull and poorly attended. Members generally wear slacks and sport shirts, including bowling- and softball-league shirts for many who can hardly wait to get out of the hall and on to an avocation that is as often as not company sponsored. (Another style note: for reasons that might require the services of a mass psychologist, the old white cotton sock has given way in Pittsburgh to one of cardinal red.) No local leader will schedule a meeting in conflict with a really popular TV program unless he deliberately wants to keep attendance down. Observes Sidney Lens: "The members still have a loyalty to the union. It's the loyalty of a man who no longer loves his wife but hasn't enough friction in his life to want a divorce."

TECHNOLOGICAL DRAG

At least as significant as the leadership lag and the spiritual sag is what some union men consider the technological drag. Too many of organized labor's leaders have set their skulls squarely against the technological revolution. Printers' Powers, for instance, made it eminently evident that he would rather let the New York Post go bankrupt than agree to permit the paper to install a computerized system. As Powers, who is far from being the blindest or the dumbest of union leaders, says: "We'll make all the wheels go the wrong way." Jimmy Hoffa has his own devilishly clever idea: "If we can find out where the components of these computers are made, we can stop the shipment of the components, and we can shut the automated plant down."

The naive, Luddite dreams of stopping progress are obviously nonsense, but labor's worries are understandable. Automation decreases the demand for employees who work with their hands and increases the need for those who use their minds. At General Electric less than half of the total employees are now on regular hourly wage scales. Thus, the blue-collar worker is falling more and more out of style. The white-collar worker, historically hard to organize, is the man of the moment. Organized labor's best chance in the future may well lie with the "grey-collar" or "faded blue-collar" worker, the one who used to wield a screw driver but has learned how to work with automated equipment.

For organized labor, another alarming effect of automation is that it blunts the strike weapon. One leader who has learned this is the Communications Workers' president Joe Beirne. Two years ago his people struck against California's General Telephone Co., which, like the rest of the industry, is overwhelmingly automated. Unorganized supervisory types easily kept the equipment working, and after more than 100 days, the union gave up without winning a single significant benefit. Beirne now says: "There will still be strikes, but they will not be the same kind of tool. The picket line will be a 'promotional' line"—meaning that the unions will have to sell their case to the community at large.

In the long run, labor, like the whole U.S. economy, is bound to win enormous benefits through the increased productivity and profits made possible by automation. The Communications Workers, despite their futile strike, were already making their peace with that fact. Because automation has helped the industry expand its services by about 170%, the union, even though fewer plug-pullers and pole-climbers are required, has also increased its membership.

Moreover, automation has already brought workers more leisure. The trend is to reduce the time that men work through longer vacations, sabbaticals, earlier retirement. Such benefits constituted nearly half of last fortnight's steel settlement. The United Auto Workers operate under a contract granting them bereavement pay, funeral leave, and Christmas bonuses. Their "supplemental allowance" scheme is known to members as the Honeydew Project—because the men can retire earlier, go home, and hear their wives say, "Honey, do this—Honey, do that." Senior auto and steelworkers get 13 weeks' annual vacation. The United Brewery Workers are contractually given the right to drink as much of the plant product as they want—without charge.

Job protection in the face of automation remains one of labor's chief concerns. Five years ago, San Francisco's Longshoreman Leader Harry Bridges signed a contract permitting shippers to automate to their heart's desire—while guaranteeing Bridges' boys an annual wage, no matter how many hours they actually worked. The agreement has turned out well for both management and longshoremen.

More reasonable and less wasteful is the contract between California's Kaiser Steel Corp. and the United Steelworkers. Under it, any worker displaced by automation goes into an employment "reserve," receives his average wage of the past while being retrained and waiting for reassignment. Kaiser also offers vacation time based on productivity gains. Variations of the Kaiser-Steelworkers' arrangement are being tried out elsewhere with success. The Electrical Workers, for instance, are organizing training courses to teach members to work in atomic energy and other advanced fields. But organized labor as a whole has hardly begun to face up to the problem—and the opportunity—of automation.

PUBLIC RELATIONS SNAG

Forward-looking labor leaders are sure that they will have to find "new markets," branching out from old-line industries, and that is not always easy. Some complain that the electronics industry, for one, is mobile to the point of being nomadic and therefore hard to organize. When one union was contemplating organizing insurance company employees, the union paper struck a note of comic despair: "Can you imagine the national reaction to a strike of insurance salesmen?" Some labor leaders expect to develop new forms of cooperation with management, such as the industry-wide boards that already function in steel and coal.

Above all, organized labor will have to become more attractive to the public. One experiment in that line, tried by the Retail Clerks, used low-keyed, soft-sell TV spots. But some of labor's public relations snags will take more than TV to solve. Union leaders have used their tremendous influence to fight Section 14(b) of the Taft-Hartley Act, which permits states to enact right-of-work laws (its repeal was passed by the House, is now before the Senate). No doubt, union membership has been held down by 14(b), particularly in the South. But the gains made, when and if it is repealed, may well be offset by adverse public sentiment; many Americans, whether or not they are accurately informed on the issue, still feel that a man should have a right to hold a job without belonging to a union.

Organized labor is less than ever a monolithic segment of a fragmented national society. No more can it afford to make purely demagogic demands of industry, and to an unprecedented degree, labor and management are forced to work together. In this sense, Labor Secretary Willard Wirtz is fond of quoting Lewis Carroll's *Hunting of the Snark:*

> *But the valley grew narrow and narrower still,*
> *And the evening got darker and colder*
> *Till (merely from nervousness, not from good will)*
> *They marched along shoulder to shoulder.*

What is actually keeping them marching along together is not nervousness, though there is still some of that, or just good will, though there is a lot more of that. It is above all a common share in America's vast affluence, a common stake in a country, as nearly classless as any in the world, that gives the worker a better life than he has known since the wheels of the industrial revolution first started to turn.

The conflicting interests of business, labor, and other groups in the United States are reflected in the operation of pressure groups and lobbies. The following series of excerpts from Jessica Mitford's *The American Way of Death* reveal vividly the efforts of florists, through the Florists' Telegraph Delivery Association, to protect their perceived interest against those of funeral directors, the clergy, and the general public. They illustrate, also, how the interests of the florists and the funeral directors may coincide and place them in opposition to the clergy and the public.

THE AMERICAN WAY OF DEATH

Jessica Mitford

The slowed-up death rate makes a big difference to an industry that gets nearly 85 percent of its $1.25 million retail business from funerals and weddings. Worse still, funeral notices in the newspapers increasingly carry the message, "Please Omit Flowers."

The funeral directors are key allies in the blitzkrieg against P.O. because they control the wording of obituary notices; according to a florists' survey, 92 percent of the death notices published in newspapers are given to the papers by funeral directors. Florists spend a good deal of time and money cementing the alliance by speaking at conclaves of funeral directors, advertising in their journals, and contributing articles to the funeral trade press. There is a certain amount of buttering up, as in an article addressed to funeral directors by the President of the Florists' Telegraph Delivery Association: "Your highest duty is creation. It is surely a function that is guided by the Great Creator, for in your hands has been placed the responsibility of creating a living Memory Picture." He warns of a common danger: "the attitude in some places that the present high standards of funeral service are unnecessary. Being close to the funeral directors in their daily work, FTD florists feel that this attitude is dangerous and strikes at the very roots of our civilization." He lists "Eleven Ways to Meet 'Please Omit' Trend," the first way being "Say they may unthinkably offend sincere friends." . . .

A campaign was launched in the late fifties, backed by a $2-million-a-year advertising budget, to erase P.O. forever from the public prints. It is described by Marc Williams in *Flowers-by-Wire, The Story of The Florists' Telegraph Delivery Association:* "Before the end of 1957, Sales and Advertising conducted a national survey on the 'Please Omit' problem, which covered all the newspapers, radio and television stations in the United States. . . . Between 75 percent and 85 percent of the country's newspapers accepted such obituary notices." Armed with this information, the Florists' Information Council "was able to send its field men into the affected areas, to hold meetings with the advertising departments of the papers and also with the funeral directors to arrive at a solution."

The field men in their sorties into the affected areas wielded both clubs and carrots, the latter consisting of "a series of 85-line ads on the obituary pages of 70 newspapers . . . for obvious reasons, *The American Funeral Director* was listed for six insertions." Success was almost instantaneous: by 1959 the executive secretary of the Society of American Florists was able to report that "because of Florists' Telegraph Delivery's financial aid, 241 cities had been visited by field men and 199 newspapers had agreed to refrain from using 'Please Omit' phrases. . . ."

The least hint that a criticism of overspending on funeral flowers may be publicly voiced brings squadrons of florists' field men on the double to the affected area. Fortunately for the occasional library browser, they sometimes allow themselves to boast in print about the results of their successful forays into potentially hostile territory. Thus, the *Florists' Review:*

> It is a rare occurrence when florists can be grateful that funeral flowers are omitted. But such was the case when an article titled "Can You Afford to Die?" appeared in the June 17 (1961) issue of the *Saturday Evening Post,* a popular consumer magazine with a circulation running into the millions. . . .
>
> The important thing here is that this omission of funeral flowers did not just happen. Derogatory references to flowers did not appear in the article because of intensive behind-the-scenes efforts of the Florist's Information Committee of the Society of American Florists. By working closely with the magazine's advertising department, the FIC successfully headed off statements which would have been extremely damaging to the industry. . . .

Frequently people do not know of the existence in their community of a publicly-owned cemetery; and few take the trouble to go there to make advance arrangements. Those who do so are prosaically just buying a grave, whereas the stay-at-homes, who wait for the Memorial Counselor to call, get so much *more* for their money: "Ideally a couple in their early years of married life will benefit by making arrangements at that time, affording them protection and economic benefits when they need it most and often creating a psychological bond that may enrich their marital relationship," says the Interment Association of America. . . .

"To the avaricious churchman there must be provided proof that a funeral investment does not deprive either the church or its pastor of revenue." This extraordinary statement appeared in the *National Funeral Service Journal* for April 1961, together with the opinion that the three most important reasons for the mounting rash of criticism of funeral service are "religion, avarice, and a burning desire for social reform."

The same idea is expressed a little more fully in another issue of the same magazine:

The minister is perhaps our most serious problem, but the one most easily solved. Most religious leaders avoid interference. There are some, however . . . who feel that they must protect their parishioners' financial resources and direct them to a more "worthy" cause. Some of these men, after finding more dimes than dollars in the collection plate, reach the point of frustration where they vent their unholy anger on the supposedly affluent funeral director. . . .

We firmly believe that there is one best way to meet this threat as well as to counter the mushrooming growth of memorial societies and the actual or threatened religious encroachments on our concept of funeral service. That is through the efforts of a highly-skilled public relations firm to conduct an extensive public relations program on a national basis. Thus, purely unselfishly on our part, we have called on all funeral service and trade organizations to join in this common endeavor.

When speaking for public consumption, the spokesmen for interest groups predictably identify their group interest with the public interest. They pose as generous promoters of the public good, whose tireless efforts to serve the public may, incidentally, return some small profit to themselves. But when talking among themselves, interest-group members often forget this altruistic pose and pursue their group interest with a single-minded dedication which reveals that their group interest and the public interest do not always harmonize. *Consumer Reports* magazine carries a regular feature, "Quote Without Comment," which reproduces some of these statements. We have given the following samples a descriptive title:

Just Between Ourselves

Raise your prices [for laundry and dry cleaning] in March. You are so busy at that time of year that the loss of a few customers will not be felt. Also, customers will not be able to get very good service from any other plant at that time, and they may come back to you.

—*Midwest Dry Cleaning and Laundry Journal.*

Most public health programs are designed by people who have never practiced medicine. . . . Most of the public health people think of treating masses of people with mass screening programs that coerce the physicians into caring for people after they have been found to have something no one, including themselves, knew about.

—A. W. Neilson, M.D., *Bulletin of the Academy of Medicine of Cleveland.*

Mr. Greer stated that if advertisers and their agencies were honest about their products, the national economy would grind to a halt. "Agencies are in business to lie effectively," he said.

—*Advertising Age.*

Sports Illustrated and *Field and Stream* have recently come to the defense of the fisherman (or is it the fish?) by publishing articles on thermal pollution. . . . It's time the utility industry confessed its anti-fish attitude. We all know that the finny little nuisances are always going around clogging up our water intakes. They mean no harm, of course, but we can't allow ourselves to get sentimental about it.

—*Power Engineering.*

We don't make them [blue suede shoes] because we couldn't give them away, laments T. W. Florsheim, president of Weyenberg Shoe Manufacturing Company in Milwaukee. Mr. Florsheim is sorry about the change. "We'd love to be selling them now," he says. "They scuff easily, can't be polished, and don't look nice for very long."

—*Wall Street Journal.*

In order to make "price leader" advertising [of used cars] pay off . . . make the price surprisingly low—but believable. The vehicle should lack something in appearance or condition so that it is not too appealing. This is an excellent means of disposing of your extra high-mileage units or units with minor collision damage! Ideally, this price leader should be a car that the customer will tire of almost as soon as he drives it off the lot.

—*Kelley Blue Book Reporter.*

The logical end result of interest- and pressure-group activity is the formation of paid professional lobbies. Virtually everyone knows these groups exist; virtually no one knows, in detail, how they work. The article below was written by a contributing editor of *Harper's Magazine* who came to know lobbies well through his work as administrative assistant to two congressmen and as a journalist covering the political scene.

WASHINGTON'S MONEY BIRDS

A guide to the Lobbyist Americanus and his predatory pursuits

Larry L. King

In all the 139,581 listings contained in the Washington *Yellow Pages,* the word "lobbyist" appears not once. One might erroneously conclude that the *Lobbyist Americanus,* like the Goldwater mystique and the whooping crane, is becoming extinct. Such is not the case, though exactly how many lobbyists are at work in Washington is a mystery. In 1962 almost 1,200 individuals and organizations filed reports with Congress of lobbying activities; on the average, however, less than 400 such reports are filed. About 500 persons or groups are currently registered under the Lobbying Act of 1946. Although the vagaries of that Act make an accurate head count impossible, the Department of Commerce lists some 4,000 national organizations now foraging on the Potomac, and another 75,000 local associations settled in grass-roots nests, whence periodic delegations descend on Washington.

Among the national groups which have *not* filed spending reports in most years are the American Bankers Association, the National Association of Manufacturers, and the American Public Power Association. Some of the nation's largest defense contractors, while maintaining more Washington suites than Alabama has outside agitators, neither register as lobbyists nor report expenditures. Yet no one has whistled for a cop because more than likely no laws are being broken.

From *Harper's Magazine* (August 1965) pp. 45–54. Reprinted by permission of Larry L. King, Contributing Editor, *Harper's Magazine.*

The law covering lobbying activity is more flab than muscle; with similar legislation on the books for homicide, Murder, Inc. would be listed on the Stock Exchange. The title, "Federal Regulation of Lobbying Act," is a misnomer. It is not regulatory, but a mere disclosure-of-expenditures requirement. No government agency is charged with seeing that lobbyists file accurate reports, if at all. Reporting is willy-nilly. Filed reports, if they come in, gather dust along with affidavits from the Bobby Baker case. Nobody is designated to report violations; nobody does.

No lobby-control legislation of any kind was introduced until 1913. Thirty-three years crawled by before our statesmen gave us a Lobbying Act. Not even Teapot Dome caused any serious official twitches toward reform. Committee reports accompanying the 1946 Lobbying Act opened escape hatches big enough to free vast multitudes to behave as they wish. "The act," the reports read, "does not apply to organizations whose efforts to influence legislation are *merely incidental* to the purpose for which formed." Congress bought the language. It was the convenient verbiage which later prompted Senator John Kennedy to judge the 1946 Act "practically worthless" and peppery Senator William Proxmire to dismiss it as "a farce." Though bills have been introduced for nineteen consecutive years to make the law more meaningful, they have quietly withered on the vine. "Nobody," says Congressman Morris Udall, Arizona Democrat, "is lobbying for them."

FROM GOLF TO THE GLAD HAND

It must be emphasized at the start that there is no "typical lobbyist." Evelyn Dubrow of the Ladies Garment Workers is a kindly little woman who you feel is on the verge of urging you to eat your chicken soup; freelance public-relations woman Lucy Cummings is a statuesque blonde who might cause male heads to turn at a quarterly conference of Methodist Bishops. Former Congressman Charles Brown of Missouri, who represents among others ASCAP and the National Education Association, is a debonair gentleman you never would suspect of having once traveled the Ozarks as agent for hillbilly singer Eddie Arnold.

Just as there is no stereotyped lobbyist, neither is there a wholly uniform approach to influencing Congress. While some outfits spend small fortunes showering Congressmen with elaborate slick-paper color brochures, others are certain these find their way promptly into wastebaskets, unseen by legislators' eyes. Where one lobbyist will angle to play a round of golf with a Congressman in the same week his special cause is coming to the floor for vote, another might consider the approach too transparent. Feminine pulchritude sometimes plays a part. A stunning redhead was introduced to the lobby game by a firm which hired her to exhibit earthmoving machines to government purchasing agents. "I didn't know a bolt from a bagpipe," she recalls, "but I sold the product." All lobbyists, however, do share one abiding principle: each is after the dollar.

In my experience as newspaperman and Administrative Assistant to two Congressmen, I encountered all known breeds of these exotic birds. Though I have personally met no one representing the Kaiser, I have known paid agents for diaper makers, Indian tribes, the International Lunar Society, and the Pitkin County (Colorado) Water Protection Association. The Washington veteran can easily identify the seven most operative varieties: the *Lame Duck Emeritus*, the *Swamp Sparrow*, the *Prairie Chicken*, the *White-bellied Booby*, the *Hawk Owl*, the *Potomac Night Flier*, and the *Kingbird*.

(1) The *Lame Duck Emeritus* flies forth each two years when his nest in the House of Representatives or the U.S. Senate has been destroyed by public hand. Among the most common of the species, he is easily flushed in the halls of the Capitol. He chirps often of old glories and traffics in past friendships. He is identified by a toothy smile, a hand perpetually at the ready for shaking, and another held in reserve for instantaneous backslapping.

Lobbying goes well with prior service in Congress. Though some former Members are hired by well-heeled concerns at five-figure sums, these constitute the cream of the crop—old birds of abundant Congressional experience or with more or less direct lines toward high station. More prevalent is the dime-store variety of ex-Congressman who lost out after serving one to four terms. Faced with returning to home mud bogs, where in accordance with prevailing mores he might be expected to take a PR job in the local glue works or become a working courtroom lawyer, he hastily prints cards ascribing unto himself talents as a "legislative counselor" or "Washington representative"—with offices in his briefcase, hatband, or rumpus room of his suburban home. If the rejected politico had foresight enough in his better days to look with special favor on some particular organization, he may be tossed a rewarding bone *ex post facto* in the form of a yearly retainer.[1]

The ordinary *Lame Duck Emeritus* trades on his personal knowledge of Capitol Hill. He buzzes about the desks of former colleagues who, asking not for whom the bell tolls, feel sympathy for their fallen comrade. This

[1] Frank Ikard, a Texan who served on the tax-law-writing Ways and Means Committee, was lured from public service by the American Petroleum Institute at salary and benefits exceeding $100,000 per year. He earns it by influencing former colleagues to retain the $27\frac{1}{2}$ percent depletion allowance, under which oil companies write off that percentage in losses or depletion before paying one Indian head penny in taxes.

breed may use old contacts to secure audience with an Assistant Deputy Under Secretary of Defense for the Procurement of Keg Nails, or to entice former colleagues to whiskey-drinks for the purpose of impressing a visiting client who, hopefully, will return to native pine thickets bedazzled over what a hail-fellow lugs his Washington water.

Largely, however, contacts are cultivated for long-range purposes and to accumulate incidental intelligence which the knowing man may convert to cash dollars. Is the Federal Power Commission favorably disposed toward granting a pipeline to a certain gas company? Will a rumored Congressional investigation cause the public to lose confidence in savings-and-loan companies? Will the Public Works Committee recommend a special tax on diesel fuels in a new highway bill?

The lot of the *Lame Duck Emeritus* grows more perilous with each season. Fledgling Congressmen come in droves each two years, and the migration forces out old friends who become competitors for the lobbying dollar. By the law of diminishing returns the longer a lobbyist is out of Congress the less influence he has with current statesmen. A former Senator, having successfully wrestled a bill through the House, quickly dropped word to his Senate contacts *not* to pass the bill in that body until the following year—a strategy enabling him to renew his contract with his client.

As faces in Congress change and old favors are lost to dust, men whose names once invoked claps of Capitol Hill thunder cool their heels in outer offices of junior Senators. "I see Senator X at a party," a *Lame Duck Emeritus* complained to me, "and he invites me to drop by his office for a chat like we used to have when I served with him. But, dammit, I can't get by the cordon of clerks!"

Not all ex-Members lose their influence. One highly regarded lobbyist is former Senator Earl Clement of Kentucky, whose numerous blue-ribbon clients include the tobacco industry. A close personal friend of President Lyndon Johnson, Clement has blood-kin highly placed in The Great Society. His daughter, Bess Abell, is White House Social Secretary. His son-in-law, Tyler Abell, is Assistant Postmaster General and also the step-son of columnist Drew Pearson.

Former Congressmen scramble for all vacant lobbying berths. In 1962, when I tried for a time to become a money bird myself, several prospective clients put it bluntly: "We can take our pick of former Members. There's little demand for you ex-staffers." [2]

---

[2] There are noted exceptions. John Holton, former AA to the late Speaker Rayburn, represents the American Bankers Association; Lyle Snader, ex-Republican Reading Clerk of the House, the American Railroad Association; Booth Mooney, onetime aide to Lyndon Johnson, is Washington representative for Texas millionnaire and right-wing poobah, H. L. Hunt; Lacey Sharp and Craig Raupe, long-time House AAs, have top lobby-oriented jobs with the American Hospital Association and Eastern Airlines respectively.

EMISSARIES FROM NATIVE BOGS

(2) The *Swamp Sparrow* migrates to Washington from the hinter-lands with the preparation of each new federal budget. He may come plumed in the feathers of his local Civic Improvement Association, Commissioners Court, or Local 123 of United Pool Hall Rack Boys of America. By day a sober worker for mighty causes (a dam on the creek, National Park designation for hometown meteorite craters, a new screwworm eradication plant), he is transformed with the setting sun into a hybrid creature, part hard-drinking conventioneer, part callow freshman at the Big Game, and part Peeping Tom-at-large. Certain to cause his Congressman loss of sleep ("Show me the bright lights, Charlie. Back home they roll up the sidewalks at sundown") and much public humiliation ("Waiter, you git Ho-Say Greco over here for a drink and I'll drop a couple bucks on ya"), he will upon return to native bogs alert everybody from the Taxpayers Protective Association to the Wednesday Ladies Against Sin about the rapid decay of morals and the sound dollar in Washington City.

Though not always housebroken, these migratory *Swamp Sparrows* exert influence on their public men which cannot be negligibly measured. The Congressman faced with this invasion may only smile while hoping that his visitors will eventually go away. The discreet statesmen who understand grass-roots power will remain patient even when the lobbying constituent warns of galloping socialism, welfare-statism, and logrolling, while personally indulging in all three.

This homegrown bird can get the working politician into trouble in numerous ways. A few years ago, one appeared to testify in behalf of a local project seeking government funds. It was sponsored by my own Congressman. Although the constituent's prepared statement was adequate, a cursory questioning touching on finer points of the proposed legislation revealed him less than prepared to undergo a sharp grilling in committee. Having worked on the project, I felt more capable of facing questions. Thus, in giving the witness the usual effusive introduction to the committee, I told the Congressmen he had "total hearing impairment" and suggested that after he had read his prepared statement, all questions be directed to me. The chairman nodded. With exaggerated lip movements and a booming voice probably heard in Formosa, he bid my constituent welcome. The statement was read, my friend settled back cozily, and I began to parry the committee's questions. While I thus performed, my visiting witness fell into a gentle slumber. All went well until a spectator ten rows behind us dropped a book on the floor. The dozing constituent jumped awake, overturning a pitcher of ice water and four glasses.

(3) The *Prairie Chicken* is the breed of money bird who heads Washington-based associations which draw their main strength from huge groups

back home. Whether representing postal worker, brain surgeon, or hod carrier, he hibernates through most Congressional business. But any bill of direct bearing on his special constituency sends him winging out with great, wounded cries. He is a shameless flexer of muscle, and good at basic voter arithmetic.

Where the *Lame Duck Emeritus* might exhibit a quick-draw hand at grog flasks, the *Prairie Chicken* on his good days will spring in one of the Capitol Hill cafeterias for one gummy grilled-cheese sandwich and a cup of tepid coffee handed down through a long line of malcontent busboys. But this bird pays due bills in other ways. Champion his causes and he will lay on heavy political rewards.

A few years ago William Doherty, then President of the National Association of Letter Carriers, established a policy of writing paeans of praise to every Congressman who voted for a bill to increase the pay of postal workers. He then reproduced the letters and mailed them by the thousands to postal workers in friendly Congressmen's districts. Nobody got mad. Almost every hamlet has a Post Office, and with it postal workers —who may be the best organized group in the nation. They send delegations to Washington to lobby their bills, they would walk barefoot in snow to the polls on election day, and postal wives, not encumbered as are their husbands by Hatch Act restrictions, are known to make enthusiastic campaign workers.

Labor unions furnish willing bodies to mail posters, stuff envelopes, and do the thousand menial tasks required in campaigns. Ken Petersen of the Hotel and Restaurant Workers says: "We can't match management in money or in opportunity for social contacts. But we can let our Congressmen know we've got a strong work force to commit in campaigns." Most Congressmen are smart enough to know that any force capable of being committed for them also could be committed against them.

Some *Prairie Chickens* offer speech-writing services to friendly Congressmen and Senators. Benefits accrue to all hands. The lobbyist gets his message told in Congressional chambers and printed in *The Congressional Record*. The solon gets credit for expertise, perhaps a newspaper headline, and surely a document handily reproduced for purposes of propagandizing voters of a particular group.

L. Dan Jones of the Independent Petroleum Association often sees his prose in Congressional documents, though the words are credited to public men. Dale Miller, the President's friend and current reigning king of lobbyists, has prepared committee testimony for countless Congressmen dead and alive. The practice is common. This kind of thing carried to extremes can be embarrassing: a Border State Congressman was indicted in 1962 for allegedly having accepted $10,000 from a finance company to make a speech on the House floor. His conviction was reversed on appeal, but in the meantime he had left Congress in disgrace.

RESPONSE FROM THE MASSES

Sometimes the tactics of the organizational lobbyists backfire. Senator Stephen M. Young received thousands of letters from Ohio urging him to oppose two bills concerning the railroads. Though the letters mentioned no organizations and the messages varied, each of them incorrectly listed the Senator's middle initial as A. It was easy to trace the pressure campaign to a lobbying group. A Minnesota Senator received nine hundred telegrams in two days for a bill favored by oil companies, and found on investigation that most of the wires were sent without knowledge of the purported senders—and had been charged to a corporate firm's telephone number. In 1956 Massachusetts Senators got dozens of telegrams opposing a social-security bill, the wires uniformly spelling "amendment" with a double m. Many of the alleged authors proved to have no idea telegrams had been sent in their names.

Though Congressmen often insist they don't make decisions "by weighing pounds of letters," Republican Representative Harold R. Collier of Illinois disagrees. "We ask other members what *their* mail is like."

The U.S. Chamber of Commerce, working through its thousands of local chapters, inundated Congress with almost a million messages favoring the Landrum-Griffin labor-reform bill. It passed by only six votes. One Southern liberal told me, "I didn't want to vote for that bill. It was punitive. But the Chamber sold Jimmy Hoffa to the public as the bogeyman. I never got so much mail in my life." Mail stimulated by the National Rifle Association and militant rightist groups this year stalled efforts to pass legislation controlling the questionable sale of firearms.

(4) The *White-bellied Booby* is largely indigenous to Southern California, Texas, the rickets-and-boll-weevil South, and selected thickets of the Midwest. This sharp-eyed creature espies in Congress's every act a sinister plot to destroy the Republic, crack the Liberty Bell, and contaminate the Amalgamated Flag Stitchers of America. Anyone blind to these dark visions is suspected of favoring peace, treason, and the reading of poetry.

Most militant rightist groups are not on registered lobby rolls. (Many, in fact, receive special tax benefits as "educational" foundations—a practice being looked upon by the Internal Revenue Service with an increasingly jaundiced eye.) But perhaps more than any other group they torment Congressmen with excess stomach acidity.

My office was once flooded by letters protesting Operation Water Moccasin—described as a hairy plot by which thousands of foreign troops ("including Congolese riflemen in loincloths") would capture the whole of Georgia under the United Nations flag. This would "preview U.S. surrender to an internationalist One World Government." The story, sounding as if

it originated with somebody full of Mexican boo smoke, came to prominence in *The Independent American*—a Louisiana-based fright-sheet published by a former New Orleans public-relations flak so far out he once
accused Barry Goldwater of being "tinged with socialism." It took speeches
in Congress, statements from the Pentagon, a network television documentary, and many weeks to establish the truth: Operation Water Moccasin
was a routine field exercise observed by about two hundred military officers from friendly foreign powers.

In 1962, rightists sent hundreds of telegrams to Washington urging
Congressmen to forgo its normal adjournment. The objective was to prevent some mysterious "they" from handing the government over to Russia
once the legislators packed off for home.

George Lincoln Rockwell, self-styled Fuehrer of the American Nazi
party, often hand carries his mimeographed sheets preaching white supremacy and anti-Semitism through Capitol corridors. Gerald L. K. Smith's
Christian Nationalist Crusade is represented by a grandmotherly little type
whose outward serenity vanishes when she begins to reveal communist
conspiracies yet unknown to Mao Tse-tung. Though persistent, these birds
have little more influence on Congress these days than Billy James Hargis
has on Vatican City. Largely their activity is confined to fund-raising dinners where the faithful exhort against wasting tax money shooting bric-a-
brac at the moon; compiling charts registering the percentage of "Americanism" of individual Congressmen; or circulating books, with titles like
My Son the Red Dupe and *Yesterday East Berlin: Tomorrow Teaneck,
New Jersey.* The *White-bellied Booby* does put in numerous appearances to
alert the House Un-American Activities Committee or the Senate Internal
Security Committee to the more fashionable menaces of the moment.[3]

THE ONES WHO MATTER MOST

Until now I have concentrated on the more common of the species,
those money birds noted primarily, though by no means exclusively, for
noise and nuisance value. The following three classifications must go in a
higher, more celestial category. More often than not they gravitate directly
to the true sources of power, conducting themselves with great efficiency
and determination. They are calmer, more confident, and usually smarter.
These are the birds who personally get things done.

(5) The *Hawk Owl,* commonly known as the lawyer-lobbyist, is a

---

[3] If rightists do nothing else they provide work for defeated Congressmen. John
H. Rousselot, ex-member from California, is an organizer for the John Birch Society;
E. Franklin Foreman, a one-termer from West Texas who once branded twenty-eight
of his colleagues "Pinkos," is a paid executive for Americans for Constitutional
Action.

Washington phenomenon. A few eminent and respected ones are active in the actual practice of law, but others come before the bar principally in the Metropolitan Club or the Mayflower cocktail lounge. Almost all of these birds are extremely affluent and gregarious.

Old New Deal and Fair Deal heads who have performed well for their country are prominent among the *Hawk Owls*. Oscar Chapman, President Truman's Secretary of Interior, represents clients ranging from the American Taxicab Association to Mexican sugar interests to a firm in Zaandam, Holland. Donald S. Dawson, Truman's one-time White House aide, heads a law firm representing insurance, finance, and transportation interests—as well as a gift shop in the Virgin Islands, sugar firms in India, and the Hilton Hotel Corporation. Clinton M. Hester (once top man in the CAA under President Roosevelt), of the law firm of Hester, Owen & Crowder (representing National Wool Growers, U.S. Brewers Association among others) for years turned his palatial southern-style mansion in the Virginia mountains over to Congressional aides for an annual weekend caper there. The working cogs of the Hill danced around the clock to alternating jazz and hillbilly bands; tables were laden with the finest cured ham, smoked oysters, shrimp, and fried chicken—with uniformed cooks standing by to work artistry on steaks prepared to individual tastes. Liquor was available in abundance. For health fanatics there were golfing and horseback riding. Columnist Drew Pearson wrote of it as a boondoggle, after which alarmed Congressmen required of their aides more plebeian tastes.

The largest lawyer-lobbyist in town these days is Abe Fortas, a bearish sort of man who once prowled among New Deal agencies in varied jobs and who is now Lyndon Johnson's most trusted adviser outside official circles. Fortas, who represents the Commissioner of Baseball, Lever Brothers, National Retail Merchants, and California Finance, is a man the President turns to in crisis. It was Fortas whom Johnson summoned to the White House during the 1964 campaign when a key aide was arrested on a morals charge; he is a frequent caller at the White House by back-door routes when the President feels need of companionship or a sounding board. Another successful lawyer-lobbyist, former Senate Majority Leader Scott W. Lucas of Illinois, says, "The Senate is a club and you're a member until you die—even if you get defeated for reelection. I can see anybody in the Senate almost anytime."

(6) The elite among Washington's money birds is the *Potomac Night Flier*. A most urbane fowl, he is extremely adaptable to the mores of the moment. He owns a set of golf clubs gathering dust since late 1960, a deflated pigskin unkicked since November 1963, and right now he is big for square dancing, barbecue, and ten-gallon hats. He is found at every social event worthy of reporting by Betty Beale in the Washington *Evening Star,* is active in at least one of the fifty state societies in Washington, holds

an associate membership in the National Press Club, and habitually chooses a mate who social climbs the way Justice Douglas goes at mountains.

The most "in" lobbyist in Washington these days is a highly social specimen. Tall, white-maned, mild-mannered Dale Miller is a genuine son-of-a-lobbyist whose father got Lyndon Johnson his first Washington job as secretary to a Congressman. He has been the President's friend for thirty years. Miller has had it all: a bridge for which he secured $600,000 in federal funds has been named after him; his daughter works on the White House staff; his wife Scooter has replaced Perle Mesta as Washington's most adept hostess; the President tabbed him to be his Inaugural chairman; and the Johnson daughters call him "Uncle Dale." When President and Mrs. Johnson arrived at the Capitol for the Inauguration last January, scuttling along only six paces behind came Dale and Scooter Miller. Appropriately, a military band struck up "Happy Days Are Here Again." In perhaps the most impressive performance of a historic day, the Millers managed not to smile.

Lobbyist Miller does not hold with the theory that friendships of persons highly placed are a big factor in successful operations on the Potomac. "I think," he says, "a person acquires influence in Washington through integrity and effort—not through contacts." Mr. Miller does not say, however, whether he believes in a flat earth and werewolves.

BILLIE SOL THE KINGBIRD

(7) It is the *Kingbird* who most frequently runs afoul of the law in Washington circles. Billie Sol Estes is the classic example of the get-rich-quick tycoon who, in over his head, misrepresents himself to public men until he drags them down with him.

I bear the personal scars of Billie Sol. I first met him on the streets of Pecos, Texas, in 1954, shortly after he began to take on affluent airs. Typically, I was campaigning with a candidate for Congress, who was elected—and without Estes' support. In intervening years Estes did not support the Congressman; one year he offered campaign funds to a county judge in the hope the judge would run against the Congressman. Suddenly, in 1960, Billie Sol began to court us.

He first hired a lawyer who had been our county manager for many years. Soon the lawyer was asking his Congressman to help untie knotty problems client Estes had with the government on cotton acreage allotment transfers and importation of bracero workers from Mexico. The Congressman was urged to ask the State Department to help the Church of Christ (in which Estes was front-pew financial angel) gain permission for its missionaries to enter Tanganyika.

The Congressman acceded to each request—and why not? He performed similar chores daily for boatloads of constituents who thought nothing of asking their public men to run errands they wouldn't require of a bellhop. Additionally, Estes came with impressive credentials. The national Junior Chamber of Commerce had named him one of the nation's Ten Outstanding Young Men; he rivaled the Ford Foundation in gifts to good works; he had been eulogized down to the bone by magazines and newspapers for his astute business practices. He piously forbade mixed bathing in the pool at his palatial home, refused all nicotine and liquor, and never used strong language. As one who was among Estes' guests at a couple of Washington dinners, I can attest they were quite dry. I am sure they had more fun at the Last Supper.

In time, Estes made a $1,500 contribution to my Congressman's campaign kitty. In politics, where one looks to friends for help, this was common. Uncommon, of course, was Estes himself. Shortly after the contribution he was revealed to have bilked many large companies and individuals of millions of dollars, and to have submitted false credit reports. Testimony at the several Estes trials disclosed that he threatened bankers, government employees, and business leaders through misuse of the names of highly placed politicians. Not everyone was Estes' innocent victim. Some government employees, a passel of businessmen, and a Midwestern Congressman accepted lavish gifts and money from Estes in questionable transactions.

NOT BY BREAD ALONE

Though the Congress may not have a monopoly on high principle, only eighteen of its number have been formally accused of corrupt practices since 1900—and of these, only seven were charged with improprieties touching lobby activities. The truth is that most national legislators, harboring visions of themselves as potential Presidents, find votes more attractive than monetary gain tied to political risk. Though 239 of the 434 Representatives and 68 of 100 Senators are lawyers, the majority pointedly shun fees or retainers for cloudy "legal work" which might make them beholden to special-interest clients.

But Congressmen do not live by bread alone. Neither do most of them manage to live on official emoluments. True, they draw a $30,000 annual salary and cash allowances for stationery, home-district office expenses, and official travel. They are accorded tax-paid staff employees, Washington office suites and attendant equipment, telephone and telegraph allowances, messenger service, charwomen, swimming pools, parking spaces—even transportation from their offices to the Capitol Building on private subways. They are also get subsidized haircuts, radio-television studios with professional technicians, meals in Capitol restaurants, medical care—even box-like olive-drab footlockers provided free, one for each new session. This means Senator Carl Hayden of Arizona has 105 footlockers, some dating back to Woodrow Wilson's Administration.

Even so, unless a Washingtonian is a Kennedy or Rockefeller, one has a hard time keeping up with the Mestas and Cafritzes. Congressmen must maintain houses in the District as well as back in the mudflats, entertain on a sizable scale, invest in wardrobes complete through fish-and-soup bibs, and contribute to every charity bold enough to beg alms. Those who live west of the Mississippi often spend up to $3,000 in personal funds for flying trips home on weekends in order to keep political fences mended. Rare is the Member who does not refurbish his public image through shows of benevolence: a scholarship to the local Tonsorial Academy (awarded In Memory of Mother or in the name of a historical figure long safe in Heaven from partisan jeers), a trip to Washington for orphaned paraplegics, Thanksgiving turkey for folks at the Poor Farm, or flags certified as having "flown over the U.S. Capitol Building" to any institution owning a pole.[4]

The big money, of course, goes into campaigning. Neither Lyndon Johnson, *The New York Times,* nor the Prophet Isaiah knows what it *really* costs to run for Congress. Our legislators have placed such miserly political-spending limitations on themselves they must form phantom committees and letterhead organizations, and even file official reports swearing lies in order to stay within the law they made. A Senator from California or New York running scared might easily spend a cool million in a campaign; some rural Pharaoh so long in Congress his constituents think he rules by right of blood might spend only a few hundred dollars. With rare exceptions, however, one cannot hope to win a Congressional race for less outlay than the job's annual $30,000 salary.

Lobbyists apply the balm to this financial sting. It is not given unto earthlings to know how much money changes hands, nor what the private understandings are, for this is largely a cash trade without checks, stamps, or money orders. Lobby money often buys tickets to fund-raising dinners where guests have anted up $10 to $1,000 per plate for eighty cents' worth of vintage roast beef, where they keep one ear closed against the honoree's two-hour declaration of personal modesty and the other hopefully cocked for the opening strains of the recessional. No Congressman's bank account in the Sergeant at Arms office in the Capitol may be viewed by anyone unless approved by majority consent of the Congress. Lobbyists prefer their gifts to be known only to the benefactors, and the law encourages false re-

---

[4] Capitol Hill policemen fly many of these flags daily on poles erected for the sole purpose. It takes thirty seconds to run up each flag, and ten days to get a letter and embossed certificate attesting the act. Congressmen pay $3.50 or $6 for the package, depending on flag size. Even the Speaker can't get certification unless the flag has actually flown.

porting. These factors make it impossible even for the best gumshoe to know much of political finance.[5]

When a Billie Sol Estes, Bernard Goldfine, or Bobby Baker comes along there is panic in the lobbying community. In 1956, when the late Senator Francis Case of South Dakota dropped the bombshell that he had been offered $2,500 to vote for the Harris-Fulbright bill to relieve natural gas of federal regulations, after which President Eisenhower vetoed the bill because "of arrogant lobbying tactics," the anguish of members of the brotherhood was genuine.

Many lobbyists feel they provide helpful information to Congressmen so harried by constituents' demands they cannot possibly know the details of more than a few of the twenty thousand bills introduced each year. Honest Congressmen admit they often vote "in the blind" because of skimpy information. Senator Gale McGee of Wyoming is so concerned he has introduced a bill to give members sabbatical leaves provided they stay out of their home districts and spend the time in reflection on the issues of our time. Texas Congressman Wright Patman would provide more staff help.

"Too frequently," Patman says, "we take the presentation of lobbyists as facts when such information is really a lopsided plea from selfish interests. Consequently, we get some legislation that never should be passed —and neved would be passed if [we] had screening specialists."

WHEN STAKES ARE HIGH

Though quick to claim they perform valid services for Congressmen and "the people," lobbyists are slow to submit supporting evidence. The contention holds no more water than the ancient cry of corporations that to tax them "is to tax all of us." Even those lobbyists appealing to what I consider my humanitarian predilections (higher wages for the working stiff, benefits for the physically or mentally handicapped, the dreamy causes of bearded "peacemongers") often turned to shrill war-hawks when glaring across my desk demanding special booty.

Perhaps this is to be expected. As the courtroom lawyer is more concerned with a favorable verdict than with the vagaries of some obscure justice, so the lobbyist is more concerned with making his point than with giving all hands a fair roll of the bones. Like the professional football player, he is paid to win in a league where moral victories are not tallied in the final standings. The game is hard-fought, and rare is the money bird who does not stray from the rule book's teachings when victory is near.

___

[5] Insiders do know that many Congressmen maintain political "slush funds" similar to the $18,000 fund which caused the great outcry against Richard Nixon in 1952.

When the Landrum-Griffin measure was before Congress, representatives of management and labor actually had fist fights in Congressional waiting rooms, Capitol corridors, and cocktail lounges. At the time that taxes were being increased to finance the National Highway Bill, railroad and trucking representatives, besides invoking God's preference, engaged in shoving matches, shouted abuse, and carried spurious tales on the enemy.

Unusual pressures are applied against Congressmen when the stakes are high. When Representative Olin E. Teague, chairman of the House Veterans' Affairs Committee, refused to go along with a $100-per-month pension to every veteran of World War I—regardless of length or condition of service, financial need, or physical condition—many veterans condemned him as a coward, traitor, and enemy of the nation's defenders, although Teague happens to be one of the nation's most-wounded and most-decorated war heroes. Representative Patman, proposing an investigation of the nation's banking institutions, was so defamed by many financial executives one might have thought he had advocated going back to animal pelts as legal tender. Congressmen who have voted for public housing are reviled by prosperous home builders. Others who voted for bills opposed by the AMA have been booed on public platforms by physicians otherwise well-versed in the social graces.

Our public men, coming to their jobs through public favor, are obsessed with the fear that withdrawal of the mandate will grind their large ambitions to dust. Few relish the idea of being opposed by lobby groups capable of turning against them hoards of dollars and voting members. The temptation to go along to get along is great. Splitting two key votes, one in favor of management and one in favor of labor, merely leaves both groups angry at different times. Thus the inclination is to cast both pearls before the same swine—a strategy which, if followed to its logical extension over the years, robs the Congressman of his ability to reach independent conclusions on many public issues. The man not constantly on guard against the trend soon winds up the captive of numerous pressure groups. This may make his reelection less painful, but it also makes his value as a public man more suspect.

A Congressman or Senator overly committed to special-interest groups soon finds himself regularly supping at their private tables to the exclusion of all others. He may at first reluctantly accept—and then come to consider his due—transportation to distant points, vacations at some plush resort, tickets to sell-out Broadway shows, liquor, vicuna rugs, mink coats, deep freezes, inside tips on the stock market, and, ultimately, under-the-table greenbacks.

Such favors may be rationalized away by recipients as tokens of admiration laid on by true friends. But any Congressman who has been defeated can attest that many Washington friendships are transitory in nature. The deposed monarch who was fawned over by lobby society when riding high may, following a downward plunge of personal fortunes, find himself very lonely indeed. Less than a week after a former Congressman of whom I was fond ran afoul of the electorate, I wrote letters to twenty-two men for whom he had done substantial favors over the years. The object was to raise $7,000 to cover the deficit from the Congressman's losing campaign. The take was a single one-hundred-dollar check and no sympathy notes.

While lobbyists have improved their "image" to some extent over the years, the taint that remains on their craft is quite often justified. Lobbyists posing as newsmen—a ploy allowing them to ask pointed questions about their special interests—have been tossed out of press conferences held by Cabinet members in recent years. They have flocked into House and Senate visitors' galleries in such numbers that Members unwilling to be recorded "yea" or "nay" before such watchful eyes have pulled all the parliamentary strings to avoid roll-call votes, thereby depriving the public of knowing how its elected men stood on vital issues disposed of by voice or teller vote. Congressional investigations have revealed that lobbyists often have misrepresented their influence and contacts with top government officials when writing confidential reports to their clients. Hardly a day passes without lobbyists persuading Congressmen to write or telephone federal agencies with which they have some problem. As Dr. George B. Galloway of the Library of Congress says,

"A telephone call from a Senator or Congressman can paralyze the will of a government executive and alter the course of national policy."

DEALING IN FALSE SKILLS

A friend of mine who is a lobbyist recently told me, over three-to-one martinis, of his hard lot. "I guess we deal in false skills," he said. "We spend half our time conning our clients in an attempt to justify our fees, and the other half trying to convince Congressmen to act against what some people call the public interest. I wrote the other day to the B—— Corporation on a little matter I'm working on for them, and I worked in something about having 'talked to Speaker McCormack yesterday.' Well, I talked to him, all right. I met him in the Capitol corridor and I said, 'How are you, Mister Speaker?' And he glanced up from some papers he'd been shuffling and said, 'Very well, thank you.'" Then, as if to convince himself, my friend said, "It won't rank with Plato's *Dialogues,* but I *did* talk to him."

I asked him why he dealt in mock shows. He was intelligent, had himself worked for a Congressman, and was once a newspaper man. He spoke of mortgages on one home, three cars, the high cost of living, his investment in time, children to raise and educate.

"Would you want your son to be a lobbyist?" I said.

He gazed into his glass. "Oh, I wouldn't object if he really wanted to." Then he gave me a sour grin. "But my daughter"—he said—"I sure wouldn't want my daughter to marry one."

We drank to that. On the B—— Corporation.

The following article, by widely respected United States senator Stephen M. Young, seeks to present a balanced analysis of the role of lobbying before Congress. He points out that lobbying is not only far from new but it is probably becoming less blatant and more responsible with the passage of time. Most lobbyists are competent, sincere, hard-working people who are exercising, for the organizations they represent, the basic American right to petition their government.

Senator Young emphasizes, also, that congressmen confront a formidable mass of proposed legislation each session, much of it in areas in which the congressman has only very limited knowledge. Lobbyists, he says, provide a service by assembling useful, reliable information on legislative matters in which they are interested. Lobbies are as likely to be involved in the passage of legislation that we approve as they are in legislation we do not approve.

Although the senator is more sanguine than many about the relatively few cases of successful abuse of lobbying, not many informed people would challenge his assertion that lobbying is inevitable in a representative government. Most would probably agree, too, that abuse by an unscrupulous minority is a small price to pay for the preservation of the basic right of petition.

THE CASE FOR LOBBIES

Stephen M. Young
U.S. Senator

I have served as a Senator of the United States since January 1959. Previously, I was elected four times to the U.S. House of Representatives; and before that, I served terms in the General Assembly of Ohio and in appointive office in the state government. I have encountered thousands of lobbyists and have known scores of them well. Most of them I respect and trust. Some I would throw out of my office on sight.

More than 50 years in public life have taught me that lobbying can be good or bad, constructive or corrosive. It's all in the eyes of the beholder and in the hand of the practitioner. Periodically, stories explode in the press charging sundry trickery and irregularities jointly to lobbyists and public officials—as in the Bobby Baker business, or in the more recent allegations concerning Senator Thomas Dodd's close relations with a lobbyist for foreign firms. Public and Congressional uproars follow. All of the abuses of lobbying—real and potential and, in some cases, imagined—are aired. Sweeping changes in the laws regulating lobbying and the registration of lobbyists are demanded and shotgun blasts are fired at the moral caliber of politicians and public officials.

I'll get to the lobbying laws in a minute. Obviously, they should be strengthened and tightened. But I'll say right now that I am fed up with thundering editorial writers who relish every occasional proof or charge of corruption in lobbyist/officeholder relationships as a golden opportunity to tarbrush all public servants as too feeble-minded or too loose morally to resist the blandishments of shrewd operators and conniving seekers of privilege. Let me straighten that out quickly. Most of us are honest people trying to serve the public as best we can. We are not sitting ducks for lobbyists on the hunt. Nor do most lobbyists think we are. Most of them are honest, too, as are most editorial writers.

Lobbying essentially is grinding an ax. It is pushing your own or someone else's cause. More frequently, lobbyists represent corporations, unions or associations. This is promotional work, public relations and advertising—bundled together to put pressure on public officials. But, let's face it: It's also the exercise of the right to petition—a right guaranteed all Americans in the First Amendment to the Constitution of our country. If inconvenience sometimes accompanies that right, I am willing to abide it.

The way some practice it, lobbying is hocus-pocus: a fat expense account and a big front; flattery and favors to score points for your client or cause. However, with most lobbyists working on Capitol Hill and concerned with legislative matters, it is a job done responsibly and with conviction. One person, or an association representing millions of persons, can constitute a lobby.

We inherited the practice of lobbying from the British. It started a good three centuries ago, when Englishmen seeking special privileges from Members of Parliament customarily gathered in the outer lobbies of the House of Commons to buttonhole various M.P.s.

As in so many things, it remained for Americans to perfect and expand the practice into an institution. It has been said, with only slight exaggeration, that there are more lobbyists in Washington than lobsters in

New England, and if lobbyists were suddenly evacuated from the nation's capital, there would be very few guests—and even fewer hosts—at cocktail parties.

The "lobbying problem," as some Members of Congress insist on calling it, is as old as our Government; indeed, older. Lobbyists fluttered around at the first sign the 13 colonies gave of seeking independence from the mother country. In those Colonial days, New England merchants opposed to separation from Great Britain wined and dined delegates en route to the First Continental Congress, hopeful that some good mutton and huge quantities of spirits would exorcise that radical spirit of independence.

The spiritual descendants of these early merchants—now banded together in the National Association of Manufacturers and United States Chamber of Commerce—still cry out against radicalism. They testify before Congressional committees and lobby among Representatives and Senators against Medicare, Federal aid to education, the war on poverty, the Great Society—against all sorts of liberal legislation and other proposals that offend their sense of good Americanism. Though this is their right, their lyrics are boring. They have been singing the same song too long.

Our patriot fathers in the Continental Congress and in succeeding Congresses also had their encounters with lobbyists. The first business lobby was Alexander Hamilton's Philadelphia Society for the Promotion of National Industry. This group was interested in tariff legislation. Long before the Civil War started, petitioning the Government was on its way to becoming the gigantic activity that it is today. Daniel Webster and other Senators of an earlier era wrote supporting letters for lobbyists that no Senator of modern days would write. At least I hope not.

Lobbying had become so entrenched in Washington and in state legislatures—and lobbyists so abundant—by the middle of the 19th Century that concerned legislators of that early date were already looking for an out. When Samuel Colt wanted to renew the patent on his revolver in 1855, he set up headquarters in various hotels. Food and wine were made available in prodigal quantities. He paid a "contingent fee" of $10,000 to a Congressman to refrain from attacking the bill that would extend his patent. Elaborately decorated revolvers were distributed to legislators. And, for those gentlemen who were not interested in guns, he kept a supply of "three charming ladies"—known as "spiritualists"—available to ply their craft for the enlightenment of Congressmen. There were also some non-spiritual types for Congressmen who knew how to vote correctly. The tradition established by Colt flourished so successfully that the lobbying scandals of the later 19th century could fill quite a number of volumes.

From that period emerged the most simple and effective solution to the lobbying problem ever proposed. The influential Senator Thomas Hart Benton of Missouri, truly a great U.S. Senator, was feeling the heat from lobbyists seeking a profitable shipbuilding subsidy. To their surprise, Senator Benton quickly agreed to help. But he pressed one condition: "When the vessels are finished, they will be used to take all such damned rascals as you out of the country."

If this was a practical idea then, it is obsolete today. There aren't enough ships. Besides, lobbying is a big business and it is here to stay. More than 5000 ex-Congressmen, lawyers, former Government officials, business representatives, union officials and public-relations men are now lobbying in Washington. There are more than 300 registered lobby groups. Nearly $5,000,000 a year is acknowledged as being paid out in direct lobbying expenses. And this is only a fraction of the total spent to influence support for various legislative proposals.

Additional thousands of individuals and millions of dollars are wrapped up in indirect lobbying—the "new lobbying"—consisting mostly of nationwide public campaigns to arouse concern over specific issues and let loose a flood of mail, telegrams and phone calls to Congressmen and Senators.

Pressure mail from citizens stirred up by the professional propagandists of the "new lobby" is, of course, easy to spot. Some time ago, I received thousands of letters from various cities in Ohio, each envelope being addressed "Hon. Stephen A. Young." The lobbyist directing the campaign was careless about my middle initial, which happens to be M. Also, inclusion of the specific legislative number of the bill in question indicates that the letter was probably written at the urging of a Washington lobbyist. (Frankly, most Senators do not know—nor do we try to know—the numbers assigned to various House or Senate bills.) Similarly, a flood of letters or postcards urging a specific position on an issue, all written in the same style and phraseology, reveals an organized pressure campaign.

Of course, 20,000 letters obviously written in response to pressure from chamber-of-commerce officials, union officials or other organizations are less effective than a few hundred letters written personally, expressing the view and belief of the writer himself. I know that my Senatorial colleagues, like myself, pay great attention to individual letters and telegrams that appear to truly represent the views of the writers. Sometimes detailed personal arguments and observations can be very convincing.

In the public mind, lobbying has a sinister association. It evokes pictures of slick promoters hovering around Congressional and Federal agency offices, the green corners of large-denomination bills poking invitingly out of their pockets to lure weak or dishonest public officials. It's a great picture and a dramatic one, occasionally buttressed by some sensational revelation. But, basically, it's wrong. Most lobbyists are scrupulous persons who confront a Congressman openly with a point of view—and often with important information on legislative matters. There is nothing sinister about them. Most lobbyists wouldn't dare offer a bribe for a vote.

The majority probably never even think of doing so. Most couldn't pull it off if they tried. Any lobbyist stupid enough to attempt a bribe would find few, if any, takers. A couple of gas-industry blockheads tried it about ten years ago on the late Senator Francis Case, a conservative, thoroughly honest South Dakota Republican. They proposed $2500 ostensibly as a campaign contribution to sew up the wrong man. Senator Case exposed them publicly. The facts are, without a doubt, that probably every U.S. Senator would have rejected such an offer instantly. The result in the gas case was that President Eisenhower was forced by the pressure of public opinion to veto the legislation the gas lobby had so heavy-handedly espoused.

Incidents like this are rare. On the whole, lobbying is a respectable practice. In fact, it is a useful one. Senators and Representatives cannot hope to know everything about all the major legislation they have to consider, unless the proposal goes through one of the two or three committees of which the legislator is a member. Scores of major bills and thousands of lesser ones are introduced each year. We are not Renaissance men. We often rely on information and recommendations of other committees—and frequently on data from lobbyists. As a Senator, I always appreciate useful, reliable information from experts, and some lobbyists are experts in their fields. They are usually devoted entirely to one issue or cause, and facts on their subject spew from them as from a computer.

Often, the contribution of lobbyists to the successful passage of important legislation is considerable. It was, after all, civil rights lobbies that developed much of the hard, factual material that helped build support for civil rights legislation. Education lobbies helped pass breakthrough programs in school aid at all levels. Advocacy by lobbies for the elderly, the trade-union movement and other liberal groups made Medicare possible— after a 20-year struggle.

Ironically, it was a lobby's bungling—not the genius of Congress— that, more than anything, made Medicare a stronger, better measure than it otherwise would have been. That the lobby in question was one of the slickest, best-financed in the nation—the American Medical Association— only heightens the irony. The AMA spent millions of dollars (it has been the "spendingest" lobby in Washington in recent years) to convince Americans that Medicare would lead them down the dreaded road to socialized medicine. This scare campaign finally lost its bite, and the AMA took a new approach. In late 1964 and early 1965, it unleashed a radio-TV-newspaper-magazine blitz, covering Capitol Hill like a fog, to convince legislators and the public that the Medicare bill advocated by the Johnson Administration should be defeated because it did not cover doctors' bills.

The AMA was right. It made its case so well that Congress, instead of killing the bill, as the AMA wished, added to the measure on optional provision covering doctors' bills. As a supporter of Medicare for more than 20 years, I found myself silently thanking the AMA for its unwitting assistance. In my opinion, over the years the AMA's House of Delegates, the lobby's ruling clique, has misrepresented most of those who comprise its membership.

Not only do the Goliaths of lobbying trip occasionally over the intricate wires of their own strategy but now and then they are felled by a determined David with a sling of justice. The powerful American Meat Institute threw all the techniques of modern lobbying into its campaign against a humane-slaughter bill in 1958—advertising, professional lobbyists, public-relations campaigns, even a suite of lavish entertainment rooms at a leading Washington hotel. Among legislators, this sort of social lobbying is called the "indigestion circuit." Its premise is that the way to a Congressman's vote is through his stomach. The lamb intended for the slaughter was the Humane Society of the United States, chief backer of the bill. With modest funds and no paid lobbyists, the Humane Society and its army of amateurs—Americans whose common cause was simple, humane concern—loosed an unprecedented flood of mail on Congress and stormed Capitol Hill with ardent, dedicated members. They reached both the public and the Congressional conscience with articles and photos of the needlessly cruel treatment of animals in slaughterhouses and packing plants; struggling, screaming hogs pulled by moving cables through the shackling pen, then aloft to the killing floor; dumb cattle stunned by the brutal poleax before the death blow. They urged, as a simple alternative, electrical stunning methods and anesthetization. Congress was impressed by their sincerity and their good sense. The House passed the Humane Slaughter Bill by an overwhelming voice vote, and the Senate quickly registered its approval, 72-9. David had flattened Goliath.

In Washington, there's a lobby for just about everything—the doctors, the businessmen, the unions, the farmers. The American Legion, when it relaxes from asserting its 150-percent red-blooded Americanism, does a responsible job for veterans. There are lobbies, too, for hundreds of smaller special-interest groups.

With so much activity and pressure directed at public officials, you might say, "there ought to be a law." As a matter of fact, there is. There has been a long history of attempts to regulate lobbies through investigation and legislation. In 1913, a committee of the House of Representatives investigated the National Association of Manufacturers. It turned up evidence that the NAM carried several Congressmen and the chief page of the House on its payroll—and influenced appointments to strategic committee posts. One Congressman, clearly culpable, resigned as a result. In 1928, a general lobbying probe led to the introduction of the Lobbyist Control Bill, a meritorious legislative proposal passed in the Senate but smothered in the House. Since then, there have been investigations of the utility lobbies, of the distribution of some publications of lunatic right-wing organizations, of the influence on military procurement of retired Army officers lobbying for defense contractors, and of the pressure brought by foreign lobbyists in connection with domestic legislation, to mention a few. There was one probe by the Senate Foreign Relations Committee that led to the introduction of a bill by the chairman, Senator William Fulbright, to tighten registration requirements under the Foreign Agents Registration Act. But the Fulbright bill, like so many others, passed one house only to die in the other.

Responsible lobbying groups themselves have instituted procedures of self-regulation and have set high standards of conduct for their representatives. On the other hand, some groups, through their lobbyists, have committed unscrupulous distortion of facts and information for shortsighted, selfish ends. Such, I believe, was the behavior of the automobile industry in attempting to suppress information on the lack of safety features in American automobiles—and in trying to prevent passage of legislation to compel manufacturers to make their automobiles and tires less dangerous. Such, also, has been the behavior of the cigarette industry—in attempting to distort findings of objective research in the relationship between smoking and such diseases as cancer and heart trouble.

The most important single piece of legislation dealing with the matter was the Federal Regulation of Lobbying Act of 1946, which required anyone engaged in lobbying to report his expenditures and activities. However, no limit was set on the amount spent or the techniques used. The secretary of the Senate and the clerk of the House of Representatives receive and publish these reports, but they lack the staff to check them out or to assure maximum compliance. It seems to me that a much more effective way of handling this problem might be to turn the entire job over to the General Accounting Office, an agency directly responsible to the Congress, which has the necessary staff and facilities to assure compliance with the law.

Complicating the picture was a United States Supreme Court ruling in 1954 that held that a lobbyist is someone who collects or receives money for the principal purpose of influencing legislators by direct contacts—leaving uncovered and unregulated the mammoth and sometimes very effective nationwide campaigns of the "new lobby," relying mostly on the media and the mails to press a cause.

The real, general abuses in political pressure today—except for occasional cases of personal corruption—stem from these spare-no-expense, no-holds-barred publicity and public-relations campaigns that excite voters to turn the heat on legislators. Abuses of distortion, exaggeration and oversimplification are inherent in such campaigns. But little can be done about them, for to prohibit or to control them rigidly would abridge the constitutionally guaranteed rights of Americans to advocate what they believe is their interest and to oppose what they believe is not. This is a right to be protected zealously. It is precious enough to be preserved intact, despite the occasional abuses it might engender.

For decades, legislators and editorial writers have bemoaned the existence of pressure groups—an exercise in futility, for they are as inevitable as daybreak. Whether we like it or not, lobbying is here to stay. Indeed, lobbies and pressure groups are now an integral part of our political process, and I'll leave it to others to inveigh against them. In a democracy, when each citizen's view is of equal importance, like-minded individuals are bound to organize to increase the volume of their voice.

At present, the individual Senator or Representative is far from powerless when he feels pressure groups threatening legitimate necessary legislation. As a United States Senator, I have access to one of the best forums in the nation—the floor of the Senate. Without abusing the right, I can rise to my feet any time during a Senate session and bring pressure of my own on a pressure group. I can wonder if a pressure group truly represents, in its propaganda statements, the sentiments of its membership. (I am convinced some of them do not.)

Large and rich lobbies are as entitled to express their views as are small and poor ones. Though we may regret the discrepancy, we cannot muffle one without gagging the other. I have enough faith in my colleagues and in other elected officials to assume they are more impressed by the rightness of an argument than by the size, wealth and membership of its protagonists.

There is no discount on democracy. While we must police and punish corruption, we cannot and should not police free expression of ideas—or the right to petition our Government. Occasional cynical misuse of these rights is part of democracy's price. It is a very small price, however; and I, for one, will run the risk of paying it.

5 Crime and Delinquency

From the many hundreds of research articles and thoughtful discussions of the crime problem, it is difficult to select only a handful. Perhaps there is no better concise statement of the crime problem than the opening summary statement of a recent presidential commission.

SUMMARY

This report is about crime in America—about those who commit it, about those who are its victims, and about what can be done to reduce it.

The report is the work of 19 commissioners, 63 staff members, 175 consultants, and hundreds of advisers. The commissioners, staff, consultants, and advisers come from every part of America and represent a broad range of opinion and profession.

In the process of developing the findings and recommendations of the report the Commission called three national conferences, conducted five national surveys, held hundreds of meetings, and interviewed tens of thousands of persons.

The report makes more than 200 specific recommendations—concrete steps the Commission believes can lead to a safer and more just society. These recommendations call for a greatly increased effort on the part of the Federal Government, the States, the counties, the cities, civic organizations, religious institutions, business groups, and individual citizens. They call for basic changes in the operations of police, schools, prosecutors, employment agencies, defenders, social workers, prisons, housing authorities, and probation and parole officers.

But the recommendations are more than just a list of new procedures, new tactics, and new techniques. They are a call for a revolution in the way America thinks about crime.

Many Americans take comfort in the view that crime is the vice of a handful of people. This view is inaccurate. In the United States today, one boy in six is referred to the juvenile court. A Commission survey shows

From "President's Commission on Law Enforcement and Administration of Justice," *The Challenge of Crime in a Free Society* (Washington, U.S. Government Printing Office, 1967), pp. v–xi.

that in 1965 more than two million Americans were received in prisons or juvenile training schools, or placed on probation. Another Commission study suggests that about 40 percent of all male children now living in the United States will be arrested for a nontraffic offense during their lives. An independent survey of 1,700 persons found that 91 percent of the sample admitted they had committed acts for which they might have received jail or prison sentences.

Many Americans also think of crime as a very narrow range of behavior. It is not. An enormous variety of acts make up the "crime problem." Crime is not just a tough teenager snatching a lady's purse. It is a professional thief stealing cars "on order." It is a well-heeled loan shark taking over a previously legitimate business for organized crime. It is a polite young man who suddenly and inexplicably murders his family. It is a corporation executive conspiring with competitors to keep prices high. No single formula, no single theory, no single generalization can explain the vast range of behavior called crime.

Many Americans think controlling crime is solely the task of the police, the courts, and correction agencies. In fact, as the Commission's report makes clear, crime cannot be controlled without the interest and participation of schools, businesses, social agencies, private groups, and individual citizens.

What, then, is America's experience with crime and how has this experience shaped the Nation's way of living? A new insight into these two questions is furnished by the Commission's National Survey of Criminal Victims. In this survey, the first of its kind conducted on such a scope, 10,000 representative American households were asked about their experiences with crime, whether they reported those experiences to the police, and how those experiences affected their lives.

An important finding of the survey is that for the Nation as a whole there is far more crime than ever is reported. Burglaries occur about three times more often than they are reported to police. Aggravated assaults and larcenies over $50 occur twice as often as they are reported. There are 50 percent more robberies than are reported. In some areas, only one-tenth of the total number of certain kinds of crimes are reported to the police. Seventy-four percent of the neighborhood commercial establishments surveyed do not report to police the thefts committed by their employees.

The existence of crime, the talk about crime, the reports of crime, and the fear of crime have eroded the basic quality of life of many Americans. A Commission study conducted in high crime areas of two large cities found that:

43 percent of the respondents say they stay off the streets at night because of their fear of crime.

35 percent say they do not speak to strangers any more because of their fear of crime.

21 percent say they use cars and cabs at night because of their fear of crime.

20 percent say they would like to move to another neighborhood because of their fear of crime.

The findings of the Commission's national survey generally support those of the local surveys. One-third of a representative sample of all Americans say it is unsafe to walk alone at night in their neighborhoods. Slightly more than one-third say they keep firearms in the house for protection against criminals. Twenty-eight percent say they keep watchdogs for the same reason.

Under any circumstance, developing an effective response to the problem of crime in America is exceedingly difficult. And because of the changes expected in the population in the next decade, in years to come it will be more difficult. Young people commit a disproportionate share of crime and the number of young people in our society is growing at a much faster rate than the total population. Although the 15- to 17-year-old age group represents only 5.4 percent of the population, it accounts for 12.8 percent of all arrests. Fifteen- and sixteen-year-olds have the highest arrest rate in the United States. The problem in the years ahead is dramatically foretold by the fact that 23 percent of the population is 10 or under.

Despite the seriousness of the problem today and the increasing challenge in the years ahead, the central conclusion of the Commission is that a significant reduction in crime is possible if the following objectives are vigorously pursued:

First, society must seek to prevent crime before it happens by assuring all Americans a stake in the benefits and responsibilities of American life, by strengthening law enforcement, and by reducing criminal opportunities.

Second, society's aim of reducing crime would be better served if the system of criminal justice developed a far broader range of techniques with which to deal with individual offenders.

Third, the system of criminal justice must eliminate existing injustices if it is to achieve its ideals and win the respect and cooperation of all citizens.

Fourth, the system of criminal justice must attract more people and better people—police, prosecutors, judges, defense attorneys, probation and parole officers, and corrections officials with more knowledge, expertise, initiative, and integrity.

Fifth, there must be much more operational and basic research into the problems of crime and criminal administration, by those both within and without the system of criminal justice.

Sixth, the police, courts, and correctional agencies must be given substantially greater amounts of money if they are to improve their ability to control crime.

Seventh, individual citizens, civic and business organizations, religious institutions, and all levels of government must take responsibility for planning and implementing the changes that must be made in the criminal justice system if crime is to be reduced.

In terms of specific recommendations, what do these seven objectives mean?

1. PREVENTING CRIME

The prevention of crime covers a wide range of activities: Eliminating social conditions closely associated with crime; improving the ability of the criminal justice system to detect, apprehend, judge, and reintegrate into their communities those who commit crimes; and reducing the situations in which crimes are most likely to be committed.

Every effort must be made to strengthen the family, now often shattered by the grinding pressures of urban slums.

Slum schools must be given enough resources to make them as good as schools elsewhere and to enable them to compensate for the various handicaps suffered by the slum child—to rescue him from his environment.

Present efforts to combat school segregation, and the housing segregation that underlies it, must be continued and expanded.

Employment opportunities must be enlarged and young people provided with more effective vocational training and individual job counseling. Programs to create new kinds of jobs—such as probation aides, medical assistants, and teacher helpers—seem particularly promising and should be expanded.

The problem of increasing the ability of the police to detect and apprehend criminals is complicated. In one effort to find out how this objective could be achieved, the Commission conducted an analysis of 1,905 crimes reported to the Los Angeles Police Department during a recent month. The study showed the importance of identifying the perpetrator at the scene of the crime. Eighty-six percent of the crimes with named suspects were solved, but only 12 percent of the unnamed suspect crimes were solved. Another finding of the study was that there is a relationship between the speed of response and certainty of apprehension. On the average, response to emergency calls resulting in arrests was 50 percent faster than response to emergency calls not resulting in arrest. On the basis of this finding, and a cost effectiveness study to discover the best means to reduce response time, the Commission recommends an experimental program to develop computer-aided command-and-control systems for large police departments.

To insure the maximum use of such a system, headquarters must have a direct link with every on duty police officer. Because large scale production would result in a substantial reduction of the cost of miniature two-way radios, the Commission recommends that the Federal Government assume leadership in initiating a development program for such equipment and that it consider guaranteeing the sale of the first production lot of perhaps 20,000 units.

Two other steps to reduce police response time are recommended:

Police callboxes, which are locked and inconspicuous in most cities, should be left open, brightly marked, and designated "public emergency callboxes."

The telephone company should develop a single police number for each metropolitan area, and eventually for the entire United States.

Improving the effectiveness of law enforcement, however, is much more than just improving police response time. For example a study in Washington, D.C., found that courtroom time for a felony defendant who pleads guilty probably totals less than 1 hour, while the median time from his initial appearance to his disposition is 4 months.

In an effort to discover how courts can best speed the process of criminal justice, the known facts about felony cases in Washington were placed in a computer and the operation of the system was simulated. After a number of possible solutions to the problem of delay were tested, it appeared that the addition of a second grand jury—which, with supporting personnel, would cost less than $50,000 a year—would result in a 25 percent reduction in the time required for the typical felony case to move from initial appearance to trial.

The application of such analysis—when combined with the Commission's recommended timetable laying out timespans for each step in the criminal process—should help court systems to ascertain their procedural bottlenecks and develop ways to eliminate them.

Another way to prevent crime is to reduce the opportunity to commit it. Many crimes would not be committed, indeed many criminal careers would not begin, if there were fewer opportunities for crime.

Auto theft is a good example. According to FBI statistics, the key had been left in the ignition or the ignition had been left unlocked in 42 percent of all stolen cars. Even in those cars taken when the ignition was locked, at least 20 percent were stolen simply by shorting the ignition with such simple devices as paper clips or tinfoil. In one city, the elimination of the unlocked "off" position on the 1965 Chevrolet resulted in 50 percent fewer of those models being stolen in 1965 than were stolen in 1964.

On the basis of these findings, it appears that an important reduction in auto theft could be achieved simply by installing an ignition system that automatically ejects the key when the engine is turned off.

A major reason that it is important to reduce auto theft is that stealing a car is very often the criminal act that starts a boy on a course of lawbreaking.

Stricter gun controls also would reduce some kinds of crime. Here, the Commission recommends a strengthening of the Federal law governing the interstate shipment of firearms and enactment of State laws requiring the registration of all handguns, rifles, and shotguns, and prohibiting the sale or ownership of firearms by certain categories of persons—dangerous criminals, habitual drunkards, and drug addicts. After five years, the Commission recommends that Congress pass a Federal registration law applying to those States that have not passed their own registration laws.

2. NEW WAYS OF DEALING WITH OFFENDERS

The Commission's second objective—the development of a far broader range of alternatives for dealing with offenders—is based on the belief that, while there are some who must be completely segregated from society, there are many instances in which segregation does more harm than good. Furthermore, by concentrating the resources of the police, the courts, and correctional agencies on the smaller number of offenders who really need them, it should be possible to give all offenders more effective treatment.

A specific and important example of this principle is the Commission's recommendation that every community consider establishing a Youth Services Bureau, a community-based center to which juveniles could be referred by the police, the courts, parents, schools, and social agencies for counseling, education, work, or recreation programs and job placement.

The Youth Services Bureau—an agency to handle many troubled and troublesome young people outside the criminal system—is needed in part because society has failed to give the juvenile court the resources that would allow it to function as its founders hoped it would. In a recent survey of juvenile court judges, for example, 83 percent said no psychologist or psychiatrist was available to their courts on a regular basis and one-third said they did not have probation officers or social workers. Even where there are probation officers, the Commission found, the average officer supervises 76 probationers, more than double the recommended caseload.

The California Youth Authority for the last 5 years has been conducting a controlled experiment to determine the effectiveness of another kind of alternative treatment program for juveniles. There, after initial screening, convicted juvenile delinquents are assigned on a random basis to either an experimental group or a control group. Those in the experimental group are returned to the community and receive intensive individual counseling, group counseling, group therapy, and family counseling. Those in the control group are assigned to California's regular institutional treatment program. The finding so far: 28 percent of the experimental group have had their paroles revoked, compared with 52 percent in the control group. Furthermore, the community treatment program is less expensive than institutional treatment.

To make community-based treatment possible for both adults and juveniles, the Commission recommends the development of an entirely new kind of correctional institution: located close to the population centers; maintaining close relations with schools, employers, and universities; housing as few as 50 inmates; serving as a classification center, as the center for various kinds of community programs and as a port of reentry to the community for those difficult and dangerous offenders who have required treatment in facilities with tighter custody.

Such institutions would be useful in the operation of programs— strongly recommended by the Commission—that permit selected inmates to work or study in the community during the day and return to control at night, and programs that permit long-term inmates to become adjusted to society gradually rather than being discharged directly from maximum security institutions to the streets.

Another aspect of the Commission's conviction that different offenders with different problems should be treated in different ways, is its recommendation about the handling of public drunkenness, which, in 1965, accounted for one out of every three arrests in America. The great number of these arrests—some 2 million—burdens the police, clogs the lower courts and crowds the penal institutions. The Commission therefore recommends that communities develop civil detoxification units and comprehensive after-care programs, and that with the development of such programs, drunkenness, not accompanied by other unlawful conduct, should not be a criminal offense.

Similarly, the Commission recommends the expanded use of civil commitment for drug addicts.

3. ELIMINATING UNFAIRNESS

The third objective is to eliminate injustices so that the system of criminal justice can win the respect and cooperation of all citizens. Our society must give the police, the courts, and correctional agencies the resources and the mandate to provide fair and dignified treatment for all.

The Commission found overwhelming evidence of institutional shortcomings in almost every part of the United States.

A survey of the lower court operations in a number of large American cities found cramped and noisy courtrooms, undignified and perfunctory procedures, badly trained personnel overwhelmed by enormous caseloads. In short, the Commission found assembly line justice.

The Commission found that in at least three States, justices of the peace are paid only if they convict and collect a fee from the defendant, a practice held unconstitutional by the Supreme Court 40 years ago.

The Commission found that approximately one-fourth of the 400,000 children detained in 1965—for a variety of causes but including truancy, smoking, and running away from home—were held in adult jails and lockups, often with hardened criminals.

In addition to the creation of new kinds of institutions—such as the Youth Services Bureau and the small, community-based correctional centers—the Commission recommends several important procedural changes. It recommends counsel at various points in the criminal process.

For juveniles, the Commission recommends providing counsel whenever coercive action is a possibility.

For adults, the Commission recommends providing counsel to any criminal defendant who faces a significant penalty—excluding traffic and similar petty charges—if he cannot afford to provide counsel for himself.

In connection with this recommendation, the Commission asks each State to finance regular, statewide assigned counsel and defender systems for the indigent.

Counsel also should be provided in parole and probation revocation hearings.

Another kind of broad procedural change that the Commission recommends is that every State, county, and local jurisdiction provide judicial officers with sufficient information about individual defendants to permit the release without money bail of those who can be safely released.

In addition to eliminating the injustice of holding persons charged with a crime merely because they cannot afford bail, this recommendation also would save a good deal of money. New York City alone, for example, spends approximately $10 million a year holding persons who have not yet been found guilty of any crime.

Besides institutional injustices, the Commission found that while the great majority of criminal justice and law enforcement personnel perform their duties with fairness and understanding, even under the most trying circumstances, some take advantage of their official positions and act in a callous, corrupt, or brutal manner.

Injustice will not yield to simple solutions. Overcoming it requires a wide variety of remedies including improved methods of selecting personnel, the massive infusion of additional funds, the revamping of existing procedures and the adoption of more effective internal and external controls.

The relations between the police and urban poor deserve special mention. Here the Commission recommends that every large department —especially in communities with substantial minority populations—should have community-relations machinery consisting of a headquarters planning and supervising unit and precinct units to carry out recommended programs. Effective citizens advisory committees should be established in minority group neighborhoods. All departments with substantial minority populations should make special efforts to recruit minority group officers and to deploy and promote them fairly. They should have rigorous internal investigation units to examine complaints of misconduct. The Commission believes it is of the utmost importance to insure that complaints of unfair treatment are fairly dealt with.

Fair treatment of every individual—fair in fact and also perceived to be fair by those affected—is an essential element of justice and a principal objective of the American criminal justice system.

4. PERSONNEL

The fourth objective is that higher levels of knowledge, expertise, initiative, and integrity be achieved by police, judges, prosecutors, defense attorneys, and correctional authorities so that the system of criminal justice can improve its ability to control crime.

The Commission found one obstacle to recruiting better police officers was the standard requirement that all candidates—regardless of qualifications—begin their careers at the lowest level and normally remain at this level from 2 to 5 years before being eligible for promotion. Thus, a college graduate must enter a department at the same rank and pay and perform the same tasks as a person who enters with only a high school diploma or less.

The Commission recommends that police departments give up single entry and establish three levels at which candidates may begin their police careers. The Commission calls these three levels the "community service officer," the "police officer," and the "police agent."

This division, in addition to providing an entry place for the better educated, also would permit police departments to tap the special knowledge, skills, and understanding of those brought up in the slums.

The community service officer would be a uniformed but unarmed member of the police department. Two of his major responsibilities would be to maintain close relations with juveniles in the area where he works and to be especially alert to crime-breeding conditions that other city agencies had not dealt with. Typically, the CSO might be under 21, might not be required to meet conventional education requirements, and might work out of a store-front office. Serving as an apprentice policeman—a substitute for the police cadet—the CSO would work as a member of a team with the police officer and police agent.

The police officer would respond to calls for service, perform routine patrol, render emergency services, make preliminary investigations, and enforce traffic regulations. In order to qualify as a police officer at the present time, a candidate should possess a high school diploma and should demonstrate a capacity for college work.

The police agent would do whatever police jobs were most complicated, most sensitive, and most demanding. He might be a specialist in police community-relations or juvenile delinquency. He might be in uniform patrolling a high-crime neighborhood. He might have staff duties. To become a police agent would require at least 2 years of college work and preferably a baccalaureate degree in the liberal arts or social sciences.

As an ultimate goal, the Commission recommends that all police personnel with general enforcement powers have baccalaureate degrees.

While candidates could enter the police service at any one of the three levels, they also could work their way up through the different categories as they met the basic education and other requirements.

In many jurisdictions there is a critical need for additional police personnel. Studies by the Commission indicate a recruiting need of 50,000 policemen in 1967 just to fill positions already authorized. In order to increase police effectiveness, additional staff specialists will be required, and when the community service officers are added manpower needs will be even greater.

The Commission also recommends that every State establish a commission on police standards to set minimum recruiting and training standards and to provide financial and technical assistance for local police departments.

In order to improve the quality of judges, prosecutors, and defense attorneys, the Commission recommends a variety of steps: Taking the selection of judges out of partisan politics; the more regular use of seminars, conferences, and institutes to train sitting judges; the establishment of judicial commissions to excuse physically or mentally incapacitated judges from their duties without public humiliation; the general abolition of part-time district attorneys and assistant district attorneys; and a broad range of measures to develop a greatly enlarged and better trained pool of defense attorneys.

In the correctional system there is a critical shortage of probation and parole officers, teachers, caseworkers, vocational instructors, and group workers. The need for major manpower increases in this area was made clear by the findings from the Commission's national corrections survey:

Less than 3 percent of all personnel working in local jails and institutions devote their time to treatment and training.

Eleven States do not offer any kind of probation services for adult misdemeanants, six offer only the barest fragments of such services, and most States offer them on a spotty basis.

Two-thirds of all State adult felony probationers are in caseloads of over 100 persons.

To meet the requirements of both the correctional agencies and the courts, the Commission has found an immediate need to double the Nation's pool of juvenile probation officers, triple the number of probation officers working with adult felons, and increase sevenfold the number of officers working with misdemeanants.

Another area with a critical need for large numbers of expert criminal justice officers is the complex one of controlling organized crime. Here, the Commission recommends that prosecutors and police in every State and city where organized crime is known to, or may, exist develop special organized crime units.

5. RESEARCH

The fifth objective is that every segment of the system of criminal justice devote a significant part of its resources for research to insure the development of new and effective methods of controlling crime.

The Commission found that little research is being conducted into such matters as the economic impact of crime; the effects on crime of increasing or decreasing criminal sanctions; possible methods for improving the effectiveness of various procedures of the police, courts, and correctional agencies.

Organized crime is another area in which almost no research has been conducted. The Commission found that the only group with any significant knowledge about this problem was law enforcement officials. Those in other disciplines—social scientists, economists and lawyers, for example— have not until recently considered the possibility of research projects on organized crime.

A small fraction of 1 percent of the criminal justice system's total budget is spent on research. This figure could be multiplied many times without approaching the 3 percent industry spends on research, much less the 15 percent the Defense Department spends. The Commission believes it should be multiplied many times.

That research is a powerful force for change in the field of criminal justice perhaps can best be documented by the history of the Vera Institute in New York City. Here the research of a small, nongovernment agency has in a very short time led to major changes in the bail procedures of approximately 100 cities, several States, and the Federal Government.

Because of the importance of research, the Commission recommends that major criminal justice agencies—such as State court and correctional systems and big-city police departments—organize operational research units as integral parts of their structures.

In addition, the criminal justice agencies should welcome the efforts of scholars and other independent experts to understand their problems and operations. These agencies cannot undertake needed research on their own; they urgently need the help of outsiders.

The Commission also recommends the establishment of several regional research institutes designed to concentrate a number of different disciplines on the problem of crime. It further recommends the establishment of an independent National Criminal Research Foundation to stimulate and coordinate research and disseminate its results.

One essential requirement for research is more complete information about the operation of the criminal process. To meet this requirement, the Commission recommends the creation of a National Criminal Justice Statistics Center. The Center's first responsibility would be to work with the FBI, the Children's Bureau, the Federal Bureau of Prisons, and other agencies to develop an integrated picture of the number of crimes reported to police, the number of persons arrested, the number of accused persons prosecuted, the number of offenders placed on probation, in prison, and subsequently on parole.

Another major responsibility of the Center would be to continue the Commission's initial effort to develop a new yardstick to measure the extent of crime in our society as a supplement to the FBI's Uniform Crime Reports. The Commission believes that the Government should be able to plot the levels of different kinds of crime in a city or a state as precisely as the Labor Department and the Census Bureau now plot the rate of unemployment. Just as unemployment information is essential to sound economic planning, so some day may criminal information help official planning in the system of criminal justice.

6. MONEY

Sixth, the police, the courts, and correctional agencies will require substantially more money if they are to control crime better.

Almost all of the specific recommendations made by the Commission will involve increased budgets. Substantially higher salaries must be offered to attract topflight candidates to the system of criminal justice. For example, the median annual salary for a patrolman in a large city today is $5,300. Typically, the maximum salary is something less than $1,000 above the starting salary. The Commission believes the most important change that can be made in police salary scales is to increase maximums sharply.

An FBI agent, for example, starts at $8,421 a year and if he serves long and well enough can reach $16,905 a year without being promoted to a supervisory position. The Commission is aware that reaching such figures immediately is not possible in many cities, but it believes that there should be a large range from minimum to maximum everywhere.

The Commission also recommends new kinds of programs that will require additional funds: Youth Services Bureaus, greatly enlarged misdemeanant probation services and increased levels of research, for example.

The Commission believes some of the additional resources—especially those devoted to innovative programs and to training, education, and research—should be contributed by the Federal Government.

The Federal Government already is conducting a broad range of programs—aid to elementary and secondary schools, the Neighborhood Youth Corps, Project Head Start, and others—designed to attack directly the social problems often associated with crime.

Through such agencies as the Federal Bureau of Investigation, the Office of Law Enforcement Assistance, the Bureau of Prisons, and the Office of Manpower Development and Training, the Federal Government also offers comparatively limited financial and technical assistance to the police, the courts, and corrections authorities.

While the Commission is convinced States and local governments must continue to carry the major burden of criminal administration, it recommends a vastly enlarged program of Federal assistance to strengthen law enforcement, crime prevention, and the administration of justice.

The program of Federal support recommended by the Commission would be directed to eight major needs:

(1) State and local planning.

(2) Education and training of criminal justice personnel.

(3) Surveys and advisory services concerning the organization and operation of police departments, courts, prosecuting offices, and corrections agencies.

(4) Development of a coordinated national information system for operational and research purposes.

(5) Funding of limited numbers of demonstration programs in agencies of justice.

(6) Scientific and technological research and development.

(7) Development of national and regional research centers.

(8) Grants-in-aid for operational innovations.

The Commission is not in a position to recommend the exact amount of money that will be needed to carry out its proposed program. It believes, however, that a Federal program totaling hundreds of millions of dollars a year during the next decade could be effectively utilized. The

Commission also believes the major responsibility for administering this program should lie within the Department of Justice.

The States, the cities, and the counties also will have to make substantial increases in their contributions to the system of criminal justice.

7. RESPONSIBILITY FOR CHANGE

Seventh, individual citizens, social-service agencies, universities, religious institutions, civic and business groups, and all kinds of governmental agencies at all levels must become involved in planning and executing changes in the criminal justice system.

The Commission is convinced that the financial and technical assistance program it proposes can and should be only a small part of the national effort to develop a more effective and fair response to crime.

In March of 1966, President Johnson asked the Attorney General to invite each Governor to form a State committee on criminal administration. The response to this request has been encouraging; more than two-thirds of the States already have such committees or have indicated they intend to form then.

The Commission recommends that in every State and city there should be an agency, or one or more officials, with specific responsibility for planning improvements in criminal administration and encouraging their implementation.

Planning agencies, among other functions, play a key role in helping State legislatures and city councils decide where additional funds and manpower are most needed, what new programs should be adopted, and where and how existing agencies might pool their resources on either a metropolitan or regional basis.

The planning agencies should include both officials from the system of criminal justice and citizens from other professions. Plans to improve criminal administration will be impossible to put into effect unless those responsible for criminal administration help make them. On the other hand, crime prevention must be the task of the community as a whole.

While this report has concentrated on recommendations for action by governments, the Commission is convinced that governmental actions will not be enough. Crime is a social problem that is interwoven with almost every aspect of American life. Controlling it involves improving the quality of family life, the way schools are run, the way cities are planned, the way workers are hired. Controlling crime is the business of every American institution. Controlling crime is the business of every American.

Universities should increase their research on the problems of crime; private social welfare organizations and religious institutions should continue to experiment with advanced techniques of helping slum children overcome their environment; labor unions and businesses can enlarge their programs to provide prisoners with vocational training; professional and community organizations can help probation and parole workers with their work.

The responsibility of the individual citizen runs far deeper than cooperating with the police or accepting jury duty or insuring the safety of his family by installing adequate locks—important as they are. He must respect the law, refuse to cut corners, reject the cynical argument that "anything goes as long as you don't get caught."

Most important of all, he must, on his own and through the organizations he belongs to, interest himself in the problems of crime and criminal justice, seek information, express his views, use his vote wisely, get involved.

In sum, the Commission is sure that the Nation can control crime if it will.

Sociologists have often noted that "situational determinants of behavior" may govern people's actions more strongly than do their moral convictions or personal habits. Business men have been acting on this knowledge for years. Instead of simply trusting the bookkeeper, books are audited; mirrors and closed-circuit television cameras watch customers and salespersons; small items are affixed to cardboard to make a bulky package that cannot be easily pocketed. University libraries are placing low-cost copying machines in the library to encourage students to photocopy instead of tearing out their library assignments.

The following item relates an experiment which demonstrates how people's actions are affected by situational determinants—in this case, whether anyone who might be looking knows them or disapproves of their actions.

DIARY OF A VANDALIZED CAR

Editors of *Time*

At 3:15 on a recent Friday afternoon, a 1959 green Oldsmobile was parked alongside the curb in a middle-class residential neighborhood of New York City. Two men got out, removed the license plates, and

Reprinted by permission from *Time,* The Weekly Newsmagazine, February 28, 1969, pp. 62–65; copyright © Time Inc. 1969.

opened the hood slightly to make the car look as if it had been stolen or left alone while its owner went for help. Then they withdrew to a nearby window, where—unseen—they could watch what was to happen.

Vice squad cops bent on entrapment? No. In fact, the two men were psychologists, interested in the varieties of human response to the sight of an obviously unguarded, abandoned car. Within ten minutes, their vehicle received its first visitors. The researchers' log reads, in chilling ellipsis: "Family of three drive by, stop. All leave car. Well-dressed mother with Saks Fifth Avenue shopping bag stands by car on sidewalk keeping watch. Boy, about eight years old, stays by father throughout, observing and helping. Father, dressed in neat sport shirt, slacks, and windbreaker, inspects car, opens trunk, rummages through; opens own car trunk full of tools, removes hacksaw, cuts for one minute. Lifts battery out and puts it in his trunk. Lifts entire radiator out, places it on back floor of his car. Family drives off."

CASUAL OBSERVERS

The whole operation took only seven minutes. While it was going on, the log notes, "A young man and woman in a car pull up behind the Olds; both get out, go up to back of Olds, inspect it while father is sawing. They watch him and then leave. Two men around 35 years old walk by and observe the father sawing. They walk on."

Scott Fraser, a social psychologist at New York University, was one of the observers who kept round-the-clock vigils over the car for 64 hours. What surprised him was that most of the car stripping took place in broad daylight. All of the theft was done by clean-cut, well-dressed middle-class people. Furthermore, the major theft and damage was always observed by someone else. "Sometimes passersby would engage in casual conversation with the miscreants," says Fraser.

By the end of the first 26 hours, a steady parade of vandals had removed the battery, radiator, air cleaner, radio antenna, windshield wipers, right-hand-side chrome strip, hubcaps, a set of jumper cables, a gas can, a can of car wax, and the left rear tire (the other tires were too worn to be interesting). Nine hours later, random destruction began when two laughing teen-agers tore off the rearview mirror and began throwing it at the headlights and front windshield.

INTO THE CARRIAGE

Eventually, five eight-year-olds claimed the car as their private playground, crawling in and out of it and smashing the windows. One of the last visitors was a middle-aged man in a camel's hair coat and matching hat, pushing a baby in a carriage. He stopped, rummaged through the trunk, took out an unidentifiable part, put it in the baby carriage, and wheeled off.

This serious version of *Candid Camera* was one of several similar experiments which have been organized recently by Philip Zimbardo, 35, a New York born psychologist now at Stanford University. His tentative conclusion is that in office, schools and streets, a big-city feeling of personal anonymity encourages destructive behavior. It is discouraged by a sense of community—an atmosphere in which vandals feel that anyone watching disapproves of what they are doing. To check his theory, Zimbardo parked a derelict car in a middle-class neighborhood of suburban Palo Alto, California. During three days of observation, he reports, it was not touched once.

> Most college students come from the secure middle class or from the upwardly-mobile sections of the working class, and are probably accustomed to viewing themselves as "decent people." Yet there is at least one type of "crime" which is a familiar part of the college scene. While not strictly a crime in that it is not forbidden by law, it is unquestionably socially injurious in that it would, if unchecked, destroy the social system within which it operates. Perhaps a brief description of this "crime" will be a healthy antidote to the smug self-righteousness of "decent people."

A STARTLING SURVEY
ON COLLEGE CRIBBING

Editors of *Life*

The most comprehensive study ever made of cheating among U.S. college students was published last month by the Bureau of Applied Research at Columbia University Here are some of its findings:

Nearly half of the 5,000 students questioned—in strict confidence at 99 colleges and universities—admitted they had engaged in some form of cheating since entering college.

From *Life* (February 5, 1965) p. 64; reprinted by permission of the Bureau of Applied Social Research, Columbia University.

More than half of the 5,000 say that they have observed cheating among other students, and that it occurs in about 8% of final exams and about 13% of homework.

Cheating is more prevalent at large schools than at small schools and occurs more often in large classes than in small ones.

Cheating is especially rife on campuses that have sororities and fraternities. It is found more often in coeducational institutions than in men's or girls' schools. It is more common among men than women.

The highest proportion of cheaters (68%) is found among mediocre students who treat grades lightly themselves but who are under great pressure from their parents to get good grades.

Students with poor grades tend to cheat more often than better students. Among those who admitted cheating, 57% had average grades of C-minus or lower.

Good students cheat, too, and 37% of the "A" students polled admitted cheating at some point in college.

The stricter the classroom rules *against* cheating—a teacher constantly watching, assigning seats, staggering seats, refusing permission to leave the room, etc.—the more students are likely to cheat.

Cheating occurs most often on tests using multiple-choice or true and false questions, least often when essay-type questions are used. And it is most prevalent in courses where frequent tests are given and where the standardized tests are given year after year or to different classes in the same year.

Cheating is most likely to occur in introductory courses—where the classes tend to be large—and in courses that rely on lectures and textbooks rather than on smaller seminars and individual research.

Cheating has a direct relationship to study habits. Only 42% of the students who study for 30 hours or more per week admitted to cheating. Among the cheaters 57% study only 19 hours a week or less.

Cheating is rampant among students with athletic scholarships—74% of whom admitted having done it. By contrast, 45% of the students who had won academic scholarships and 41% of those with scholarships based on financial need admitted to cheating.

The students' reasons for being in college are also factors in their tendency to cheat. Of those who stated they entered college "to provide a basic education and appreciation of ideas," 45% turned out to be cheaters. But 54% of those who said they were in college for social reasons and 52% of those seeking vocational training admitted to cheating.

Students in career-oriented fields like business and engineering are more likely to cheat than students majoring in history, the humanities or language. In between are students specializing in the sciences or the arts.

The social life of the students has a bearing on their tendency to cheat. Only 41% of the students who said they did not play cards or watch TV wound up in the cheating category, while 56% of those who spend five or more hours a week in these pursuits admitted to cheating. Students who date regularly cheat more than those who don't.

Ninety percent of the students—including many who admit to cheating—said they are opposed to the practice on moral grounds. And over half of the students—again including some cheaters—believe that it is far worse to cheat than to report another student for cheating. Of those who hold this view, 16% would report even a close friend to the authorities if they caught him cheating. And 51% said they would either ignore a friend or turn him down if he asked for help during an exam.

Cheating is most prevalent at schools which try to control it by a joint student-faculty system of monitoring. It is slightly less common at schools where the faculty alone tries to cope with the problem. And it occurs far less often at colleges with an honor system, in which the students themselves do the policing and enforcing.

After noting that nearly everyone is somewhat criminal and after surveying the imperfections in our determination of "criminal," it remains true, of course, that some persons are far more dangerously criminal than others. A necessary first step in dealing with the crime problem is ot learn just how the dangerously criminal differ from the "somewhat criminal." Two sociologists reveal in the following research article that even this first step has not been definitively taken.

PERSONALITY ATTRIBUTES OF THE CRIMINAL:

An analysis of research studies, 1950-1965

Gordon P. Waldo   Simon Dinitz

Assistant Professor of Sociology   *Professor of Sociology*
University of California at Los Angeles   *Ohio State University*

During the last forty years numerous presonality tests varying in quality and validity have been developed and utilized to measure different aspects of personality and have been administered to every conceivable type of "abnormal" and deviant individual, with criminals and juvenile delinquents receiving their fair share of attention.

From the *Journal of Research in Crime and Delinquency* 2 (July 1967) pp. 185–202. Reprinted by permission.

A large number of such studies had been reported by 1950 when Schuessler and Cressey presented the first summary and review of findings regarding personality characteristics of criminals.[1] The principal focus of their review concerned the presence or absence of differences in the personality characteristics of criminals and noncriminals.

They found that thirty different personality tests measuring emotional stability and maturity, temperament, character, and total personality had been used in 113 reported studies.[2] Of these, only forty-seven (42 percent) differentiated criminals from noncriminals. However, even those tests which did discriminate manifested considerable discrepancy in differentiation and the particular components of personality differentiated. To compound the difficulties, repetition of the tests quite often did not yield the same results.

After their essentially negative findings, Schuessler and Cressey concluded:

When the results are considered chronologically, there is nothing to indicate that the personality components of criminal behavior are being established by this method. On the contrary, as often as not the evidence favored the view that personality traits are distributed in the criminal population in about the same way as in the general population.[3]

Vold was properly critical of this total dismissal of personality components in criminality, largely on methodological grounds:

Unfortunately, [the Schuessler-Cressey] survey threw together indiscriminately a jumble of well, badly, and indifferently controlled studies, so that percentages computed on the total are of quite uncertain meaning.[4]

Clinard has also been critical of the Schuessler-Cressey study and of its impact upon sociologists:

Unfortunately, some sociologists have assumed that the negative findings reported by Schuessler and Cressey have virtually terminated the discussion. . . . Several criticisms of this finding can be made. First, the studies on which the conclusions are based used thirty different personality tests, some of them long since out of date. Secondly, few of the studies made up to the time of this analysis employed the relatively sophisticated MMPI test. . . . Thirdly, although the studies evaluated by Schuessler and Cressey viewed personality

---

[1] Karl F. Schuessler and Donald B. Cressey, "Personality Characteristics of Criminals," *American Journal of Sociology* (March 1950) pp. 476–484.

[2] Ibid., p. 476. Because the concept of "personality" is quite vague, they used this term "simply to refer to whatever it is that a given test of personality claims to measure."

[3] Ibid., p. 483.

[4] George B. Vold, *Theoretical Criminology* (New York: Oxford University Press, 1958), p. 127.

traits as separate entities, the traits may be more closely related to some syndromes of behavior or types of criminal behavior than to others.[5]

Anderson, one of Schuessler's students, attempted to update the Schuessler-Cressey study for 1950 through 1959.[6] Although his work is not directly comparable to the original study, most of the criticisms of the Schuessler-Cressey evaluation also apply to this more recent study. Even more recently, in *Juvenile Delinquency,* Quay evaluated a number of attempts to clarify this issue of the role of personality trait differences in delinquency.[7] However, his analysis is far from exhaustive and includes no studies which failed to find differences between delinquents and nondelinquents. Again, the Quay results cannot be directly contrasted with the Schuessler-Cressey findings because of differences in approach, objectives, and method of analysis.

METHODOLOGY

The present study tried to avoid some of the problems cited by Vold and Clinard and still remain sufficiently true to the approach used by Schuessler and Cressey so comparisons could be drawn between the two time periods. The primary sources of data for this study were *Psychological Abstracts, Sociological Abstracts,* and the computer files of the National Clearinghouse for Mental Health Information. Undoubtedly, some studies which should have been included were inadvertently overlooked, but the review is relatively complete and any additional studies would not greatly alter the general pattern of findings.

Since we wanted to make as accurate an assessment of the studies as possible and more direct comparisons with the Schuessler-Cressey study, we excluded from this analysis all investigations conducted outside the United States. Because of the inaccessibility of material in foreign languages and problems of translation, we felt that a bias might be introduced if only those foreign articles were used which appeared in United States journals and publications. Unfortunately, this criterion excluded a number of interesting and significant studies. Generally speaking, however, studies conducted in other countries were found to follow the same pattern as the

[5] Marshall B. Clinard, "Criminological Research," *Sociology Today,* Robert Merton, Leonard Broom, and Leonard Cottrell, eds. (New York: Basic Books, 1959), p. 518.

[6] Robert G. Anderson, III, "Applications of Objective Tests of Personality to Criminal Populations, 1950–1959: A Review and Appraisal," unpublished master's thesis, 1961, Indiana University.

[7] Herbert C. Quay, *Juvenile Delinquency* (Princeton, N.J.: Van Nostrand, 1965), pp. 139–169.

studies included in this analysis, so percentages would have been changed only slightly had they been included.[8]

The present investigation divided the various studies completed in the United States since 1950 into three major categories: objective, projective, and performance. They were further subdivided according to whether sound or unsound methodological procedures had been used. The criteria for "sound methodology" were (1) use of both a "criminal" or "delinquent" group and a comparison or a control group of "normals" or, in cases of a well-established test, comparison with a standardized norm; (2) sample size of fifty or more cases in both groups, delinquent and normal; (3) control of at least some relevant background variables, usually age, sex, race, intelligence, and socio-economic status.

The rationale for the first criterion is that studies lacking a comparison group or standardized norm are of little value in clarifying the relationship of personality traits and criminality. The results of epidemiological studies are difficult to evaluate even when the research is conducted under the most rigorous of conditions; uncontrolled epidemiologic studies are often worthless. Since a very large number of personality studies had been reported, it was possible to retain the sounder ones.

Eliminated from analysis were studies comparing specific categories of criminals (alcoholics or sex offenders) with "normals" since the inclusion of these studies might bias the results in an unpredictable manner. Also excluded were studies concerned with differences within the criminal population and making no comparison with normals. Some of these compared different offense categories on personality measures and some examined a particular classification (rapists), using other inmates as "normal prisoners" for comparison. Others attempted to distinguish between recidivists and first offenders, parole violators and nonviolators, escapees and nonescapees, Negroes and whites, or males and females. This does not imply these studies are not of importance but only that they deal with somewhat different issues.

A major difficulty was identification of studies concerned with "personality." If the study used a recognized measure of personality (MMPI or Rorschach) or if its concern was "personality," either directly or indirectly, then it was included in the analysis. Excluded were studies dealing with such factors as "self-concept," attitudes, perceptions, and cognitive processes. The rationale for these exclusions was that most sociologists distinguish these factors from traditional personality characteristics. Finally,

---

[8] One of the most outstanding of these studies was by Harrison Gough, "Cross-Cultural Validation of a Measure of Asocial Behavior," *Psychological Reports* (October 1965) pp. 378–387. In this study the So scale was administered in eight languages in ten countries to 21,772 nondelinquents and 5,052 delinquents. The results support the findings presented in the present analysis for studies conducted in the United States with the So scale.

EEG studies were omitted because there is very little agreement on whether the EEG, as a measure of physiological processes, is, at the same time, a measure of personality.

In devising rules for counting the various studies, we came up against various problems. When several articles reporting only one set of data appeared in various journals, the additional studies were eliminated to avoid inflating the number of studies. A few studies utilized more than one instrument, at times giving contradictory results. In such cases each instrument was counted as a separate administration. The one exception to this approach was an article which listed sixteen separate instruments that had been utilized. Only one of these instruments (Bender-Gestalt) was used in other studies. Since very little information was included concerning the results with these instruments, it was counted as one study.[9]

The studies which met the criteria for inclusion were distributed into four categories based on sample size and control of background variables. These were studies (1) with a large sample size and demographic controls, (2) with small sample size and demographic controls, (3) with a large sample size and no demographic controls, and (4) with small samples and no demographic controls.

RESULTS

Tests before and after 1950

The most important difference between the Schuessler-Cressey and the present study is the remarkable increase in the frequency of discrimination between criminals and noncriminals of the various tests and measures. In the Schuessler-Cressey review, only 42 percent of the studies were found to differentiate the two populations. The present survey indicates that 81 percent of the studies since 1950 reported significant differences between criminals and noncriminals. This increase can be explained primarily in terms of the differences in instruments employed during the two periods. Schuessler and Cressey found thirty different instruments utilized before 1950; of these, only four were in use after 1950. In the present study, twenty-nine different instruments were used, with considerably better outcomes.

The Minnesota Multiphasic Personality Inventory (MMPI), used only four times in the earlier period, was used twenty-nine times in the later period and was, by far the most widely used test (31 percent of the studies) during this period. Dropped completely since 1950 were tests used in 101 of the 113 previous studies. These included the Bell Adjust-

---

[9] See Theodore Sarbin and Donald Jones, "Intra-Personal Factors in Delinquency: A Preliminary Report," *Nervous Child* (October 1955) pp. 23–27.

TABLE 1.   Summary of Personality Tests Used and Results Obtained in Studies Reviewed by Schuessler-Cressey and in Present Study

Test Employed	Schuessler-Cressey		Present Study	
	Total Times Used	Times Found Diff.	Total Times Used	Times Found Diff.
Authoritarian Scale	—	—	2	1
B. P. C.	1	0	—	—
Bell Adjustment Inventory	4	0	—	—
Bender-Gestalt	—	—	5	4
Bernreuter Personality Inventory	7	0	—	—
Brown Personality Inventory	1	1	—	—
California Test of Personality	1	0	1	1*
California Psychological Inventory	—	—	8	8
Cassel Group Level of Aspiration Test	—	—	3	3*
Cattell Character-Temperament Test	1	1	—	—
Character Tests	13	6	—	—
Downey Will-Temperament Tests	3	0	—	—
Edward Personal Preference Schedule	—	—	2	1
Famous Sayings Test	—	—	2	1
Furfey Developmental Age Test	3	2	—	—
Goodenough Drawing Test	1	1	—	—
Gordon's Conformity Scale	—	—	2	2**
Guilford Martin Inventory	1	0	—	—
Holtzman Inkblot Technique	—	—	1	1
House-Tree-Person Test	—	—	1	0
Humm-Wadsworth Temperament Scale	1	0	—	—
IES Arrow Dot Test	—	—	1	1
Kent-Rosanoff Word Association Test	3	2	—	—
Laslett Word Association Test	3	2	—	—
Machover Draw-A-Person Test	—	—	2	1
Maller Case Inventory	1	0	—	—
Mental Health Analysis Test	—	—	1	0
Mirror Drawing Test	1	0	—	—
Minnesota Multiphasic Personality Inventory	4	2	29	28
Murray Psychoneurotic Inventory	2	2	—	—
Neyman-Kohlstedt Introversion-Extraversion	3	0	—	—
Objective-Analytic Personality Test	—	—	1	1
Personal Opinion Inventory	—	—	1	1
Picture Identification Test	—	—	1	1
Porteus Maze Test	4	4	3	3
Pressey Interest-Attitude Test	4	2	—	—
Pressey X-O Test	8	2	—	—
Psychomotor Test II	—	—	1	1
Rogers Test of Personality Adjustment	2	0	—	—
Rorschach Test	3	0	5	2
Rosenzweig Picture-Frustration Test	—	—	6	3*
Sentence Completion Test	—	—	2	2
Situational Interpretation Test	—	—	1	1
Street Gestalt Completion Test	—	—	1	1
Sweet Personal Attitudes Test	6	3	—	—
Symond Picture Story Test	—	—	2	1*

* Each asterisk represents one study in the category which found differences opposite the direction anticipated.

TABLE 1.   (Cont.)

Test Employed	Schuessler-Cressey		Present Study	
	Total Times Used	Times Found Diff.	Total Times Used	Times Found Diff.
Szondi	—	—	3	2
Thematic Apperception Test	—	—	3	1
Thurstone Personality Schedule	3	2	—	—
Vineland Social Maturity Scale	3	1	—	—
Washburn Social Adjustment Inventory	2	1	—	—
Woodworth Personal Data Sheet	19	9	—	—
Other Objective Tests	—	—	3	3
Other Projective Tests	—	—	1	1
Totals	113	47(42%)	94	76(81%)

ment Inventory (4–0),[10] Bernreuter Personality Inventory (7–0), Character Tests (13–6), Pressey X-0 Test (8–2), and the Woodworth Personal Data Sheet (19–9).

When the studies were divided into those using projective, performance, or objective instruments, considerable differences were apparent (Table 2). Studies using objective tests gave fairly consistent results: fifty-one of fifty-six (91 percent) showed significant difference between delinquents and comparison populations. Four of these studies, however, produced results in a direction opposite the one expected. Six of eight (75 percent) of the performance tests indicated significant differences. Only nineteen of thirty projective test investigations (63 percent) showed differences; of these, two were in a direction opposite to the one anticipated.

When the studies were further subdivided in terms of the methodological criteria of sample size and use of demographic controls, four types were obtained as discussed above (Table 3). The pattern that emerges is not clear; nevertheless, all studies using a large sample and controlled demographic variables found significant differences between criminals and noncriminals. Of those which used a large sample but failed to control demographic variables, fifty-one out of fifty-eight (88 percent) found significant differences; however, a large difference was found between objective instruments in this category. Of those using projective instruments and demographic controls, regardless of sample size, six out of seven (86 percent) found differences. For those using large and small samples and no demographic controls, only thirteen of twenty-three (56 percent) found differences. Thus, in those studies included in the present review, major differences were found between the use of objective and projective tests rather than the methodological criteria invoked.

[10] Figures in parentheses represent the use of the instrument in this earlier period. The first number represents the number of times the test was used and the second the number of times a difference was found.

TABLE 2. Type of Test and Frequency of Significant Differences Obtained between Criminal and Noncriminal Samples

Test	Times Used	Times Found Diff.
Objective Tests		
California Psychological Inventory	8	8
Cassel Group Level of Aspiration Test	3	3*
Edwards Personal Preference Test	2	1
Famous Sayings Test	2	1
Minnesota Multiphasic Personality Inventory	29	28
Other objective tests [a]	12	10***
Total objective tests	56	51(91%)
Performance Tests		
Machover Draw-A-Person Test	2	1
Porteus Maze Test	3	3
Other performance tests [a]	3	2
Total perforance tests	8	6(75%)
Projective Tests		
Bender-Gestalt	5	4
Rorschach	5	2
Rosenzweig Picture-Frustration Test	6	3*
Sentence Completion Test	2	2
Symond Picture Story Test	2	1*
Szondi	3	2
Thematic Apperception Test	3	1
Other projective tests [a]	4	4
Total projective tests	30	19(63%)
Total for all tests	94	76(81%)

* Each asterisk represents one study in the category which found differences opposite the direction anticipated.

[a] "Other" tests are those in which the instrument was used on only one occasion.

Results of Objective Test

When the results of the studies using objective tests are evaluated, conclusions are far more consistent than those presented in the Schuessler-Cressey study. A large number of different objective tests have been developed in recent years, but only a few studies have been reported for most of them. Two exceptions are the Minnesota Multiphasic Personality Inventory (MMPI) and the California Psychological Inventory (CPI). Gough and Peterson developed a Socialization Scale (So or De) from the California Psychological Inventory and used this instrument extensively

TABLE 3.   Type of Test and Frequency of Significant Differences Obtained between Large and Small Samples with and without Control of Demographic Variables

Test	Large Sample, Demographic Controls		Small Sample, Demographic Controls		Large Sample, No Demographic Controls		Small Sample, No Demographic Controls	
	Times Used	Times Found Diff.	Times Used	Times Found Diff.	Times Used	Times Found Diff.	Times Used	Times Found Diff.
Objective	3	3	4	2	44	42***	5	4*
Performance	2	2	0	0	3	3	3	1
Projective	3	3*	4	3	11	6*	12	7
Total tests	8	8	8	5	58	51	20	12

* Each asterisk represents one study in the category which found differences opposite the direction anticipated.

with large delinquent and nondelinquent samples.[11] Samples of 960 male delinquents and 168 male controls and 124 female delinquents and 178 female controls were used in the development of this scale; the results were cross-validated with 1,092 Army recruits and ninety-nine stockade prisoners and again later with 353 stockade prisoners. In all cases significant differences in the responses of delinquents and nondelinquents were found. The authors assess the meaning of the higher and lower scores:

The social stimulus value of higher scores on the De scale appears to include an emphasis on characteristics such as dissatisfaction, rebelliousness, defensiveness, etc. On the other hand, lower scores "come through" socially as consideration, dependability, moderateness, patience, and tactfulness.[12]

Gough [13] later used different samples of 1,295 male delinquents and 9,001 nondelinquent males, 784 delinquent females and 9,776 nondelinquent females. He used samples of high-school students with disciplinary problems, county-jail inmates, prison inmates, and training-school inmates, as well as eighteen different groups of normals. The mean score for normals was 36.74 while the mean score for delinquents was 27.98. None of the eighteen normal groups scored as low as the highest delinquent group.

Peterson, Quay, and Anderson used the So scale with 239 male delinquents and 428 nondelinquent males. They found differences not only between delinquents and normals, but also between "good citizens" and

[11] Harrison G. Gough and Donald R. Peterson, "The Identification and Measurement of Predispositional Factors in Crime and Delinquency," *Journal of Consulting Psychology* (April 1954) pp. 207–212.
[12] Ibid., p. 212.
[13] Harrison Gough, "Theory and Measurement of Socialization," *Journal of Consulting Psychology* (February 1960) pp. 23–30.

"disciplinary problems" in the normal group and between first offenders and recidivists in the delinquent group.[14] Reckless and Dinitz used the So scale with both police contacts and teachers' nominations as the measures of delinquency and found significant differences in several different applications of the scale.[15] Knapp used the same instrument with a sample of ninety-two Navy brig confinees and a sample of high-school students.[16] He found differences between these groups comparable to those found by Gough and Peterson and by Reckless and Dinitz.

Hinkleman used the California Test of Personality on a group of thirty delinquents in a special rehabilitation school and a control group subdivided according to socio-economic status into thirty-seven upper-, twenty-three middle-, and forty lower-class nondelinquents.[17] The results favored the upper-class control group on eleven of twelve subtests at the .01 level and similar results were obtained for the lower-class control group. In the middle-class comparison with the delinquent boys, however, the results were not nearly as significant. This inconsistency in regard to findings on middle-class delinquents is not at all clarified by his conclusions:

> Differences between the middle class and the upper and lower classes were as significant as those between the delinquent and these groups. . . . There are decidedly significant differences between delinquents and nondelinquents and these differences may have been obscured by socio-economic differences.[18]

The major instrument used in recent years is the Minnesota Multiphasic Personality Inventory (MMPI). This has replaced many of the instruments previously utilized in personality measurement. The MMPI was used in twenty-nine of the studies reviewed since 1950 in the measurement of personality characteristics of criminals or delinquents. Although the test, as a whole, has not been consistent in discriminating between criminals and noncriminals, one of its subscales, psychopathic deviate (Pd), has been fairly consistent. The Pd scale differentiated twenty-eight of the twenty-nine times it was administered. On the one occasion a statistically significant difference was not obtained, the scores were in the expected direction.

[14] Donald Peterson, Herbert Quay, and Arthur Anderson, "Extending the Construct Validity of a Socialized Scale," *Journal of Consulting Psychology* (April 1959) p. 182.

[15] Simon Dinitz, Barbara Kay, and Walter Reckless, "A Self-Gradient among Potential Delinquents," *Journal of Criminal Law, Criminology and Police Science* (September–October 1958) pp. 230–233; Walter Reckless, Simon Dimitz, and Barbara Kay, "The Self-Component in Potential Delinquency and Potential Non-Delinquency," *American Sociological Review* (October 1957) pp. 566–570.

[16] Robert Knapp, "Personality Correlates of Delinquency Rate in a Navy Sample," *Journal of Applied Psychology* (February 1963) pp. 68–71.

[17] Emmet Arthur Hinkleman, "A Comparative Investigation of Differences in Personality Adjustment of Delinquents and Non-Delinquents," *Journal of Educational Research* (April 1953) pp. 595–601.

[18] Ibid., pp. 597, 601.

The MMPI is designed to provide scores on all of the more clinically important aspects of personality. It consists of 550 statements covering a wide range of subject matter, including the physical condition of the individual and his moral and social attitudes. The subject responds to all of the statements as "true," "false," or "cannot say." These responses are counted and scores derived for four validity scales and ten clinical scales. Time required for completion of all statements normally ranges from thirty to ninety minutes. Scores are converted into T scores with a mean of fifty and a standard deviation of ten. This means a score of seventy is two standard deviations from the mean and should occur among normal subjects only five times out of one hundred. Consequently, scores above seventy are usually interpreted as being "abnormal" and clinically "interesting."

In most studies comparing criminals with noncriminals, the Pd scale has consistently shown differences. Hathaway and Monachesi have used the MMPI extensively with delinquents and nondelinquents.[19] They have gathered protocols on large samples of males and females and their total sample now includes more than fifteen thousand students tested while in the ninth grade. After several studies with smaller cohorts, they began their large study in 1948 by administering the instrument to 3,971 ninth-grade students in the Minneapolis public schools. They have systematically followed this cohort for a number of years. In 1954 they tested an additional 11,329 ninth-graders in forty-seven of Minnesota's eighty-seven counties.

The 1948 Minneapolis sample showed statistically significant differences on the Pd scale. Mean scores of 57.7 and 61.9 were obtained for the normal and delinquent groups. Significant differences were also found on the schizoid (Sc) and the hypomania (Ma) scales. The Sc and Ma scales did not differentiate in as many studies as the Pd scale. In another study, Monachesi found that the Pd, hysteria (Hy), and the depression (D) scales differentiated delinquents from nondelinquents.[20] In still another study,[21] he used four different groups consisting of fifty-six nondelinquents and forty-nine delinquents who were not institutionalized (all of whom were residents of the same area), 123 boys in an academy for boys from higher socio-economic families, and eighty delinquents in training school. Most of the scales showed consistent results. On the Pd scale, however, the training school group had a mean score of 72.5; the noninstitutionalized delin-

[19] Starke R. Hathaway and Elio D. Monachesi, *Analyzing and Predicting Juvenile Delinquency with the MMPI*, Minneapolis, 1953. Also *Adolescent Personality and Behavior*, Minneapolis, 1963.

[20] Elio Monachesi, "Personality Characteristics and Socioeconomic Status of Delinquents and Nondelinquents," *Journal of Criminal Law, Criminology and Police Science*, January–February 1950) pp. 570–583.

[21] Elio Monachesi, "Personality Characteristics of Institutionalized and Non-Institutionalized Male Delinquents," *Journal of Criminal Law, Criminology and Police Science* (July–August 1950) pp. 167–179.

quents, 68.2; nondelinquents residing in the same area, 60.5; and the academy cohort, 59.4. Although attempts were made to control for socioeconomic status among the delinquents and nondelinquents living in the same area, the nondelinquents were drawn from higher socio-economic status background than were the delinquents.

Clark conducted a study of 136 soldiers committed to disciplinary barracks and compared them with "normal" soldiers.[22] The prison group was subdivided into those the psychiatrist had diagnosed as (1) no psychiatric disorder, (2) emotional instability, and (3) antisocial personality. All these groups differed significantly from the normal group on *all* of the MMPI scales. Pd scores for the groups were: normals, 47.0; no psychiatric disorder, 62.4; emotional instability, 69.2; and antisocial personality, 73.7. The difference between the normals and the "no psychiatric disorder" group was rather large and an even greater difference was obtained when the "antisocial personality" group was compared with the normals.

Silver used the MMPI as well as the Thematic Apperception Test (TAT) on a sample of twenty serious recidivists in training school ("primarily environmental delinquents excluded"), twenty mild offenders, twenty orphanage boys, and twenty high-school boys.[23] The TAT did not discriminate very well but the MMPI discriminated between the two extreme groups on the Pd scale. The orphanage boys, however, scored only .2 of one raw score unit less than the mild offenders.

Jackson and Clark used the MMPI with 111 college students apprehended for theft and a group of 111 normal college students.[24] They found significant differences on the Pd, Ma, and Sc scales in the expected direction. The Pd score of the theft group, however, was not as high as was found in most of the other delinquent groups reported in this review.

Caditz used the MMPI with ninety-four training-school boys and ninety-seven high-school boys at the beginning and at the end of the training-school experience.[25] She found significant differences on the Pd, Pa, and Ma scales at both time periods.

Ball found significant differences on the MMPI between a group of thirty-eight delinquents and 224 nondelinquents.[26] He controlled for sex, race, socio-economic status, achievement, broken homes, and teachers' ratings of maladjustment. He concluded personality maladjustments were

[22] Jerry H. Clark, "The Relationship between MMPI Scores and Psychiatric Classification of Army General Prisoners," *Journal of Clinical Psychology* (January 1952) pp. 86–89.

[23] Albert W. Silver, "TAT and MMPI Psychopathic Deviate Scale Differences between Delinquent and Non-Delinquent Adolescents," *Journal of Consulting Psychology* (August 1963) p. 370.

[24] Karma Jackson and Selby Clark, "Thefts among College Students," *Personnel and Guidance Journal* (April 1958) pp. 557–562.

[25] Sylvan Caditz, "Effect of a Training School Experience on the Personality of Delinquent Boys," *Journal of Consulting Psychology* (December 1959) pp. 501–509.

[26] John C. Ball, *Social Deviancy and Adolescent Personality* (Louisville: University of Kentucky Press, 1962).

associated with delinquency even when other relevant variables were controlled.

Volkman criticized most of the studies using the MMPI for failing to control adequately many significant variables in their analysis.[27] He made a study of twenty-seven delinquents on probation and twenty-seven nondelinquents, controlling for age, race, intelligence, and father's occupation. His conclusions were negative since the only scale that discriminated was hypochondriasis, on which the nondelinquents scored higher. The Pd scores were in the expected direction but were not statistically significant. His use of controls was much better than in most of the other studies that used the MMPI. However, the smallness of his sample and the fact that his data were in the expected direction make it difficult to use this study to refute the others which found significant differences on the Pd scale.

Results of Performance Tests

The most consistent performance test utilized in the period under study was the Porteus Maze (3–3), used primarily as a nonverbal measure of intelligence. It has also been used to measure personality characteristics. Its ability to discriminate between delinquents and nondelinquents is explained by its measurement of *impulsivity,* supposedly related to ego control. Docter and Winder used the Porteus Maze Test and matched sixty delinquents and sixty nondelinquents for age, intelligence, race, and socio-economic status.[28] They found significant differences in the "Q scores," some of which reached the .0001 level. Fooks and Thomas studied fifty delinquents diagnosed as psychopathic and fifty nondelinquents.[29] They attempted to control for age, sex, intelligence, and socio-economic status, but the normals actually were of higher socio-economic status than the delinquents. They found significant differences on the "Q scores" between delinquents and nondelinquents, but none by race or intelligence.

Gibbens used the "Q scores" of the Porteus Maze with two hundred male delinquents and fifty-two nondelinquents.[30] He found significant differences between the two groups and also a relationship of high "Q scores" to low intelligence, truancy, and other variables. The latter result contradicts the findings of Fooks and Thomas in regard to intelligence.

[27] Arthur P. Volkman, "A Matched Group Personality Comparison of Delinquents and Non-Delinquent Juveniles," *Social Problems* (Winter 1958–59) pp. 238–245.

[28] Richard F. Docter and C. L. Winder, "Delinquent versus Non-Delinquent Performance on the Porteus Qualitative Maze Test," *Journal of Consulting Psychology* (February 1954) pp. 71–73.

[29] Gilbert Fooks and Ross R. Thomas, "Differential Qualitative Performance of Delinquents on the Porteus Maze," *Journal of Consulting Psychology* (August 1957) pp. 351–353.

[30] T. C. N. Gibbens, "The Porteus Maze Test and Delinquency," *British Journal of Educational Psychology* (November 1958) pp. 209–216.

The Gibbens study also used the Minnesota Multiphasic Personality Inventory. Although the "psychopathic deviate" scale of the MMPI differentiated between delinquents and nondelinquents, it did not correlate with the Porteus Maze "Q scores." The only scale on the MMPI correlating with the "Q scores" was hypomania. Since this scale and the "Q scores" are both considered measures of impulsivity, they should logically correlate. However, the hypomania scale did not differentiate between delinquents and nondelinquents. In sum, the "Q scores" differentiated between delinquents and nondelinquents and correlated with the hypomania scale, which did not differentiate between delinquents and nondelinquents. The "Q score," however, did not correlate with the psychopathic deviate scale, which did differentiate between the two groups.

Baugh and Carpenter studied forty-one delinquent boys and fifty-two nondelinquent boys using the Machover Draw-A-Person Test (2–1).[31] They controlled for age, sex, race, and socio-economic status. However, the delinquents were all institutionalized recidivists; therefore, not a typical delinquent sample. Baugh and Carpenter obtained a significant difference in the personality patterns of the two groups and concluded that "delinquents project graphically their warped ego and retarded personality development." [32] Moreover, "thirty-two out of the forty-one delinquents were reflecting either an open psychosis or a latent underlying one with passive infantile needs." [33]

Craddick, however, who used the Machover with twenty male "psychopathic" prisoners and twenty male college students, failed to find any significant differences [34] and concluded that "no features differentiated except for shading, and here it was in the opposite direction from that expected." [35]

Naar used the House-Tree-Person test (similar to the Machover) with thirty delinquent and thirty nondelinquent white boys from similar neighborhoods and matched for intelligence.[36] He found no difference in terms of "hostility," "suspiciousness," or "impulsiveness." He did find a difference in "lack of anxiety," but in the wrong direction. He states, "Contrary to expectations, however, delinquents were found to be more anxious than nondelinquents." [37]

[31] Verner S. Baugh and B. L. Carpenter, "A Comparison of Delinquents and Non-Delinquents," *Journal of Social Psychology* (February 1962) pp. 73–78.

[32] Ibid., p. 74.

[33] Ibid., p. 75.

[34] R. A. Craddick, "Draw-A-Person Characteristics of Psychopathic Prisoners and College Students," *Perceptual and Motor Skills* (August 1962) pp. 11–13.

[35] Ibid., p. 13.

[36] Ray Naar, "An Attempt to Differentiate Delinquents from Non-Delinquents on the Basis of Projective Drawings," *Journal of Criminal Law, Crimonology and Police Science* (March 1964) pp. 107–110.

[37] Ibid., p. 109.

Results of Projective Tests

While projective tests as a group did not give as consistent results across studies as did the objective tests, some were more consistent than others. The Bender-Gestalt (5–4) was the most consistent. Nonetheless, the results were far from conclusive. Zolik compared forty-three delinquents with forty-three nondelinquents matched for age and intelligence [38] and found that the two groups differed significantly on all comparisons made:

It can be concluded that . . . errors which appear in the reproduction of the B-G figures are not attributable to chronological age or intelligence but to other psychological differences. . . . The Pascal and Suttell scoring method of the B-G test has proved valid for differentiating between delinquents and nondelinquents.[39]

A study conducted by Curnatt and Corotto,[40] however, found no differences on the Bender-Gestalt:

The results indicated poor prediction in terms of differentiating delinquent behavior from nondelinquent behavior whether one utilized the higher cut-off score suggested by Pascal and Suttell or the lower cut-off score of Zolik.[41]

Schuessler and Cressey considered the Rorschach (5–2) to have the potential to solve the problem of the role of personality attributes as etiologic factors in criminality; however, results obtained thus far are still very inconclusive. The Gluecks, in *Unraveling Juvenile Delinquency,* used the Rorschach with five hundred delinquents and five hundred nondelinquents matched for age, intelligence, ethnic origin, and place of residence.[42] They concluded the delinquent is more socially assertive, more defiant, more ambivalent to authority, more resentful of others, more hostile, more suspicious, more destructive, more impulsive, and more extroversive. The delinquent is also less submissive to authority, suffers less from fear of

[38] Edwin S. Zolik, "A Comparison of the Bender-Gestalt Reproductions of Delinquents and Non-Delinquents," *Journal of Clinical Psychology* (January 1958) pp. 24–26.

[39] Ibid., p. 26.

[40] Robert Curnatt and Loren V. Corotto, "The Use of Bender-Gestalt Cut-off Scores in Identifying Juvenile Delinquents," *Journal of Projective Techniques* (September 1960) pp. 353–354.

[41] Ibid., p. 354.

[42] Sheldon Glueck and Eleanor Glueck, *Unraveling Juvenile Delinquency* (New York: Commonwealth Fund, 1950). For a more detailed analysis of the Gluecks' data, see Ernest G. Schacter, "Notes on Rorschach Tests of 500 Juvenile Delinquents and a Control Group of 500 Non-Delinquent Adolescents," *Journal of Projective Techniques* (June 1951) pp. 144–172.

failure, is less cooperative and dependent on others, less conventional in ideas and behavior, less masochistic and self-controlled.

It is clear that the delinquent group is strikingly different from the non-delinquent in respect to those traits and dynamisms of personality-character structure and functions which the Rorschach Test is designed to reveal.[43]

Swenson and Grimes studied a group of forty-five male sex offenders and found the Rorschach showed no strong difference in content abnormality from a group of normals.[44] In another study of sixty-three "sexual psychopaths" and a comparison group of hospital employees, Guertin and Trembath found no difference between the groups on the Rorschach test.[45] They concluded that the only difference was that the prisoners acted out their psychosexual problems while normals only thought about theirs, and that the Rorschach is "too sensitive and reflects psychosexual immaturity too well" since it does not distinguish between the two groups.[46]

Uehling used the Rorschach with fifty inmates, fifty guards, and fifty clients at a Jewish Community Service Society.[47] He concluded the inmates did not differ significantly from the guards on any aspect of the Rorschach; however, both the guards and inmates were greatly inferior to the clients. One interpretation of these findings would be that both guards and inmates have personality disturbances; however, the society's clients were actively seeking guidance and therapy, apparently for some form of personality maladjustment.

Although the Gluecks' results appear impressive, the negative results of other studies leave the issue of the ability of the Rorschach to differentiate between criminals and noncriminals very much in doubt.

The Rosenzweig Picture-Frustration Test (6–3) was the projective instrument utilized the most frequently. Gatling used a sample of twenty-five delinquents and twenty-five nondelinquents, controlled for age, race, sex, and nativity.[48] He concluded that delinquents give more extrapunitive responses (take their frustrations out on others), while the nondelinquents give more impunitive responses (take their frustrations out on themselves). Vane studied ninety-five delinquent girls and fifty nondelinquent girls

[43] Glueck and Glueck, op. cit. supra note 42, p. 241.
[44] W. M. Swenson and B. P. Grimes, "Characteristics of Sex Offenders Admitted to a Minnesota State Hospital for Pre-Sentence Psychiatric Investigation," *Psychiatric Quarterly Supplement* (January 1958) pp. 110–123.
[45] Wilson H. Guertin and William Trembath, "Card VI Disturbance of the Rorschachs of Sex Offenders," *Journal of General Psychology* (July 1953) pp. 221–227.
[46] Ibid., p. 226.
[47] Harold F. Uehling, "Rorschach 'Shock' for Two Special Populations," *Journal of Consulting Psychology* (June 1952) p. 224.
[48] F. P. Gatling, "Frustration Reaction of Delinquents Using Rosenzweig's Classification System," *Journal of Abnormal and Social Psychology* (October 1950) pp. 749–752.

matched for age, intelligence, and socio-economic status and found the two groups differed greatly.[49] The delinquents were *less aggressive* than the nondelinquents and tended to turn their aggressions inward rather than outward:

> That the delinquents differed from norms and nondelinquents was not surprising, but it was not expected that they would respond in a manner which would indicate that they were less aggressive than either the norms or nondelinquents.[50]

Holzberg and Hahn used the Rosenzweig Picture-Frustration Test with seventeen institutionalized psychopaths and twenty-five normal highschool boys, matched for age, intelligence, reading level, and socio-economic status.[51] They were unable to find any differences between the two groups in terms of more or less frustration.

Scott used the Szondi Test with a large sample of three hundred delinquent boys, three hundred delinquent girls, three hundred nondelinquent boys and three hundred nondelinquent girls [52] and found significant differences on almost all possible comparisons:

> Regarding personality, delinquents seem to need more affection (+H), are less apt to recognize their daily needs and deeper underlying emotions (−P), and hence there is a tendency to compensate by oral activity (open M). Nondelinquents appear better adjusted socially (+).[53]

At the same time, however, some of the differences anticipated between delinquents and normals either did not occur or were in the opposite direction. "Deri's prediction that delinquency would be indicated by −E and −Hy and −M fails to receive confirmation."

The Szondi Test (3–1) was used by Caston with fifty prisoners, fifty controls, and thirty-two Aid Force prisoners.[54] Some aspects of the test discriminated while others did not. The test, as a whole, showed differences between the groups, and "clusters of positive signs indicated criminality." [55] Coulter used a delinquent and a control group of six hundred

[49] Julia R. Vane, "Implications of the Performance of Delinquent Girls on the Rosenzweig Picture-Frustration Study," *Journal of Consulting Psychology* (August 1954) p. 414.

[50] Ibid.

[51] J. D. Holzberg and F. Hahn, "The Picture-Frustration Technique as a Measure of Hostility and Guilt Reactions in Adolescent Psychopaths," *American Journal of Orthopsychiatry* (October 1952) pp. 776–795.

[52] Edward M. Scott, "An Investigation of Juvenile Profiles on the Szondi Test," *Journal of Clinical Psychology* (January 1955) pp. 46–50.

[53] Ibid., p. 50.

[54] William F. Caston, "The Szondi Test and Criminality," *Dissertation Abstracts* (July 1954) p. 1096.

[55] Ibid.

each and attempted to distinguish between the groups on fourteen basic indicators of the Szondi.[56] The fourteen indicators as a group were unable to distinguish and only two of these indicators were able to distinguish separately. One of these indicators was in a direction opposite to that hypothesized.[57]

SUMMARY AND CONCLUSIONS

Since the results of objective tests provide the greatest support for the view that criminals differ from noncriminals in personality characteristics, most of the summary comments apply primarily to these instruments, particularly the MMPI. Although the MMPI results are impressive, several cautions should be noted.

First, a difference in T scores between fifty and sixty on the Pd scale of the MMPI, which would be highly significant, actually represents a difference in response of the two groups to four items out of the fifty in the scale.[58] Although this represents statistical significance, it is difficult to ascertain the degree of theoretical significance involved. Since one item in the scale is "I have never been in trouble with the law," a positive response to this item alone would tend to discriminate statistically between delinquents and nondelinquents if the sample were of sufficient size. As Vold states:

Personality diagnosis on the basis of objective tests or scales has not yet developed to such a degree of specificity that differences established as statistically significant for particular groups may then be extended to correspondingly significant theoretical formulations about personality deviation and delinquency.[59]

Second, as Volkman pointed out, the failure to control other variables adequately is a serious limitation in interpreting the results. Silver's findings, showing the orphanage boys had Pd scores almost identical with those of the mild offenders, and the work of Monachesi indicate that socioeconomic status has a marked effect on MMPI scores.

Third, exactly what does the MMPI measure? If our definition of personality is "that which the personality test measures," then we might be satisfied to call this entity "personality." However, it would appear that Volkman's comment has some relevance:

[56] Walter Coulter, "The Szondi Test and the Prediction of Antisocial Behavior," *Journal of Projective Techniques* (March 1959) pp. 24–29.

[57] (This footnote lists 48 research articles included but not previously cited in the review; for reasons of brevity, this lengthy footnote is deleted).

[58] W. Grant Dahlstrom and George Welsh, *An MMPI Handbook, A Guide to Use in Clinical Practice and Research* (Minneapolis, 1960) p. 438.

[59] Vold, op. cit. supra note 4, pp. 137–138.

The existing body of sociological knowledge furnished adequate grounds for expecting responses to many of the MMPI items to vary in accordance with certain sociological factors associated with the respondent. In the MMPI manual (p. 5), the 550 items comprising the instrument are classified under 26 headings, at least eight of which may be assumed to have sociological correlates: habits, 19 items; family and marital factors, 12 items; sexual attitudes, 16 items; religious attitudes, 19 items; political attitudes, including law and order, 46 items; social attitudes, 72 items.[60]

Fourth, many of the studies did not use random samples of delinquents. Hathaway and Monachesi's work, which probably utilized the best sampling techniques, shows the smallest difference on the Pd scale between the delinquent and nondelinquent groups. The T score means of 57.7 and 61.9 on this scale represent a difference in response between the two groups of less than two questions of the fifty in the scale.

Fifth, the differences *within* delinquent and nondelinquent populations are often greater than the differences *between* the two groups. In the various studies the mean scores on the Pd scale for "nondelinquents" ranged from 47.0 to 65.0, whereas the "delinquents" ranged from 58.0 to 72.3. It is difficult to interpret results of this nature since it would seem that the "normals" or "nondelinquents" in one study are more "psychopathic" than the "delinquents" in other studies.

Sixth, there is a problem inherent in the use of criterion group analysis in scale development when the scale is used for future hypothesis testing. The Pd scale originally was constructed from those items which distinguished a cohort of patients diagnosed as psychopathic personalities. Most were aged seventeen to twenty-two and a large number were delinquent.[61] If the instrument is to be utilized entirely for diagnostic purposes, this may be a valid technique for scale development. However, if it is to be used for hypothesis testing, as it was in all of the studies in this article, then success has been built into the instrument.

Psychopathy (Pd scale) was operationally defined as those items which discriminated between a group of young delinquents and a normal group. If the researcher proceeds to administer the Pd scale to groups of criminals and noncriminals, he finds differences on this scale and concludes that criminals are more psychopathic than noncriminals. This is a tautological argument since the manner in which the scale was developed insures that differences will be found between the two groups. Schuessler makes a similar point in a book review:

60 Volkman, op. cit. supra note 27, p. 240.
61 J. C. McKinley and S. R. Hathaway, Article 9, Scale 3 (hysteria), 9 (hypomania), and 4 (psychopathic deviate), *Basic Readings on the MMPI in Psychology and Medicine,* George Welsh and Grant Dahlstrom, eds. (Minneapolis: University of Minnesota Press, 1956).

The consistent differences yielded by scale 4, psychopathic deviate, must be construed in light of the fact that this scale was derived from persons who were "often young and delinquent." This scale is to a certain extent, then, a "delinquency scale" in the sense that it measures aspects of delinquency itself. Measurement from such a scale cannot be used to explain delinquency, since they are not independent of the object to be explained.[62]

Finally, a criticism made by Schuessler and Cressey would appear still pertinent:

The results of this method do not indicate whether criminal behavior is the result of a certain personality trait or whether the trait is the result of criminal experiences. In other words, whether a given trait was present at the onset of a delinquent career or whether the trait was developed during that career is not shown.[63]

Although the results appear more positive than they did a few years ago, in terms of the number of studies showing differences between criminals and noncriminals, the findings are far from conclusive. The conflict over the role of personality in criminality has not been resolved. The results of this review indicate that "personality" cannot be dismissed readily, as it is by many sociologists, and its etiologic role cannot be assumed casually, as it is by many psychiatrists and psychologists.

If laws are to be enforced, violators apprehended, and the public protected, someone must perform these tasks. Police officers are authorized to carry deadly weapons for use as necessary, and the decision to use them must be made instantly. If an officer fails to use deadly force when it is necessary, he, or a citizen, may be killed. If he overreacts, he commits an act of "police brutality." Yet a police officer is a human being, subject to the full range of human emotions and frailties. To empower police officers to use force and deadly weapons is to guarantee that these will sometimes be used unwisely.

How often does "police brutality" occur? Who are its victims? Many impassioned debates about police brutality are based upon a remarkable absence of reliable knowledge about its incidence. The following article is the only responsible study we know which attempts to measure the incidence of police brutality.

[62] Karl Schuessler, "A Review of *Analyzing and Predicting Juvenile Delinquency with the MMPI*"; *American Journal of Sociology* (November 1954) pp. 321–322.
[63] Schuessler and Cressey, op. cit. supra note 1, p. 483.

POLICE BRUTALITY—
ANSWERS TO KEY QUESTIONS

Albert J. Reiss, Jr.

Professor of Sociology
University of Michigan

"For three years there has been through the courts and the streets a dreary procession of citizens with broken heads and bruised bodies against few of whom was violence needed to effect an arrest. Many of them had done nothing to deserve an arrest. In a majority of such cases, no complaint was made. If the victim complains, his charge is generally dismissed. The police are practically above the law."

This statement was published in 1903, and its author was the Hon. Frank Moss, a former police commissioner of New York City. Clearly, today's charges of police brutality and mistreatment of citizens have a precedent in American history—but never before has the issue of police brutality assumed the public urgency it has today. In Newark, in Detroit, in Watts, in Harlem, and, in fact, in practically every city that has had a civil disturbance, "deep hostility between police and ghetto" was, reports the Kerner Commission, "a primary cause of the riots."

Whether or not the police accept the words "police brutality," the public now wants some plain answers to some plain questions. How widespread is police mistreatment of citizens? Is it on the increase? Why do policemen mistreat citizens? Do the police mistreat Negroes more than whites?

To find some answers, 36 people working for the Center of Research on Social Organization observed police-citizen encounters in the cities of Boston, Chicago, and Washington, D.C. For seven days a week, for seven weeks during the summer of 1966, these observers, with police permission, sat in patrol cars and monitored booking and lockup procedures in high-crime precincts.

Obtaining information about police mistreatment of citizens is no simple matter. National and state civil-rights commissions receive hundreds of complaints charging mistreatment—but proving these allegations is difficult. The few local civilian-review boards, such as the one in Phila-

From *TRANS-action*, 5 (July–August 1968) pp. 10–19. Copyright by TRANS-action Magazine, New Brunswick, New Jersey. Reprinted by permission.

delphia, have not produced any significant volume of complaints leading to the dismissal or disciplining of policemen for alleged brutality. Generally, police chiefs are silent on the matter, or answer charges of brutality with vague statements that they will investigate any complaints brought to their attention. Rank-and-file policemen are usually more outspoken: They often insinuate that charges of brutality are part of a conspiracy against them, and against law and order.

THE MEANING OF BRUTALITY

What citizens mean by police brutality covers the full range of police practices. These practices, contrary to the impression of many civil-rights activists, are not newly devised to deal with Negroes in our urban ghettos. They are ways in which the police have traditionally behaved in dealing with certain citizens, particularly those in the lower classes. The most common of these practices are:

the use of profane and abusive language,
commands to move on or get home,
stopping and questioning people on the street or searching them and
    their cars,
threats to use force if not obeyed,
prodding with a nightstick or approaching with a pistol, and the actual
    use of physical force or violence itself.

Citizens and the police do not always agree on what constitutes proper police practice. What is "proper," or what is "brutal," it need hardly be pointed out, is more a matter of judgment about what someone did than a description of what police do. What is important is not the practice itself but what it means to the citizen. What citizens object to and call "police brutality" is really the judgment that they have not been treated with the full rights and dignity owing citizens in a democratic society. Any practice that degrades their status, that restricts their freedom, that annoys or harasses them, or that uses physical force is frequently seen as unnecessary and unwarranted. More often than not, they are probably right.

Many police practices serve only to degrade the citizen's sense of himself and his status. This is particularly true with regard to the way the police use language. Most citizens who have contact with the police object less to their use of four-letter words than to *how* the policeman talks to them. Particularly objectionable is the habit policemen have of "talking down" to citizens, of calling them names that deprecate them in their own eyes and those of others. More than one Negro citizen has complained:

"They talk down to me as if I had no name—like 'boy' or 'man' or whatever, or they call me 'Jack' or by my first name. They don't show me no respect."

Members of minority groups and those seen as nonconformists, for whatever reason, are the most likely targets of status degradation. Someone who has been drinking may be told he is a "bum" or a "shitty wino." A woman walking alone may be called a "whore." And a man who doesn't happen to meet a policeman's standard of how one should look or dress may be met with the remark, "What's the matter, you a queer?" A white migrant from the South may be called a "hillbilly" or "shitkicker"; a Puerto Rican, a "pork chop"; a young boy, a "punk kid." When the policeman does not use words of status degradation, his manner may be degrading. Citizens want to be treated as people, not as "nonpersons" who are talked about as if they were not present.

That many Negroes believe that the police have degraded their status is clear from surveys in Watts, Newark, and Detroit. One out of every five Negroes in our center's post-riot survey in Detroit reports that the police have "talked down to him." More than one in ten says a policeman has "called me a bad name."

To be treated as "suspicious" is not only degrading, but is also a form of harassment and a restriction on the right to move freely. The harassing tactics of the police—dispersing social street-gatherings, the indiscriminate stopping of Negroes on foot or in cars, and commands to move on or go home—are particularly common in ghetto areas.

Young people are the most likely targets of harassing orders to disperse or move on. Particularly in summer, ghetto youths are likely to spend lots of time in public places. Given the inadequacy of their housing and the absence of community facilities, the street corner is often their social center. As the police cruise the busy streets of the ghetto, they frequently shout at groups of teenagers to "get going" or "get home." Our observations of police practices show that *white as well as Negro youths* are often harassed in this way.

Frequently the policeman may leave the car and threaten or force youths to move on. For example, one summer evening as the scout car cruised a busy street of a white slum, the patrolmen observed three white boys and a girl on a corner. When told to move on, they mumbled and grumbled in undertones, angering the police by their failure to comply. As they slowly moved off, the officers pushed them along the street. Suddenly one of the white patrolmen took a lighted cigarette from a 15-year-old boy and stuck it in his face, pushing him forward as he did so. When the youngsters did move on, one policeman remarked to the observer that the girl was "nothing but a whore." Such tactics can only intensify resentment toward the police.

Police harassment is not confined to youth. One in every four adult

Negroes in Detroit claims he has been stopped and questioned by the police without good reason. The same proportion claim they have been stopped in their cars. One in five says he has been searched unnecessarily; and one in six says that his car was searched for no good reason. The members of an interracial couple, particularly a Negro man accompanying a white woman, are perhaps the most vulnerable to harassment.

What citizens regard as police brutality many policemen consider necessary for law enforcement. While degrading epithets and abusive language may no longer be considered proper by either police commanders or citizens, they ofen disagree about other practices related to law enforcement. For example, although many citizens see "stop and question" or "stop and frisk" procedures as harassment, police commanders usually regard them merely as "aggressive prevention" to curb crime.

PHYSICAL FORCE—OR SELF-DEFENSE?

The nub of the police-brutality issue seems to lie in police use of physical force. By law, the police have the right to use such force if necessary to make an arrest, to keep the peace, or to maintain public order. But just how much force is necessary or proper?

This was the crucial problem we attempted to answer by placing observers in the patrol cars and in the precincts. Our 36 observers, divided equally between Chicago, Boston, and Washington, were responsible for reporting the details of all situations where police used physical force against a citizen. To ensure the observation of a large number of encounters, two high-crime police precincts were monitored in Boston and Chicago; four in Washington. At least one precinct was composed of primarily Negro residents, another primarily of whites. Where possible, we also tried to select precincts with considerable variation in social-class composition. Given the criterion of a high-crime rate, however, people of low socioeconomic status predominated in most of the areas surveyed.

The law fails to provide simple rules about what—and how much—force that policemen can properly use. The American Bar Foundation's study *Arrest,* by Wayne La Fave, put the matter rather well, stating that the courts of all states would undoubtedly agree that in making an arrest a policeman should use only that amount of force he reasonably believes necessary. But La Fave also pointed out that there is no agreement on the question of when it is better to let the suspect escape than to employ "deadly" force.

Even in those states where the use of deadly force is limited by law, the kinds of physical force a policeman may use are not clearly defined. No kind of force is categorically denied a policeman, since he is always permitted to use deadly force in self-defense.

This right to protect himself often leads the policeman to argue self-defense whenever he uses force. We found that many policemen, whether or not the facts justify it, regularly follow their use of force with the charge that the citizen was assaulting a policeman or resisting arrest. Our observers also found that some policemen even carry pistols and knives that they have confiscated while searching citizens; they carry them so they may be placed at a scene should it be necessary to establish a case of self-defense.

Of course, not all cases of force involve the use of *unnecessary* force. Each instance of force reported by our observers was examined and judged to be either necessary or unnecessary. Cases involving simple restraint—holding a man by the arm—were deliberately excluded from consideration, even though a policeman's right to do so can, in many instances, be challenged. In judging when police force is "unwarranted," "unreasonable," or "undue," we rather deliberately selected only those cases in which a policeman struck the citizen with his hands, fist, feet, or body, or where he used a weapon of some kind—such as a nightstick or a pistol. In these cases, had the policeman been found to have used physical force improperly, he could have been arrested on complaint and, like any other citizen, charged with a simple or aggravated assault. A physical assault on a citizen was judged to be "improper" or "unnecessary" only if force was used in one or more of the following ways:

If a policeman physically assaulted a citizen and then failed to make an arrest; proper use involves an arrest.

If the citizen being arrested did not, by word or deed, resist the policeman; force should be used only if it is necessary to make the arrest.

If the policeman, even though there was resistance to the arrest, could easily have restrained the citizen in other ways.

If a large number of policemen were present and could have assisted in subduing the citizen in the station, in lockup, and in the interrogation rooms.

If an offender was handcuffed and made no attempt to flee or offer violent resistance.

If the citizen resisted arrest, but the use of force continued even after the citizen was subdued.

In the seven-week period, we found 37 cases in which force was used improperly. In all, 44 citizens had been assaulted. In 15 of these cases, no one was arrested. Of these, 8 had offered no verbal or physical resistance whatsoever, while 7 had.

An arrest was made in 22 of the cases. In 13, force was exercised in the station house when at least four other policemen were present. In two cases, there was no verbal or physical resistance to the arrest, but force was still applied. In two other cases, the police applied force to a hand-cuffed offender in a field setting. And in five situations, the offender did resist arrest, but the policeman continued to use force even after he had been subdued.

Just how serious was the improper use of force in these 44 cases? Naturally there were differences in degree of injury. In about one-half of the cases, the citizens appeared little more than physically bruised; in three cases, the amount of force was so great that the citizen had to be hospitalized. Despite the fact that cases can easily be selected for their dramatic rather than their representative quality, I want to present a few to give a sense of what the observers saw and reported as undue use of force.

OBSERVING ON PATROL

In the following two cases, the citizens offered no physical or verbal resistance, and the two white policemen made no arrest. It is the only instance in which the observers saw the same two policemen using force improperly more than once.

The police precinct in which these incidents occurred is typical of those found in some of our larger cities, where the patrolmen move routinely from gold coast to slum. There are little islands of the rich and poor, of old Americans and new, of recent migrants and old settlers. One moves from high-rise areas of middle- and upper-income whites through an area of the really old Americans—Indians—to an enclave of the recently arrived. The recently arrived are primarily those the policemen call "hillbillies" (migrants from Kentucky and Tennessee) and "porkchops" (Puerto Ricans). There are ethnic islands of Germans and Swedes. Although there is a small area where Negroes live, it is principally a precinct of whites. The police in the district are, with one exception, white.

On a Friday in the middle of July, the observer arrived for the 4 to 12 midnight watch. The beat car that had been randomly chosen carried two white patrolmen—one with 14 years of experience in the precinct, the other with three.

The watch began rather routinely as the policemen cruised the district. Their first radio dispatch came at about 5:30 P.M. They were told to investigate two drunks in a cemetery. On arriving they found two white men "sleeping one off." Without questioning the men, the older policeman began to search one of them, ripping his shirt and hitting him in the groin with a nightstick. The younger policeman, as he searched the second, ripped away the seat of his trousers, exposing his buttocks. The policemen then prodded the men toward the cemetery fence and forced them to climb it, laughing at the plight of the drunk with the exposed buttocks. As the drunks went over the fence, one policeman shouted, "I ought to run you fuckers in!" The other remarked to the observer, "Those assholes won't be back; a bunch of shitty winos."

Not long after they returned to their car, the policemen stopped a woman who had made a left turn improperly. She was treated very politely, and the younger policeman, who wrote the ticket, later commented to the observer, "Nice lady." At 7:30 they were dispatched to check a suspicious auto. After a quick check, the car was marked abandoned.

Shortly after a 30-minute break for a 7:30 "lunch," the two policemen received a dispatch to take a burglary report. Arriving at a slum walkup, the police entered a room where an obviously drunk white man in his late forties insisted that someone had entered and stolen his food and liquor. He kept insisting that it had been taken and that he had been forced to borrow money to buy beer. The younger policeman, who took the report, kept harassing the man, alternating between mocking and badgering him with rhetorical questions. "You say your name is Half-A-Wit [for Hathaway]? Do you sleep with niggers? How did you vote on the bond issue? Are you sure that's all that's missing? Are you a virgin yet?" The man responded to all of this with the seeming vagueness and joviality of the intoxicated, expressing gratitude for the policemen's help as they left. The older policeman remarked to the observer as they left, "Ain't drunks funny?"

For the next hour little happened, but as the two were moving across the precinct shortly after 10 P.M., a white man and a woman in their fifties flagged them down. Since they were obviously "substantial" middle-class citizens of the district, the policemen listened to their complaints that a Negro man was causing trouble inside the public-transport station from which they had just emerged. The woman said that he had sworn at her. The older policeman remarked, "What's a nigger doing up here? He should be down on Franklin Road!"

With that, they ran into the station and grabbed the Negro man who was inside. Without questioning him, they shoved him into a phone booth and began beating him with their fists and a flashlight. They also hit him in the groin. Then they dragged him out and kept him on his knees. He pleaded that he had just been released from a mental hospital that day and, begging not to be hit again, asked them to let him return to the hospital. One policeman said: "Don't you like us, nigger? I like to beat niggers and rip out their eyes." They took him outside to their patrol car. Then they decided to put him on a bus, telling him that he was returning to the hospital; they deliberately put him on a bus going in the opposite direction. Just before the Negro boarded the bus, he said, "You police just like to shoot and beat people." The first policeman replied, "Get moving, nigger, or I'll shoot you." The man was crying and bleeding as he was put on the bus. Leaving the scene, the younger policeman commented, "He won't be back."

For the rest of the evening, the two policemen kept looking for drunks and harassing any they found. They concluded the evening by being dispatched to an address where, they were told, a man was being held for the police. No one answered their knock. They left.

The station house has long been suspected of harboring questionable police practices. Interrogation-room procedures have been attacked, particularly because of the methods the police have used to get confessions. The drama of the confession in the interrogation room has been complete with bright lights and physical torture. Whether or not such practices have ever existed on the scale suggested by popular accounts, confessions in recent years, even by accounts of offenders, have rarely been accompanied by such high drama. But recently the interrogation room has come under fire again for its failure to protect the constitutional rights of the suspect to remain silent and to have legal counsel.

BACKSTAGE AT THE STATION

The police station, however, is more than just a series of cubicles called interrogation rooms. There are other rooms and usually a lockup as well. Many of these are also hidden from public view. It is not surprising, then, that one-third of all the observations of the undue use of force occurred within the station.

In any station there normally are several policemen present who should be able to deal with almost any situation requiring force that arises. In many of the situations that were observed, as many as seven and eight policemen were present, most of whom simply stood by and watched force being used. The custom among policemen, it appeared, is that you intervene only if a fellow policeman needs help, or if you have been personally offended or affronted by those involved.

Force is used unnecessarily at many different points and places in the station. The citizen who is not cooperative during the booking process may be pushed or shoved, have his handcuffs twisted with a nightstick, have his foot stomped, or be pulled by the hair. All of these practices were reported by policemen as ways of obtaining "cooperation." But it was clear that the booking could have been completed without any of this harassment.

The lockup was the scene of some of the most severe applications of force. Two of the three cases requiring hospitalization came about when an offender was "worked over" in the lockup. To be sure, the arrested are not always cooperative when they get in the lockup, and force may be necessary to place them in a cell. But the amount of force observed hardly seemed necessary.

One evening an observer was present in the lockup when two white policemen came in with a white man. The suspect had been handcuffed and brought to the station because he had proved obstreperous after being arrested for a traffic violation. Apparently he had been drinking. While waiting in the lockup, the man began to urinate on the floor. In response, the policemen began to beat the man. They jumped him, knocked him down, and beat his head against the concrete floor. He required emergency treatment at a nearby hospital.

At times a policeman may be involved in a kind of escalation of force. Using force appropriately for an arrest in the field seemingly sets the stage for its later use, improperly, in the station. The following case illustrates how such a situation may be develop:

Within a large city's high-crime rate precinct, occupied mostly by Negroes, the police responded to an "officer in trouble" call. It is difficult to imagine a call that brings a more immediate response, so a large number of police cars immediately converged at an intersection of a busy public street where a bus had been stopped. Near the bus, a white policeman was holding two young Negroes at gun point. The policeman reported that he had responded to a summons from the white bus-driver complaining that the boys had refused to pay their fares and had used obscene language. The policeman also reported that the boys swore at him, and one swung at him while the other drew a screwdriver and started toward him. At that point, he said, he drew his pistol.

The policemen placed one of the offenders in handcuffs and began to transport both of them to the station. While driving to the station, the driver of one car noted that the other policeman, transporting the other boy, was struggling with him. The first policeman stopped and entered the other patrol car. The observer reported that he kept hitting the boy who was handcuffed until the boy appeared completely subdued. The boy kept saying, "You don't have any right to beat me. I don't care if you kill me."

After the policemen got the offenders to the station, although the boys no longer resisted them, the police began to beat them while they were handcuffed in an interrogation room. One of the boys hollered: "You can't beat me like this! I'm only a kid, and my hands are tied." Later one of the policemen commented to the observer: "On the street you can't beat them. But when you get to the station, you can instill some respect in them."

Cases where the offender resists an arrest provide perhaps the most difficulty in judging the legitimacy of the force applied. An encounter that began as a dispatch to a disturbance at a private residence was one case about which there could be honest difference in judgment. On arrival, the policemen—one white, the other Negro—met a white woman who claimed that her husband, who was in the back yard and drunk, had beaten her. She asked the policemen to "take him in." The observer reported that the police found the man in the house. When they attempted to take him, he resisted by placing his hands between the door jamb. Both policemen then grabbed him. The Negro policeman said, "We're going to have trouble, so let's finish it right here." He grabbed the offender and knocked him down. Both policemen then wrestled with the man, handcuffed him, and took him to the station. As they did so, one of the policemen remarked, "These sons of bitches want to fight, so you have to break them quick."

A MINIMAL PICTURE?

The reader, as well as most police administrators, may be skeptical about reports that policemen used force in the presence of observers. Indeed, one police administrator, indignant over reports of undue use of force in his department, seemed more concerned that the policemen had permitted themselves to be observed behaving improperly than he was about their improper behavior. When demanding to know the names of the policemen who had used force improperly so he could discharge them —a demand we could not meet, since we were bound to protect our sources of information—he remarked, "Any officer who is stupid enough to behave that way in the presence of outsiders deserves to be fired."

There were and are a number of reasons why our observers were able to see policemen behaving improperly. We entered each department with the full cooperation of the top administrators. So far as the men in line were concerned, our chief interest was in how citizens behave toward the police, a main object of our study. Many policemen, given their strong feelings against citizens, fail to see that their own behavior is equally open to observation. Furthermore, our observers are trained to fit into a role of trust—one that is genuine, since most observers are actually sympathetic to the plight of the policeman, if not to his behavior.

Finally, and this is a fact all too easily forgotten, people cannot change their behavior in the presence of others as easily as many think. This is particularly true when people become deeply involved in certain situations. The policeman not only comes to "trust" the observer in the law-enforcement situation—regarding him as a source of additional help if necessary —but, when he becomes involved in a dispute with a citizen, he easily forgets that an observer is present. Partly because he does not know what else to do, in such situations the policeman behaves "normally." But should one cling to the notion that most policemen modify their behavior in the presence of outsiders, one is left with the uncomfortable conclusion that our cases represent a minimal picture of actual misbehavior.

Superficially it might seem that the use of an excessive amount of force against citizens is low. In only 37 of 3826 encounters observed did the police use undue force. Of the 4604 white citizens in these encounters,

27 experienced an excessive amount of force—a rate of 5.9 for every 1000 citizens involved. The comparable rate for 5960 Negroes, of whom 17 experienced an excessive amount of force, is 2.8. Thus, whether one considers these rates high or low, the fact is that the *rate of excessive force for all white citizens in encounters with the police is twice that for Negro citizens.*

A rate depends, however, upon selecting a population that is logically the target of force. What we have just given is a rate for *all* citizens involved in encounters with the police. But many of these citizens are not logical targets of force. Many, for example, simply call the police to complain about crimes against themselves or their property. And others are merely witnesses to crimes.

The more logical target population consists of citizens whom the police allege to be offenders—a population of suspects. In our study, there were 643 white suspects, 27 of whom experienced undue use of force. This yields an abuse rate of 41.9 per 1000 white suspects. The comparable rate for 751 Negro suspects, of whom 17 experienced undue use of force, is 22.6 per 1000. If one accepts these rates as reasonably reliable estimates of the undue force against suspects, then there should be little doubt that in major metropolitan areas the sort of behavior commonly called "police brutality" is far from rare.

Popular impression casts police brutality as a racial matter—white police mistreating Negro citizens. The fact is that white suspects are more liable to being treated improperly by the police than Negro suspects are. This, however, should not be confused with the chances a citizen takes of being mistreated. In two of the cities we studied, Negroes are a minority. The chances, then, that any Negro has of being treated improperly are, perhaps, more nearly comparable to that for whites. If the rates are comparable, then one might say that the application of force unnecessarily by the police operates without respect to the race of an offender.

Many people believe that the race of the policeman must affect his use of force, particularly since many white policemen express prejudice against Negroes. Our own work shows that in the police precincts made up largely of Negro citizens, over three-fourths of the policemen express prejudice against Negroes. Only 1 percent express sympathetic attitudes. But as sociologists and social psychologists have often shown, prejudice and attitudes do not necessarily carry over into discriminatory actions.

Our findings show that there is little difference between the rate of force used by white and by Negro policemen. Of the 54 policemen observed using too much force, 45 were white and 9 were Negro. For every 100 white policemen, 8.7 will use force; for every 100 Negro policemen, 9.8 will. What this really means, though, is that about one in every 10 policemen in high-crime rate areas of cities sometimes uses force unnecessarily.

Yet, one may ask, doesn't prejudice enter into the use of force? Didn't some of the policemen who were observed utter prejudiced statements toward Negroes and other minority-group members? Of course they did. But the question of whether it was their prejudice or some other factor that motivated them to mistreat Negroes is not so easily answered.

Still, even though our figures show that a white suspect is more liable to encounter violence, one may ask whether white policemen victimize Negroes more than whites. We found, for the most part, that they do not. Policemen, both Negro and white, are most likely to exercise force against members of their *own* race:

67 percent of the citizens victimized by white policemen were white.
71 percent of the citizens victimized by Negro policemen were Negro.

To interpret these statistics correctly, however, one should take into account the differences in opportunity policemen have to use force against members of their own and other races. Negro policemen, in the three cities we studied, were far *less* likely to police white citizens than white policemen were to police Negroes. Negro policemen usually policed other Negroes, while white policemen policed both whites and Negroes about equally. In total numbers, then, more white policemen than Negro policemen used force against Negroes. But this is explained by the fact that whites make up 85 percent of the police force, and more than 50 percent of all policemen policing Negroes.

Though no precise estimates are possible, the facts just given suggest that white policemen, even though they are prejudiced toward Negroes, do not discriminate against Negroes in the excessive use of force. The use of force by the police is more readily explained by police culture than it is by the policeman's race. Indeed, in the few cases where we observed a Negro policeman using unnecessary force against white citizens, there was no evidence that he did so because of his race.

The disparity between our findings and the public's sense that Negroes are the main victims of police brutality can easily be resolved if one asks how the public becomes aware of the police misusing force.

THE VICTIMS AND THE TURF

Fifty years ago, the immigrants to our cities—Eastern and Southern Europeans such as the Poles and the Italians—complained about police brutality. Today the new immigrants to our cities—mostly Negroes from the rural South—raise their voices through the civil-rights movement, through black-nationalist and other race-conscious organizations. There is no comparable voice for white citizens since, except for the Puerto Ricans, they now lack the nationality organizations that were once formed to promote and protect the interests of their immigrant forbears.

Although policemen do not seem to select their victims according to race, two facts stand out. All victims were offenders, and all were from the lower class. Concentrating as we did on high-crime rate areas of cities, we do not have a representative sample of residents in any city. Nonetheless, we observed a sizable minority of middle- and upper-status citizens, some of whom were offenders. But since no middle- or upper-class offender, white or Negro, was the victim of an excessive amount of force, it appears that the lower class bears the brunt of victimization by the police.

The most likely victim of excessive force is a lower-class man of either race. No white woman and only two Negro women were victimized. The difference between the risk assumed by white and by Negro women can be accounted for by the fact that far more Negro women are processed as suspects or offenders.

Whether or not a policeman uses force unnecessarily depends upon the social setting in which the encounter takes place. Of the 37 instances of excessive force, 37 percent took place in police-controlled settings, such as the patrol car or the precinct station. Public places, usually streets, accounted for 41 percent, and 16 percent took place in a private residence. The remaining 6 percent occurred in commercial settings. This is not, of course, a random sample of settings where the police encounter suspects.

What is most obvious, and most disturbing, is that the police are very likely to use force in settings that they control. Although only 18 percent of all situations involving suspects ever ended up at the station house, 32 percent of all situations where an excessive amount of force was used took place in the police station.

No one who accepts the fact that the police sometimes use an excessive amount of force should be surprised by our finding that they often select their own turf. What should be apparent to the nation's police administrators, however, is that these settings are under their command and control. Controlling the police in the field, where the policeman is away from direct supervision, is understandably difficult. But the station house is the police administrator's domain. The fact that one in three instances of excessive force took place in settings that can be directly controlled should cause concern among police officials.

The presence of citizens who might serve as witnesses against a policeman should deter him from undue use of force. Indeed, procedures for the review of police conduct are based on the presumption that one can get this kind of testimony. Otherwise, one is left simply with a citizen complaint and contrary testimony by the policeman—a situation in which it is very difficult to prove the citizen's allegation.

In most situations involving the use of excessive force, there were witnesses. In our 37 cases, there were bystanders present three-fourths of the time. But in only one situation did the group present sympathize with the citizen and threaten to report the policeman. A complaint was filed on that incident—the only one of the 37 observed instances of undue force in which a formal complaint was filed.

All in all, the situations where excessive force was used were devoid of bystanders who did not have a stake in being "against" the offender. Generally, they were fellow policemen, or fellow offenders whose truthfulness could be easily challenged. When a policeman uses undue force, then, he usually does not risk a complaint against himself or testimony from witnesses who favor the complainant against the policeman. This, as much as anything, probably accounts for the low rate of formal complaints against policemen who use force unnecessarily.

A striking fact is that in more than one-half of all instances of undue coercion, at least one other policeman was present who did not participate in the use of force. This shows that, for the most part, the police do not restrain their fellow policemen. On the contrary, there were times when their very presence encouraged the use of force. One man brought into the lockup for threatening a policeman with a pistol was so severely beaten by this policeman that he required hospitalization. During the beating, some fellow policemen propped the man up, while others shouted encouragement. Though the official police code does not legitimate this practice, police culture does.

VICTIMS—DEFIANT OR DEVIANT

Now, are there characteristics of the offender or his behavior that precipitate the use of excessive force by the police? Superficially, yes. Almost one-half of the cases involved open defiance of police authority (39 percent) or resisting arrest (9 percent). Open defiance of police authority, however, is what the policeman defines as *his* authority, not necessarily "official" authority. Indeed in 40 percent of the cases that the police considered open defiance, the policeman never executed an arrest— a somewhat surprising fact for those who assume that policemen generally "cover" improper use of force with a "bona-fide" arrest and a charge of resisting arrest.

But it is still of interest to know what a policeman *sees* as defiance. Often he seems threatened by a simple refusal to acquiesce to his own authority. A policeman beat a handcuffed offender because, when told to sit, the offender did not sit down. One Negro woman was soundly slapped for her refusal to approach the police car and identify herself.

Important as a threat to his authority may appear to the policeman, there were many more of these instances in which the policeman did *not* respond with the use of force. The important issue seems to be whether the policeman manages to assert his authority despite the threat to it. I suspect that policemen are more likely to respond with excessive force when they define the situation as one in which there remains a question as to who is "in charge."

Similarly, some evidence indicates that harassment of deviants plays a role in the undue use of force. Incidents involving drunks made up 27 percent of all incidents of improper use of force; an additional 5 percent involved homosexuals or narcotics users. Since deviants generally remain silent victims to avoid public exposure of their deviance, they are particularly susceptible to the use of excessive force.

It is clear, though, that the police encounter many situations involving deviants where no force is used. Generally they respond to them routinely. What is surprising, then, is that the police do not mistreat deviants more than they do. The explanation may lie in the kind of relationships the police have with deviants. Many are valuable to the police because they serve as informers. To mistreat them severely would be to cut off a major source of police intelligence. At the same time, deviants are easily controlled by harassment.

Clearly, we have seen that police mistreatment of citizens exists. Is it however, on the increase?

Citizen complaints against the police are common, and allegations that the police use force improperly are frequent. There is evidence that physical brutality exists today. But there is also evidence, from the history of our cities, that the police have long engaged in the use of unnecessary physical force. No one can say with confidence whether there is more or less of it today than there was at the turn of the century.

What we lack is evidence that would permit us to calculate comparative rates of police misuse of force for different periods of American history. Only recently have we begun to count and report the volume of complaints against the police. And the research reported in this article represents the only attempt to estimate the amount of police mistreatment by actual observation of what the police do to citizens.

LACK OF INFORMATION

Police chiefs are notoriously reluctant to disclose information that would allow us to assess the nature and volume of complaints against the police. Only a few departments have begun to report something about citizen complaints. And these give us very little information.

Consider, for example, the 1966 Annual Report released by the New Orleans Police Department. It tells us that there were 208 cases of "alleged police misconduct on which action was taken." It fails to tell us whether there were any allegations that are *not* included among these cases. Are these all the allegations that came to the attention of the department? Or are they only those the department chose to review as "police disciplinary matters"? Of the 208 cases the department considered "disciplinary matters," the report tells us that no disciplinary action was taken in 106 cases. There were 11 cases that resulted in 14 dismissals; 56 cases that resulted in 72 suspensions, fines, or loss of days; and 35 cases involving 52 written or verbal "reprimands" or "cautionings."

The failure of the report to tell us the charge against the policeman is a significant omission. We cannot tell how many of these allegations involved improper use of force, how many involved verbal abuse or harassment, how many involved police felonies or misdemeanors, and so on. In such reports, the defensive posture of the nation's police departments is all too apparent. Although the 1966 report of the New Orleans Police Department tells us much about what the police allege were the felonies and misdemeanors by citizens of New Orleans, it tells us nothing about what citizens allege was misconduct by the police!

Many responsible people believe that the use of physical brutality by the police is on the wane. They point to the fact that, at least outside the South, there are more reports of other forms of police mistreatment of citizens than reports of undue physical coercion. They also suggest that third-degree interrogations and curbstone justice with the nightstick are less common. It does not seem unreasonable, then, to assume that police practices that degrade a citizen's status or that harass him and restrict his freedom are more common than police misuse of force. But that may have always been so.

Whether or not the policeman's "sense of justice" and his use of unnecessary force have changed remains an open question. Forms may change while practices go on. To move misuse from the street to the station house, or from the interrogation room to the lockup, changes the place but not the practice itself.

Our ignorance of just what goes on between police and citizens poses one of the central issues in policing today: How can we make the police accountable to the citizenry in a democratic society and yet not hamstring them in their legitimate pursuit of law and order? There are no simple answers.

Police departments are organizations that process people. All people-processing organizations face certain common problems. But the police administrator faces a problem in controlling practice with clients that is not found in most other organizations. The problem is that police contact with citizens occurs in the community, where direct supervision is not possible. Assuming our unwillingness to spend resources for almost one-to-one supervision, the problem for the police commander is to make policemen behave properly when they are not under direct supervision. He also faces the problem of making them behave properly in the station house as well.

Historically, we have found but one way—apart from supervision—that deals with this problem. That solution is professionalization of workers. Perhaps only through the professionalization of the police can we hope to solve the problem of police malpractice.

But lest anyone optimistically assume that professionalization will eliminate police malpractice altogether, we should keep in mind that problems of malpractice also occur regularly in both law and medicine.

> The foregoing article shows that, while *most* police officers rarely, if ever, use unnecessary force, a small but significant minority use unnecessary force in a manner both brutal and unjust, generally without interference or reprimand from their fellow officers. Although such acts of brutality may be relatively infrequent, they tend to exert a disproportionate influence on public attitudes toward the police, especially among the groups most affected. In the following article a popular magazine writer gives some idea of why such incidents occur.

POLICE IN CRISIS

Fletcher Knebel

The profile of the average cop is etched from studies amassed by the President's Commission on Law Enforcement and Administration of Justice. The surveys the Commission gathered supply other insights into the character and career of the average police officer. Among them: While his job requires that he make instant street decisions of the wisest and least provocative caliber, he was not tested for emotional stability before going on the police force.

He also has an ambivalent view of his work. He thinks that some of his colleagues are incompetent, corrupt and abusive. He often contemplates quitting. He feels that he is only a cog in a machine. He believes that much of the public regards him with hostility and contempt.

Attitude samplings show, too, that he is prejudiced against Negroes and other minority groups and that he tends to be tougher in his dealings with nonwhites. He has little appreciation of the psychology and culture of the poor, minorities or juveniles. He is aware that some fellow officers treat minority citizens with rudeness, abuse and even physical roughness. He opposes full integration of his own police department.

His feelings warp the facts. For instance, it is not true that the prevailing view of him is one of disdain. Polls show that about 70 percent of *all* people respect him. But it is true that a majority of Negroes dislike him, and about one-third believe he is guilty of outright brutality. Half of the Negro population thinks he is corrupt. Negro teenagers view him as the enemy. Puerto Ricans and Mexican-Americans also hold him in low regard.

He finds few compensations in his work. He feels stifled by the police seniority system, believes his superiors desert him under political pressure, thinks society expects an impossible performance from him and feels harassed by the courts for recent decisions that hobble him in gaining convictions. He is disheartened by the increasing difficulty of making a case against criminals he feels certain are guilty.

Each policeman is charged with protecting about 600 people. He faces a constantly rising crime rate. He manages to solve only about one quarter of the crimes he encounters—a lower proportion than he used to.

Many of his emergency calls involve domestic squabbles, in which he acts as arbiter. He seldom arrests either party. Actually, he makes few arrests a month, and half of these are for such minor offenses as vagrancy, loitering and drunkenness. Two-thirds of his time is consumed by noncrime duties, many of them irksome. Criminal investigation occupies few of his hours.

Still, he confronts danger constantly. In addition to a one-in-eight chance of being assaulted during the year, he faces one chance in 22 of being injured and one chance in 3,500 of being killed. He is, however, in less danger of losing his life than if he worked in mining, farming, construction or transportation.

He is reasonably secure financially. He is covered by life, health and disability insurance, gets three weeks' vacation a year, participates in a decent pension plan and can retire after 23 years on the job.

His education has not fitted him to master the enormous social-worker chores that are thrust upon him. The complexities of his job would tax a superman. He is supposed to be familiar with and help enforce a staggering 30,000 local, state and Federal laws. His career becomes a long march of frustration. He is expected to embody the compassionate qualities of priest, nurse, Boy Scout, physician, father and friend—but he is also supposed to galvanize himself into an instant commander, disciplinarian, keen shot and military genius. He may be pardoned if he fails.

This is the man—the average policeman in the United States—who patrols the streets at a time when lawlessness, riots, racial strife, juvenile unrest and the depredations of the organized Cosa Nostra combine to produce an era of social disorder unmatched in the nation's history.

The police of the United States—350,000 men and women of the municipal, county and state forces—are in a state of crisis. Resignations are rising. Recruiting lags. Morale plunges. Technology trails far behind that of Europe. Police training, despite stellar exceptions in such cities as New York, Chicago and Los Angeles, remains poor. Educational standards are low. A new crusade for police professionalism collides with entrenched politics, corruption and the torpor of administrators encrusted with out-worn traditions. Crime rates rise. Crime solutions recede. Police retreat from rioters, looters and snipers in one city while exploding with indiscriminate and excessive force in another.

In Newark, N.J., Negroes demand that the politics-ridden force be placed in receivership. In Detroit, Negroes complain that police responded too slowly to quell last summer's riot—yet some Detroit cops were charged with brutality, even murder. A storm of 300 bills, all seeking to improve local police forces, pelted the last session of Congress. Charges of police brutality, some justified, most fancied, rain down on city departments. Police chiefs are accused of mistreating minorities. In some cities, anti-poverty officials and the police are locked in angry battle.

A shower of new orders, directives and advice, much of it conflicting and confusing, descends on the daily police roll calls about the nation. "Don't draw your guns." . . . "Be firm." . . . "Address everyone as Mister, Miss or Mrs." . . . "Clean out and isolate Fourth Street." . . . "Attend community-relation classes."

A key factor in the crisis is that police in the United States wear the face, prejudice and culture of the white man at a time when the big Northern cities shift heavily toward a black population, the ugly ghettos spill over with raging violence and the Negro revolution sweeps the land. Save in a few cities, Negro policemen are only token black spots on a field of white, reviled in the streets as "Uncle Toms" or accused of man-handling members of their own race. In cities with more than 20 percent Negro population, here are some samples of the number of Negro officers on the force: Oakland, Calif., two percent; Detroit, four percent; New Orleans, four percent; Birmingham, Ala., 0.2 percent. Even in Washington, D.C., where Negroes comprise more than a majority of the population, black officers constitute but one-fifth of the force despite accelerated Negro recruiting in recent years. In county sheriffs' offices, the percentage of Negro deputies is even smaller than in the cities. State police forces remain almost all white. Of 1,200 New Jersey state policemen, only five are Negro. South Carolina this year selected its first Negro for training for the state-highway patrol.

The police today resemble toy soldiers buffeted by a hurricane. The nation is being hammered by immense social changes, the most pronounced of which are: the growing youthfulness of the population (and juveniles account for a majority of all crimes against property); the massing of more and more people in the crime-breeding slums; the expanded use of drugs; the rise of the great civil-disobedience movements; the dissolution of family and religious disciplines; swiftly increasing personal mobility and rootlessness; riots in the black city cores, with their weary trail of looting, arson, sniping and murder. Society itself has not decided how to grapple with these baffling, rapid changes. The policeman, a sentinel without an army, stands alone on the street, equipped with old attitudes, weapons and training, charged with maintaining the kind of order that his employers are not even sure they want.

The result is a mood of bitter, often sullen, frustration among policemen. Sol Littman, police expert of the Anti-Defamation League, terms the mood one of hopelessness and despair. *Look*'s interviews with patrolmen illustrate the point: "Garbage on my head and abuse all day long. I'm ready to pack it in." . . . "For this kind of pay, who needs it?" . . . "Everything you do now is wrong, either too much or too little. Now, I flag [evade] as much as I can. All I want is to get by for my last eight years."

Sen. Robert C. Byrd (D., W. Va.) recently questioned 50 Washington policemen with a promise of anonymity. Here are representative answers:

Officer J.: "You get a stock question from most of your Negro citizens, which is, 'Why are you picking on me?' and then from your white citizens, 'Why don't you stop all the crime?' "

Officer Y.: ". . . Morale is nil. I don't think morale exists."

Officer AE: "It seems everybody resents you, and they don't want you; and when you are called, they even tell you they don't want you there; and they don't need you, and so why bother?"

Officer AL: "You have to be afraid [that] if you lock this person up, you will have to sit down and write letters [because of protests of unfair arrest]. You figure sometimes it is best to let them go. If he goes through a red light, let him go. God willing, if he is a bad enough driver, maybe he will be killed without killing an innocent person. It is a bad attitude to take, but you feel you will get yourself and your family involved."

Officer AQ: "It is not a personal matter, but once you go to lock them up, the first thing they throw at you is that 'You are locking me up because I am colored.' Now, most of our population is colored. Most of our police department is white. . . . We are getting walked on."

As the old attitudes clash with the vast new social forces, the shock unnerves many a cop. "Since the time of the pyramids," observes one veteran police reporter, "the police have been the protectors and the agents of those in power." This is a truism of all societies, the great American democracy not excepted. Police in this country traditionally have reacted not so much to race as to economic and social status. When the president of the local bank, in dinner jacket and black tie, is stopped for tipsy driving on the way home from the country club dance, he is driven home by the officer. But the drunk in the dirty sport shirt and battered car, white or Negro, is hauled to the station, given a test for intoxication and booked on charges that may bring a jail term or revocation of his license.

Now, the policeman's world is changing with startling rapidity. Black Power in the big cities has become a political fact of life. The black, the poor, the slum-tied demand to be treated like the resident of New York's Sutton Place or Detroit's Grosse Point. The "clout" is there. It manifests itself either through the politician or the Molotov cocktail. The policeman, skilled at discriminating in a manner society seemed to want or at least to tolerate, suddenly finds himself without guideposts. He is puzzled, bewildered, frustrated. He thinks the majority wants one thing, but its leaders seem to be saying another.

"The average police officer is confused and hurt," says George O'Connor, professional-standards expert of the International Association of Chiefs of Police. "The public expects the moon of him, but will give him neither the authority nor the responsibility. Not knowing what it wants in a time of swiftly changing values, the public has insured itself against all risks by stripping the policeman of authority."

In his own fraternity, the cop is caught in a squeeze between the traditionalists who occupy most of the chiefs' offices in the nation and a sprinkling of new "police professionals," for the most part college-trained, who challenge the old ways. The traditionalist chief voices opposition to the U.S. Supreme Court, champions unfettered use of gun and club, believes in tough, instant response to lawbreakers.

The new breed supports the decisions of the Supreme Court relating to the rights of the accused, thinks gun and club should be used with utmost restraint, deplores racial bias on the force, urges understanding of Negro culture, advocates more social work by police and enjoins patrolmen to approach every citizen, regardless of race or economic status, with tact and sympathy.

The new breed demands that bribery and payoffs be rooted out of the station houses. The traditionalists prefer to deny that corruption exists—or to avoid all discussion of it. A clash of attitudes at a secret police meeting last year emphasized the division. When the President's crime commission prepared its task-force volume on police, some chiefs brought pressure on the staff to eliminate or water down a section that criticized departments for graft and corruption. The staff refused. After the report was published, James Vorenberg, a Harvard Law School professor and the commission's executive director, met with a group of big-city police chiefs. The chiefs bitterly rebuked Vorenberg for the corruption charges. They contended that the police had been denigrated by baseless accusations and that Vorenberg's critical credentials were suspect, since he was an academic who had never been a policeman. One chief of a majority force came to the director's aid at the peak of the wrangle. "Listen," he said, "maybe Jim wasn't a policeman, but I am. And you guys all know what I know. Graft is a way of life in an awful lot of departments in this country."

The most severe criticism of American police heard by this writer came not from a black militant or a civil libertarian but from one of the new police breed. He rose from patrolman to command one of the country's most progressive police units. He asked for and was accorded anonymity.

"There is a continuity of corruption in many police departments," he said. "It is bound up in the nature of police work, primarily in the enforcement of incompatible and largely unwanted laws. There is no moral fervor underlying most of these laws. They become but lip service to the Protestant ethic. Take gambling. In a sense, the average city wants gambling restricted—so that only the affluent are allowed to indulge in it. So the cop, testing for reality as opposed to formal pronouncements, begins taking payoffs to let gamblers operate. The corruption moves upward from patrolman to sergeant, to lieutenant and captain. Soon, there is a web of corruption, ensnarling the whole force. This means that soon, no patrolman can be disciplined for anything—such as harsh treatment of minorities—because all police are implicated in payoffs. The average police executive can't face this sitution, so he shrugs and says it doesn't exist. The honest but ineffectual administrator knows what goes on, but he's afraid to lose the support of his men by cracking down. This is the situation in most of the major police departments in this country.

"Aside from corruption, the young police officer is in a dilemma of values. He sees the struggle between his own superiors and the Supreme Court, and then he wonders what his own posture should be. He sees arbitrary, capricious and even corrupt local judges, and he becomes cynical and discouraged.

"As for police brutality, he senses a prevailing attitude in favor of some violence by the police, despite the admonitions of his commissioner. Negroes themselves want other Negroes beat up. Whites want Negroes mauled and vice versa. Look at Milwaukee. The Negro senses that the Milwaukee cop is antiblack, and he despises him. But also, the white scream at the cop for not unleashing them on the Negroes. These pressures are intense, and, in one form or another, they're countrywide. Everybody hates the cop now. Like society itself, the police officer is groping for some absolute standard and can't find it."

The torment of the policeman in his crisis of morale can be best understood through an examination of the police dilemma segment by segment. Here are the major problems:

Recruiting

Few middle-class youths have ever looked upon a police career with envy. Rather, in the words of one professional expert, "Police work has been the traditional avenue for upward mobility by the last and lowest immigrants to the city." The once-embattled and scorned Irish became the cops of the Eastern cities. Then came the Italians, the Poles and the Slavs. Now, it would seem to be the turn of the Negroes to take over big-city police departments; but to young blacks, the policeman is the white foe, even if the face in the nearest patrol car happens to be black. Civil service examinations for a police career draw only a scattering of black applicants, and most of them fail because of poor preparation.

Even the white response to the police image is dismaying to chiefs. A recent Western Michigan University survey of attitudes among 2,000 junior high school students revealed strong antagonism to the police. More than half are convinced that the police treat people unequally in different sections of a city. Many stated they would not seek out the police themselves if they were in trouble.

White apathy, coupled with black antipathy, has reduced police recruitments to a dangerously low level. The President's crime commission put this year's police deficit at 50,000 men.

Pay

While pay scales have moved up recently, the average is still too low to be competitive with industry. The trouble is not so much starting salaries but the depressing top pay that a patrolman can anticipate after years on the beat. In its latest annual survey of police salaries, the Kansas City (Mo.) Police Department finds that the average beginning salary for patrolmen in cities of the 300,000–1,000,000 population bracket is $114.41 a week, while the top attained by an average patrolman is $142.59 a week.

To bolster incomes, tens of thousands of policemen moonlight in such jobs as factory security agents, bank guards, taxi drivers and racetrack cashiers. One expert estimates that a third to a half of all patrolmen in the country hold second jobs. This fact rankles in the impoverished black areas. "I can't get one job," said a young Negro. "Whitey, especially if he's a cop, has two."

Standards

Thirty percent of the nation's police departments still do not require that applicants have a high school diploma. Only about 20 departments, chiefly in California, require some college credits. And only one of the nation's 40,000 local and state police units, the 235-man force of Multnomah (Portland) County, Ore., insists on a college degree for recruits.

Many departments require men to be five feet nine inches tall, thus effectively barring many Puerto Ricans and Mexican-Americans. Imposing physique is more highly prized than mental stability. Only one-fourth of all departments screen men for emotional fitness. Relatively few units require psychiatric tests to spot racial bias, sadism or panic response under stress. In departments that do have psychological screening, an amazing number of applicants are dropped. In the Portland, Ore., city police department, as a sample, 25 percent flunk the psychiatric tests.

High qualifications mean far fewer recruits, especially Negroes from ghetto schools. In some departments where requirements are stiff, only about three new policemen make it out of every 100 applicants. But in departments where low standards prevail, there is always the chance that the man put on the street to enforce the law with a .38 pistol is not only poorly educated, with questionable tolerance and understanding, but perhaps is psychotic. The brutal, sadistic police stereotype of fiction is still being enlisted on some American forces.

Training

Police training varies from none to excellent. At one end of the scale are such cities as New York, where recruits spend four months in a rigorous academy course. At the other end is the small town where a boy dons uniform and gun and goes out to keep the peace after a brief lecture from his chief.

The most serious indictment of police training comes from the International Association of Chiefs of Police. Staffer Norman Kassoff compared minimum state requirements for selected professions. The median minimum is more than 11,000 hours of training for physicians; 9,000 for attorneys; 7,000 for teachers; 5,000 for embalmers; 4,000 for barbers; 1,200 for beauticians; and less than 200 hours for policemen. Yet, of these occupations, only those of physician and policeman entail split-second decisions that can mean life or death. The average physician has nine years of training. Only a quarter of all police officers go on the street with as much as five weeks' training.

Kassoff notes that most professionals are licensed by the states, while the police officer begins work under a probation system. "In over 31 percent of the police agencies," says Kassoff, "the officer is on the street with *little or no training* of any type. The concept of probation permits an individual officer to practice his 'skills' under a system that in effect is still testing him to determine if his training has been successful—his 'guinea pigs' are the public he is supposed to serve. Obviously, it follows that some of America's law-enforcement problems are created by the police themselves."

Attitudes

The Negro revolution roars across the land, with the cop in the teeth of the gale. Yet few white police officers understand, know or care about the Negro or other ethnic minorities. In a belated attempt to cope with crisis before it erupts, a number of police departments have created divisions of "community relations" to labor for police-minority understanding in the slums. Some, including those of New York City, San Francisco and Atlanta, involve major efforts. Atlanta, under the bold leadership of an imaginative veteran policeman, Chief Herbert T. Jenkins, has 43 officers, almost ten percent of the force, working in a "crime-prevention bureau." The men circulate in Negro areas on such tasks—historically alien to police work—as persuading dropouts to return to school, directing people to appropriate social agencies, helping job hunters and delaying rental evictions. The emphasis is on help rather than hard-nosed law enforcement. Chief Jenkins seeks to establish his officers as friends, not foes. The goal of most such programs is to gain Negro confidence and respect as insurance against the militant who cries "police brutality" on slight provocation.

Other innovations are being tried. A few cities, such as Tampa, Fla., enlist young Negroes to help dampen riots. New Haven, Conn., hit by unexpected rioting last summer, is opening neighborhood police centers in Negro areas, where young blacks and the police will work together to solve problems short of arrest and handcuffs. In New Rochelle, N.Y., young Negroes, paid $2.25 an hour, patrol the night streets as "police partners."

But such efforts are foreign to most departments. Typically, a police academy will include one or two hours of "community relations" lectures in its curriculum. A minister, priest, rabbi or academic delivers a discourse on tolerance and the plight of the poor, and the unimpressed recruit goes on to more pertinent instruction, such as how to shoot, wield his nightstick and eject obstreperous drunks from gin mills. If his superiors care so little about racial attitudes and social issues, the beginner sees no reason why he should bother.

The Presidential police task force says that a 1952 observation by Charles Reith still applies in 1967: "It can be said of police training schools that the recruit is taught everything except the essential requirements of his calling, which is how to secure and maintain the approval and respect of the public. . . ." Too often, the chief sees community relations as a public relations gimmick to improve the "police image" without altering his men's behavior. As long as the policeman remains aloof and alienated from the ghetto Negro, that long will he be seen as the armed tool of the white "enemy," and that long will he be the first target of riot snipers.

Riots

Today's policeman is poorly equipped to make the swift, drastic shift from lone operator to disciplined member of a military unit. One minute, he is patrolling his district, responsive only to his own judgment and experience. The next minute, as the riot flares, he must merge quickly into a military force under strict orders of a unit commander. It is as though a forest ranger were suddenly plummeted into a Marine battalion in Vietnam and expected to exhibit the precise responses under fire that took months to soak into the brain and blood of the soldier. Police riot training in this country lags far beyond techniques employed in some European countries.

Cosa Nostra

Organized crime is winning its own war with the police. The Cosa Nostra, with a tight hold on rackets in the teeming cities, murders, pillages, terrorizes and expands its empire into once-legitimate businesses. Local police departments lack the manpower, records and intelligence techniques to fight the Mafia. In Washington, intelligence fails to pass freely between Federal enforcement agencies. Very little of it filters down to local police, chiefly because the Feds have learned through rude experience that the Mafia has paid pipelines into many police departments. What is needed is a broad national organization, as centrally directed and as sophisticated as the Cosa Nostra itself, with cooperating units manned by trusted, security-cleared officers in every major police department. Such an elite organization would sift and coordinate intelligence, gather evidence and plan arrests and indictments.

Trivia

Even if he were geared to handle organized crime, the police officer would find little time to wage the fight. His days are steeped in trivia. He may have to enforce the town ordinance against burning leaves before 4 P.M.; scatter the boys shooting craps in an alley; pacify battering husbands and wives who, when they sober up, will forget he was ever called; or reassure the mother whose daughter is an hour overdue from school. I rode with two officers on a rush mission to the home of a distracted housewife. Purpose: to allay panic. Method: transporting a ground mole, which had alarmed the housewife, to a nearby vacant lot.

Some such chores are inevitable on a policeman's rounds, and the next call may as easily be a lunatic threatening a family with a shotgun or burglars fleeing from a gas station. But why should a trained peace officer spend hour after hour placing parking tickets on car windshields? Some cities employ meter maids or high school boys for this innocuous and placid task, but many others burden veteran motorcycle patrolmen with it. The harrying of drunks is another time-consuming encumbrance for police. One-third of all arrests in the United States are for public drunkenness. In only a small minority of cases are the pedestrian drunks either dangerous or in danger, yet local law demands that the policeman clear the streets. One, two or thirty nights later, depending on the mood of the judge, the drunk is back, and the dreary routine begins all over again. Prostitution falls in the same category, and follows a monotonous rhythm of arrest, fine and back to work.

Some police thinkers urge a complete reevaluation of the policeman's job. Police concern with petty gambling and prostitution either proves a weary vexation to no permanent avail or invites corruption through swift, easy payoffs. And the 2,000,000 arests each year for drunkenness appear to change the complexion of city streets not a whit. As for parking meters, experts ask: "Why send a man to do a boy's job?" Changes are under way to free police of routine duties. New York may use civilians, instead of police, to tow away cars from no-parking zones. Los Angeles Chief Thomas Reddin is experimenting with civilians to direct downtown traffic.

Some method must be found to channel police energies into the crucial battles for law and order.

Bright, New Gadgets

The United States, well behind Europe in police technology, is about to witness a sunburst of advances. Within a few years, every major police department will be linked in a computerized maze to the FBI's National Crime Information Center, where records of felonies, wanted persons and stolen property will be instantly available for the cop on the beat. Already, about 20 departments are connected on the initial loop. Some results have been spectacular. Cars halted in one state have been identified within 90 seconds as having been stolen in another. The national computer answers inquiries within 15 seconds. The remainder of the 90 seconds is consumed in radio relays from squad car to city or state police headquarters.

This sudden leap is somewhat like vaulting across an entire century of police procedure; for today, many police units have no more idea than 100 years ago of what is contained in criminal records of a police department a few miles away.

Another promising area is the substitution of nonlethal, immobilizing sprays, liquids and gas for the deadly gun of the police officer. One of these, Mace, renders the human target helpless for about 15 minutes, enabling an officer to brave an assailant armed with knife or club without risking a shot that could prove fatal. It is already in use in a number of departments. The advantage in tense racial areas, where the shooting of a Negro suspect by a policeman touches off a flaming riot, is obvious. New devices for civil disorders include immobilizing foams, a spray that renders a street too slick to stand upon and a squirted dye that is used to mark fleeing suspects. In Los Angeles, searchlight helicopters track nighttime burglars. Traffic control by sensors and closed-circuit TV is still another avenue for advance. Quiet direction of downtown traffic by television has been used for some time in West German cities. American police technology is finally awakening after two centuries of slumber.

But no brave new world of police science will change the stance of the officer on the beat. Like the infantry soldier, he remains the heart and the essence of the battle. Today, he is asked to fill an almost superhuman role with ancient tools, outmoded skills and crustacean attitudes. He neds more education, better training, new weapons, more pay, vastly more status and, above all, a new outlook toward his fellow citizens. "The Los Angeles Police Department," says a prominent police executive, "is one of the most professional in the world—and one of the most heartless. What I want are police officers who combine L.A.'s professionalism with heart, sympathy and understanding."

The American policeman will continue to be confused, disillusioned, frustrated and hostile until he learns to see the people he serves—of all races—as fellow human beings and until the bulk of the people on his beat call him friend, not foe.

It is obvious that the average community's police, often carelessly selected and usually understaffed and undertrained, have been given an impossible job—impossible in view of their selection, training, and staffing. If the public expects professional responsibility from the police, the public must support a truly professional police force, which it has been unwilling to do. Some of this unwillingness may stem from the fact that part of the police officer's task is "dirty work." This point of view is developed in the following article by one of the editors of *Trans-action.*

THE REVOLT OF THE DIRTY-WORKERS

Lee Rainwater

Professor of Sociology
Harvard University

Schoolteachers, social workers, and policemen in a number of major cities have recently gone on strike, or resigned en masse, or taken mass sick leaves. These events bring to mind the works of Everett C. Hughes, the man who established the investigation of work, occupations, and professions as a major area of social research. In "Good People and Dirty Work," Everett Hughes analyzed some of the societal and social-psychological factors in Germany that fostered the mass murder of concentration-camp victims. He was particularly concerned with the link between the cadre that actually carried out the dirty work and the Germans in general, who were "ignorant" of and silent about what went on in the concentration camps. As in much social-science research, Hughes was able to use an extreme, almost unique social event to advance our understanding of much more common processes. The German murderers raised much more general questions about how societies go about handling situations in which repressive action is considered necessary, but few citizens are willing to do what they want done.

The Germans' anti-Semitism made them feel that "something must be done about the Jews," which in turn led them to covertly delegate to the S.S. the task of doing that something. It then became important to the Germans to fuzz over the gory details, to conceal from themselves, as well as from others, exactly what was being done. Hughes suggested that this is a typical way societies deal with out-groups:

The greater their social distance from us the more we leave in the hands of others a sort of mandate by default to deal with them on our behalf. . . . Perhaps we give them an unconscious mandate to go beyond anything we ourselves would care to do, or even to acknowledge. I venture to suggest that the higher and more expert functionaries who act in our behalf represent something of a distillation of what we may consider our public wishes, while some of the others show a sort of concentrate of those impulses of which we are, or wish to be, less aware.

This shameful work that nevertheless must be done is, then, (morally) "dirty work."

It is easy to see the same processes operating in the deeply-felt American ambivalence toward the police. But the process operates much more broadly. In our world, there is a large out-group—a separate nation of ghetto Negroes whom most white Americans feel must be controlled and confined. Yet those same white Americans are deeply ashamed and uncertain about *how* Negroes are controlled and confined, and they prefer to conceal from themselves much of the detail of how the doers of this dirty work actually go about their assigned tasks.

As the urban ghettos have grown, so has the cohort of functionaries who receive the covert assignment to "keep the colored out of our way." In the process, many institutions officially designed to further well-being and opportunity have become perverted into institutions of custody and constraint. Social-welfare workers find that their profession, designed to help, has been perverted into one designed to spy and to punish. More dramatically, the schools have become custodial institutions in which less and less learning takes place. To conceal their failure, year-in and year-out the schools promote students who have learned less than they should. The proliferation of policemen in schools, of special schools for "incorrigible" children, and the like, testify to the prison-like functions that undergird the educational rhetoric and increasingly call into question the national ideology that "education" cures all ills.

Americans are, in general, indifferent to the welfare of their public functionaries—witness the notoriously poor prestige and salaries of these functionaries. This indifference has been so great that those recruited for many public-service jobs tend to be people who are not the main breadwinners of their families, or who regard public-service work as temporary, or who are motivated more by a desire for security than by the usual American expectation of affluence. And, in the same way, society's indifference has served to blunt the drive of public-service workers for equitable compensation and for a reasonable recognition of their right to collective bargaining.

As the ghettos in this country grow, a new dimension is added, a dimension of silence and ignorance about exactly what these functionaries are expected to do, and how in fact they do carry out society's covert orders to control and cool out those who must be excluded from ordinary society. If the teachers, social workers, and cops were ever to spell out in detail what their duties are in order to justify their wage demands, they would threaten the delicate balance preserved by silence about their assigned dirty work—no one wants to learn that they are striking for "combat pay."

But the dirty-workers *are* striking—for increased pay, of course, but also for other demands that are more directly related to the dangers of dirty work, and to the disrespect society insists on giving to those who do its tacit bidding. The New York teachers, for example, openly and directly challenged the implicit understanding that it is more important for them to be custodians than for them to be teachers. It is gradually dawning on all of these public servants that both their official public tasks (to educate, to protect the citizens, to look after the welfare of the dependent) and their covert tasks (to control Negroes and make them as invisible as possible) are impossible to achieve.

The dirty-workers are increasingly caught between the silent middle class, which wants them to do the dirty work and keep quiet about it, and the objects of that dirty work, who refuse to continue to take it lying down. Individual revolts confront the teachers with the problems of the "blackboard jungle," the police with the problem of "disrespect for law and order," and the welfare workers with the problem of their charges' feigned stupidity and real deception. These civilian colonial armies find their right to respect from their charges challenged at every turn, and often they must carry out their daily duties with fear for their physical safety.

Equally ominous for the dirty-workers is the organized Negro challenge to their legitimacy. Not only must they cope with individual resistance to their ministrations, but also, more and more, with militant and insistent local civil-rights groups that expose their failures and tax them with their abrogation of their professional responsibilities to teach, to protect, to help.

It is encouraging that those expected to do the dirty work are rebelling. But it is really too much to expect that they will admit their own individual culpability, at least as long as the rest of us won't. Even so, the more the teachers, the police, and the welfare workers insist on the impossibility of their tasks, the more that society at large, and its political leaders, will have to confront the fact that our tacit understandings about the dirty work that is to be done are no longer adequate.

Of course there are dangers, too. The police are our internal hawks, and they might win—and there are also hawks among schoolteachers (they want unruly children kicked out of school) and welfare workers (who want to escalate the attack on welfare chiselers). As dangerous in the long run, perhaps, are the doves—the teachers and the social workers who want to save the ghetto through education and casework (or that form of neighborhood casework called "community action"). Should either the ghetto hawks or doves carry the day, their victory could become the basis for a new tacit understanding about dirty work, one that would save the country from paying the price it is apparently most reluctant to pay—the price of providing economic resources and open, decent housing to Negroes, so there is no longer a ghetto that requires dirty-workers.

One of the most perplexing difficulties in law enforcement arises from the great suspicion and distrust of the police, especially among the very classes of people who are most often the victims of crime and whose need for protection is the greatest. This problem is treated in the final chapter of Donald H. Bouma's *Kids and Cops,* a research study of attitudes held toward each other by ten thousand junior high school students and three hundred police officers in several Michigan cities. The section reprinted below includes a number of generalizations which are not accompanied by any supporting data—these data were presented in earlier chapters of his study.

NARROWING THE HOSTILITY GAP

Donald H. Bouma
Professor of Sociology
Western Michigan University

Widespread violence, urban riots, student demonstrations, and a rising crime rate dramatize both the enhanced need for police action and the disenchantment and hostility toward the activity of the police. Our studies of the attitudes of youth toward the police and law enforcement and of the attitudes of the police toward inner-city youth, cited in the previous chapters, reveal a horrendous chasm of antagonism.

Failure to narrow the gap between the police and the citizenry, and that right early, portends the possibilities of either foundering in the chaos of anarchy or suffocating under the regimen of a police state. To argue whether it is the police who need to change or the community is to dissipate energies and waste time. Programs aimed at both are needed.

The starkly negative feelings that students have toward the police, and the fact that they become more antagonistic as they advance through the junior high years, is a grim challenge to both the schools and the police.

Quoted from *Kids and Cops,* Chap. 6 (1969), by Donald H. Bouma and used by permission of the Eerdmans Publishing Co., Grand Rapids, Michigan.

While they are learning the average rainfall in Chile, the capitals of the banana republics, how to diagram a complex sentence, the rhyming scheme of the Elizabethan sonnet, the names of the President's cabinet, and the like, they are also learning to think negatively about the police. . . .

There is growing awareness that the present state of police-community relations is a threat to both personal and social values. The studies reported in the previous chapters, as well as others which have just been completed or are now in progress, will facilitate analyzing the problem into constituent segments. By focusing on the identified ingredients of the problem, it becomes possible to tailor programs for the specific segments. One does not design programs to get at illness, but for specific illnesses, each with its unique symptomology and idiosyncratic remedial possibilities. Similarly, one does not get at the problem of police-community relations by attacking it *en masse*. Our studies have indicated that the problem is particularly acute in certain segments of the population and in certain particular aspects of the police-citizen relationship. With both police and citizen groups aware of the problem and with both concerned to take corrective action, it becomes more likely that the gap between the two can be narrowed.

To the extent that citizen antagonism rises out of defects in the police operation, suggestions for changes in these specific and specified areas can be made. To the extent that the antagonisms are generated by misperceptions each has of the other, programs for improving understanding can be formulated. Clearly, understanding is a two-way street. The community must work as hard for it as the police.

TWIN DANGERS OF OVERACTING AND UNDERACTING

Ramsey Clark, former attorney general of the United States, calls police-community relations the most important law enforcement problem of today and the years ahead. "As never before, the policeman needs full community support. And as never before, the community needs him. It is both ironic and tragic that we have given so little to the support of those on whom so much depends." Clark claims that the policeman is the most important American today, working in a highly flammable environment where a spark can cause an explosion. If he overacts, he can cause a riot. If he underacts, he can permit a riot.[1]

Our studies have indicated that those youth who reported having police contact had much more negative attitudes toward law enforcement than the others. Although it is not known whether the hostility feelings

---

[1] Foreword by Ramsey Clark in George Edwards, *The Police in the Urban Frontier* (New York, Institute of Human Relations Press, 1968), p. viii.

were the cause of, or the consequence of, police contact, clearly the way police handle juveniles is an important aspect of the problem. More than one million young people come to the attention of the police each year, according to Lynn D. Swanson, consultant on police services for the U.S. Children's Bureau.[2] Some are involved because of parental neglect and abuse, but most of them because of violations of local, state, and federal statutes. The majority are between the ages of 10 and 17. How the police handle children in these situations undoubtedly has an effect on not only the attitudes of the youngsters involved but also those of parents and the larger public toward all police activities.

In recent decades police have become more protective and understanding in their handling of delinquent and neglected children. There has been an increased recognition that what the police officer does or fails to do may have a lasting influence upon the child's life and also upon his respect for authority. Yet, wide variations exist between police departments in the way they handle youth. Some departments require that all children coming to police attention be referred immediately to a specialized unit assigned to work with children. Others expect the police generalist to handle most of the youth cases and to refer to the specialized youth unit only cases which pose special problems.

Since the initial contact with the juvenile is particularly critical, and since this contact is apt to be with any member of the police department, it is apparent that a special juvenile unit specially trained in handling problems of youth is not sufficient, but that all police officers must have some preparation in this area. Swanson sees the greatest contribution of the special youth division as being that of consultant to other police officers in matters dealing with children and youth, disseminating knowledge about juveniles to the entire department through in-service and recruit training programs. Beyond that, he sees the youth unit members as being specially trained in the basic understanding of adolescent behavior, the causes of delinquent behavior and possible controls for it, and as having a working knowledge of community resources and agencies that may be of assistance in particular cases.

One of the suggestions for improving police-community relations in general, and for increasing the effectiveness of police operations in the inner city particularly, is to increase the number of Negro officers in police departments. There is a good deal of consensus on this point. Our studies indicated that the vast majority of police officers are in favor of this goal. Achievement of this goal, however, is made difficult because of the increasingly negative value placed on police work in the black community and because of disagreements as to how this can be achieved within the

2 Lynn D. Swanson, "Police and Children," *The Police Chief* (June 1958) p. 18.

framework of present standards of eligibility for police work, or some changed set of standards.

While the recruitment of additional Negro police officers is acknowledgedly difficult, one of the communities in our study found that it was not impossible. Since the disturbances of 1967, when only one of the 160-member Kalamazoo Police Department was a Negro, five new black officers were added in the next 14 months. All have been educated beyond high school, four of them in universities, and only one of them grew up in the local community.

Despite pressures to the contrary, two of the black officers said they wanted to become policemen all their lives. One of them admitted he had an ulterior motive. "White people need an education," he said, "and I am going to teach them that I can be just as good a cop as anybody else." One reason given for the success of the recruitment efforts was a new police pay scale whereby a patrolman now makes between $7,400 and $9,300 a year. . . .

The black officers claim that they face less discrimination from co-workers in the police department than they did in their previous jobs where they worked primarily with whites. All agree that in a difficult situation any of their white comrades would rush to their aid without hesitation. . . .

A number of police departments have used short-contact public relations programs in the schools in an attempt to develop early positive feelings toward the police. Illustrative of such programs is the "Policeman Bill" program established in the first, second and third grades of the public elementary schools of Los Angeles as a joint effort of the police department and the school officials. One significant aspect of the program was that an attempt to evaluate its effectiveness was made.

In the program an officer in uniform makes a half-hour presentation to the youngsters, describing the functions of the police and explaining in a non-threatening manner the purposes of various items of police equipment. Students get a chance to sit in the squad car, blow the siren, blink the lights, and listen to the police radio. In a before-and-after evaluative study, it was found that the children displayed significantly less antipathy toward the police after the contact with the police program.

The evaluation, designed by Robert L. Derbyshire, involved having third grade students representing three divergent ethnic and social class categories draw pictures of "the policeman at work." [3] Four raters then compared each picture on a seven-point scale indicating the degree that each picture expressed aggressiveness, authoritarianism, hostility, kindness,

[3] Robert L. Derbyshire, "Children's Perceptions of the Police: A Comparative Study of Attitudes and Attitude Change," *Journal of Criminal Law, Crimonology and Police Science* (June 1968) pp. 183–190.

goodness, strength, and anger. The findings showed that lower-class Negro and lower-middle-class Mexican-American third-grade children see the policeman's tasks as aggressive, negative, and hostile, while upper-middle-class white children see the tasks as being neutral, non-aggressive, and assisting. In the Watts district of Los Angeles the third graders were asked to draw "policeman at work" pictures both before and after the "Policeman Bill" presentation. A statistically significant change in the direction of less antipathy toward the police was found. Derbyshire reports that the major change for the Watts children was drawing pictures to indicate assistance positive when previously they drew pictures demonstrating aggressive, assistance negative, and neutral behavior.

How long the more favorable attitudes persisted is not known. The "after" study was done just four days following the program presentation. A much more extensive evaluation study is needed to assess the relative impact of confounding variables and the persistence of attitude change with and without reinforcement mechanisms. At least, this represents a beginning in the more systematic approach to the problem of building better relationships between the police and young pupils.

POLICE COUNSELORS IN THE SCHOOLS

A more systematic and sustained effort to improve relationships between the police and students involves the placement of a police officer as a counselor in the school system. Police-school liaison programs have been instituted in a number of cities, most of them patterned after the pioneering effort of the Mott Program of the Flint (Michigan) Board of Education which has been in existence for over ten years. The police counselor is not in uniform, does not patrol corridors to maintain order, is not a punitive agent of last resort, and must be distinguished from those police officers increasingly assigned to schools to prevent or handle disturbances and disorder.

While the structure and function of programs vary considerably, five purposes of the school-liaison policeman's role are often identified:

1. To establish collaboration between the police and school in preventing crime and delinquency.
2. To encourage understanding between police and young people.
3. To improve police teamwork with teachers in handling problem youth.
4. To improve the attitudes of students toward police.
5. To build better police-community relations by improving the police image.

The cooperative effort in placing officers with capacity for understanding squarely in the midst of the daily academic scene and making them a functioning part of it is viewed as an important step toward breaking through the barriers of hostility and suspicion, kid to cop and cop to kid, which have so long perpetuated themselves. By making the policeman a familiar part of the everyday learning experience, the program seeks to establish genuine rapport between youth and those who represent the law enforcement function. Hopefully, the law officer now becomes something more than a symbol of a badge, a bludgeon, and a screaming siren. He becomes somebody to turn to rather than to run from, a person to be trusted rather than feared.

In Flint the police liaison detective is a member of a five-man counseling team which uses a multi-disciplinary approach to children's problems much like that traditionally used in child guidance clinics. Each team is composed of a dean of counseling, dean of students, visiting teacher (school social worker), police counselor, and nurse counselor. The team meets regularly to consider referrals from school personnel, parents, or a community agency. It makes a preliminary study of a problem, places the case on a priority list for further handling, and arranges for the accumulation of data on the problem case from all of the specialties involved.

The police counselor has his office in the school but remains an employee of the police department, and the costs of the program are typically shared by the school and the department. Important to the success of the program is the officer's relationship with faculty, students, and parents. He attends school functions and becomes known in the school neighborhood, to merchants, and members of civic and church organizations. While he has no authority for discipline within the school, he is in a position to make early identification of delinquent behavior and to become familiar with trouble spots in the neighborhood.

In some programs he also checks on complaints that come in from the police juvenile bureau relating to youth in his school district. The officer likely knows something about the youth already, has ready access to school background on the person involved, and spares the youth the trauma of any more official police contact.

In such programs the purpose is double-barreled. Through close cooperation between the police and the school a joint approach is possible for understanding problems of youth and for working with delinquents. Also, to the extent that the officer can develop close personal relationships with all students, a greater respect for the police and law enforcement is created.

In other police-liaison programs, notably those recently instituted by the Michigan State Police, the sole purpose is to develop better relationships between youth and the police and a greater respect for the law enforcement function. Efforts to achieve this purpose are vitiated, it is maintained, by attempting to combine it with a delinquency and problem behavior control function. Hence, any deviant behavior by school pupils coming to the attention of the police liaison officer is not handled by him but referred to regular police agencies. Clearly, the difference between the two programs is quite fundamental. Regrettably, there have been no evaluations of extant programs to determine their effectiveness or to provide a basis for assessment of relative merit. Provisions for evaluation are built into the three most recently launched Michigan State Police programs.

School-liaison officers in the expanding programs of the Michigan State Police are carefully selected and must complete a specially-designed training program before placement in a school. Officers must have some formal college education and be interested in continuing college courses while on the job. This is considered essential because of the close working relationship with teachers, counselors, administrators, social workers, and probate (juvenile) court personnel. Officers are to be young enough to identify readily with the school children and be acceptable to them. Other qualities emphasized in the selection process are the ability to work independent of close supervision, ability to develop and present public relations programs and lectures, an unbiased attitude toward juvenile offenders, an absence of racial prejudice, and an understanding of the social problems involved in minority group relationships.

The school liaison officer is paid and equipped by the state police, while the school provides office space and finances the continuing education of the officer. The men are assigned to the police post having jurisdiction over the school area and are responsible to the post and district commander for their deportment, work schedule reports, and the like. They receive staff direction from the juvenile section of the central state police headquarters. During the summer months the officers remain to some extent within the school area, continuing to maintain liaison with the students and their parents. They work complaints from the post involving that school area and are also used for other regular police duties.

The goal of the program is basically one of prevention of juvenile misbehavior through the establishment of improved police-citizen relationships. Some of the approaches used by the officers include:

1. Acting as an instructor before various school groups and classes, explaining the reason for pertinent laws, their meaning, consequences of violation, and the police function. Through discussion, negative feelings can be identified, adequate perspective provided, and misinformation corrected.

2. Acting as a counselor to students apart from, or in conjunction with, school personnel. Many students have been found to be concerned

about problems that are related to laws and their enforcement. Some students prefer to talk with someone not completely identified with the school program.

3. Maintaining contacts with the parents or guardians of students exhibiting anti-social behavior patterns, advising them of the acts, offering his assistance and soliciting theirs in coping with the problems that lie at the cause of the trouble. In doing this the officer is opening up new avenues of communication, and changing the image of the police officer from one of being strictly effect-oriented to one of being cause-oriented, from punishment to prevention, from negative to positive.

4. Making appearances before various community organizations to demonstrate police concern with the prevention of delinquency through the determination of the causes and treatment of the causes, rather than through apprehension because of the effects of delinquency. By indicating their sympathetic concern for the problems of everyday life, they may help to create within parents an increased awareness and sense of responsibility toward the laws and their enforcement.

5. Working with school personnel and the law enforcement agencies of the community in bridging the gap which so often impeded the efforts of both groups to effectively carry out their mutual responsibilities in reference to the youth of the area. Role misconceptions on the part of both the school and law enforcement agencies have undoubtedly produced disjunctions and even antagonistic feelings. Through joint efforts school personnel come to see that police agencies, too, are interested in education as a preventive tool; and law enforcement personnel come to see that educators, too, are concerned with developing respect for and obedience to laws of the community.

Police-school liaison programs continue to spread in cities throughout the country. Both school and police officials generally claim them to be successful, public support is usually present at the outset or comes after a trial period, and the first national police-school workshop was held last year in Flint under Mott Foundation auspices. However, there has also been considerable and organized opposition to the programs.

Some individuals and organizations believe the dangers of inserting a law enforcement officer into everyday school routine far outweigh the benefits. Criticism has come from churches, parent-teacher organizations, and civil rights agencies. In Tucson a public furor was spearheaded by the Arizona Civil Liberties Union, fearful that stationing police in school buildings and empowering them to interrogate children would almost certainly lead to intrusions on their civil liberties and could be a long step toward a "police school."

Sensitive to these criticisms, the U.S. Department of Justice, in announcing a federal grant in support of the Tucson police counselor program, indicated that careful procedures will be developed to protect the rights of students in all investigative interviews, including advance notification to parents, advice on the voluntary nature of the interview, and the presence of parents or school representatives at all interviews. . . .

The police-school cadet program is another technique designed to develop more positive attitudes toward the police and law enforcement. Typically, it is an after-school club activity, often sponsored by a police officer. The boys structure their organization like a police department with captains, lieutenants and sergeants, and wear badges and arm patches to indicate their membership in the program. Activities may involve the study of gun safety, bicycle operation, court procedures, crime detection, city government, community relations, and the like. At times it is combined with school safety work. The value of such programs obviously depends on the way they are organized and the enthusiasm of the directors. Again, evaluations of the effectiveness of such programs are lacking. If the concern for improved police-youth relationships becomes serious enough, the potentials of such programs should be carefully explored.

New York City has a police-school program in teacher education in which members of the police department conduct an in-service training program for teachers. The course informs teachers of police problems, rationale for procedures, legal limitations, and the like. The teachers are then able to convey this information to their classes and more realistically discuss the police role with the students.

Other programs involve police personnel with neighborhood groups to discuss mutual problems and to share concern for the difficulties of the young people. Free-wheeling discussions with the youth themselves, traumatic as they often become, generate a greater depth of understanding all ways around.

DESIGN FOR CHANGING YOUTH ATTITUDES

One of the most highly organized approaches to the problem is the project developed by Robert Portune at the University of Cincinnati, aimed at increasing the understanding of police of problems of early adolescence, and at the same time directed toward improving youth attitudes toward the police.[4] The program brings together teachers and policemen to cooperatively develop methods and materials for the training of police in the comprehension of youth problems. The two groups also work on a curriculum which can be used in the school to inculcate in the children better attitudes toward law enforcement agencies. . . .

[4] Robert G. Portune, "Early Adolescent Attitudes Toward the Police," unpublished manuscript, University of Cincinnati, 1967.

Portune also notes that the obligation to develop favorable attitudes toward law enforcement is especially crucial in the junior high school. These students are in a transition period, breaking away from the opinions of their parents, trying to fit society to their own personalities and egos, developing their own attitudes toward the world in which they live. He reports that school people are increasingly coming to the awareness that early adolescence is a key period in life, especially with respect to attitude formation. With the school's growing responsibility for attitude formation and the junior high school youngster's growing importance, it appears that efforts to improve attitudes toward the police could profitably be focused on the junior high years.

In a number of communities growing awareness of public apathy, ignorance, and hostility concerning the police operation has led to the formation of citizen groups aimed at the improvement of understanding between the police and the public. In San Francisco a group composed of members of various ethnic, racial, and religious sub-cultures has been operating for several years to narrow the gap in understanding. Its purpose is to collect, analyze, and channel to appropriate governmental and social agencies accurate and reliable reports growing out of charges of police misbehavior, including brutality, harassment, and unequal enforcement and applications of the law. Recognizing that law enforcement bodies need the full cooperation of all citizens, the group alerts the public to the problems of the police and educates people to both their rights and obligations under the law.

To implement these purposes the San Francisco group, calling itself Citizens Alert, receives and records complaints of police brutality, harassment, and intimidation. The complaints are investigated. If unsupported, community fears and hostilities are quickly allayed. Because it is not officially a part of city government, the investigative conclusion of the group is apt to be more readily accepted as legitimate. If supported, complaints are filed with the community relations unit of the police department, and, if warranted, suits are filed against the city and the police department.

To open up additional channels of communication with the community, and especially to facilitate the registering of complaints about the police, the Kalamazoo department has recently made available an addressed, ready-to-mail form on which citizens can register their dissatisfactions. Entitled "We Welcome Your Complaint," the forms are placed at the police information center, in various social and community service agencies, and in public offices.

The new community-relations effort is aimed at making it as easy as possible for a citizen to express himself on any problem he has with the department, and to make suggestions for improvement. The blank informs the writer that the police chief is the only one who will open it, that each criticism and complaint received will be investigated thoroughly and appropriate action taken when warranted by the facts obtained, and that the writer will be informed of the results of the investigation when completed. The more channels of communication that are opened and the easier it is to register a complaint, the less likelihood that smoldering grievances will be ignited, the greater opportunity to correct defects in policy and procedure, and the increased capability of sorting out the legitimate critics from the rest.

THE POLICE-CITIZEN CONFRONTATION TECHNIQUE

A relatively new technique for developing improved relations between the police and the community involves an organized and intensive confrontation between small groups of officers and citizens, particularly those from the minority neighborhoods. The program throws hostile groups together—hour after hour and day after day—and forces them into intimate, brutally frank, emotion-spilling discussions. It is variously called "laboratory confrontation," "eyeball-to-eyeball technique," "sensitivity training," "group therapy," and the like.[5]

Since the development of the laboratory confrontation method of dealing with dysfunctional forces within communities and their various institutions is of fairly recent origin, evaluative research on its effectiveness is practically non-existent. Research evaluating related, but by no means identical, techniques which have been fairly common training tools of business and industry for the past decade is inconclusive, serving to intensify the growing debate over the contribution of laboratory confrontation in effectuating behavioral and attitudinal changes.[6]

The data presented in previous chapters revealed that in most areas there was great similarity in the police departments studied. However, in some areas there was a significant difference in the sophistication of racial attitudes held by members of the Grand Rapids Police Department and those of other departments studied. For example, while Grand Rapids experienced a major riot in the summer of 1967, and the other cities had only minor skirmishes, the attitudes of Grand Rapids officers toward inner-city residents had deteriorated much less. For six months prior to the riot (and ten months prior to the field work for our study), the Grand Rapids police were involved in a series of laboratory confrontations primarily with members of the Negro and Spanish-American communities. Thus there

[5] This description of the laboratory confrontation program was written with the assistance of Holly Porter, who has participated in the utilization of this technique in training sessions with police departments throughout the midwest for MARC (Metropolitan Area Resources Company) of New York City. With Irving Goldaber, she has recently established Community Confrontation and Communication Associates, which specializes in the laboratory confrontation approach.

[6] Symposium, "Laboratory Training," *Industrial Review* (October 1968) p. 32.

seems to be supportive evidence to suggest that involvement in the laboratory confrontations did contribute toward more tolerant and sensitive attitudes.

At the instigation of citizen groups in Grand Rapids, an experimental program was designed in early 1967 to improve relationships between the police department and the members of the community, particularly members of minority groups. The concept of laboratory confrontation was the core of the program, representing the first instance of the intensive utilization of this technique to improve police-community relations. Since the Grand Rapids experiment first attracted national attention, the technique has been used in other cities across the country, with some significant changes in program design based on the Grand Rapids experience.

The laboratory confrontation program brings together in a controlled setting and for a scheduled period of time representatives of two or more identifiable conflict groups whose attitudes and behavior have proved to be dysfunctional to the harmonious, productive working relationships of the total group. Group relations techniques are utilized to produce a functional system of interaction.

Specifically, the hostilities felt by each side and by each individual are permitted and actually encouraged to be expressed openly and freely. Then, with exposure to planned group dynamics exercises, the conflict groups specify their grievances, large and small. Many of the problem areas are thus minimized with communication, information, and clarification.

Some disagreements persist, and the group is then introduced to problem-solving techniques. In the process of developing problem-solving skills, the group addresses itself to the areas of disagreement which still exist and jointly conceives a workable plan for dealing with the remaining problems.

During the confrontation laboratory the members of the groups move from positions of polarized antagonism to collaboration through a process which encourages "gut level" venting of hostilities, builds in the development of communication skills and problem-solving techniques, and introduces a new behavioral norm previously unthinkable, or at least impractical—that of cooperatively preparing a rationale and a scheme by which to operate harmoniously and productively in the particular community.

This technique differs from the traditional kind of police-community relations program in that it provides for an intensive and direct confrontation between police personnel and representatives of the community groups who feel aggrieved. Trained consultants are present to sustain the neutral atmosphere, to provide the in-put necessary to develop group skills essential to a functional relationship, and to facilitate movement of the dysfunctional groups of hostile individuals to the point of effective collaboration. . . .

If in a police-community laboratory confrontation strategically located leaders from an aggrieved segment of the community are in confrontation with police personnel who occupy positions of authority, or who are in constant contact with that segment of the community, the impact of the project can be significantly increased out of proportion to sheer numbers of people involved. The trust and understanding achieved by the participant group presumably facilitates the establishment of important new networks of communication within and between the inner-city communities and the police departments. Implementation of the confrontation approach in conflict resolution and social change could be expected to enhance law enforcement efforts.

For an effective confrontation to take place several basic requirements are deemed vital:

1. It is important that there be at least the *potential* of identifying a goal or goals shared by the participants, although they might not initially recognize the goal or goals as being mutually held. There can be very little hope of a meaningful, jointly conceived plan of action if, for instance, some participants are dedicated to the destruction of the societal system or of particular institutions involved, while others are dedicated to creating a better or more effective society or institution. There may be much conflict over how the improvements should be made but there should be a minimum of disagreement over the essential value of making the improvements.

2. Participants should be sensitive representatives of all the identifiable conflict groups within the affected community or institution. The laboratory participants should approximate as much as possible a microcosm of the total group involved to insure expression of all the feelings and attitudes contributing to the climate within the community or institution in question.

3. There must be a realistic expectation among participants that their efforts will eventually effect change in a significant way.

4. There must be a willingness on the part of the community or institutional leadership to make changes in response to the laboratory group's final product or plan of action.

In addition to meeting these basic requirements, the effectiveness of the actual laboratory confrontation depends to a great degree on thorough preliminary planning involving representatives of all concerned parties—the sponsoring groups, appropriate community members, the professional training team, and others—in order that the unique nature of a particular community and its problems be brought to the surface. With sagacious selection of program participants and flexibility of program design to meet idiosyncratic local needs and freshly developing situations, the possibilities of achieving meaningful improvements in police-community relations are increased.

While the effectiveness of the laboratory confrontation technique has not been carefully evaluated, it has gained respect where it has been used and is increasingly being utilized in police training programs. It is much more costly, in terms of both time investment and money, than other approaches to narrowing the gap between the police and the public. Given the aggravated hostilities rampant in so many communities and the lack of demonstrated effectiveness of other techniques which have been tried, plus the availability of new federal funds for the improvement of local law enforcement efforts, it seems that the confrontation approach should be given careful consideration by those seriously concerned to improve police-community relations.

CONCLUSION

Where the antagonism toward the police is the greatest—in the inner city—there the need for the police is also the greatest. No segment of our society has a greater stake in effective, vigorous law enforcement than do Negroes. All the statistics dramatize the fact that blacks are more likely to be victims of crime, particularly crimes of violence, than are whites.

Yet, the policeman, whose mission it is to guard the peace, walks uneasily in the ghetto. According to George Edwards, U.S. Court of Appeals Judge and former police commissioner of Detroit, what worries the policemen is not so much the "ordinary criminal; usually he feels he can cope with lawbreakers, whose apprehension is his main job. He fears, rather, the very people he is there to protect. For many otherwise law-abiding ghetto dwellers are openly hostile to him: many refuse to cooperate with him in maintaining law and order; and on occasion some may attack him." [7]

Ghetto residents, on the other hand, complain of mistreatment by the police. Edwards observes that in every major city police brutality is a familiar complaint and that this charge cannot be "dismissed as empty talk by irresponsible elements. It has been effectively documented by three authoritative national commissions over a period of four decades and is a matter of deep concern to many sensible, law-abiding citizens, both Negroes and whites."

Optimism about the possibilities of narrowing the gap between the black community and the police will have to be tempered by the realization that the hostility between these two groups has deep roots in the past—in the long years of legally prescribed and popularly supported second-class citizenship for Negroes. The system of two-class citizenship, based not on conduct but simply on color, was enforced by the police, who ob-

[7] Edwards, *The Police in the Urban Frontier* (New York, Institute of Human Relations Press, 1968) p. 20.

viously, since color was the determinant, did not have to make distinctions between the law-abiding and lawless Negro. Thinking and acting in terms of stereotypes—THE POLICE and THE NEGRO—has always been a major impediment to honest and realistic relationships between people. Any effective program for improving the quality of interaction between these two groups will have to recognize the importance of achieving specification and particularization instead of generalization, and differentiation instead of stereotyping.

And this is a concern not only of the police and the ghetto community, but of the entire community. The National Advisory Commission on Civil Disorders (February 29, 1968) put it this way:

The abrasive relationship between the police and the ghetto community has been a major—and explosive—source of grievance, tension and disorder. The blame must be shared by the total society. . . . Police administrators, with the guidance of public officials, and the support of the entire community, must take vigorous action to improve law enforcement and to decrease the potential for disorder.

Few policemen understand why in ghetto neighborhoods hostility results from even their most routine actions—arrest for a traffic violation or responding to a disorderly dispute between husbands and wives—and they respond with resentment of their own. As Michael Harrington has noted, ". . . for the urban poor, the police are those who arrest you. In almost any slum there is a vast conspiracy against the forces of law and order." [8] The contrast between their hopes and the reality gives rise to frustration and anger, which are often turned against the police.

At the same time, police responsibilities in the ghetto have grown as other institutions of social control have lost much of their authority: the schools, because so many are old and inferior; religion, which has become meaningless to many who have shifted hopes from the hereafter to the here, rather than the after; career aspirations, which for many young Negroes are totally lacking; the family, because its bonds are so often broken. It is the policeman, along with a few others, who must fill this institutional vacuum, and is then resented for the presence this effort demands.

Alone, the policeman in the ghetto cannot solve these problems, as noted by the U.S. Commission of Civil Disorders. "His role is already one of the most difficult in our society. He must deal daily with a range of problems and people that test his patience, ingenuity, character, and courage in ways that few of us are ever tested. Without positive leadership, goals, operational guidance, and public support, the individual policeman can only feel victimized. Nor are these problems the responsibility only of

[8] Michael Harrington, *The Other America* (New York, Macmillan, 1962) p. 16.

police administrators; they are deep enough to tax the courage, intelligence, and leadership of mayors, city officials, and community leaders," the Commission concludes.[9]

Many other suggestions have been made for the improvement of police-community relations. They include:

1. Strong department rules against the use of epithets such as "wop," "kike," "nigger," "polack," etc., or "boy," "girl," etc., when addressed to adults.

2. Assign police officers known to be strongly prejudiced against Negroes to noncritical jobs. The assumption here is that there is no way of knowing of this prejudice prior to employment and only his record on the force will reveal it.

3. Honest and effective investigation of civilian complaints together with appropriate correction. Whether this is best achieved through civilian control of police departments, through an internal community-relations bureau, or through an outside civilian review board is widely debated.

4. Police cadet programs where high-school-age boys are apprenticed to police departments with the hopes both of building better attitudes and of interesting young men, especially minority youth, to make police work their career.

5. Increasing the pay of police officers so that it will be more realistic to expect and to achieve a higher level of professionalization. A police officer in Michigan at the present time is not required to have as much training as a barber, a beautician, or a mortician. And yet police work requires men to make split-second decisions in settings charged with emotion. As has often been observed, a community gets just about the quality of police service it deserves.

6. Much more intensive and much more professionalized in-service training programs for police departments, with heavy emphasis on human relations, on how and why peoples differ, and the unique cultural qualities of the varieties of groups, who never were completely melted down in the American melting pot.

The police officer in America finds himself today on the grinding edge between the increasing demands for law and order and the strident charges of police brutality, mixed with new epithets of "fascist pigs." Fears of anarchy, on the one hand, and fears of a police state, on the other, have produced an ambivalence in the citizenry that makes the definition of the police role the most difficult in the history of this country.

New demands for social change, sharpened awareness of the distance still to be traveled to make the American dream come true for all people,

[9] *Report of the National Advisory Commission on Civil Disorders* (Washington, D.C., Government Printing Office, 1968) p. 300.

genuine concern for the surge of violence in the 1960's, quickened consciences guiltily aware of the bitter fruits of long-established racism in our society, fresh realization that we have asked much of the police and given them little in either prestige or money, shocking knowledge of police sins of omission and commission in both behavior and attitudes—all of these and others have fueled the ambiguity.

Defining the goal for adequate, effective, and necessary police-community relations is really not difficult. Just one sentence from the Police Officers' Code of Ethics provides the blueprint:

With no compromise for crime and with relentless prosecution of criminals, I will enforce the law courteously and appropriately without fear or favor, malice or ill will, never employing unnecessary force or violence.

There will be honest debate as to how best this goal may be actualized. That it is a responsibility of both the police and the community and its various institutions, particularly the schools, should be the platform of agreement from which significant programs for better police-community relations can be launched.

6 Problem Families and Family Problems

The American family is both a greatly revered and a much maligned institution. Perhaps because so much sentiment surrounds it, problems besetting the family receive almost universal attention. Among the many problems confronting American families at the third quarter of the twentieth century are high divorce rates, sex outside of marriage, controversies over birth control and abortion, and perplexity over changing roles for women.

Traditionally, divorce and rising divorce rates have been regarded as major social problems. They still are, but as Americans become more accustomed to high divorce rates, attention is shifting somewhat to the consequences, not merely of divorce, but of unhappy marriages and present divorce laws.

THE SORRY STATE OF DIVORCE LAW

Editors of *Time*

Americans do just about everything a bit more spectacularly than most other people. That includes marriage and divorce. The U.S. has the world's highest divorce rate, but it also leads in the rate or remarriage after divorce, an occurrence that frequently boosts the statistics by leading to yet another breakup. Americans, in short, appear to be marrying more and enjoying it less. This situation distresses clergymen, sociologists and anthropologists, who rightly regard stable marriage as the foundation of society. But it is only half the tragedy of divorce in America. The real scandal is not that so many Americans resort to divorce. It is that so many of the laws of the land are sadly out of step with the growing recognition that, for both married couples and society, divorce is often preferable to a dead marriage.

The most significant happening in the divorce field is a widespread and growing attack on those laws. Whatever else marriage may be, the state regards it as a public contract that only the state can dissolve. The laws that govern that dissolution in the U.S., however, are not only widely conflicting and confusing—all 50 states have their own laws—but are based on notions that are out of touch with the changing realities of modern society. Most of them tend to embitter spouses, neglect the welfare of the children, prevent reconciliation and produce a large measure of hypocrisy, double-dealing and perjury. Looking at the welter of divorce laws in the U.S., David R. Mace, executive director of the American Association of Marriage Counselors, can only call it "an absolutely ghastly, dreadful, deplorably messy situation." Across the U.S., judges, lawyers and marriage experts are raising an urgent cry that it is time to reform and humanize the divorce system.

A CONFESSION OF FAILURE

The system has not only succeeded in making divorce unpleasant, complicated and expensive; it has been woefully ineffective in its original aim of holding down divorce and protecting society from the problems that breakups produce. Roughly 400,000 U.S. couples are being divorced each year. About 40% of them are childless; the rest have some 500,000 children, two-thirds of them under the age of ten. More than 6,000,000 Americans are now divorced or separated, and divorce seems to breed divorce: probably half of all divorced Americans are the children of divorced parents. Divorce or separation occurs most among the poor, the least educated and Negroes, least among the affluent (who usually get most of the publicity), the well-educated and couples with three or more children. Increasingly, it is a problem of the young: 46% of all divorces involve girls who marry in their teens, and 74% those who marry under 25. Conversely, an estimated 85% of Americans who marry at the age of 25 or over stay married. Even so, there is a growing trend for couples to split up in middle age after the kids have left home and husband and wife have discovered that they no longer can, or want to, get along. Though Roman Catholics get fewer divorces than others because of their church's proscriptions, they are not very far behind the Protestant breakup rate because of desertions, separations and annulments.

Most Americans still agree with Dr. Lawrence S. Kubie, clinical professor of psychiatry at the University of Maryland, that "divorce is always a tragedy no matter how civilized the handling of it, always a confession of human failure, even when it is the sorry better of sorry alternatives." But Americans are more relaxed, tolerant and realistic about divorce than they used to be. Though vestiges of social stigma because of divorce still remain in small U.S. communities, most of the nation long ago decided that a happy divorce, when such can be accomplished, is better than an unhappy marriage, or what British Author A. P. Herbert called "holy deadlock."

Because of this attitude, many of the attacks that used to be directed at divorce itself have now shifted to the law. The pressure to make divorce laws more humane also draws strength from the realization that the divorce rate, while hardly anything to boast about, is not really as alarming as it is often made out to be. The rate of divorce in the U.S. has actually held rather steady for 15 years, and the vast majority of Americans still stay married "until death do us part." The rate hit an all-time high of 18.2 divorces per 1,000 existing marriages in 1946, when many hasty wartime marriages were dissolved. Since then it has dropped to 9.2 per 1,000, not much above the 6.6-per-1,000 figure that was the norm in 1920.

MATING AT RANDOM

Another reason for a more realistic appraisal of divorce laws is a deeper understanding of what causes marital breakups. While sex, money and incompatibility are the traditional reasons for divorce, a mobile and changing urban society has loosened many of the bonds that once held marriage together, depriving men of their absolute dominance, giving women a large measure of economic independence and weakening the sense of kinship. Marriage means happiness to Americans—and its inevitable problems seem to catch them by surprise. Mistakes are also easier to make in a day when mating is more random than ever. Unlike the divorce laws, the laws of marriage are simplicity itself: a girl can marry at 18 in most states without parental consent, and 20 states do not even bother with the normal three-day wait after a blood test. Many who get married do not seem to know quite what it is all about; a survey showed that U.S. teen-agers agree widely on only one marital duty: that the man should take out the garbage.

The argument that children suffer most by a divorce no longer seems to be a deterrent; many psychiatrists believe that they can adjust nicely to an orderly divorce. "Divorce is not the costliest experience possible to a child," says Child Psychiatrist J. Louise Despert. "Unhappy marriage without divorce can be far more destructive." The gradual weakening of religious strictures against divorce has also tended to make it more acceptable; all but the most fundamental U.S. Protestants now accept civil divorce—and the "new moralists" go further. In destructive family situations, says the Rev. Dr. Joseph F. Fletcher, professor of Christian social ethics at the Episcopal Theological School in Cambridge, Mass., "divorce is the good thing to do: not merely excusable, but rather the greatest of all goods. The divorce rate is a social symptom of increased respect for personal freedom and for genuine marriage commitment."

That is a far cry from Christ's unequivocal condemnation of the Mosaic right of Jewish husbands to banish their wives at will: "What therefore God hath joined together, let not man put asunder." Still, it is hardly a surprise. The bonds of Christian matrimony have been slowly loosening ever since the twelfth-century church began granting annulments and separations. At Luther's urging, the Protestant Reformation approved secular divorce for grounds of adultery or desertion. Such Catholic countries as Italy and Argentina still ban divorce, but many others, from Japan to Sweden, have reached the point of permitting divorce by mutual consent.

U.S. divorce laws theoretically shun the idea of mutual consent because it offends religious tradition and raises the specter of too many marriages being dissolved by whim or passing despair. In practice, however, 90% of U.S. divorces actually involve mutual consent that is disguised by legal hocus-pocus or outright perjury. Reason: the whole U.S. approach begins with a disastrous premise. Instead of recognizing that both parties are almost always partly to blame, U.S. law demands verified proof of "fault" by one partner—and only one. The insistence seems almost sadistic: the "innocent" party must prove his or her mate "guilty" of offenses for which divorce is the punishment.

The result is that the typical U.S. divorce trial is a farce that totally abdicates society's interest in salvaging marriage whenever possible. Most couples hammer out a collusive pretrial agreement in which one consents to accept the fault. The couple may sue on any of 47 assorted grounds, depending on the state. All 50 states recognize adultery as grounds for divorce, 44 accept cruelty, 47 desertion, 29 nonsupport, 40 alcoholism, 43 the commission of a felony and 32 impotence. By far the most common ground is the vague "cruelty," a catchall that conceals more than it reveals. The harried judge, in fact, rarely hears the true story, usually signs the divorce agreement after only perfunctory questioning. The defendant in the case has every reason to lie: the size of the alimony, the custody of the children and even the right to remarry may well depend on what the agreement says about his guilt.

The real combat takes place in lawyers' offices as the parties bargain —and punish each other. Now the woman scorned makes the cad pay: alimony may cost the husband one-third of his income, in some cases may continue even after his wife remarries. Children become pawns in the bargaining process: if he holds down alimony, she holds down visiting privileges. The hotter the fight, the higher the fees; some unscrupulous lawyers even inflame the sides to inflate the charges. Meanwhile, no one represents the children. They are commonly awarded like trophies to the "innocent" party, who is not necessarily the best parent. The spouses usually part more bitterly than they began.

A PROFESSIONAL "OTHER WOMAN"

The tougher the state, the bigger the lies. New York is the only state with only one ground for divorce: adultery as proved by third-party testimony.[1] As a result, divorces that are contested by one of the parties roil in perjury and mudslinging. In uncontested cases, New Yorkers can get divorced by hiring a professional "other woman," but many childless couples prefer to seek annulments based on phony claims of refusal to bear children; New York has more annulments than any other state. Whatever their other disagreements, affluent couples usually agree to flee to divorce in easier states. A strong drive is being conducted in the New York legislature to reform the state's 1787 divorce law, a reform that has long been opposed by spokesmen of the Catholic Church. This time, though church spokesmen have asked for a delay in consideration of the reform bill, a group of Catholic laymen has urged its passage, and the prospects look better.

In theory, U.S. marriages can be ended only by the state of domicile —the state in which the parties really live. Actually, such states as Idaho and Nevada permit divorce after only six weeks' residence, and solemnly accept the visitor's lie that he or she aims to stay. The other states, including New York, accept such divorces because the Constitution commands all states to give "full faith and credit" to one another's court judgments. On the other hand, no state is required to recognize the highly popular 24-hour Mexican divorce, which shuns the domicile lie and mainly involves mutual consent. The only state that fully recognizes Mexican divorce is New York—all because its own archaic law has forced more than 250,000 New Yorkers to get Mexican divorces.

Even U.S. "migratory divorces" can be challenged when the divorcing state does not have proper jurisdiction over the divorcing couple. For this reason, reformers have long urged a uniform federal divorce code. Congress has no power to enact one without a constitutional amendment, and every proposed amendment since 1884 has failed because states jealously guard their right to marriage and divorce laws based on local conditions and moral attitudes. In fact, a federal law that would supersede local law is not necessary. The states ideally should get together and work out a uniform divorce code that would be agreeable to all of them, with local options where necessary.

There are still many things that states can do individually to make divorce a more civilized process, including broader grounds and inter-

[1] Since this article was written, the law in New York has been changed. New York now permits divorce on five different grounds. It is too early to tell whether the new law will make much difference in divorce practice.

locutory decrees that give couples several months to think things over before divorce becomes final. But even such healthy changes are not enough to cure the nation's sick divorce laws. What the U.S. really needs is something far more drastic: a complete new approach that totally banishes "fault" and all its sleazy consequences. The most sensible solution would be a system that readily grants divorce only after skilled clinicians confirm that a marriage is beyond repair. In many cases, divorce might be harder to get; in all, it would be far more humane.

While insisting that divorce be made a more rational process, most marriage experts also believe that many of the divorces that now take place can be prevented. One of the most effective, though not yet widespread, ways of helping to prevent divorce is the conciliation court. Eighteen states have already set up more than three dozen such courts, many of which try to mend marriages with the aid of full-time staff psychologists and social workers. The courts have an overall record of intact marriages in 33% of the cases voluntarily brought before them. They try to get the couple to communicate with each other once more, to concentrate on what they have in common rather than what separates them and to analyze for themselves the problems that are interfering with their marriage.

In Toledo, Judge Paul W. Alexander's much-admired conciliation court averts divorce in 44% of the cases it tackles. In Los Angeles, Judge Roger A. Pfaff's conciliation court gets 50% of its business from lawyers who refer unhappy spouses even before they file divorce suits. With the aid of eleven highly trained counselors who must have at least ten years' experience, Pfaff's court helps more than 4,000 volunteer couples a year, gets 60% of them to make up and sign detailed "husband-wife" agreements that have the force of law. "Divorce courts throughout America are burying marriages that are still alive," says Meyer Elkin, Pfaff's supervising counselor. The success of conciliation courts proves that it is perfectly possible to create a rational divorce system that saves as well as severs—if the U.S. wants it.

MORE IMPORTANT, LESS CERTAIN

In a culture addicted to romance, few legislators are likely to propose the ultimate solution to fewer divorces: make marriage tougher. Even a month's wait would probably cut the divorce rate quite a bit, but education in what to expect of marriage seems a more likely solution. Many experts are working to get courses in marriage in the schools. Most engaged Catholic couples now get premarital counseling at pre-Cana conferences (named for the Cana wedding feast at which Christ miraculously turned water to wine), and Protestant churches are increasingly offering some form of premarital advice; both offer talks by doctors, clergymen and counselors.

In addition, the new art of family therapy has made impressive gains in analyzing the complex psychological equations that create U.S. marriage. When frustration jars the equation, warring couples often become blinded by hostility and feel so unique and helpless that they wind up divorcing. Today a skilled therapist may well save the marriage—or at least keep an inevitable divorce from becoming too bitter.

The new realism about divorce in the U.S. is thus combined with a new optimism about reconciliation under the law. In modern America, as elsewhere, marital happiness is at once more important and less certain than ever before. To the couples involved, a marital breakup is an intensely personal affair, full of anguish, doubt and a sense of failure. By insisting on the public character of divorce as well, U.S. law takes upon itself certain responsibilities that it has not yet fulfilled. The time has come for a compassionate law that would prevent divorce when it honorably could and, when it could not, leave an unhappy couple with a maximum of dignity and a minimum of bitterness.

Perhaps the only family problem that receives more attention than divorce is illicit sex. A brief wire service story reveals one facet of the problem.

PREGNANCIES UP IN SCHOOLS

NEW YORK (UPI)—Nearly 150,000 teenaged schoolgirls, some as young as 12 or 13, get pregnant each year and the number is expected to increase by 30,000 a year during the next decade.

The statistics were cited by *Education News,* a biweekly magazine for school administrators. The magazine said federal statistics indicate the number of illegitimate births is increasing in the suburbs even though abortions, outnumbering such births by an estimated four-to-one, are more easily available for more prosperous suburban families.

Social workers and educators have "suddenly and spontaneously begun to realize that some form of schooling during pregnancy and education for jobs after the child is born must be provided if the girl is to build a productive life for herself," the magazine said.

Cities which have begun providing special courses and medical, recreational and psychological services for pregnant schoolgirls are San Francisco, Minneapolis, Detroit, St. Louis, and Buffalo, N.Y.

Few would argue that 150,000 schoolgirl pregnancies are anything but a very serious problem. The tragedy is evident. The expectation of a thirty thousand per year increase over the next decade may indicate to many people that a serious breakdown of sexual morality is occurring. Before jumping to that conclusion, however, two other facts should be noted. First, in a rapidly growing United States population, the number of teenage pregnancies will increase even if the teenage pregnancy rate stays exactly the same. Second, the risk of teenage pregnancy is a function of the proportion of teenagers to the total population. The high birth rates of the twelve years from 1946 to 1958 mean a very large teenage population over the next ten years.

That illicit sex behavior is not a simple function of moral standards is demonstrated by the next item. Ordinarily, senior citizens are not thought of as being especially prone to living in sin. Yet, as this article makes clear, lonely old people of the most conservative upbringing are being forced into illicit relationships by unthinking government policy.

FLORIDA SENIOR CITIZENS
SINNING ON SOCIAL SECURITY

MIAMI, Fla. (AP)—The president of the Florida Council for Senior Citizens says thousands of old people are living together out of wedlock in the Miami area because marriage would mean loss of Social Security payments.

And Mayor Melvin Richard of Miami Beach wants the law changed so these couples can marry.

Max Friedson, head of the Senior Citizens Council, said the law is forcing these old people "to live in sin—or what they think is sin."

The problem, he said, is so pressing that one rabbi has agreed to give unofficial blessing to such unions.

"Many couples even come to me for moral comfort," Friedson said, "and I give it to them."

When a woman outlives her husband, she gets part of his Social Security only as long as she stays single. She loses the money on remarriage, on the theory that her new husband is responsible for her support.

A retired man living on $85 a month, authorities agreed, can't afford the theory.

Richard wrote U.S. Social Security Commissioner Robert M. Ball asking if the law could be changed to permit widows over 65 to continue receiving benefits through their former husbands.

"This would solve the problem immediately," Richard said. "Of course, it might mean disaster to the Social Security system. That's what I have to find out."

The Rev. Benjamin Schumacker, president of the State Council on Aging, said he tries to comfort the old couples who come to him.

"There's always somebody around to shake his Victorian head," Mr. Schumacker said, "but I see no moral or religious problem.

"It's platonic. When I see them hold hands while they listen to a sermon, I don't feel any sin is committed in the church."

Henry Gillman, secretary of the Florida Senior Citizens League of Voters, says the sin is committed by "a society that causes them to do something wrong."

Over the past decade hundreds, and probably thousands, of articles have been written that refer to the "sexual revolution." That relationships between men and women are changing rapidly is obvious. If there are 150,000 pregnant teenagers and thousands of sinning grandparents in Florida, the suspicion grows that young people are rejecting their parents' standards and openly sanctioning promiscuous sexual behavior. The only thing wrong with the argument is that it appears not to be true.

WHAT SEXUAL REVOLUTION?

Most people believe that America, especially its college youth, is going through a "sexual revolution." There seems to be a tremendous increase in premarital sexual relations, the abandonment of old reticences to talk about sex openly, and a marked change in the laws about pornography, nudity and sex in books, movies, colleges, and public life.

Yet, whatever increased public *attention* there may be to sex, *there is no hard evidence whatsoever,* write Robert V. Sherwin and George C. Keller, "that there has been anything amounting to a revolution in American sexual practices, attitudes or legal codes in the past several decades." Their report—the senior author is a lawyer, an authority on laws relating to sex

Reprinted by permission of Robert Veit Sherwin and George Keller from *Columbia College Today* (Fall 1967). Above synopsis from *The Public Interest* 2 (Spring 1968) pp. 93–95. © National Affairs, Inc. 1968.

and administrative director of the Society for the Scientific Study of Sex and his collaborator an official of Columbia College—entitled "Sex on the Campus," occupies most of the Fall 1967 issue of *Columbia College Today*.

The most important fact, the authors point out, is that there is "pitifully" little information about human sexual behavior that allows one to gauge its range and extent. The language itself is quite inexact and ambiguous. Although "there may be over 50 million acts of sexual intercourse in the world daily, the English language possesses no socially acceptable verb for the act of coitus. The verb 'copulate' comes close, but it does not necessarily imply vaginal penetration, only a union of coupling *with* someone." The difficulty of description itself thus hinders the collection of accurate data.

Then, too, the definition of the sexual act is a further complicating problem. Is a girl who engages in heavy petting, including orgasm, but without being penetrated still a virgin, while a quiet lonely girl who has had one furtive encounter of actual intercourse "not." This is further compounded by William Masters and Virginia Johnson's argument in *Human Sexual Response* (1966) that the female orgasm is largely a matter of clitoral, not vaginal, stimulation.

Given all these problems, the authors have scoured the literature and, in addition, conducted interviews on several college campuses to come up with the following conclusions:

First, all the evidence indicates that there has been no radical increase in the incidence of premarital relations in America in this century.

The closest thing to a "revolution' is the substantial rise in *female* involvement that occurred in the 1920s. While male participation has apparently climbed slowly from roughly 55 percent at the turn of the century to over 65 percent in the 1960's, female premarital activity was a relatively low 30 percent or so around 1900 but jumped to over 50 percent in the 1920s, where it has remained approximately to this day. The strong feminist feelings of the 1920's were apparently expressed in sexual terms by many women.

Of great importance is that a major portion of premarital sex, particularly among college students, occurs among *engaged* couples intending to marry. For example, nearly half of all women who have premarital intercourse do so *only with their fiances* or persons they eventually marry. . . . The engagement period has become, in effect, a trial marriage among a greater number of people. . . . Also of importance is the evidence that only two-thirds of the males and one-half of the females who engage in premarital coitus are under 20 years of age or teenagers. A high proportion of premarital sex is done, therefore, by *consenting adults,* not just experimenting college students and adolescents. Contrary to popular beliefs, about 40 percent of all American male college students and over 55 percent of the coeds still graduate as virgins, according to most indications.

Second, education and socioeconomic position, not religion or geography, are the major determinants in American sexual behavior. Those in the upper socio-educational level are astonishingly different—one might say almost a world apart—in their sexual practices from those in the lower socio-educational level.

Upper level young people are must less sexually active, but they pet more. They tend to reserve sex for someone for whom they feel affection. Their sexual play usually has more prolonged foreplay, a greater readiness to use a variety of coital positions, a higher incidence of oral-genital contact. The males tend to treat women more as equals, and women tend to take a more active role, with the result that females at this level have a greater frequency of orgasms. Possibly because of the greater number of sexual postponements, masturbation is higher; college men masturbate twice as often as those with only a grade school education. . . .

Persons at the lower socio-educational levels have a radically different style. The frequency of male premarital sex is much higher; nearly one half of the boys who do not go to college have intercourse by the age of 15. Many fewer females participate, but those who do, do so with greater frequency. Persons at the lower level, especially the males, tend not to see sex as having a close relation with affection or love. They are usually impatient with mere petting. Among this group sexual play has greater simplicity and directness; there is less foreplay, less variety, greater speed. It tends to be male-oriented and women at this level experience fewer orgasms and less emotional satisfaction. Masturbation is lower, but homosexuality, especially among high school graduates without college education is higher. . . .

Third, since 1900 there have been two noteworthy changes in sexual behavior:

a slight increase in extramarital intercourse and a marked increase in the quality of marital sexual life. About 35 percent of American married males have had an adulterous encounter, compared with perhaps 25 percent in the 1920's. Less than 10 percent are *regularly* adulterous though. Among married women the figures are still lower: around 15 percent have had coitus outside their marriage, and very few of them regularly. Adultery is not widespread in America, or increasing rapidly. Both men and women have more premarital intercourse in the few years prior to marriage than they have extramarital intercourse in the 40 years after.

As for the quality of sexual life inside marriage, there seems to be a change toward much less frigidity and impotence. The satisfaction of females especially has increased substantially. Female orgasm was an unusual thing in the first quarter of this century. . . . As late as 1948, according to Kinsey's figures, 10 percent of American married women had *never* had an orgasm. This percentage is probably lower now because the feeling that women have a right to satisfaction is spreading, partly as a result of higher education levels. . . .

Fourth, there has been some change in sexual attitudes, but no real "revolution." If anything, what has happened is that attitudes which were once held privately are now discussed openly. This new frankness is most apparent in language and characteristics. Boys and girls in college who used to refer to each other

and their friends principally in terms of their geographical background, religion, color, nationality, career aim, character structure, or personality—"Californian," "Baptist," "Oriental," "Swede," "scientist," "square shooter," or "good-time Charlie"—now more frequently refer to each other in terms of their sexual attitudes and behavior—"livewire," "swinger," "gentleman," "slut," "cold fish," "Casanova," "tease," "animal," "wolf," "square," "sex fiend." . .

As a result of the greater frankness of discussion there is a growing sense among parents, the press, and the students themselves that much more is happening than ever before. The change in *attitude* is mistaken for the change in *behavior*. Among the college girls we interviewed, two-thirds of whom were virgins, nearly all of them believed that "most" of the other college girls were engaging in intercourse and many of them guessed that between 10 and 20 percent of their college mates were promiscuous. (Less than 2 percent of the college students actually are promiscuous, even at the most notoriously "liberal" institutions.) . . .

The attitudes men and women hold toward one another and toward themselves have been changing. So have many of the actual conditions of living. Change both creates social problems and sharpens awareness of problems; yet aspects of some problems seem impervious to change. Witness the following perceptive article on the "new" woman.

THE NEW WOMAN

Ruth Hill Useem

Professor of Sociology and Education
Michigan State University

For more years than I am willing to own up to, I, along with a number of other women who are also social scientists, have been reacting to

Remarks prepared for delivery to The Society for the Study of Social Problems, San Francisco, California, August 27, 1967. Used by permission.

generalizations, theoretical formulations, interview schedules, with a "yes, but"—yes, but they don't apply to women.

Those of us who have said this have been put into the unenviable position of being asked, "All right, now *you're* a woman; tell us why the analysis is wrong" or "Why do you think the women answered the questionnaire this way?" And just as often as the question is asked, we have had to stand mute or plead guilty to ignorance. For although we have an identification with this segment of mankind which makes us sensitive to the problem, we have not reflected on it, studied it, intellectualized it, documented or conceptualized it—and hence are often as ignorant as our questioners. In this respect, we are in a position similar to the upper-class, ivy-league-educated specialist in international relations who is asked, "Now, you're a Negro. Tell me why the Negroes rioted in Detroit." And when we have turned to those studies which have been made of women (and there are some excellent ones), we have come to know more about women but we are still in doubt as to how to integrate the materials into an overall theoretical framework of human behavior.

Then there are some of us who are wearied with being asked to talk about one type of woman—the type most troublesome to the men and women in the circles in which we move—and that is the highly educated woman who has trouble combining career, marriage, and motherhood, or the highly educated woman whose trouble is having neither marriage nor motherhood to combine with her career. We are wearied because the perspectives on this issue have become polarized into breast-beating advocates of equal rights for women and soft-headed proponents of the "little mother and wife." Consequently, we have to spend so much time dissociating ourselves from one or the other position that we never get on with a sociological analysis of the topic. . . .

Because this is The Society for the Study of Social Problems, I presume that in some way the new woman is considered a social problem; that the problem of the new woman can be conceptualized, studied, and somehow improved. I should like to set forth some of my reflections on the question then, "In what way is the new woman a social problem?" In the usual academic style, I will get to this question by asking another.

What is the order of phenomena we are talking about, who is the new woman? I would answer this by saying:

The new woman is a Negro mother of three small children, standing in line for food or clothing in Detroit, Buffalo, Newark, while the genitor of her last child is being held in jail for looting.

The new woman is an American ambassador to a foreign country, an Indian Prime Minister, a televised analyst of United Nations deliberations, a widowed, world-wide figure who personifies a new generation's interpretation of an old American dream.

The new woman is a once-married but now divorced mother of two, returning to college to get her teaching certificate so she can support her children.

The new woman is an aged widow in a nursing home, kept alive by the miracles of modern medicine and the personal services of another new woman, the second-career, middle-aged, licensed practical nurse.

The new woman is the mother of an American Marine in Vietnam, the streetwalker who picks up the Marine and his American dollars while he is on a weekend in Saigon, the Viet Cong mother whose husband was killed by the Marine's bullet and who clutches her little ones to her as she walks into a refugee camp.

The new woman is the bewigged, bedecked and bedeviled wife of an affluent white professional, a cultural museum piece whose education and looks have been frozen for twenty years. Having been denied the opportunity to come alive as well as look alive, she has mothered the long-haired, sandaled, turned-on hippie of superficially indeterminate sex in the Haight-Ashbury, Greenwich Village, Kathmandu, Mexico City, or Paris scene.

The new woman is the wife of an American technician overseas, teaching in a parent-sponsored school, coping with servants and hepatitis.

The new woman is the American wife of an American-educated Pakistani, Indian, Dane, Japanese, residing far from her extended kin and with too many of her husband's, trying to live with strange stoves, languages, clothing, and bazaars.

The new woman is the foreign wife of an American serviceman, businessman or Peace Corpsman.

The new woman is the unmarried college student, the wife supporting a graduate student, the secretary, the worker on the line, the mother of six children, the schoolteacher.

The new woman is the mother of the population explosion, a contributor to and consumer of the knowledge explosion, the consumer and producer of material goods, the voice of the rising tide of aspirations and exasperations.

In short, the new woman is roughly half, or gently half, of what is happening today, and that half is inextricably related to the other half. The new woman is a real, living person, and altogether composes that segment of the 1.2 billion people in the world who have multiple selves and multiple social identities and happen to be encapsulated in a female body. To infer from the body the multiple selves and identities is to repeat the classic error pointed out by Whitehead of misplaced concreteness. On a less classic scale, it invokes the naive French world view of mankind— vive le difference! A goodly proportion of these women have troubles, personally unresolvable troubles. And not the least of the troubles which real, live people in trouble have is that their troubles are *not* defined as social problems.

I should like to argue that the trouble with women is that they have had imposed upon them or have carried in the past and in considerable part of the world today, more of the unexamined, unresolved, "fate-assigned" troubles of what we term the human condition than have men.

As a result of this fairly widespread reality, there are some who consider the status of women a good index of the quality of a society, an index of the degree to which a society has solved its troubles. I think there may be something to this argument—but not much. For it does not follow that improving the status of women by shifting their troubles to husbands and children, or shifting their troubles to another segment of mankind defined as something less than human such as slaves, servants, lower castes or classes, improves the overall quality of the society. At any rate, we have run out of people upon whom to impose troubles in this last third of the twentieth century. What we mean by the "rising tide of aspirations" of the developing nations, the Negro, and the young, is the explicit objection to carrying the troubles of mankind. Of course one way to shift the troubles is to put them on the yet-unborn generations. This may be part of what we are doing.

The answer then, to the question which I originally asked, "In what way is the new woman a social problem," is, "in no way." The new woman is no more a social problem than the new man is. It cannot be made into a social problem because it is not a sociological problem or economic problem or psychological problem. The question as posed cannot be answered, and I think we ought to stop wasting our time and effort trying to solve an unsolvable problem. The question which we ought to ask is, "How can we conceptualize the troubles which people have so that they can be redefined as social problems and hence might be amenable to some sort of solution?"

To do this, I suppose we have to have some notion of the nature of human nature that includes the fact that humans come in male and female bodies. Notions about the nature of woman vary all the way from women are the same as men, to women are totally different from men. Sometimes the same data and observations are used to buttress widely different conceptualizations. We can only conclude that the notions about the nature of men and women reflect the orientation of the behavioral science analysts. This, of course, leads each one of us into being a bit anxious and sometimes guilty, for no matter what our notions are, each and every one of us daily experiences some uneasiness over the notions we hold. In contrast to some other phenomena which we conceptualize, this is an area in which no individual is unaffected. Each one of us is related actually and potentially to a member of the other sex. Secondly, we all confront this problem within ourselves; we daily make concrete decisions about the expression of our own femaleness or maleness, manhood or womanhood, motherhood or fatherhood.

The question about the nature of women and men is simply a new rhetoric for the same old unresolvable question of the relationship of psyche and soma, mind and body, individual and society, heredity and environment, ideal and real, or what I have summarized as the tender-hearted and toughminded aspects of mankind. No era, society, generation, or individual can give ultimately true and right answers to these questions. But it is mandatory on every era, society, generation, and individual to give answers—no one can be indifferent.

Any attempts then to analyze the questions of men, women, body, and sex are subject to the distortions of the particularistic attachments of social scientists to the answers which have been made individually and collectively. The results of the analyses, in turn, affect the social identities of the scientists not only in their daily behavior but also in their definition of social problems. In short, I think that the troubles which women have are going to resist easy redefinition into social problems. Nevertheless, I would like to seek a degree of detachment rather than be polemical.

Everyday life is so intricate, messy, complex and vast, that what gets known, summarized, and analyzed reflects the preoccupation of the analysts rather than the reality that exists, and how it gets analyzed depends upon the theoretical framework of the analyst.

Therefore I need to state explicitly, in an oversimplified way, my own assumptions about the human condition and how I think it works. I will leave to the anthropologists the analysis of how it was in the beginning and the McLuhans, Riesmans, and Aries to detail how we got this way, and to the Kahns, Bells, and all the new committees on the future to tell us where we are going.

I shall assert my assumptions as though I were sure of them—but I am less certain of them than I may sound:

1. Man is the only animal which knows he can have a collective future despite his individual mortality, and furthermore makes decisions which shape the outlines of that future. Images of the future may be couched in terms of a remembered past, a replication or improvement of the present, or a destruction of parts, or all of what is now known. These are decision-making roles or what I term the blueprinting roles; roles in which the decisions are made which have implications for the social life and organization of human behavior.

2. Social life is always carried by real, live individuals who are born, age, and sooner or later die. These individuals have year-round sexuality, come in two kinds of bodies (male and female). One of these types of bodies, the female, bears the young. In order for any society to survive, some must produce viable offspring.

3. Offspring at birth are ignorant, uncaring individuals who can learn with varying degrees of efficacy what they are exposed to and can learn to care for those who care for them in a tenderhearted but non-genital, sexual way. Roles of teaching and caring for the learning individual are the imprinting roles of society. Since this is a rather basic assumption and one which is highly debatable, I shall state it in another way. These are gender roles which take into account the fact that those who are interacting with each other come in bodies with sexual needs, but the overt expression of erotic sexuality is denied. In the family we call the denial of overt sexuality the incest tabu. Using the term incest tabu to apply only to kin has caused us to overlook the very important function of the tabu against erotic or genital sexuality, and that is that any complex social system carried by three or more people and which is based on sustained thinking is always disrupted by the expression of overt sexuality. It is a bit difficult for men and women to keep their mind on their work and objectives when sexually excited.

4. Although the bodies of mankind come in two sexes and a variety of sizes, colors and shapes, the forebrain of man is seemingly without sexuality or color and can be trained to think and to be toughminded, provided that the individual with that brain does not have to pay attention to major or prolonged troubles from the body or by threatening social definitions of his body. This is where a computer has it all over man—it is an unembodied brain. The products of thinking—summaries of information and knowledge—can be disembodied into symbols and stored in other minds and in tools of varying degrees of complexity, from digging sticks to computers. Knowledge gives power for the allocation of life chances.

These are not the only roles in social life, but they are the ones most crucial to our discussion here. Every society has blueprinters or decision-makers, imprinters or socializers, thinkers who create new knowledge and individual actors who come in one of two sexes, attractive to each other on a one-to-one basis and who carry the roles of a society in various combinations.

In preliterate societies, these various roles were usually ascribed by age, sex, and kinship. Knowledge was stored in the minds of its members, imprinted on succeeding generations by the show-and-tell method. The blueprinters of the future were the wise old men and women. In societies in which everyone was a do-it-yourself intellectual, it is not surprising that the sick, ignorant, and stupid died early. The only activities which were not easily imprinted or blueprinted were sexuality and thinking. Females were often given to or taken by the males of friendly and hostile outgroups. (Diffusion has never struck me as a curiously disembodied process.) And then there was reward for thinking. It helped men and women stay alive in a precarious world.

Lest we become enamored by the idyllic state of affairs in which persons were whole people in a whole society, let me hasten to say that these preliterate groups did not create the thinkers or blueprinters which would enable them to compete with, stand up to, or be unaffected by the literate, post-literate, technological, scientific societies which have kept alive large numbers of actors through specialization and differentiation of the roles of blueprinting, imprinting, and thinking. At any rate, we are in a state today in which a relatively few blueprinting roles based on the disembodied, toughminded knowledge brought about by thinking specialists can produce societal changes in fractions of the time which it earlier took societies to bring about comparable changes. Thus we have quickened societal time and societal generations. Societal time now comes in mini-generations.

But imprinting still has to be done where the bodies are, and human beings live on body time which has been pretty much the same for millennia. We have increased the number of years that people live in this body time so that each individual has to live in more societal generations. A lot of human beings are in trouble, therefore, because the blueprinters are producing social conditions which impinge on people imprinted to live by norms which are quickly obsolescent or irrelevant or disfunctional to mankind such as: mother loyalties or kinship loyalties or tribal loyalties, or ethnic loyalties, or national loyalties, or most recently no loyalties except to one's body. People are in trouble if that with which they are imprinted does not enable them to live emotionally satisfying lives in those social conditions which are blueprinted. At one time we were able to isolate and segregate those in trouble from those not in trouble, but the blueprinters have produced an instantly visible, instantly impinging, and totally interdependent world in which there is no place for the successful actors to hide from the failures.

I think, in short, that the trouble with women is that the thinkers do not know how to think about the human condition, that the mystery of the new woman reflects the overriding commitments of the social scientists, the thinkers of our time, to an inappropriate notion of social life and human nature.

Let me illustrate this specifically. One notion of the world is that it is composed of variables but not people, which leads to what might be called the error of the indiscrete use of the discrete variable, sex. One would think that we knew a lot about women because the variable appears on the face data sheet of almost every sociological study of our own and other societies: Sex: M_____ F_____ (check one).

There is a lot of confusion perpetrated by this process. First, sex of mankind is not a variable, not even a dichotomous variable. Even symbolically male and female cannot be put on a continuum, nor can sex be used as an independent variable or dependent variable. Maleness is one independent variable and femaleness is another independent variable. To meet the logic of dichotomous variables, it means that maleness must be measured by its presence, or absence, it must be given a value of 1 or 0, and that femaleness must be measured by its presence or absence and given a value of 1 or 0. But usually what we do is measure maleness and give it a value of 1, and call its absence, femaleness. But anyone, man or woman, can tell you that being female is more than being nothing or nonmale. For some purposes, I presume that knowing the presence or absence of maleness or presence or absence of femaleness is important—but for social scientists it is not the presence or absence of maleness or femaleness, but the meaning which each has for the individual. In short, every individual has a sexual identity. This is still not a variable but falls into three categories: maleness—I am male; femaleness—I am a female; and confused— I don't know whether I am male or female. Knowing a person's sexual identity seems important to social scientists. People act in terms of it and there is some reason to think that having a confused or transsexual identity leads to a heightened overt sexuality of bizarre and deviant types by those who are in either kind of body, and an excessive need to be perennially pregnant by those who come in female bodies. A number of studies suggest that by the age of three or so, sexual identity based on both physiological and social components is firmly established.

In contrast to sexual identity, gender identity or what we call masculine behavior or feminine behavior derives not from the type of body which an individual has but from social definitions of what is appropriate behavior for a person who comes in one or the other kind of body. In contrast to sexual identities which have a physiological component, gender identities are not precipitated by hormones or physiology, but by imprinting through interpersonal experiences and especially early familial encounters. On the basis of fragmentary evidence, it is thought that each person has a gender role fairly well imprinted by the age of three, which may be irreversible. That is, a child has a gender identity—"I am a boy" or "I am a girl" or "I don't know if I am a boy or girl." Most children have a congruent sexual identity and gender identity, but an increasing number do not. Some think they are girls in a male body and some think they are boys in a female body and some are just confused. We are not certain that gender roles have to be imprinted early, but of one thing we are fairly certain—and that is that with the mobility of mankind today and with the male, masculine blueprinters at work, and with the female, feminine imprinters isolated from the blueprinters, a whole lot of people are in trouble when it comes to mixing the two gender roles together as adults or trying to match adult gender role expectations with early gender role expectations. In an empirical study of cross-cultural marriages done by Ann Baker Cottrell, it was not the sexual roles which gave married couples trouble but the gender roles— what behavior was expected of a husband–wife–mother–father, etc.

Again then, gender roles which are significant for social science studies are not arrived at by checking one: Sex: M_____ F_____.

Third, in addition to a sexual identity and a gender identity, there is also a thinking identity. Sexual identity does have hormonal and physiological components, gender identities are socially derived, but thinking identity has neither and yet both, it is the creative thrust of putting old and new ideas together in new ways. On the basis of as yet insufficient evidence, we are of the provisional opinion that individuals cannot think if they have not resolved the problem of sexual identity or gender identity or if changes in societal generations produce confusion in the minds of the potential thinkers.

Despite the theoretical separability of sexual identity, gender identity, and thinking identity, we precipitate for ourselves considerable confusion by the indiscrete use of the discrete variable, sex, by analyzing thinking roles which are based on ideational or thought processes in which sex and gender are irrelevant as though such roles *had* to have sex and gender. In this it may simply be that we are caught in the web of our own culture and language and the historical answers of the past. The English language has no third person singular pronouns which can be used to refer to a role occupant of either sex without being insulting or introjecting thoughts of sex. English has only three genders—masculine, feminine and neuter. I can remember several years ago in colleges of education, the discussion which went on about how to refer to high school teachers. Early in our history, we had separation of secondary schoolteachers into the schoolmaster, he and the schoolmistress, she. Then, as the high school teacher role became predominantly held by females, we spoke of the teacher, she. Subsequently, as men entered and now are in the majority in high school teaching, the question arises do you say the high school teacher, he, or the high school teacher, she. It is also inherent in the illogic of the question often asked me, "Do you think women should be scientists?" My answer is, "No, men shouldn't be scientists either; only those educated in science should be scientists." But how does one refer to a scientist in the generic sense—he, she, *it*?

These linguistic codings of thought have led to considerable illogic in many studies. All of us who are women and sociologists have had the experience of being gratuitously offered the collected but unanalyzed data on women left over from somebody's study. It goes something like this. Someone has undertaken a study of a theoretical problem related to, say, talent and performance, aspirations of high school students, the self-concept of graduate students, the productivity of the line worker. The hypotheses are stated, assuming a masculine gender role, the questionnaire worded, the independent variable Sex: M_____ F_____ put on the face data sheet, the data collected, cards punched and sorted by sex. Lo and behold, the hypotheses are confirmed or disconfirmed for the males but are inconclusive for the females, even holding other variables constant. Usually the hypotheses are salvaged by throwing out the females or giving them to some nice, unsuspecting woman graduate student to analyze. No amount of analysis of questions which were asked can produce answers which should have been asked in the first place, had there been an adequate theoretical framework. This is tantamount to explaining masculine behavior by theory and feminine behavior by physiology.

Sometimes, however, we go even further and explain the differences between men and women by the physiological differences between males and females, which is the way we conceived the variable in the first place. For example, whole school systems have been revamped to accommodate to the fact that girls are better school achievers than boys presumably because of physiological differences in maturational processes—the only trouble is that it doesn't hold up in England or India or Israel, and their children come in two sexes also.

To summarize more generally, we do not know what the variable Sex: M_____ F_____ stands for in a modern world. We are still using it as an index for behavior for which at one time there was a high correlation between the gender roles and the sex of an individual. But we do not know now of what it is an index. Similar arguments could be made for the other variables on the face data sheet—e.g., occupation: housewife; using the occupation of the male head of household as an index of socio-economic status when in at least a third of the cases the wife is employed. The variables which we use have reference to a society which no longer exists and yet we go on using the variables as though that which they reflect remains the same—that we just have a different incidence, or that the variables are patterned in a different way. Does divorce mean the same today as it did thirty years ago, does geographical mobility and land-measured distance indicate social mobility and social distance in our world of instant communication and fast travel? Sociologists must therefore ask the meaning of housewife, the meaning of divorce, the meaning of employment, and the meaning of Sex: M_____ F_____.

But let us return to the main burden of the argument. I think there are physiological differences between males and females and there are different socially defined gender roles of masculine and feminine. And there are nonsexual, nongender thinking roles. But what it most leaves out is how these attributes and variables get embodied and acted upon by real, live human beings. Which brings us to the systems analysts who are the joy of the blueprinters.

System analysts take one part of the totality of human existence to analyze. We have social scientists who analyze the family as a social system, the university as a social system, the ghetto as a social system, the church as a social system, marketing as a social system, the academic marketplace as a social system, the factory as a social system, medical care as a social system, even a nation as a social system. I have no quarrel with taking a part of existence for analysis; in fact I don't see any alternative, but it does get us into difficulties if we want to use the analyses for redefining the troubles which people, especially women, have as social problems.

First, basic to systems analysis is the implicit and often explicit assumption that a system can be made to work more efficiently and effectively in terms of the ends or goals of that particular system, never mind the meaning and implications this may have for people. The most effective and efficient way to make the system work is to automate the role and throw away the role holder. Which, of course, spells success for the system but trouble for the individuals. But if the role cannot be automated, we are in different kinds of troubles. Blueprinters who make decisions using the systems model often make an error in logic that because a role, a basic unit of analysis, is enacted by a person, that role is all there is to a person. Consequently anyone who has roles in multiple, differentiated systems (and who hasn't in a complex society), and who wants to behave responsibly in terms of the expectations of others, is caught in a web of overcommitments which cannot possibly be successfully fulfilled. The resulting feelings of frustrations, guilt, anger, and stress we have never been able to automate. Social systems have no emotions, only human beings feel. This state of affairs is especially compounded for women who in modern society have been assigned many of the tenderhearted, caring-for individual imprinting roles, the substantive contents of which are not easily made more efficient and predictable. I am not saying they couldn't be, it is just that we have not given our thought to it. We need to have some thought given as to how human beings can put multiple roles together, what kinds of external resources are necessary, what kinds of internal resources are required, what new systems need to be put together to enable individuals to aggregate their roles more meaningfully and how much inefficiency should be built into a particular system to allow the multiple role holder who comes in but one body to perform to his own and to others' satisfaction.

Secondly, the world view of the systems analysts is that the social life of mankind is made up of disembodied, interlinking social systems, and that somehow one can blueprint a world order by connecting the systems without imprinting the feelings, emotions, loyalties, commitments—in short, the tenderhearted, body time aspects which would sustain such a system.

Thus two of the dominant overriding theoretical models of the nature of human social life—variable analysis and systems analysis—are not likely to give us help in retranslating the troubles which women have into social problems amenable to more reasonable, rational, humane solutions. Both help us diagnose, predict, and blueprint. But as far as I can see, the blueprinters using these theoretical orientations are just blueprinting troubles, and the imprinters operating on unanalyzed, unknown assumptions are imprinting troubles—and often these are the same persons!

Hence, to me it is ironic that some women are stridently asking for substantive equality with American upper middle class men when what men have is not good enough for men or women or children or the family of mankind. As I see it, the new woman, that half of mankind encapsulated in a female body, is primarily a do-it-yourself imprinter of the next generation who has neither the skills nor the resources for doing a good job. As such, she is already being blamed for "causing" the ills of our times, she is becoming the scapegoat for our failures, she is being pinpointed as the source of our own inadequacies in thinking about the family of mankind. She has become the object of cheap moralization. That kind of trouble women don't need. It is what I sometimes call the "little woman" theory of societal change, and it gives us about as much knowledge as the "great man" theory of societal change.

We live in a complex, intricate world; we live in it as real, living, feeling, thinking, sexual beings. We are in deep trouble, and the new woman is carrying some of those troubles, but so are men and children. If we are not to dump them onto unborn actors, we shall somehow have to solve the basic problems of blueprinting and imprinting by *thinking* in a new theoretical framework. The troubles of the new woman dramatize the theoretical shortcomings in the social sciences, but the new woman is not the social or the sociological problem.

Part of the trouble which mankind is in and which leads to societies in trouble, and to men, women, and children in trouble, is that the present thinkers in general and the social scientists in particular are lacking in a theoretical definition of the possible which takes into account that any society, to be a society, is lived by human beings who come in two sexes, who live on body time, and who possess in common a brain which is sexless, which can be imprinted with new images of a viable future—if the blueprinter takes it into account.

Change also creates demand for solution to problems that have long been tolerated. In the United States, harsh laws that permit abortion only when continuation of pregnancy would jeopardize the mother's life finally are being challenged. Religious groups including The National Council of Churches, Episcopal Bishops, and the Unitarian Universalist Association have taken stands in favor of more liberal legislation. So have civil groups such as the American Civil Liberties Union. A few states have passed laws that take the general welfare of mother and family into account, but in most states the old repressive legislation holds fast. New light on the problem is cast by a University of California biologist in his article, "Abortion—or Compulsory Pregnancy?"

ABORTION—OR COMPULSORY PREGNANCY?

Garrett Hardin

Professor of Biology
University of California, Santa Barbara

The year 1967 produced the first fissures in the dam that had prevented all change in the abortion-prohibition laws of the United States for
three-quarters of a century. Two states adopted laws that allowed abortion
in the "hardship cases" of rape, incest, and probability of a deformed child.
A third approved the first two "indications," but not the last. All three
took some note of the mental health of the pregnant woman, in varying
language; how this language will be translated into practice remains to be
seen. In almost two dozen other states, attempts to modify the laws were
made but foundered at various stages in the legislative process. It is quite
evident that the issue will continue to be a live one for many years to
come.

The legislative turmoil was preceded and accompanied by a fast-
growing popular literature. The word "abortion" has ceased to be a dirty
word—which is a cultural advance. However, the *word* was so long under
taboo that the ability to think about the *fact* seems to have suffered a sort
of logical atrophy from disuse. Popular articles, regardless of their conclusions, tend to be over-emotional and to take a moralistic rather than
an operational view of the matter. Nits are picked, hairs split. It is quite
clear that many of the authors are not at all clear what question they are
attacking.

It is axiomatic in science that progress hinges on asking the right
question. Surprisingly, once the right question is asked the answer seems
almost to tumble forth. That is retrospective view; in prospect, it takes
genuine (and mysterious) insight to see correctly into the brambles created
by previous, ill-chosen verbalizations.

The abortion problem is, I think, a particularly neat example of a
problem in which most of the difficulties are actually created by asking the
wrong question. I submit further that once the right question is asked the
whole untidy mess miraculously dissolves, leaving in its place a very simple
public policy recommendation.

From *Journal of Marriage and the Family* 30(2) (May 1968) pp. 246–251. Reprinted by permission.

RAPE AS A JUSTIFICATION

The wrong question, the one almost invariably asked, is this: "How can we justify an abortion?" This assumes that there are weighty public reasons for encouraging pregnancies, or that abortions, per se, somehow threaten public peace. A direct examination of the legitimacy of these assumptions will be made later. For the present, let us pursue the question as asked and see what a morass it leads to.

Almost all the present legislative attempts take as their model a bill proposed by the American Law Institute which emphasizes three justifications for legal abortion: rape, incest, and the probability of a defective child. Whatever else may be said about this bill, it is clear that it affects only the periphery of the social problem. The Arden House Conference Committee [1] estimated the number of illegal abortions in the United States to be between 200,000 and 1,200,000 per year. A California legislator, Anthony C. Beilenson,[2] has estimated that the American Law Institute bill (which he favors) would legalize not more than four percent of the presently illegal abortions. Obviously, the "problem" of illegal abortion will be scarcely affected by the passage of the laws so far proposed in the United States.

I have calculated [3] that the number of rape-induced pregnancies in the United States is about 800 per year. The number is not large, but for the woman raped the total number is irrelevant. What matters to her is that she be relieved of her unwanted burden. But a law which puts the burden of proof on her compels her to risk a second harrowing experience. How can she *prove* to the district attorney that she was raped? He could really know whether or not she gave consent only if he could get inside her mind; this he cannot do. Here is the philosopher's "egocentric predicament" that none of us can escape. In an effort to help the district attorney sustain the illusion that he can escape this predicament, a talented woman may put on a dramatic performance, with copious tears and other signs of anguish. But what if the raped woman is not an actress? What if her temperament is stoic? In its operation, the law will act against the interests of calm, undramatic women. Is that what we want? It is safe to say also that district attorneys will hear less favorably the pleas of poor women, the general assumption of middle-class agents being that the poor are less responsible in sex anyway.[4] Is it to the interest of society that the poor bear more children, whether rape-engendered or not?

[1] Mary Steichen Calderone, ed., *Abortion in the United States* (New York: Hoeber-Harper, 1958) p. 178.

[2] Anthony C. Beilenson, "Abortion and Common Sense," *Per/Se,* 1 (1966) p. 24.

[3] Garrett Hardin, "Semantic Aspects of Abortion," *ETC.,* 24 (1967) p. 263.

[4] Lee Rainwater, *And the Poor Get Children* (Chicago: Quadrangle Books, 1960) p. ix and Chap. 1.

A wryly amusing difficulty has been raised with respect to rape. Suppose the woman is married and having regular intercourse with her husband. Suppose that following a rape by an unknown intruder she finds herself pregnant. Is she legally entitled to an abortion? How does she know whose child she is carrying anyway? If it is her husband's child, abortion is illegal. If she carries it to term, and if blood tests then exclude the husband as the father, as they would in a fraction of the cases, is the woman then entitled to a *delayed* abortion? But this is ridiculous: this is infanticide, which no one is proposing. Such is the bramble bush into which we are led by a *reluctant* consent for abortion in cases of rape.

HOW PROBABLE MUST DEFORMITY BE?

The majority of the public support abortion in cases of a suspected deformity of the child [5] just as they do in cases of rape. Again, however, if the burden of proof rests on the one who requests the operation, we encounter difficulties in administration. Between 80,000 and 160,000 defective children are born every year in the United States. The number stated depends on two important issues: (a) how severe a defect must be before it is counted as such and (b) whether or not one counts as birth defects those defects that are not *detected* until later. (Deafness and various other defects produced by fetal rubella may not be detected until a year or so after birth.) However many defective infants there may be, what is the prospect of detecting them before birth?

The sad answer is: the prospects are poor. A small percentage can be picked up by microscopic examination of tissues of the fetus. But "amniocentesis"—the form of biopsy required to procure such tissues—is itself somewhat dangerous to both mother and fetus; most abnormalities will not be detectable by a microscopic examination of the fetal cells; and 96 to 98 percent of all fetuses are normal anyway. All these considerations are a contra-indictation of routine amniocentesis.

When experience indicates that the probability of a deformed fetus is above the "background level" of 2 to 4 percent, is abortion justified? At what level? 10 percent? 50? 80? Or only at 100 percent? Suppose a particular medical history indicates a probability of 20 percent that the baby will be defective. If we routinely abort such cases, it is undeniable that four normal fetuses will be destroyed for every one abnormal. Those who assume that a fetus is an object of high value are appalled at this "wastage." Not uncommonly they ask, "Why not wait until the baby is born and then suffocate those that are deformed?" Such a question is unquestionably rhetoric and sardonic; if serious, it implies that infanticide has no

[5] Alice S. Rossi, "Abortion Laws and Their Victims," *TRANS-action* 3 (September–October, 1966) p. 7.

more emotional meaning to a woman than abortion, an assumption that is surely contrary to fact.

SHOULD THE FATHER HAVE RIGHTS?

Men who are willing to see abortion-prohibition laws relaxed somewhat, but not completely, frequently raise a question about the "rights" of the father. Should we allow a woman to make a unilateral decision for an abortion? Should not her husband have a say in the matter? (After all, he contributed just as many chromosomes to the fetus as she.)

I do not know what weight to give this objection. I have encountered it repeatedly in the discussion section following a public meeting. It is clear that some men are disturbed at finding themselves powerless in such a situation and want the law to give them some power of decision.

Yet powerless men are—and it is nature that has made them so. If we give the father a right of veto in abortion decisions, the wife has a very simple reply to her husband: "I'm sorry, dear, I wasn't going to tell you this, but you've forced my hand. This is not your child." With such a statement she could always deny her husband's right to decide.

Why husbands should demand power in such matters is a fit subject for depth analysis. In the absence of such, perhaps the best thing we can say to men who are "hung up" on this issue is this: "Do you really want to live for another eight months with a woman whom you are compelling to be pregnant against her will?"

Or, in terms of public policy, do we want to pass laws which give men the right to compel their wives to be pregnant? Psychologically, such compulsion is akin to rape. Is it in the public interest to encourage rape?

"SOCIO-ECONOMIC"—AN ANEMIC PHRASE

The question "How can we justify an abortion?" proves least efficient in solving the real problems of this world when we try to evaluate what are usually called "socio-economic indications." The hardship cases—rape, incest, probability of a deformed child—have been amply publicized, and as a result the majority of the public accepts them as valid indicators; but hardship cases constitute only a few percent of the need. By contrast, if a woman has more children than she feels she can handle, or if her children are coming too close together, there is little public sympathy for her plight. A poll conducted by the National Opinion Research Center in December, 1965, showed that only 15 percent of the respondents replied "Yes" to this question: "Please tell me whether or not you think it should be possible for a pregnant woman to obtain a legal abortion if she is married and does not want any more children." Yet this indication, which received the lowest rate of approval, accounts for the vast majority of instances in which women want—and illegally get—relief from unwanted pregnancy.

There is a marked discrepancy between the magnitude of the need and the degree of public sympathy. Part of the reason for this discrepancy is attributable to the emotional impact of the words used to describe the need. "Rape," "incest," "deformed child"—these words are rich in emotional connotations. "Socio-economic indications" is a pale bit of jargon, suggesting at best that the abortion is wanted because the woman lives by culpably materialistic standards. "Socio-economic indications" tugs at no one's heartstrings; the hyphenated abomination hides the human reality to which it obliquely refers. To show the sort of human problem to which this label may be attached, let me quote a letter I received from one woman. (The story is unique, but it is one of a large class of similar true stories.)

I had an illegal abortion 2½ years ago. I left my church because of the guilt I felt. I had six children when my husband left me to live with another woman. We weren't divorced and I went to work to help support them. When he would come to visit the children he would sometimes stay after they were asleep. I became pregnant. When I told my husband, and asked him to please come back, he informed me that the woman he was living with was five months pregnant and ill, and that he couldn't leave her—not at that time anyway.

I got the name of a doctor in San Francisco from a Dr. friend who was visiting here from there. This Dr. (Ob. and Gyn.) had a good legitimate practice in the main part of the city and was a kindly, compassionate man who believes as you do, that it is better for everyone not to bring an unwanted child into the world.

It was over before I knew it. I thought I was just having an examination at the time. He even tried to make me not feel guilty by telling me that the long automobile trip had already started a spontaneous abortion. He charged me $25. That was on Fri. and on Mon. I was back at work. I never suffered any ill from it.

The other woman's child died shortly after birth and six months later my husband asked if he could come back. We don't have a perfect marriage but my children have a father. My being able to work has helped us out of a deep financial debt. I shall always remember the sympathy I received from that Dr. and wish there were more like him with the courage to do what they believe is right.

Her operation was illegal, and would be illegal under most of the "reform" legislation now being proposed, if interpreted strictly. Fortunately some physicians are willing to indulge in more liberal interpretations, but they make these interpretations not on medical grounds, in the strict sense, but on social and economic grounds. Understandably, many physicians are unwilling to venture so far from the secure base of pure physical medicine. As one Catholic physician put it:

Can the patient afford to have another child? Will the older children have sufficient educational opportunities if their parents have another child? Aren't two, three or four children enough? I am afraid such statements are frequently made in the discussion of a proposed therapeutic abortion. [But] we should be doctors of medicine, not socio-economic prophets.[6]

To this a non-Catholic physician added: "I sometimes wish I were an obstetrician in a Catholic hospital so that I would not have to make any of these decisions. The only position to take in which I would have no misgivings is to do no interruptions at all." [7]

WHO WANTS COMPULSORY PREGNANCY?

The question "How can we justify an abortion?" plainly leads to great difficulties. It is operationally unmanageable: it leads to inconsistencies in practice and inequities by any moral standard. All these can be completely avoided if we ask the right question, namely: *"How can we justify compulsory pregnancy?"*

By casting the problem in this form, we call attention to its relationship to the slavery issue. Somewhat more than a century ago men in the Western world asked the question: "How can we justify compulsory servitude?" and came up with the answer: *"By no means whatever."* Is the answer any different to the related question: "How can we justify compulsory pregnancy?" Certainly pregnancy is a form of servitude; if continued to term it results in parenthood, which is also a kind of servitude, to be continued for the best years of a woman's life. It is difficult to see how it can be argued that this kind of servitude will be more productive of social good if it is compulsory rather than voluntary. A study [8] made of Swedish children born when their mothers were refused the abortions they had requested showed that unwanted children, as compared with their controls, as they grew up were more often picked up for drunkenness, or antisocial or criminal behavior; they received less education; they received more psychiatric care; and they were more often exempted from military service by reason of defect. Moreover, the females in the group married earlier and had children earlier, thus no doubt tending to create a vicious circle of poorly tended children who in their turn would produce more poorly tended children. How then does society gain by increasing the number of unwanted children? No one has volunteered an answer to this question.

[6] Calderone, ed., op. cit., p. 103.

[7] Ibid., p. 123.

[8] Hans Forssman and Inga Thuwe, "One Hundred and Twenty Children Born after Application for Therapeutic Abortion Refused," *Acta Psychiatrica Scandinavica,* 42 (1966) 71.

Of course if there were a shortage of children, then society might say that it needs all the children it can get—unwanted or not. But I am unaware of any recent rumors of a shortage of children.

ALTERNATIVES: TRUE AND FALSE

The end result of an abortion—the elimination of an unwanted fetus—is surely good. But is the act itself somehow damaging? For several generations it was widely believed that abortion was intrinsically dangerous, either physically or psychologically. It is now very clear that the widespread belief is quite unjustified. The evidence for this statement is found in a bulky literature which has been summarized in Lawrence Lader's *Abortion* [9] and the collection of essays brought together by Alan Guttmacher.[10]

In tackling questions of this sort, it is imperative that we identify correctly the alternatives facing us. (All moral and practical problems involve a comparison of alternative actions.) Many of the arguments of the prohibitionists implicitly assume that the alternatives facing the woman are these:

Abortion—No Abortion

This is false. A person can never do nothing. The pregnant woman is going to do something, whether she wishes to or not. (She cannot roll time backward and live her life over.)

People often ask: "Isn't contraception better than abortion?" Implied by this question are these alternatives:

Abortion—Contraception

But these are not the alternatives that face the woman who asks to be aborted. She *is* pregnant. She cannot roll time backward and use contraception more successfully than she did before. Contraceptives are never foolproof anyway. It is commonly accepted that the failure rate of our best contraceptive, the "pill," is around one percent, i.e., one failure per hundred woman-years of use. I have earlier shown [11] that this failure rate produces about a quarter of a million unwanted pregnancies a year in the United

9 Lawrence Lader, *Abortion* (Indianapolis: Bobbs-Merrill, 1966).
10 Alan F. Guttmacher (ed.), *The Case for Legalized Abortion* (Berkeley, California: Diablo Press, 1967).
11 Garrett Hardin, "A Scientist's Case for Abortion," *Redbook* (May 1967) p 62.

States. Abortion is not so much an alternative to contraception as it is a subsidiary method of birth control, to be used when the primary method fails—as it often does.

The woman *is* pregnant: this is the base level at which the moral decision begins. If she is pregnant against her will, does it matter to society whether or not she was careless or unskillful in her use of contraception? In any case, she is threatening society with an unwanted child, for which society will pay dearly. The real alternatives facing the woman (and society) are clearly these:

Abortion—Compulsory Pregnancy

When we recognize that these are the real, operational alternatives, the false problems created by pseudo-alternatives vanish.

IS POTENTIAL VALUE VALUABLE?

Only one weighty objection to abortion remains to be discussed, and this is the question of "loss." When a fetus is destroyed, has something valuable been destroyed? The fetus has the potentiality of becoming a human being. A human being is valuable. Therefore is not the fetus of equal value? This question must be answered.

It can be answered, but not briefly. What does the embryo receive from its parents that might be of value? There are only three possibilities: substance, energy, and information. As for the substance in the fertilized egg, it is not remarkable: merely the sort of thing one might find in any piece of meat, human or animal, and there is very little of it—only one and a half micrograms, which is about a half of a billionth of an ounce. The energy content of this tiny amount of material is likewise negligible. As the zygote develops into an embryo, both its substance and its energy content increase (at the expense of the mother); but this is not a very important matter—even an adult, viewed from this standpoint, is only a hundred and fifty pounds of meat!

Clearly, the humanly significant thing that is contributed to the zygote by the parents is the information that "tells" the fertilized egg how to develop into a human being. This information is in the form of a chemical tape called "DNA," a double set of two chemical super-molecules each of which has about three billion "spots" that can be coded with any one of four different possibilities, symbolized by *A, T, G,* and *C.* (For comparison, the Morse code offers three possibilities in coding: dot, dash, and space.) It is the particular sequence of these four chemical possibilities in the DNA that directs the zygote in its development into a human being. The DNA constitutes the information needed to produce a valuable human being. The question is: is this information precious? I have argued elsewhere [12] that it is not:

Consider the case of a man who is about to begin to build a $50,000 house. As he stands on the site looking at the blueprints a practical joker comes along and sets fire to the blueprints. The question is: can the owner go to the law and collect $50,000 for his lost blueprints? The answer is obvious: since another set of blueprints can be produced for the cost of only a few dollars, that is all they are worth. (A court might award a bit more for the loss of the owner's time, but that is a minor matter.) The moral: *a non-unique copy of information that specifies a valuable structure is itself almost valueless.*

This principle is precisely applicable to the moral problem of abortion. The zygote, which contains the complete specification of a valuable human being, is not a human being, and is almost valueless. . . . The early stages of an individual fetus have had very little human effort invested in them; they are of very little worth. The loss occasioned by an abortion is independent of whether the abortion is spontaneous or induced. (Just as the loss incurred by the burning of a set of blueprints is independent of whether the causal agent was lightning or an arsonist.)

A set of blueprints is not a house; the DNA of a zygote is not a human being. The analogy is singularly exact, though there are two respects in which it is deficient. These respects are interesting rather than important. First, we have the remarkable fact that the blueprints of the zygote are constantly replicated and incorporated in every cell of the human body. This is interesting, but it has no moral significance. There is no moral obligation to conserve DNA—if there were, no man would be allowed to brush his teeth and gums, for in this brutal operation hundreds of sets of DNA are destroyed daily.

The other anomaly of the human information problem is connected with the fact that the information that is destroyed in an aborted embryo *is* unique (unlike the house blueprints). But it is unique in a way that is without moral significance. A favorite argument of abortion-prohibitionists is this: "What if Beethoven's mother had had an abortion?" The question moves us; but when we think it over we realize we can just as relevantly ask: "What if Hitler's mother had had an abortion?" Each conceptus is unique, but not in any way that has a moral consequence. The *expected* potential value of each aborted child is exactly that of the average child born. It is meaningless to say that humanity loses when a *particular* child is not born, or is not conceived. A human female, at birth, has about 30,000 eggs in her ovaries. If she bears only 3 children in her lifetime, is there any meaningful sense in which we can say that mankind has suffered a loss in those other 29,997 fruitless eggs? (Yet one of them might have been a super-Beethoven!)

People who worry about the moral danger of abortion do so because they think of the fetus as a human being, hence equate feticide with mur-

[12] Garrett Hardin, "Blueprints, DNA, and Abortion: A Scientific and Ethical Analysis," *Medical Opinion and Review*, 3:2 (1967) p. 74.

der. Whether the fetus is or is not a human being is a matter of definition, not fact; and we can define any way we wish. In terms of the human problem involved, it would be unwise to define the fetus as human (hence tactically unwise ever to refer to the fetus as an "unborn child"). Analysis based on the deepest insights of molecular biology indicates the wisdom of sharply distinguishing the information for a valuable structure from the completed structure itself. It is interesting, and gratifying, to note that this modern insight is completely congruent with common law governing the disposal of dead fetuses. Abortion-prohibitionists generally insist that abortion is murder, and that an embryo is a person; but no state or nation, so far as I know, requires the dead fetus to be treated like a dead person. Although all of the states in the United States severely limit what can be done with a dead human body, no cognizance is taken of dead fetuses up to about five months' prenatal life. The early fetus may, with impunity, be flushed down the toilet or thrown out with the garbage—which shows that we never have regarded it as a human being. Scientific analysis confirms what we have always known.

THE MANAGEMENT OF COMPULSORY PREGNANCY

What is the future of compulsory pregnancy? The immediate future is not hopeful. Far too many medical people misconceive the real problem. One physician has written:

Might not a practical, workable solution to this most difficult problem be found by setting up, in every hospital, an abortion committee comprising a specialist in obstetrics and gynecology, a psychiatrist, and a clergyman or priest? The patient and her husband—if any—would meet with these men who would do all in their power to persuade the woman not to undergo the abortion. (I have found that the promise of a postpartum sterilization will frequently enable even married women with all the children they can care for to accept this one more, final pregnancy.) If, however, the committee members fail to change the woman's mind, they can make it very clear that they disapprove of the abortion, but prefer that it be safely done in a hospital rather than bungled in a basement somewhere.[13]

What this author has in mind is plainly not a system of legalizing abortion but a system of managing compulsory pregnancy. It is this philosophy which governs pregnancies in the Scandinavian countries,[14] where the experience of a full generation of women has shown that women do

[13] H. Curtis Wood, Jr., "Letter to the Editor," *Medical Opinion and Review,* 3:11 (1967) p. 19.
[14] David T. Smith, ed., *Abortion and the Law* (Cleveland: Western Reserve University, 1967) p. 179.

not want their pregnancies to be managed by the state. Illegal abortions have remained at a high level in these countries, and recent years have seen the development of a considerable female tourist trade to Poland, where abortions are easy to obtain. Unfortunately, American legislatures are now proposing to follow the provably unworkable system of Scandinavia.

The drift down this erroneous path is not wholly innocent. Abortion-prohibitionists are showing signs of recognizing "legalization" along Scandinavian lines as one more roadblock that can be thrown in the way of the abolition of compulsory pregnancy. To cite an example: on February 9, 1966, the *Courier,* a publication of the Winona, Minnesota Diocese, urged that Catholics support a reform law based on the American Law Institute model, because the passage of such a law would "take a lot of steam out of the abortion advocate's argument" and would "defeat a creeping abortionism of disastrous importance." [15]

Wherever a Scandinavian or American Law Institute type of bill is passed, it is probable that cautious legislators will then urge a moratorium for several years while the results of the new law are being assessed (though they are easily predictable from the Scandinavian experience). As Lord Morley once said: "Small reforms are the worst enemies of great reforms." Because of the backwardness of education in these matters, caused by the long taboo under which the subject of abortion labored, it seems highly likely that our present system of compulsory pregnancy will continue substantially without change until the true nature of the alternatives facing us is more widely recognized.

[15] Anonymous, *Association for the Study of Abortion Newsletter,* 2:3 (1967) p. 6.

7 Religious Problems and Conflicts

Religious institutions in the United States are in a period of rapid change. Some deplore this, believing that the church should embody a system of eternal truths and unchanging principles. This viewpoint is neatly phrased in the motto of one church, "A changeless Christ for a changing world." Others believe that the church *must* change, not only in its operating techniques but also in its fundamental message, if it is to remain relevant to the concerns of a changing world. This view, strongly endorsed by the National Council of the Churches of Christ in the United States and by the World Council of Churches, calls for active church involvement in social action and social ethics.

Stark and Glock, after a highly sophisticated interview study of a national sample of nearly two thousand church members, reach some dramatic conclusions about the consequences of church involvement in social ethics. They believe that the shift from an emphasis upon personal religious salvation to a concern for ethics and social action has been accompanied by a decline in religious commitment. They do not attempt to answer the possibly unanswerable question—which of these developments is the cause and which is the effect—but they do suggest that the church as we know it may be doomed.

ARE WE ENTERING A
POST-CHRISTIAN ERA?

Rodney Stark

Survey Research Center
University of California

Charles Y. Glock

Professor of Sociology
University of California, Berkeley

Perhaps at no prior time since the conversion of Paul has the future of Christianity seemed so uncertain. Clearly, a profound revolution in religious thought is sweeping through the churches. But where will it lead: is this a moment of great promise or peril for the future of Christianity?

Some observers believe we have already entered a post-Christian era and that the current upheavals are the death throes of a doomed religion. Yet many theologians interpret these same signs as the promise of an era of renewed religious vigor. They foresee the possibility of a reconstructed and unified church which will recapture its relevance to contemporary life. A great many others, both clerical and lay, are simply mystified. In the face of rapid changes and conflicting claims for the future they hardly know whether to prepare for the church to rise triumphant or to administer the last rites to the faith. Probably the majority of Christians think the whole matter has been greatly exaggerated; that the present excitement too shall pass away and the churches will continue pretty much as before. . . .

What then are the main features of the changing character of American Christianity? The evidence leads us to two conclusions: the religious beliefs which have been the bedrocks of Christian faith for nearly two millennia are on their way out; this may very well be the dawn of a post-Christian era.

While many Americans are still firmly committed to the traditional supernatural conceptions of a personal God, a Divine Saviour, and the promise of eternal life, the trend is away from these convictions. Although

A number of our colleagues made careful and extensive criticisms of the initial draft of this chapter. We are indebted to Jay Demerath, Langdon Gilkey, Andrew J. Greeley, Phillip E. Hammond, Benton Johnson, Gerhard Lenski, Martin E. Marty, James A. Pike, David Riesman, Guy E. Swanson, and Milton Yinger. They deserve credit for many improvements and for saving us from several important errors. We alone are responsible for all errors of judgment and interpretation which remain.

From *American Piety: The Nature of Religious Commitment* (Berkeley: University of California Press, 1968) pp. 204–224. Reprinted by permission of The Regents of the University of California.

we must anticipate an extended period of doubt, the new reformation in religious thought reflects the fact that a demythologized modernism is overwhelming the traditional, Christ-centered, mystical faith. . . .

Although only a minority of church members so far reject or doubt the existence of some kind of personal God or the divinity of Jesus, a near majority reject such traditional articles of faith as Christ's miracles, life beyond death, the promise of the second coming, the virgin birth, and an overwhelming majority reject the existence of the Devil. This overall picture is subject to considerable variation among the denominations. Old-time Christianity remains predominant in some Protestant bodies such as the Southern Baptists and the various small sects. But in most of the mainline Protestant denominations, and to a considerable extent among Roman Catholics, doubt and disbelief in historic Christian theology abound. In some denominations the doubters far outnumber the firm believers. . . .

More direct evidence of an erosion in orthodox belief is provided by contrasts in the proportions of orthodox believers in different age groups. In an analysis reported elsewhere, based on our church-member sample, it was found that age made very little difference in the proportion subscribing to traditional beliefs among respondents fifty years of age or older.[1] Similarly, among those *under* fifty, orthodoxy differed little by age. But Christians over fifty are considerably more likely than younger persons to hold orthodox views. The difference occurs in every denomination and is quite substantial. These findings suggest an important generational break with traditional religion and that it occurred rather recently.[2]

The existence of a growing erosion in religious commitment is further corroborated by a Gallup Poll report issued just as this book was going to press.[3] The most recent Gallup findings indicated a continuation of the downward trend in American church attendance which began in the late 1950's. This decline has been particularly sharp among young adults; the proportion of them who attend weekly dropped 11 percentage points between 1958 and 1966. Furthermore, the Gallup interviewers found that Americans overwhelmingly *believe* that religion is losing its influence in contemporary life. While in 1957 only 14 percent of the nation's Christians thought religion was losing its influence and 69 percent thought it was increasing, ten years later 57 percent thought religion was losing and only 23 percent perceived faith to be gaining. Obviously, these appraisals could be inaccurate, for the respondents were being asked to make an expert judg-

[1] Rodney Stark, "Age and Faith," *Sociological Analysis,* 29:1–10 (Spring, 1968).

[2] The intergenerational break consistently occurs between those who grew up since the beginning of World War II, those who were 25 or less in 1940, and those who were raised in a prewar America. In this and in many other ways World War II seems to mark a watershed between the older America of small town and rural living (or stable urban neighborhood), and the contemporary America of highly mobile, urban life and the development of a mass culture.

[3] American Institute of Public Opinion, press release of April 11, 1967.

ment. Still, taken as a reflection of their own personal attitudes towards religion, this would seem to mark an enormous loss of confidence in religious institutions during the past decade. . . .

It is the discrepancy between institutional inertia and theological revolution which we suspect presents the churches with growing peril. Can the old institutional forms of the church continue to elicit commitment and support from persons whose theological outlook is no longer represented in these forms—or as least maintain sufficient support until such time as the theological revolution is so widespread that it is possible to make institutional changes? But perhaps an even more serious question is whether a Christianity without Christ as a literal Saviour can survive in *any* institutional form.

Our data provide no final answer to these questions. They do, however, provide some important clues as to what will happen should future developments follow the present course. As they are now constituted, it is evident that belief in traditional Christian doctrines is vital to other kinds of religious commitment. While the churches continue to be organized on the basis of traditional orthodoxy, persons who lack the beliefs which are needed to make such organization meaningful are falling away from religious institutions: *a general corrosion of commitment presently accompanies the acceptance of a modernized, liberal theology.*

Table 1 shows that among both Protestants (in every instance but one) and Roman Catholics, other aspects of religious commitment are very strongly related to orthodoxy. The highly orthodox are also much more likely to be ritually involved in the church, and far surpass the less orthodox on devotionalism, religious experience, knowledge, and particularism. Only on ethicalism among Protestants is the pattern reversed. By a slight margin it is the least orthodox who are more likely to hold the ideals of Christian ethics. Clearly, a loss of orthodoxy is very powerfully related to a loss of religiousness on these other aspects of piety as well.

Nevertheless, we recognize the fact that it could be convincingly argued that devotionalism, religious experience, knowledge, particularism, and perhaps even ritual involvement are not intrinsically necessary to the existence of Christian institutions. The fact that these forms of commitment decline as traditional belief is eroded could be interpreted as reflecting changes in modes of religious expression rather than a decline in commitment to religious institutions. After all, the new theology implies not only a departure from old time supernaturalism, but from other forms of commitment which are undergirded by supernaturalism. The clergy of the new reformation hardly expect to produce an outbreak of speaking in unknown tongues among their adherents.

However, it is quite implausible to speak simply of change rather than of decline unless religious institutions retain a laity committed in *some* fashion. On purely practical grounds, the churches cannot survive as formal

TABLE 1. The Impact of Orthodox Belief on Other Aspects of Commitment (Church-Member Sample)

	Orthodoxy Index		
	Low	Medium	High
Percentage high on ritual involvement			
Protestants	19	39	71
Catholics	19	36	55
Percentage high on devotionalism			
Protestants	20	49	79
Catholics	18	58	80
Percentage high on religious experience			
Protestants	25	57	86
Catholics	29	49	70
Percentage high on religious knowledge			
Protestants	15	19	46
Catholics	0	5	7
Percentage high on particularism			
Protestants	9	25	60
Catholics	15	28	40
Percentage high on ethicalism			
Protestants [a]	47	46	42
Catholics	48	48	56
Number of cases on which percentages are based [b]			
Protestants	595	729	705
Catholics	64	115	304

[a] Members of some minor Protestant sects are excluded from these computations.
[b] With trivial variations all computations in these tables are based on this same number of cases.

organizations unless a sufficient proportion of persons participate in the life of the church and provide it with financial support. Without funds or members surely the churches would be empty shells awaiting demolition.

The data in Table 2 suggest that this is at least a plausible version of the future. Among both Protestants and Catholics, church attendance is very powerfully related to orthodoxy. Only 15 percent of those Protestants with the most fully modernized religious beliefs attend church every week, while 59 percent of those who have retained traditional orthodox views do so. Among Catholics the contrast is 27 percent versus 82 percent. Similarly, the table shows that membership in one or more church organizations is strongly related to orthodoxy. Finally, financial support for the churches is mainly provided by those with orthodox views. These findings are powerful within all Protestant denominations as well, and when the social class of church members was taken into account the relationships between orthodoxy and institutional support for the churches were even stronger.

These data strongly testify that the institutional church, predicated as it is on traditional theological concepts, tends to lose its meaning and its ability to move men as these concepts become outmoded. Consequently, if

TABLE 2.   The Impact of Orthodox Belief on Organizational Support for the Church (Church-Member Sample)

	Orthodoxy Index		
	Low	Medium	High
Percentage who attend church every week			
Protestants	15	31	59
Catholics	27	60	82
Percentage who belong to one or more church organizations			
Protestants	46	61	72
Catholics	14	24	46
Percentage who contribute $7.50 or more per week to their church			
Protestants	17	23	44
Catholics	2	4	8
Percentage of Catholics who contribute $4 or more per week to their church	13	19	26

Note: With trivial variations all computations are based on the number of cases shown in Table 1.

the erosion of traditional beliefs continues, as presumably it will, so long as the church remains locked in its present institutional forms it stands in ever-increasing danger of both moral and literal bankruptcy. At the moment, the liberal denominations are particularly vulnerable because the demise of traditional theology and a concomitant drop in other aspects of commitment is already considerably widespread in these bodies.

However, it seems clear that the solution is not a return to orthodoxy. In coming days many conservative Christians will undoubtedly argue and work for such an about-face. We judge their prospects for success as minuscule. The current reformation in religious thought appears irrevocable, and it seems as likely that we can recover our innocence in these matters as that we can again believe the world flat or that lightning is a palpable manifestation of God's wrath.

Is there any way the likely impending triumph of liberal theology can be translated into the regeneration of religious institutions, anticipated by the liberal clergy? Or must it inevitably lead to the demise of organized faith? It is here the future is most murky. The alternatives to orthodoxy being advocated by the new theologians and their supporters are still relatively formless and inchoate. It is too soon to know just how they will evolve. However, their central thrust seems to be towards the ethical rather than the mystical.

But this is more than a change in emphasis. The ethics of the new theologies differ sharply from the old. No longer are Christian ethics defined as matters of personal holiness or the rejection of private vices, but they are directed towards social justice, with the creation of a humane society. As Langdon Gilkey put it recently, there has been a "shift in Christian ethical concern from personal holiness to love of neighbor as the central obligation, if not the essence, of Christianity . . . [a concern] with a man's attitudes and behavior in relation to his neighbor in the social community." [4] In the new ethical perspective the individual is not neglected for the sake of the group, but the whole question of what is ethical is freed from the confines of the individual and seen as integral to the social situation in which persons are embedded. The long Christian quest to save the world through individual salvation has shifted to questions of how to reform society directly.

Consequently, the new theology is manifested less in what one believes about God than in what one believes about goodness, justice, and compassion. A depersonalized and perhaps intuitively understood God may be invoked by these theologies, but what seems to count most is not how one prepares for the next life—the reality of which the new theology seems to deny—but what one does to realize the kingdom of God on earth.

As we have seen earlier, ethicalism may provide a substitute for orthodoxy among some modern Christians. Ethicalism—the importance placed on "Loving thy neighbor" and "Doing good for others"—is more prevalent in denominations where orthodoxy is least common. Furthermore, individual Christian church members whose religious beliefs are the least orthodox are slightly more inclined to score high on ethicalism than are the most orthodox (Table 1).

But from an institutional point of view, is ethicalism a satisfactory substitute for orthodoxy? Can ethical concern generate and sustain the kinds of practical commitment—financial support and personal participation—which the churches need to survive?

If the churches continue their present policy of business as usual, the answer is probably no. The ethically oriented Christian seems to be deterred rather than challenged by what he finds in church. The more a man is committed to ethicalism the less likely he is to contribute funds or participate in the life of the church. We suspect he is also less likely, in the long run, to remain a member.

As we interpret our data, a decline in church support and participation is a function both of a decline in orthodoxy and a reaction against the present nature of the churches by those who have taken up an ethical conception of Christianity. Tables 3 and 4 show the joint effects of orthodoxy and ethicalism on financial contributions and church attendance. Table 3 shows that among Protestants the more a church member is committed to ethics the less likely he is to contribute money to his church, regardless of

[4] Langdon Gilkey, "Social and Intellectual Sources of Contemporary Protestant Theology in America," *Daedalus* (Winter 1967) p. 73.

TABLE 3.   Orthodoxy, Ethicalism, and Contributions to the Church (Church-Member Sample)

| | Ethicalism Index | | |
	High	Medium	Low
	Percentage who contribute $7.50 or more per week to their church		
Protestants Orthodoxy index			
High	38 (304)	43 (240)	58 (111)
Medium	18 (333)	25 (321)	43 (44)
Low	18 (241)	20 (251)	12 (34)
	Percentage who contribute $4 or more per week to their church		
Catholics Orthodoxy index			
High	27 (150)	45 (122)	* (4)
Medium	16 (48)	18 (56)	* (4)
Low	7 (30)	21 (28)	* (1)

* Too few cases for a stable percentage.

his level of orthodoxy.[5] The best contributors are those with unwavering orthodoxy, who reject the religious importance of loving their neighbors or doing good for others. A similar relationship exists among Roman Catholics, the higher the score on the ethicalism index the less likely a parishioner is to give money to the church regardless of orthodoxy. At the present moment, member commitment to Christian ethics seems to cost the churches money.

Table 4 shows the joint impact of ethicalism and orthodoxy on church attendance. Here again among Protestants it is clear that the higher their ethicalism the less likely they are to attend church regularly. The best attenders are the highly orthodox who reject ethical tenets. Among Roman Catholics it is unclear from these data whether or not ethicalism has any effect at all upon church attendance.

These findings were rechecked within liberal, moderate, and conserv-

[5] The one exception to this generalization occurs among Protestants who are low on both ethicalism and orthodoxy. However, the relatively small number of cases on which the percentage is based makes it difficult to know whether or not to take it seriously. In any event it is of minor interest.

TABLE 4. Orthodoxy, Ethicalism, and Church Attendance (Church-Member Sample)

	Ethicalism Index		
	High	Medium	Low
	Percentage who attend church every week		
Protestants Orthodoxy index			
High	55 (328)	58 (247)	67 (113)
Medium	29 (347)	31 (331)	52 (44)
Low	19 (255)	22 (165)	10 (39)
Catholics Orthodoxy index			
High	82 (161)	82 (124)	* (4)
Medium	65 (51)	60 (57)	* (4)
Low	30 (30)	27 (30)	* (2)

* Too few cases for a stable percentage.

ative Protestant groups, and within specific denominations as well. In all cases a concern with ethics tended to be incompatible with church attendance and contributions. Furthermore, these same relationships were observed for participation in church organizations and activities.[6]

These findings strongly suggest that the churches are presently failing to engage the ethical impulses of their members: regardless of whether or not they have retained orthodox religious views, to the extent that persons have accepted the ethical preachments of Christianity they seem inclined to treat the church as irrelevant. Obviously, this bodes ill for the future of the churches. It means, in effect, that the churches have yet to find a substitute for orthodoxy which will guarantee their organizational survival. While some form of ethicalism might provide a theological substitute for orthodoxy, the present efforts along these lines have not succeeded.

Sooner or later the churches will have to face these facts. This will require a forthright admission that orthodoxy is dead and, more important, a refusal to compromise with orthodoxy either theologically or institutionally. But it will also require (and here perhaps is the impediment) a clear articulation of an alternative theology, ethically based or otherwise, and radical changes in forms of worship, programs, and organization to make them consistent and relevant with this new theology.

But even successfully fulfilling these tasks would not insure the survival

[6] Nor did controls for social class alter the findings.

of the churches. Indeed, the immediate effect would almost certainly be to alienate those members committed to old-time orthodoxy and thus sharply reduce the base of support on which the churches presently depend.[7] The gamble would be that these people could be replaced by renewing the commitment of those members whose interest in the church is presently waning, and by winning new adherents from the unchurched.

Such a radical change of posture is clearly not a present prospect for the more conservative churches. The impact of modernized theology on these bodies has so far been indirect, in the loss of members who change to more liberal denominations. To the extent that these losses remain endurable, and the clergy and laymen remain relatively impervious to modernism they can delay their crisis. Thus if institutional reforms are to come, obviously the liberal churches must lead the way. The data suggest that not only are the liberal churches in the best position to make such changes, but their existence may well depend on it.

At the present time the liberal bodies are functioning as way stations for those who are moving away from orthodoxy, and who are as yet unwilling to move outside the churches entirely. But this influx of new members may prove only a passing phenomenon unless the liberal churches can find a way to keep them and activate them. Their current practices are clearly unequal to this task. For it is the liberal churches who are currently in the poorest organizational health. As can be seen in Table 5, in contrast to conservative denominations, the majority of members of liberal bodies are dormant Christians. They have adopted the theology of the new reformation, but at the same time they have stopped attending church, stopped participating in church activities, stopped contributing funds, stopped praying, and are uninformed about religion. Furthermore, only a minority of members of the liberal bodies feel that their religious perspective provides them with the answers to the meaning and purpose of life, while the overwhelming majority of conservatives feel theirs does supply the answers. Finally, the liberal congregations resemble theater audiences, their members are mainly strangers to one another, while conservative congregations resemble primary groups, united by widespread bonds of personal friendships.

In the light of these data the liberal churches do not seem organizationally sound by comparison with the conservatives.

Although all these signs point to the need for a radical break with traditional forms in the liberal churches, it seems quite unlikely that they will do any such thing, at least in the immediate future. For one thing there is no sign that the leaders of these bodies recognize the situation that confronts them. Here and there one hears a voice raised within the clergy,

---

[7] See the discussion in Charles Y. Glock, Benjamin B. Ringer, and Earl Babbie, *To Comfort and to Challenge* (Berkeley and Los Angeles: University of California Press, 1967), especially Chap. 9.

TABLE 5.   Denominational Patterns of Religious Commitment (Church-Member Sample)

	Members of Liberal Protestant Churches [a]	Members of Moderate Protestant Churches [b]	Members of Conservative Protestant Churches [c]	Members of Roman Catholic Parishes
	(982)	(894)	(450)	(545)
Percentage high on orthodoxy	11	33	81	61
Percentage high on ritual involvement	30	45	75	46
Percentage high on devotionalism	42	51	78	65
Percentage high on religious experience	43	57	89	58
Percentage high on religious knowledge	17	25	55	5
Percentage who feel their religious perspective provides them with the answers to the meaning and purpose of life	43	57	84	68
Percentage who attend church weekly	25	32	68	70
Percentage who have 3 or more of their 5 best friends in their congregation	22	26	54	36
Percentage who contribute $7.50 or more per week to their church	18	30	50	6

[a] Congregationalists, Methodists, Episcopalians.
[b] Disciples of Christ, Presbyterians, American Lutherans, American Baptists.
[c] Missouri Synod Lutherans, Southern Baptists, sects.

but such spokesmen are a minority with little power to lead. However, leadership is not the only thing that is lacking. There is no clearly formulated theological and institutional alternative to provide the blueprint for renovating the churches. The critical attack on orthodoxy seems a success, but now what? The new theologians have developed no consensus on what it is they want people to believe, or what kind of a church they want to erect.

What we anticipate is that all of the churches (liberal, moderate and conservative; Catholic and Protestant) will continue a policy of drift, with a rhetoric of hope, and a reality of business as usual. There will be more mergers and more efforts to modernize classical interpretations of the faith, but these will go forward as compromises rather than as breaks with the past. Perhaps more radical change will come eventually, when the trends we see have caused greater havoc, for institutions, like people, have a strong will to survive. Still, institutions do die, and often salvage efforts come too late.

Only time will reveal the eventual destiny of Christianity. As matters now stand we can see little long-term future for the church as we know it. A remnant church can be expected to last for a long time if only to provide the psychic comforts which are currently dispensed by orthodoxy. However, eventually substitutes for even this function are likely to emerge leaving churches of the present form with no effective rationale for existing.

This is hardly to suggest that religion itself will die. Clearly, so long as questions of ultimate meaning persist, and so long as the human spirit strives to transcend itself, the religious quest will remain alive. But whether or not the religion of the future is in any sense Christian remains to be seen. Clearly it will not be if one means by Christian the orthodoxy of the past and the institutional structures built upon that theology. But if one can conceive of Christianity as a continuity in a search for ethics, and a retention of certain traditions of language and ritual, then perhaps Christianity will remain alive.

The institutional shape of the religion of the future is as difficult to predict as its theological content. Conceivably it may take on a public character, as suggested recently by Robert Bellah, or the invisible form anticipated by Thomas Luckmann. Or it may live on in a public witness conducted by priests without parishes similar to religions in Asia. Quite possibly, religion in the future will be very different from anything we can now anticipate. The profound portents of what is to come could easily seem trivial and unintelligible today. As Yeats put it:

> And what rough beast, its hour come round at last,
> Slouches toward Bethlehem to be born?

Should the church engage in "social action"? A half-century ago, the Federal Council of Churches (now the National Council of the Churches of Christ in the United States) began an energetic campaign against the twelve-hour-day, seven-day-week in the steel industry, which culminated in its abolition in 1923. In the 1930's, church councils and some (not all) clergymen supported labor's bid for union recognition. The civil rights legislation of the 1960's probably would not have passed without church support, and mounting opposition to the Vietnam war in the late 1960's was fed by considerable church support. But when the clergy lead, do the members follow? The religious editor of *The New York Times* raises some interesting questions.

CLERGY AND CIVIL RIGHTS

Edward B. Fiske

Do Protestant clergymen speak for their constituents when they join picket lines and take liberal positions on social issues?

Last week a sociologist at Western Reserve University in Cleveland released a study confirming that a wide gap does in fact exist between the views of Protestant clergy and laymen on at least one key issue: race.

The sociologist, Jeffrey K. Hadden, based his conclusions on a national sampling of clergymen in six major Protestant denominations and a survey of 1,500 non-clergymen of all faiths. The full results will be published in January by Doubleday in "A House Divided."

Mr. Hadden found that, as a group, Protestant clergymen, especially younger ministers and theological liberals, are "overwhelmingly sympathetic to the general principle of achieving social justice for Negroes in America." Depending on denomination, only four to nine percent said that they disapprove of the civil rights movement.

Among laymen, however, a radically different picture emerged.

Approximately 45 percent of regular churchgoers, for instance, declared that they "basically disapprove of the civil rights movement in America."

In addition, although regular churchgoers, like the population as a whole, overwhelmingly believed that clergymen should "speak out as the moral conscience of the nation," they nevertheless expressed rigid opposition to this in practice on the race issue.

Three out of four, for instance, said that they would be upset if their minister were to participate in a picket line or demonstration. One-half agreed that "clergy should stick to religion and not concern themselves with social, economic and political questions."

In all cases, Protestants were more vigorous in their opposition to social action by clergymen than either Roman Catholics or Jews.

One possible explanation is that Protestant clergymen have been more visible than Catholic priests in social protest activities, especially the peace movement. In addition, Jews have traditionally made less distinction between secular and religious activities.

Mr. Hadden's research dovetails with other recent findings by social scientists.

Charles Y. Glock and Rodney Stark, two sociologists at the University of California in Berkeley, released a report three weeks ago indicating that the view of church members on social questions does not differ significantly from those of the population as a whole and that, if anything, churchgoers tend to be slightly more prejudiced.

Lay opposition to social change can probably be ascribed largely to middle class conservatism. The explanation of why a gap exists between clergy and laymen, however, is considerably more difficult to interpret.

One possibility is that clergymen are more concerned about social justice than laymen because they take their religion more seriously and are more involved than laymen in questioning traditional religious beliefs. This does not appear to be true among devout laymen, however.

One ironic effect of lay opposition to social involvement has been to drive frustrated liberal clergymen out of local parishes into teaching or denominational positions. In these posts they then become influential in training young clergymen and drafting the official church pronouncements that irritate conservatives.

The dangers inherent in the split between clergy and laity are substantial. One is the growth of anticlericalism. Another is schism or weakening of religious institutions that are important in establishing national values.

"Apparently what clergymen are saying just isn't being absorbed by laymen," said Canon W. Ebert Hobbs, an official of the National Council of Churches. "I think we had better do some careful questioning of our methods."

Clergymen often meet bitter objections when they enter the field of social action. Some of their members insist that the church should concentrate on personal salvation and not "meddle in politics." There is no way to know whether their objections are based on genuine religious conviction or on use of the church to sanctify private prejudices and vested interests. When the church engages in social action, it challenges powerful and profitable vested interests or perhaps makes people uncomfortable in the enjoyment of their pet prejudices. One way for parishioners to express their opposition is to firmly close their checkbooks!

THE PRICE OF CONVICTION

Editors of *Time*

U.S. churchgoers have a tradition of generous giving—more than $3 billion in 1964 alone. Normally, pledges are made with no strings attached and without regard to the minister's policies or convictions, but the churches' strong commitment to civil rights has been a divisive issue. In anger, some givers have withheld pledges; in respect for this kind of contemporary Christian witness, others have donated with even greater enthusiasm.

This new passion for selective giving reached a peak last month when New York's Episcopal Bishop Horace Donegan, at a ceremony marking his fifteenth year as head of the diocese, announced that a parishioner had stricken from his will a pledge of $600,000 toward completion of the Cathedral of St. John the Divine.[1] Although he named no names, Donegan said that two other rich benefactors were threatening to withdraw bequests much larger than that. The purpose of withholding the money, said Donegan, was to show disapproval of his stand on civil rights—including speeches, sending priests to Selma, installing a Negro canon at the cathedral, and integrating parishes.

RESCINDED GIFTS

Other clergymen have received similar threats. Although controversial Bishop James A. Pike of San Francisco has given Episcopalians numberless reasons for withholding donations, gifts to the diocese of California appear to be down 15 percent in 1965 chiefly because he opposed the constitutional amendment that repealed the state's fair housing act. Methodist Bishop Gerald Kennedy, who also opposed the amendment, says that some of his Los Angeles churches "had a harder time than usual meeting the budget" for the same reason. When Episcopal Father James Jones of

From *Time*, November 19, 1965, p. 118. Reprinted by permission from Time, The Weekly Newsmagazine. Copyright Time, Inc., 1965.

[1] Long known to New Yorkers as "St. John the Unfinished," the massive, somewhat Gothic structure was begun in 1891, still lacks towers and transepts. In length, it is the world's second largest church—601 ft., compared to 718 ft. for St. Peter's Basilica in Rome.

Chicago, the director of diocesan charities, was jailed last June for taking part in a civil rights demonstration, one layman rescinded a $750,000 pledge to the church's charitable agencies.

More often than not, however, ministers have found that a strong stand on civil rights pays off in the collection plate. A common experience is that attempts to silence the church through financial pressure inspire more sympathetic laymen to make up for any lost pledges.

REVERSE BACKLASH

In Nashville one parishioner canceled a $500 pledge to Calvary Methodist Church after the pastor, the Rev. Sam R. Dodson Jr., led a protest march of ministers against segregation; another layman at once raised his pledge by $500. In Alabama, when one Presbyterian church cut off the minister's car allowance because he had helped out-of-state civil rights demonstrators, a group of laymen within the church formed a committee to make up the difference out of their own pockets. Presbyterian Frank H. Stroup, chief executive of the Philadelphia presbytery, acknowledges opposition to his church's allowing the use of its Corinthian Avenue Chapel as a gathering place for demonstrators who oppose segregation at Girard College, but notes: "We are in the middle of collecting $1,125,000, and everyone is coming through on their pledges."

Even when churchgoers do withhold gifts, the gesture often proves empty. A rich woman who refused a donation to East Texas Baptist College after it desegregated was asked where she expected to find any segregated institution worthy of her beneficence. "That's what's worrying me," she said.

Chicago's Father Jones is convinced that sooner or later his angry benefactor will eventually come to see things in a different light. "I am confident that if you can weather the immediate storm you can usually finish up on top," he says. "It's just a matter of letting these people see for themselves the implications and consequences of their decisions. In the end they see the point."

Although some clergymen are critically assessing the capitalist system, others are energetically engaged in mining it! One critic has estimated that under present tax exemptions, a church with a one-million-dollar kitty could parlay this capital into ownership of the entire United States in only sixty years! Just how this might be done is described in the following article.

SHOULD THE CHURCH
BE IN THE GIRDLE BUSINESS?

Edward B. Fiske

The Real Form Girdle Company of Brooklyn is owned by the Cathedral of Tomorrow, a 2,200–member Protestant church in Akron, Ohio. In New Orleans, the local CBS television outlet is owned by the Jesuit–run Loyola University.

In both cases profits are exempt from the normal 52 percent Federal corporate income tax that their competitors pay because the companies happen to be owned by religious organizations.

With pressure building for a major overhaul of the nation's tax policies, such special treatment for churches is coming under increasing fire. Last week Mortimer M. Caplin, the former Commissioner of Internal Revenue, attacked the practice as a "plain inequity" in testimony before the House Ways and Means Committee.

"A number of churches have entered into active and aggressive commercial endeavors," he stated. "One, for example has become a wholesale distributor of popular phonograph records. Another has acquired at least seven sportswear and clothing manufacturing businesses."

CHURCHES EXEMPTED

At issue is a 1950 revision of the Federal tax laws that requires secular non-profit organizations to pay corporate profit taxes on their "unrelated business income," but specifically exempts churches from this obligation.

The law, which was spurred by New York University's ownership of the Mueller Macaroni Company, owes its present form largely to the reluctance of Congress to give the impression of attacking religion. Last year there was a bill in Congress to tax church income accruing from outside business activity financed by borrowed funds. The bill died in committee.

Ironically, such fears apparently contradict the body of public opinion both inside the churches and out.

Several major Protestant denominations, including the United Presbyterians, United Methodists and American Lutherans, have officially opposed the exemption. Roman Catholic officials have rarely raised the issue, but several Catholic publications, including the Jesuit weekly *America,* have editorialized against treating churches differently from other nonprofit groups.

A recent survey by the Columbia Broadcasting System found that taxation of unrelated business income of churches was favored by 84 percent of the general public, 93 percent of clergymen—and 96 percent of Congressmen!

The basic argument against the exemption is its inherent "unfairness" in allowing some businesses to plow all of their profits back into their operations while others must give a large proportion to the government.

UNCONSTITUTIONAL

A minority also maintains that the exemption is not so much unfair as unconstitutional. In January, Protestants and Other Americans United for Separation of Church and State filed suit in Federal District Court here against an exemption granted the Stratford Retreat House, an organization that has been given the legal status of a church in New York State, and which owns a number of businesses that allegedly have a sales volume of $15-million to $20-million a year. The suit charged that the exemption amounted to government support of a particular religion.

The most imaginative use of the present law is the situation in which churches purchase businesses at the market value or even higher and then pay for it out of the tax savings.

A spokesman for the Cathedral of Tomorrow, for instance, said last week that his church has not put any of its own money into its businesses. Rather, it is using the untaxed profits—which have been as high as $188,000 a year—to pay for the firms over a twelve-to-fifteen-year period while the former owners stay on the payroll to run the company.

Although it is difficult to find churchmen who will defend the present tax law, some are afraid that the act of closing the unrelated business income loophole could lead to re-examination of other exemptions that the churches share with other nonprofit organizations.

At this point there is virtually unanimous agreement that churches should be exempt from property taxes on buildings used for religious purposes and from income tax on contributions. The arguments are that nonprofit groups provide a useful social function and that, in cases of churches, taxation of their essential operations would constitute a violation of the principle of separation of church and state.

8   Population Problems

Since the end of World War II, the Western world has been plagued by mounting fears of the "population explosion." Death rates, almost everywhere, have declined while birth rates have soared. National populations have been doubling in as few as twenty-three years, and whimsical writers have been calculating such dates as when the people on earth will come to outweigh the earth itself.

Public concern has perhaps been greatest in the United States, which has shared in the explosive growth. The United States took the lead, both at home and abroad, in promoting contraceptive and family-planning programs.

To what end? In 1957, the United States birth rate began to drop. It has continued to drop ever since. Shallow thinkers often ascribe the drop to the introduction of the "pill," but oral contraceptives were not really marketed until 1960. What has caused the drop? How far will it go? What does it mean in terms of the future growth of the U.S. population?

The article, " 'Boom Babies' Come of Age: The American Family at the Crossroads," was prepared by the Population Reference Bureau, an organization devoted to lowering the birth rate, particularly among lower-income groups. It summarizes, in terms of two recent national surveys, the history of American population growth, the factors which regulate growth, and the situation facing the United States in the immediate future. It poses a choice between relatively uncontrolled fertility and accompanying population disaster, and the possibility of general limits on family size and the maintenance of a genuinely habitable world.

"BOOM BABIES" COME OF AGE:

The American family at the crossroads

Population Reference Bureau

Nearly all American parents would ridicule the idea that having one additional child could contribute to a national calamity. Yet this is the situation today. Within recent years American women have averaged slightly over three children each. Were they to achieve an average of 3.5 and maintain it to the end of the century, the U.S. population would total 400 million, twice what it is today. So sudden a doubling would have dire effects on the American scene. Famine would not be a threat, of course. But the asphalt and the concrete jungles would grow relentlessly. Congestion and pollution would prevail. The psychological effects of crowding —in crime and violence—would be more prevalent than they are today. After a second generation of such growth, the population would approach the billion mark and the American dream, as we now envision it, would be on the way to becoming a nightmare.

Ten years ago, this alarming prospect seemed much more likely than it does today. The U.S. birth rate has shown a downward trend since 1957, which, if it continues, would reduce the average family by one child to about 2.5. Such a cutback would shrink the national increase by 70 million for a total of 330 million Americans by the end of the century. A further reduction to 1.5 children would slice the population to 260 million by the year 2000. This last figure would still be a substantial increase over the present 200 million total, but the rate of growth would be far more manageable.

Short range, however, there is little likelihood of a further downswing in the birth rate. If anything, the coming of age of boom babies will bring an unprecedented number of couples into parenthood, thus boosting the birth rate.

Were the fertility consensus to tilt the other way and were the four- or five-child family to become the popular ideal—fortunately, a most un-

From " 'Boom Babies' Come of Age: The American Family at the Crossroads," *Population Bulletin* (August 1966). Population Reference Bureau, Inc. used by permission. (This *Bulletin* was written from a report prepared by Goody Solomon.) From *Population Bulletin*, Vol. 24, No. 3 (August 1966) pp. 61–79. Used by permission of Population Reference Bureau, Inc.

likely prospect—the United States would definitely be on the economic toboggan, snowed under with burgeoning population.

The intriguing aspect of such reflections is that in the United States at the present time the level of fertility is predominantly determined by a multitude of individual decisions: some couples cannot have any children for a variety of physiological reasons; another cadre of couples overshoot their ideal by one or even two children. But the record proves that an impressive majority of couples are highly competent sharpshooters when it comes to calling the shots on how many children they want to have. If they have a problem, it is one of timing their marksmanship so that they are able to space their children more comfortably.

This record, over the past century, proves that even though befogged in ignorance of population dynamics, and shrouded in reactionary laws, the people of the United States have managed to make astonishingly wise decisions. Now in the age of increased enlightenment, that excellent record of past performance will hopefully be sustained.

The fertility transition which has already taken place is truly phenomenal. In the early decades of the Republic, the number of children ever born per woman is believed to have been between 8 and 10. In compensating for ever declining death rates, the American people, with very little statistical enlightenment and no governmental nudging, cut the children-per-woman ratio from 8 to 10 to about 3 by 1920 and to just over 2 in the parlous days of the great depression.

Such a level of fertility dips toward the long-pull replacement level which necessitates that each woman average a fraction over two children. To keep population growth in balance, each woman must have one adult daughter who lives through the childbearing age.

Whatever the future brings, there are several paradoxes in the population situation in the United States at the present moment. Though the birth rate has been declining for a decade, the population continues to grow substantially. Even with a further decline in the birth rate, the population will continue to grow. Recent alarmist statements have been published warning that the United States is approaching an actual population decline. This opinion is not justified by any realistic appraisal of the present situation.

The future welfare of the United States is intimately related to population pattern. And no better indicator of the future exists than the national birth rate, because it represents an integral part of a vast number of decisions regarding family size and made by millions of individual couples, particularly the growing number entering on their years of maximum fertility. The attitudes of these young marrieds toward family planning are crucial as a major determinant of social and economic growth of this nation. Unfortunately, reliable information as to what they are thinking is not easy to come by. More than 15 years ago, two major university research institutes in the population field joined forces to initiate a sophisticated and statistically adequate survey that sheds light on this important point. The study was set up under the title, "Growth of American Families," shortened to GAF as a convenient label. The first study was initiated in 1955 and published in 1959. The June 1960 *Population Bulletin* summarized this report.

The second sampling was undertaken five years later and was only recently made available. This *Bulletin* is devoted to a summary of the findings of the second GAF study published by Princeton University Press this year under the title *Fertility and Family Planning in the United States*. The book explores the fertility performance and attitudes of young couples. Their decisions as to the size of the ideal family have far-reaching influence on the future development of the nation.

The factors on which their decisions are based are those which differentiate American couples from their neighbors, most important are religious background and educational level. Even these, the GAF authors discovered, are being masked by American mass culture and the need to conform, to fit the ideal of the normal, happy American couple.

Perhaps the most important finding of the current GAF report is that the younger married couples are definitely opting for smaller families, more than were those interviewed in the 1955 survey.

LOOKING BACK

That a low birth rate can produce large population increases is less of a paradox than it seems. Since the early days of the Republic, American population has multiplied impressively despite a steady decline in the birth rate. And although this has been dubbed a "nation of immigrants," considerably less of this expansion came from immigration than is popularly imagined. More, in fact, came from the offspring of fecund American couples aided by a death rate that has decreased from 20–25 to 9 since the nation began.

In 1790, the year of the first census and a time of colonization, 90 percent of the population was native born. Even after a century of resettling the oppressed from Europe, the nation remained substantially native born. In 1890, with more than 9 million foreign born in its population, the United States was still 85.3 percent native. In 1920, before the flow was dammed by barriers to immigration, this percentage rose to 86.9, with nearly 14 million immigrants.

All the while the nation was filling with people, the birth rate was changing drastically. It is estimated to have been 55 per 1,000, or near the physiological upper limits in the beginning of the nineteenth century. Americans numbered over 5 million then, and were increasing at a high rate. In the years between 1810 and 1820, they netted a 2.4 million gain in population, adding another 3.2 million by 1830. This was at a time when life expectancy was around 35 and the death rate ran between 20 and 25 per 1,000.

Total growth per decade in the early years of the nation was comparable to the annual growth today when more than 4 million infants are born each year and the net gain in population runs around 2.8 million. Between 1960 and 1965 the nation grew by 14.1 million, and the birth rate fell from 23.7 per 1,000 to 19.4.

HOW MANY MOTHERS?

What influences both the birth rate and the absolute number of births is the number of actual and potential mothers, and the relative size of the infant and aged groups. The slide in the birth rate has in effect been offset by a continued increase of mothers, who have reproduced in such numbers that annual births set records in most years from 1791 to 1921, when the first period of sustained decline began. This downtrend in the birth rate lasted until 1933, picked up again, though with less intensity than before, and showed small increases into the 1940's. After World War II new records were set. The crude birth rate was higher in 1947 than in any recent year, but a new record for the largest annual number of births was scored in 1957.

A comparison of 1932 with 1965 emphasizes the effects of the number and structure of the population on low birth rate. In both years, the birth rate was about the same, 19.5 and 19.4 per 1,000, respectively. Yet in 1932, the number of births was a mere 2.4 million compared with 3.8 million in 1965. The difference results from the combination of different numbers of women of childbearing age, 15–44, and their varying fertility rates. The fertility rate is the annual number of live births per 1,000 women of childbearing age. In 1932, the fertile group constituted 23.9 percent of the population and their fertility rate was 81.7. Hence the birth rate was 19.5 or 81.7 $\times$ .239. In 1965, women of comparable age were only 20 percent of the population, but their fertility rate was 96.8, making a birth rate of 19.4 or 96.8 $\times$ .20.

The composition of the population has changed very considerably in the past three decades. In 1935, 36 percent were under 20 and 6 percent were over 64. At present, a larger proportion are very old or very young. Half are less than 25 years old, 40 percent are under 20, and more than 9 percent are over 64. Fewer men and women are in the intermediate age groups. In absolute numbers, the age categories are shown in Table 1.

The age structure of today's population is such, that in a very few years, numbers of potential mothers will soar rapidly to a new high. Oddly

TABLE 1.   Age Categories in U.S. Population

	1935		1965	
	(millions)	(%)	(millions)	(%)
Under 20	46.2	36.3	77.0	39.6
20–64	73.3	57.6	99.4	51.1
65 and over	7.8	6.1	18.2	9.3
Total U.S.	127.3	100.0	194.6	100.0

enough, the number of women in the prime reproductive years, 20–29, has not changed much in the last 30 years by reason of the low fertility of the depression years. There were 11.1 million of them in this age group in 1935, and 11.0 million of these women in 1960. By 1970, this fertile group will number 15.5 million; by 1980, 20 million. At the same time all potential mothers, those aged 15–44, will grow at a moderate pace. They totaled 36 million in 1960, 39 million in 1965. By 1970, they are expected to increase 3 million more for a total of 42 million.

Taking the youngest women, 15–19 years old, as a point of comparison, the last time they approached their present roster of more than 8.4 million was in 1939. In 1947 the postwar baby boom peaked and the birth rate reached its highest point since the 1920's (26.6).

It is these boom babies who are now coming to the reproductive roost, causing an enormous increase in potential fertility and placing the nation at a demographic crossroads. The young men and women born immediately after World War II are now reaching marriageable age.

Both the number of children they have and the age at which they have them hold the key to the future population trends. If the fashion of early marriage and early motherhood is perpetuated, the fertility potential can be vastly compounded and the signs for this are already posted. In 1961, mothers averaged 21.8 years old when their first offspring arrived. In 1940, the comparable age was 23.2. In the late 50's and early 60's young mothers were having second and third children sooner than women a generation earlier. Furthermore, since the average American wife has been having her last child while still in her 20's, after giving birth to from two to four children, her period of excess pregnancy risk is longer. How she handles total fertility during this time holds the key to future population growth.

Fortunately, the fertility rate of women between 20 and 24 years of age has declined in the last few years from 257.5 per 1,000 in 1959 to 219.8 in 1964. This means that seven years ago, one quarter of these women bore children each year. Two years ago, the figure was dropped towards one fifth.

This trend may lead demographers to believe that the average size of the American family will decline still further.

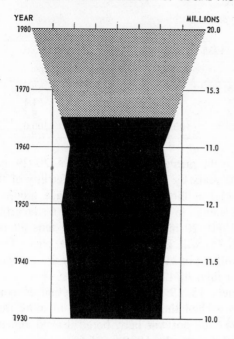

FIGURE 1.
Increase in women of child-bearing ages, 20–29, from 1930 to 1980.

Since 1957, wives over 24 have also been having fewer births than during the baby boom years. A decline occurred because many wives over 30, and some between 25 and 30, had already completed their families. In other words, they had timed births early, spaced them close together, and called a halt to fertility.

"The unusually high rates observed at the older childbearing ages (30 years of age and over) during the 1950's were due to the making up of births postponed by couples who were in the early childbearing ages during the late 1930's and the early 1940's," reported the U.S. Public Health Service in February, 1966. "Most of these couples are no longer having children. The couples who followed them are now having lower birth rates at the older childbearing ages because they tended to marry earlier and have their children sooner after marriage."

THE CRUX: CHILDREN EVER BORN

In the long run, the number of children born to each woman will be the most significant factor contributing to population increase. Most recent statistics show that the present childbearers on the average have been producing larger families than did their mothers. That previous generation composed of "depression wives," born between 1906 and 1915, bore the lowest average number of children, 2.4 to 2.5. Those born in the 1930's appear to be reaching an average of 3.1 to 3.6.

What will be the average for women born in 1940's, especially for women born during the years immediately after World War II? This is a pivotal question about which revolves much conjecture on future trends. The future direction of fertility trends greatly depends on those women now moving into the marriageable ages and beginning to reproduce. Their family aims and plans will determine the amount and rate of population growth.

Because the birth rates of young couples have been declining in the last few years, some demographers suggest that a new fashion of small families may be in the making. There is a possibility that the new vogue is one of widely spaced births rather than small families. This could mean as high an ultimate fertility spread over a longer period.

Obviously, projecting past and current statistics into the future gives an inadequate picture of possible developments. This type of activity does not take into account the thoughts and intentions of today's young married couples regarding family planning. Nor does it measure the profound effect economic changes can have on their attitudes and intentions. An awareness of the inadequacy of this failing in statistical population projections, based on past performance and purely speculative assumption, stimulated the *Growth of American Families* (GAF) studies, two unique national surveys of attitudes and practices of American women with regard to childbearing.

They are the work of the Survey Research Center of the University of Michigan and the Scripps Foundation for Research in Population Problems, Miami University, Oxford, Ohio. Professors Ronald Freedman and Pascal K. Whelpton, who unfortunately did not live to see the second study completed, were the moving spirits behind the undertaking. They were assisted by Arthur A. Campbell and, in the second survey, by John E. Patterson. The first was conducted in 1955 and the findings were reported in 1959 in the book *Family Planning, Sterility and Population Growth.* The second survey comprised a larger and more comprehensive sample than the first. Like the first it used an interview-in-depth technique on a probability sampling of married women 18–39 years old. The 1955 study was limited to white women; the 1960 sequel included a sampling of the non-white population.

A unique feature of the studies was the use of cohort analysis, a method developed by Dr. Whelpton. It was adopted by the U.S. Census Bureau in 1964 in preparing its projections. A cohort, in this study, is a group of women born in a 12-month period with January 1 in the center. For example, the women born between July 1, 1919, and June 30, 1920, constitute the 1920 cohort. The reproductive histories of women in each cohort are followed from the beginning to end of their child-bearing periods, with fertility treated as a cumulative process.

The advantage of the cohort system lies in forecasting. The GAF authors, in 1955, explained it this way:

By focusing attention on the childbearing of real groups of people as they live through the reproductive ages, statements can be made which are understandable in terms of the behavior of individuals and married couples. For example, one can readily comprehend what is meant by the assumptions that 95 percent of the women born in 1931–35 and living to age 45 will have married before age 45 and that the average number of births to those who marry will be 3. In contrast, it is difficult to interpret in terms of the behavior of individuals or married couples the assumptions that during 1956–65 the birth rate will remain at 24 per 1,000 (the 1955 figure) and that it will then decline to 20 per 1,000 in 1980.

The 1960 GAF sampling also included women aged 40–44 as representative survivors of those who were 35–39 years old in 1955. The later participants, however, were not the same women who were interviewed five years earlier. The newer sampling was most carefully selected, however, to assure a close matching of characteristics.

A primary objective of the 1960 survey was to determine how well wives interviewed in 1955 predicted the number of children that women the same age would have during the ensuing five years. The results were uncanny in their accuracy. In 1955, wives of fecund couples, those with normal ability to have children, expected an average of almost one birth, .90 to .93, in the next five years. In that period, comparable married women averaged precisely .92 births.

Whether such precision will hold over the long haul is yet to be determined. Not only are future GAF surveys planned, but others of a similar nature are also under way. For one, in 1962, the Population Studies Center of the University of Michigan began collecting data on the number of births in the U.S. to date and the total number of births expected in light of information on the racial, religious, socio-economic, and demographic characteristics of married couples. Relevant questions about fertility were asked in various nationwide surveys conducted by the University's Survey Research Center. The answers will be used to update available information concerning the family-building expectations of American couples.

What is more, analyses of the American family's growth are under way at Princeton's Office of Population Research. In a 1962 Population Studies Center report based on the replies of 1,383 respondents, the results of the 1960 GAF study were generally confirmed. Certainly the high correlation between expectations and performance is a tribute to the thoroughness of the two studies. The interviews on which both GAF reports are based involved approximately 200 questions with interviews running from one to one and one half hours in length. Questions posed involved the number of children the wife had at the time of interview, the total number of children she and her husband wanted, the number she actually expected to have, and the physiological ability of the wife and the husband to have children in the future. Couples were also asked about their attitudes toward family planning, effectiveness of family planning practices, religion, level of education, husband's occupation, and whether the wife was presently working.

The 1960 study verified the prevalence of some of the 1955 practices and attitudes, and indicated changes in others. Many of the findings of the earlier survey tend to have been confirmed by other more specialized studies and by official U.S. statistics. But when all data are integrated and analyzed, what trend appears in family formation in the United States, first for the white population and then for the nonwhite?

IDEAL FAMILIES ARE BIGGER

Most U.S. married women no longer think of the ideal average family as a foursome composed of mother, father, and two children—as they did in 1940. "An overwhelming majority of these wives (about 9 out of 10)" report the GAF authors, "said they thought two, three, or four children are ideal for the average American family, with four clearly being the most popular number." In 1941, the most popular ideal was two children; in 1945, three; and in 1955 and 1960, four.

Taking an average of minimum and maximum replies over a 19-year interval, the ideal family has increased from an average of three to an average of 3.5 children. That "half" child, if realized, could boost population to about the billion mark within a century. If families average three children, this country could expect 600 million people within a century. To maintain the population at the current size, an average of 2.1 children per woman is required.[1]

On the average, the ideal (3.5) is higher than the number desired— between 3.1 and 3.4. Desires are conditioned by income, health, ability to care for more children, size of home, and marital happiness.

If women bore the average number of children they desired (between 3.1 and 3.4), the American population in the next 100 years would climb to between 600 million and 1 billion.

In gauging expectation of family size, the report incorporated the number of children married women had at the time of their interviews with the additional births they actually anticipated. In this way, the report allows for successes and failures in family planning. Some women expect fewer children than they want because of fecundity impairments, some expect more because of unwillingness or inability to prevent unwanted conceptions, and others expect fewer or more than they themselves want because of the family size preferences of their husbands.

[1] The assumptions made in these projections and estimates are that there will be no major wars, severe economic depressions, or other catastrophies. They assume decreasing mortality, increasing life expectancy, and minimal immigration.

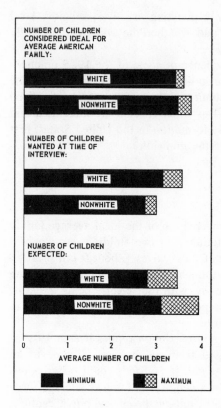

FIGURE 2.
NUMBER OF CHILDREN CONSIDERED IDEAL, WANTED AT TIME OF INTERVIEW, AND EXPECTED; FOR WIVES, BY COLOR.

Source: After 1960 GAF Report, from Pascal K. Whelpton, Arthur A. Campbell, and John E. Patterson, *Fertility and Family Planning in the United States* (Princeton, N.J.: Princeton University Press, 1966).

On the whole, the American married couple has been harmonizing its childbearing with the desired family size to a surprising degree. Expectations in 1960 came close to the ideal. Wives aged 18 to 39 who were queried in 1955 expected between 2.7 and 3.3 children. In 1960, wives in the same age bracket expected between 2.9 and 3.5 children. The average total number of expected births per woman increased from 3.0 to 3.1. Part of the increase was due to a sizeable number of wives anticipating five or six children and fewer expecting one, two, or four children.

Analysis of expectations, according to the ages of the wives, reveals an element of declining fertility. In the 1955 GAF study, the youngest wives (18–24) expected the largest families—an average of 3.2 children. *But*—and, as noted, this is the big But to demographers—in 1960, the wives 18–24 years old expected the smallest families, 3.0. It was the wives aged 25–29 who then had the highest expectations: 3.4 births.

"This is one of our most important findings," say the 1960 GAF authors. "The lower expectations of the younger wives may forecast a reversal of the postwar trend toward larger families, and the childbearing of these wives will have an important influence on the birth rate during most of the 1960's. Wives who were 18–24 account for 43 percent of the additional births expected by all wives who were 18–39 years of age." This conservative trend of the younger wives, if it is maintained, would considerably affect the rate of future population growth.

The 1960 GAF study also signalled that the trend toward earlier childbearing may be slowing down. It found that many wives are delaying initial pregnancies. This pause may account for the 1962–1965 decline in the birth rates among wives 18–24 and 25–29. However, there is activity running counter to the trend. Offsetting it is the tendency of more wives in the same cohort to increase their expectations. This could result in a fertility higher than current expectations; still, "Unless the pattern differs substantially from wives aged 18–24 in 1955, the expectations of wives 18–24 in 1960 will remain lower," say the GAF authors. Relevant here is the fact that older wives tell the number of children they actually have while younger wives generally tell of their intentions.

DISAPPEARANCE OF VOLUNTARY CHILDLESSNESS

There is one component missing in this demographic picture. The childless couple has become all but extinct. Rare indeed is the married couple who chooses to have no children. For the most part, childless couples today are frequently the consequence of one spouse suffering an impairment to the reproductive system.

Using women ever married aged 30–34 for comparison, the proportion of childlessness has dropped by two-thirds from 23 percent in 1940 to 17 percent in 1950, to 10 percent in 1960, and to 7 percent in June 1964. Many of these women postponed childbearing until well after the war.

It is possible that women who were 25–29 years old in 1964 will record an even lower percent of childlessness by the end of their fertile period. In 1964, about 11 percent of women 25–29 years old and over married had no children. This represents a drop from 30 percent of childless women in that age category in 1940.

To an extent, a woman's age when she marries and when she has her first child affects plans for family size. But then, so do religious and socioeconomic background factors. Rural-urban residence, levels of education and income, occupation, and whether or not the wife works do not affect fertility to the extent that they once did. The nation has grown more uniform as a result of rapid urbanization, a sophisticated national communications system, widespread prosperity, mobility, and improved education. In short, by experiencing similar working and living conditions, Americans en masse have acquired like desires, hopes, and drives despite diverse backgrounds.

RELIGIOUS DIFFERENCES

Religion is perhaps the strongest influence affecting the number of children couples want and the question as to whether they are willing to control fertility. The average expected number of births in 1960 was 3.7 for Catholics, 2.9 for Protestants, and 2.5 for Jews. Because of increased expectations among Catholic families, the differences seem to have been widening. Thus, while average expectations for Protestants were the same in 1955 and 1960, Catholics increased their expectations from 3.4 in 1955 to 3.7 in 1960. The report on the 1960 study explained:

First, the wives who were 18–34 in 1955 and thus 23–39 in 1960—and eligible for both studies—tended to revise their expectations upward as they grew older during 1955–1960, and this tendency may have been somewhat more pronounced for Catholics than for Protestants. Second, the Catholics who were included in the 1960 sample of 18–39-year-old wives, but were not eligible in 1955, expected to have larger families than those who were included in 1955, but were not eligible in 1960. In other words, the Catholics who entered the sample between the 1955 and 1960 studies thought they would have more children than those who left it. The Protestants who moved into the sample, on the other hand, expected *fewer* children than those who moved out of it.

Among Catholics, there is a direct relationship between expected fertility and expressed faithfulness to the Church. For example, those who receive the sacraments at least once a week expect an average of 4.4 children compared to an average of 3.2 births anticipated by those who do not receive the sacraments regularly.

Protestants differed from Catholics in that no significant relationship was found between frequency of church attendance and number of births expected.

Between Protestants and Jews, the differences in actual and expected births are fewer for urban residents with more education, income, and occupational status than for Protestants and Jews overall.

Between Protestants and Catholics, differences are larger in higher socio-economic levels than at the lower levels. It is at the upper levels that differences have grown, for Catholics with higher education and income expect more children than they did in the past—for example, they desired 3.7 in 1960 against 3.4 in 1955. Among Protestants the reverse is true. Expectations decline as education, income, and occupational status rise. Among Catholics, in contrast, the highest expectations are characteristics of the highest and the lowest socio-economic groups. This finding seems to invalidate the assumption that as Catholics become more like the rest of the population socio-economically they will copy their fertility patterns.

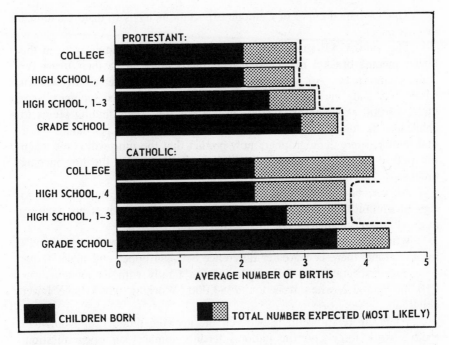

FIGURE 3.   Births by 1960 and total number expected; for wives, by education and religion.

Source: After 1960 GAF Report, from Pascal K. Whelpton, Arthur A. Campbell, and John E. Patterson, *Fertility and Family Planning in the United States* (Princeton, N.J.: Princeton University Press, 1966).

EDUCATION AND FERTILITY

More than any single characteristic, education seems to determine a wife's abilities to control fertility. The young and newly married with little schooling think they will have better fertility control than they do; hence they underestimate the size of their families. The better educated, knowing more about physiology and birth control methods, do a more effective job of planning family size.

Expectations, however, do not decline consistently from grade school through college. Among Protestants they decrease as the level of education advances through the third year of high school, then remain equal for high school graduates and college graduates.

What is true for the Protestant spouse is not true for Catholics. Catholic wives with college educations expect almost as many children as wives with grade school education; Catholics with high school education have lower expectations.

This U-shaped curve of Catholic expectations tends to distort national averages.

The 1960 GAF study found that wives whose husbands were in the higher income bracket expect almost as many children as their lower income counterparts. An average of 3.1 children was expected by women whose husbands earned $10,000. Those whose husbands' incomes were under $3,000 expected an average of 3.2 children. This finding seems to challenge the adage that "the rich get richer and the poor get babies." For that matter, some demographers now predict that the time will come when the well-to-do will average more children than those in the low income brackets.

As yet, however, procreation among low-income groups shows no sign of diminishing. At the same time, higher-income wives are bearing more children and increasing their expectations.

When the basis of comparison is family income rather than husband's income alone, there is a greater difference between upper and lower levels —average expectation is 2.8 children for a family with an income over $10,000 and 3.2 when it is under $3,000. Working wives have fewer children.

What the relationship is between the growing number of women in today's work force and the nation's fertility remains an open question. Furthermore, an increasing number have been returning to the labor force after they have completed their families.

Fertility differences which are associated with the husband's occupation are sharper than those related to his income, but they are substantially smaller than they were before World War II. This is most true for nonfarm occupations.

Wives of husbands in blue-collar jobs anticipate 7 percent more births than wives of husbands in white-collar jobs. According to the U.S. Census Bureau, white-collar workers with moderate incomes tend to limit the size of their families because of desire for status and for a high standard of living.

In the GAF studies, the gap between farm and nonfarm occupations seemed to be shrinking. The 1960 survey found a decrease in expectations among farm wives and an increase among wives in the nonfarm group. Even so, farm population is more fertile than nonfarm population, and according to the U.S. Census Bureau, "Between 1960 and 1964, the number of children ever born per 1,000 women 15 to 44 years old, standardized for age, increased by about the same amount in the farm population as in the nonfarm population."

Notable in this connection is that the farm population continues to decrease. In 1960, 7.5 percent of the nation's people lived on farms; in 1965, the total had shrunk to 6.4 percent.

RURAL-URBAN AND REGIONAL DIFFERENCES

One influence on the fertility rate is the size of cities and towns. Wives in cities of less than 150,000 people statistically expect more children than those in the larger metropolises.

In addition, wives in rural farm areas differ in their anticipations from wives in rural nonfarm communities. In 1960, it was found that wives who lived in rural areas but not on farms did not anticipate significantly larger families than wives who lived in cities and towns. Yet wives who had lived on farms at some time since they were first married, but were not living on farms at the time they were interviewed, expected almost as many births as wives still living on farms. However, women who left farm life before they were married expected fewer births.

Since the 1930's, the rise in fertility has been sharper in the cities and towns than in the rural communities. As the rural-urban differences of the past are lessening, so too are the traditional fertility variations between regions of the country. In the old South, a high proportion of the rural, farm, and nonwhite population produced the nation's highest level of fertility. Now, along with industrialization, emigration of Negroes, integration, and civil rights movements, have come better incomes, more widespread education, and urban-type sophistication—in short, life in the South is experiencing an upheaval. According to the GAF study, this sector of the country had not only the lowest birth rate, but the lowest birth expectancy.

White wives who lived in the South—where Catholics are fewer— had borne fewer children by 1960 and expected to have smaller completed families than those who lived in the remainder of the country. The north-central region has overtaken the South as the region with both the highest fertility and the highest expectancy.

NONWHITE FERTILITY

The nonwhite American population in 1960 was 11.4 percent of the total. It included American Indians, Japanese, Chinese, Filipinos, Koreans, Hawaiians, Asian Indians, Eskimos, Aleuts, Malayans and Negroes, who predominated comprising 10.5 percent of the total population.

In at least three respects, fertility among nonwhites parallels trends among the white population:

1. There is far less childlessness—only 9 percent among nonwhite women 30–34 years old in 1964 compared with 22.6 percent in 1962, or a sharp drop by more than half in two years.

2. Families are larger: about 36 percent of nonwhite women ever married 30–34 years old in 1964 had borne five or more children; in 1962, that figure was 31 percent.

3. Fertility seems to be declining among nonwhites under 25 years of age.

In addition, nonwhite fertility, like white, rose in the 1950's, then fell in the 1960's. However, in the 1950's, nonwhite births rose at a greater rate than among the white couples. During the ten-year period 1951–60, the crude birth rate of nonwhites ranged between 32 and 35 per 1,000, which is roughly 10 points higher than the rate for whites and marks a larger difference than at any time since the 1920's.

Significant to nonwhite fertility is the fact that since World War II, the prevalence of venereal disease has rapidly diminished among nonwhites and it is thought to be an important cause of both the increase in their birth rate and the decrease in childlessness. Overall, not only is the average fertility of nonwhites higher than whites, but also a high proportion of non-

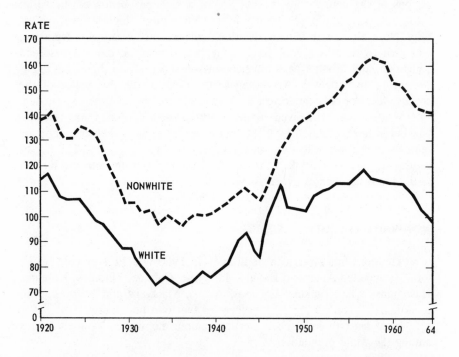

FIGURE 4.   Births per 1,000 women 15–44 years old, for whites and nonwhites, United States, 1920–1964.

Source: After 1960 GAF Report, from Pascal K. Whelpton, Arthur A. Campbell, and John E. Patterson, *Fertility and Family Planning in the United States* (Princeton, N.J.: Princeton University Press, 1966).

whites have had and expect large numbers of births. In 1960, 19 percent of the nonwhite wives expected six or more births compared with only 6 percent of a group of matched whites and 7 percent of all whites.

The 1960 GAF study revealed a significant difference between whites and nonwhites. The nonwhites set the ideal number of children higher than whites, 3.6–3.8 as against 3.4–3.5 for whites. But nonwhites actually want fewer children, 2.7–3.0 compared with 3.1–3.5. Nonwhites' average expectations—3.4–4.1—considerably exceed their preferences. The GAF study found that nonwhite couples have a higher prevalence of excess fertility (unplanned children) than whites; 31 percent vs. 17 percent.

A group of wives was selected in order to determine the extent to which fertility differences are related to racial and socio-economic backgrounds. The white and nonwhite wives were matched in certain characteristics: duration of marriage, wife's religion, region of residence, size of place of longest residence since marriage, farm background, and husband's occupation.

In comparing white and nonwhite fertility patterns, regional factors are important. The greatest differences among whites and nonwhites are in the South.

Below the Mason-Dixon Line, in 1960, nonwhites had 50 percent more births than whites; elsewhere in the country, the excess was merely 10 percent. In addition, fertility of Southern nonwhites on farms was more than double that of whites living on farms—an average of 4.5 children against an average of 2.1. Southern nonwhites also expected twice as many children as Southern whites—5.9 vs. 2.9.

The GAF authors say:

Such differentials suggest that the traditional patterns of marriage and family life that developed in the rural South during and after the period of slavery still influence nonwhite fertility perceptibly. Informal and often temporary unions between men and women beginning in adolescence, relatively ineffective sanctions against illegitimacy among the economically deprived, a genuine affection for children, and the existence of customary arrangements to provide for their care in case the mother cannot do so all contribute to high birth rates.

These trends are arrested in part by urbanization and education. The proportion of nonwhites living in cities of 50,000 or more jumped from 32 percent in 1940 to 50 percent in 1960. In that period, the proportion of nonwhites with a high school education sprang from 9 percent to 24 percent.

The sooner and further away from Southern farm life the nonwhites move and the higher the education they attain, the more their fertility resembles that of the white population. The result is a growing educated Negro middle class with relatively few children.

SOURCES

Ronald Freedman, Pascal K. Whelpton, and Arthur A. Campbell, *Family Planning, Sterility, and Population Growth* (New York: McGraw-Hill, 1959).

Institute of Life Insurance. *Family Security Feature Service* (August 1965). New York City.

Emily H. Mudd, speech delivered at conference organized by the Population Reference Bureau at Hotel Roosevelt in New York City, April 14, 1966. (See Population Profile, "300 or 400 Million in 35 years? The Nation's Young Married Couples Will Decide." April 15, 1966. Population Reference Bureau.)

Pascal K. Whelpton, Arthur A. Campbell, and John E. Patterson, *Fertility and Family Planning in the United States* (Princeton, N.J.: Princeton University Press, 1966).

Few other nations have yet shared the recent birth-rate drop in the United States. Most are still experiencing runaway growth. Significant signs of change are present, however. One noted demographer has gone so far as to predict that the population explosion will prove to be a uniquely twentieth-century phenomenon—that, in as few as thirty years, it will be over.

THE END OF THE POPULATION EXPLOSION

Donald J. Bogue

Professor of Sociology
University of Chicago

Recent developments in the worldwide movement to bring runaway birth rates under control are such that it now is possible to assert with considerable confidence that the prospects for success are excellent. In

From *The Public Interest*, 7 (Spring 1967) pp. 11–20. Copyright © National Affairs 1967. Reprinted by permission.

fact, it is quite reasonable to assume that *the world population crisis is a phenomenon of the twentieth century, and will be largely if not entirely a matter of history when humanity moves into the twenty-first century.* No doubt there will still be problematic areas in the year 2000, but they will be confined to a few nations that were too prejudiced, too bureaucratic, or too disorganized to take action sooner, or will be confined to small regions within some nations where particular ethnic, economic, or religious groups will not yet have received adequate fertility control services and information. With the exception of such isolated remnants (which may be neutralized by other areas of growth-at-less-than-replacement), it is probable that by the year 2000 each of the major world regions will have a population growth rate that either is zero or is easily within the capacity of its expanding economy to support.

The implications of these assertions for the feeding of the human race are obvious. Given the present capacity of the earth for food production, and the potential for additional food production if modern technology were more fully employed, mankind clearly has within its grasp the capacity to abolish hunger—within a matter of a decade or two. Furthermore, it is doubtful whether a total net food shortage for the entire earth will ever develop. If such a deficit does develop, it will be mild and only of short duration. The really critical problem will continue to be one of maldistribution of food among the world's regions.

These optimistic assertions are not intended to detract from the seriousness of the present population situation. Some years of acute crisis lie immediately ahead for India, China, the Philippines, Indonesia, Pakistan, Mexico, Brazil, Egypt, and other nations. Severe famines quite probably will develop within local areas of some of these nations unless emergency international measures are taken. My purpose here is to emphasize that the engineers and the agricultural technicians striving to increase the output of material goods in these nations are not working alone. Paralleling their activity is a very ambitious international fertility control program which is just starting to "pay off."

These remarks are certainly not intended to cause the participants in this international fertility control program to relax their efforts and be lulled into complacency. The successful outcome anticipated above is not one that will come automatically, but only as a result of a continued all-out "crash program" to make the widest and most intensive use of the medical, sociological, and psychological knowledge now available, and of the practical experience that has recently emerged from experimental family planning programs. It also anticipates a continued flow of new research findings and enriched practical experience that is promptly fed back into programs of fertility reduction.

This view is at variance with the established view of many population experts. For more than a century, demographers have terrorized themselves, each other, and the public at large with the essential hopelessness and inevitability of the "population explosion." Their prophecies have all been dependent upon one premise: "If recent trends continue. . . ." It is an ancient statistical fallacy to perform extrapolations upon this premise when in fact the premise is invalid. It is my major point that *recent trends have not continued, nor will they be likely to do so.* Instead, there have been some new and recent developments that make it plausible to expect a much more rapid pace in fertility control. These developments are so new and so novel that *population trends before 1960 are largely irrelevant in predicting what will happen in the future.*

In times of social revolution, it often is fruitless to forecast the future on the basis of past experience. Instead, it is better to abandon time series analysis and study the phenomenon of change itself, seeking to understand it and to learn in which direction and how rapidly it is moving. If enough can be learned about the social movement that is bringing about the change, there is a hope that its eventual outcome can be roughly predicted. This procedure is followed here. The result is subjective and crude, but I believe it to be nearer the future course of demographic history than the official population projections now on record.

Limitations of space permit only a listing of major social developments which, in my view, justify the relatively optimistic prospect I have set forth.

1. Grass-roots approval. All over the world, wherever surveys of the attitudes of the public with respect to fertility have been taken, it has uniformly been found that a majority of couples with three living children wish to have no more. Of these, a very large proportion approve of family planning in principle and declare they would like to have more information about it. They also approve of nationwide health service that includes family planning. In other words, active objections among the masses on cultural, moral, or religious grounds are minor rather than major obstacles. This is true both in Asia and Latin America, and seems to be developing rapidly in Africa. Thus, at the "grass-roots" level, the attitudinal and cultural conditions are highly favorable. Previously, it had been feared that traditionalism and religious attitudes would prove to be almost insuperable blocks to rapid fertility control. But the more sociologists study the situation, the more they accept as correct the generalization that, in most places where there is a population problem, the attitude toward family planning among the mass of the people is strongly positive.

2. Aroused political leadership. Whereas fertility control was regarded as a subversive, immoral, and sinful program during the 150 years of fertility decline in Europe and the United States, in the nations with a population problem today the national political leadership openly accepts family planning as a moral and rational solution. Heads of state in India, Pakistan, Korea, China, Egypt, Chile, Turkey, and Colombia, for example, have made fertility control an integral part of the national plan for economic development. In this, they have followed the lead of Japan. The national ministers of health and welfare not only are permitted but are expected to provide family planning services. National health services are adding family planning to their clinic services, financed by public tax funds. The mass media are increasingly carrying official endorsements, public encouragements, and specific information.

3. Accelerated professional and research activity. Professional groups in the developing countries (as well as in the rest of the world) are rapidly losing whatever antipathy or prejudice against family planning they may have had. Everywhere, the medical profession is rapidly giving it a solid endorsement—even in nations where there have been problems of religious objection. Within religious groups where there formerly was a hard inflexible prohibition against the use of chemical or mechanical contraceptive appliances, there is now a great deal of difference of opinion. Gradually, the laity is reaching the belief that the control of natality is a matter for the individual conscience, or a medical matter to be discussed with a physician —but not with the priest. Physicians and priests alike tend to accept this interpretation without forthright challenge.

Universities, both in the United States and abroad, have undertaken large-scale and sustained research activities in the fields of family planning. Their activities cover the entire range of topics—medical, sociological, and psychological. Most of the nations with a national family planning program are sponsoring research into the problem. This includes not only projects to discover new and improved ways of promoting fertility control, but also the evaluation of present programs. These activities are not amorphous, but within a remarkably short time have been coordinated. The process of integration was greatly facilitated by the holding in Geneva in 1965 of an International Conference on Family Planning Programs.

Much of the credit for the development described above is due to the activities of not-for-profit organizations that have taken population control as a focus of their activities: the Ford Foundation, Rockefeller Foundation, Population Council, and International Planned Parenthood are the leaders. The Swedish Government, the Milbank Memorial Fund, the Planned Parenthood Association of America, and the Pathfinder Fund have also been highly important sponsors of these activities. These organizations have provided unprecedented financial and technical support.

4. The slackening of progress in death control. Immediately after World War II, the industrialized nations of the world realized that there was a series of public health and medical programs that could be accomplished quickly and cheaply to bring about a reduction in mortality. These have now been largely carried out—there have been campaigns against malaria, smallpox, cholera, yellow fever, and other diseases that can be brought under control with an injection, a semiannual house spraying, etc.

The results have been dramatic, and death rates have tumbled. However, further progress in death control will be slower, because the remaining problems are those for which a solution is more difficult or is as yet unknown. For example, the death rate in Latin America stands at about 14 per thousand now. Modern medicine could bring it, at best, only to about 8 per thousand—a fall of 6 points. But a very much greater investment must be made, and over a considerably longer span of time, to achieve these 6 points than was required to obtain the preceding 6 points. In Asia the death rate still stands at about 20, even after the advent of the "miracle drugs" and the mass-inoculation and mass-treatment programs. It may be expected to drift lower, but at a slower pace than before.

This slackening of death control has a most important implication—a decline in the birth rate would be more directly reflected in a decline in the rate of population growth. During the past two decades, even if birth rates were declining, death rates were declining still faster, so that the population growth rate increased. That trend now appears to be reaching the end of a cycle: the cycle appears to be on the verge of reversing itself.

5. A variety of sociological and psychological phenomena, previously unknown or underappreciated, are promoting the rapid adoption of family planning by the mass of the people. Here we can only list them, without explanation:

a. Privation is itself a powerful motivating force for fertility control.

b. Private communication about family planning is far greater than had been thought, and can easily be stimulated to attain flood proportions.

c. "Opinion leaders"—indigenous men and women who are knowledgeable about birth control and freely undertake to influence others to adopt it—can be mass-produced cheaply and very rapidly by means of mass media and other action programs. Thus, in this area just as in economic development, there is a "multiplier effect" which, if capitalized upon, can greatly hasten "takeoff" into rapidly declining fertility.

d. It is becoming evident that fathers are very nearly equally as interested and responsible in controlling fertility as are wives. Programs aimed at couples, instead of at females, are highly effective.

e. We are discovering that illiterate rural populations will make use of the traditional methods of family planning—condom, suppositories, etc. —very nearly as readily as urban populations, after a brief period of information and trial. They will also adopt the newer methods as—or even more—readily.

6. Improved technology in contraception promotes massive adoption by uneducated people at a rapid pace. Oral contraceptives and the intra-uterine devices have both proved to be highly acceptable after only short periods of instruction and familiarity. Even illiterate rural villagers make sustained use of these methods where they have been given unprejudiced trial. These developments are only half a decade old, but they already have had a profound impact upon fertility control programs and plans. As yet there is still a great deal of prejudice against the oral compounds in Asia, so that the advantages of a two-method assault have not been fully realized there. In Latin American experiments, where the "pills" and intrauterine devices are used side by side as alternative methods, the results are highly impressive.

We are repeatedly being told by the physiologists, however, that our so-called "modern" methods of contraception are crude and barbarous— each with unpleasant side-effects and unsuitable for as much as one quarter of the population. They insist that much superior methods are on the horizon—that soon there will be dramatic improvements, that costs will be cheaper, and that the need for "sustained motivation" to practice contraception will be greatly reduced. Millions of dollars are being poured into experimental research on this front each year. This activity is taking place both in the public and the private sector. The giants of the drug industry know that huge markets can be gained by improving upon present contraceptive technology—and that huge markets will be lost if a competitor discovers and markets a superior product. As a result, all of the leading motives that bring about frenzied activity for progress among scientists have been harnessed and are at work in behalf of improving contraceptive technology—prestige, economic gain, anxiety, compassion.

In order to illustrate the above points, let us take as an example the recent experience of Korea. In 1962, the Republic of Korea formally adopted family planning as one of its national policies. In 1965, a National Survey of Family Planning was conducted. Following are some points from that survey:

1. Eighty-nine percent of the wives and 79 percent of the husbands approved of family planning.

2. The rate of approval was only slightly lower in the rural than in the urban areas (88 percent for rural women and 77 percent for rural men).

3. Of the minority who disapproved, only 8 percent mentioned religion or morals. Traditional resistance was as low in rural as in urban areas.

4. Inability to read was no barrier; 81 percent of those unable to read nevertheless approved of family planning.

5. On the verbal level, the population declared itself willing to practice family planning if given services. Seventy-seven percent of the urban women and 71 percent of the rural women made such a declaration. Among

husbands, 71 percent of the urban and 65 percent of the rural made such a declaration.

6. Unwillingness to practice family planning was concentrated primarily among young couples who had not yet had the number of children they desired and older couples (past 40 years of age) who were approaching the end of their childbearing. Couples in the years of prime importance for birth control, 25–40, were most positive in their attitudes. Moreover, the greater the number of living children, the greater the willingness to practice.

7. As a result of the national information program, 85 percent of the urban and 83 percent of the rural population had heard of family planning. Moreover, 67 percent of the urban and 64 percent of the rural population had knowledge of at least one contraceptive method. Even among the illiterate, 51 percent knew of one method or more. Knowledge of the more reliable methods—oral pill, IUCD, condom—was only very slightly less widespread in rural than in urban areas.

8. At the time of the interview, 21 percent of the urban and 14 percent of the rural couples were practicing family planning. Even among the illiterate population, 10 percent were currently practicing family planning. Although small, these percentages very obviously have sprung from a condition of near zero within a span of three years. If only 2 percent are added each year, within 35 years population growth would be near zero.

9. The methods used by rural families were equal to or superior to those of the urban population in terms of reliability, as shown in Table 1.

TABLE 1.   Reliability of Contraceptive Methods

Method	Percent of Those Using a Method	
	Rural	Urban
Condom	51.1	61.1
IUCD	18.4	27.0
Oral pill	8.5	3.5
Foam tablet	34.5	42.2

Note: Figures add to more than 100 because some couples employed more than one contraceptive.

10. In April of 1965 there were 2207 field workers in the national family planning service, stationed in the health centers or in local offices. This is only the first wave of a rapid buildup to a point where there will be one field worker for each 10,000 population. The medical and social science departments of Seoul National University are actively engaged in research, evaluation, and participation in the national program. A private organization, Planned Parenthood Federation of Korea, has a branch in

each province and is providing service and information through its office. Yonsel Medical College is conducting special experiments in rural areas, with assistance from the Population Council.

11. The progress of the national program in giving family planning services is most impressive. The progress that results when a well-designed family planning program is carried out in a population of low education is illustrated by the Sungdong Gu Action-Research Project on Family Planning, conducted by Seoul National University School of Public Health under the sponsorship of the Population Council. This program started in July, 1964. It included the use of mass media (TV, radio, newspaper, posters, pamphlets, leaflets), group meetings, and home visiting. During the first 15 months of the program, of a total of 44,900 eligible (married women in the ages 20–44), 9,809 visited the family planning station for family planning information. About 85 percent of these visitors (19 percent of all the eligible women) accepted a method of family planning. Acceptance was divided roughly equally between condoms and other traditional methods and the IUCD's. Within the period, a total of 5,722 insertions (13 percent of the eligible women) were made. Even when allowance is made for the fact that the first year's experience would "skim off" the accumulated group of already motivated people, the fact that one-fifth of the fertile population could be induced to adopt family planning within such short time is most impressive. It suggests the potential progress that can be made when a well-balanced program of information and service is provided, making use both of the mass media and personal contact.

The above brief notes on the progress of fertility control in Korea are not isolated instances. A recent report from the Pakistan Family Planning Programme suggests that more than one million families in that nation of 100 million (about 5 percent of the eligible population) now are currently contracepted through this program alone. In India, more than a million insertions of IUCD's are being made annually—in addition, the use of other methods of contraception is rising. In Colombia in Latin America, the oral pills and the IUCD both are being accepted at phenomenal rates; it is estimated that more than 120,000 couples in this nation of 18 million persons are using the oral pills alone; this is roughly 3 percent of the eligible population. In addition, large quantities of other methods are known to be used. In Santiago, Chile, the IUCD is so well known and widely used that it is a part of the medical service throughout the metropolitan area.

To summarize: wherever one looks in the underdeveloped segments of the world, one finds evidence of firmly established and flourishing family planning activity. By whatever crude estimates it is possible to make, it is quite clear that a sufficiently large share of the population already is making use of modern contraceptives to have a depressing effect upon the birth rate. Even conservative evaluation of the prospects suggests that *instead of a "population explosion" the world is on the threshold of a "contraception adoption explosion."* Because of lack of adequate vital statistics, the effects of this new "explosion" will not be readily measurable for a few years, but they will start to manifest themselves in the censuses of 1970 and will be most unmistakable in 1980.

Given the situation that has just been described, what can be said concerning the future population of the world? If we insist on extrapolating past trends, we are making the unrealistic assertion that conditions have remained and will continue to remain unchanged. If we predict a slow change of the type that was typical of Europe and Northern America before 1960, we are implicitly asserting that the current programs are having zero effect: this assertion is contrary to fact. The course taken here has been to try to comprehend the nature of the change that is taking place, and to predict its probable course and speed, so that its impact may be guessed. As crude and subjective as this procedure is, it appears to offer more valid predictions than conventional population projections.

Looking at the developments listed above, realizing that they are only 5 years old or less, knowing that accomplishments in this area are cumulative and grow by exponential curves, and appreciating that new discoveries and improvements will accrue promptly along all fronts—medical, social, and psychological—both from basic research and from accumulating experience and evaluation—the following generalizations appear to be justified:

The trend of the worldwide movement toward fertility control has already reached a state where declines in death rates are being surpassed by declines in birthrates. Because progress in death control is slackening and progress in birth control is accelerating, the world has already entered a situation where the pace of population growth has begun to slacken. The exact time at which this "switch-over" took place cannot be known exactly, but we estimate it to have occurred about 1965. From 1965 onward, therefore, the rate of world population growth may be expected to decline with each passing year. The rate of growth will slacken at such a pace that it will be zero or near zero at about the year 2000, so that population growth will not be regarded as a major social problem except in isolated and small "retarded" areas.

In evaluating these conclusions, it must be kept in mind that the topic is a deadly serious one, and the penalties for misjudgment may be very great. There is one set of penalties that results from overoptimism. But there is another set of penalties that results from overpessimism. It is quite possible that nothing has sapped the morale of family planning workers in the developing countries more than the Malthusian pessimism that has been radiated by many demographic reports. It is like assuring soldiers going into battle that they are almost certain to be defeated. If the comments made here should be so fortunate as to fall into the hands of these same family planning workers, it is hoped that those who read them will appreciate just how close they actually are to success. They have it within their grasp to improve dramatically their countries' fortunes. Coupled with the companion programs of industrialization and modernization, the effects could appear almost miraculous as they unfold in the 1970's and 1980's.

Prediction of future rates of population growth has not been the least hazardous of the many problems confronting social scientists. In making such sweeping predictions, Bogue certainly cannot be accused of temerity. Yet, even the Population Reference Bureau, not known for its sanguine views in this area, presents an analysis of guarded optimism.

Behind gross statistics countless human dramas unfold. One such drama will be unfolded briefly here, which deals with a third factor—beyond births and deaths—in population growth: immigration.

With the passage of the Immigration Act of 1965, the United States gave up the national origins concept that had been basic to its immigration policy for almost half a century. Some old problems were lessened—and some new ones were created. Victoria's view of population problems seldom finds expression in textbooks or scholarly treatises.

IMMIGRATION BRINGS A SHIFT IN MAIDS

John Corry

Victoria said she had been fortunate. Her lawyer had charged $450 to arrange her emigration from Jamaica, and most of the maids she knew had paid far more.

"Because I can tell you something," she said. "The Jamaican lawyers recruit the girls and they charge them $250, and then when the girls get here another lawyer tells them they must pay, oh, $750."

Victoria, who refuses to be further identified, is a sleep-in maid for a family on the East Side. She grew up on a farm in the back country of Jamaica, and before she emigrated she was a dressmaker.

In the past, the family she works for might have had a maid from Britain, say, or Sweden. But changing immigration laws, which will take their full effect on July 1, have virtually closed Europe as a source of domestic help.

Consequently, women like Victoria are arriving in this country in increasing numbers to work for white families, and quite often to be victimized by lawyers, travel agents and the families themselves.

Furthermore, an increasing number of women like Victoria, abetted by lawyers, quasi-employment agencies and American housewives are breaking Federal laws by working as domestics while they are here on visitors' visas. These visas are granted for indeterminate periods, perhaps six months or a year, at the discretion of immigration authorities. No one knows, even approximately, how many women are working while they are here on these visas, but there are indications.

One immigration official said there were perhaps 20,000 illegal maids in the metropolitan area alone.

P. A. Esperdy, the district director of the Immigration and Naturalization Service, said only that the number was "sizable."

A woman in Roslyn, L.I., who also said, "My husband would kill me if he knew what I'm going to do." She was going to get a maid on a visitor's visa because all her friends had one. "Besides," she said, "you hardly have to pay them anything."

Robert S. Shuster, who operates the Windsor Employment Agency in Great Neck, L.I., said that in the past he arranged the emigration and subsequent employment as domestics of perhaps 50 women each month. For this he charged the women about $95 and their employers about $200.

UNEXPECTED BYPRODUCT

Now, he said, he feels fortunate to place five women a month. Unscrupulous operators, who may charge a West Indian woman $1,000 or more for what Mr. Shuster did for $95, have shrunk his business.

The problem is an unexpected byproduct of the new immigration laws. Before October, 1965, immigration was governed by the national origins quota system, which sought to preserve the ethnic balance that existed in the United States when the 1920 census was taken. As a practical matter, this meant that white Anglo-Saxons could, if they chose to, dominate emigration.

Asians, meanwhile, were virtually excluded from entry, although no numerical limitation was placed on emigration from Canada and Latin America.

In October, 1965, the national origins system was revised. The revision provided that, until July 1, 1968, no country would have its quota of potential immigrants reduced, but that the unused portion of each quota would be assigned to a pool from which immigrants from all nations would be drawn.

The distribution of the unused quota numbers was done under a complicated preference system that gave most of the new visas to relatives of United States residents. A lesser number was distributed on the basis of talents and skills that were needed in the United States.

After July 1, this preference system will govern emigration from the Eastern Hemisphere almost entirely, and the last of the national origins system will fade away. The preference system, however, will not apply to Latin America and Canada, although a limit of 120,000 emigrants a year will be imposed on the Western Hemisphere.

RULE FOR THE UNSKILLED

What has agitated Mr. Esperdy, wrecked Mr. Shuster's business and brought grief to Victoria's friends has been the rule under which unskilled persons may emigrate.

No more than 17,000 persons a year may emigrate from the Eastern Hemisphere under what is called the sixth preference—skilled and unskilled labor.

(Furthermore, at the behest of organized labor, the Labor Department has circumscribed this preference by listing occupations that theoretically are oversupplied in the United States. A bartender or laborer, for example, may not come to the United States because there are allegedly too many unemployed bartenders and laborers here.)

The result is that the sixth preference is oversubscribed, with more people applying for visas under it than are available. Consequently, there is a backlog, and if the lady in Roslyn were to insist on an English maid she might now have to wait two to four years for the maid to get her visa.

For Western Hemisphere emigrants, however, there is no problem because there is no preference system, only the 120,000 numerical limitation. A prospective sleep-in maid can get a visa processed within months.

This, and American affluence, which allows the lady from Roslyn to even consider having a maid, is altering the flow of emigration from the Western Hemisphere. A fair guess is that half the 120,000 visas that will be granted to Latin Americans in the year after July 1 will be granted to prospective sleep-in maids.

OVER 17,000 THIS YEAR

In the 1965 fiscal year—from July 1, 1964, to June 30, 1965—which was the last full year under the old rules of immigration, 1,685 Jamaicans emigrated to the United States. In 1967, the number was 11,204 and this year it will be something in excess of 17,000.

The majority of these immigrants are here as domestics. Last March, for example, 1,504 United States visas were issued in Jamaica. Of these, only 358 were assigned to persons who would join relatives here. The others were given to those who had jobs awaiting them in the United States, which meant that most of them were domestics.

Although there is some grumbling about this in the Labor Department, few persons connected with immigration appear to be greatly concerned about it. There is concern, however, that the laws governing the immigration of sleep-ins are flagrantly violated.

For one thing, the Labor Department says that a new immigrant working in the metropolitan area as a sleep-in maid must be paid $66 a week. A random check found few housewives paying that much.

For another, entrepreneurs are openly peddling the services of women who are here on visitors' visas in the classified advertising sections. In New York, these operators are said to include a Harlem chauffeur, a former employe of the immigration service and a lawyer whose wife runs an employment agency.

Then, too, immigration authorities complain, a considerable number of women emigrate legally to work here as sleep-in maids and then simply disappear or quit their maid's jobs in search of other work. There are no legal restraints to prevent this.

There seems to be little consensus in immigration circles on how to resolve the problem of the sleep-ins. A Senate source said that eventually a solution would be found through administrative rather than legislative measures.

Welles C. Klein, the director of the American Branch of International Social Service, a worldwide social agency, suggested that pre-migration counseling in foreign countries would help to steer the sleep-in maids away from unscrupulous operators and better equip them for American life.

This, however, would cost money. In Jamaica alone, he said, the cost of setting up a training program would be about $150,000 over three years.

"Getting a visa to this country is like getting ready to go heaven," said Victoria, who is a Seventh-day Adventist. "But then some of the things that happen to you, oh, it is so discouraging."

9 Educational Problems and Conflicts

With hundreds of publications on educational problems appearing each month, the task of making a few selections is a sobering one. Merely to list some of the problem areas is impressive: school finance and the growing taxpayer revolt against school taxes, controversy over tax support for parochial schools, school desegregation conflicts, failure of schools to educate children of the poor, the issue of "neighborhood control," student protests, curriculum controversies, and many others.

For this chapter, we have selected items on school organization, job training, and student protests. In the first of these, Vanfossen challenges a number of educational sacred cows by proposing a national public school system.

QUALITY EDUCATION IN AMERICA:

Why not?

Marion G. Vanfossen
Associate Professor of Sociology
College of William and Mary

Few would disagree that the American public school system is somehow not fulfilling well its primary function of education. The list of specific complaints, both those empirically demonstrated and others more broadly sensed in books, articles, and even art forms, is extensive and sufficiently familiar not to require repetition here. The flavor of the list, however, is quite consistent: it emphasizes incompetency and inadequacy. Incompetent students, teachers, administrators, and organization; inadequate funds, facilities, structure, and purpose. On one level, perhaps no one is more directly aware of the shortcomings of public education than the teachers and administrators themselves. After all, they live with it, day

Paper delivered before Southern Sociological Society, New Orleans, April 10, 1969. Used by permission.

in and day out. The conscientious ones are frustrated and either leave the profession or come to settle for a modicum of order and operationally defined success (they graduate students). Since these well-intentioned people are not in a position to effect structural changes, tenure seems to generate resignation or indifference.

There is, however, no *crisis in our schools*. This myth has been widely perpetrated for at least the last decade, and as all myths, generally serves to shield its subject from detailed and prosaic analysis. For there to be a crisis someone beyond a handful of teachers and powerless intellectuals would have to be seriously concerned about the state of affairs, regardless of how generally recognized and conventionally lamented that state may be.[1] We might, in fact, be better off if there were one generalized overall crisis. At least it would demand attention, and perhaps ultimately the type of concern out of which some realistic national prognosis could emerge. The eruption of long-festering urban problems and the intensified struggle for civil rights, especially of the Negro, has recently focused some public attention on the school system which at least in some ways and in some communities has been approaching a crisis situation. For the most part, however, this public attention has not been on our nation's school system per se but upon specific attempts of the Negro and other disenfranchised sectors of our population to participate more fully in the system more or less as is. Such attempts have and will produce some changes; however, I can not agree with those who upon reviewing present societal trends give the optimistic impression that structural lags and inconsistencies will produce desirable changes which "have a kind of dynamic of their own," independent of decision making, and which will lead inevitably to sound educational policy. On the basis of present trends, one could more readily assume and amass evidence supporting the proposition that the system will continue to fall even further behind our society's increasing need for a well-educated populace. . . .

I am convinced that should we ever become serious about education in American society, something approaching the following proposals would have to be accomplished.

First, we would have to have a *coordinated and integrated nationwide system of public education, centrally administered*. The arguments for such a system are numerous and obvious to anyone familiar with the trends of modern society.[2] The most immediate is that it would allow a more equitable distribution of educational resources. The quality of the present

---

[1] As early as 1950 the write-up of a Roper Survey which found that most people were dissatisfied with their local school concluded that "when Americans think about education, they are complacent as a whole and dissatisfied in particular." "What U.S. Thinks About Its Schools," *Life,* October 16, 1950.

[2] For one of the most persuasive arguments for such a system see James B. Conant, *The American High School Today* (New York: McGraw-Hill, 1959).

system is not uniformly low, it is much poorer in some areas than in others for all kinds of social and economic reasons.[3] Our single constancy is the educability of our youth regardless of region, race, or local resources, and it is that given constancy (and no other) to which our school system should conform. The high and increasing rate of horizontal mobility necessitates an ease of movement from school to school without loss of time or normal progression and without abrupt shifts in quality and content of subject matter. Our increasing specialization in all areas of the division of labor requires a coordinated and diversified system to supply the changing demand. And finally, we simply need a system through which our rapidly expanding knowledge in all realms can be disseminated to our youth as effectively and efficiently as possible.

Perhaps more significant at this point than a full elaboration of the reasons why such a system is necessary are the arguments which are usually marshalled against it. Besides the practical aspects of organization and coordination which such a proposal would entail (and incidentally, which we have demonstrated in spheres of real value, such as the economic, that we do have the knowledge and resources to accomplish), there are three immediate and related ideological objections to this basic proposal which arise as far more significant than the organizational ones. The first, not to be lightly dismissed, is that this proposal smacks of extending governmental control of education. The second is that it would foster conformity, standardization, and even regimentation. The third is that it would take what our children are taught out from under the control of the local community and place it in the hands of some distant inhuman bureaucracy, thus wrenching away what some may consider the last clear guardian of freedom the local citizen has.

The tendency of many writers who have supported some form of centrally administered system has been to ignore or impatiently dismiss these objections either as conservative backwardness or as emphasizing other values to the disadvantage of education, thus in a sense granting the legitimacy of the objections, at least on their own terms. I should like to take a somewhat different approach and (1) where an objection would seem to have some validity, attempt to offer some reasonable alternative to in effect saying "don't have those values," and (2) try to meet the objection head on where it is logically suspect. First, the fear that such a system would extend *governmental* control. I would contend that a system could be instituted which would actually reduce the likelihood of governmental interference and control as many people imagine and fear it. Anyone who believes that government's role in education is not rapidly increasing under the present system is simply unaware of the facts. It is increasing at all levels, but I think we can assume that it is the federal government which

[3] See National Education Association, *Ranking of the States,* issued annually (Washington: National Education Association).

is seen as the major nemesis.[4] An oft-heard sentiment is that "with the purse strings goes control," and there is certainly some evidence that this has been true of the present arrangement.[5] There is no logical or structural reason, however, why a national system of public education would have to be an appendage of the federal government. There is an operational alternative to the either/or federal-private dichotomy which we implicitly tend to think in terms of. This would be a system independently controlled and administered by a body of the nation's most revered scholars, scientists and educators, representative of major disciplinary areas. Though they would need the counsel of urban planners, teachers, politicians, and community leaders at all levels of our society, their judgment would not be subject to direct governmental influence except, as is also true of any private corporation, that they would be subject to the laws of the land. This system would thus be private in the sense of control but financed through public funds. If one combines what the federal government now spends for public education with the total spent by state and local sources, the money is already available to support a coordinated and efficient centrally administered system at a much higher level of effectiveness than we now have. The problem is thus not so much the cost of such a system as it is one of getting the funds into and out of the national treasury with no strings attached, and providing for the increments which would be necessary as both the quality of education and the general needs of the society expanded. To accomplish this, some kind of sliding formula would have to be worked out, and would have to be protected by law from infringement. Such a system would certainly not be completely free of the pressures of the federal government, neither however is any private corporation. There are several operational ways in which the top personnel could come to occupy their positions, but the actual procedure arrived at would probably not be as important as the criteria for eligibility for consideration. Their number should be kept relatively small, perhaps ten or twelve, their tenure should be of some duration, and once established, they should probably be a self-perpetuating body, selecting from among the most outstanding men in each area as the present man in that area retires, resigns, or is rotated out. Such a procedure would avoid some of the problems inherent in political appointment or regional election; nevertheless, the standards for eligibility for consideration should probably be incorporated into law to guarantee that demonstrated excellence in science or scholarship be the essential criterion, thus minimizing the possibility of the body becoming packed or

[4] Whether or not people in a democratic society *should* fear their government, particularly when it has become the most staunch defender of their private rights and public welfare, is not at issue. The fact is that many seem to.

[5] Though one may support governmental involvement in the system as it now operates, as for example the tactic of withholding federal funds to enforce desegregation laws, the point being pursued here is that a centralized national system *without* direct governmental control *is* possible.

weighted in terms of other considerations. Some form of public impeach-
ment potential might even be built into the procedure such as now exists
in regard to political offices.

Though to visualize such a system as I have just indicated may only
move the basis of opposition from what I listed above as the first to the
third category of objection, the point to be made here is that regardless
of what other problems might be invited, it is possible to conceive of a
centrally administered system of national public education without the
nemesis of big government, an objection beyond which the discussion
seldom proceeds. A further point, which should at least be mentioned, is
that such a coordinated national system could much better withstand unwanted pressures from any source than can the present isolated local
school boards.

The second objection is that such a system would increase conformity
and standardization. There are several things wrong with this objection.
The most obvious is that it assumes that the present system does not do
this very much. However, it might be argued that one of the most significant functions of the present system as it actually operates is the in-
doctrination of local standards. Neither students nor teachers are now free
of conformity or standardization, only to have these *forced upon them* by
a national system. The question is much more one of what standards are
going to be conformed to, ones that more nearly represent a specific region
and community or ones which reflect a broader perspective. The people
who offer this objection do not really seem to be against conformity in our
schools so long as it is local conformity. Were they against conformity
per se, they should in fact be in support of some form of national educational system, since there is no question that such a system would expand
what Lazarsfeld and Thielens have termed the "effective scope" of many
students.[6]

Standardization is an equally slippery term with several meanings.
Offered as an objection to a national system of education, it seems to bring
forth a picture of students all following an identical curriculum administered
in a highly regimented style with overtones of brown-shirted Nazi youth.
Such fantasies obfuscate the unavoidable fact that any operating system
must by definition have reasonably stable and integrated organization.
That there be some standardization, some consistency in both the quality
and broad range of courses which make up the various possible curricula,
is of course at the heart of trying to improve American education. With an
increasingly mobile population, we sorely need this. But it would be a
standardization that would enable a wider range of subjects and programs
(of higher quality) to be offered than all except perhaps a few of the
more wealthy suburban schools could now even attempt. The children of

[6] Paul Lazarsfeld and Wagner Thielens, Jr., *The Academic Mind* (Glencoe: The
Free Press, 1958).

both the northern urban ghetto and the small rural village in South Carolina are presently subject to both conformity and standardization, and very little else at least in the way of quality education. Once again, it would seem that this objection actually reduces to the third and perhaps most meaningful one, that such a system would take the control of what and how the children are taught away from the local community and place it in the hands of a distant bureaucracy.

This, finally, is the only valid objection. Such a system *would* take the schools out from under local control. However, the simple fact is that the local community does not and can not educate its youth to the demands of modern society. If local citizens continue to be willing to sacrifice their children as well as the nation's future to the principle of keeping control of a job they can not do, then we are all in serious trouble that will become worse as the incompetency and inefficiency of local education increases in the face of our society's exploding need for knowledge and reality judgments at all levels in all spheres. Local school boards are made up of local citizens, predominantly small businessmen, who run the nation's schools in their spare time and who know nothing about education and very little about the complexities of modern society. We are stuck with a system which emerged in frontier America as an alternative to no schools at all. Even if we could somehow finance education locally, we can not administer it locally. We are no longer a vast continent of isolated communities in which son replaces father in the scheme of things needing only the most rudimentary skills and local folklore.

Yet, even admitting their community's inability to do the job satisfactorily, many people conceive of the local control of the public schools as the last clear hope of guaranteeing a legacy of freedom to their children. This is the most curious stance of all. "As a citizen I shall guarantee my child's right to freedom by sacrificing his right to education." If freedom were thus so easily won, it might be worth it. But like it or not, freedom is less and less an individual matter (if it ever were) and more and more a collective one. The chance for freedom resides not so much in the implantation of vague local values supporting it as in the possibility of perpetuating and developing a social structure into which the concept is built as the very fabric of its materials. The creation of a free and democratic society is a gargantuan task which our faltering efforts this far well illustrate. It is a task which requires knowledge, not ignorance. It is a task which will require the very best education we can provide for all our children.

All remaining proposals follow the primary one of a centralized system of public education, and in themselves, should raise only the objections of specific vested interests. The second proposal is that *major alterations be effected in our college and university schools and departments of educa-*

tion, and that a new set of criteria emphasizing competence in subject matter areas replace the long list of dreary and essentially useless education courses now required for certification. Though some training in educational techniques, especially for elementary school teachers, may be justifiable, the absence of adequate training in subject matter is not. Neither is the low level of quality of the profession generally. Education departments are almost always among the largest and poorest departments on any campus. They have the worst students, they spread a very thin content over a proliferation of courses, and ironic as it may seem, there is no evidence that education professors are any better teachers than other college professors, though most of the latter have never had an education course. Our continuing toleration of this condition reflects two things. One is the general lack of importance given to public education in American society. The other is the rather impressive success, in the face of this indifference, which the educationists have had in tying up not just the training of teachers but the pacing of the whole system in their drive to professionalize and buttress their own and the teacher's status.

The third proposal is that *the concept of public education be expanded to include a wide variety of different types of schools* ranging from those which are completely college preparatory to those which are engaged in specialized job training. Movement in either direction between adjacent schools on such a continuum should be made as effortless and automatic as possible for the student who wants to and is able. However, all students would begin a program which could lead to college preparation. But no student would flunk out or be retained as a vegetable until he reached the legal age to quit. With all students starting relatively even, the college preparatory program could be mildly rigorous. Those who could not or would not wish to continue in that direction would be transferred, ordinarily to the next adjacent school. The last school on the continuum should be, in effect, compulsory on-the-job training for learning some line of work.[7] The object of such a system is of course that all be trained at the highest level of their ability and motivation. That the continuum of schools is not a completely horizontal one insofar as social status is concerned would be obvious without any needed attempts to make it so. This is desirable however if student scholarship is ever to become revered in American society. Our present technical schools are generally less prestigious than more academic institutions without apparent dire effect or challenge to the concept of equality, and the present system neither gives all an even

[7] This may be far removed from our usual idea of "school." However, such a program would be invaluable to the many young and not so young people who now lounge about on the corners of our urban slums, unprepared for even the most unskilled employment. See Elliot Liebow *Talley's Corner,* Boston: Little, Brown and Company, 1967, especially Chapter II, "Men and Jobs."

chance nor allows much flexibility of moving from more technical training back into the more academic.

The fourth proposal is that *the gap between high school and college be more effectively bridged*. This is essentially an organizational and financial problem. With a centrally administered program of public education, it should not be difficult to institute a central clearing house to provide ready, accurate, evaluative information on the nation's colleges. Every student who graduates from the college preparatory schools, and many who graduate from schools further down the continuum, should be encouraged (it should be the public expectation) to go on to college, and provided with the funds to do so. Probably the most effective way to do this, at least initially, would be with an automatic and very liberal payback system for those who can not afford any or all of the costs of their higher education.

The problems involved in gaining public support for the establishment of such a system of education as I have proposed are momentous. At the same time it seems clear to me that the increasing random dissatisfaction with our present public school system, and the growing awareness of the importance of substantive and honest education for the maintenance and perpetuation of a democratic society, will soon focus in a general public groping for another way. I propose a nationwide system, supported by public funds and administered by a body of independent professional scholars, a reorientation in our colleges and universities to training teachers in subject matter areas and adjusting certification accordingly, a greater range and number of types of schools from college preparatory to job-training with flexibility of movement among them, and a closer, easier step from high school to college with financial assistance to those who can not afford college on their own. In terms of the inadequacy and incompetency of the present system, and the perhaps irrecoupable loss resulting from its long tenure, I do not feel these to be either radical or unrealistic proposals.

Many people are unemployed or underemployed because they are uneducated. There are exceedingly few jobs which can be filled satisfactorily by a worker who cannot read, write, and do simple arithmetic. But it has recently been noted that far greater educational requirements or far more exacting qualifying examinations are specified for many jobs than are actually required. Many who could do the work satisfactorily are thus excluded and the jobs are filled by workers who are overeducated for the jobs they hold. This situation and its consequences are discussed in the following article.

RICH MAN'S QUALIFICATIONS
FOR POOR MAN'S JOBS

Ivar Berg
Professor of Sociology
Graduate School of Business
Columbia University

It is now a well-known fact that America offers more and more jobs to skilled workers while the increase in unskilled jobs has slowed down. Newspaper articles regularly remind us that we have a shortage of computer programmers, and, at the same time, too many unskilled laborers. The conventional solution is to correct the shortcomings of the labor force by educating more of the unemployed. Apart from its practical difficulties, this solution begs the important question: Are academic credentials important for *doing* the job—or just for *getting* it?

My studies of manpower use indicate that although in recent years requirements for many jobs have been upgraded because of technological and other changes, in many cases education requirements have been raised arbitrarily. In short, *many employers demand too much education for the jobs they offer.*

Education has become the most popular solution to America's social and economic ills. Our faith in education as *the* cure for unemployment partly reflects our inclination as a society to diagnose problems in individualistic terms. Both current and classical economic theories merely reinforce these attitudes; both assume that the labor supply can be significantly changed by investments in education and health. Meanwhile private employers, on the other side of the law of supply and demand, are held to be merely reacting to the imperatives that generate the need for better educated manpower.

Certainly the government cannot force private employers to hire people who have limited educations. Throughout our history and supported by our economic theory, we have limited the government's power to deal with private employers. According to law and the sentiments that support it, the rights of property owners and the protection of their property are essential

From *TRANS-action*, March 1969, pp. 45–50. Copyright © by TRANS-action Magazine, New Brunswick, New Jersey. Reprinted by permission.

functions of government, and cannot or should not be tampered with. In received economic doctrine, business stands apart as an independent variable. As such, business activity controls the demand for labor, and the best way the government has to reduce unemployment is by stimulating business growth.

Some of the methods the government uses to do this are direct subsidies, depreciation allowances, zoning regulations, fair-trade laws, tax holidays, and credit guarantees. In return for these benefits, governments at all levels ultimtely expect more jobs will be generated and more people employed. But when the market for labor does not work out according to theory, when employer demand does not increase to match the number of job seekers, attention shifts to the supply of labor. The educational, emotional, social, and even moral shortcomings of those who stand outside the boundaries of the social system have to be eliminated, we are told—and education seems to be the best way of doing it.

Unfortunately, economists and public planners usually assume that the education that employers require for the jobs they offer is altogether beneficial to the firm. Higher education, it is thought, means better performance on the job. A close look at the data, however, shows that here reality does not usually correspond with theory.

In recent years, the number of higher-level jobs has not increased as much as personnel directors lead us to believe. The big increase, rather, has been in middle-level jobs—for high-school graduates and college dropouts. This becomes clear when the percentages of jobs requiring the three different levels of education are compared with the percentages of the labor force that roughly match these categories. The comparison of census data with the U.S. Employment Service's descriptions of 4,000 different jobs also shows that (1) high-education jobs have expanded somewhat faster for men than for women; (2) those jobs in the middle have expanded faster for women than for men; and (3) that highly educated people are employed in jobs that require *less* education than these people actually have.

The fact is that our highly educated people are competing with lesser educated people for the jobs in the middle. In Monroe County, N.Y. (which includes Buffalo), the National Industrial Conference Board has graphically demonstrated this fact. Educational requirements for most jobs, the board has reported, vary with the academic calendar: Thus, requirements rise as the end of the school year approaches and new graduates flood the market. Employers whose job openings fall in the middle category believe that by employing people with higher-than-necessary educations they are benefiting from the increasing educational achievements of the work force. Yet the data suggest that there is a "shortage" of high-school graduates and of people with post high school educations short of college degrees while there is a "surplus" of college graduates, especially females.

The economic and sociological theories that pour out of university computers have given more and more support to the idea that we, as a society, have more options in dealing with the supply side of employment —with the characteristics of the work force—than with demand.

These studies try to relate education to higher salaries; they assume that the income a person earns is a valid measure of his job performance. The salaries of better-educated people, however, may not be closely related to the work they do. Female college graduates are often employed as secretaries; many teachers and social workers earn less than plumbers and others who belong to effective unions. What these rate-of-return studies lack is productivity data isolated according to job and the specific person performing the job.

In any event, it is circular reasoning to relate wage and salary data to educational achievements. Education is often, after all, the most important criterion for a person's getting a job in the first place! The argument that salaries may be used to measure the value of education and to measure the "value added" to the firm by employees of different educational backgrounds, may simply confirm what it sets out to prove. In jobs for which educational requirements have not been thoughtfully studied, the argument is not an argument at all, but a self-fulfilling prophecy.

Despite the many attempts to relate a person's achievements to the wages he receives, researchers usually find that the traits, aptitudes, and educational achievements of workers vary as greatly *within* job categories as they do *between* them. That is, people in job A differ as much from one another as they differ from people in job B. Only a small percentage of the labor force—those in the highest and those in the lowest job levels— are exceptions. And once workers become members of the labor force, personal virtues at even the lower job levels do not account for wage differences—intelligent, well-educated, low-level workers don't necessarily earn more than others at the bottom of the ladder. Marcia Freedman's study of employment patterns for Columbia's Conservation of Human Resources project indicates that, although many rungs of the organizational ladder are linked to differences in pay, these rungs are not closely related to differences in the employees' skills and training.

Educational requirements continue to go up, yet most employers have made no effort to find out whether people with better educations make better workers than people with inferior educations. Using data collected from private firms, the military, the federal civil service, and public-educational systems, and some collected from scratch, I have concentrated on this one basic question.

Business managers, supported by government leaders and academics interested in employment problems, have well-developed ideas about the value of a worker's educational achievement. They assert that with each increment of education—especially those associated with a certificate, diploma, or degree—the worker's attitude is better, his trainability is greater, his capacity for adaptation is more developed, and his prospects for promotions are rosier. At the same time, those workers with more modest educations, and especially those who drop out of school, are held to be less intelligent, less adaptable, less self-disciplined, less personable, and less articulate.

The findings in my studies do not support these assertions.

A comparison of 4,000 insurance agents in a major company in the Greater New York area showed that an employee's productivity—measured by the dollar value of the policies he sold—did not vary in any systematic way with his years of formal education. In other words, those salesmen with less education brought as much money into the company as their better educated peers. When an employee's experience was taken into account, it was clear that those with *less* education and *more* experience sold the most policies. Thus, even an employer whose success in business depends on the social and psychological intangibles of a customer-client relationship may not benefit from having highly educated employees. Other factors such as the influence of colleagues and family obligations were more significant in explaining the productivity of agents.

In another insurance agency, the job performances of 200 young female clerks were gauged from the number of merit-salary increases they had received. Researchers discovered that there were *no* differences in the performance records of these women that could easily be attributed to differences in their educational backgrounds. Once again, focusing on the educational achievements of job applicants actually diverted attention from characteristics that are really relevant to job performance.

At a major weekly news magazine, the variation in educational achievement among over 100 employees was greater than among the insurance clerks. The magazine hired female college graduates, as well as high-school graduates, for clerical-secretarial positions. While the employers argued that the girls needed their college degrees to qualify for future editorial jobs, most editorial positions were *not* filled by former secretaries, whether college graduates or not, but by college graduates who directly entered into those positions. And although the personnel director was skeptical of supervisors' evaluations of the secretaries, the supervisors determined the salary increases, and as many selective merit-pay increases were awarded to the lesser-educated secretaries as to the better-educated secretaries.

Executives of a large well-known chemical company in New York told me that the best technicians in their research laboratory were those with the highest educational achievement. Therefore, in screening job applicants, they gave greater weight to a person's educational background than to his other characteristics. Yet, statistical analysis of relevant data revealed that the rate of turnover in the firm was positively associated with the employees' educational achievement. And a close look at the "reasons for leaving" given by the departing technicians showed that they intended to continue their educations. Furthermore, lesser-educated technicians earned higher performance evaluations than did their better-educated peers. Understandably, the employer was shocked by these findings.

OVEREDUCATED ARE LESS PRODUCTIVE

The New York State Department of Labor's 1964 survey of employers suggests that technicians often possess educational achievements far beyond what employers themselves think is ideal for effective performance. Thousands of companies reported their minimal educational requirements to the Labor Department, along with their ideal requirements and the actual educators of the technicians they employed. In many industries and in respect to most types of technicians, the workers were better educated than they were required to be; in 10 out of 16 technical categories they were even better educated than their employers dared hope, exceeding the "ideal" requirements set down by the employers.

Upper- and middle-level employees are not the only ones who are overqualified for their jobs. Nor is the phenomenon only to be observed in metropolitan New York. In a study of eight Mississippi trouser plants, researchers found that the more education an employee had, the less productive she was. Several hundred female operators were paid by "piece work" and their wages therefore were a valid test of workers' productivity. Furthermore this study showed that educational achievement was positively associated with turnover: The better-educated employee was more likely to quit her job.

Education's negative relationship to jobs can be measured not only by the productivity and turnover of personnel, but also by worker satisfaction. It may be argued that dissatisfaction among workers leads to a desirable measure of labor mobility, but the funds a company spends to improve employee morale and make managerial personnel more sensitive to the needs of their subordinates strongly suggest that employers are aware of the harm caused by worker dissatisfaction. Roper Associates once took a representative sample of 3,000 blue-collar workers in 16 industries in all parts of the United States. Among workers in lower-skilled jobs, dissatisfaction was found to increase as their educational achievements increased.

These studies of private firms suggest that many better-educated workers are assigned to jobs requiring low skills and that among the results are high turnover rates, low productivity, and worker dissatisfaction. Nonetheless, the disadvantages of "overeducation" are best illustrated by employment practices of public-school systems.

EDUCATED TEACHERS OPT OUT

Many school districts, to encourage their teachers to be highly educated, base teachers' salaries upon the number of credits they earn toward
higher degrees. However, data from the National Opinion Research Center
and the National Science Foundation's 1962 study of 4,000 teachers show
that, like employees elsewhere, teachers become restless as their educational
achievements rise. Elementary and secondary school teachers who have
master's degrees are less likely to stay in their jobs than teachers with
bachelor's degrees. And in a similar study done by Columbia Teachers
College, it was evident that teachers with master's degrees were likely to
have held jobs in more than one school system.

Thus, for school systems to tie pay increases to extra credits seems
to be self-defeating. Teachers who earn extra credits apparently feel that
their educational achievements reach a point beyond which they are over-
trained for their jobs, and they then want to get administrative jobs or
leave education for better paying jobs in industry. The school districts are,
in a sense, encouraging teachers not to teach. This practice impedes the
upgrading of teacher qualifications in another way. Thanks to the extra-
credit system, schools of education have a steady supply of students and
therefore are under little pressure to furnish better and more relevant
courses.

For the most part, though, employers in the public sector do not
suffer from problems of unrealistic educational requirements. For a variety
of reasons, they do not enjoy favored positions in the labor market and
consequently have not been able to raise educational requirements nearly
so fast as the private employer has. But for this reason alone, the experiences of government agencies are significant. How well do their employees with low-education backgrounds perform their job?

The pressure on the armed forces to make do with "what they get"
has forced them to study their experiences with personnel. Their investigations clearly show that a person's educational achievement is not a good
clue to his performance. Indeed, general tests developed for technical, military classifications and aptitude tests designed to screen individual candidates for training programs have turned out to be far better indicators of
a person's performance.

In a 1948 study of Air Force personnel, high-school graduates were
compared with nongraduates in their performance on the Army Classification Tests and on 13 tests that later became part of the Airman Classification Battery. The military's conclusion: "High-school graduates were not
uniformly and markedly superior to nongraduates. . . . High-school grad-
uation, unless supplemented by other screening measures such as tests or

the careful review of the actual high-school record, does not insure that a basic trainee will be of high potential usefulness to the Air Force."

In 1963, the Air Force studied 4,458 graduates of eight technical courses. Comparing their performances in such courses as Reciprocating Engine Mechanic, Weather Observer, Accounting, and Finance Specialist with the education they received before entering the service, the Air Force found that a high-school diploma only modestly predicted the grades the airmen got in the Air Force courses. In other Air Force studies, aptitude tests were consistently found to correlate well with a person's proficiency and performance, while educational achievement rarely accounted for more than 4 percent of the variations.

These Air Force data do not conclude that education is unimportant, or that formal learning experiences are irrelevant. Rather, it points out the folly of confusing a man's driver's license with his driving ability. Just as different communities have different safety standards, so schools and school systems employ different kinds of teachers and practices. It should surprise no one that a person's credentials, by themselves, predict his performance so poorly.

Army and Navy studies confirm the Air Force findings. When 415 electronic technicians' scores on 17 concrete tasks were analyzed in conjunction with their age, pay grades, and education, education was found to be negatively associated with performance. When the Navy updated this study, the outcome was the same. For high performance in repairing complicated electronic testing equipment, experience proved more significant than formal education.

Perhaps the military's most impressive data came from its experiments with "salvage" programs, in which illiterates and men who earn low scores on military classification tests are given remedial training. According to research reports, these efforts have been uniformly successful—as many graduates of these programs develop into useful servicemen as the average, normal members of groups with which they have been regularly compared.

NAVAL MANPOWER SALVAGE

In a 1955 study done for the Navy, educational achievements were not found to be related to the performance of 1,370 recruits who attended "recruit preparatory training" courses. Neither were educational achievements related to the grades the recruits received from their company commanders and their instructors, nor to their success or failure in completing recruit training. In some instances, the low-scoring candidates with modest educational backgrounds performed at higher levels than better-educated men with high General Classification Test scores. The military recently expanded its "salvage" program with Project 100,000, and preliminary results tend to confirm the fact that training on the job is more important than educational credentials.

Military findings also parallel civilian studies of turnover rates. Reenlistment in the Navy is nearly twice as high among those men who have completed fewer than 12 years of school. But reenlistment in the military, of course, is related to the fact that the civilian economy does not particularly favor ex-servicemen who have modest educational achievements.

Wartime employment trends make the same point. During World War II, when demand for labor was high, both public and private employers adapted their recruiting and training to the labor supply. Productivity soared while a wide range of people mastered skills almost entirely without regard to their personal characteristics or previous circumstances. Labor's rapid adjustment on the job was considered surprising; after the war, it was also considered to be expensive. Labor costs, it was argued, had gone up during the war, and unit productivity figures were cited as evidence. These figures, however, may have been misleading. Since the majority of wartime laborers were employed in industries with "cost-plus" contracts—where the government agreed to reimburse the contractor for all costs, plus a certain percentage of profit—such arrangements may have reduced the employer's incentives to control costs. The important lesson from the war period seems to be that people quickly adjust to work requirements once they are on the job.

A 5 percent sample of 180,000 men in the federal civil service shows that while the number of promotions a person gets is associated with his years of education, the link is far from complete. Education has a greater bearing on a person's rank at *entry* into the civil service than on his prospects for a promotion. Except for grades 11–15, in accounting for the promotion rates of civil servants, length of service and age are far more significant than education. A closer look at one government agency will perhaps clarify these points.

Few organizations in the United States have had to adapt to major technological changes as much as the Federal Aviation Agency has. Responsible among other things for the direction and control of all flights in the United States, it operates the control-tower facilities at all public airports. With the advent of jet-powered flights, the FAA had to handle very quickly the horrendous technical problems posed by faster aircraft and more flights. Since no civilian employer requires the services needed by the FAA in this area, the agency must train its own technicians and control-tower people. The agency inventively confronted the challenge by hiring and training many new people and promoting those trained personnel it already had. Working with the background data on 507 men—all the air-traffic controllers who had attained grade 14 or above—it would seem that, at this high level, education would surely prove its worth.

ON-THE-JOB TRAINING FOR TOWER CONTROLLERS

Yet in fact these men had received very little formal education, and almost no technical managerial training except for the rigorous on-the-job training given by the FAA itself. Of the 507 men in the sample, 211, or 42 percent, had no education or training beyond high school. An additional 48, or 10 percent, were high-school graduates who had had executive-training courses. Thus, more than half of the men had had no academic training beyond high school. There were, however, no patterns in the differences among the men in grades 13 or 15 with respect to education. That is, education and training were *not* related to the higher grade.

The FAA's amazing safety record and the honors and awards given to the tower controllers are good indicators of the men's performance. The FAA's Executive Selection and Inventory System records 21 different kinds of honors or awards. Only one-third of the men have never received any award at all. Half of the 77 percent who have been honored have been honored more than once. And a relatively high percentage of those with no education beyond high school received four or more awards; those with a BA degree were least likely to receive these many honors. Other breakdowns of the data confirm that education is not a factor in the daily performance of one of the truly demanding decision-making jobs in America.

The findings reported in these pages raise serious questions about the usefulness of raising educational requirements for jobs. They suggest that the use of formal education as a sovereign screening device for jobs adequately performed by people of lower educational achievements may result in serious costs—high turnover, employee dissatisfactions, and poorer performance. Programs calculated to improve employees' educations probably aim at the wrong targets, while programs calculated to reward better-educated people are likely to miss their targets. It would be more useful to aim at employers' policies and practices that block organizational mobility and seal off entry jobs.

THERE ARE MORE OPENINGS IN THE MIDDLE

Given the facts that there are more job openings in the middle, and that many people are overqualified for the jobs they do have, policies aimed at upgrading the educational achievements of the low-income population seem at best naïve. It would make better sense to upgrade people in the middle to higher jobs and upgrade those in lower-level jobs to middle positions, providing each group with an education appropriate to their age, needs, and ambitions. The competition for lower-level jobs would then be reduced, and large numbers of dropouts could move into them. (Only after young people, accustomed to a good income, develop middle-class aspirations are they apparently interested in pursuing the balance of their educations.) Current attempts to upgrade the labor supply also seem questionable in light of what psychologists and sociologists have to say. Changing people's attitudes, self-images, and achievements is either enormously time-consuming—sometimes requiring half a generation—or it is impossible. At any rate, it is always risky.

If the much-maligned attitudes of low-income Americans were changed without establishing a full-employment economy, we might simply be adding fuel to the smoldering hatreds of the more ambitious, more frustrated groups in our urban ghettos. And if we wish to do something about the supposed shortcomings in the low-income Negro families, it will clearly require changes in those welfare arrangements that now contribute to family dissolution. The point is that rather than concentrate on the supply of labor, we must reconsider our reluctance to alter the *demand* for labor. We must have more realistic employment requirements.

Unfortunately, attempts to change people through education have been supported by liberal intellectuals who place great value upon education and look appreciatively upon the economic benefits accruing to better-educated Americans. Indeed, one of the few elements of consensus in present-day American politics may well be the reduction of the gap between the conservative and liberal estimate of the worth of education.

Obviously, the myths perpetuated about society's need for highly educated citizens work to the disadvantage of less-educated people, particularly nonwhites who are handicapped whatever the state of the economy. Information obtained by economist Dale Hiestand of Columbia does not increase one's confidence that educational programs designed to help disadvantaged people over 14 years old will prove dramatically beneficial. Hiestand's studies show that even though the best-educated nonwhites tend to have more job mobility, they are more likely to enter occupations that are *vacated* by whites than to compete with whites for *new* jobs. Since the competition for middle-education jobs is already very intense, it will be difficult to leapfrog Negroes into jobs not yet vacated by whites, or into new jobs that whites are likely to monopolize.

Now, nothing in the foregoing analysis should be construed as suggesting that education is a waste of time. Many jobs, as was stated at the outset, have changed, and the need for education undoubtedly grows quite aside from the monetary benefits individuals derive from their educations. But I think it is fundamentally subversive of education and of democratic values not to see that, in relation to jobs, education has its limits.

As the burden of evidence in this article suggests, the crucial employment issue is not the "quality of the work force." It is the overall level of employment and the demand for labor in a less than full-employment economy.

> Once upon a time there was an ivory tower: a calm, secluded retreat where attentive students sat respectfully at the feet of learned scholars who gravely introduced them to the wisdom of the ages—supposedly. *Actually,* the university has often been a scene of raucous clamor and riotous disorder. Student protest is nothing new. Among student protest leaders of not too long ago were Chief Justice Charles Evans Hughes, President Calvin Coolidge, and Governor Ronald Reagan. There is, however, one important difference between the protesting students of some decades ago and protesting students today. The earlier students were alienated from their university administrations but were not alienated from their society. They sought to bring antiquated administrations into step with the rest of the society but were not attacking the university as a means of attacking the social system. The more extreme student protest leaders of today are at war not only with their university administrators but with the entire social and cultural system which the university serves.
>
> In the following essay, a university vice president discusses the roots of student protest and makes some suggestions.

TOWARD A STUDENT-FACULTY CONFRONTATION

Steven Muller
Vice President for Public Affairs
Cornell University

There is a good deal of talk these days about student power, but the truly striking fact on the American university scene is the total absence of student power in the context we have sketched here. Of late, students have been allowed increasing authority over their own affairs, but unhappily this

From "Thoughts on University Government," address before seminar on higher education at Cornell University, Summer, 1968. Reprinted by permission of the author.

is not as healthy and progressive a development as it sounds. To some extent the growing willingness to let students make their own rules and live by them does indeed reflect the view that they are young adults entitled to their own dignity and democracy as citizens of the university community. To at least an equally large extent, however, this willingness also reflects a destructive or patronizing indifference on the part of the faculty. The corollary of the axiom that published research comes first is that students— especially undergraduates—are a necessary nuisance. . . .

This is comprehensible. What is astonishing is that students play no role whatsoever in the selection of their professors or in the determination of curricula in most of American higher education. The justification is easy and venerable, but not necessarily convincing. Students are, so runs the accepted doctrine, incapable of valid judgment in these matters. First, because they are too young, too impressionable, too ignorant, too unstable, and too lazy. In other words, they can't be trusted. They are apt to confuse entertaining popularization with sound instruction; to seek the easiest way rather than the tough challenge; they want to be trained but they do not yet know the subject in which they are being trained, so they are the last to know whether they are being trained well or not; they respond to the dramatic rather than to necessary drudgery; they are not mature of purpose —look at the way they change their majors and how much trouble they have defining themselves; their tastes are those of children at play—look at their parties and their football games. This type of thinking implies a contempt for undergraduates which can only be labelled insulting. Were it true, one would ask whether students are worth teaching at all—by the way, a question sometimes explicitly asked by faculty. The doctrine is not persuasive because most undergraduates at major universities today are in fact noticeably mature, earnest, hard-working, ambitious, and sophisticated. Their judgments about their instructors and the instruction they receive generally are acute, informed, and sound.

The second kind of reasoning that discounts the validity of student judgment in academic matters simply asserts the fact that they are short-term transients. By the time they know anything they are on their way out. They care only about themselves, and are not interested in making long-range decisions that affect only their successors. Their rapid transit prevents establishment of continuity from their participation in decision-making because there is no provision for memory. What any one class may learn each new class has to learn again, and agreements with any one class not only fail to bind succeeding classes but are not even known to them. Their useful academic life-span is so short that they are unable to tackle really significant problems that cannot be resolved in weeks but demand months or even years. Furthermore, the faculty thinks about these matters during the summers, when students are not around. This set of considerations contains much truth, but it, too, is not wholly persuasive.

For one thing, faculty commitment often lasts no longer than a student's four undergraduate years; often short-term department members make vital decisions on academic matters. In today's world, students easily could be around during the summer if anyone really wanted them. The lack of continuity is a most serious problem and probably does disqualify students from some decisions, but not all of them. As for the length of time given over to consideration of crucial matters, this is more of a vice than a virtue. It could well be argued that academic renovation would prosper more if decisions had to be taken rapidly before the student participants graduated, than if they continued to be carried on at the current comfortable snail's pace.

In any event, it is true that students have no power in the academic establishment. And in contemporary American higher education the consequences are devastating. The quality of undergraduate instruction has declined severely. This is a factor not only of who still teaches, but also of what is taught. Undergraduate curricula in universities presently suffer from three distortions. First, undergraduate instruction in the hands of a research-oriented faculty has become increasingly pre-professional, even in the liberal arts. With some justification, undergraduates are viewed as pre-graduate students and are taught as such. Variety and a sense of fullness are sacrificed for an ever-larger dose of intensive, specialized, professional preparation. Second, the undergraduate departmental curriculum is frequently a composite compromise with the research interests of the faculty. Professors who do teach undergraduates teach their specialty, often almost as narrowly as they do in their graduate seminars. The total discipline as presented to undergraduate majors is therefore distorted in favor of the tastes of the resident faculty—what no one wants to teach is sometimes simply not offered. Third, the relevance of undergraduate courses to the world's and society's problems is not usually a major consideration in the determination of curricula. The stress is, legitimately, on fundamentals, on theory, on technique, and on the abstract. The effort to link this vital knowledge to reality is very frequently omitted altogether, on the assumption either that this little task is the student's very own to accomplish or that the linkage will be made later, most often only at the stage of professional practice. Seen in these terms, undergraduate students at American universities are a disenfranchised proletariat in the fullest sense in which Marx used this ugly word, alienated in the very process of their education both from the world they live in and their mentors on the faculty.

An alienated proletariat is ripe for revolution, and today one speaks not of potential, but actual, revolt. No longer content with the bread and circuses of improved student housing, intercollegiate athletics and more liberal parietal rules, American university undergraduates are already rebels, but confused as to their cause. They have begun to move in two directions: the first, in search of relevance, has largely led them off the campus. Feeling their campus life to be sterile and isolated from the real problems of society, they have plunged into civil rights and lately a growing range of social and political problems. Understandably they have also begun to drag these problems back to the campus as a means of pushing the universities into a meaningful relationship with society. The second direction has led them into assaults on the central administration of their universities. Here, after all, is management, and an alienated mass, conscious of a pervasive discontent, finds management an obvious and irresistible target. The confrontations between student rebels and administrators produce a dismaying paradox: students vent their unformed grievances; administrators either throw them out, dismiss them, or try to understand; when the latter stage is reached, administrators explain that they are really not the ones who can solve most of these problems; student rebels regard this as buck-passing or getting the old runaround and become angrier; administrators, who are pressed by alumni and faculty and everyone else to keep the students in line, become more intransigent. Then, in a marvelous blend of a-plague-on-both-your-houses and holier-than-thou, the faculty stirs itself to mediate. If it has occurred to students that their real grievances are with the faculty—and there are few signs of such awareness—the thought has been put aside because the faculty is too massive, diffuse and dangerous a target.

To say all this is not to condone the various forms of student rebellion that have occurred. Too often the leadership has been in the hands of malevolent extremists; too often the grievances specifically put forward have been absurd rather than profound; too often the behavior has been that of a mob at its worst. It is necessary to recognize that these minority outbreaks are symptoms of a deeper discontent of far greater significance. They erupt repeatedly because a large majority of all undergraduates are at least willing to tolerate these excesses. They constitute a warning to those who are waiting hopefully for the great mass of undergraduates to assert their basic loyalty to their universities. An alienated proletariat is not likely to rise to the defense of its exploiters, and the total impact of the flight from teaching in the American universities of the post-World War II era clearly represents the exploitation of undergraduates who spend more and more of their time and money for less and less specific attention to their problems. American university faculties as a whole bear a heavy burden of guilt for their growing neglect of their undergraduate students. It is no accident that the most virulent student rebellions of the recent past have occurred at such urban universities as Berkeley, Columbia and San Francisco State, where faculty relationships with students are attenuated not only by faculty preoccupation with research but also by the fact that professors tend to be away from the campus except for classes and fixed appointments, commuting from homes randomly scattered over enormous urban areas.

Finally, to say all this is also to reach a conclusion: that central university administrations, concerned about the university as a community, and students, concerned with reasserting the importance of their own undergraduate education in all its significance, each have more reason to make common cause than to indulge in fundamentally pointless confrontations.

This conclusion must be put, not in rhetorical terms, but in the context of constitutional revision in the government of American universities. The purpose is to redress the internal balance of the university community by the application of student power as a countervailing force to faculty pressures that central university management has found itself unable to govern. The means is an internal political reorganization to link students directly to the critical decision-making bodies within the faculty, namely the disciplinary departments, at least to a point that would institutionalize a continuing dialogue between faculty and students about the teaching process. For this purpose, each group of undergraduate departmental majors—at most institutions these would be sophomores, juniors, and seniors—would constitute an identifiable constituency. Small departments with a small group of undergraduate majors could then practice a form of direct democracy simply by scheduling regular meetings at which faculty and students meet together to review the departmental program and to discuss change. In most cases, however, the departmental student constituency will be so large as to require a representative system. One could carry such a scheme one step farther and conceive of the whole group of departmental student councils within a single school or college as a college council, which could in turn elect representatives to meet regularly with the Dean and faculty committees of the college as a whole. And of course the ultimate step would be the composition of a university-wide student academic senate, consisting of all of the student college representatives. Such a senate could meet both with committees of the university faculty, and with central administrators directly concerned with university academic affairs.

The scheme is sufficiently simple so that it might be worth trying without a preliminary effort to work out all the niceties of detail, crucial as they will prove to be. For instance, there might be endless discussion of whether students should have the right to vote on curricular matters and on academic appointments, but practice might well indicate that the question will never be explicitly raised because the process of regular discussion with students would create a climate of mutual understanding and sympathy. This is the type of question best resolved only when actual issues arise. . . .

Certainly experiments in this direction would have the advantage of lending more substance to student government. Student self-government over extracurricular affairs would continue, but the addition of a new academic ingredient would require the creation of a second system of student political organization. The way would be open to a wider application of student interest and talents to internal university affairs. At a number of universities, the president and some of his fellow administrators now meet regularly with a group of student leaders, but the range of topics at such meetings normally does not include academic matters. Meetings of this type with a student academic senate, and including faculty as well as administration might prove to have far greater substance.

Above all, these suggestions point to the need for institutionalizing a new and continuing confrontation between students and faculty. Student participation in central adminstrative deliberations and on boards of trustees would be, on the whole, less meaningful and irrelevant. To a considerable degree, students already participate in central administrative decisions relating directly to student residential, dining, athletic, entertainment, and extracurricular activities. Boards of trustees, on the other hand, do not ordinarily deal in detail with the academic matters that should be of the greatest concern to undergraduates. The central point remains that the end of student exploitation and alienation must be sought in a new political relationship between students and faculty, and that central university administration would be well advised to assist this process before the university community is further threatened by a student proletariat that has not yet focused on a real cause and therefore remains at the mercy of demagogues.

> Muller's suggestions will not satisfy the campus revolutionaries, who would view his recommendations as an insidious attempt to patch up a corrupt and oppressive establishment. For those who feel that nothing can take the place of a good campus revolt, a philosophy professor of Berkeley, who was a faculty leader in the Free Speech Movement in 1964, offers some helpful suggestions.

A FOOLPROOF SCENARIO
FOR STUDENT REVOLTS

John R. Searle
Professor of Philosophy
University of California, Berkeley

In several years of fighting for, fighting against and simply observing student revolts in the United States and Europe, I have been struck by certain recurring patterns of action and internationally common styles in the rhetoric of confrontation. Leaving out student revolts in Turkey, Czechoslovakia and Spain—all of which have rather special features—and confining ourselves to the U.S. and the advanced industrial democracies of Western Europe, it seems to me to be possible to discern certain family resemblances in the successful campus rebellions. In general, successful student revolts in these countries tend to occur in three identifiable phases or stages.

THE CREATION OF THE ISSUE

In the beginning, the revolt always has—at least in the mythology of local administrations—the same two features: there is only "a very small minority" of troublemakers, and "they have no legitimate grievances." These conditions, I have found in visits to campuses all over the U.S. and Western Europe, are, by common administrative consent, universal. They are also the reasons why "it won't happen here"; that is, they are always the reasons why "this campus won't become another Berkeley" or, lately, "another Columbia." I have discovered, incidentally, that a legitimate grievance is defined as one in which the students win. If you win, it turns out that your grievance was legitimate all along; if you lose, then alas for you, you had no legitimate grievance.

"The small minority with no legitimate grievance" starts out by selecting an issue. Curiously, almost any old issue will do. At Berkeley it concerned the campus rules on political activity; at Columbia it was the location of a gym; at Nanterre, a protest at the offices of TWA and the Chase

From *The New York Times Magazine*, December 29, 1968, pp. 4ff. © 1968 by The New York Times Company. Reprinted by permission.

Manhattan Bank; at Essex it was a visit by a representative of the Ministry of Defense, and many places have used recruiters from the Dow Chemical Company and other variations on the theme of the war in Vietnam.

Almost any issue will do, provided it has two crucial features: (1) It must be an issue that can be somehow related to a Sacred Topic. In the United States, the Sacred Topics are the First Amendment, race and the war in Vietnam—in that order, though I believe that in the last year race has been pulling ahead of the First Amendment. (In France, *la révolution* is itself a Sacred Topic.) If the issue can be related to a Sacred Topic, then the majority of students even though they would not do anything about it themselves, will at least be sympathetic to the demonstrators' position in the early stages. (2) The issue has to be one on which the university authorities cannot give in. The authorities must initially refuse your demands. If you win, you have lost. If the authorities give in to your demands there is nothing for it but to pick another issue and start all over.

The demand, therefore, has to be presented in the maximally confrontationalist style. This usually requires a demonstration of some sort, and sit-ins are not uncommon at this stage, though a "mass meeting" or march to present your demands will often do as well. The number of people in Stage One is usually small, but they serve to "educate" the campus, to "dramatize" the issue. It is a good idea, though not always necessary in Stage One, to violate as many campus rules or civil laws as you possibly can, in as visible a manner as you possibly can, during the initial presentation of your demands. In other words, you should challenge the authorities to take disciplinary action against you, and generally they will oblige by suspending a few of your leaders.

Stage One closes when the administration rejects your demands, admonishes you to better behavior in the future and, if possible, brings some of your leaders to university discipline for rule violations in the demonstrations. Berkeley 1964 and Paris 1968 are the models of a well-managed Stage One. . . .

THE CREATION OF A RHETORICAL CLIMATE

In Stage Two the original issue is transformed so that the structure of authority in the university is itself the target. This is achieved by the following method. The fact that the university rejected the original demands and, even more, the fact that the university disciplined people for rule violations in making those demands are offered as conclusive proof that the university is the real enemy of the forces of truth and justice on the Sacred Topic. Thus, if the original demand was related to the war in Vietnam, the fact that the university disciplined a student for rule violation in making the demand is proof that the university is really working for the war and that it is out to "crush dissent." If, for example, the demonstrations were against Dow Chemical Company recruiters on campus, the fact of university discipline proves that the university is really the handmaiden (or whore) of the military-industrial complex. And the fact that the university refuses to cancel plans for the gym (Columbia) or *does* cancel plans for the Cleaver course (Berkeley) demonstrates that the university is really a racist institution. Why would anybody try to discipline our fellow students and refuse our just demands if they weren't racists, warmongers or dissent-crushers, as the case might be? And, indeed, can't we now see that the university is really just a part of much larger forces of oppression (imperialism, racism) in our American society? In the face of such proof, only the most callous or evil would fail to join us in our struggle to make this a livable university, a place where we can be truly free.

If this attempt to make the university the primary target is successful, the number of people involved in Stage Two will increase enormously. Large numbers of students who will not demonstrate illegally against the war in Vietnam or for free speech will demonstrate illegally if they can demonstrate against someone's being disciplined for illegally demonstrating against the war in Vietnam or for free speech. The original issues is made much more personal, local and "relevant" to their life as students by being redefined, with the university authorities as the main enemy. The war in Vietnam is a long way off, but Grayson Kirk's office is just across the campus. This redefinition of the issue so that the university authorities become the main target is crucial to the success of the entire operation and is the essential characteristic of a successful Stage Two.

Speeches, leaflets, meetings and articles in student papers all serve to create a certain rhetorical climate in which charges that would normally be thought to verge on the preposterous can gain currency and acceptability. Thus, the president of the university is a racist, the board of regents is trying to run the university for its personal profit, the university is fundamentally an agent of the Pentagon and so on. Anyone who remembers the witch hunts of the nineteen-fifties will recognize the distinctive features of this rhetorical atmosphere: the passionate conviction that our side is right and the other side not only wrong but evil, the urgency of the issue, the need for all of us to stand united against the threat (of Communism or the military-industrial complex, depending on your choice of era) and, most important, the burning sincerity of all but the most intelligent.

In Stage Two certain new and crucial elements enter the fray—television and the faculty. It sounds odd to describe the jobs television does but here they are: it provides a leader and it dignifies the proceedings. The mechanisms by which television provides the movement with a leader are not generally well understood. It looks like the movement chooses a leader and he addresses the TV cameras on its behalf. But that is rarely what happens; in fact, that almost never happens.

What happens is that among the many speakers who appear at rallies and such, some are more telegenic than others; and the TV reporters and cameramen, who can only use a small amount of footage anyway, are professional experts at picking the one who will make the most interesting news shots. The man they pick then becomes the leader or spokesman or symbol of the movement. Of course, his selection has to be approved by the movement, so any TV selection is subject to ratification by the crowd. If they don't like him, the TV people have to find somebody else, but among the many leaders who are acceptable to the demonstrators, television plays an important role in the eventual success of one or another.

Thus Mario Savio in Berkeley, Daniel Cohn-Bendit in Paris and Mark Rudd at Columbia were poeple with relatively little leadership position prior to Stage One, but who, as a result of their own qualities and the fact that the television people chose them to present as leaders, were elevated to the status of leaders, at least symbolically. . . .

In a crazy kind of way, television also dignifies the proceedings. If you are at a demonstration at noon and you can go home and watch yourself on the 6 o'clock news, it suddenly means that the noon behavior is lifted out of the realm of juvenile shenanigans and becomes genuine historical stuff. If you are there on the box it must be pretty serious, an authentic revolutionary event.

This is a McLuhanite generation, raised with a feel for publicity in general and TV in particular. When I was an undergraduate, if you got kicked out of school you went somewhere else and tried to forget about it; nowadays you would immediately call a TV news conference and charge that you did not get due process. As a news medium, television requires the visually exciting, and campus demonstrations are ideal telegenic events; they are dramatic, colorful, often violent, and in slack moments the cameras can rest on the bearded, barefoot hippies or the good-looking, long-haired girls. In return for useful footage, the media men provide the dignity and self-respect that ordinary people derive from mass publicity.

It is very important in Stage Two that a few faculty members side with the demonstrators "on the issues." In general, they will not directly condone rule violations, but by supporting the issues of Stage One they add a stamp of approval to the whole enterprise and thus have the effect of indirectly excusing the rule violations: "It is unfortunate that there should be any disruption of the university, but it really is awful that the administration should kick poor Smith out just for sitting peacefully and nonviolently on the dean's desk for a few hours, especially when Smith was only trying to end racisim and the war in Vietnam."

More important, the approval of faculty members provides a source of security and reinforcement of convictions. An undergraduate engaging in a disruption of university operations is not (at least, not yet) engaging in a conventional and established form of political behavior. He feels deeply insecure, and the stridency of his rhetoric should not conceal from us the depth of his insecurity. The apparent passionate convictions of most university demonstrators are in fact terribly fragile, and when away from the crowd many of them are fairly easily talked out of their wildest fantasies. A few faculty members can provide security and reinforcement, and are therefore a great aid in recruiting more student support. Old-fashioned people, Freudians and such, would say that the student needs the faculty member to play the role of an older sibling in his revolt against the administration-parent.

At the end of Stage Two, there is a large-scale demonstration against the university on the issue of Stage One as transformed by the rhetorical impact of Stage Two. In the United States it takes the form of a large sit-in, though this has recently been developing into the seizure ("liberation") of a building, complete with barricaded doors and windows. (In Paris, it was also a matter of building street barricades, but street barricades are a French tradition, not easily exportable, that somehow seems to survive; the survival is aided by the presence of small cars that can be used as building material.) When the sit-in or seizure occurs, the university authorities are strongly inclined to—and usually do—call out the police to arrest the people who are sitting in. When that happens, if all has gone according to the scenario, we enter Stage Three, and we enter in with a vengeance.

THE COLLAPSE OF AUTHORITY

The first characteristic of Stage Three is an enormous and exhilarating feeling of revulsion against the calling of the police. The introduction of hundreds of policemen on the campus is regarded as the ultimate crime that any university administration can commit, and a properly led and well-organized student movement will therefore direct all of its efforts in Stages One and Two to creating a situation in which the authorities feel they have no choice but to call the police. Large numbers of faculty members who have so far watched nervously from the sidelines, vaguely sympathetic with the students' rhetoric but unwilling condone the rule violations, are suddenly liberated. They are rejuvenated by being able to side with the forces of progress against the forces of authority; the anxieties of Stages One and Two are released in a wonderful surge of exhilaration: we can hate the administration for calling the cops instead of having to tut-tut at the students for their bad behavior. On the students' side, there is a similar euphoria. In Berkeley, the student health service reported in 1964 a sharp decline in the number of students seeking psychological and psychiatric help during Stage Three.

In the transition to Stage Three, the more police brutality you can elicit by baiting and taunting (or the more the police are able to provide by themselves in the absence of such incitement), the better, but, as any competent leader knows, police brutality is not, strictly speaking, necessary because any large-scale mass arrest will produce accusations of police brutality no matter what happens.

In the face of the sheer horror of the police on campus, the opposition to the movement, especially the opposition among the liberal and moderate students, becomes enfeebled and usually collapses altogether. At this point, there is a general student strike with fairly strong faculty support, and quite often the campus will be completely shut down.

Furthermore, the original demands of Stage One are now only a small part of a marvelously escalated series of demands. Sometimes, as in Paris, the Stage One demands may be pretty much forgotten. Who, for example, could remember on the barricades what Cohn-Bendit was agitating for back in Stage One? A typical list of Stage Three demands would comprise the following:

The president must be fired (he usually is, in fact).

There must be amnesty for all.

The university must be restructured so as to give the students a major share in all decision-making.

The administration has to be abolished, or at any rate confined to sweeping sidewalks and such.

The university must cease all cooperation with the Defense Department and other official agencies in the outside community.

Capitalism must end—now.

Society must be reorganized.

Meanwhile, interesting things are happening in the faculty: committees are meeting and drafting resolutions, alliances are being formed and petitions circulated. The faculty government, by tradition a sleepy and ill-attended body that gently hassles about parking and by-laws, is suddenly packed with record numbers of passionate and eloquent debaters. There are endless amendments and fights over the symbolism of a "whereas" clause. Great victories are won and symbolic defeats sustained. Also, in the general unhinging of Stage Three many faculty members discover all sorts of long-forgotten grievances they have against the administration. There is simply no end of good grievances; indeed, in our best universities I believe this could be one of the conditions of continued employment: if you can't think up half a dozen really good grievances against the place you are probably not intelligent enough for continued employment in a university of top caliber. . . .

So now we have come from the halcyon days of Stage One, in which there was "only a small minority with no legitimate grievances," to the full-blown revolutionary ecstasy of Stage Three; the place is shut down, the president is looking for a new job and the *effective* authorities are a handful of fairly scruffy-looking and unplausible-sounding student leaders. How does it work? What is the fuel on which the mechanism functions?

Before I answer that, I need to make the usual academic qualifications about the model: it is intended only as an analytical framework and not a complete empirical generalization. Certainly, not all successful student revolts go through these three stages, and I can think of many counterexamples, and so on. Furthermore, I do not mean to imply that anybody on either side actually plans his behavior with these three stages in mind; I am not suggesting that student leaders sit in cellars asking themselves, "Are we in Stage Two yet?" Furthermore, I am not saying that the demonstrators are either in the right or in the wrong on the demands they make. Student demonstrators, like university administrators, are sometimes right, sometimes wrong; on some occasions, such as the Free Speech Movement in Berkeley, the demonstrators have, in my view, been overwhelmingly in the right. I am just trying to describe a common pattern of events that has recurred in many places and with quite different issues, but it will be obvious from what I have said that I find it at least an *inefficient* method of resolving campus disputes.

Getting back to the question—What makes it work?— the unique feature of the present situation in universities is the pervasive dislike and distrust of authority. Far more students in the Western democracies today —more than, say, 10 years ago—hate their governments, police forces and university administrations (there are complex historical reasons for this, most of which have nothing to do with universities). I can, for example, remember when it was quite common for university presidents to be respected and admired, even on their own campuses. Now it is almost unheard of (except after they have been fired).

The strategy of a successful student movement is to unite this existing mistrust of authority with genuinely idealistic impulses on one of the Sacred Topics in such a way that assaults on university authority become a method of expressing that idealism. Each new exercise of authority then becomes further proof that the administration is an enemy of the idealism, and this serves to undermine authority even more. The transition from each stage to the next, remember, is produced by the exercise of authority, and eventually—with the use of masses of policemen—if all has gone according to plan, campus authority collapses altogether. The strategy, in short, is to pit "the students" (and not "the radicals" or "the small minority") against "the administration" in a fight that appears to concern a Sacred Topic, and then to undermine the administration by provoking exercises of authority that will serve to discredit it. The three stages, then, should be seen as a continuous progression, beginning with the creation of an issue (or issues) and ending with the collapse of authority.

The demonstrators are always puzzled by the hostility they arouse among the liberal intelligentsia outside the university. But what the demonstrators perceive as the highest idealism often looks from the outside like a mixture of vandalism and imbecilic dogmatism. Though they can convince *themselves* that, say, Columbia, Stanford and Berkeley are racist institutions, few on the outside ever accept this view.

When administrations are defeated, they almost invariably go down as a result of technical mistakes, failure to grasp the nature of the struggle they are engaged in and, most important, their own demoralization. A confident administration bent on defending intellectual values, and consequently determined to destroy the power of its essentially anti-intellectual adversary, can generally win. Victory for the administration requires a readiness to deal with each of the three stages on its own terms and certain overall strategies involving internal university reforms and the intelligent use of discipline (even including the police when it comes to the crunch). Curiously, many college administrations in America don't yet seem to perceive that they are all in this together. Like buffaloes being shot, they look on with interest when another of their number goes down, without seriously thinking that they may be next.

Although Searle recognizes that student revolts arise from genuine grievances, his tone indicates he is annoyed at their arrogance and irrationality. The question, "When is disorderly protest good?" is an interesting one. We revere the memory of the Boston Tea Party, but elect law-and-order candidates today. We applaud Negro protest riots —in South Africa. In the following brief item, a newspaper columnist comments on our double standard for evaluating public disorder.

UNREST ON CAMPUS FINE,
EXCEPT AT "OUR" SCHOOLS

Art Buchwald

It is generally agreed that the student unrest going on these days is worldwide. It doesn't matter if the students live in a permissive society or a totalitarian one—they're still raising Cain. And for that reason, those of us watching from the sidelines are divided as to whether the unrest is a good thing or a bad thing.

At the University Club the other day, I was having a brandy and cigar with some very nice chaps when the question of student demonstrations came up.

"I see they still haven't solved the problem at Columbia," Liverwhistle said.

"It's appalling, absolutely appalling," Cartwright sputtered.

"The students should all be booted out on their ears. You can't have a university if you're going to have children running around locking up the faculty."

Conrad said, "Did you read what's going on in Paris? The French students have tied up the city."

"Ah, yes," said Cartwright. "One can't help admiring the French students' gumption. They've certainly put De Gaulle in his place."

"You have to respect their attitude," Liverwhistle said. "At least the students can see through De Gaulle, if the rest of the French people can't."

"I don't think things have cooled off at Stanford," Studsdale commented. "They're still holding the administration building."

"If you ask me," said Cartwright, "it's a Communist plot. These things don't just happen. There's nothing the Commies wouldn't do to shut down the schools in this country. The only answer is force. It will make those radicals sing another tune."

"Did you read where the students in Czechoslovakia not only demonstrated, but caused the downfall of the Soviet-backed regime?"

"God bless them," said Conrad. "If we're ever going to see the end of tyranny behind the Iron Curtain, it's going to be the students who accomplish it."

"I understand the same thing could happen in Poland," Liverwhistle said, "and perhaps even East Germany. They're a new breed, those students, and a credit to the human race."

"You know, of course," said Studsdale, "that the administration completely collapsed at Northwestern and gave in to every demand of the students there."

Cartwright said, "My blood boiled when I read the story. Those damn kids don't know up from down and they're telling us how to run the country. I say we have to act now and act firmly. We ought to cut off all funds to any student who demonstrates or strikes against a university administration."

"The students in Franco's Spain have been agitating for a year now. No one knows how many are in jail," Conrad said.

"The poor kids," Liverwhistle said. "They're only trying to make a better world, and they're thrown in jail for it. I think we should get up a petition and send it to the Spanish ambassador."

"I see they're having another sit-in at Berkeley," Liverwright commented.

"They're always having a sit-in at Berkeley," Studsdale said.

Cartwright, who was flipping through a newspaper, said, "It says here that the students in Communist China are thinking about having another Red Guard revolution."

"Great," said Liverwhistle. "Old Mao won't be able to take another one of those."

Liverwright agreed. "I must say one thing for the students abroad. They sure have a lot of class."

When students protest, it sometimes appears that anything the administration does is wrong. If it does nothing and waits for the protest to "blow over" things are likely to blow *up*. Granting all demands is like cutting off the heads of Hydra; new ones keep sprouting. Calling in the police radicalizes the students. What are faculties and administrators to do?

In the following essay, three sociologists propose some policy guidelines.

ON KEEPING OUR COOL
IN THE HALLS OF IVY

Thomas Ford Hoult   John W. Hudson

Albert J. Mayer

Professors of Sociology
Arizona State University

Current student protest movements have raised the question—"Who should control the university?" Answers to the question vary with the values of those answering it. *Our* values are such that we answer thus:

Any university should be controlled by those persons and groups, and in such a way, that the university's function is most expeditiously fulfilled.

Since we base our answer on the function of the university, the obvious next question is: "What is the basic function of the university?" Our answer, gleaned from a wide range of historical experience, is that the university exists to preserve, extend, and disseminate accurate knowledge. This idealistic conception of the university's function is, of course, not acceptable to those who would like the university to be a handmaiden to the establishment or become (as one observer put it) an "all-purpose brothel." But when a university is thus made to serve specific interests, it is diverted from the task of helping to meet society's critical need for knowledge. This need is met systematically and adequately in the university setting alone, and only to the degree that the university is permeated with a sense of freedom from partisan ideological control, whether such control emanates from left or right, black or white, business or labor. This means, in turn, that we disagree with Christian Bay's view that the university should be politically active. He has asserted:

We want . . . to extricate the university from its present stance of indifference and passive or active support to ugly government policies like the war in Viet Nam.[1]

From *Bulletin of the American Association of University Professors*, 55 (Summer 1969) pp. 186–191. Reprinted by permission of the authors and of the American Association of University Professors.

[1] Christian Bay, "Academic Citizenship in a Time of Campus revolt," *Trans-Action*, Vol. 6, No. 3 (January 1969) pp. 4–7, see p. 4.

We agree that the U.S. Viet Nam policy is unwarranted and, *as individuals,* we have strongly opposed it. But we have not asked the university, as such, to join us in this protest because we know that the politically committed university almost always degenerates so that it becomes little more than a tool for whoever is in power at any given time. It is unfortunate that the politically neutral university unavoidably lends indirect support to an existing regime, but the consequences of active commitment appear to be worse, as illustrated by the sad state of schools which have proscribed all but "Aryan science," "free enterprise economics," or "Marxian dialectic."

Those accepting the foregoing point of view—the view that the university's purpose is cultivation of the life of the mind and that control of the university should be such as to facilitate its purpose—have, in effect, a general guide for making appropriate responses when various individuals or groups make demands on the university. The guide can be summarized as a question to be asked and answered when a demand is made: "If this demand is acceded to, will the functioning of the university be enhanced?"

We are convinced that much of the chaos now gripping so many campuses can be alleviated or avoided only to the degree that those concerned adopt, and firmly and consistently adhere to, a guide such as that suggested above. To clarify the important implications of this point, we have formulated a number of relevant assertions, ranging from pure value judgments to factual observations; we list these assertions below, together with conclusions that appear to follow logically. By "relevant assertions" we mean those particularly applicable to "the university," the latter phrase being used here to designate universities and liberal arts colleges in general. A few of the conclusions will, at first glance, seem to contradict others; but further thought will indicate that this is only superficially so, since a rational approach to a subject as complex as the campus crisis calls for an attitudinal set that is a unique blend of realism and idealism.

I. ASSERTION

Aside from the restrictions imposed by relevant aspects of the requirements of academic freedom and the democratic process, ultimate control over the university should logically be exercised by the most knowledgeable members of the university community.

Conclusion

Faculty members and administrative officials should strenuously resist the various moves to implement total student control over the university.

If, in comparison to students generally, faculty members and other senior participants in the university community do not have a better grasp of the educational process and of historical perspective, then the faculty are being paid under false pretenses. Students who do not agree with this point of view are wasting their time, energy, and money, since the basic premise of almost every school is that the faculty has special know-how which can be acquired by students who apply themselves adequately.

The knowledge and campus privilege differential between faculty and students does not, of course, imply that faculty are "better" than students; it implies only that members of the two groups temporarily have different tasks in the division of labor. Thus, there is no master-slave relationship between students and faculty, as claimed in Perry Farber's "The Student as Nigger." [2] Students become teachers, but slaves never become masters.

Varying time-involvement is another justification for faculty-administration control of academic affairs. Unlike faculty members in general, students do not have to live with the results of various changes that can be made. Furthermore, youthful students typically have transitory interests that alter before they can be implemented. "Hurry up and grant my non-negotiable demands before I forget what they are," shouts the protester in a recent Hugo cartoon.

Faculty-administrative control over academia need not, however, be arbitrary or absolute. Students quite properly want and should have control over their own day-to-day concerns—the activity funds they subsidize, the student news media, their own private lives, and so on. In addition, the student point of view should be well represented on all appropriate university committees, in the formulation of new programs, and even—along with that of faculty—on controlling boards or regents or trustees.

But the student views represented should obviously be those of genuine students in general, not the pseudo-students whose aim is destruction rather than growth. "Student power will take over the universities; we will wreck them or we will burn them down," the 1968–69 president of the 365,000 member Canadian Union of Students has declared publicly.[3] Giving such a person an official voice on campus is equivalent to choosing Nasser as spokesman for the Israelis. Modern society is, after all, the accumulated wisdom of the ages, and this wisdom is stored in the facilities and professional personnel of the university community. Destroying the university, thus, promises nothing but a return to the conditions prevailing during the dark ages.

---

[2] Originally an article in the *Los Angeles Free Press,* date unknown; we have seen a mimeographed copy only.

[3] Quoted in a 19 September speech made by Donald Cameron in the Canadian Senate, First Session, 1968; the transcript we used was in the form of a mimeographed release by the Department of Social Science, Lansing (Michigan) Community College.

II. ASSERTION

When more than a relatively small number of participants in a social system become seriously alienated from the system, the latter will usually not survive unless the extent of the alienation is sufficiently reduced by appropriate and timely reforms.

Conclusion

On any given university campus, responsible administrative officials must carefully ascertain the real nature of local student protest movements and activity. If such study indicates that particular difficulties are almost solely due to a few noisy nihilists, then it is reasonable to conclude that the troublemakers can be handled without undue complication—although, in the interests of justice, some reforms may be appropriate.

On the other hand, if a proper survey indicates that readily visible protest activities are outward symbols of widespread unrest, then suitable fundamental changes are necessary and should be instituted immediately —a conclusion which is prompted by the obvious fact that the basically undermined social organization can hardly accomplish its purpose. This point has been illustrated all too graphically at San Francisco State College. Presently available information suggests that, months before serious difficulty surfaced at San Francisco State, various student groups were given the classic runaround when they made legitimate requests such as that more students be included on appropriate committees, that courses dealing realistically with black Americans be inaugurated, etc. Finally, repeated frustration resulted in the various explosions and absurd demands about which we now know more than we really want to know.

For those willing to learn, the San Francisco State story has two important lessons: one is that orderly dissent, ignored, readily becomes disorderly; the other is that, in the modern Western world, any social system will function effectively and peaceable only to the degree that a large majority of those expected to abide by the system's norms are convinced that they have both a say and a stake in the norms. These principles can be given meaningful expression in the campus setting by involving students in various appropriate decision-making processes. Putting the point more bluntly, senior members of the university community need to share some of the power that has always been exclusively theirs. This will pain a number of those who feel nothing should ever be done the first time, but realists will see that the alternative to such sharing can easily become a breakdown of the whole system followed by a power reshuffle that is unlikely to leave any prerogatives in the hands of those representing the old establishment.

So—faculty members and administrative officials, awake! You have nothing to lose but your livelihoods if you continue in a blissful unawareness that students will no longer tolerate the sense of being used. As one student wrote in a recent letter to the editor: "We are angry because we are powerless. We have no voice in the forces which so completely control our lives." [4]

III. ASSERTION

A university's limited funds and energies are needlessly depleted when university officials, performing as such, engage in activities that are not reasonably related to the creation and dissemination of knowledge.[5]

Conclusion

Universities should publicly disavow the doctrine of *in loco parentis* and should therefore cease the attempt to regulate the personal life of students. If students violate the law, they can pay the attendant penalties; but it is no direct concern of the university that its students, when off campus, smoke marijuana, engage in legally prohibited sexual behavior, consume alcoholic beverages, etc. When the university's basic function is kept in mind, it becomes clear that the university's concern with nonacademic behavior is properly confined to doing research on, and teaching about, the likely consequences of any given kind of action.

IV. ASSERTION

Arbitrary categorization of men, such as on the basis of race, is one of the root causes of human misery.

Conclusion

Demands for Jim Crow dormitories, student unions, and curricula should be resisted vigorously. Racism on the part of whites has always been reprehensible; it does not achieve respectability when it is manifested by blacks. University officials should not be misled by irrational guilt feelings

[4] *Arizona Republic,* January 27, 1969.
[5] We interpret "reasonably related" to include a number of leisure-time artistic and athletic endeavors that can have both recreational and public relations value.

arising from the customary treatment of blacks by whites. This treatment has obviously been almost totally deplorable, but it is not mitigated in any meaningful way by new forms of the very evil underlying the treatment.

For these same reasons, proposals for courses teaching "race pride" should be opposed. It is particularly unfortunate that black Americans have, in effect, accepted the prevailing general value that "black is bad" —but the answer to this sad result is cultivation of self-acceptance, not racism in a new form. If race pride on the part of blacks is acceptable—e.g., black is beautiful *because* it is black—then the logical grounds for opposing white racism are removed.

A related matter is the current cry on the part of some militants that a separate black world would somehow lead to a better life for the average black man. But this is a misleading idea and, if historical experience is any guide, quite inaccurate. It is therefore obligatory for knowledgeable members of the university community—in line with the university's function of disseminating *accurate* information—to tell it like it really is when it comes to the question of black separatism. And this is the way it really is: It would be a violation of constitutional principles to block those who wish to withdraw from participation in society at large, but the present distribution of power, knowledge, and resources is such that creation of separate black and white worlds would very likely condemn the vast majority of blacks to a state of permanent inferiority. The black world would almost certainly become a case of *Emperor Jones* writ large. According to Roy Wilkins, NAACP head:

Racial separatism is but a comforting delusion for those who impose it. It is a hell in a thousand different big and little ways for those upon whom it is imposed.[6]

The American Indian reservation experience is relevant—there we can see the consequences of separatism for those who have long and sadly been dominated: an illiteracy rate of 75 percent, alcoholism as a way of life, and, for many participants, a degraded and hopeless existence that makes a mockery of the separatist claim, "At least we'll have dignity." It would be telling it like it is to assert, "If that is dignity, then the word has lost all meaning."

The foregoing does not mean that a black studies curriculum—as distinguished from "autonomous" Jim Crow schooling—is inappropriate. Surely there is as much justification for black studies as for the Latin American and Asian studies that already exist in so many schools. In addition, a well-run black studies curriculum can serve the dual purpose of providing a more familiar academic home-away-from-home for particular students, and it can help to compensate for the devastating sense of having

[6] *The Phoenix Gazette,* January 23, 1969.

no place-in-the-sun that underlies the self-rejection so common among black Americans.

V. ASSERTION

Students are misled when they are not taught in the United States today one can become occupationally successful in the best jobs only to the extent that one manifests what may roughly be termed middle-class behavior (willingness to postpone reward, diligent and systematic attention to tasks, clock orientation, etc.—in short, the Puritan work ethic).

Conclusion

We should resist the pressure to apply lower standards to students who, because of their membership in a disadvantaged minority group, are ill prepared for traditional college life. Students so treated inadvertently learn something that is erroneous and potentially damaging to them— namely, that moaning about the past gets the same results as hard work in the present, or that one can make it in American life simply by pleading one is a victim of historical injustice. This may work with softhearted instructors, but it gains nothing but tokenism in the harsh world of business.

However, the university helps to perpetuate injustice if it does not have well-staffed and financed remedial programs designed to aid the culturally disadvantaged meet normal requirements. A university which does not have such programs is contributing to the conditions that spark revolution since it is saying, in effect, "Successful participation in the general social system now requires a university education, but numerous people must be denied such education because they unfortunately chose the wrong kind of forebears." Such a statement is equivalent to saying, "Let them eat cake," and promises the same type of consequences.

Programs set up to help system outsiders become insiders do not, of course, insure positive results. Indeed, it is only realistic to observe that a distressingly large number of persons reared in ghetto circumstances probably cannot be trained to meet ordinary academic standards. This observation applies particularly to those presons who have been doubly damned— i.e., those who not only face the usual disadvantages arising from segregation and discrimination, but who have also become long-term victims of the stultifying effects of deficient health conditions.

The logical answer for such life-time victims of a social system that has deprived them of chances for normal development is an appropriate social-welfare and technical-training program that is accompanied by related massive social changes designed to eliminate the factors presently dooming whole categories of people to become second-class citizens. But since logic does not always prevail, harassed college officials—fearing censure for the continued racial imbalance in the student body—often admit to conventional programs some persons who clearly cannot become qualified for traditional academic work. Such a response to the problem subverts the university's function and is no help to those who can't possibly make the regular grade, academically speaking. The latter typically become dropouts, thus giving false substance to prevailing negative stereotypes; and they quite understandably become more frustrated and bitter than ever since they have been given a teste of a sweet life that they know is forever barred to them. Who can reasonably blame them for then listening sympathetically to extremists that vow to wreck the system that has wrecked them?

The technical-training program referred to above could well be a college-sponsored and degree-granting parallel to the vocational high school. This would accommodate to the reality that a four-year college degree is now the social equivalent to the high school diploma of yesteryear—and, just as public high schools had to find ways to admit and graduate virtually all students, so must tax-supported undergraduate colleges.

VI. ASSERTION

Education is not, strictly speaking, something that is done to people; it is something they do to themselves.

Conclusion

Many of the protests about "poor teaching," "irrelevant classes," and lack of meaningful courses are based on the false premise that education is something that is injected into people if teachers are clever enough to know how to wield the appropriate type of instrument. Actually, however, education that is truly significant for any given individual is the information he seeks out and integrates into a personal philosophy. In the words of the first president of Arizona State University (Territorial Normal School then), "Self-effort educates." [7] The best universities are those which provide a setting such that they attract the type of student who is most inclined to dig out the facts and work out the relationships for himself. Even in the lesser universities, the enterprising student can, with an assiduous reading and library program, compensate for all manner of poor teaching, irrelevant subject matter, or nonexistent curricula dealing with this and that. Such self-help programs will, of course, not seem attractive to the complainers

[7] Ernest J. Hopkins and Alfred Thomas, Jr., *The Arizona State University Story* (Phoenix: Southwest Publishing, 1960) p. 88.

whose demands suggest that they think there must be a gimmick making it possible to get a degree without serious effort, or alternatively, that education is something which can somehow be silver-plattered to the passive.

VII. ASSERTION

The essence of the university is that it is a place for the conduct of various forms of *reasoned* debate, but such debate cannot take place when there is serious physical interference with the usual academic activities of members of the university community.

Conclusion

Those responsible for the operation of the university must use all necessary measures to block any who wish to impede the regular functioning of the university. If, in some rare instances, "all necessary measures" must include 24-hour guards and a closed campus protected much like a restricted-access air base, then so be it. The even less savory alternative may be another kind of closed campus—the one that is completely ruined by shouting nihilists who proclaim that the whole social system must be overturned because only thus can adequate reforms be instituted.

The use of physical force is understandably repugnant to scholars whose commitment is to the life of the mind. But timid academicians should keep two interrelated points in mind: First—If, in any local situation, the use of illegitimate force is not adequately countered, then the chances are great that social control will gravitate to the most unscrupulous persons in the community. Second—At most colleges today there are a few campus hangers-on whose primary interest is not to get an education, but to foment a revolution that will give them total power. They focus on universities because it is there that they find their most implacable enemy *and* their fundamental tool.

The deadly enemy of the revolutionist, as of every extremist—whether from the far left or far right—is the university tradition of free thought which throws the cold light of scholarship on the extravagant claims of self-proclaimed messiahs. Such scholarship has repeatedly found something that revolutionists must, at all costs, keep from their followers—namely, that reforms carried out by wildly impatient true-believers always end as exploitation of the many by the unprincipled few. In the words of George Kennan:

I have seen more harm done in this world by those who tried to storm the bastions of society in the name of utopian beliefs, who were determined to achieve the elimination of all evil and the realization of the millennium within their own time, than by all the humble efforts of those who have tried to create a little order and civility and affection within their own intimate entourage, even at the cost of tolerating a great deal of evil in the public domain.[8]

The basic tool of the campus revolutionist is the mass of students whose general innocence, youth, and sincere interest in building a better world make many of them so easy to excite into a thoughtless frenzy of destructive behavior. In addition, every campus has a large number of adolescent types who, seeking any excuse not to attend class, will gleefully join in the forcible occupation of buildings—especially since experience suggests that good old mother university, so often staffed by the timid and the uncertain, will not really reject her errant children no matter what they do. With such help, a few arrogant anarchists have been able to bring particular schools to a complete halt. Halts of this sort could probably be eliminated, or at least sharply curtailed, if university administrators and faculty members would make it clear, in advance, that teaching of various classes will go on even if classes must meet off campus, and that students not meeting the normal requirements of attendance and scholarship will be graded as appropriate. Meanwhile, back at the ranch, so to speak, building invaders can be left to stew in an isolation that will soon be as satisfying as is the temper tantrum to the child who is ignored but who knows he will somehow have to compensate for any damage he does.

The other side of the coin which has just been examined is that the views of an unchallenged establishment too easily become unchallengeable dogma; and law and order based on anything other than a widespread sense of justice is, at best, only a temporary respite from chaos. Therefore, to the end that justice and orderly change shall prevail, the university must encourage and support constitutionally protected methods of dissent and protest. This support and encouragement, to be meaningful, must be systematized so there is little chance it can be stifled. Indeed, the wise administrator will officially sponsor forums for the expression of dissent. Such forums have the doubt merit of releasing pressure and providing information that can contribute to the making of wise decisions. As Bay has written, ". . . radical intellectual and political inquiry . . . are more essential than ever in a world that changes so fast. . . . Only sheltered societies can depend on the unchallenged wisdom of their elders."[9] Communication lines should be kept open, even to youths so disaffected we cannot reach them—" . . . we should give them the opportunity to reach us," Bertram Davis has observed, "for by attending carefully we may see

8 George F. Kennan, *Democracy and the Student Left* (Boston: Little, Brown, Bantam Books, 1968) p. 8.

9 Bay, "Academic Citizenship," p. 7.

some flashes of insight which will shed some light upon our institutions and ourselves." [10]

VIII. ASSERTION

Despite all their admitted limitations, the American social system generally, and the university social system particularly, have produced some very admirable results.

Conclusion

Little consideration need be given to the few irrational students and faculty who cry that nothing good has been produced by American society and universities, and therefore both must be destroyed. Faculty members who speak thus, obviously exempt themselves; and students testify to their own irrationality if they continue to go to class, yet genuinely believe a modern university education is unalterably trivial or irrelevant. That such a belief is often not genuine is suggested by the number of youths who decry the workaday world in favor of meditating with their favorite guru, but—when afflicted with a gut ache—are eager to partake of the benefits of the work and research done in university laboratories or by university-trained medical personnel.

As for the social system at large, the United States has one of the highest standards of living known to man, and a governmental organization that is democratic enough and flexible enough to weather constant loud-spoken New Left charges that there is no free speech and that totalitarianism abounds—which, if true, would of course preclude making such charges more than once. But on the other hand, it is equally true that the government is often insensitive and that the benefits of American life are mal-distributed in the sense that some large categories of citizens enjoy almost no privileges—two realities which, it bears repeating, can undermine the entire social system if adequate reforms are not quickly instituted.

Those who claim that current difficulties on the campus are a temporary aberration which can best be handled by simple repression alone unwittingly confess to the narrowness of their vision. It seems more realistic to view many aspects of the campus revolt as part of a world-wide revulsion against all that is implied by the term "colonialism." Everywhere, people who have been thoughtlessly exploited, and who have accepted such exploitation virtually without protest, are now saying *Enough!*

[10] Bertram H. Davis, "From the General Secretary," *AAUP Bulletin* (Autumn 1968) pp. 292–294; see p. 293.

In Viet Nam, in Algeria, in black ghettos, in India, South America, and Africa—and on those campuses where students have long been treated in a cavalier fashion—the downtrodden have indicated they will no longer tolerate arbitrary control by outsiders who clearly want to *use* people rather than help them develop. This is no temporary movement! It is the shape and cry of the future, and it will be joined by all who have a sense of justice or a grasp of the direction of historical forces. It was these same forces that produced the American revolution, the Magna Charta, and the Bill of Rights. But the rights secured by these magnificent instruments have largely been restricted to the privileged few. They can now be extended to the many, thus creating widespread commitment to social order—if we take the proper steps. Taking the proper steps, however, is dependent upon having accurate information, which it is the function of the university to provide, hence the critical need to protect the university from those who would alter its fundamental nature.

Defense against attackers from the far right has always been necessary; now the direction of attack is more often from the extreme left. But the essential battle remains precisely the same—namely, to keep the university free of partisan control so it can increasingly serve mankind in general rather than particular men. It is not easy to counter the activities of the modern Robespierres who stalk the campuses of the land and mouth slogans such as "Freedom! Brotherhood! Peace!" while they shout down opponents and destroy laboratories and libraries. Coping with such tactics is difficult, but by no means impossible. As Bertram Davis has pointed out

. . . colleges and universities have strong sustaining powers. For all their faults, they are the freest of American institutions and a bulwark of freedom and progress in society. They are at once the preservers of an old culture and the outposts of a new, the very root and vine of our growth.[11]

11 Ibid., p. 294.

10 Poverty in the Land of Plenty

Poverty has many faces—rural Anglo-Saxons in Appalachia where mining is a dying industry and farming is unprofitable; large numbers of blacks, from the Mississippi delta country to the countless tenements of New York City; the very old and very young married persons—the list goes on and on.

Some of the faces of poverty are revealed not in groups of people but in the institutional structure of American society. The vast bureaucratic system which is called "welfare" has been putting its roots deeper into the nation for thirty years, alleviating *and* perpetuating poverty. The welfare system, created before the advent of automation, has shown little disposition to change with the technological revolution. Elimination of poverty calls for radical change in these collective social arrangements.

The first brief selection in this chapter comes from Harry M. Caudill's *Night Comes to the Cumberlands: A Biography of a Depressed Area*. The people portrayed do not fit into any familiar stereotypes of lazy, shiftless poor. Instead, we see a once proud and industrious people who have become apathetic and demoralized through poverty.

NIGHT COMES TO THE CUMBERLANDS

Harry M. Caudill

About 3:30 in the afternoon the county truant officer (known officially by the horrendous title of Director of Pupil Personnel) made his appearance. A warrant had been sworn out charging a father with failing to send his children to school and the trial was set for that hour. The defendant was already present in the little courtroom. A few moments later the county attorney appeared to prosecute the case for the state. The truant officer explained that the defendant was the father of six children, all of whom were of elementary school age. They had not been to school in the preceding month despite his pleas that the father keep them in regular attendance. The county attorney asked the Court to impose a fine or jail sentence. The judge asked the defendant why he had not been sending his children to school. The man stalked forward and gazed around him with the uncertainty of a trapped animal. He was dressed in tattered overalls to which many patches had been affixed. He was approximately forty-five years old and it was obvious from his huge hands and stooped shoulders that he had spent many years under the low roof of a coal mine. He pleaded his defense with the eloquence of an able trial lawyer. With powerful conviction he said:

I agree with everything that's been said. My children have not been going to school and nobody wants them to go any more than I do. I've been out of work now for four years. I've been all over this coalfield and over into Virginia and West Virginia looking for work. I've made trip after trip to Indianny, Ohio and Michigan and I couldn't find a day's work anywhere. I drawed out my unemployment compensation over three years ago and the only income I've had since has been just a day's work now and then doing farm work for somebody. I sold my old car, my shotgun, my radio, and even my watch to get money to feed my family. And now I don't have a thing in the world left that anybody would want. I'm dead-broke and about ready to give up. I live over a mile from the schoolhouse and I simply don't have any money to buy my children shoes or clothes to wear. I own a little old four-room shanty of a house and twenty acres of wornout hillside land. Last spring the coal company that owns the coal augered it and teetotally destroyed the land. I couldn't sell the whole place for five hundred dollars if my life depended on it. Me and my oldest boy have one pair of shoes between us, and that's all. When he wears 'em I don't have any and when I wear 'em he don't have any. If it wasn't for these rations the gover'ment gives us, I guess the whole family would of been starved to death long afore now. If you want to fine me I ain't got a penny to pay it with and I'll have to lay it out in jail. If you think puttin' me in jail will help my young-'uns any, then go ahead and do it and I'll be glad of it. If the county attorney or the truant officer will find me a job where I can work out something for my kids to wear I'll be much abliged to 'em as long as I live.

At the conclusion of this declaration the judge looked uneasily around, eying the county attorney and the truant officer in the hope that some help would come from that quarter. Both gentlemen remained silent. At length the judge plied the defendant with questions. The man had a third-grade education. He had worked in the mines for a total of twenty years and had spent three years as an infantry soldier in the war against Japan. He had been fortunate, however, and had received no wounds. Consequently, he drew no pension or compensation from the Veterans' Administration. The factories to which he had applied for employment had insisted on men with more education than he possessed. They also wanted younger men. Finally the county attorney demanded to know whether he had any skill except mining coal. The answer was an emphatic "No." Then he blurted out:

Judge, I'm not the only man in this fix on the creek where I live. They's at least a dozen other men who ain't sent their children to school for the same reason mine ain't a-goin'. They can't send 'em cause they can't get hold of any money to send 'em with. Now the county attorney and the truant officer are trying to make an example out of me. They think that if I go to jail for a week or two the rest of 'em will somehow find the money to get their kids into the schoolhouse.

He looked intently at the truant officer and demanded, "Ain't that so?" to which the truant officer hesitantly assented.

The judge mulled the problem over for a moment or two and then "filed away" the warrant. He explained that it was not being dismissed, but was being continued upon the docket indefinitely. "If the case is ever set for trial again I will write you a letter well in advance of the trial date and tell you when to be here," he said. "In the meantime go home and do the best you possibly can to make enough money to educate your children. If they don't go to school they'll never be able to make a living and when they get grown they'll be in just as bad a fix as you are in now."

The defendant thanked the judge, picked up his battered miner's cap and walked to the door. There he paused and looked back at judge, attorney and truant officer for a long moment, as though framing a question. Then he thought better of it and closed the door behind him. His Honor had had enough for one day, and decided to go home. While he was locking the door I glanced at the headlines on the newspapers the morning mail had brought to his desk:

FEDERAL AID TO EDUCATION BILL DIES IN HOUSE COMMITTEE

BILLIONS APPROVED FOR FOREIGN AID

JOBLESS MINER KILLS SELF IN HARLAN

In spite of the fact that the miner's family probably would have starved to death except for rations doled out by the government, few people believed that starvation really existed in the United States until the summer of 1967 when a subcommittee of the United States Senate held hearings on hunger and malnutrition in America. The report of those hearings, which ran over three hundred pages, has been ably summarized and interpreted by the chairman of the subcommittee, then Senator Joseph S. Clark.

STARVATION IN THE AFFLUENT SOCIETY

Joseph S. Clark

Former United States Senator

Gloria Palmer, a round-eyed, solemn-faced little girl of ten, stood shyly outside her slum home in Washington, D.C. and shifted her six-months-old baby brother from one arm to another, while two other tots leaned against her and stared up at the two United States Senators. Curiosity and childish bafflement were written across their faces. They did not know what Senators were or why they should be asking questions, nor did they recognize Senator Robert Kennedy or me. As we talked in front of the dilapidated and condemned tenements on Defrees Street, five blocks away could be seen the gleaming white dome of the Capitol.

I asked Gloria—one of eleven children of Wilhelmina Palmer—what she had eaten for lunch. "We didn't have any lunch," said Gloria quietly, and added, "But we have black-eyed peas for supper a lot." I asked her little brother, George, aged seven, "What did you have for lunch yesterday?" George replied, "Soup." "And what did you have for breakfast?" "Soup," George said.

A community action worker who accompanied Senator Kennedy and me on this personal inspection of slums in the shadow of the Capitol, commented: "There are hundreds of others in this neighborhood who are hungry, kids and adults who get up in the morning hungry and who go to bed at night hungry. It's been that way ever since I've been here, years and years."

When Senator Kennedy remarked that Gloria should have been in school during the neighborhood visit of our Senate Subcommittee on Employment, Manpower and Poverty, my thoughts suddenly whirled back two weeks to another group of youngsters who were also hungry and also not in school.

This time the Subcommittee, which I serve as chairman, was walking along the dusty, sun-seared country roads of the Mississippi Delta. Here in ramshackle homes of one or two rooms holding families of eight and ten, we encountered children who were not sent to school by their mothers because they had no shoes. Later on, doctors suggested to us a more

Reprinted by permission of the publisher and author. From *The Progressive*, Madison, Wisconsin (October 1967) pp. 13–16.

shocking reason: "bloated stomachs, chronic sores of the upper lip, and extreme lethargy—all tragic evidence of serious malnutrition."

In Belzoni, heart of the Delta, a mother of four told me that she and her brood had bologna sandwiches for breakfast and this would be the big meal of their day. Other times they have rice or grits, she told me in an infinitely tired voice, "but we never have any milk or fruit or fresh meat." Over and over again I was told that the staple diet for Belzoni's poor was beans, rice, margarine, lard, meal, peanut butter, raisins, powdered milk, and one can of meat for each person in the family per month. The can lasts, at the most, a week and a half.

The children we saw were visibly underweight, their bodies spotted with sores and untreated lesions.

Mrs. Ollie May Chapman and her nine children live in a tar-paper shack in Belzoni. On the day she was interviewed the family had gone without breakfast; for lunch they had soup made from a meat bone and cornmeal bread. For supper they would have beans—and a rare treat, a can of peaches.

We found a mother of fifteen children nursing a three-day-old child which she had delivered herself. There was no food in the house, she said, and no money. She didn't know what she would do.

Near Greenville, Mississippi, I came across a tumbledown collection of shacks ironically called Freedom City, housing the families of displaced plantation workers. Surviving, somehow, in this appalling squalor were forty-eight children who subsisted entirely on grits, rice, soybeans, and "whatever is donated," plus the customary one can of meat per month. Eggs, milk, and fruit juice, the mothers told me, were unknown.

There is no way in which you can prepare yourself for the overpowering effect of hunger and starvation seen close up. No matter how familiar you may be with the facts and figures of malnutrition, nothing can avert the feeling of stunned, disbelieving horror at the sight of little children with swollen bellies, shriveled limbs, and open sores that disfigure the small, bewildered faces and weakened bodies.

One reaches desperately for comparisons to give some semblance of reality to an experience that is essentially unreal and irrational. The mind rejects the evidence that innocent children *can and do* starve in this most abundant and fruitful of all nations, or go hungry in the Delta which contains 6,000,000 acres of the richest land on the continent. The visitor reaches for analogies. Senator Kennedy remarked that what he saw on our visit to the Mississippi Delta was as bad as anything he encountered in Latin America. A former British Army doctor with extensive experience in Africa told us that what he saw in Mississippi was comparable only to what he had observed in primitive parts of Kenya. Another doctor who worked for the World Health Organization in Asia told me, "I've been in India and I've seen famine and starvation. What we have seen in Mississippi and places in the north is slow starvation."

Yes, the North, too, allows its citizens, including its children, to waste away with hunger and to starve. Hunger, we discovered, is no respecter of area or region. No state is free of hunger any more than any state is free of poverty and deprivation. There is hunger, for example, in prosperous Illinois, which admits that 1,281,100 people, or twelve per cent of the state's population, have incomes below the poverty line.

The Subcommittee recently reported that in a small Appalachian town, near the border between Virginia and Tennessee, five small children tore apart and devoured a chicken before it could be cooked. It was the first meat the family had eaten in three months.

"In the San Joaquin Valley of California," our report continued, "fifty yards off a seldom-traveled road, a migrant family of seven, the youngest child not yet two, were living in a pick-up truck abandoned by a small stream. They had had no breakfast and did not know where they would find food for lunch. In other years they could have fished, but the stream had dried up."

As such specific cases as these came increasingly to the attention of the Subcommittee, we were struck by the discovery that these instances could not be projected against an overall picture of malnutrition and hunger in the United States. The fact is we simply do not know the extent or severity of malnutrition in this country today. Newspapermen were shocked when the U.S. Surgeon General told the Subcommittee that we know more about malnutrition in Pakistan and other poor countries than in the United States. He said such studies have not been made in this country and, if they were to be made, he was not sure which agency should make them.

How vague our information is can be judged by the fact that the Subcommittee was forced to report, after soliciting the best opinion available, that "estimates of the number of American citizens in serious need of food vary from as few as 400,000 to more than 4,000,000." Twelve years ago a Federal study estimated that twenty-three percent of America's poor —those with incomes under $3,000—had "poor diets." In 1955 that meant 7,500,000 Americans had insufficiently nutritious diets.

Nor do we know with any degree of accuracy the minimum cost of an adequate diet. An Office of Economic Opportunity official told me a tentative conclusion had been reached that an average of $16 a month or $192 a year would provide one person with a "minimum low standard diet —enough to hold body and soul together."

On the basis of other figures compiled by the Department of Agriculture, it seemed more realistic to assume an annual minimum food cost per individual of $225, about twenty-one cents a meal.

Manifestly what is needed before the Government can deal decisively with hunger and malnutrition is a comprehensive and incisive study of the problem. We must know the number of Americans who suffer from malnutrition and, next, what can be done to correct their inadequate diets.

Let us return to Mississippi because here surveys and studies have been made and possibly they may provide clues to the nationwide dimensions of the hunger problem.

A study this year by the Department of Agriculture covered 509 poor families in two wealthy Delta counties. At least sixty percent of these families had diets providing less than two-thirds of the *minimum* dietary requirements recommended by the National Research Council. Moreover, these family diets were seriously deficient in milk, vegetables, and fresh fruits. The value of all the meals consumed by the average individual in the study was a miserable four dollars a week, or fifty-seven cents a day, including the foods distributed free by the Federal Government.

A spot-check study in seven Delta counties was made by the Mississippi Council on Human Relations and reported to us by its Executive Director, Kenneth L. Dean. Here are brief excerpts from the report:

Using an economic standard, Mississippi is the poorest state in the republic. The fact that we receive more Office of Economic Opportunity poverty program funds per capita than any other state, and that during the month of March, 1967, 405,000 people received food assistance, indicate that there is a widespread problem of poverty that could, at any given moment, turn into acute hunger or a slow starvation if Federal programs are not upgraded in keeping with population trends. . . .

The most acute problem of hunger, and the most common situation, is the middle-aged mother, without a husband, in a small two-room shack, caring for somewhere between four and fifteen children. Most of the children will be of school age but many will not be attending school. . . .

The diet of such a family usually consists of a breakfast of grits, molasses, and biscuit. For lunch the adults will eat nothing, and the children who are at home will be given a piece of bread and a drink of Kool-aid or water. The evening meal usually consists of boiled beans and corn bread. Sometimes boiled rice, dry peanut butter, or a canned meat substitute from the commodity program will supplement the evening meal.

These people, while not starving in the extreme sense of the word, are suffering from acute hunger. This hunger could be called starvation in that people's bodies actually are being denied proper sustenance, which causes the mortality rate of the [Negro] children to be much higher than that of whites, and which also shortens the life span of adults considerably. Medical doctors who work among these people say they never know the depth of their hunger for, from the time of birth on, they never have enough to eat.

Any consideration of hunger, in Mississippi or elsewhere, must take cognizance, as does the Council's report, of the distribution of surplus foods. One-fifth of Mississippi's entire population is now being fed through the Federal food distribution programs. But the too-seldom recognized fact is that surplus foods were never intended to comprise full meals or adequate diets. Nevertheless, they have become almost the only source of food for hundreds of thousands of Americans. The meaning of this for nutrition and health can be perceived in the fact that the total value of the commodities distributed amounts to about five dollars per person per month. They consist chiefly of flour, cornmeal, dry milk, and shortening. Only recently was the one can of meat per person per month added to the diet.

Appalling as this situation was it became worse when a shift from surplus commodities to food stamps in just eight Mississippi counties in one year's time deprived 36,000 poor residents of their commodity allotments. The result simply had to be more hunger and more malnutrition since these people could not afford to buy food stamps to exchange for groceries.

By far the most impressive testimony on hunger was given to the Senate Subcommittee by a group of six doctors who made a first-hand investigation of malnutrition and starvation in the Delta. Sponsored by the Field Foundation, the doctors comprised a distinguished panel of medical experts: Dr. Joseph Brenner, Medical Department, Massachusetts Institute of Technology; Dr. Robert Coles, Harvard University Health Service; Dr. Alan Mermann, Department of Pediatrics, Yale University; Dr. Milton J. E. Senn, Sterling Professor of Pediatrics, Yale University; Dr. Cyril Walwyn, Medical Adviser to Friends of the Children of Mississippi and a private practitioner in Mississippi; and Dr. Raymond Wheeler, a private practitioner of Charlotte, North Carolina.

Their report emerged as a unique document, unique in its fusion of professional and humanitarian shock and profound concern. Here is part of their findings on hunger among the Delta's children:

We saw children whose nutritional and medical condition we can only describe as shocking—even to a group of physicians whose work involves daily confrontation with disease and suffering. In child after child we saw evidence of vitamin and mineral deficiencies; serious untreated skin infections and ulcerations; eye and ear diseases; also unattended bone diseases; the prevalence of bacterial and parasitic diseases as well as severe anemia with resulting loss of energy and ability to lead a normally active life; diseases of the heart and lung—requiring surgery—which have gone undiagnosed and untreated; epileptic and other neurological disorders; severe kidney ailments that in other children would warrant immediate hospitalization; and finally, in boys and girls in every county we visited, obvious evidence of severe malnutrition, with injury to the body's tissues—its muscles, bones, and skin as well as an associated psychological state of fatigue, listlessness, and exhaustion.

We saw homes with children who are lucky to eat one meal a day—and that one inadequate so far as vitamins, minerals, or protein are concerned. We saw children who don't get to drink milk, don't get to eat fruit, green vegetables, or meat. They live on starches—grits, bread, Kool-aid. They are living under such primitive conditions that we found it hard to believe we were examining American children in the twentieth century.

In some we saw children who are hungry and who are sick—children for whom hunger is a daily fact of life and sickness, in many forms, an inevitability. *We do not want to quibble over words, but "malnutrition" is not quite what we found; the boys and girls we saw were hungry—weak, in pain, sick, their lives are being shortened; they are, in fact, visibly and predictably losing their health, their energy, and their spirits. They are suffering from hunger and disease and directly or indirectly they are dying from them—which is exactly what "starvation" means.*

The charge of starvation was supported by all six of these eminent doctors.

In their individual testimony before the Senate Subcommittee, the doctors presented other observations and conclusions, some of them almost heartbreaking.

DR. WHEELER: Only one of the [Delta] families I visited ever had milk at all and this was reserved for the "sickliest" ones. One mother summed up the question of diet in a single, poignant sentence: "These children go to bed hungry and get up hungry and don't ever know nothing else in between." Thin arms, sunken eyes, lethargic behavior, and swollen bellies were everywhere to be seen.

DR. BRENNER: What is it that makes these Negro children so vulnerable to diseases that ordinarily are no longer considered killers in the United States? These children are vulnerable because their bodily resistance is so low they don't have ability to cope with infections the way healthy children have. The main cause of lack of resistance is malnutrition. The food available to them lacks the vital components that are necessary to build healthy bodies that can develop resistance against disease. . . . I would estimate that among the many families that I saw and I visited, with 150 or 160 children, at least three-quarters of them get less than the vital amount of animal protein per day—at least three-quarters, and I think I am being very conservative. Increasing evidence has come from different countries to suggest that infants both before birth and after birth, deprived of the kinds of foods which are necessary for normal bodily growth, suffer not only visible damage to their bodies but also to the central nervous system, to the brain.

DR. COLES: I would like to speak briefly about the psychiatric aspect of my work. . . . I am describing in detail what it means for a child and his or her parents to be sick, more or less all the time, and hungry, more or less regularly. From all that one can learn, the aches and sores of the body become, for a child of four or five, more than a concrete physical factor of life; they bring in the child's mind a reflection of his worth and a judgment upon him and his family by the outside world. They ask themselves and others what they have done to be kept from the food they want or what they have done to deserve the pain they feel.

In my experience with families in the Delta, their kind of life can produce a form of withdrawal, sullen behavior. I have some of the families I knew in the South go North and carry with them that state of mind and I am now working with them in Boston. They have more food, more welfare money, and, in the public hospitals of the Northern city, certain medical services. But one sees how persistently sickness and hunger in children live on into adults who doubt any offer, mistrust any goodness or favorable turn of events.

I fear that we have among us now in this country hundreds of thousands of people who have literally grown up to be and learned to be tired, fearful, anxious, and suspicious. . . . The children need food, the kind of food that will enable their bones to grow, their blood to function as it should, their vital organs to remain healthy, and their minds to stay alert. It is inconceivable to us that children at this stage of American history, and in the context of American wealth, continue to live like this in Mississippi, in Alabama, in Kentucky, in West Virginia, in the Southwest, and, indeed, carry this condition of life to all of our Northern cities.

Later I asked Dr. Coles, a vital young psychiatrist who has not become insensitized by repeated trips into the most poverty-stricken areas of the Deep South and Appalachia, how many children suffering from malnutrition live in the Delta region today.

"There is no way, at present, of knowing for certain," he replied. "There are thousands and thousands of children in the Delta we didn't see, out of sight, out of reach, out of mind, out of access to white doctors and Negro doctors. There must be between 50,000 and 100,000 children suffering from malnutrition in the Delta."

Dr. Coles agreed on the use of the word "starvation" rather than "malnutrition." "The kind of starvation we observed," he said, "is the kind of starvation in which the body is slowly consuming itself. The body is victimized by diseases which definitely can shorten life. We saw severe malnutrition, hunger, and starvation in the sense that the body is irretrievably going downhill."

I am convinced from what I saw that among the great number of Negroes who have moved from the Deep South to Northern ghettos are some who knew starvation in the South as children, and that this bitter experience makes some of them potential recruits for the riots in cities.

I wish to reemphasize, as would the doctors, that hunger, malnutrition, and slow starvation are not confined to the Deep South nor to any other part of the country. There is, certainly, widespread hunger and malnutrition in all the Negro ghettos, North and South.

Washington, D. C., for example, is no better nor any worse than any other American city, although undoubtedly, as the center of Federal Government, it should be better. One-third of the population of the nation's capital exists at little more than subsistence level.

Under the District of Columbia's Headstart program, for example, 4,200 children recently received physical examinations. Between forty and fifty percent of these youngsters were found to have low hemoglobin counts, a condition (when not caused by infection) reflecting a food deficiency which produces nutritional anemia.

Deficient diets among Washington children are also indicated in the School Free Lunch Program which provides free lunches in elementary and secondary schools *only on application by the family, certifying need.* Nationally, a total of eleven percent of all school children receive free school lunches, but in Washington they are provided to fifty-one percent of all school youngsters.

Students may wonder if the foregoing account is exaggerated. Does anyone actually go hungry in the richest nation on earth, which ships food all over the world to the hungry? The following brief item dramatizes an affirmative answer. And it should be noted that this news item is critical of a proposed program which would be far more generous than programs presently in effect.

HOW TO EAT ON WELFARE

Women's News Service

Mrs. Philip A. Hart, wife of the Democratic Senator from Michigan, invites you to eat on welfare for the week of Dec. 1–7.

Jane Briggs Hart, who has been called a "Joan of Arc in Slacks," is heading a campaign by the National Welfare Rights Organization to tell the American public just what it's like to live on welfare, especially welfare as proposed by the Nixon administration. It has proposed federal welfare payments of a minimum of $1,600 a year for a family of four.

Since the Labor Department has calculated that a low-income family

From Women's News Service, release of November 15, 1969. Reprinted by permission.

must spend 39 percent of its income for food, that allows a family of four on welfare 19 cents a meal per person.

Mrs. Hart and the welfare rights organization have prepared a day's menu at 19 cents per person. It is:

BREAKFAST
1 glass water
1 slice toast with margarine
1 cup coffee

LUNCH
1 peanut-butter-and-jelly sandwich
1 glass Kool-aid

DINNER
1 helping macaroni and cheese
1 cup tea
or
1 helping collard greens and rice
1 cup tea
or
1 bowl chili con carne
1 cup tea or 1 glass Kool-aid

That's it, seven times a week.

The Nixon proposal would provide that no state could cut its present minimum payments to welfare clients, so in most states they would get a little more. But in 21 states the $1,600 for a family of four would be the maximum. . . .

The following article by Daniel Moynihan is in quite a different vein. It deals with the whole system of public welfare in the United States, which has been growing and changing since its inauguration during the New Deal days of the 1930's. Mr. Moynihan points out that the heart of the program involves Aid to Families of Dependent Children, which currently has over five million recipients. Originally a program for widows and their children, it has become significantly transformed into a program for the support of lower-class Negroes. As such, it is extremely controversial politically and is widely believed to hinder improvement of the basic life situations of its recipients.

Moynihan does not believe that the system is amenable to fundamental change, but he does believe that it can be improved significantly through income equalization. He makes a convincing case for the United States to adopt what all other industrial democracies in the world already have—a system of family allowances.

IMPROVING SOCIAL WELFARE:

The bankrupt welfare system

Daniel P. Moynihan

Advisor on Urban Affairs to President Nixon

In the course of the Second Session of the 90th Congress, the House of Representatives by near-unanimous action approved what must surely be the first purposively punitive welfare legislation in the history of the American national government. On the initiative of the Ways and Means Committee, the House inserted provisions in the Social Security amendments of 1967 which deny Federal funds for any further proportionate rise in the number of children being supported by the Aid to Families of Dependent Children [AFDC] program, thus placing enormous pressure on the mothers of such children to go to work, and which also institute formal investigations to determine who and where are the fathers. Inasmuch as no effort was made to conceal the fact that these provisions were designed to halt the rise in *Negro* dependence on the AFDC program, the House action might also be considered the first deliberate anti-civil rights measure of the present era.

The targets of the legislation—weak and abandoned women, helpless and surely innocent children—are equally without precedent. Dickens would have been hard put to invent a credible sponsor. The Mayor of New York declared that, if enacted, the legislation would cause a "thundering crisis" in his city. The same would be true of a dozen cities, half of them even now going through the shudders of near insurrection. . . . But for all this, on balance, the House move was probably a useful one, since it brought into the open the mounting crises in the . . . welfare system, all of which were worsening as a result of the general disinclination to acknowledge that they even existed.

The arithmetic of the present situation is clear enough. The 1960's have seen an economic expansion in the United States of all but unimagined proportions. The *increase* in the Gross National Product each year now routinely matches the *total* GNP of the early 1930's. Yet with each year of growing affluence the number of persons dependent on public charity

From Daniel P. Moynihan, "The Crisis in Welfare," *The Public Interest* (Winter 1968), as excerpted by *Current* (April, 1968), No. 94, pp. 40–51. Copyright © National Affairs, Inc., 1968. Reprinted by permission.

also grows. In many cities the growth has been quite startling. New York is now at the point where 10 percent of its population and 20 percent of its children live on welfare. The relationship of mounting dependency to escalating violence demands further explanation, while the prospect that both will lead to a massive withdrawal of support for programs to eliminate poverty and break down racial barriers is rapidly becoming a reality. After a generation of something less than benign neglect, the time is at hand for a thorough reassessment of public welfare.

The *first* of five general points this paper will make about the welfare situation is that the rising incidence of dependency in the United States has not been distributed evenly across the full spectrum of welfare categories. Anything but. Old age assistance, for example, once the central activity of the Federal welfare program, has shown a steady relative decline, in direct response to increasing national wealth and the widening coverage of social security insurance programs.

In 1966, a particularly strong year for the economy, there were declines in the number of recipients for almost all welfare programs, with one conspicuous exception—Aid to Families of Dependent Children.

In 1940, there had been 891,000 children supported by this Federal program. By the end of 1966 there were 3,526,000. With parents and caretakers the total came to 4,666,000. (It has now passed 5 million.) The recipient rate for children had risen from 22 per 1,000 population under 18 years of age to 48. . . . At a monthly cost of $184.6 million, the AFDC program had now passed Old Age Assistance as the most expensive Federal welfare program, and had become perhaps the leading conundrum of American domestic policy. . . . [In October 1966] *The New York Times* noted that the number of dependent children in the city exceeded the entire population of Omaha or Akron. . . .

On May 10, 1967, New York City Welfare Commissioner Ginsberg went before a Senate subcommittee and declared that the nation's welfare system was "bankrupt" as a social institution.

Just so. What then are the prospects for reorganizing the system? This raises the *second* general point about the existing welfare system, namely that the nation is not likely to do anything much to change it. What we can do is to improve it somewhat. . . .

The idea that the welfare system is not working is gaining currency among the elite groups in business, politics, labor, churches, and universities that in normal circumstances legitimatize and direct government-managed social change in the United States. This means there is an opportunity to make a number of important, incremental advances. . . .

The problem with changing the welfare system is not that the present system does not work, but rather that it does. It maximizes the advantages and conveniences of almost all the parties involved. It would be difficult, nigh impossible, to point to another government program of comparable importance—and equivalent potential for conflict and controversy—that works as smoothly as does welfare, or that makes as few difficult or dangerous demands on those who run the society. The present welfare system is the social equivalent of an automated factory: the input goes in and the output comes out untouched by human hands. If anything goes wrong, it is the machinery that is to blame. Moreover, the system is not costly. As a percentage of Gross National Product, social welfare expenditures are quite low in the United States as compared with other Western nations, and public assistance has consistently used up only about 1 percent of the national income. . . .

THE STRUCTURAL BASIS OF DEPENDENCY

Economists speak of structural unemployment, and the concept is similarly useful with respect to welfare dependency. For some time the national government has acknowledged the former and has taken, not total, but tentative steps to deal with the problem in terms of manpower retraining and the like. It is reasonable to think similar measures are in the offing with respect to structural problems in the field of welfare. But it is necessary to insist that we are no more likely to make a total effort with regard to welfare than with regard to unemployment. It may be useful here as well to draw a list of what such a total commitment would involve in order to understand, if not to accept this point.

Much, much less is known about the sources of welfare dependency than those of structural unemployment, so that any list must be tentative to the point of speculation; but, for the very reason that dependable knowledge is lacking, any serious total effort would have to take the unavoidably inefficient form of testing all probable approaches. A total effort to put an end to mass welfare dependency, then, would require something as follows:

(1) An end to structural unemployment and the achievement of consistently low levels of cyclical unemployment.

(2) Universal coverage for all social insurance programs, universal application of minimum wage standards, and the adoption of a nationwide system of disability insurance such as now exists in New York and three other states. The length of unemployment compensation should be permanently extended and should provide, far better than is now the case, for workers with large families.

(3) Systematic and rigid enforcement of national minimum standards of social and educational services throughout the nation, and especially in the rural South, Puerto Rico, Appalachia, Indian reservations, and the Alaskan interior.

(4) A system of income supplements for workers with families, such as now exist in most parts of the world.

(5) A massive dissemination of birth control knowledge and practice among low-income groups.

(6) Greatly increased levels of social service, directed particularly at the needs of female-headed households, combined with a greater willingness on the part of the state to remove children from homes deemed improper, and on the part of the community to encourage interracial adoption of children.

(7) Significant diminishment in racial discrimination against Negroes, especially in the area of private housing.

(8) A sharp curtailment of the freedom now by and large enjoyed by low-income groups to produce children they cannot support and, in the case of family heads, to abandon women and children they are no longer willing to live with.

In the context of such a list, it is possible better to appreciate the implications of the thought that welfare dependency is a structural problem in American society. This means it is a problem with markedly different impact on different ethnic, racial, and religious groups. To resolve it will require the imposition of uniformities of behavior in a society that has vigorously resisted anything of the sort, and has done so in the name of values a great deal more important to it than the size of the welfare rolls.

These issues, moreover, involve not just group values, but group power as well. The resistance of Southern whites to improvements in social services that would benefit Negroes is commonly understood as resistance to changes that might potentially threaten white dominance of Southern society. But not dissimilar considerations exist outside the South. Thus the United States is the only industrial democracy in the world that does not have a family allowance, a system of flat grants to all parents of dependent children. This program, which might be expected to have great support among white liberals, has so far had little—and for the openly (if mistakenly) declared reason that it would encourage the poor to have children; that it would be, in common usage, a baby bonus. White liberals are in favor of birth control, which will enable the poor to have not more but fewer children. Now at one level these are entirely benevolent attitudes. But at another they amount to nothing more or less than the view that a family allowance will increase the number of Negro votes, or Puerto Rican, or whatever, while a birth control program will decrease the number of such votes. And minority group leaders are beginning to suspect as much.

Similarly, while minority group spokesmen are increasingly protesting the oppressive features of the welfare system, and liberal scholars are actively developing the concept of the constitutional rights of welfare recipients with respect to such matters as man-in-the-house searches, it is nonetheless the fact that the poor of the United States today enjoy a quite unprecedented de facto freedom to abandon their children in the certain knowledge that society will care for them, and, what is more, in a state such as New York, to care for them by decent standards. . . . Much attention is paid the fact that the number of able-bodied men receiving benefits under the AFDC program is so small. In February 1966 Robert H. Mugge, of the Bureau of Family Services of HEW, reported that of 1,081,000 AFDC parents, there were but 56,000 "unemployed but employable fathers." But in addition to 110,000 incapacitated fathers, there were some 900,000 mothers, of whom far the greatest number had been divorced or deserted by their presumably able-bodied husbands. A working-class or middle-class American who chooses to leave his family is normally required first to go through elaborate legal proceedings and thereafter to devote much of his income to supporting them. Normally speaking, society gives him nothing. The fathers of AFDC families, however, simply disappear. Only a person invincibly prejudiced on behalf of the poor will deny that there are attractions in such freedom of movement. . . .

The third general point about the welfare situation is that the political leaders of the nation have [shunned these issues and] more or less consistently avoided any serious involvement with the problems of welfare. Which is not to say that welfare has been kept out of politics: on the contrary, it has become increasingly involved, but normally at the instance of minor figures seeking to make an impact on the public by charges of abuse and fraud, or by extreme conservative leaders who see in the rising welfare rolls a symbol of developments they generally disapprove of. But since the establishment of the present welfare system under the New Deal, the major national political leaders . . . have only rarely allowed themselves to become involved with the subject. . . . What they have done is to leave the matter to the professionals, and in so doing have given rise to an extraordinary chapter in the history of American professionalism.

For roughly a quarter century . . . the management and direction of the welfare system was kept "out of politics." This was possible largely because of a technicality in the Social Security Act that was little noticed at the time, but which was decisive later on. *Welfare costs are a charge on the Treasury which are automatically disbursed.* Neither the President nor the Congress has any but a *pro forma* say in the matter—which made it not only possible, but almost necessary to leave matters to the administrators, and this is what happened. . . .

Matters might have gone on peaceably enough, save that about halfway through this period the character of the welfare program began to change in somewhat inexplicable ways. . . . Some [systems] are able to respond creatively [to change]; some are not. Welfare was not. That is why the present crises exist.

What happened, of course, was that the nature of the AFDC program changed profoundly, and its size commenced growing at a wholly un-expected rate. The major thrust behind the Social Security Act had been the mounting Congressional support for an old-age assistance program. Little attention was paid to the ADC [Aid to Dependent Children] pro-vision, which was modeled directly on the widow's laws that had been enacted by the States. . . .

In his classic study, *The Negro Family in the United States,* published in 1939, E. Franklin Frazier of Howard University forecast that, as the bankrupt system of Southern agriculture forced more and more of the rural Negro proletariat into the cities, the problem of welfare dependency of Negro families would become increasingly acute. . . . Frazier was per-fectly correct in his forecast, and the AFDC program responded by changing, almost abruptly, from a widow's program to what in certain important respects became a Negro program.

Because this is an extremely sensitive subject, it is necessary to be explicit and somewhat detailed. Until the present moment, at least, the majority of families receiving AFDC support have been white. However, the Negro proportions have been rising steadily. A special HEW study in 1948 showed that only 29 percent of ADC families were Negro. By 1961 the proportion had increased to 44 percent, and accounted for 60 percent of the increase in the total number of AFDC families from 449,154 to 921,102. Because Negro families were larger, 1,112,106 or almost half the children supported by the program in 1961 were Negro, as against 1,165,308 whites. Moreover, 72 percent of white children receiving AFDC support in 1961 were living in rural nonfarm areas, whereas 75 percent of the Negro children were living in central cities.

It must be insisted that these proportions are functions of class far more than of race. . . . However, Americans are accustomed to thinking in categories of race, rather than class, and the AFDC program began to acquire this cast. Just as importantly, the nature of the families changed. In 1940, in the nation as a whole, 42 percent of the fathers of AFDC children were dead. By 1963 this proportion had declined to 6 percent. A good two-thirds of the children were, for practical purposes, simply abandoned. . . .

Probably this development was at least in part due to a rise in illegiti-macy. Between 1940 and 1965 the estimated *rate* of illegitimate births (per 1,000 unmarried women aged 15–44) rose from 7.1 to 23.4 for the nation as a whole. For whites the increase was from 3.6 to 11.6. For nonwhites it was from 35.6 to 97.7. The estimated illegitimacy *ratio* (per 1,000 births) rose from 19.5 to 39.6 for whites, and from 168.3 to 263.2 for nonwhites. . . . Only a minority of illegitimate children receive public assistance, and they are a distinct minority of AFDC children. . . . How-ever, there was an increasing number of such children, and they must have had an impact on the welfare program.

In short: from being a program designed to aid unfortunate *individuals,* AFDC gradually turned into a subsistence program for both individuals and for a *class.* Robert Mugge has calculated that for youths reaching 18 in 1963 approximately one white child in ten, and *six* nonwhite children in ten, had at some point in their life been supported by AFDC.

This silent transformation is the essential fact behind the present crises in welfare. The public is beginning to see it as a crisis in public expenditure. Social scientists are beginning to see it as a crisis in socal structure: the development of a permanently dependent class. And the members of that class are beginning to see in the inadequacies of the system the source of their dependency, to the point that an even greater crisis must be created in order to force the larger society to change the system.

A principal reason that these crises have crept into being is that somewhere along the line the social welfare professionals decided, in effect, to say nothing about them. In effect, to cover up. This was in some respects a consequence of the political climate of the times. . . . But it has also to do with the nature of the role of nonpolitical professionals in government.

The ADC program began with the least controversial of objectives: to aid the children of widows. . . . Gradually the typical recipient became an urban Negro or a member of some other minority group, the source of whose dependency the larger society not infrequently classified as grossly immoral conduct. It was unlikely in the extreme that the Congress would ever have enacted a program *de novo* to serve such a clientele, and even less likely that it would be moved to improve the program if greater attention were drawn to its new dimension. Lee Rainwater has suggested that, finding they could do little to improve the conditions of the welfare population, the social welfare professional opted instead to protect its good name. . . .

A circular process took effect: despairing of the public being willing to improve matters if it were told the truth, the professionals opted more or less to conceal the truth, which left the public with the impression that matters were not particularly in need of improvement.

The heart of the matter is as follows: Developments in the 1950's would have made it apparent to anyone closely involved that, despite burgeoning prosperity, patterns of income, employment, housing discrimination, and social services—*very possibly including the welfare system itself*—were somehow undermining stability of family life among the poor, particularly the urban Negro poor. There was, moreover, growing evidence that the more prestigious forms of casework and counseling had relatively little effect on the clients, however much they enhanced the status of the counselors. . . .

POLITICIZING THE WELFARE ISSUE

The fourth general point about the welfare situation is that the period of nonpolitical professional direction appears to be coming to an end. Welfare is becoming politicized. The events of 1967 in the House of Representatives settled that.

The reasons for this are various, although convergent. A principal one is that the transformation of the program and its increasing size is becoming a matter of wider public knowledge and concern. Here and there in the nation more conservative political leaders have been able to exploit the issue with some success. Terms such as "welfare mothers" and demands for residency requirements have emerged as effective forms in which to exploit anti-Negro sentiment among voters to whom raw racism would appear vulgar, even immoral. . . .

Negro and other minority groups have found it difficult to respond to these attacks. The dilemma of the Negro groups is clear enough, and would perhaps be less painful and paralyzing if it were better understood and more readily acknowledged. It is this: From one point of view the conditions of family life among the Negro lower class constitute the strongest possible indictment of the social conditions that have been imposed upon that class by the larger American society. The fact that a large group of persons is reduced to such conditions declares that the system under which they live is unjust. Period.

But from another point of view the conditions of family life among the lower class poor constitute ammunition for the charge that the people involved are worthless, are responsible for their own plight, and should expect nothing from society save ostracism and perhaps punishment. When directed against Negroes, this attitude may be based on nothing more than race prejudice. But it would be greatly mistaken to suppose that it is derived solely or even largely from racial considerations. Ironically it is every bit as likely to be associated with religious or moral convictions as is the very opposite view. In the United States, a conspicuous streak of this kind of thinking is to be found among a certain type of Catholic, preoccupied with problems of contraception and dirty magazines to a point perhaps injurious to spiritual life. But the central tradition is that of Protestant fundamentalism, and most especially *Southern* Protestant fundamentalism.

It is necessary to consider whether Negro Americans, being themselves permeated with this tradition, find it particularly excruciating to deal with the subject of disorganized family life for the very reason that their own religious inheritance is so remorselessly unforgiving of it. In truth, the inheritance of slavery—certainly a hateful thing for Negro Americans to consider—may be a relatively minor consideration in this matter when compared with the inheritance of Bible Belt Fundamentalism. This inheritance is, of course, especially marked among the Negro leadership groups, who by and large come from long-established Southern families whose domestic standards appear to have been as rigid as anything a hard shell Baptist could hope for, and indeed a rebuke to their neighbors, white and black.

Yet another convolution must be explored. Family morality or, specifically, sexual morality is such an obsession among religious conservatives in the United States that those who are in rebellion against religious conservatism tend to lump the two together. As it happens, it is just such persons, notably liberal white ministers, who have provided much leadership and support for civil rights activities. These activists and militants have been especially active in national church organizations, and by and large have resisted any examination of family problems among the poor as both an insult to a class of persons already sufficiently stigmatized and as a concession to the very forces of conservative religiosity which, in truth, in the South, are very much part of the racist coalition.

In general, many persons active in the civil rights movements, as in most social reform efforts in recent American history, bring to the undertaking a considerable disenchantment with the traditional "middle-class" values of the society. Although they are likely to be—or because they are —the products of quite successful families, ideas of family stability and morality tend to be seen by such persons as part of the bourgeois *apparat.* And they say to hell with it. . . . Somehow or other, the idea that sexual repression is bad has gotten mixed up with the idea that illegitimacy, or whatever, is good. . . .

Minority group spokesmen, when the subject is raised, tend to respond with arguments about their group values being different from those of the larger society, which is a way of saying "Let's not talk about it." Which in effect declares "Let's not do anything about it." The response is perfectly human, but not much help save to a policy of laissez-faire. Nevertheless, despite an occasional reference in NAACP literature to the fact that in the South welfare laws require families to break up in order to receive assistance, in the main the established Negro organizations, and the only now emerging organizations of Puerto Ricans and Mexican Americans, have been silent and essentially obstructionist about the subject. This of course can change, but to the present moment welfare has been a subject that civil rights leaders have chosen to ignore for the essential fact that to confront it would seem to give ammunition to their worst enemies. Not surprisingly then, the issue has been raised by militant civil rights activists who (regardless of their own color) are in revolt, not only against white American society, but also against the established Negro leaders whom they regard as mere appendixes of the larger system. Greatly stimulated by the Federal government's poverty program, with its emphasis on organizing the poor and its frequently avowed contempt for "social workers," these militants are seeking to transform welfare recipients into a powerful interest group that will no longer be forced to accept whatever bargain the welfare establishment could strike with the larger society, but rather will themselves become a party to the negotiations.[1] . . .

The aims of these groups are as yet indeterminate and not without a measure of inconsistency. Many of those involved seek nothing more than to improve the situation of welfare recipients, responding to the conviction that the existing system inculcates and perpetuates precisely the dependency that it nominally seeks to overcome. This is an essentially conservative goal, comparable in many ways to that of traditional trade unionism. (And, of course, as likely as not to be seen as radical and threatening by more comfortable parties.) . . .

There is as yet no great evidence that the welfare population has accepted their message. But the very notion that there is a welfare population—and the spectacle of the riot-torn streets of the American cities where, by and large, it lives—suggests that welfare will become an increasingly prominent political issue in the years ahead. And an ugly one. A most powerful member of the United States Senate, the man in charge of the legislation involved, openly refers to the Poverty/Rights mothers as "Black Brood Mares, Inc.," and in truth their tactics have invited such racial slurs.

The *fifth* and final general point is that, by and large, the proposals now being made for improving the welfare system would, in the first instance at the very least, have the effect of enlarging it rather than utterly transforming it.

The features of the existing system that are most objected to (and indeed are most objectionable) arise from what is almost a conflict of interest on the part of welfare agencies: they want to help their clients, but they must also strive to keep costs down. There is the added internal conflict that, within the human species, dependency evokes disdain. "Cold as charity" is the old and accurate description. . . .

Two general approaches to this dilemma have been suggested, and deserve close attention. The first is an administrative approach which seeks to eliminate the complexities and built-in tensions of the present system, involving as it does cost sharing by three levels of government in a literal maze of programs defined by category. . . . [In the proposed system,] . . . government would ask not *why*, but simply *whether* a person needed assistance, and then provide it in a context of national minimum levels. This would eliminate much confusion, and dickering—but also . . . it would increase the number of persons receiving public assistance. In 1966

[1] See *Current*, July 1966, p. 44.

only an estimated one-fifth of those families with annual incomes under $3,000 were being helped by public assistance; presumably many more would be if a single-criterion system took effect.

In another vein, a number of legal scholars and social scientists have proposed that the harassment and humiliation of welfare recipients will never end until welfare is established as a *right,* a new form of property that entitles the individual to receive benefits quite apart from his meekness, moral worth, or lack thereof. In order to achieve this, there should be a guarantee of counsel in relations between the recipient and the welfare agency, and a heightened concern by all involved for the constitutional rights of recipients in such matters as unannounced visits, without benefit of search warrant, to determine if welfare mothers are cohabiting without benefit of clergy.[2] Again it may be noted that these are proposals that in the instance will tend to increase the number of persons on welfare. It should also be noted that they may also serve to lower the public's acceptance of the program. . . . The strategy of politicizing the welfare issue is risky, indeed. It could easily serve to divide rather than unify American society, and would do so along . . . lines of race and ethnicity. . . .

On the other hand, in a state such as New York welfare has every reason, as it were, to become a political issue in that it profoundly affects the distribution of power and wealth among groups in the society. *The true issue about welfare is not what it costs the taxpayers, but what it costs the recipients.* Evidence—as usual—is practically nonexistent, but the probability is strong that the present welfare system is serving to maintain the poorest groups in society in a position of impotent fury. . . .

The new militancy is likely to have some effect, and the number of welfare recipients will be affected accordingly. It is at least possible that part of the recent rise in AFDC rates has reflected not so much a change in the size of the eligible population—no one has the foggiest idea what that size might be—but rather an increased willingness and ability on the part of eligible persons to claim what are indeed their rights. It may be assumed that this process will continue. But the larger question for public policy is, of course, how to set in motion forces that will gradually diminish the size of the population that *needs* public assistance. For some special groups—the blind, the aged, the disabled—there is likely always to be a measure of need, and this will no doubt grow somewhat with the population. But these groups are not now, and are never likely to be, either a threat to social stability or a serious charge on public resources. Indeed, in the case of the blind and the disabled it is reasonably clear that investment of public resources brings ample returns, with benefits all around. *The heart of the problem is dependent children from broken families.* The swelling number of such children must be reversed if we are

2 See *Current,* October 1967, p. 21.

not to create out of our very affluence the "under class" of which Gunnar
Myrdal has warned.

And the first point to be made is that we do not know how. . . . We
simply do not know the answers to most of the basic questions as to what
forces people into dependency and what liberates them from it. . . . [But]
we have at least brought that all-important fact out into the open.

One further point has also become clear. A high level of welfare dependency appears to have become a *normal* function of American society.
What is more, if normal social functioning will not solve the problem, then
it is required that the notion of what is normal be redefined. In a word,
what is required is social change. Unhappily, this brings on the question of
theory. What works?

In the main, efforts to bring about social change on behalf of the
American poor, and especially the Negro poor, have been dominated by
two theories, that of legal action and that of services. . . . "In [legal]
theory," James S. Coleman writes, "the arena of social action is the court,
and any advocate of social change implements his advocacy by obtaining
court rulings." The movement to establish the rights of welfare recipients
and to provide them legal counsel is derived from this theory. Coleman
argues that the evidence on the theory is quite mixed, and from his analysis
it would appear particularly difficult to apply to a highly decentralized
system such as those under which education and welfare are administered.

The second theory is that of services—providing advice, counsel, and
assistance to needy persons to enable them to function better. This has been
a dominant theme in social welfare practice and, as Lee Rainwater argues,
the "principal thrust" of the community action programs of the Federal
antipoverty program. . . .

Clearly neither of these theories is without value, and efforts to implement them must continue, but by themselves they appear to be inadequate
to the present task. What is needed now is a strategy of *income equalization.* . . . The problem of the poor is that they are excluded from the
larger society because they do not have the income needed to sustain an
"average" life. As a result we have built up a dual system under which the
goods and services—from food stuffs to marriage counseling—which most
persons purchase in the market place are provided the welfare population
by the government. The poor get their victuals from a massive company
store, and it may be doubted how much the essence of things will be
changed by transforming it into a supermarket. There will be no end of
this until the incomes of the poor are brought up to average levels. American income distribution for the past several decades has resembled an
elongated diamond—widest in the middle ranges, but reaching both far
above and below the average. Rainwater proposes a triangle-shaped distribution in which great heights may be reached, but with no one below
the base. He is right.

It might be imagined that the goal of full employment would be much more politically feasible than that of income redistribution, but it may prove just the opposite. The reason for this is that full employment requires structural changes in the economy—in the society—that impinge on a whole range of great and petty sovereignties, and in truth it may prove easier to redistribute money than power. . . . Proposals [for income maintenance] abound, most of them associated with the idea of providing a national minimum income for all. The attractions of such programs are considerable, but it must be said that so also is their cost. If they have one crucial failing, however, it relates to the present political climate of the nation, rather than to any intrinsic defect. The Negative Income Tax, and similar arrangements, would divide the nation between those who receive the benefit and those who pay for it. In the present state of race relations, and the mounting radicalism of both the left and the right, it may be argued that what is needed is a program that will benefit everyone, rather than emphasizing those qualities that divide it. For this purpose the family allowance would seem an ideal solution. . . . The advantages of a family allowance are many. It is paid automatically, requiring no means test, nor a great bureaucracy. . . . The principal disadvantage of the family allowance is that a large portion of the payments would go to families that are not now defined as poor. But this is also an advantage! The greatest number of these families are working class or lower middle class people, earning incomes in the $5,000 to $8,000 range. This is the group that by and large has been left out of the recent spate of government programs: if not forgotten, it is at least ignored. . . . This—majority—group of Americans . . . is anything but affluent. . . . The average industrial wage in the United States today does not provide even half the income necessary to meet the City Worker's Family Budget as calculated by the Bureau of Labor Statistics [for a moderate standard of living for an urban family of four]. . . .

Two other significant measures appear to be in the realm of practicable possibility for the near future: the establishment of national standards for welfare payments under the Social Security Act, and the beginning of serious research efforts to try to find out what is going on.

The case for national standards in welfare assistance is in ways a close one, although given the recent trends in welfare dependency it is at least possible that the Congressional delegations of the industrial states outside the South will organize themselves to bring about some change. The essential facts are out. First, that a large proportion of the poorest people in the nation are located in states whose welfare payments are miserable to the point of being punitive, with the result that the children dependent on them certainly suffer and very possibly are hurt in lasting ways. Second, the differential in payments between jurisdictions, however, *has* to encourage *some* migration toward urban centers in the North. . . .

In the matter of research, two general areas cry out for support. In the first instance there is a need for sustained, longitudinal studies of poverty populations to try to determine which factors lead into welfare dependency, and which lead out. . . . (An elemental question: is it a good or bad thing for AFDC mothers to go to work? In what circumstances? No one knows. Many prescribe.)

In the second instance, after three generations of professional casework, it is time we learned how genuinely to give help to those deepest in poverty. It is the judgment of such researchers as Oscar Lewis and Jane C. Kronick that there are vast numbers of families caught up in poverty who *cannot* get out by themselves and need intensive help. . . . In any case, the argument for research is compelling.

> The final article in this chapter deals with the respective roles of technological know-how and political pressures in the amelioration not only of poverty but of a variety of other problems in modern life. Based upon the Report of the Presidential Commission on Technology, Automation, and Economic Progress, the article lauds the report for its forthright advocacy of a negative income tax and expanded government employment, but criticizes it for assuming that available technological capacity will be used rationally. Experience to date indicates that tax cuts which favor the relatively well-to-do may continue to get priority over social welfare programs.

THE AUTOMATION REPORT

Robert Lekachman

Professor of Economics
State University of New York
Stony Brook

As a public document, the Report of the National Commission on Technology, Automation, and Economic Progress possesses rare virtue. The search for consensus by distinguished academics like Daniel Bell and

From *Commentary*, 41:5 (May 1966), by permission of the author and publisher. Copyright © 1966 by the American Jewish Committee.

Robert Solow, labor leaders like Walter Reuther and Joseph Bierne, and businessmen like Philip Sporn and Thomas J. Watson, Jr. has not been permitted to blunt an unusually vigorous intellectual thrust toward sharp diagnosis and effective remedy.

In order to appreciate the full value of the Report, it is wise to recall something of the context in which the Commission began its short life. The Commission was the federal government's response to the general sense of uneasiness and apprehension which has accompanied the rapid introduction into factories and offices of the computers and automatic control devices usually grouped together under the name of automation. At about the same time as the members of the group received their Presidential appointments (December 1964), the Ad Hoc Committee on the Triple Revolution issued its apocalyptic diagnosis of a forthcoming condition in which much or most work (as work is currently defined) would be rendered otiose by the new computer technology. The portion of the Ad Hoc Committee's recommendations which received the most public attention was a guaranteed minimum income payable to all members of the population either unemployed, unemployable, or earning sums below a decent minimum. Closely related to this proposal was an extreme position in the argument that has been raging for some years among economists, sociologists, and public officials—a controversy over the actual rate at which technological change has been occurring and the actual numbers of men and women who either have already been displaced by automation or are likely in the near future to be displaced. . . .

One of the virtues of the [National Commission's] Report is a well-argued resolution of the automation controversy. As the Commission interprets present rates of productivity change, the United States is not trembling on the "verge of a glut of productivity sufficient to make our economic institutions and the notion of gainful employment obsolete"—the central claim of the Triple Revolutionaries. Nevertheless, "the pace of technological change has increased in recent decades, and may increase in the future, but a sharp break in the continuity of technical progress has not occurred, nor is it likely to occur in the next decade." To this conclusion is attached an important qualification. The present acceleration in annual per capita productivity gains (excluding agriculture) from 2.0 percent before World War II to 2.5 percent since World War II, entails a doubling of total output in 28 years instead of in 36 years as in the past. The shortened time scale, judges the Report, "is quite enough to justify the feeling of continuous change that is so much a part of the contemporary environment." And, one might add, is a political fact of considerable significance.

All the Report's predictions are for the next decade only, but it is plain that the Commission is skeptical about the possibility that major technological novelties (either now in development or in earlier stages of evolution) will significantly alter present rates of technical change even beyond the next decade. Studies made for the Commission indicate that, in spite of an acceleration in the rate at which novelties are diffused, it still takes some fourteen years before inventions are translated into consumer or producer goods and a further 1–15 years before as many as half of the firms in an industry emulate the innovating leader. The inference drawn is this: "It seems safe to conclude that most major technological discoveries which will have a significant economic impact within the next decade are already at least in an identifiable stage of commercial development."

On this critical issue the Commission's argument is convincing. The Report thus reinforces the confidence of most economists in the efficacy of federal stimulation of aggregate demand as the best way to reduce unemployment. Although 4 percent is still a high rate of unemployment, it is a rate that compares favorably with the 5–7 percent range of the 1950's and early 1960's Moreover, unemployment in 1966 may well descend to 3 percent—a figure which is very close to most definitions of full employment. During the last five years, "automation" has indeed displaced workers, and quite probably at the 20,000-per-week clip so often cited in alarm, but most of those displaced have secured other jobs. The Commission has a point when it says that "the basic fact is that technology eliminates jobs, not work," at least when sensible public policy directs itself to the maintenance of high levels of aggregate demand.

This out of the way, the Report turns to the issues involved in managing social and economic policy in such a manner as to make full use of gains in productivity and full provision for a decent existence for all members of the community. What the Commission recommends to start with is familiar enough to readers of Kennedy-Johnson messages to Congress and the *Economic Reports* of the Council of Economic Advisers. Above all, it is essential that budgetary and interest-rate policy be directed toward the support at high levels of the total spending of consumers, businessmen, and public bodies. In a glancing reference to current discussions, the Commission affirms its disbelief in the idea that the "toleration of unnecessary unemployment is an acceptable way to relieve inflationary pressure." In a time of incipient inflationary pressure, what is appropriate instead is an intensification of efforts to retrain displaced workers, upgrade the semiliterate, encourage the shift of workers from less productive to more productive occupations—in short, a commitment to those elements of manpower policy which have already demonstrated their worth even according to the newly fashionable criteria of cost-benefit analysis. "Manpower policy," the Commission assures us, "is triply productive as it enriches the prospects of the disadvantaged, adds to the productive capacity of the nation, and helps relieve inflationary pressures."

As the Commission sees it, a sensible, enlightened manpower policy would facilitate desirable shifts in the occupational and the geographic job structure—movements from farms to cities, South to North, blue-collar to white-collar production of goods to production of services. It would meet the special national obligation to diminish the dangerously high rate of unemployment among the young. It would undertake a serious national mission to tackle Negro unemployment. Here the Commission makes one projection which deserves wide attention: "If nonwhites continue to hold the same proportion of jobs in each occupation as in 1964, the nonwhite unemployment rate in 1975 will be more than five times that for the labor force as a whole." The moral could not be plainer: ". . . nonwhites must gain access to the rapidly growing higher-skilled and white-collar occupations at a faster rate than in the past eight years if their unemployment rate is to be brought down to the common level." This is possible in a buoyant economy, but only if manpower measures do their job, as an indispensable supplement to aggregate measures.

All this is forthcoming and convincing, but still little more than an expression of the conventional wisdom of the 1960's, a brew which even though infinitely preferable to the insipid beverages of the Eisenhower era, is still rather low-proof. But the Report does pass beyond these fiscal, monetary, and manpower recommendations in its advocacy of two major new policies. The first emerges from the recognition that there are some people whose skills and aptitudes are simply insufficient, even after training, to enable them to compete successfully in contemporary labor markets even when these markets operate within a prosperous economy. For such unfortunates, the Commission quietly proposes that the federal government turn itself into an employer of last resort. A striking set of numbers estimates the jobs which need to be filled in order to bring public services up to *present* levels of acceptable operation. The Commission's estimates are shown in Table 1.

For the most part, these are jobs which require the simplest variety of manual skill. They are the custodial, personal-service, and public-improvement jobs, the scamping of which in our society has much to do with the filth of the cities, the inhumanity of the hospitals, the limited hours

TABLE 1.   Potential Sources of New Jobs through Public Service Employment

Source of Employment	Job Potential
Medical institutions & health services	1,200,000
Educational institutions	1,100,000
National beautification	1,300,000
Welfare and home care	700,000
Public protection	350,000
Urban renewal and sanitation	650,000
Total	5,300,000

during which museums are open, and the lack of amenity that characterizes our public places. There is a refreshing simplicity in the combination of unfilled national needs and unwanted human beings. With admirable aplomb, the Commission suggests an initial appropriation of $2-billion, enough to support possibly 500,000 additional full-time jobs.

There is a group still more unfortunate than the candidates for public-service employment. Of the 20 million people who in the fiscal year 1964–65 received $28 billion in welfare benefits, perhaps half subsist below the poverty line. They include the widowed, the disabled, the elderly, the totally incapacitated. For the genuinely needy, our welfare arrangements are woefully inadequate. As Nathan Glazer has recently emphasized, insofar as the assault on poverty is intended to raise incomes, it is in large part misdirected. We could drastically reduce the number of individuals who fall below the poverty line simply by reconstructing and enlarging our welfare benefits.

For some of the unemployed, there is at least the hope of a job sometimes. But consider the size of the average payment per person under the aid to dependent children program (ADC): it is $34 per month. As the Report summarizes the entire welfare situation: "Less than one-quarter of the 35 million people now living in poverty receive any type of public assistance payment and less than one-third of the 15 million children living in poverty benefit from public assistance." Such as it is, all assistance is administered under the most humiliating conditions, complete with means tests, detailed regulations, invasions of privacy, and incessant surveillance. The social workers, who in a more rational society might assist their clients, instead spend the bulk of their time checking up on them and filling out the endless forms which are the testimonials to their diligence, if not the mark of their own servitude.

To its great credit, the Commission proposes *not* a patching of the system alone but a negative income tax, whereby those whose income falls below a certain level would receive supplementary payments from the government. The tax is not designed as a substitute for all social-welfare programs—as Professor Milton Friedman, one of the tax's proponents, hopes—but as a valuable income supplement to the rehabilitation and sympathetic support of a better social-welfare program. For a mere $5–8 billion, it is possible to go 50 percent of the way toward the elimination of poverty-level incomes. Employing existing income-tax mechanisms, it is easy to adjust rates for negative as well as positive returns. The Commission proposal is coupled with a useful note of amplification from the labor members: federal standards should be established to prevent the more ungenerous states from seizing the opportunity to reduce their already exiguous welfare payments.

For accepting unrhetorically in a matter-of-fact manner both income maintenance and expanded government employment, the Commission deserves the very highest praise. In particular, the negative income tax, promoted by this Report and aided by the unusual concurrence (for different reasons) of liberal economists like James Tobin and conservative economists like Milton Friedman, may stand a real chance of enactment within the next five or ten years, particularly if the Vietnam war contracts in scale. At the least, the Commission has set in motion two proposals which not so very long ago had a most radical aspect to them. If it helps achieve public familiarity and then public acceptance of these proposals, the Report will deserve an honorable place as an important document of American social progress.

After saying this much, is there any reason to do other than dismiss the members of the Commission with thanks for a job far better performed than one could reasonably have anticipated of a semipublic body representing diverse interests? The answer, I think, is yes, and I shall devote the remainder of this essay to saying why.

The Report's shortcomings are closely related to its objectives, and these in turn are *not* comprehended by the fiscal, monetary, manpower, welfare, and income-maintenance programs which I have already discussed. There is no question that a society which pursued these policies and adopted these programs would be a considerably more humane society than the United States in 1966; oddly enough, it would also be a much more efficient society. Nevertheless, the thrust of the Commission's argument stretches far beyond a mere transformation of existing economic policy and social care. In the Commission's words and italics, ". . . we are being asked, *what can our society have, how can it get what it wants?* In short, we are being asked to deal with the quality of human life in the years ahead." It is according to the adequacy of the Commission's answers to its own questions that one can appropriately evaluate its work.

The Report approaches the issue of the shape of a better society in a special manner, by asking whether any means are available to us for identifying human and community needs. To this question, the Report returns a negative answer. We lack the rational mechanisms we require to tell us what is wrong with ourselves. Social policy is generally made "piecemeal." It is distorted by "vested interests" which often use their power to "obtain unjust shares." There are at hand "few mechanisms" of the kind which are necessary "to see the range of alternatives and thus enable us to choose with a comprehension of the consequences of our choice."

If we accept the Commission's reasoning, much of the explanation for the critical weaknesses of our social decisions is to be found in the division of economic goods between public and private production. For the latter, free markets are the means by which preference scales are organized. Where competition is even reasonably effective, producers who sense the tastes and inclinations of their customers flourish; those who do not, falter and fail. Thus the pattern of output corresponds broadly to the preferences of individual consumers. Not so with public goods. For "we cannot individually buy in the marketplace our share of unpolluted air," or, for that matter, our share of national defense or space exploration. If we limited higher education to those families able to purchase it for their children, we should frustrate the talents of many young people and deny the fruits of these talents to the community. Hence nobody would apply unqualified market tests to government output. Nevertheless, public production requires some acceptable justification, and it is a deficiency of our society that we lack "an effective social calculus to give us true valuations of the entire costs and benefits of individual and social purchases." So long as we lack the calculus, we cannot tell with any assurance just what the optimum combination of private consumption and public services is.

It is possible to quarrel with the Report's statement of the condition. As economists have known for a long time, private production often entails some unregistered costs. For example, Consolidated Edison's pollution of the metropolitan air raises expenditures for window cleaning, building rehabilitation, dry cleaning, medical attendance, and hospital care: in short, electrical energy costs more than the bill from the utility declares it does. And there are people who seriously question the efficiency of a private sector in which oligopoly, monopoly, and the conscientious distortion of consumer tastes by advertising are so prominent. To be really certain of the rational consequences of private markets, we should fragmentize giant corporations, ban advertising, and destroy trade unions— not a program for tomorrow.

However, for purposes of orderly exposition, let us accept the Commission's position and see where we are taken next. The Commission wants above all to improve the rationality of public choice and public expenditure. With that goal in mind, it makes three suggestions. The first is research into community needs: "For example, a research effort which resulted in a new, integrated concept of water supply, desalination, and waste disposal might prompt political action, just as the potential space and rocketry research resulted in the decision to embark on the man-to-the-moon project." (In America, the Commission seems to say, what *can* be done, soon gets done.) A second suggestion goes to the heart of the problem of estimating costs. "Efforts should be made to improve our capability to recognize and evaluate social costs and social benefits more adequately and to supply better information to the public and to political leaders on cost-benefit relationships." Finally, the Report, in an ominous throwback to the Eisenhower Commission on National Goals, recommends a commission "of high prestige and distinction which would engage in the study of national goals and in the evaluation of our national performance in relation to such goals."

On the issues raised by these proposals, the Report has much to say that is interesting and a good deal that is novel. Thus, in a discussion of health care, the Commission sees possibilities in automated multiphasic screens, diagnosing the condition of hundreds of patients each hour, and in regional health computer centers capable of storing the medical histories of 12–20 million persons; it also advances more conventional proposals for expanded training of doctors, nurses, and ancillary personnel. When it approaches the massive difficulties of creating an attractive urban environment out of our traffic-dogged, dirt-covered, and slum-defaced cities, the Commission concentrates on transportation, air and water pollution, and housing. It is convinced that federal support of a "systems research program directed toward particular multi-state regions" holds the largest promise of success. Since information about the causes of air and water pollution, and particularly about the costs of its control and prevention, is comparatively meager, the Commission is led to "urge an enlargement of current research," and more quickly a fee system designed to promote the construction of waste-disposal systems and the federal creation of river-basin authorities on a regional basis.

As for housing, the Commission regards it as the most recalcitrant of urban problems, the most antique in its techniques, the most afflicted by racial prejudice (both in construction and sale), and the most corrupted by special alliances (of contractors, unions, and politicians). Even more than usual, the Report relies here on federal action as the catalyst. The role of the federal government is crucial as the patron of basic research, the market for experimental housing, the standard-setter in its own housing programs, the leader in the modernization of obsolete building codes, and the natural promoter of a new industry centered upon mass-production techniques and massive urban reconstruction.

We have, says the Commission, the technology to do almost anything we collectively decide we want to do to improve the quality of our common environment. We simply lack the knowledge about how best to apply the technology. In social affairs, as in rocketry and military weapons systems, knowledge leads to action, even if sometimes a technology-infatuated culture does not pause to ask the consequences of the action. But just as Robert McNamara has used cost effectiveness and program budgets to rationalize the $50–60 billion which the Department of Defense annually expends, we can apply cost-benefit and systems analysis to the programming of social spending.

As a proposition, this is exceedingly seductive. It amounts to a recipe for cool research rather than hot politics, orderly university training rather than untidy street demonstrations, and the forging of a consensus out of rational thought rather than out of conflicts of ideologies and interests. Even if the picture misrepresents reality, one would like to believe that its central premise can be turned into a creative social myth of the sort which persuades people to behave in new ways.

This is why it is a pity that so little in our recent experience or our immediate prospects lends plausibility to such a vision of orderly social change. As it happens, our technology has been quite adequate for a long time to achieve certain social goals—and without any help from systems analysis. We do not need systems analysis to send larger checks to welfare clients; nor are there any technical obstacles in the way of liberalizing training allowances, educational grants to the talented sons and daughters of poor families, and unemployment compensation payments. No advance in cost-benefit analysis is required to extend the protection of workmen's compensation, unemployment insurance, and old-age benefits to migrant farm laborers. Or, to return to the shortage of health facilities: granted that computer diagnosis and sophisticated computer retrieval methods can generate vast economies in medical care, these potential gains still do not explain why in 1966 we have too few doctors. After all, we know how to train them; it is a profession endowed with high prestige: why then don't youngsters flock into medical schools, some years later to staff hospitals now largely served by foreign interns and residents? Everybody knows the familiar answers—the trade-union attitudes of the American Medical Association, the vast cost of training facilities, and the inadequate scholarship aid available for medical students. What impedes expansion is existing institutional interests and existing inequities of income distribution.

A similar observation applies to urban slums. The disgrace of their existence will persist even if building technology is modernized, craft-union sabotage defeated, and ancient building codes discarded. Given the racial prejudice which has prevented public construction of low-income housing in the suburbs and which has confined growing numbers of Negroes and Puerto Ricans to central city ghettos, not even six thousand computers deployed in serried array can bring decent housing to minorities.

What these comments imply about the Commission's approach to social change is simple enough. Change takes place either when the interests of politically potent groups are allied to change, or when such groups accept change in preference to riot and revolt. In the 1960's, the triumph of Keynesian public finance was the consequence of the belated perception by a not-very-bright business community of the benefits that government-supported prosperity offered the businessman in his search for sales and profits. Support for federal aid to higher education grew with the ascent of college tuition charges. The conservative middle classes saw their interest in higher quality education only when its costs hit them personally.

Thus, it is quite possible that in the next decade there will be general public support for federal auto-safety standards, meaningful control of pesticides, and genuine assaults upon water and air pollution. These are environmental hazards which afflict everybody. It is here, no doubt, that systems analysis, computer science, and cost-benefit analysis stand their best chance of influencing events. But it should be plain that not all the measures which the Commission supports coincide so obviously with the interests of the large prosperous majority of Americans whose incomes place them far above the poverty line and whose skin color protects them against the continuing discriminations which their less fortunately pig-mented fellow-citizens continue to encounter.

The most massive evidence of the familiar human reluctance to set the public good above personal advantage is the obvious national preference in 1963, 1964, and 1965 for general tax reductions over large social-welfare expenditures. In the last five years, federal taxes have been slashed something like $20 billion. This sum, available each year, could easily have paid for the $2 billion public-employment program the Commission recom-mends, and a generous negative income tax into the bargain. The tax-cut choice had very little to do with social valuations and a great deal to do with the political force and influence of the businessmen and middle- and upper-income families—who derived the bulk of the gains—as against the relative lack of such force and influence among the poor and the unem-ployed—who benefited only slightly from the successive tax slashes.

The remedies of poverty, like its causes, are in substantial degree political and not technical. Public transportation is more likely to become available in Watts because of last year's riots than because of the general-ized good will—a chancy emotion—of more affluent Californians. Negro schools in the South will be integrated more rapidly as Negroes become a political force to be reckoned with. As Saul Alinsky has repeatedly demon-strated, militancy on the part of the poor improves garbage collection, housing inspection, school services, even police manners. It is no accident that the Community Action Program of the War on Poverty has run into so much trouble. The dimmest mayor realizes that when the poor organize they are bound to ask for a great many inconvenient things.

It does not detract from the general intellectual value of systems and cost-benefit analysis to point out that political pressures and political choices will determine the sphere of application of the techniques. Indeed, even when these instruments of rational choice are employed, we should be wary of the results. Cost-benefit analysis can help compare the relative virtues of various job-training programs, various approaches to pollution control, or even various ways of expanding the supply of low-cost housing. But cost-benefit analysis is most unlikely to demonstrate persuasively that it is better to raise taxes than to reduce social-welfare expenditures (one of 1966's possible issues), and it is even less likely to explain just how to distribute the pains of tax increases or the pleasures of tax cuts. One wonders just how useful to Mayor Lindsay a cost-benefit analysis of com-muter payments and receipts would be. Would the triumphant conclusion that the commuters are paying less than their fair share toward city services (which everybody knows anyway) really persuade them to accept a city income tax with good grace? It is not cynical to conclude that they would continue to resist such a tax to the full extent of their political power and personal influence.

Thus at its center, the Report is flawed. Implicitly, its authors assume a basic harmony of interests among the major orders of American society. We know that this harmony has severe limits which are defined by self- and group-interest. The Report evinces a lingering confidence in the appeal to authority, here personified by "some national body of distinguished private citizens representing diverse interests and constituencies and devoted to a continuing discussion of national goals." From such a body, the Commission expects a "monitoring" of social change, an identification of "possible social trends," and a suggestion of "policy alternatives to deal with them." What it is likely to receive are either the windy platitudes of Eisenhower study groups or a series of minority reports.

Worst of all is the Commission's excessive dependence upon technique and method as the solvents of social change. Here, it seems to me, the Commission has things the wrong way around: it is not so much that social needs can be fulfilled when the technical prerequisites to their fulfillment are present; it is rather that urgently-enough felt social needs will produce the technical tools required to relieve them. This is the lesson of military technology. The commitment to social change precedes the methods by which change can be rationally evaluated; it does not follow them.

In sum, this Report deserves general gratitude and respect for what it has recommended and for the platitudes it has refrained from emitting. One hopes that it will be widely read and discussed. Its very merits entitle it to criticism for its neglect of the politics of social change, and for the optimism which leads to the hope that important social changes can be the result of amicable discussion and intelligent measurement. Even in America, even in the 1960's, significant alteration in the way we conduct our lives seems mainly to come about through social and political conflict, extralegal action, riots in the streets, and the death of martyrs.

11 Races in Conflict

Difficulties between racial and ethnic groups are worldwide. In South Africa the native black population lives under a white police state, while people speculate how long race war can be postponed. In Malaysia, Chinese are massacred by the Malays. In Northern Scandinavia the Lapps are victims of discrimination justified by rationalizations familiar to any American. In several of the new African states, native tribes, who may be identical in racial origin, are seeking to exterminate each other. In the Soviet Union, anti-Semitism revives after several decades of relative quiescence. There are a few spots, such as Hawaii and Brazil, where two or more races live quite harmoniously, but they are few indeed.

In almost all parts of the world where different racial or ethnic groups meet, varying degrees of intermittent conflict and accommodation are the norm. Will group conflict be the norm as long as different racial or ethnic groups endure? Possibly. Yet those rare groups living in comparative harmony show that race conflict is not unavoidable. We have not yet succeeded in establishing any general, universally applicable "laws" for the attainment of racial harmony, but we have learned something about the situations which make race conflict a predictable certainty. For example, the American experience demonstrates that the practice of discrimination and racial inequality amid the rhetoric of democratic equalitarianism is a certain road to race conflict. A quarter-century ago, Myrdal (*An American Dilemma*) perceived that we must surrender either the ideals of democracy or the practice of discrimination, or, failing to do either, resign ourselves to perpetual race conflict and possible race war.

Race problems in the United States involve several groups—Negroes, Puerto Ricans, Mexican-Americans, American Indians, Jews, Orientals, and possibly others. Discussion centers heavily on the black-white problem, probably because it is most threatening to white people. But if successful means of resolving the black-white problem can be found, they will probably apply, with some modifications, to most other minority problems as well.

There must be agreement upon the goals of social policy before the question of means can be intelligently discussed. Until recently, a racially integrated society was the goal agreed upon by both white liberals and most minority leaders. In recent years a militant black leadership has arisen to question both the attainability and the desirability of racial integration. They argue that whites will never permit any more than token integration and that even if integration were genuine and complete, it would destroy the black man's identity, creating a black white man.*

The following article is a sophisticated analysis of the integrationist and separatist alternatives, of the research basis for making a choice, and of the probable consequences of each.

RACIALLY SEPARATE OR TOGETHER?[1]

Thomas F. Pettigrew

Professor of Social Psychology
Harvard University

America has had an almost perpetual racial crisis for a generation. But the last third of the twentieth century has begun on a new note, a change of rhetoric and a confusion over goals. Widespread rioting is just one expression of this note. The nation hesitates; it seems to have lost its confidence that the problem can be solved; it seems unsure as to even the direction in which a solution lies. In too simple terms, yet in the style of the fashionable rhetoric, the question has become: Shall Americans of the future live racially separate or together?

This new mood is best understood when viewed within the eventful sweep of recent years. Ever since World War I, when war orders combined with the curtailment of immigration to encourage massive migration to industrial centers, Negro Americans have been undergoing rapid change as a people. The latest product of this dramatic transformation from southern peasant to northern urbanite is a second- and third-generation northern-born youth. Indeed, over half of Negro Americans alive today are below twenty-two years of age. The most significant fact about this "newest new Negro" is that he is relatively released from the principal social controls recognized by his parents and grandparents, from the restraints of an extended kinship system, a conservative religion and an acceptance of the inevitability of white supremacy.

---

* See Robert S. Browne, "The Case for Two Americas—One Black, One White," *The New York Times Magazine,* August 11, 1968, pp. 12 ff.

From the *Journal of Social Issues,* 25 (January 1969) pp. 43–69. Reprinted by permission.

[1] This paper was the author's presidential address to the Society for the Psychological Study of Social Issues, delivered at the annual convention of the American Psychological Association in San Francisco, California on September 1, 1968. Its preparation was facilitated by Contract No. OEC 1-6-061774-1887 of the United States Office of Education.

Consider the experience of the twenty-year-old Negro youth today. He was born in 1948; he was an impressionable six years old when the highest court in the land decreed against *de jure* public school segregation; he was only nine years old at the time of the Little Rock, Arkansas desegregation confrontation; he was twelve years old when the student-organized sit-ins began at segregated lunch counters throughout the South; and he has fifteen when the dramatic March-on-Washington took place and seventeen when the climactic Selma march occurred. He has literally witnessed during his short life the initial dismantling of the formal structure of white supremacy. Conventional wisdom holds that such an experience should lead to a highly satisfied generation of young Negro Americans. Newspaper headlines and social psychological theory tell us precisely the opposite is closer to the truth.

Relative Deprivation Theory

The past three decades of Negro American history constitute an almost classic case for relative deprivation theory.[2] Mass unrest has reoccurred throughout history after long periods of improvement followed by abrupt periods of reversal.[3] This pattern derives from four revolt-stirring conditions triggered by long-term improvements: (a) living conditions of the dominant group typically advance faster than those of the subordinate group; (b) the aspirations of the subordinate group climb far more rapidly than actual changes; (c) status inconsistencies among subordinate group members increase sharply; and (d) a broadening of comparative reference groups occurs for the subordinate group.[4]

Each of these four conditions typifies the Negro American situation today.[5] (a) Though the past few decades have witnessed the most rapid gains in Negro American history, these gains have generally not kept pace with those of white America during these same prosperous years. (b) Public opinion surveys document the swiftly rising aspirations of Negro Americans, especially since 1954. Moreover, (c) status inconsistency has been increasing among Negroes, particularly among the young whose educational level typically exceeds the low status employment offered them. Finally, (d) Negro Americans have greatly expanded their relevant reference

[2] T. F. Pettigrew, *A Profile of the Negro American* (Princeton, N.J.: Van Nostrand, 1964); ———, "Social Evaluation Theory: Convergences and Applications," in D. Levine, ed., *Nebraska Symposium on Motivation,* 1967 (Lincoln: University of Nebraska Press, 1967).

[3] J. C. Davies, "Toward a Theory of Revolution," *American Sociological Review,* 27 (1962) pp. 5–19.

[4] Pettigrew, "Social Evaluation Theory."

[5] J. A. Geschwender, "Social Structure and the Negro Revolt: An Examination of Some Hypotheses," *Social Forces,* 43 (1964) pp. 248–256; Pettigrew, *Negro American;* ———, "Social Evaluation Theory."

groups in recent years; affluent referents in the richest country on earth are now routinely adopted as the appropriate standard with which to judge one's condition. The second component of unrest involving a sudden reversal has been supplied, too, by the Vietnam War. Little wonder, then, that America's racial crisis reached the combustible point in the late sixties.

The young Negro surveys the current scene and observes correctly that the benefits of recent racial advances have disproportionately accrued to the expanding middle class, leaving further behind the urban lower class. While the middle-class segment of Negro America has expanded from roughly five to twenty-five percent of the group since 1940,[6] the vast majority of Negroes remain poor. Raised on the proposition that racial integration is the basic solution to racial injustice, the young Negro's doubts grow as opportunities open for the skilled while the daily lives of the unskilled go largely unaffected. Accustomed to a rapid pace of events, many Negro youth wonder if integration will ever be possible in an America where the depth of white resistance to racial change becomes painfully more evident: the equivocation of the 1964 Democratic Party Convention when faced with the challenge of the Mississippi Freedom Democratic Party; the Selma bridge brutality; the summary rejection by the 1966 Congress of antidiscrimination legislation for housing; the repressive reaction to riots from the Chicago Mayor's advocacy of police state methods to the New Jersey Governor's suspension of the Bill of Rights in Plainfield; and, finally, the wanton assassinations within ten weeks of two leading symbols of the integration movement. These events cumulated to create understandable doubts as to whether Dr. Martin Luther King's famous dream of equality could ever be achieved.

Shift in Militant Stance and Rhetoric

It is tempting to project this process further, as many mass media accounts unhesitantly have done, and suggest that all of Negro America has undergone this vast disillusionment, that Negroes now overwhelmingly reject racial integration for separatist goals. As we shall note shortly, this is emphatically not the case. Nevertheless, the militant stance and rhetoric *have* shifted, and many whites find considerable encouragement in this new Negro mood. Indeed, strictly separatist solutions for the black ghettos of urban America have been most elaborately and enthusiastically advanced not by Negroes at

---

[6] These figures derive from three gross estimates of "middle class" status: $6,000 or more annual family income, high school graduation or white-collar occupation. Thus, in 1961 roughly a fifth of Negro families received in excess of $6,000 (a percentage that now must approach a fourth even in constant dollars), in 1960, 22 percent of Negroes over 24 years of age had completed high school, and in 1966, 21 percent of employed Negroes held white-collar occupations.

all but by such white writers as newspaper columnist Joseph Alsop (1967a, 1967b) and W. H. Ferry (1968) of the Center for the Study of Democratic Institutions.[7] Nor should we confuse "black power" ideas as such with separatism, since there are numerous variants of this developing ideology, only a few of which portray a racially-separate United States as the desirable end-state. As a presumed intervening stage, black separatism is more concerned with group pride and "local control," more a retreat from whites than an attempt to dominate them. This contrasts with the traditional attempts at racial supremacy of white segregationists. Black separatism and white separatism present the danger that they might well congeal to perpetuate a racially separate nation; but they are otherwise somewhat different phenomena as a cursory examination of their basic assumptions readily reveals.

SEPARATIST ASSUMPTIONS

White segregationists, North and South, base their position upon three bedrock assumptions. First, they maintain that separation benefits both races in that each feels awkward and uncomfortable in the midst of the other.[8] Whites and Negroes are happiest and most relaxed when in the company of "their own kind." We shall call this *the comfortable assumption.*

The second assumption of white segregationists is blatantly racist. The underlying reality of the nation's racial problem, they unashamedly maintain, is that Negroes are inherently inferior to Caucasians. The findings of both social and biological science place in serious jeopardy every argument put forward for *"the racial inferiority assumption,"* and an ever decreasing minority of white Americans subscribe to it.[9] Yet it remains the essential substrata of white segregationist thinking; racial contact must be avoided, according to this reasoning, if white standards are not to be diluted. Thus, Negro attendance at a predominantly white school may

---

[7] See, too, replies to Alsop by Schwartz. R. Schwartz, T. Pettigrew, and M. Smith, "Fake Panaceas for Ghetto Education," *The New Republic,* 157 (September 23, 1967) pp. 16–19,———, "Is Desegregation Impractical?" *The New Republic,* 157 (January 6, 1968) pp. 27–29. Alsop eagerly calls for giving up the effort to integrate schools racially in order to put all efforts into achieving separate but improved schools in the ghetto. Ferry goes further and advocates "black colonies" be formally established in American central cities, complete with treaties enacted with the federal government. Black militants, in sharp contrast, complain of being in a colonial status now but do not endorse it as a desired state of affairs.

[8] Clairette P. Armstrong and A. J. Gregor, "Integrated Schools and Negro Character Development: Some Considerations of the Possible Effects," *Psychiatry,* 27 (1964) pp. 69–72.

[9] Pettigrew, *Negro American.*

benefit the Negro children, but it is deemed by segregationists as inevitably harmful to white children.[10]

The third assumption flows from this presumption of white racial superiority. Since contact can never be mutually beneficial, it will inevitably lead to racial conflict. The White Citizens' Councils in the deep South, for example, stoutly insist that they are opposed to violence and favor racial separation as the primary means of maintaining racial harmony. As long as Negroes "know their place," as long as white supremacy remains unchallenged, *"the racial conflict assumption"* contends strife will be at a minimum.

Coming from the opposite direction, black separatists fundamentally base their position upon three parallel assumptions. They agree with *"the comfortable assumption"* that both whites and Negroes are more at ease when separated from each other. Some of this agreement stems from the harsh fact that Negroes have borne the heavier burden of desegregation and have entered previously all-white institutions where open hostility is sometimes explicitly practiced by segregationist whites in order to discourage the process. Yet some of this agreement stems, too, from more subtle situations. The demands by a few black student organizations on interracial campuses for all-black facilities have been predicated on *"the comfortable assumption."*

A second assumption focuses directly upon white racism. Supported by the chief conclusion of the National Advisory Commission on Civil Disorders (1968),[11] black separatists label white racism as a central problem which so-called white liberals should confine their energies to eradicating. *"The white-liberals-must-eradicate-white-racism-assumption"* underlies two further contentions: namely, that "white liberals" should stay out of the ghetto save as their money and expertise are explicitly requested, and that it is no longer the job of black militants to confront and absorb the abuse of white racists.

The third assumption is the most basic of all, and is in tacit agreement with the segregationist notion that interracial contact as it now occurs makes only for conflict. Interaction between Negro and white Americans, it is held, can never be truly equal and mutually beneficial until Negroes gain personal and group autonomy, self-respect and power. *"The autonomy-before-contact assumption"* often underlies a two-step theory of how to achieve meaningful integration: the first step requires separation so that Negroes can regroup, unify and gain a positive self-image and

[10] Analysis specifically directed on this point shows this contention not to be true for predominantly white classrooms as contrasted with comparable all-white classrooms (U.S. Commission on Civil Rights, 1967; Vol. I, p. 160).

[11] National Advisory Commission on Civil Disorders *Report* (Washington, D.C.: U.S. Printing Office, 1968).

identity; only when this is achieved can the second step of real integration take place. Ron Karenga, a black militant leader in Los Angeles, states the idea forcefully: "We're not for isolation, but interdependence. But we can't become interdependent unless we have something to offer. We can live with whites interdependently once we have black power." [12]

Each of these ideological assumptions deserves examination in light of social psychological theory and findings.

SOCIAL PSYCHOLOGICAL CONSIDERATIONS OF SEPARATIST ASSUMPTIONS

The Comfortable Assumption

There can be no denying the reality of initial discomfort and ill-ease for many Negro and white Americans when they encounter each other in new situations. This reality is so vivid and generally recognized that both black and white separatists employ it as a key fact in their thinking, though they do not analyze its nature and origins.

The social science literature is replete with examples of the phenomenon. Kohn and Williams, for instance, studied New York State facilities unaccustomed to Negro patronage.[13] Negro researchers would enter a tavern, seek service and later record their experiences, while white researchers would observe the same situation and record their impressions for comparison. Typically the first reaction of waitresses and bartenders was embarrassment and discomfort; they turned to the owner or others in authority for guidance. When this was unavailable, the slightest behavioral cue from anyone in the situation was utilized as a gauge of what was expected of them. And if there were no such cues, confusion often continued until somehow the tense situation had been structured. Needless to add, the tension was at least as great for the potential Negro patron.

Other examples arise from small group and summer camp research. Irwin Katz has described the initial awkwardness in biracial task groups in the laboratory; white partners usually assumed an aggressive, imperious role, Negro partners a passive role.[14] Similarly, Yarrow found initial tension and keen sensitivity among many Negro children in an interracial summer camp, much of which centered around fears of rejection by white camp-

[12] B. E. Calame, "A West Coast Militant Talks Tough, But Helps Avert Racial Trouble," *The Wall Street Journal,* 172 (July 26, 1968) p. 15.

[13] M. L. Kohn and R. M. Williams, Jr., "Situational Patterning in Intergroup Relations," *American Sociological Review,* 21 (1956) pp. 164–174.

[14] Irwin Katz, "Review of Evidence Relating to Effects of Desegregation on the Performance of Negroes," *American Psychologist,* 19 (1964) pp. 381–399.

ers.[15] Not all Negroes and whites, of course, manifest this discomfort. Furthermore, such tension does not continue to pervade a truly integrated situation. Katz noted that once Negroes were cast in assertive roles behavior in his small groups became more equalitarian and this improvement generalized to new situations. Yarrow, too, observed a sharp decline in Negro anxiety and sensitivity which occurred after two weeks of successful integration at the summer camp. Similar increments in cross-racial acceptance and reductions in tension have been noted in new interracial situations in department stores,[16] the merchant marine,[17] the armed forces,[18] public housing,[19] and even among the Philadelphia police.[20]

Contact Effects Limited to the Situation

This is not to say that new interracial situations invariably lead to acceptance. As we shall note, the *conditions* of the interracial contact are crucial. Moreover, even under optimal conditions, the cross-racial acceptance generated by contact is typically limited to the particular situation. Thus, white steelworkers learn to work easily with Negroes as co-workers and vote for them as union officers; but this acceptance does not carry over to attitudes and action concerning interracial housing.[21] A segregated society restricts the generalization effects of even truly integrated situations; and at times like the present when race assumes such overwhelming salience, the racial tension of the larger society may poison previously successful interracial settings.

[15] Marian R. Yarrow, ed., "Interpersonal Dynamics in a Desegregation Process," *Journal of Social Issues,* 14 (1) (1958) pp. 3–63.

[16] J. Harding and R. Hogrefe, "Attitudes of White Department Store Employees toward Negro Coworkers," *Journal of Social Issues,* 8 (1952) pp. 18–28; G. Saenger and Emily Gilbert, "Customer Reactions to the Integration of Negro Sales Personnel," *International Journal of Opinion and Attitude Research,* 4 (1950) pp. 57–76.

[17] I. N. Brophy, "The Luxury of Anti-Negro Prejudice," *Public Opinion Quarterly,* 9 (1946) pp. 456–466.

[18] S. A. Stouffer, E. A. Suchman, L. C. DeVinney, Shirley A. Star, and R. M. Williams, Jr., *The American Soldier: Adjustment During Army Life,* Studies in Social Psychology in World War II, vol. I (Princeton, N.J.: Princeton University Press, 1949).

[19] M. Deutsch and Mary Collins, *Interracial Housing: A Psychological Evaluation of a Social Experiment* (Minneapolis: University of Minnesota Press, 1951); Marie Jahoda and Patricia West, "Race Relations in Public Housing," *Journal of Social Issues,* 7 (1951) pp. 132–139; D. M. Wilner, Rosabelle Walkley and S. W. Cook, *Human Relations in Interracial Housing: A Study of the Contact Hypothesis* (Minneapolis: University of Minnesota Press, 1955); E. Works, "The Prejudice-Interaction Hypothesis from the Point of View of the Negro Minority Group," *American Journal of Sociology,* 67 (1961) pp. 47–52.

[20] W. M. Kephart, *Racial Factors and Urban Law Enforcement* (Philadelphia: University of Pennsylvania Press, 1957).

[21] D. C. Reitzes, "The Role of Organizational Structures: Union Versus Neighborhood in a Tension Situation," *Journal of Social Issues,* 9 (1953) pp. 37–44.

Acquaintance and similarity theory helps to sort out the underlying process. Newcomb states the fundamental tenet as follows:

Insofar as persons have similar attitudes toward things of importance to both or all of them, and discover that this is so, they have shared attitudes; under most conditions the experience of sharing such attitudes is rewarding, and thus provides a basis for mutual attraction.[22]

Rokeach has applied these notions to American race relations with some surprising results. He maintains that white American rejection of Negro Americans is motivated less by racism than by assumed belief and value differences. In other words, whites generally perceive Negroes as holding contrasting beliefs, and it is this perception and not race per se that leads to rejection. Indeed, a variety of subjects have supported Rokeach's ideas by typically accepting in a social situation a Negro with similar beliefs to their own over a white with different beliefs.[23]

Additional work specifies the phenomenon more precisely. Triandis and Davis have shown that the relative importance of belief and race factors in attraction is a joint function of the interpersonal realm in question and personality.[24] Belief similarity is most critical in more formal matters of general personal evaluation and social acceptance, where racial norms are ambiguously defined. Race is most critical in intimate matters of marriage and neighborhood, where racial norms are explicitly defined. For interpersonal realms of intermediate intimacy, such as friendship, both belief and race considerations appear important. Moreover, there are wide individual differences in the application of belief similarity and race, especially in contact realms of intermediate intimacy.

(This resolution of the earlier Triandis and Rokeach controversy [25] takes on added weight when the data from studies favorable to the Rokeach

22 T. M. Newcomb, R. H. Turner, and P. E. Converse, *Social Psychology: The Study of Human Interaction* (New York: Holt, Rinehart and Winston, 1965).

23 M. Rokeach, Patricia W. Smith and R. I. Evans, "Two Kinds of Prejudice or One?" in M. Rokeach, ed., *The Open and Closed Mind* (New York: Basic Books, 1960); M. Rokeach and L. Mezei, "Race and Shared Belief as Factors in Social Choice," *Science*, 151 (1966) pp. 167–172; Carole R. Smith, L. Williams, and R. H. Willis, "Race, Sex, and Belief as Determinants of Friendship Acceptance," *Journal of Personality and Social Psychology*, 5 (1967) pp. 127–137; D. D. Stein, "The Influence of Belief Systems on Interpersonal Preference," *Psychological Monographs*, 80 (1966) whole no. 616; D. D. Stein, Jane A. Hardyck, and M. B. Smith, "Race *and* Belief: An Open and Shut Case," *Journal of Personality and Social Psychology*, 1 (1965) pp. 281–290.

24 H. C. Triandis and E. E. Davis, "Race and Belief as Determinants of Behavioral Intentions," *Journal of Personality and Social Psychology*, 2 (1965) pp. 715–725.

25 H. C. Triandis, "A Note on Rokeach's Theory of Prejudice," *Journal of Abnormal and Social Psychology*, 62 (1961) pp. 184–186; M. Rokeach, "Belief Versus Race as Determinants of Social Distance: Comment on Triandis' Paper," *Journal of Abnormal and Social Psychology*, 62 (1961) pp. 187–188.

position are examined carefully. That different interpersonal realms lead ta varying belief-race weightings is borne out by Table 4 in Stein, et al., "Race *and* Belief"; that intensely prejudiced subjects, particularly in environments where racist norms even extend into less intimate realms, will act on race primarily is shown by one sample of whites in the deep South of Smith, et al., "Race, Sex, and Belief as Determinants.")

Isolation's Negative Effects

Seen in the light of this work, racial isolation has two negative effects both of which operate to make optimal interracial contact difficult to achieve and initially tense. First, isolation prevents each group from learning of the common beliefs and values they do in fact share. Consequently, Negroes and whites kept apart come to view each other as so different that belief dissimilarity typically combines with racial considerations to cause each race to reject contact with the other. Second, isolation leads in time to the evolution of genuine differences in beliefs and values, again making interracial contact in the future less likely.

A number of pointed findings of social psychological research support this extrapolation of interpersonal attraction theory. Stein et al. noted that relatively racially-isolated ninth-graders in California assumed an undescribed Negro teen-ager to be similar to a Negro teen-ager who is described as being quite different from themselves.[26] Smith, et al. found that belief similarity relative to racial similarity was more critical in desegregated settings, less critical in segregated settings.[27] And the U.S. Commission on Civil Rights, in its study of *Racial Isolation in the Public Schools,* found that both Negro and white adults who as children had attended interracial schools were more likely today to live in an interracial neighborhood and hold more positive racial attitudes than comparable adults who had known only segregated schools.[28] Or put negatively, those Americans of both races who experienced only segregated education are more likely to reflect separatist behavior and attitudes as adults.

Racial separatism, then, is a cumulative process. It feeds upon itself and leads its victims to prefer continued separation. In an open-choice situation in Louisville, Kentucky, Negro children were far more likely to select predominantly white high schools if they were currently attending predominantly white junior high schools.[29] From these data, the U.S. Com-

[26] Stein, et al., "Race *and* Belief."

[27] Smith, et al., "Race, Sex, and Belief as Determinants."

[28] U.S. Commission on Civil Rights, *Racial Isolation in the Public Schools,* Vols. I and II (Washington, D.C.: U.S. Government Printing Office, 1967).

[29] For twelve junior highs, the Spearman-Brown rank order correlation between the white junior high percentage and the percentage of Negroes choosing predominantly white high schools is $+.82$ (corrected for ties)—significant at better than the one percent level of confidence.

mission on Civil Rights concluded: "The inference is strong that Negro high school students prefer biracial education only if they have experienced it before. If a Negro student has not received his formative education in biracial schools, the chances are he will not choose to enter one in his more mature school years." [30]

Similarly, Negro adult products of segregated schools, the Civil Rights Commission finds, are more likely to believe that interracial schools "create hardships for Negro children" and less likely to send their children to desegregated schools than Negro products of biracial schools.[31] Note that those who most fear discomfort in biracial settings are precisely those who have experienced such situations least. If desegregation actually resulted in perpetual and debilitating tension, as separatists blithely assume, it seems unlikely that children already in the situation would willingly opt for more, or that adults who have had considerable interracial contact as children would willingly submit themselves to biracial neighborhoods and their children to biracial schools.

A Social Cost Analysis Is Needed

A social cost analysis is needed. The question becomes: What price comfort? Racially homogeneous settings are often more comfortable for members of both races, though this seems to be especially true at the start of the contact and does not seem to be so debilitating that those in the situation typically wish to return to segregated living. Those who remain in racial isolation, both Negro and white, find themselves increasingly less equipped to compete in an interracial world. Lobotomized patients are more comfortable, too, but they are impaired for life.

There is nothing inevitable, then, about the tension that characterizes many initial interracial encounters in the United States. Rather it is the direct result of the racial separation that has traditionally characterized our society. In short, separation is the cause, not the remedy, for interracial awkwardness.

THE ASSUMPTIONS OF RACIAL INFERIORITY AND WHITE-LIBERALS-MUST-ERADICATE-WHITE-RACISM

The second set of separatist assumptions raises related issues. Indeed, both of these assumptions also afford classical cases of self-fulfilling prophecies. Treat a people as inferior, force them to play subservient

[30] U.S. Commission on Civil Rights, *Civil Rights, USA: Public Schools, Southern States, 1962* (Washington, D.C.: U.S. Government Printing Office, 1963).
[31] U.S. Commission on Civil Rights, *Racial Isolation.*

roles,[32] keep them essentially separate and the products will necessarily support the initial racist notions. Likewise, assume whites are unalterably racist, curtail Negro efforts to confront racism directly, separate from whites further, and the result will surely be continued, if not heightened, racism.

The core of racist attitudes, the assumption of innate racial inferiority, has been under sharp attack from social science for over three decades.[33] Partly because of this work, white American attitudes have undergone massive change over these years. For example, while only two out of five white Americans regarded Negroes as their intellectual equals in 1942, almost four out of five did by 1956—including a substantial majority of white Southerners.[34] Yet a sizable minority of white Americans, perhaps still as large as a fifth, persist in harboring racist attitudes in their most vulgar and naive form. This is an important fact in a time of polarization such as the present, for this minority becomes the vocal right anchor in the nation's social judgment process.

Racist assumptions are not only nourished by separatism but in turn rationalize separatism. Equal-status contact is avoided because of the racist stigma branded upon Negro Americans by three centuries of slavery and segregation. Yet changes are evident in social distance attitudes, too. Between 1942 and 1963, the percentage of white Americans who favored racially desegregated schools rose from 30 to 63; and those with no objections to a Negro neighbor from 35 to 63.[35] Nor has this trend abated during the recent five years of increasing polarization—a period which the mass media misinterpreted with the vague label of "backlash." [36] The most dramatic shifts have occurred in the South; the proportion of white Southern parents who stated that they would not object to having their children attend classes with "a few" Negro children rose from only 38 percent in 1963 to 62 percent by 1965.[37] Consistently favorable shifts also

[32] For a role analysis interpretation of racial interactions in the United States, see Pettigrew, *Negro American*.

[33] One of the first significant efforts in this direction was the classic intelligence study by Klineberg. O. Klineberg, *Negro Intelligence and Selective Migration* (New York: Columbia University Press, 1935). For a summary of current scientific work relevant to racist claims in health, intelligence, and crime, see Pettigrew, *Negro American*.

[34] H. H. Hyman and P. B. Sheatsley, "Attitudes toward Desegregation," *Scientific American*, 195 (December 1956) pp. 35–39; ———, "Attitudes toward Desegregation," *Scientific American*, 211 (July 1964) pp. 16–23.

[35] Hyman and Sheatsley, "Attitudes toward Desegregation"; P. B. Sheatsley, "White Attitudes toward the Negro," in T. Parsons and K. B. Clark, eds., *The Negro American* (Boston: Houghton Mifflin, 1966).

[36] The incorrect interpretation of present white animosities toward the Negro as a "backlash" is a classic case of the ecological fallacy; see Pettigrew, "Parallel and Distinctive Changes in Anti-Semitic and Anti-Negro Attitudes," in C. H. Stember, ed., *Jews in the Mind of America* (New York: Basic Books, 1966).

[37] American Institute of Public Opinion, press release, May 22, 1965.

characterized white opinion in the North. Here, a school with "a few" Negro children was declared unobjectionable by 87 percent of white parents in 1963, by 91 percent in 1965; a school where the student body was one-half Negro was acceptable to 56 percent in 1963, to 65 percent in 1965; and a school with a majority of Negro students found no objection among 31 percent in 1963, among 37 percent in 1965. Similar changes are evident in white attitudes in other realms and in more current surveys, though shifts in attitudes toward intimate contact have remained limited.

This slow but steady erosion of racist and separatist attitudes among white Americans has occurred during years of confrontation and change. To be sure, the process has been too slow to keep pace with the Negro's rising aspirations for full justice and complete eradication of racism. Yet this relentless trend parallelling the drive for integration should not be overlooked.

In a Period of Confrontation

Thus, in a period of confrontation, dramatic events can stimulate surprisingly sharp shifts in a short period of time. Consider the attitudes of white Texans before and after the tragic assassination of Martin Luther King, Jr., the riots that followed his murder, and the issuance of the forthright Report of the National Advisory Commission on Civil Disorders.[38] Table 1 shows the data collected prior to the assassination in November 1967 and February 1968 and following the assassination in May 1968.

Observe the especially large change in the four realms of relatively formal contact—desegregation in busses, jobs, restaurants and hotels; the moderate change in realms of relatively informal contact—the desegregation of schools and churches; and the lack of significant change in realms of intimate contact—desegregation of social gatherings, housing, swimming pools, house parties and college dormitories. Despite the ceiling effect, approval increased greatest for those items already most approved. One is reminded of the Triandis and Davis breakdown of racial realms by degree of intimacy.[39] The attitude change also varied among different types of white Texans; the young and the middle class shifted positively the most, again despite ceiling effects.[40] The tentative generalization growing out of

[38] National Advisory Commission *Report.*
[39] Triandis and Davis, "Race and Belief as Determinants."
[40] That the post-King murder data do not reflect merely temporary shifts is demonstrated by further data collected in Texas in August of 1968. Similar to these results was an overall shift of approximately five percent toward favoring the racial desegregation of public schools noted among white Texans between two surveys taken immediately before and after the 1957 crisis in Little Rock. And, once again, the most positive shifts were noted among the young and the middle class (R. Riley and T. F. Pettigrew, "Dramatic Events and Racial Attitude Change." Unpublished paper, Harvard University, 1968.)

TABLE 1.   Percent of White Texans Who Approve

Area of Desegregation	November 1967	February 1968	May 1968	May − Nov. + Feb. / 2 Change
Same busses	65.6	66.6	75.6	+9.5
Same jobs	68.5	70.7	77.3	+7.7
Same restaurants	60.7	62.5	69.2	+7.6
Same hotels	55.2	55.4	62.5	+7.2
Same schools	57.1	60.4	64.3	+5.6
Teach your child	53.1	53.6	57.7	+4.4
Same churches	61.5	62.9	66.2	+4.0
Same social gatherings	42.1	42.4	45.3	+3.1
Live next door	34.2	36.2	36.8	+1.6
Same swimming pools	35.1	30.9	34.2	+1.2
Same house party	29.4	30.0	30.3	+0.6
College roommate of your child	21.4	21.5	21.4	−0.1

These results are taken from R. T. Riley and T. F. Pettigrew, "Dramatic events and racial attitude change," unpublished paper, Harvard University, August 1968. The data are from probability samples of white Texans drawn and interviewed by Belden Associates of Dallas, Texas specifically for the U.S. Office of Education Contract No. OEC 1-6-061-774-1887 to Harvard University.

these data is: In times of confrontation, dramatic events can achieve positive attitude changes among those whites and in those realms least subject to separatist norms.

Contact Studies

The most solid social psychological evidence of racial attitude change comes from the contact studies. Repeated research in a variety of newly desegregated situations discovered that the attitudes of both whites and Negroes toward each other markedly improved. Thus, after the hiring of Negroes as department store clerks in New York City, one investigation noted growing acceptance of the practice among the white clerks [41] and another noted rapid acceptance among white customers.[42] And a series of studies concentrating on public housing residents found similar results,[43] as did studies on servicemen,[44] the merchant marine,[45] government work-

[41] Harding and Hogrefe, "White Department Store Employees."
[42] Saenger and Gilbert, "Customer Reactions."
[43] Deutsch and Collins, Interracial Housing; Jahoda and West, "Race Relations"; Wilner, et al., "Human Relations"; Works, "Prejudice-Interaction Hypothesis."
[44] Stouffer, et al., Social Psychology in World War II; Barbara MacKenzie, "The Importance of Contact in Determining Attitudes toward Negroes," Journal of Abnormal and Social Psychology, 43 (1948) pp. 417–441.
[45] Brophy, "Luxury of Anti-Negro Prejudice."

ers,[46] the police,[47] students,[48] and general small town populations.[49] Some of these results can be interpreted not as the result of contact, but as an indication that more tolerant white Americans seek contact with Negro Americans. A number of the investigations, however, restrict this self-selection factor, making the effects of the new contact itself the only explanation of the significant alterations in attitudes and behavior.

A major study by Deutsch and Collins illustrates this important literature.[50] These investigators took ingenious advantage of a made-to-order natural experiment. In accordance with state law, two public housing projects in New York City were desegregated; in all cases, apartment assignments were made irrespective of race or personal preference. In two comparable projects in Newark, the two races were assigned to separate buildings. Striking differences were found between the attitudes toward Negroes of randomly selected white housewives in the desegregated and segregated developments. The desegregated women held their Negro neighbors in higher esteem and were considerably more in favor of interracial housing (75 percent to 25 percent). When asked to name the chief faults of Negroes, they mentioned such personal problems as feelings of inferiority and oversensitivity; the segregated women listed such group stereotypes as troublemaking, rowdy and dangerous.

As discussed earlier, however, improvements in social distance attitudes are often limited to the immediate contact situation itself. Yet basic racist stereotypes are often affected, too. One white housewife in an interracial development put it bluntly: "Living with them my ideas have changed althogether. They're just people . . . they're not any different." Commented another: [51] "I've really come to like it. I see they're just as human as we are." And a Negro officer on an interracial ship off Korea summed it up candidly: "After a while you start thinking of whites as people."

On a National Scale

Recent surveys bear out these contact findings on a national scale. Hyman and Sheatsley found that the most extensive racial attitude changes among whites have occurred where extensive desegregation of

---

[46] MacKenzie, "Importance of Contact."

[47] Kephart, "Racial Factors."

[48] MacKenzie, "Importance of Contact."

[49] R. M. Williams, Jr., *Strangers Next Door: Ethnic Relations in American Communities* (Englewood Cliffs, N.J.: Prentice-Hall, 1964).

[50] Deutsch and Collins, *Interracial Housing*.

[51] Deutsch and Collins, *Interracial Housing*.

public facilities had already taken place.[52] And data from the Equal Educational Opportunity Survey—popularly known as "the Coleman Report" —indicate that white students who attend public schools with Negroes are the least likely to prefer all-white classrooms and all-white "close friends"; and this effect is strongest among those who began their interracial schooling in the early grades.[53] Recall, too, the similar findings of the U.S. Commission on Civil Rights for both Negro and white adults who had attended biracial schools as children.[54]

Not all intergroup contact, of course, leads to increased acceptance; sometimes it only makes matters worse. Gordon Allport,[55] in his intensive review of this research, concluded that four characteristics of the contact situation are of the utmost importance. Prejudice is lessened when the two groups: (a) possess equal status in the situation, (b) seek common goals, (c) are cooperatively dependent upon each other, and (d) interact with the positive support of authorities, laws or custom. Reviewing the same work, Kenneth Clark came to similar conclusions, and correctly predicted one year prior to the Supreme Court ruling against *de jure* public school segregation that the process would be successful only to the extent that authorities publicly backed and rigorously enforced the new policy.[56]

The Allport statement of contact conditions is actually an application of the broader theory of interpersonal attraction. All four of his conditions maximize the likelihood of shared values and beliefs being evinced and mutually perceived. Rokeach's belief similarity factor is apparently, then, a key agent in the effects of optimal contact. Thus, following the Triandis and Davis findings,[57] we would anticipate the attitude alterations achieved by intergroup contact, at least initially, to be greatest for formal realms and least for intimate realms—as with the changes wrought in white Texan attitudes by the dramatic events of early spring 1968.

Accordingly, from this social psychological perspective, the black separatist assumption that "white liberals" should eliminate white racism is an impossible and quixotic hope. One can readily appreciate the mili-

[52] Hyman and Sheatsley, "Attitudes toward Desegregation." This is, of course, a two-way causal relationship. Not only does desegregation erode racist attitudes, but desegregation tends to come first to areas where white attitudes are least racist to begin with. The Hyman-Sheatsley finding cited, however, specifically highlights the former phenomena: "In those parts of the South where some measure of school integration has taken place official action has *preceded* public sentiment, and public sentiment has then attempted to accommodate itself to the new situation."

[53] J. S. Coleman, E. Q. Campbell, C. J. Hobson, J. McPartland, A. M. Mood, F. D. Weinfeld, and R. L. York, *Equality of Educational Opportunity* (Washington, D.C.: U.S. Government Printing Office, 1966). See p. 333.

[54] U.S. Commission on Civil Rights, *Racial Isolation.*

[55] Gordon W. Allport, *The Nature of Prejudice* (Cambridge, Mass.: Addison-Wesley, 1954).

[56] Kenneth B. Clark, "Desegregation: An Appraisal of the Evidence," *Journal of Social Issues,* 9 (1953) pp. 1–76.

[57] Triandis and Davis, "Race and Belief as Determinants."

tants' desire to avoid further abuse from white racists; but their model for change is woefully inadequate. White liberals can attack racist attitudes publicly, conduct research on racist assertions, set the stage for confrontation. But with all the will in the world they cannot accomplish by themselves the needed Negro push, the dramatic events, the actual interracial contact which has gnawed away at racist beliefs for a generation. A century ago the fiery and perceptive Frederick Douglass phrased the issue pointedly:

I have found in my experience that the way to break down an unreasonable custom is to contradict it in practice. To be sure in pursuing this course I have had to contend not merely with the white race but with the black. The one has condemned me for my presumption in daring to associate with it and the other for pushing myself where it takes it for granted I am not wanted.[58]

THE ASSUMPTIONS OF RACIAL CONFLICT AND AUTONOMY-BEFORE-CONTACT

History reveals that white separatists are correct when they contend that racial change creates conflict, that if only the traditions of white supremacy were to go unchallenged racial harmony might be restored. One of the quietest periods in American racial history, 1895–1915, for example, witnessed the construction of the massive system of institutional racism as it is known today—the nadir of Negro American history as Rayford Logan calls it.[59] The price of those two decades of relative peace is still being paid by the nation. Even were it possible in the late twentieth century, then, to gain racial calm by inaction, America could not afford the enormous cost.

But if inaction is clearly impossible, the types of action called for are not so clear. Black separatists believe that efforts to further interracial contact should be abandoned or at least delayed until greater personal and group autonomy is achieved by Negroes. This is the other side of the same coin that leaves the struggle against attitudinal racism completely in the hands of "white liberals." And it runs a similar danger. Racism is reflected not only in attitudes but more importantly in institutionalized arrangements that operate to restrict Negro choice. Both forms of racism are fostered by segregation, and both have to be confronted directly by Negroes. Withdrawal into the ghetto, psychologically tempting as it may be for many,

[58] Frederick Douglass, *Life and Times of Frederick Douglass: The Complete Autobiography* (New York: Collier Books, 1962). See pp. 366–367. (Original edition in 1892.)

[59] Rayford L. Logan, *The Negro in the United States: A Brief History* (Princeton, N.J.: Van Nostrand, 1957).

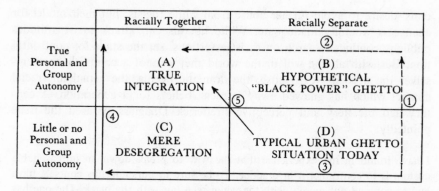

FIGURE 1.   Schematic diagram of autonomy and contact-separation.

Note: The author is indebted to Professor Karl Deutsch, of Harvard University, for several stimulating discussions out of which came this diagram. Dotted lines denote hypothetical paths, solid lines actual paths.

essentially gives up the fight to alter the racially discriminatory operations of the nation's chief institutions.

The issues involved are highlighted in the schematic diagram shown in Figure 1. By varying contact-separation and an ideologically vague concept of "autonomy," four cells emerge that represent various possibilities under discussion. Cell "A", true integration, refers to institutionalized biracial situations where there is cross-racial friendship, racial interdependence, and a strong measure of personal autonomy (and group autonomy, too, if group is defined biracially). Such situations do exist in America today, but they are rare imbattled islands in a sea of conflict. Cell "B" represents the autonomous "black power" ghetto, relatively independent of the larger society and with a far more viable existence than is commonly the case now. This is an ideologically-derived hypothetical situation, for no such urban ghettos exist today. Cell "C" stands for merely desegregated situations. Often misnamed as "integrated," these institutionalized biracial settings include both races but little cross-racial acceptance and often patronizing legacies of white supremacy. Cell "D" represents today's typical Negro scene—the highly separate urban ghetto with little or no personal or group autonomy.

To Get from "D" to "A"

Save for white separatists, observers of diverse persuasions agree that the achievement of true integration (cell "A") should be the ideal and ultimate goal. But there are, broadly speaking, three contrasting ways of getting there from the typical current situation (cell "D"). The black separatist assumes only one route is possible: from the depressed ghetto today to the hypothetical ghetto of tomorrow and then, perhaps, on to true integration (lines numbered 1 and 2 on Figure 1). The desegregation-ist assumes precisely the opposite route: from the present-day ghetto to mere desegregation and then, hopefully, on to true integration (lines num-bered 3 and 4 in Figure 1). But there is a third, more direct route right across the diagonal from the current ghetto to true integration (line 5 in Figure 1). Experience to date combines with a number of social psycho-logical considerations to favor the last of these possibilities.

The black separatist route has a surprising appeal for an untested theory; besides those whites who welcome any alternative to integration, it seems to appeal to cultural pluralists, white and black, to militant black leaders searching for a new direction to vent the ghetto's rage and despair, and to Negroes who just wish to withdraw as far away from whites as possible. Yet on reflection, the argument involves the perverse notion that the way to bring two groups together is to separate them further. One is reminded of the detrimental consequences of isolation in economics, through "closed markets," and in genetics, through "genetic drift." In social psychology, isolation between two contiguous groups generally leads to: (a) diverse value development, (b) reduced intergroup communication, (c) uncorrected perceptual distortions of each other, and (d) the growth of vested interests within both groups for continued separation. American race relations already suffer from each of these conditions; and the pro-posal for further separation, even if a gilded ghetto were possible, aims to exacerbate them further.

No Access to the Tax Base

Without pursuing the many economic and political difficulties inherent in the insulated ghetto conception, suffice it to mention the meager resources immediately available in the ghetto for the task. Recognizing this limitation, black separatists call for massive federal aid with no strings attached. But this requires a national consensus. Some separatists scoff at the direct path to integration (line 5 in Figure 1) as idealistic dreaming, then turn and casually assume the same racist society that resists integration will un-hesitantingly pour a significant portion of its treasure exclusively into ghetto efforts. Put differently, "local control" without access to the necessary tax base is not control. This raises the political limitations to the black separatist route. The Irish-American model of entering the mainstream through the political system is often cited as appropriate to black separatism —but is it really? Faster than any other immigrant group save Jewish-Americans, the Irish have assimilated via the direct diagonal of Figure 1. Forced to remain in ghettos at first, the Irish did not settle for "local control" but strove to win city hall itself. Boston's legendary James Michael Curley won "Irish power" not by becoming mayor of the South Boston ghetto, but by becoming mayor of the entire city. There are serious problems with immigrant analogies for Negroes, since immigrants never suffered from slavery and legalized segregation. But to the extent an analogy is appropriate, Mayor Carl Stokes of Cleveland and Mayor Richard Hatcher of Gary are far closer to the Irish-American model than are black separatists.

Fate Control

A critical part of black separatist thinking centers on the psychological concept of "fate control"—more familiar to psychologists as Rotter's internal control of reinforcement variable. "Until we control our own destinies, our own schools and areas," goes the argument, "blacks cannot possibly achieve the vital sense of fate control." [60] And Coleman Report data are cited to show that fate control is a critical correlate of Negro school achievement.[61] But no mention is made of the additional fact that levels of fate control among Negro children were found by Coleman to be significantly higher in interracial than in all-Negro schools. Black separatists brush this important finding aside on the grounds that all-Negro schools today are not what they envision for the future. Yet the fact remains that interracial schools appear to be facilitating the growth of fate control among Negro students now, while the ideological contention that it can be developed as well or better in uniracial schools remains an untested and hypothetical assertion.

Despite the problems, black separatists feel their route (lines 1 and 2 in Figure 1) is the only way to true integration in part because they regard the indirect desegregation path (lines 3 and 4 in Figure 1) as an affront to their dignity. One need only know the blatantly hostile and subtly rejecting racial acts that typify some interracial situations to know to what this repudiation of nonautonomous desegregation refers (cell "C" in Figure 1.[62]) But it is conceptionally and practically useful to make a clear distinction between true integration (cell "A" in Figure 1) and mere desegregation (cell "C" in Figure 1). The U.S. Commission on Civil Rights,[63] in reanalyzing Coleman's data, found this distinction provided the tool for separating empirically between effective and ineffective biracial schools

[60] J. B. Rotter, "Internal Versus External Control of Reinforcement," *Psychological Monographs,* 80 (1966) whole no. 609.

[61] Coleman, et. al., *Equality of Educational Opportunity.*

[62] M. Chessler, *In Their Own Words* (Atlanta, Ga.: Southern Regional Council, 1967).

[63] U.S. Commission on Civil Rights, *Racial Isolation.*

where whites form the majority. Negro student achievement, college aspirations and sense of fate control proved to be highest in truly integrated schools when these schools are independently defined as biracial institutions characterized by no racial tension and widespread cross-racial friendship. Merely desegregated schools, defined as biracial institutions, typified by racial tension and little cross-racial friendship have scant benefits over segregated schools.

Allport Conditions for Optimal Contact

This civil rights commission finding reflects the Allport conditions for optimal contact.[64] Truly integrated institutions afford the type of equal status, common goal, interdependent and authority-sanctioned contact that maximizes cross-racial acceptance and Rokeach's belief similarity.[65] They apparently also maximize the positive and minimize the negative factors which Katz has carefully isolated as important for Negro performance in biracial task groups.[66] And they also seem to increase the opportunity for beneficial cross-racial evaluations which may well be critical mediators of the effects of biracial schools.[67] Experimental research following up these leads is now called for to detail the precise social psychological processes operating in the truly integrated situation.[68]

The desegregation route (lines 3 and 4 in Figure 1) has been successfully navigated, though the black separatist contention that Negroes bear the principal burden for this effort is undoubtedly true. Those southern institutions that have attained integration, for example, have typically gone this indirect path. So it is not as hypothetical as the black separatist path, but it is hardly to be preferred over the direct integrationist route (line 5 in Figure 1).

[64] Allport, *The Nature of Prejudice.*

[65] Another white observer enthusiastic about black separatism even denies that the contact studies' conclusions are applicable to the classroom and other institutions which do not produce "continual and extensive equal-status contact under more or less enforced conditions of intimacy." Stember (C. H. Stember, "Evaluating Effects of the Integrated Classroom," *The Urban Review,* 2 [June 1968] pp. 30–31) selectively cites the public housing and armed forces contact investigations to support his point; but he has to omit the many studies from less intimate realms which reached the same conclusions—such as those conducted in schools (See F. 68), employment situations (see Fs. 16, 20, 44, 49), and even one involving brief clerk and customer contact (see F. 16).

[66] I. Katz, "Effects of Desegregation on Performance"; ———, "The Socialization of Competence Motivation in Minority Group Children," in D. Levine, ed., *Nebraska Symposium on Motivation,* 1967 (Lincoln: University of Nebraska Press, 1967).

[67] Pettigrew, "Social Evaluation Theory."

[68] Thomas F. Pettigrew, "Race and Equal Educational Opportunity," *Harvard Educational Review,* 38 (1968) pp. 66–76.

The Self-Fulfilling Prophecy

So why not the direct route? The standard answer is that it is impossible, that demographic trends and white resistance make it out of the question in our time. The self-fulfilling prophecy threatens once more. Secretary of Health, Education and Welfare, Wilbur Cohen, insists integration will not come in this generation—hardly a reassuring assertion from the chief of the federal department with primary responsibility for furthering the process.[69] The Secretary adopts the Alsop separatist argument and opts for programs exclusively within the ghetto, a position that makes extensive integration unlikely even a generation hence. One is reminded of the defenders of slavery who in the 1850's attacked the Abolitionists as unrealistic dreamers and insisted slavery was so deeply entrenched that efforts should be limited to making it into a benign institution.

If the nation acts on the speculations of Cohen, Alsop and Ferry, then, they will probably be proven correct in their pessimistic projections. For what better way to prevent racial change than to act on the presumption that it is impossible?

Urban Racial Demography

The belief that integration is impossible is based on some harsh facts of urban racial demography. Between 1950 and 1960, the average annual increment of Negro population in the central cities of the United States was 320,000; from 1960 to 1966 the estimated annual growth climbed to 400,000. In the suburbs, however, the average annual growth of the Negro population has declined from 60,000 between 1950 and 1960 to an estimated 33,000 between 1960 and 1966. In other words, it would require about thirteen times the present trend in suburban Negro growth just to maintain the sprawling central city ghettos at their present size. In the nation's largest metropolitan areas, then, the trend is forcefully pushing in the direction of ever-increasing separatism.

But these bleak data are not the whole picture. In the first place, they refer especially to the very largest of the metropolitan areas—to New York City, Chicago, Los Angeles, Philadelphia, Detroit, Washington, D.C., and Baltimore. Most Negro Americans, however, do not live in these

[69] Consistent with the thesis of this paper, a number of leading black separatists attacked the Cohen statement. For example, Bryant Rollins, separatist spokesman in Boston, called Cohen's statement "a cop-out" and described it as typical of "white bureacratic racists who don't want to do anything." (R. A. Jordan, "Go-slow Integration Draws Retorts," *The Boston Globe* (August 8, 1968), p. 2.

places, but reside in areas where racial integration is in fact possible in the short run were a good faith attempt to be made. The Harlems and Wattses, especially during this period of urban riots, have blinded some analysts into thinking of the entire Negro population as residing in such ghettos. Put differently, there are more Berkeleys and White Plainses—small enough for school integration to be effectively achieved—than there are New York Cities.

In the second place, the presumed impossibility of reversing the central city racial trends are based on antimetropolitan assumptions. Without metropolitan cooperation, central cities—and many suburbs, too—will find their racial problems insoluble. So need we assume such cooperation impossible? Effective state and federal incentives are being proposed, and a few established, to further this cooperation. Moreover, some large Negro ghettos are already extending into the suburbs (e.g., Pittsburgh and soon in Chicago); the first tentative metropolitan schemes to aid racial integration are emerging (e.g., Boston, Hartford, and Rochester); and several major metropolitan areas have even consolidated (e.g., Miami-Dade County and Nashville-Davidson County). Once the issue is looked at in metropolitan terms, its dimensions become more manageable. Negro Americans are found in America's metropolitan areas in almost the same ratio as white Americans; about two-thirds of each group resides in these 212 regions, so that on a metropolitan basis Negroes are not significantly more metropolitan than their one-ninth proportion in the nation as a whole.

POLICY IMPLICATIONS

Much of the policy confusion seems to derive from the assumption that since *complete* integration in the biggest cities will not be possible in the near future, present efforts toward opening integration opportunities for both Negro and white Americans are premature. This thinking obscures two fundamental issues. First, the democratic objective is not total racial integration and the elimination of the ghetto; the idea is simply to provide an honest choice between separation and integration. This separation side of the choice is available today; it is integration that is closed to Negroes who would choose it. The long-term goal is not a complete obliteration of cultural pluralism, of distinctive Negro ghettos, but rather the transformation of these ghettos from today's racial prisons to tomorrow's ethnic areas of choice. Life within ghettos can never be fully satisfactory as long as there are Negroes who reside within them only because discrimination requires them to.

Second, the integrationist alternative will not become a reality as long as we disparage it, as long as we abandon it to future generations. Exclusive attention to within-ghetto enrichment programs is almost certain, to use Kenneth Clark's pointed word, to "embalm" the ghetto, to seal it in even further from the rest of the nation (making line 2 in Figure 1 less likely yet). This danger explains the recent interest of conservative whites in exclusive ghetto enrichment programs. The bribe is straightforward: "Stop rioting and stop demanding integration, and we'll minimally support separatist programs within the ghetto." Even black separatists are understandably ambivalent about such offers, as they come from sources long identified with opposition to all racial change. Should the bargain be struck, however, American race relations will be dealt still another serious blow.

What Is Possible

The outlines of the situation, then, are these: (a) widespread integration is possible everywhere in the United States save in the largest central cities; (b) it will not come unless present trends are reversed and considerable resources are provided for the process; (c) big central cities will continue to have significant Negro concentrations even with successful metropolitan dispersal; (d) large Negro ghettos are presently in need of intensive enrichment; and (e) some ghetto enrichment programs run the clear and present danger of embalming the ghetto further.

Given this situation and the social psychological considerations of this paper, the overall strategy needed must contain the following elements:

(a) A major effort toward racial integration must be mounted in order to provide genuine choice to all Negro Americans in all realms of life. This effort should envisage by the late 1970's complete attainment of the goal in smaller communities and cities and a halting of separatist trends in major central cities with a movement toward metropolitan cooperation.

(b) A simultaneous effort is required to enrich the vast central city ghettos of the nation, to change them structurally, and to make life in them more viable. In order to avoid embalming them, however, strict criteria must be applied to proposed enrichment programs to insure that they are productive for later dispersal and integration. Restructuring the economics of the ghetto, especially the development of urban cooperatives, is a classic example of productive enrichment. The building of enormous public housing developments within the ghetto presents a good illustration of counterproductive enrichment. Some programs, such as the decentralization of huge public school systems or the encouragement of Negro business ownership, can be either productive or counterproductive depending upon how they are focused. A Bundy Decentralization Plan of many homogeneous school districts for New York City is clearly counterproductive for later integration; a Regents Plan of a relatively small number of heterogeneous school districts for New York City could well be productive. Likewise, Negro entrepreneurs encouraged to open small shops and expected to prosper with an all-Negro clientele are not only counterproductive but are probably committing economic suicide. Negro businessmen encouraged to pool resources to establish somewhat larger operations and to appeal to white as well as Negro customers on major traffic arteries in and out of the ghetto could be productive.

A Mixed Integration-Enrichment Strategy

In short, a mixed integration-enrichment strategy is called for that contains safeguards that the enrichment will not impede integration. Recent survey results strongly suggest that such a mixed strategy would meet with widespread Negro approval. On the basis of their extensive 1968 survey of Negro residents in fifteen major cities, Campbell and Schuman conclude:

Separatism appeals to from five to eighteen percent of the Negro sample, depending on the question, with the largest appeal involving black ownership of stores and black administration of schools in Negro neighborhoods, and the smallest appeal the rejection of whites as friends or in other informal contacts. Even on questions having the largest appeal, however, more than three-quarters of the Negro sample indicate a clear preference for integration. Moreover, the reasons given by respondents for their choices suggest that the desire for integration is not simply a practical wish for better material facilities, but represents a commitment to principles of nondiscrimination and racial harmony.[70]

Young men prove to be the most forthright separatists, but even here the separatist percentages for males sixteen to nineteen years of age ranged only from eleven to twenty-eight percent. An interesting interaction between type of separatism and educational level of the respondent appears in the Campbell and Schuman data.[71] Among the twenty-to-thirty-nine-year-olds, college graduates tended to be the more separatist in those realms where their training gives them a vested interest in competition-free positions— Negro-owned stores for Negro neighborhoods and Negro teachers in mostly Negro schools; while the poorly educated were most likely to believe that whites should be discouraged from taking part in civil rights organizations and to agree that "Negroes should have nothing to do with whites if they can help it" and that "there should be a separate black nation here."

[70] A. Campbell and H. Schuman, "Racial Attitudes in Fifteen American Cities," in The National Advisory Commission on Civil Disorders, Supplemental Studies (Washington, D.C.: U.S. Government Printing Office, 1968), p. 5.
[71] Campbell and Schuman, "Racial Attitudes," p. 19.

Negroes Want Both Integration and Black Identity

But if separatism draws little favorable response even in the most politicized ghettos, positive aspects of cultural pluralism attract wide interest. For example, forty-two percent endorse the statement that "Negro school children should study an African language." And this interest seems rather general across age, sex, and education categories. Campbell and Schuman regard this as evidence of a broadly supported attempt ". . . to emphasize black consciousness *without* rejection of whites . . . A substantial number of Negroes want *both* integration and black identity." [72] Or in the terms of this paper, they prefer cell "A" in Figure 1—"true integration."

The Campbell and Schuman data indicate little if any change from the prointegration results of earlier Negro surveys.[73] And they are consistent with the results of recent surveys in Detroit, Miami, New York City, and other cities.[74] Data from Bedford-Stuyvesant in Brooklyn are especially significant, for here separatist ideology and a full-scale enrichment program are in full view. Yet when asked if they would prefer to live on a block with people of the same race or of every race, eighty percent of the Negro respondents chose an interracial block.[75] Interestingly, the largest Negro segment choosing integration—eighty-eight percent—consisted of residents of public housing where a modest amount of interracial tenancy still prevails.

A final study from Watts links these surveys to the analysis of this paper. Ransford found that Negro willingness to use violence was closely and positively related to a sense of powerlessness, feelings of racial dissatisfaction, and limited contact with whites.[76] Respondents who indicated that they had no social contact with white people, "like going to the movies together or visiting each other's homes," were significantly more likely to feel powerless and express racial dissatisfaction as well as to report greater

[72] Campbell and Schuman, "Racial Attitudes," p. 6. This is not a new position for Negro Americans, for their dominant response to Marcus Garvey's movement in the 1920's was essentially the same. Garvey stressed black beauty and pride in Africa and mounted a mass movement in the urban ghettos of the day, but his "back to Africa" separatist appeals were largely ignored.

[73] W. Brink and L. Harris, *The Negro Revolution in America* (New York: Simon and Schuster, 1964); ———, *Black and White: A Study of U.S. Racial Attitudes Today* (New York: Simon and Schuster, 1967).

[74] P. Meyer, *A Survey of Attitudes of Detroit Negroes After the Riot of 1967* (Detroit: Detroit Urban League, in press); ———, *Miami Negroes: A Study in Depth* (Miami, Florida: The Miami Herald, 1968); Center for Urban Education, "Survey of the Residents of Bedford-Stuyvesant," unpublished paper, 1968.

[75] Center for Urban Education, "Residents of Bedford-Stuyvesant."

[76] H. E. Ransford, "Isolation, Powerlessness, and Violence: A Study of Attitudes and Participation in the Watts Riot," *American Journal of Sociology*, 73 (1968) pp. 581–591.

willingness to use violence. The personal, group, and national costs of racial separatism are great.

A FINAL WORD

Racially separate or together? Our social psychological examination of separatist assumptions leads to one imperative: the attainment of a viable, democratic America, free from personal and institutional rascism, requires extensive racial integration in all realms of life. To prescribe more separation because of discomfort, racism, conflict, or autonomy needs is like getting drunk again to cure a hangover. The nation's binge of *apartheid* must not be exacerbated but alleviated.

It has often been noted that one of the difficulties in relations between races (and classes) is communication. Differing backgrounds and word usages make communication difficult. Pupil and teacher often speak a different language, and learning suffers. Many standard tests—IQ tests, aptitude tests, admission tests, job qualification tests— are composed by middle-class whites, and generally discriminate against the poor in general and the Negro poor in particular. As a reverse illustration of such tests, Negro sociologist Adrian Dove composed a "Soul Folks Chitlings Test." A few items are reproduced below.

SOUL FOLKS CHITLINGS TEST

Adrian Dove

Most testmakers conceded that their own cultural backgrounds impose a distinct bias on their questions. Arguing that all U.S. employment and IQ tests reflect the culture of white, middle-class America, Negro Sociologist Adrian Dove, 33, a program analyst for the U.S. Budget Bureau, devised his own quiz. Wryly known as the "Soul Folk Chitlings Test," it is cast with a black, rather than a white, bias. Some of his 30 black imponderables prove extremely difficult for Whitey:

1. Whom did "Stagger Lee" kill (in the famous blues legend)? (a) His mother, (b) Frankie, (c) Johnny, (d) His girl friend, (e) Billy.

2. If a man is called a "Blood," then he is a (a) Fighter, (b) Mexican-American, (c) Negro, (d) Hungry Hemophile, (e) Redman or Indian.

3. If you throw the dice and seven is showing, what is facing down? (a) "Seven," (b) "Snake eyes," (c) "Boxcars," (d) "Little Joes," (e) "Eleven."

4. In "C.C. Rider," what does "C.C." stand for? (a) Civil Service, (b) Church Council, (c) Country Circuit (Preacher), (d) Country Club, (e) "Cheatin' Charlie" (the "Boxer Gunsel").

5. Cheap "Chitlings" (not the kind you purchase at a frozen-food counter) will taste rubbery unless they are cooked long enough. How soon can you quit cooking them to eat and enjoy them? (a) 15 minutes, (b) eight hours, (c) 24 hours, (d) one week (on a low flame), (e) one hour.

6. Hattie Mae Johnson is on the County. She has four children and her husband is now in jail for nonsupport, as he was unemployed and was not able to give her any money. Her welfare check is now $286 per month. Last night she went out with the biggest player in town. If she got pregnant, then nine months from now, how much more will her welfare check be? (a) $80, (b) $2, (c) $35, (d) $150, (e) $100.

7. The "Hully Gully" came from (a) East Oakland, (b) Fillmore, (c) Watts, (d) Harlem, (e) Motor City.

8. Many people say that "Juneteenth" (June 19) should be made a legal holiday because this was the day when (a) The slaves were freed in the U.S., (b) The slaves were freed in Texas, (c) The slaves were freed in Jamaica, (d) The slaves were freed in California, (e) Martin Luther King was born, (f) Booker T. Washington died.

Answers:

5)c 6)c 7)c 8)b
1)e 2)c 3)a 4)c

Many white people, impressed by the "rapid gains" Negroes have made in recent years, are puzzled and incensed to find that they are not at all grateful; instead, Negro leaders are presenting a rapidly escalating series of new demands, often in a manner most whites consider arrogant and insulting. "Why," they ask, "should Negroes act this way when we have done so much for them?"

There are several explanations given: gratitude is rare in group relations; when finally granted a long overdue *right*, the recipient is less likely to be grateful for receiving it at last than to be angered at having had to wait so long; "rapid gains" have been too few, too spotty, and too late. But none of these is very convincing. The following is a brief excerpt from an essay describing the frustrations lying behind the 1967 riots in Detroit. It may give some insight into why so many black people are not very grateful and why recent gains have been accompanied by increasing discontent.

POSTSCRIPT ON DETROIT:

"Whitey hasn't got the message"

J. Anthony Lukas

Twelfth Street today is not what it was in its kosher days. Some of the apartment buildings, where Jewish widows used to tend goldfish and philodendron, are now packed with low-income Negro families in $18-a-week apartments. But never, even in the shabbiest, does one feel trapped in a prison of asphalt, brick and cast iron as one does in Harlem.

For the 12th Street area, also known as Virginia Park, is at most only a "pocket slum" about eight blocks long and one or two blocks wide in the midst of a pleasant middle-class Negro neighborhood. A block or two away mulberry and maple trees spread dappled canopies over neatly-clipped lawns and hedges around tile-roofed bungalows.

"The cat on 12th Street can look a hundred yards away and see another black cat living in an eight-room house with a 1967 Pontiac and a motorboat on Lake Michigan," says a Negro schoolteacher. "For that matter, General Motors itself is only a few blocks away. I've seen kids from my school walk over to the showroom and sit down in a new model Cadillac, sort of snuggle their little rear ends into the soft leather, slide their hands over the slick plastic steering wheel and say, 'Man, feel that.' It's all so close, and yet it's all so far away, and the frustration just eats them up."

Nowhere in the country does a low-income Negro feel so close to affluence as he does in Detroit, because nowhere is there so much Negro affluence.

The credit, of course, goes largely to the auto industry, which pays among the highest industrial wages in the country. In the Cadillac plant,

Excerpted from J. Anthony Lukas, "Postscript on Detroit: 'Whitey Hasn't Got the Message,'" *The New York Times Magazine,* August 27, 1967, pp. 24ff. Reprinted by permission.

janitors and other unskilled workers get $2.99 an hour, assembly line men and other semiskilled workers get $3.24 and skilled workers get $3.99.

The auto industry sets the pace for all industrial wages in Detroit. If 100 is the average national wage for unskilled manufacturing positions, then Detroit's wages are 120, second only to San Francisco with 121. The figure for Cleveland is 111, Newark and Los Angeles, 110; New York, 105; Chicago, 99; Miami, 71, and San Antonio, 67.

Each Fourth of July there is a speedboat race on the Detroit River. This year, at least 30 of the yachts which lined up to watch the race were owned by Negroes. From the shore one could see Negro men in yacht caps sipping cocktails on the fantail while their daughters sunbathed.

Detroit has the country's largest chapter of the National Association for the Advancement of Colored People—18,000 members. It is also the most successful fund-raising chapter. It collected $130,000 last year, most of it at the ananul "Fight for Freedom Dinner," one of Detroit's most fashionable events.

In 1960, more than 57 percent of Detroit's Negroes owned automobiles (11.4 percent had two). About 41 percent owned their own homes in 1960, and that figure is expected to reach 48 percent by 1970. These homes are spread through such a large area of the city that it is difficult to talk of a Negro ghetto in Detroit. "If there's a ghetto, I live in it," says a white banker.

"Detroit has opened the Golden Door to the Negro," says one Negro poverty worker. "But only a relatively few Negroes can get through that door at any one time. That's the real trouble. In Jackson, Miss., no Negro can get through the door, and strangely enough that can be kind of reassuring. He can always say it's a white door and so there's no use a black man even trying. Some call it Negro laziness or apathy, but it's the disease of the ghetto. In Detroit the door is open—at least to the prepared Negro and even to some half-prepared ones. The guy who doesn't get through no longer can find solace in saying, 'I can't make it because I'm black.' He has to face the black pain."

It can be particularly painful if, just when a man thinks he's moving toward the Golden Door, the door begins to close. Despite Detroit's great opportunities, this happens repeatedly here. For the auto industry responds with particular sensitivity to fluctuations in the national economy. "When the rest of the country sneezes, we come down with pneumonia," they say here.

The auto industry had a prolonged bout of pneumonia from 1958 to 1961, made a spectacular recovery from 1962 through 1965; but from mid-1966 on, it has had a mild relapse. Employment fell 16,000 from October, 1966, to May, 1967. But May is normally the peak employment month, usually followed by a sharp drop until the new models go into production in September. Last year 36,000 men were laid off from May through August. It is a fair guess that the drop was even more severe this year.

The impact on the Negro is unquestionably greater than on the white man because whites got into most industries earlier and therefore have greater job security. No figures are available for Negro unemployment in Detroit. However, last October, when the over-all Detroit unemployment rate was 2.2 percent, a Wayne State University survey showed that the rate for Negro men in the inner city was 7.2 percent. When the overall rate reached 4 percent in May, the Negro rate was almost certainly correspondingly higher.

Although men laid off qualify for unemployment compensation, they must often stop payments on the car or TV set they were buying, and the Golden Door suddenly seems to be closing again. There is nothing much to do but stand on the corner and watch the Thunderbirds go by on 12th Street.

"You're sitting on the stoop with your head down and the man comes along and lifts it up and you begin to see some sky and then—whop—he lets it fall again," said Wilbert Martin, a 28-year-old auto worker who was laid off two months ago. Martin, who served a year in Vietnam, displays a small gash on his scalp which he says he got from a police billy on 12th Street during the trouble "although I wasn't doin' nothin.' " He calls the riot "sweet, sassy, filled with meaning whether whitey accepts it or not."

"To raise levels of expectation without providing corresponding opportunity is psychologically devastating," says George Henderson, a Negro who is an assistant to the superintendent of the Detroit public schools. "As people get a little off the bottom, they want more from life and they don't want to wait," says Philip Rutledge, another Negro who is director of Detroit's antipoverty program. "There's lots of Negro prosperity here, but too many guys aren't getting a piece of the action," says Al Dunmore, managing editor of The Michigan Chronicle, Detroit's Negro weekly. "The hopeless don't revolt because revolution is an act of hope," said Kropotkin, speaking of the Russian revolution.

All of these men are saying much the same thing—and there is a widespread suspicion here that it has something to do with what happened early that Sunday morning on 12th Street. . . .

Major developments in race relations are often precipitated by a trivial incident which triggers release of long-suppressed resentments and hostilities. The Montgomery bus boycott, which brought Martin

Luther King into national prominence, began when a weary Negro cleaning woman, ordered to give up her seat to a white person, simply said, "No."

The following report tells how an incident of unfairness provoked the Negro garbage collectors' strike in Memphis, Tennessee, which eventually claimed the national limelight. Shortly after this report was published, Martin Luther King was assassinated in Memphis. The immediate effect of his death was to insure passage of the Civil Rights Act of 1968. Another effect was to weaken the case for nonviolent solution of race problems by silencing its most effective advocate.

IN MEMPHIS: MORE THAN A GARBAGE STRIKE

J. Edward Stanfield

This report is written and published as the strike and accompanying Negro protest—the old civil rights movement still alive—in Memphis continues. Perhaps by the time this report reaches the reader, the strike and turmoil will have been settled. This is to be wished—but only if the settlement is honorable, if it reaches honestly to the issues, from the surface economic ones to the deep-lying ones of human dignity. Otherwise—as in the past in Memphis and all too many other Southern and American locales —the time of danger and of disaster will have only been postponed, with an ever-increasing store of anger and loss of faith. There is the real possibility, too, that the situation in Memphis may have deteriorated into violence and repression. If so, this report can only contribute to the record, so badly misread and misunderstood in America, of how such tragedy comes about, and of how it might be averted. In simplest terms, avoiding such tragedy was in Memphis and across America merely a matter of government and society living up to their responsibilities to all citizens.

There have been at work through the time of tension in Memphis forces and influences for positive and intelligent action meeting the highest obligations of society and government. Such forces and influences come from both races of men in Memphis. It remains a problem in all of American life how such positive people and institutions might be supported and encouraged. . . .

On Monday, Feb. 12, 1,375 men (mostly sanitation workers but also

Special Report, Southern Regional Council, March 22, 1968. Reprinted with the permission of the Southern Regional Council.

other employees of Memphis' Department of Public Works) went out on strike.

The walkout originated over a sewer worker's grievance. Twenty-two employees of that department who reported for work on Jan. 31 were sent home when it began raining. White employees were not sent home and, when the rain stopped after an hour or so, were put to work and paid for the full day. The Negro workers complained. The city then paid them two hours' "call up pay." When they saw their pay envelopes at the end of the week, they called a meeting of Memphis Local 1733 of the American Federation of State, County, and Municipal Employees (A.F.L.-C.I.O.). Local 1733 is all Negro. The local had no official status, a result of the city of Memphis' policy of not recognizing a particular union as bargaining agent for municipal employees. The question of recognition of the union was to become a central issue in the strike.

Mayor Henry Loeb, who was elected in October 1967, took the position that the strike was illegal and that the strikers had to return to work before their grievances could be discussed. He declared that he would never sign a contract, that the city could not recognize a particular union as bargaining agent for municipal employees, and that he would not agree to a dues check-off. The union insisted that Federal precedent supported its demand for recognition. Indications were that the Mayor would not be adamant on any of the other points. Coming even as it did in the shadow of the devastating, nine-day sanitation strike in New York City, the Memphis strike received little notice outside the state. It did not create a "newsworthy" crisis as the New York strike did. . . .

A cartoon published in the *Commercial Appeal* on Friday, Feb. 23, after the sit-in at City Hall on Thursday, silhouetted a fat Negro sitting atop a garbage can surrounded by a pile of rubbish and overturned receptacles. The garbage can was labeled "City Hall Sit-In." Wavy lines indicated an odor rising from the garbage heap and the black man. Above his head these fume-lines formed the legend, "Threat of Anarchy." The cartoon was titled, "Beyond the Bounds of Tolerance."

"Memphis garbage strikers have turned an illegal walkout into anarchy," said an accompanying editorial, "and Mayor Henry Loeb is exactly right when he says, 'We can't submit to this sort of thing!' . . . When the Council deals with the problem today it should not be intimidated or stampeded into imprudent decisions by yesterday's belligerent show of force." (Ironically, on Wednesday evening, scarcely twenty-four hours before that cartoon and editorial were published, *Commercial Appeal* Editor Frank R. Ahlgren had received a brotherhood award at the annual affair of the local National Conference of Christians and Jews.) . . .

The use of Mace and billy clubs by the police (during the Feb. 23rd march) resulted in unprecedented unity among Memphis Negroes. According to residents, Negro ministers who in other years were often leaders of divisive factions were virtually unanimous in calling for support of the sanitation workers and the union.

The ministers canceled a demonstration scheduled for Saturday (Feb. 24) and had a strategy meeting instead. Next day they went into their pulpits and called for a boycott of (1) all downtown stores; (2) the two daily newspapers; and (3) every establishment doing business under the name of "Loeb." (Mayor Henry Loeb's brother, William, owns a chain of barbecue and fried chicken restaurants, and a laundry chain.) They also announced downtown marches in support of the strikers and the boycott for both Monday morning and Monday afternoon, and a mass meeting at Clayborn Temple AME Church on Monday night.

The action of the police greatly strengthened the strikers. It made the preachers mad, and preachers still have influence among Negroes in the South. . . . The boycott was effective, and again the actions of the police had helped. Downtown streets and stores were virtually empty throughout the next week. . . .

In spite of Friday's bitter experience, marches were conducted daily throughout the following week (Feb. 26–Mar. 2). In Monday's march, which was typical of others during the week, most of the demonstrators were adults and nearly all were Negroes. . . . On Saturday, Mar. 2, 400 to 500 college and high-school students picketed downtown stores all day. That afternoon there was a joint march by the young people, the ministers and their followers, and the sanitation men. The papers estimated 1,000 people in that march; again observers sympathetic to the strikers guessed twice that many.

Meanwhile, on the day after the use of Mace on marchers, Mayor Loeb and City Attorney Frank B. Gianotti decided to seek an injunction against the strike in Chancery Court. Chancellor Robert Hoffman issued an injunction prohibiting engaging in a strike against the city; causing, authorizing, or inducing employees to strike against the city; picketing city property and coercing the city by striking, picketing, or other means to recognize the union as bargaining agent. Officials explained that it would be difficult to enforce the injunction so as to require the men to return to work, but 23 persons specifically named could be cited for contempt and jailed for up to ten days. These included Jerry Wurf, president of the union international; P. J. Ciampa, the union's field director; T. O. Jones, president of the local; and other national and local officers. . . .

In the state capitol at Nashville, meanwhile, Senators Joe Pipkin and Hugh Stanton of Memphis had introduced three bills aimed at the strike. The bills were rushed through the Senate committee system and scheduled for a vote in only three legislative days. One bill, passed by 21–10, provided a five-year prison sentence for persons disrupting public communication with police and fire departments. (There had been some talk in Memphis of tying up police and fire department telephone lines.)

The other two bills would have outlawed strikes against police, fire, and sanitation departments and prohibited union dues check-offs from government paychecks. Little opposition had been expressed to them, perhaps because of the speed with which they were sent through the legislative machinery. Then, on the night of the 26th, according to the Nashville *Tennessean* "Organized labor . . . descended on the legislative halls . . . and appealed to each senator." Matt Lynch, president of the State Labor Council, said "all elements of organized labor" opposed the two measures. The bills were defeated, in effect, by referring them to a committee.

Thus, in the first two weeks, a pattern was set which was not in significant degree to change through subsequent meetings of the City Council, protest confrontations of strikers and their sympathizers with police, and negotiating sessions with city officials. In effect, the Negro community, unified as probably never before around the issue of the garbage strike, met and became increasingly aware of stubborn resistance from the city's top official, and less stubborn but vacillating and ineffective responses from the City Council, this accompanied by abrasive encounters with police and harsh criticism from the press. A measure of support unprecedented in the South had come from white union members who marched some 500 strong with the strikers on Mar. 4. But beyond that, the other elements of white power, including clergy and businesses, the latter hard-hit by the boycott, had not effectively entered the crisis on either side, a not unusual situation in the South. With each passing day of inability of the city (and beyond it, the state and the nation) to deal realistically with the simple terms of the strike and the larger issues of rightful Negro demands, tension in Memphis mounted.

By Mar. 7, such whites as Baxton Bryant (Executive Director of the Tennessee Council of Human Relations), who had played a valuable role as a trusted intermediary between the Negro community and the city, began to doubt the utility of their function. It seemed to them that the city officials retained the imperturbable, immemorial Southern charm and willingness to discuss the problem, but that in fact they were not yielding an inch. Perhaps he should cease walking through open doors which led only to closed minds, Bryant suggested to the Reverend Starks, president of the black Interdenominational Ministers Alliance, over breakfast that morning. "Oh, no," responded Starks. "Somebody's got to talk to them; some channels have got to stay open. And *we* can't do it. We've got nothing to say to them any more."

But a man as positively disposed toward life as Reverend Starks has difficulty in persuading himself of his own counsel of despair. He decided to join Bryant and a reporter in interviews with the Mayor and Downing Pryor. In both interviews, Bryant tried to convey his sense of the dangerously escalating hostility between the solidified Negro community and the city officialdom. He cited the report of the National Advisory Commission on Civil Disorders. Memphis was becoming a perfect example of two alienated, antagonistic communities tensely confronting one another, he said. The Mayor responded with great personal warmth, repeated his unalterable opposition to dues check-off, now the crux of the conflict. In the large, beautifully appointed, softly-shaded office, the anguish expressed by Bryant and reflected in the tense face of Starks, seemed incapable of passing to the other side of the executive desk.

But if the Mayor was unmoved, he was not inactive. He wanted so much to "keep talking" to the Negro leadership and he was so happy Starks had come. Could he not return later? The Mayor would be happy to clear his calendar. Was it not of the utmost importance "that we keep talking to each other?" The group was rising to leave, but it looked as if Starks were rising alone. He drew himself up to his full height and said, "No, Mayor. I cannot come to see you. Our community has taken a position and I stand with them. You have to talk to all of us." There was no sign that the Mayor had heard the death knell of plantation politics for the duration of this crisis.

Councilman Downing Pryor tried to express his personal concern, and the helplessness of the Council. Any action by the City Council would require six weeks to hurdle a mayoral veto—surely that was too late? But Starks did not let him off so easy. A prounion resolution by the Council would not only hearten the Negro community, but show them that there was now an independent agency at city hall, capable of redressing their grievances. Pryor evaded this challenge, describing instead the bold new fair employment resolution promulgated by the Council: Increased hiring of Negroes until their number in city jobs equals their percentage in the population, accompanied by the necessary placement and training services. It sounded like a serious piece of legislation and there was little doubt that it had been hastened, if not inspired, by the mobilization of the black community behind the sanitation workers.

The objectives of the strike were outlined by Jerry Wurf, president of the AFSCME (AFL-CIO) as follows: (1) Union recognition and a contract with the city. (2) Effective grievance procedures ("So if it rains they don't send a man home like a dog without wages—or worse, send you home and give the white man wages.") (3) Union payroll deduction, or dues check-off. (4) Merit promotion—without regard to race. (5) Equal treatment in the retirement system. (6) Payment of overtime. (7) Decent wages.

Something like accord was reached early in the strike on all of the strikers' demands except union recognition and dues check-off. . . .

After the Negro community, led by the preachers, got into the fight other issues were defined. Dr. Ralph Jackson, director of the Department of Minimum Salary of the African Methodist Episcopal Church, was principal speaker at the mass meeting on Monday night, Feb. 26. "We're going to march until the sanitation workers say 'Satisfied!' " he told the crowd. . . . "But I have news for you: We're going to march *after that!*" And again the crowd let it be known that he was speaking for them.

He listed the following issues: (1) Police treatment. (2) Housing. ("The housing authority has announced plans for 12,000 units—8,000 for whites and 4,000 for Negroes. Well, they'll never get off with it!") (3) Jobs. ("And the days of the *one* Negro are over. You know what I mean,—one here, one there, and one over yonder—and look what we've done for you!") (4) Wage scales. (5) Justice in the schools. . . .

The police were always very much in evidence before and during the marches downtown or when workers and sympathizers attended meetings at city hall. They talked back and forth on walkie-talkies. They cruised in police cars with shotgun muzzles visible above the dashboards. Little wonder the crowds were sparse for the marches. Rumor had it that the Mayor was greatly pleased at the report that only 120 people showed up for one of the marches, and concluded that the strike would play out. But at the mass meetings in Negro churches and at the rallies in the union hall, when no police were in evidence, the meeting places were packed and jammed. . . . The past record of the Memphis Police Department in this crucial area of relations with Negro citizens has not been a notably bad one, as these things go in the South and the nation. . . . Incredibly, albeit incidentally, it was reported on Feb. 27 that 3,000 Tennessee National Guardsmen were to bivouac in Memphis on Mar. 9 for one day of riot control practice. Other drills were to be staged simultaneously in Nashville and Knoxville. The practice was planned to acquaint Guardsmen with the topography of the city and identify potential trouble spots. Details were not revealed. The Guardsmen would be outfitted, the report said, in full field gear, including weapons.

The drill took place on schedule, but without incident. The Guard avoided "areas of existing tension."

Negro citizens' complaints against police and the newspapers were only a part of the problem in Memphis. The attitude of public officials was the common denominator of the preachers and the garbage collectors in their struggle. If one were required to say in a word what the strike and the marches and the mass meetings in Memphis were all about, that word would have to be *dignity*. One can read in the narrative of events of those days in Memphis a chronicle of indignities suffered by Negroes at the hands of the Public Works Department, of the City Council, and of the Mayor. Early in the strike, the people began calling him "King Henry."

Dr. Ralph Jackson was by his own admission a conservative minister. But he happened to be marching in support of the strikers when the police broke up that march and his ministerial standing meant nothing: he was gassed with all the others. Preaching at one of the mass meetings, he let it be known that the Mace had opened his eyes: "I have a confession to make. For thirty years I have been training to hold myself in check. I couldn't understand what made some people lose control of themselves and fly off the handle. I never thought it would happen to me. But I lost thirty years of training in just five minutes last Friday!" . . . Jesse Epps is the AFSCME's staff man in charge of the southern region. Highly capable, he is a union organizer who recites poetry ("Heaven is not reached at a single bound. . . .") and quotes the Bible accurately. In one of those quiet, two-men-in-a-room conversation that do not lend themselves to posturing, he said matter-of-factly and with a far-away look, "I don't think I've ever been so hurt as I was when the City Council walked out last Friday afternoon without hearing the people." This was Jesse Epps the man, the black man, talking—not Jesse Epps the union organizer. "The basic issue," he continued, "is not pay, but recognition of the union. There has never been the unity in the Negro community of Memphis that there is now, and the reason is that recognition of the union involves recognition of the workers as *men*. The Mayor wants to say, 'Go on back to work and then we'll do right about your complaints; you know our word is as good as our bond.' Just as if Memphis were a Delta plantation."

There is much talk these days about coalitions, and particularly a coalition of the labor movement and the civil rights movement. What happened at Memphis seems, at first glance, anyway, to be an example of the kind of coalition that is so much discussed. Union men readily acknowledge that, if it were not for the Negro ministers and the unity of the Negro community behind them, the sanitation workers "wouldn't have the chance of a snowball in hell." On the other hand, the union has provided the sort of know-how (and money) that seems to be necessary these days to come to grips with a not-so-simple issue around which to rally liberal and minority-group forces. AFSCME officials did this without preempting —and, in fact, encouraging—local leadership of the strike. . . .

In Memphis, labor forces were standoffish at first. The rank and file were all for better wages and working conditions for the sanitation men, but did not care for the civil rights overtones. As late as the fifteenth day of the strike, an AFSCME official commented that he had heard from only three white men representing local labor unions. There had been a few relatively small checks for the strike fund, he said, but helpful as that was, he needed some white faces at the union hall rallies to let the sanitation men know that they had labor's support. The evidence of support came on Mar. 4, at the beginning of the fourth week of the strike. . . . Five hundred white labor unionists joined Negro ministers and sanitation workers in the daily downtown march. It was a red-letter day for the strikers.

It remained to be seen whether the AFSCME or other unions will find in the Memphis experience anything like a standard procedure for organizing in the South. Perhaps conditions in Memphis were unique. . . . Nevertheless, the coalition of civil rights forces with organized labor in Memphis, however brief or singular, was noteworthy. President Wurf had the candor to acknowledge at one mass meeting that some parts of the AFL-CIO have given Negroes less than a fair shake. . . .

It was unusual, labor observers said, for a national president of a union to put so much of his personal prestige on the line in a situation as unsure of victory and unpredictable in tone as that in Memphis. Mr. Wurf's union does have a large number of Negro members across the nation, and they might be expected to be pleased with his role in Memphis. But beyond that, he seemed genuinely involved in the demand for dignity that transcended the practical and pragmatic aspects of the struggle in Memphis.

The outcome of the strike remains doubtful. At the end of the fourth week, both city officials and strikers were standing firm. . . .

In the midst of all the drama in Memphis, the excursions and alarums, one sensed tragedy waiting in the wings. For one thing, there was a strong undertone of alienation, even among the ministers, whose basic attitude toward the society is positive. . . . (With a few exceptions) the white churches and churchmen of Memphis were not notably involved. . . .

(One) preacher (at a church meeting) said that the ministers were committed to nonviolence as a way of life. "But if we ministers, leading the people our way, cannot get results, we have no alternative but to withdraw and. . . ." The end of his sentence was lost in an approving roar, in the midst of which he turned and pointed into the balcony where three or four young black men, self-proclaimed radicals, stood watching. They broke into broad grins. . . .

When he had finished his sermon, Dr. Jackson came to the pulpit to direct the taking of a collection for the strike fund. . . . "When Dr. Brewster was up here talking about loving Loeb," he said, "Bishop Patterson passed me a note that said, 'He didn't get a whiff of that gas, did he?' " . . . "You better be careful, Doctor," he concluded. "You might be up here calling for water while the rest of us are calling for fire!"

With that he pulled an object out of his pocket and held it up for the crowd to see. It was a gold-plated cigar lighter. . . .

And so at this writing, with the strike a month old, the tension mounting (in the fourth week, there were incidents of brick throwing by Negroes, of garbage being set afire, of a sit-in at City Council with 121 Negroes arrested and released on their recognizance, of a policeman brandishing an oversized billy club gleefully and just as gleefully being laughed at scornfully by Negroes), the outcome was highly uncertain in Memphis—both as to the immediate issues of the strike, the deeper one of dignity, and the awesome one hanging over America in 1968 involving the danger of massive violence and police-state repression.

Out of the impasse, these points, with meaning not merely in Memphis but for all the nation, seemed clear:

1. Spiritual as well as physical needs are imbedded in Negro protest and agitation and, indeed, anger. The demand for dignity as well as better pay was the most profound and moving quality of the Memphis garbage strike. In all of its floundering with the problems of race and poverty, America has seemed unable to grasp that there are hurts in deprivation to the psyche as well as the stomach. Organized labor, in many of its modern manifestations, has seemed to miss this point, also, concerning itself with economic security rather than social needs of people. . . .

2. Black Power, for all its ambiguity and sometimes irrationality, is a psychological force at work in such a situation as that in Memphis, not by any means all negatively. Indeed, the most positive, constructive meanings of the phrase were implicit in Negroes' demand for dignity. That this demand was made in a context of nonviolence and in the traditional framework of a labor strike should serve to give new insight into the semantics and psychology of black power as an influence on Negro thinking and emotion.

3. The impetus to violence by Negroes is also a factor to be reckoned with in such a situation as that in Memphis. In the simplest terms of human anger, the capacity and ability of Negroes in such a situation to espouse and practice nonviolence was extraordinary. For here as in nearly all other Southern locales, there had been the beautiful spirit of the Negro movement of the early 1960's met with hostility and force and arrests when all that had been demanded was the most basic rights of American citizenship.

And here as in nearly all other Southern locales, eight years after the sit-ins and four years after passage of the 1964 Civil Rights Act, the demands were the same ones of basic rights—for an end to discrimination in education, jobs, housing.

Those who have pronounced the civil rights movement dead and buried may want to take a second look at such phenomena as Memphis. . . . The tone and much of the spirit of the old movement was newly alive in Memphis, and its impetus still lives in Negro communities and hearts across the South's cities, towns, and farmlands. One of the very most hopeful things about such new manifestations of the movement as Memphis has been the absence of exploitation from afar, for less than local interests, of the braveness and beauty and belief of the local people who are the strength of the movement. It was to be hoped that such exploitation would not be attempted in Memphis.

Maintaining nonviolence among masses of untrained and volatile demonstrators was never easy. The implicit threat of the nonviolent leaders in Memphis to "go fishing" and leave things in the hands of "radicals" was a mark of the loss of faith, the frustration and the despair that has come to so many Americans of goodwill and pragmatic common sense out of the failures on every level of government and through all elements of American society to answer the most elemental needs of race and poverty. . . .

4. Failure was on prominent display in Memphis. The city government, the press, the business community, the white church, all the institutions, seemed for the first month simply incapable of coping with what was at once a fairly clear-cut demand, and also a highly dangerous situation. . . . But it was a paralysis of the normal function of the city and society to resolve the strike and its issues and its dangerous potential, rather than a will to confront basic problems that characterized the first month of the strike in Memphis. An observer felt that those in positions of power never seemed to grasp the reality of the situation, its danger, or its promise. And this same sort of paralysis seemed to afflict the other agencies of government, state and Federal, which might be expected to act toward mediation and reconciliation when a city did not.

Only when the tragedy of violence occurs, the situation seemed to say, could these governments act, and the record has been all too clear that harshness and repression, weaponry and killing, have been most often their answer.

Whether in Memphis, Orangeburg, Harlem, or Watts, America needed —most desperately—to find out of its great natural and human resources a better answer to the cry of its own people.

"Letters to the Editor" in newspapers and magazines contain a great deal of interesting data on current social problems. The writers are not a representative sample of the public; they are a self-selected sample of people sufficiently aroused and sufficiently assertive to compose and mail a letter. Consequently these letters probably represent polar extremes more often than the moderate majority. For the publisher, they are a popular feature with high reader interest. For the observer of social controversy, they are an indication of what some people think about current issues.

In the following two letters, a Negro college student bitterly indicts American society, and an older member of another minority, who has also suffered hardship and discrimination, replies that Negroes should work more and complain less. Do you agree with this youth's indictment? Is the rejoinder sound? Do you believe the handicaps faced by poor Jewish boys in America are basically similar to those faced by poor Negro boys? What similarities and differences do you see?

WHY AM I ANGRY?

Calvin Mitchell, Jr.

1. Because I am a Black Man in a White society.

Why does my struggle for equality have to be peaceful? I seem to recall that all of the revolutions in the history were violent. The Black man's struggle for freedom is a revolution because we are revolting against a system; a system that has done innumerable wrongs from stealing us from our homeland, to telling us that we are inferior. Why should I be passive while being spat upon, kicked, mutilated, castrated, and assassinated because all I want is a few stinking rights that should have been mine the moment I was born. I am angry because thousands of white people can congregate each year in Florida, overloading Ft. Lauderdale, acting rowdy and have it called a disturbance while my Black brothers can enter a downtown restaurant and have the police called down on them for no reason at all. Now you say I must go to Vietnam and fight for freedom. My fight is in the streets of this racist nation. I will fight much harder for the same cause than on the other side of the world where nobody even knows what they are fighting for. What is so terrifying about Black people having what white Americans have had all their lives? Power does grow out of the barrel of a gun. The reason that white people are where they are today is because they have always had the guns.

2. Because I do not know myself.

The Black man cannot trace his ancestry more than three or possibly four generations because of the splitting, selling, and forced rape of our people. Therefore, in order for the Black man to be proud of his heritage, he must know that his forefathers were men of great pride, stature, and wealth. He should be proud of being Black and therefore he can respect himself and he can command respect from others.

3. Because I have been taught a racist-oriented history.

Before three or four years ago, I didn't know that any Black men besides George Washington Carver and Booker T. Washington had ever done anything constructive besides picking cotton and footshuffling. Why is it that the race whose blood and sweat built this country is not recognized? Why do I have to read "Huckleberry Finn" and face the snickers

From Battle Creek (Michigan) *Enquirer and News,* May 1, 1968. Reprinted by permission.

of my white classmates as they laugh at the "Nigger Jim"? Why can't I read things written by Black people, my people? Believe it or not, we can write!

4. Because I am a young man eager to fight for what I believe in while my older brothers condemn me.

Older people in this nation are so willing to let things progress at a snail's pace so nobody will get hurt. Well, passive attitudes won't change the racist system that killed the three civil rights workers, the four little girls who were killed in the church bombing, Medgar Evers, or Dr. King. This American society is a violent society. Every peaceful race trying to get along with this society has been met with violence. The Chinese were using gunpowder for fireworks. It was taken from them and made into dynamite and put into bullets and used to conquer the people who initially invented it. The Indians welcomed the white man with open arms, who was "discovering" them. They hadn't lost it in the first place. So next came the settlers moving in and claiming ownership for something they didn't even know existed a few years earlier. Is the Black man to be added to the list of conquered people who couldn't make it in white man's society? I am quite aware of the fact that I haven't seen the gaping prejudice that my parents have seen, but the little prejudice I have seen is just as big to me as the great misdeeds they have seen. Young people today are unwilling to watch things go by, and we are not about to settle for a token once in a while. There is a "new breed of cats" on the scene and we are a Winner.

5. Because I am told that I am wrong to want to live with my Black brothers and own my own business establishments.

Even if all of my rights were granted tomorrow, Black people wouldn't go flocking out into white neighborhoods to "integrate." My friends are Black and I want to live where I want to. If I like the house I now live in, I won't move just because I want to integrate. All I want is the potential to be able to say "I want that house," and go right out and buy it. Most business establishments in the Black community are white owned. The Black people in some ghettoes must sometimes pay up to 25 percent more at the neighborhood grocery to the white merchants who are steadily taking the money out of the Black community and socking it away downtown somewhere. Why not Black owned stores and banks?

6. Because the Black church has furnished me no leadership in this nation.

The most powerful organization in the Black community has failed to provide the leadership and or participation needed by the Black man. Preachers seem to stay out of public issues even though their churches' members are directly concerned. The Black youth, in certain instances (this community included), have received more aid by certain white ministers than from their own clergymen.

7. Because it takes the death of great men like Dr. Martin Luther King, Jr. to bring about changes even at Battle Creek Central.

Before the disturbances last spring at this city's High School, efforts were made to form a human relations commission. All efforts were futile and the subject was dropped. Right after the disturbances last spring, there was a hurried attempt toward better understanding. This year, it took the death of Dr. King, plus the threat of possible violence to crack the shell of the administration where discrimination is imposingly evident.

8. Because there are Black citizens in this nation using their Blackness to get ahead so that they can forget their brothers in the grass roots.

People so often point out the fact that there are Black people in this nation who have "made it" and are representing the Black man. Their so-called leaders were not chosen by the Black man, but put where they are by whites who think they will do the "right thing" when they are needed. These so-called "Good Negroes" or "Toms" as they are called by the Black community, will do any amount of foot-kissing and-or shuffling to gain the favor of the white power structure. These individuals are the traitors who would sell out their own people.

9. Because some people figure that just because we are up North things are different.

Unbelievably, there are places in the South where conditions are better than here. At least the South admits their problem. Northern whites and Blacks are so busy pointing the blame on the Southerners that they fail to realize that there is a problem right under their noses. This is why most of the riots occur in the North.

10. Because your so-called freedom of speech, press, and right to bear arms are so distorted as to infect the rights of a supposedly free people.

America's news media is so wrapped up in selling news to the viewers, that often things are given far out of context. Stokely Carmichael has said "Arm yourselves," so right away the press gives the impression that all of the Blacks are going to take up arms and destroy whole white communities as did the settlers to the Indians years ago. The press didn't mention the "in self-defense" part of the statement. They also seem to omit the fact that Carmichael preaches Black unity and undying love for Black brothers in the streets. He said "If and when you make it, pull up your Black brothers also. How many of your so-called white liberals are willing to sit down to a good old round-table discussion and talk and argue your points out? This is why the older generation is in the position it's in today. Because there was never any real exchange of ideas between the two races. Out of the arguing and sweating come new ideas, different views, and most of all respect for one another.

11. People are under the fallacy that Black men sold their brothers into slavery.

Maybe in some cases this is true, but for the most part the slaves were stolen. What was there for the white man to buy us with? The brothers in Africa already had all of the gold, diamonds, and natural resources they wanted. Their women were wearing the gold, silver, and the diamonds. Already owning the precious resources, what did the white man have to bargain with? The Black man was stolen and oppressed.

Why do I call myself Black?

Because I am no longer ashamed of being what I am. If you say that I am colored to a person who does not know what I look like, I could be colored with a green crayon or anything. Negro means virtually nothing to me. What does the term Negro describe? There are many variously dark-shaded races in the world, but there is only one Black race. When the Black man was free we were called Black race. When the Black was forced into slavery, we were "Negro, darkie, boy, Sunshine, and colored." Now I am again Black.

What do I intend to accomplish by all this?

Through my re-awakening of myself, I have learned the truth. And it is the truth that will make us free.

White America, unless a change comes about in this society (Battle Creek included), a violent upheaval will occur. The Black man in America hasn't been violent yet because if the majority of Black men in this country were violent, Vietnam would look like a church service. I am not threatening, but just making sure that somebody knows the facts. Right or wrong, these are my feelings and I don't foresee a change in them until white America changes. The Black man is having a revolution with his own leaders and in his own way and there will be no leadership by or chosen by whites. To my Black brothers, all I can say is that it is up to you to get yourself and your brothers together because this is our thing and whether or not you like it, you are Black and this is your fight too. Can you dig it?

AN ANSWER TO
"ANGRY BLACK STUDENT"

Sheldon B. Frank

Mr. Mitchell, listen well, you and your followers who have embarked upon a racist path to gain the age-old goal of something for nothing. The American public has just about reached the limits of endurance. Upon reading your article I could not help but relive my past and contrast it to the plight of the militant such as yourself.

I was born into a family that suffered from abject poverty during the 1930's. I did not have the opportunity to pick my parents either. A nickel candy bar was a luxury. My parents both worked over 56 hours a week to pay for the bare essentials of life. The home that was mortgaged was re-possessed while I was still a baby and I had the supreme joy of growing up in a crowded apartment with a cement backyard and narrow, junk-laden alley. Parks existed in memory only. My parents were poor yet they did not form a rebellion or ally themselves with divergent groups for power. They followed the only acceptable path toward economic and social improvement: hard work and self education.

In addition to being poor we held close to the Jewish faith. If you feel that you had it tough, just try growing up in a large city during the 1930's with the label of JEW. It is truly regrettable that documentary films were not made of the problems of the minority groups in America. German, Italian, Greek, Irish, Slav, Pole, etc., have all suffered from the rejection of the affluent segments of the population. It was natural for the "haves" to want to suppress and isolate the "have nots"; they were a threat to their social and economic security. All of the minority groups are part of the so-called white race but how wrong you are to assume that they can be classified as one united entity.

You speak of rights, and at that I must laugh. How many times were you chased home after school by a gang of children who were throwing rocks at you and calling you names because of your religion? You may not recall the signs that existed in the early 1940's that read, "No Jews Allowed." Where were my rights during the years when I was growing up?

Vietnam is a real threat to you and your friends who are on student

From Battle Creek (Michigan) *Enquirer and News,* May 10, 1968. Reprinted by permission.

deferments. At the age of 16 I graduated from high school and enlisted in the U.S. Army while World War II was still in progress; yes, in spite of the unfair treatment I had as a second class citizen. This is my country, as well as that of the persons who oppressed me. I knew then that my future would be a result of my aspirations and determined efforts and no amount of bigoted resistance would contain my energies.

I recall many instances in my youth where trouble occurred at sporting events, neighborhood stores and upon street corners. If a person broke a window he was hauled into jail and his parents came out and made proper restitution. The hoax of lawlessness and looting that has swept this nation in the guise of "civil rights" is nothing less than mob rule or anarchy. The question is not color of skin or level of social acceptance; it is one of moral and legal action. This is either a nation of laws that are imperfect and can be redressed through proper channels, or it is a nation of sheep who will allow themselves to be coerced by demagogy and threats.

You speak of power and in that light I must agree that your salvation as well as any member of a minority group lies in the acquisition of power, but legislative, economic and social power, not the kind that comes "from the barrel of a gun." No group, let it be green-skinned or yellow, will gain prominence of a lasting nature through physical force. You scorn the members of your group who have "made it" by their talents, ability and hard work. They are Uncle Toms? By what right do you have the audacity to judge the accomplishments and contributions to mankind of persons such as Ralph Bunche, Sammy Davis Jr., Thurgood Marshall, Carl Stokes, Marion Anderson, John H. Johnson and the like?

The problem of family history and heritage seems to bother you. My father came from Russia at the age of 3 with relatives because his parents could not afford the cost of the boat passage. He never knew his father or mother. To this date my family lineage can only be traced back to my father. So what? We live in the present and look toward the future. What is the value of a family tree? I cannot remember one page in a history book that had a good word for the Russian peasant or the Jewish faith. If textbooks are to be rewritten, then I believe that your approach is extremely selfish. What about the Puerto Rican? the Eskimo? the Mexican?

Now let us get to the subject of persecution and bodily harm. Though you may wish to negate history or moral judgment, it would be well for you to examine the plight of the Jew in Germany during the Hitler regime. Over six million persons were killed under a policy of systematic genocide. Where were you and your friends at that time, Mr. Mitchell? Are rights for you and your kind only? If any ethnic group has a claim to public sympathy it is the Jews, but where is their militancy? Where are their demonstrations? Where are their demands? Many Jews went to Israel; many more remained in their native lands and dedicated themselves to the lawful fight against discrimination and bigotry. If you feel that your future lies in a distant land then a passport can be arranged. If you decide to remain in America, then I suggest that you learn the effective methods of change and embark upon those pathways of endeavor. If you want economic and social well-being then earn it and do not spend your time and efforts in demanding what is not ours to give.

Do you believe that success comes for the asking? I was denied entrance to a major university upon discharge from service. The reason given was religion quota. There were no demonstrations, I enrolled at another school and graduated magna cum laude and then entered the original school as a graduate student. Prejudice can only be overcome by accomplishments, not by wishes. In many of my business endeavors I met every form of obstacle and resistance. The courts cannot legislate consumer action; only service and satisfaction will earn his dollar vote. You want results but you are not willing to sacrifice the slightest inconvenience for their achievement.

A college education cost me several thousands of dollars back in the 1940's as there were few publicly-supported colleges or scholarship programs available. Your position is badly compromised by the fact that many citizens of Battle Creek and the State of Michigan including myself are paying for the majority of your educational costs at Kellogg Community College.

Economic and social success can be yours, as well as they can come to any person in America. This is the great strength of our system, and I for one will not let you or any fallaciously-thinking group deny my children or myself that prerogative. In spite of your insistence upon racism and discrimination, I find that you are the racist and are engaging in the dangerous game of national blackmail against a lethargic public. But heed this warning—blackmail is a touchy practice and can be disastrous.

How your ancestors came to America is irrelevant and immaterial. My father and many more like him came over on a cattle boat. So what? It is what you make of your life that is important and if you feel that another political or social system would serve you better, so be it. Many people left their homelands due to oppression and persecution. The Russians, the Germans, the Irish, the Polish, the Dutch and many others did. Is it true that you can find another place on the face of the earth that offers more opportunity, more benefits, more security than America? If so, what is keeping you here?

Thoughout this article I have never referred to you as a Black man, or Negro, as you are an American and that is how I treat my fellow man. If you insist upon separation of ethnic or cultural groups, then speak for yourself and take appropriate action but do not sentence Americans to your warped sense of values. This nation is not homogeneous in any way, shape or form and the sooner you recognize that you and your group are another minority like hundreds of others, you will realize the impossibility of your demands. It is you who are discriminating.

In my classroom or in my business a person is respected for his membership in the human race and beyond that fact it is his accomplishments and actions that count. If you deny me that right as you want to do, then the American society will be a sad place to dwell. I refuse to treat you or any citizen in a special manner, and in the final analysis that is what you are demanding.

12 Cities in Crisis

Cities have become such an overwhelming feature of modern society that it is difficult to identify where urban problems begin or end, to separate problems of cities from those of the nation. Moreover, urban problems are unbelievably varied and complex. They include problems of housing, zoning, municipal government, suburbanization, traffic, pollution, congestion, and so on. They also include problems of poverty and racial segregation that take special form and have special impact when they appear in the urban environment.

The first selection in this chapter is not an article, or even a selection from an article. It is an excerpt from a book review. The book itself, *Megalopolis Unbound,* was written by United States Senator Claiborne Pell of Rhode Island in protest of the idea that the self-interests of transportation industry lobbyists should prevail over the public welfare. The senator argues that we spend hundreds of millions of dollars in senseless expansion of air and highway travel while an obvious solution, expansion of rail travel, is ignored.

Getting Nowhere

Since 1956, the Federal government has spent more than one hundred times as much on highways as on mass transit and is currently spending thirty times as much.

In the decade 1962–72, urban freeways will devour an estimated 205 square miles of urban land, more than the combined areas of Washington, Boston, San Francisco, and Buffalo, effectively removing $4 billion worth of property from our cities' tax rolls.

Railroads pay some $200 million annually in property taxes, assessed at more than double normal rates on facilities whose counterparts for highways and airlines are generally provided at public expense.

In 1963, as its share of the long-established local airlines' operating subsidies, Allegheny Airlines received $6 million in Federal aid, while the bankrupt New Haven Railroad struggled on with no comparable subsidy to serve twenty-three times as many passengers in the same area.

From a review by C. W. Griffin in *The Reporter*, March 23, 1967. Copyright 1967 by *The Reporter* Magazine Company. Reprinted by permission.

As transportation presents both social and engineering problems, the contamination and defilement of the environment poses problems that go beyond social, financial, and engineering problems to threaten the existence of life itself. Those problems are cogently summed up in the following essay, "The Age of Effluence," from *Time* Magazine.

THE AGE OF EFFLUENCE

Editors of *Time*

What ever happened to America the Beautiful? While quite a bit of it is still visible, the recurring question reflects rising and spreading frustration over the nation's increasingly dirty air, filthy streets and malodorous rivers—the relentless degradations of a once-virgin continent. This man-made pollution is bad enough in itself, but it reflects something even worse: a dangerous illusion that technological man can build bigger and bigger industrial societies with little regard for the iron laws of nature.

The problem is much bigger than the U.S. The whole industrialized world is getting polluted, and emerging nations are unlikely to slow their own development in the interest of clearer air and cleaner water. The fantastic effluence of affluence is overwhelming natural decay—the vital process that balances life in the natural world. All living things produce toxic wastes, including their own corpses. But whereas nature efficiently decays —and thus reuses—the wastes of other creatures, man alone produces huge quantities of synthetic materials that almost totally resist natural decay. And more and more such waste is poisonous to man's fellow creatures, to say nothing of himself.

Man has tended to ignore the fact that he is utterly dependent on the biosphere: a vast web of interacting processes and organisms that form the rhythmic cycles and food chains in which one part of the living environment feeds on another. The biosphere is no immutable feature of the earth. Roughly 400 million years ago, terrestrial life consisted of some primitive organisms that consumed oxygen as fast as green plants manufactured it. Only by some primeval accident were the greedy organisms buried in sedimentary rock (as the source of crude oil, for example), thus permitting the atmosphere to become enriched to a life-sustaining mix of 20% oxygen, plus nitrogen, argon, carbon dioxide and water vapor. With miraculous precision, the mix was then maintained by plants, animals and bacteria, which used and returned the gases at equal rates. About 70% of the earth's oxygen is thus produced by ocean phytoplankton: passively floating plants. All this modulated temperatures, curbed floods and nurtured man a mere 1,000,000 or so years ago.

To primitive man, nature was so harsh and powerful that he deeply respected and even worshiped it. He did the environment very little damage. But technological man, master of the atom and soon the moon, is so aware of his strength that he is unaware of his weakness—the fact that his pressure on nature may provoke revenge. Although sensational cries of impending doom have overstated the case, modern man has reached the stage where he must recognize that real dangers exist. Indeed, many scholars of the biosphere are now seriously concerned that human pollution may trigger some ecological disaster.

CONSUMING NOTHING

For one thing, the impact of human pollutants on nature can be vastly amplified by food chains, the serial process by which weak creatures are typically eaten by stronger ones in ascending order. The most closely studied example is the effect of pesticides, which have sharply improved farm crops but also caused spectacular kills of fish and wildlife. In the Canadian province of New Brunswick, for example, the application of only one-half pound of DDT per acre of forest to control the spruce budworm has twice wiped out almost an entire year's production of young salmon in the Miramichi River. In this process, rain washes the DDT off the ground and into the plankton of lakes and streams. Fish eat the DDT-tainted plankton; the pesticide becomes concentrated in their bodies, and the original dose ultimately reaches multifold strength in fish-eating birds, which then often die or stop reproducing. DDT is almost certainly to blame for the alarming decrease in New England's once flourishing peregrine falcons, northern red-shouldered hawks, and black-crowned night herons.

In the polluting sense, man is the dirtiest animal, and he must learn that he can no longer afford to vent smoke casually into the sky and sewage into rivers as he did in an earlier day, when vast reserves of pure air and water easily diluted the pollutants. The earth is basically a closed system with a waste-disposal process that clearly has limits. The winds that ventilate earth are only six miles high; toxic garbage can kill the tiny organisms that normally clean rivers. Today, industrial America is straining the limits.

One massively important factor is that the U.S. consumer actually consumes nothing; he merely uses things, and though he burns, buries, grinds, or flushes his wastes, the material survives in some form, and technology adds to its longevity. The tin can used to rust away; now comes the immortal aluminum can, which may outlast the Pyramids. Each year, the U.S. produces 48 billion cans, plus 28 billion long-lived bottles and jars. Paced by hardy plastic containers, the average American's annual output of 1,600 lbs. of solid waste is rising by more than 4% a year. Disposal already costs $3 billion a year.

All this effluence is infinitely multiplied in big cities—and 70% of Americans live on only 10% of the country's total land area. Every day, New York City dumps 200 million gallons of raw sewage into the Hudson River. Each square mile of Manhattan produces 375,000 lbs. of waste a day; the capital cost of incinerating that 1-sq.-mi.-output is $1.87 million, and 30% of the residue drifts in the air as fly ash until it settles on the citizens.

The sheer bulk of big cities slows the cleansing winds; at the same time, rising city heat helps to create thermal inversions (warm air above cold) that can trap smog for days—a crisis that in 1963 killed 400 New Yorkers. Cars complete the deadly picture. While U.S. chimneys belch 100,000 tons of sulfur dioxide every day, 90 million motor vehicles add 230,000 tons of carbon monoxide (52% of smog) and other lethal gases, which then form ozone and peroxyacetyl nitrate that kill or stunt many plants, ranging from orchids to oranges. Tetraethyl lead in auto exhausts affects human nerves, increasing irritability and decreasing normal brain function. Like any metal poison, lead is fatal if enough is ingested. In the auto's 70-year history, the average American's lead content has risen an estimated 125-fold, to near maximum tolerance levels. Arctic glaciers now contain wind-wafted lead.

AIR, WATER, AND THE SEWER

By the year 2000, an estimated 90% of Americans will live in urban areas and drive perhaps twice as many cars as they do now. The hope is that Detroit will have long since designed exhaust-free electric or steam motors. Another hope is nuclear power to generate electricity in place of smoggy "fossil fuels" (oil, coal), but even with 50% nuclear power, U.S. energy needs will so increase by 2000 that fossil-fuel use may quadruple. Moreover, nuclear plants emit pollution: not only radioactive wastes, which must be buried, but also extreme hot water that has to go somewhere and can become a serious threat to marine life.

Industry already devours water on a vast scale—600,000 gal. to make one ton of synthetic rubber, for example—and the resultant hot water releases the dissolved oxygen in rivers and lakes. This kills the oxygen-dependent bacteria that degrade sewage. Meanwhile, the country's ever-mounting sewage is causing other oxygen-robbing processes. By 1980, these burdens may well dangerously deplete the oxygen in all 22 U.S. river basins. The first massive warning is what happened to Lake Erie, where overwhelming sewage from Detroit and other cities cut the oxygen content of most of the lake's center to zero, turning a once magnificently productive inland sea into a sink where life is catastrophically diminished. With state and federal aid, the cities that turned Erie's tributaries into open sewers are now taking steps to police the pollution, and if all goes well, Erie may be restored to reasonable life in five or ten years.

But the problem goes on. Though one-third of U.S. sewage systems are below health standards, improving them may also kill lakes. The problem is that treated sewage contains nitrate and phosphate, fertilizing substances widely used in agriculture that make things worse in overfertilized lakes. Though nitrate is normally harmless in the body, intestinal bacteria can turn it into nitrite, a compound that hinders hemoglobin from transporting oxygen to the tissues, causing labored breathing and even suffocation.

THE SYSTEMS APPROACH

It seems undeniable that some disaster may be lurking in all this, but laymen hardly know which scientist to believe. As a result of fossil-fuel burning, for example, carbon dioxide in the atmosphere has risen about 14% since 1860. According to Ecologist Lamont C. Cole, man is thus reducing the rate of oxygen regeneration, and Cole envisions a crisis in which the amount of oxygen on earth might disastrously decline. Other scientists fret that rising carbon dioxide will prevent heat from escaping into space. They foresee a hotter earth that could melt the polar icecaps, raise oceans as much as 400 ft., and drown many cities. Still other scientists forecast a colder earth (the recent trend) because man is blocking sunlight with ever more dust, smog and jet contrails. The cold promises more rain and hail, even a possible cut in world food. Whatever the theories may be, it is an established fact that three poisons now flood the landscapes: smog, pesticides, nuclear fallout.

Finding effective antidotes will take a lot more alertness to ecological consequences. What cities sorely need is a systems approach to pollution: a computer analysis of everything that a total environment—greater Los

Angeles, for example—is taking in and giving out via air, land, water. Only then can cities make cost-benefit choices and balance the system. Equally vital are economic incentives, such as taxing specific pollutants so that factories stop using them. Since local governments may be loath to levy effluence charges, fearing loss of industry, the obvious need is regional cooperation, such as interstate river-basin authorities to enforce scientific water use. Germany's Ruhr River is ably governed this way. A shining U.S. example is the eight-state Ohio River Valley Water Sanitation Commission, which persuaded 3,000 cities and industries to spend $1 billion diverting 99% of their effluent to sewage plants.

Similar "air shed" action is starting between some smog-bound states and is considered preferable to federally imposed air standards, which might not fit local climate conditions. Still, far greater federal action— especially money—is urgently needed to help cities build all kinds of waste-treating facilities. In fact, the Secretary of the Interior really ought to be the Secretary of the Environment. To unify federal leadership, he might well be given charge of the maze of rival federal agencies that now absurdly nibble only at their own slice of the pollution mess.

One of the prime goals in attacking pollution ought to be a vast shrinkage of the human impact on other creatures. The war on insects, for example, might actually go a lot better without chemical pesticides that kill the pests' natural enemies, such as birds. One of the best strategies is to nurture the enemies so they can attack the pests; more insect-resistant crops can also be developed. Florida eliminated the screw-worm fly not by spraying but by sterilizing hordes of the male flies, then liberating them to produce infertile eggs. A still newer method is the use of sex attractants to lure male insects into traps and thus to their death.

Above all, man should strive to parallel natural decay by recycling —reusing as much waste as possible. Resalvaging already keeps 80% of all mined copper in circulation. But U.S. city incinerators now destroy about 3,000,000 metric tons of other valuable metals a year; magnetic extractors could save the metal and reduce incineration by 10%. The packaging industry could do a profound service by switching to materials that rot—fast. The perfect container for mankind is the edible ice-cream cone. How about a beer container that is something like a pretzel? Or the soft-drink bottle that, when placed in the refrigerator, turns into a kind of tasty artificial ice? Soft drinks could also come in frozen form, as popsicles with edible sticks.

To cut air pollution, a Japanese process can be used to convert fly ash into cinder blocks. Since the market is too small for commercial success, public subsidies would make sense; recovering waste at the source is almost always cheaper than cleanup later. There are some real prospects of profit in reconstituting other waste. Take sulfur, for example, which is in short supply around the world. While 26 million tons are mined a year, smokestacks belch 28 million tons of wasted sulfur dioxide, which could easily be trapped in the stack and converted to sulfuric acid or even fertilizer. Standard Oil of California is already profitably recovering the refinery sulfur waste that pollutes streams.

To reduce smog over cities, one of the most visible and worst forms of pollution, smog-causing power plants might be eliminated from densely populated areas. Why not generate electricity at the fuel source—distant oil or coal fields—and then wire it to cities? On the other hand, industrialization must not be taken to distant places that can be better used for other purposes. Industrializing Appalachia, for example, would smogify a naturally hazy region that settlers aptly named the Smokies. The right business for Appalachia is recreation; federal money could spur a really sizable tourist industry.

Sometimes pollution can even help recreation. In flat northeastern Illinois, for instance, the handsomest recreation area will soon be Du Page County's fast-rising 118-ft. hill and 65-acre lake—artfully built on garbage fill. One form of pollution could even enhance—rather than spoil—water sports. Much of the nation's coastline is too cold for swimming; if marine life can be protected, why not use nuclear plant heat to warm the water? Or even create underwater national parks for scuba campers?

IN HARMONY WITH NATURE

Ideally, every city should be a closed loop, like a space capsule in which astronauts reconstitute even their own waste. This concept is at the base of the federally aided "Experimental City" being planned by Geophysicist Athelstan Spilhaus, president of Philadelphia's Franklin Institute, who dreams of solving the pollution problem by dispersing millions of Americans into brand-new cities limited to perhaps 250,000 people on 2,500 acres of now vacant land. The pilot city, to be built by a quasi-public corporation, will try everything from reusable buildings to underground factories and horizontal elevators to eliminate air-burning cars and buses. The goal is a completely recycled, noise-free, pure-air city surrounded by as many as 40,000 acres of insulating open countryside. "We need urban dispersal," says Spilhaus, "not urban renewal."

In the search for solutions, there is no point in attempting to take nature back to its pristine purity. The approach must look forward. There is no question that just as technology has polluted the country, it can also depollute it. The real question is whether enough citizens want action. The biggest need is for ordinary people to learn something about ecology, a humbling as well as fascinating way of viewing reality that ought to get more attention in schools and colleges. The trouble with modern man is that he tends to yawn at the news that pesticides are threatening remote penguins or pelicans; perhaps he could do with some of the humility toward animals that St. Francis tried to graft onto Christianity. The false assumption that nature exists only to serve man is at the root of an ecological crisis that ranges from the lowly litterbug to the lunacy of nuclear proliferation. At this hour, man's only choice is to live in harmony with nature, not conquer it.

The size and the complexity of the problems confronting Americas' cities deeply involves physical scientists, engineers, and many other specialists in the development of solutions. That is even more true in the more apparently "social" problems, such as poverty and racial segregation. The interests of sociologists, however, are more primary in social problems and it is to them that the major selections in this chapter are addressed.

The first of these selections was written by Lee Rainwater, who has been deeply involved in research in a federal public housing area (Pruitt-Igoe) in St. Louis. In "The Services Strategy vs. the Income Strategy," he hits at the bankruptcy of the traditional American "services" approach to the problems of urban poor and makes a case for lifting family incomes as the only real solution to the problem.

THE SERVICES STRATEGY
VS. THE INCOME STRATEGY

Lee Rainwater
Professor of Sociology
Harvard University

There seem to me to be two different kinds of urban problems, although each deeply affects the other. Efforts to solve the general problems of *urban management* will forever be frustrated—or at least much, much more costly—without a solution to the *problem of poverty,* both urban and rural. Unless the poverty problem is solved, every urban service will have to be seriously distorted and fragmented in order either to avoid or to take special account of the problems posed by having an "other America." For this reason, as well as for reasons of simple human justice, first priority in dealing with urbanization as our major domestic problem should be given to the elimination of poverty.

The elimination of poverty has a very simple referent. It means that the present income distribution in the nation—in which a small group of the population earns a great deal of money, a large proportion earns a more moderate amount of income, and a small proportion earns very little —must be changed by moving that bottom portion up into the middle category. In short, the current diamond-shaped income distribution must be changed into one which has the shape of a pyramid. I'm speaking here about family income rather than individual income.

There is certainly nothing wrong with a teenage boy earning $1.50 an hour while he goes to school or while he learns a trade. But there is something very wrong about that kind of income for a head of a family with two or three children, or for a man who would like to be the head of a family but cannot afford to be.

This redistribution would channel national income, particularly the yearly increment in national income, to families in the lower 30 to 40 percent of the population, so that a family income floor is established which is not too far below the median income for American families as a whole. If we can accomplish this, we will have succeeded in creating an urban society in which, while problems may still be difficult, they will not seem nearly so insoluble, because we will not have to plan for two kinds of Americans, the average American and the deprived American, as we do now.

It seems to me that there are basically two strategies implicit in the various programs and suggested plans for doing something about poverty: One, by far the most entrenched at present, might be called the *services strategy,* and the other, the *income strategy.*

The services strategy involves the design of special services for the poor. The problem with the services approach is that to a considerable extent it carries the latent assumption that either the poor are permanently poor and, therefore, must have special services, or that the poor can be changed while they are still poor, and that once they have changed, they will then be able to [function] in ways that will do away with their poverty. I think these assumptions are extremely pernicious ones.

One problem with the services approach is that the priority of needs of the poor is categorically established when the service programs are set up and funded. For example, the federal public housing program provides a service to each household in Pruitt-Igoe in the form of a subsidized apartment that costs about $545 a year—that is the subsidy. This subsidy amounts to a fifth of the mean family income of the tenants in the project.

It is very likely that from the point of view of the needs of many of the families who live in Pruitt-Igoe that $545 could be put to much better use.

For another example, the Council of the White House Conference "To Fulfill These Rights" recommended that one program to help do away with Negro disadvantage could be to increase the average school expenditure per child $500 per year. Consider a poor family with three or four school children. Such an increase would mean devoting $1,500 to $2,000 a year to better educational facilities for that family's children. Yet, might it not be that, because of its effect on the family environment, an increase of $1,500 to $2,000 in that family's income would have as much or more educational effect on those children than would a comparable expenditure of resources in the school?

Finally, special programs for the poor are extremely difficult to design so that they do not have the effect of furthering the stigmatized status of the poor. To design services which do not stigmatize at the same time that they try to serve seems to pose tremendous political, administrative, and human engineering tasks, for which past experience gives us little reason to believe we have the skills.

Most of those who have studied the actual operation of service programs catering to an exclusively lower class clientele have been impressed by the demeaning and derogation of the poor that goes along with the service. The principal power that the poor want is the power of money in their pockets to make these choices as they see fit and as the needs of their families dictate.

The second poverty elimination strategy, the income strategy, goes a long way toward avoiding the difficulties that past experience suggests are inherent in the services strategy. Here the task is to develop a set of economic programs that have the direct result of providing poor families and individuals with an adequate income. There are good reasons from the social science information now available to us for believing that the most powerful and immediate resource to assist the poor to cope with their problems, not only the problems of economic disadvantage, but all of the dependent problems of community pathology, individual lack of motivation, and the like—the most powerful resource is income.

We know, for example, that when a man has a job and an adequate income, he is more respected in his home, and he is less likely to desert or divorce his wife. If one wishes to reverse those effects of lower class adaptations that are unconstructive, the most direct way of doing it is to strike at the root of the problem—at the lack of an income sufficient to live out a stable "good American life" style.

Having said this, I leave the field of sociological expertise because the problems are then ones that require the technical competence of an economist. Those economists who have pursued this line of thinking in studying the problem of poverty have suggested that an income strategy requires three elements:

An aggregational approach—that is, tight full employment—with a low, a very low, real unemployment rate—that is, an unemployment rate that takes into account labor force dropouts.

Second, a structural approach, which compensates the tendency for unemployment among low skilled workers to remain at high levels even when overall unemployment is low. Such an approach would require that federal programs to bring about full employment be tied to guarantees of labor force entry jobs for unskilled men, and guarantees of training on the job to upgrade those skills. In this context, a high minimum wage would also be necessary and would not have the negative effect of hastening the replacement of men by machines.

Finally, an income maintenance program, which fills in the income gap not touched by the tight full employment programs. The income maintenance program would be required for families with a disabled or no male head, and where the wife should not work because of the ages or numbers of the children.

Such a program could take the form of family allowances or a negative income tax or an annual guaranteed income, but in any case should involve a major reorganization of the government's current income maintenance programs, notably ADC and other types of public assistance, since these current programs are by far the most stigmatizing poverty programs now in existence.

If the first two employment strategies were as successful as some economists feel they might be, the dollar investment in an income maintenance program could be quite small. However, such a program would have considerable long-run importance, since it would serve as proof of a more permanent national commitment to a more equal income distribution, and as a yearly goal to the federal government to plan the economy in such a way that no more than a very small number of families are without an adequate bread-winner. . . .

The final, and longest, selection in this chapter builds nicely upon Rainwater's thesis. Herbert Gans, a sociologist at the Joint Center for Urban Studies in Cambridge, Mass., describes the increasing racial and class polarization in our cities and suburbs. He shows how and why traditional approaches to the problem have not worked; he then proposes solutions that proceed from the same general assumptions Rainwater makes.

THE FUTURE OF THE SUBURBS

Herbert J. Gans

Joint Center for Urban Studies
Harvard University and M.I.T.

In this unpredictable world, nothing can be predicted quite so easily as the continued proliferation of suburbia. Not only have American cities stopped growing for more than a generation, while the metropolitan areas of which they are a part were continuing to expand lustily, but there is incontrovertible evidence that another huge wave of suburban home building can be expected in the coming decade.

Between 1947 and about 1960, the country experienced the greatest baby boom ever, ending the slowdown in marriages and childbirths created first by the Depression and then by World War II. Today, the earliest arrivals of that baby boom are themselves old enough to marry, and many are now setting up housekeeping in urban or suburban apartments. In a few years, however, when their first child is two to three years old, and the second is about to appear, many young parents will decide to buy suburban homes. Only simple addition is necessary to see that by the mid-seventies, they will be fashioning another massive suburban building boom, provided of course that the country is affluent and not engaged in World War III.

The new suburbia may not look much different from the old; there will, however, be an increase in the class and racial polarization that has been developing between the suburbs and the cities for several generations now. The suburbs will be home for an ever larger proportion of working-class, middle-class and upper-class whites; the cities, for an ever-larger proportion of poor and nonwhite people. The continuation of this trend means that, by the seventies, a great number of cities will be 40 to 50 percent nonwhite in population, with more and larger ghettos and greater municipal poverty on the one hand, and stronger suburban opposition to open housing and related policies to solve the city's problems on the other hand. The urban crisis will worsen, and although there is no shortage of rational solutions, nothing much will be done about the crisis unless white America permits a radical change of public policy and undergoes a miraculous change of attitude toward its cities and their populations.

Another wave of suburban building would develop even if there had been no post-World War II baby boom, for American cities have always grown at the edges, like trees, adding new rings of residential development every generation as the beneficiaries of affluence and young families sought more modern housing and "better" neighborhoods. At first, the new rings were added inside the city limits, but ever since the last half of the nineteenth century, they have more often sprung up in the suburbs. . . .

Moreover, studies of housing preferences indicate that the majority of Americans, including those now living in the city, want a suburban single family house once they have children, and want to remain in that house when their children have grown up. This urge for suburban life is not limited to the middle class or just to America; the poor would leave the city as well if they could afford to go, and so would many Europeans. . . .

Obviously, the popular antisuburban literature, which falsely accuses the suburbs of causing conformity, matriarchy, adultery, divorce, alcoholism, and other standard American pathologies, has not kept anyone from moving to the suburbs, and even the current predictions of land shortages, longer commuting, and urban congestion in the suburbs will not discourage the next generation of home buyers. Most, if not all, metropolitan areas still have plenty of rural land available for suburban housing. Moreover, with industry and offices now moving to the suburbs, new areas previously outside commuting range become ripe for residential development to house their employees. . . .

Of course, all this leads to increasing suburban congestion, but most suburbanites do not mind it. They do not leave the city for a rural existence, as the folklore has it; they want a half acre or more of land and all their favorite urban facilities within a short driving distance from the house. . . .

It goes without saying that almost all the new suburbanites—and the developments built for them—will be white and middle-income for, barring miracles in the housing industry and in Federal subsidies, the subdivisions of the seventies will be too expensive for any family earning less than about $7,000 (in 1967 dollars). Thus, even if suburbia were to be racially integrated, cost alone would exclude most nonwhites. Today, less than 5 percent of New York State's suburban inhabitants are nonwhite, and many of them live in ghettos and slums in the small towns around which suburbia has developed.

Nevertheless, the minuscule proportion of nonwhite suburbanites will increase somewhat in the future, for, if the current affluence continues, it will benefit a small percentage of Negroes and Puerto Ricans. Some of them will be able to move into integrated suburban communities, but the majority will probably wind up in existing and new middle-class ghettos.

If urban employment is available, or if the ongoing industrialization of the South pushes more people off the land, poverty-stricken Negroes will continue to come to the cities, overcrowding and eventually enlarging the inner-city ghettos. Some of the better-off residents of these areas will move to "outer-city" ghettos, which can now be found in most American cities; for example, in Queens. And older suburbs like Yonkers and Mount Vernon will continue to lose some of the present residents and attract less affluent newcomers, as their housing, schools and other facilities age. As a result of this process, which affects suburbs as inevitably as city neighborhoods, some of their new inhabitants may be almost as poor as inner-city ghetto residents, so that more and more of the older suburbs will face problems of poverty and social pathology now thought to be distinctive to the city.

That further suburban growth is practically inevitable does not mean it is necessarily desirable, however. Many objections have been raised, some to suburbia itself, others to its consequences for the city. For example, ever since the rise of the postwar suburbs, critics have charged that suburban life is culturally and psychologically harmful for its residents, although many sociological studies, including my own, have shown that most suburbanites are happier and emotionally healthier than when they lived in the city. In addition, the critics have charged that suburbia desecrates valuable farm and recreation land, and that it results in "suburban" sprawl.

Suburbia undoubtedly reduced the supply of farm acreage, but America has long suffered from an oversupply of farmland, and I have never understood why allowing people to raise children where other people once raised potatoes or tomatoes desecrates the land. Usually, the criticism is directed to "ugly, mass-produced, look-alike little boxes," adding a class bias to the charges, as if people who can only afford mass-produced housing are not entitled to live where they please, or should stay in the city. . . .

The harmful effects of suburbia on the city are a more important criticism. One charge, made ever since the beginning of suburbanization in the nineteenth century, is that the suburbs rob the city of its tax-paying, civic-minded and culture-loving middle class. Actually, however, middle-class families are often a tax liability for the city; they demand and receive more services, particularly more schools, than their taxes pay for. Nor is there any evidence that they are more civic-minded than their non-middle-class neighbors; they may be more enthusiastic joiners of civic organizations, but these tend to defend middle-class interests and not necessarily the public interest. Moreover, many people who live in the suburbs still exert considerable political influence in the city because of their work or their property holdings and see to it that urban power structures still put middle-class interests first, as slum organizations, whose demands for more antipoverty funds or public housing are regularly turned down by city hall, can testify.

The alleged effect of the suburbs on urban culture is belied by the vast cultural revival in the city which occurred at the same time the suburban exodus was in full swing. Actually, most suburbanites rarely used the city's cultural facilities even when they lived in the city, and the minority which did, continues to do so, commuting in without difficulty. Indeed, I suspect that over half the ticket buyers for plays, art movies, concerts and museums, particularly outside New York, are—and have long been—suburbanites. Besides, there is no reason why cultural institutions cannot, like banks, build branches in the suburbs, as they are beginning to do now. Culture is no less culture by being outside the city.

A much more valid criticism of suburbanization is its effect on class and racial segregation, for the fact that the suburbs have effectively zoned out the poor and the nonwhites is resulting in an ever-increasing class and racial polarization of city and suburb. In one sense, however, the familiar data about the increasing polarization are slightly misleading. In years past, when urban census statistics showed Negroes and whites living side by side, they were actually quite polarized socially. On New York's Upper West Side, for example, the big apartment buildings are de facto segregated for whites, while the rotting brownstones between them are inhabited by Negroes and Puerto Ricans. These blocks are integrated statistically or geographically, but not socially, particularly if white parents send their children to private schools.

Nor is suburbanization the sole cause of class and racial polarization; it is itself an effect of trends that have gone on inside the city as well, and not only in America. When people become more affluent and can choose where they want to live, they choose to live with people like themselves. What has happened in the last generation or two is that the opportunity of home buyers to live among compatible neighbors, an opportunity previously available only to the rich, has been extended to people in the middle- and lower-middle-income brackets. This fact does not justify either class or racial segregation, but it does suggest that the polarization resulting from affluence would have occurred even without suburbanization.

Class and racial polarization are harmful because they restrict freedom of housing choice to many people, but also because of the financial consequences for the city. For one thing, affluent suburbia exploits the financially bankrupt city; even when payroll taxes are levied, suburbanites do not pay their fair share of the city's cost in providing them with places of work, shopping areas and cultural facilities and with streets and utilities, maintenance, garbage removal and police protection for these facilities.

More important, suburbanites live in vest-pocket principalities where they can, in effect, vote to keep out the poor and the nonwhites and even the not very affluent whites.

As a result, the cities are in a traumatic financial squeeze. Their ever more numerous low-income residents pay fewer taxes but need costly municipal services, yet cities are taking in less in property taxes all the time, particularly as the firms that employ suburbanites and the shops that cater to them also move to the suburbs. Consequently, city costs rise at the same time as city income declines. To compound the injustice state and Federal politicians from suburban areas often vote against antipoverty efforts and other Federal funding activities that would relieve the city's financial troubles, and they also vote to prevent residential integration.

These trends are not likely to change in the years to come. In fact, if the present white affluence continues, the economic gap between the urban have-nots and the suburban haves will only increase, resulting on the one hand in greater suburban opposition to integration and to solving the city's problems, and on the other hand to greater discontent and more ghetto rebellions in the city. This in turn could result in a new white exodus from the city, which, unlike the earlier exodus, will be based almost entirely on racial fear, making suburbanites out of the middle-aged and older middle-class families who are normally reluctant to change communities at this age and working-class whites who cannot really afford a suburban house. Many of them will, however, stay put and oppose all efforts toward desegregation, as indicated even now by their violent reaction to integration marches in Milwaukee and Chicago, and to scattered-site public housing schemes which would locate projects in middle-income areas in New York and elsewhere.

Ultimately, these trends could create a vicious spiral, with more ghetto protest leading to more white demands, urban and suburban, for repression, resulting in yet more intense ghetto protests, and culminating eventually in a massive exodus of urban whites. If this spiral were allowed to escalate, it might well hasten the coming of the predominantly Negro city.

Today, the predominantly Negro city is still far off in the future, and the all-Negro city is unlikely. Although Washington, D.C.'s population is already about 60 percent Negro, and several other cities, including Newark, Gary and Richmond, hover around the 50 percent mark, recent estimates by the Center for Research in Marketing suggest that only 5 of the country's 25 largest cities and 10 of the 130 cities with over 100,000 population will be 40 percent or more Negro by 1970. (New York's Negro population was estimated at 18 percent in 1964, although in Manhattan, the proportion of Negroes was 27 percent and of Negroes and Puerto Ricans, 39 percent.)

Moreover, these statistics only count the nighttime residential population, but who lives in the city is, economically and politically, a less relevant statistic than who works there, and the daytime working population of most cities is today, and will long remain, heavily and even predominantly white.

Still, to a suburbanite who may someday have to work in a downtown surrounded by a black city, the future may seem threatening. A century ago, native-born WASPs must have felt similarly, when a majority of the urban population consisted of foreign-born Catholics and Jews, to whom they attributed the same pejorative racial characteristics now attributed to Negroes. The city and the WASPs survived, of course, as the immigrants were incorporated into the American economy, and suburban whites would also survive. . . .

Unfortunately, present governmental policies, local, state and Federal, are doing little to reverse the mounting class and racial polarization of city and suburb. Admittedly, the strong economic and cultural forces that send the middle classes into the suburbs and bring poor nonwhite people from the rural areas into the city in ever larger numbers are difficult to reverse even by the wisest government action.

Still, governmental policies have not been especially wise. The major efforts to slow down class and racial polarization have been these: legislation to achieve racial integration; programs to woo the white middle class back to the city; plans to establish unified metropolitan governments, encompassing both urban and suburban governmental units. All three have failed. None of the open housing and other integration laws now on the books have been enforced sufficiently to permit more than a handful of Negroes to live in the suburbs, and the more recent attempt to prevent the coming of the predominantly black city by enticing the white middle class back has not worked either.

The main technique used for this last purpose has been urban renewal, but there is no evidence—and, in fact, there have been no studies —to show that it has brought back a significant number of middle-class people. Most likely, it has only helped confirmed urbanites find better housing in the city. The attractions of suburbia are simply too persuasive for urban renewal or any other governmental program to succeed in bringing the middle class back to the city. . . .

Metropolitan government is, in theory, a good solution, for it would require the suburbs to contribute to solving the city's problems, but it has long been opposed by the suburbs for just this reason. They have felt that the improvements and economies in public services that could be obtained by organizing them on a metropolitan basis would be offset by what suburbanites saw as major disadvantages, principally the reduction of political autonomy and the loss of power to keep out the poor and the nonwhites.

The cities, which have in the past advocated metropolitan government, may become less enthusiastic as Negroes obtain greater political power. Since the metropolitan area is so predominantly white, urban Negroes would be outvoted every time in any kind of metropolitan government. Some metropolitanization may nevertheless be brought about by Federal planning requirements, for as Frances Piven and Richard Cloward point out in a recent New Republic article, several Federal grant programs, particularly for housing and community facilities, now require a metropolitan plan as a prerequisite for funding. Piven and Cloward suggest that these requirements could disfranchise the urban Negro, and it is of course always possible that a white urban-suburban coalition in favor of metropolitan government could be put together deliberately for precisely this purpose. Under such conditions, however, metropolitan government would only increase racial conflict and polarization.

What then, can be done to eliminate this polarization? One partial solution is to reduce the dependence of both urban and suburban governments on the property tax, which reduces city income as the population becomes poorer, and forces suburbs to exclude low-income residents because their housing does not bring in enough tax money. If urban and suburban governments could obtain more funds from other sources, including perhaps the Federal income tax, parts of the proceeds of which would be returned to them by Washington, urban property owners would bear a smaller burden in supporting the city and might be less opposed to higher spending. Suburbanites would also worry less about their tax rate, and might not feel so impelled to bar less affluent newcomers, or to object to paying their share of the cost of using city services.

Class polarization can be reduced by rent- or price-supplement programs which would enable less affluent urbanites to pay the price of suburban living and would reduce the building and financing costs of housing. But such measures would not persuade the suburbs to let in Negroes; ultimately, the only solution is still across-the-board residential integration.

The outlook for early and enforceable legislation toward this end, however, is dim. Although election results have shown time and again that Northern white majorities will not vote for segregation, they will not vote for integration either. I cannot imagine many political bodies, Federal or otherwise, passing or enforcing laws that would result in significant amounts of suburban integration; they would be punished summarily at the next election.

For example, proposals have often been made that state and Federal governments should withdraw all subsidies to suburban communities and builders practicing de facto segregation, thus depriving the former of at least half their school operating funds, and the latter of Federal Housing Authority (FHA) insurance on which their building plans depend. However desirable as such legislation is, the chance that it would be passed is almost nil. One can also argue that Washington should offer grants-in-aid to suburban governments which admit low-income residents, but these grants would often be turned down. Many suburban municipalities would rather starve their public services instead, and the voters would support them all the way.

The best hope now is for judicial action. The New Jersey Supreme Court ruled some years back that builders relying on FHA insurance had to sell to Negroes, and many suburban subdivisions in that state now have some Negro residents. The United States Supreme Court has just decided that it will rule on whether racial discrimination by large suburban developers is unconstitutional. If the answer turns out to be yes, the long, slow process of implementing the Court's decisions can at least begin.

In the meantime, solutions that need not be tested at the ballot box must be advanced. One possibility is new towns, built for integrated populations with Federal support, or even by the Federal Government alone, on land now vacant. Although hope springs eternal in American society that the problems of old towns can be avoided by starting from scratch, these problems seep easily across the borders of the new community. Even if rural governments can be persuaded to accept new towns in their bailiwicks and white residents could be attracted, such towns would be viable only if Federal grants and powers were used to obtain industries—and of a kind that would hire and train poorly skilled workers.

Greater emphasis should be placed on eliminating job discrimination in suburban work places, particularly in industries which are crying for workers, so that unions are less impelled to keep out nonwhite applicants. Mass transit systems should be built to enable city dwellers, black and white, to obtain suburban jobs without necessarily living in the suburbs.

Another and equally important solution is more school integration— for example, through urban-suburban educational parks that will build up integrated student enrollment by providing high-quality schooling to attract suburban whites, and through expansion of the bussing programs that send ghetto children into suburban schools. Although white suburban parents have strenuously opposed bussing their children into the city, several suburban communities have accepted Negro students who are bussed in from the ghetto; for example, in the Boston area and in Westchester County.

And while the Supreme Court is deliberating, it would be worthwhile to persuade frightened suburbanites that, as all the studies so far have indicated, open housing would not mean a massive invasion of slum dwellers, but only the gradual arrival of a relatively small number of Negroes, most of them as middle-class as the whitest suburbanite. A massive suburban invasion by slum dwellers of any color is sheer fantasy. Economic studies have shown the sad fact that only a tiny proportion of ghetto residents can even afford to live in the suburbs. Moreover, as long as Negro workers lack substantial job security, they need to live near the center of the urban transportation system so that they can travel to jobs all over the city.

In addition, there are probably many ghetto residents who do not even want suburban integration now; they want the same freedom of housing choice as whites but they do not want to be "dispersed" to the suburbs involuntarily. Unfortunately, no reliable studies exist to tell us where ghetto residents do want to live, but should they have freedom of choice, I suspect many would leave the slums for better housing and better neighborhoods outside the present ghetto. Not many would now choose predominantly white areas, however, at least not until living among whites is psychologically and socially less taxing, and until integration means more than just assimilation to white middle-class ways.

Because of the meager success of past integration efforts, many civil rights leaders have given up on integration and are now demanding the rebuilding of the ghetto. They argue persuasively that residential integration has so far and will in the future benefit only a small number of affluent Negroes, and that if the poverty-stricken ghetto residents are to be helped soon, that help must be located in the ghetto. The advocates of integration are strongly opposed. They demand that all future housing must be built outside the ghetto, for anything else would just perpetuate segregation. In recent months, the debate between the two positions has become bitter, each side claiming only its solution has merit.

Actually there is partial truth on both sides. The integrationists are correct about the long-term dangers of rebuilding the ghetto; the ghetto rebuilders (or separatists) are correct about the short-term failure of integration. But if there is little likelihood that the integrationists' demands will be carried out soon, their high idealism in effect sentences ghetto residents to remain in slum poverty.

Moreover, there is no need to choose between integration and rebuilding, for both policies can be carried out simultaneously. The struggle for integration must continue, but if the immediate prospects for success on a large scale are dim, the ghetto must be rebuilt in the meantime.

The primary aim of rebuilding, however, should not be to rehabilitate houses or clear slums, but to raise the standard of living of ghetto residents. The highest priority must be a massive antipoverty program which will, through the creation of jobs, more effective job-training schemes, the negative income tax, children's allowances and other measures, raise ghetto families to the middle-income level, using outside resources from government and private enterprise and inside participation in the planning and decision-making. Also needed are a concerted effort at quality compensatory education for children who cannot attend integrated schools; federally funded efforts to improve the quality of ghetto housing, as well as public services; some municipal decentralization to give ghetto residents the ability to plan their own communities and their own lives, and political power so that the ghetto can exert more influence in behalf of its demands.

If such programs could extend the middle-income standard of living to the ghetto in the years to come, residential integration might well be achieved in subsequent generations. Much of the white opposition to integration is based on stereotypes of Negro behavior—some true, some false —that stem from poverty rather than from color, and many of the fears about Negro neighbors reflect the traditional American belief that poor people will not live up to middle-class standards. Moreover, even lack of enthusiasm for integration among ghetto residents is a result of poverty; they feel, rightly or not, that they must solve their economic problems before they can even think about integration.

If ghetto poverty were eliminated, the white fears—and the Negro ones—would begin to disappear, as did the pejorative stereotypes which earlier Americans held about the "inferior races"—a favorite nineteenth-century term for the European immigrants—until they achieved affluence. Because attitudes based on color differences are harder to overcome than those based on cultural differences, the disappearance of anti-Negro stereotypes will be slower than that of anti-immigrant stereotypes. Still, once color is no longer an index of poverty and lower-class status, it will cease to arouse white fears, so that open-housing laws can be enforced more easily and eventually may even be unnecessary. White suburbanites will not exclude Negroes to protect their status or their property values, and many, although not necessarily all, Negroes will choose to leave the ghetto.

Morally speaking, any solution that does not promise immediate integration is repugnant, but moral dicta will neither persuade suburbanites to admit low-income Negroes into their communities, nor entice urbane suburbanites to live near low-income Negroes in the city. Instead of seeking to increase their middle-income population by importing suburban whites, cities must instead make their poor residents middle-income. The practical solution, then, is to continue to press for residential integration, but also to eliminate ghetto poverty immediately, in order to achieve integration in the future, substituting government antipoverty programs for the private economy which once created the jobs and incomes that helped poorer groups escape the slums in past generations. Such a policy will not only reduce many of the problems of the city, which are ultimately caused by the poverty of its inhabitants, but it will assure the ultimate disappearance of the class and racial polarization of cities and suburbs. . . .

13 Communication Problems in Mass Society

It would be easy to find a hundred articles dealing with some controversial aspect of communications problems. One familiar theme is the helplessness of the individual citizen, who is pictured as utterly powerless to influence the floods of words and images which roll heedlessly over him. But is the consumer's lack of influence over media content a measure of his powerlessness, or of his laziness?

In the following essay, a former law professor and present member of the Federal Communications Commission suggests that the private citizen *can* exert real influence over the communications barons —but only if the citizen is interested enough to mount a protest, and intelligent enough to find out how to make his protest effective.

WHAT YOU CAN DO TO IMPROVE TV

Nicholas Johnson
Federal Communications Commission

Critics of radio and television are generally agreed that the Federal Communications Commission is a far from effective guardian of the "public interest" in broadcasting. It has failed—according to one widely accepted view—because it has, in effect, been "captured" by the industry it was established to regulate. How did this come about? And what can you do about it? Many people have written me letters asking essentially that question. This article is an attempt at an answer.

So far as I know, the problem is not that sinister forces staged a coup one dark night in the FCC's headquarters at 20th and M Street in Washington. The problem is much more subtle, and common to virtually all regulatory agencies. As James Landis put it in his devastating report to President Kennedy: ". . . it is the daily machine-gun-like impact on both agency and its staff of industry representatives that makes for industry orientation on the part of many honest and capable agency members as well as agency staffs."

The remedy, in my view, is not going to come from spontaneous government action. Ordinary citizens can, must—and upon occasion do— influence those administrative decisions. But *effective* citizen representation requires considerably more sophistication than has been generally evidenced.

One basic principle, which I will call "the law of effective reform," is this: in order to get relief from legal institutions (Congress, courts, agencies) one must assert, first, the factual basis for the grievance and the specific parties involved; second, the legal principle that indicates relief is due (Constitutional provision, statute, regulation, court or agency decision); and third, the precise remedy sought (new legislation or regulations, license revocation, fines, or an order changing practices). When this principle is not understood, which is most of the time, the most legitimate public protests from thousands of citizens fall like drops of rain upon lonely and uncharted seas. But by understanding and using the right strategy the meekest among us can roll back the ocean.

Here is an illustration of both points.

The health hazards of cigarette smoking and, especially, the impact of TV cigarette commercials on teen-agers, have been matters of wide concern for a good many years. Yet despite ominous government reports, and despite the warning notice now printed on cigarette packages, the commercials continued, cigarette consumption increased, and more and more teen-agers picked up a habit which TV told them was the road to sexual prowess and a fun-packed adult world. A Federal Trade Commission report deplored the impact of cigarette commercials. Senator Robert Kennedy had suggested legislation outlawing them. Hundreds of thousands of Americans wrote letters to everybody they could think of—Senators, Congressmen, the networks, advertisers, the FTC—and the FCC. Most got replies; some did not. But nothing happened.

This protest failed I believe, because it ignored "the law of effective reform." Vague feelings rather than facts were presented. The letter writers were not specific about who had done something wrong. They did not refer to any legal principle that had been violated. And, finally, they did not seek a precise remedy. Indeed, many such letters begin, "Can't the FCC do something about . . . ?" The answer is that it can't—or at least that it won't—until you tell it just what you want it to do.

Fortunately, however, there was one young man who understood the "law of effective reform" and attacked the problem accordingly. He was John Banzhaf, a New York lawyer in his twenties. Mr. Banzhaf, too, wrote to "Washington." But his "letter" was different. He called it a "Fairness Complaint." In it he specified an offender: the CBS-owned flagship station in New York City, WCBS. He said the station ran great quantities of cigarette commercials. He then referred to a legal principle, the "fairness doctrine," which has evolved over the years from the Communications Act, FCC regulations, and FCC and court decisions.[1] It provides, in summary, that a broadcaster has an obligation to treat "controversial issues of public importance" fairly, and to present all sides of such issues during the course of his programming. The remedy it provides, and which John Banzhaf sought, is that the FCC can order a station complained of to present the omitted points of view. (The FCC generally leaves it up to the station to decide how this is to be done.) In this case, said Mr. Banzhaf, the debate about cigarette smoking is "a controversial issue of public importance." Cigarette commercials constitute the presentation of a particular point of view. (Cigarette smoking is associated with vigor, success, and good times.) WCBS had failed, he said, to present the other point of view. (Cigarette smoking is also associated with gruesome lingering illnesses and death.) The "fairness doctrine" requires, therefore, that the FCC order WCBS (and, by implication, all other stations) to present information about the health hazards of cigarette smoking.

Mr. Banzhaf won. A potential of some fifty to one hundred million dollars' worth of free antismoking commercials are now being presented in the course of a year over radio and television. As a result of his rather simple act and investment in a six-cent stamp he has produced a result that federal officials and hundreds of thousands of concerned Americans had been unable to bring about: cigarette consumption has declined in our nation for the first time in its history.

The point of this story is not that "one man can make a difference" (although he can, and did), or that the "fairness doctrine" is the magic solution to all complaints about broadcasting (although it has not been used as much as it might). The point is that for each citizen grievance (about broadcasting or other matters) there is one particular course of action suggested by "the law of effective reform" that will bring the quickest and most thorough results in the most efficient and cheapest way. Any effective reformer must spend at least as much energy planning that optimum strategy as executing it. You *can* fight city hall, the "little man" *can* do effective battle with massive corporate and governmental institutions, the government *can* be made to be responsible to an individual citizen's desires. The individual's frustration in our institutionalized society comes only from ignorance, not impotence. Those who preach the necessity for revolution in this country might do better to study and practice the strategy of utilizing presently available techniques of reform.

[1] A pamphlet known as "The Fairness Primer" is available free on request from the FCC, Washington, D.C. 20554. Other free pamphlets describe the rules concerning the right of rebuttal to personal attacks and the equal-time rights of political candidates. Such rules of responsible conduct are under almost constant legal challenge by the networks and broadcasters, as they are now.

It is obviously impossible to spell out in advance all potential grievances about broadcasting, let alone the optimum remedy for each, especially
in a short article. But a few more examples may be useful.

Though you may not know it, you can, and should, have a voice in
deciding who will operate radio and TV stations in your community. This
is the citizen's ultimate control over broadcast programming. A broadcast
station "owner" is using the public's property—the airwaves—and Congress
has provided that he cannot "own" this property in the sense that the
corner druggist owns his drugstore. A broadcaster is like an elected official,
and his license entitles him to no more than a three-year term, after which
he must either have his license renewed by the FCC or be turned out of
office. You—his constitutents—who are supposed to vote in this election
often do not even know it is being held. All the licenses in each state expire
at the same time. (For example, New York broadcasters' licenses are renewed June 1, 1969. Other expiration dates can be obtained from the
FCC.) Any local organization with a stake in the quality of broadcasting
(church, union, civil-rights group, or civic club) can appear as a party in
a license-renewal proceeding by writing the FCC that it wishes to be a
party, expressing its views in writing, or requesting an oral hearing. It can
not only participate in the FCC proceeding, but—often more important—
it can appeal to a court for reversal if the FCC grants the renewal un-
justifiably.

This right was first established five years ago, when the United
Church of Christ, along with two leaders of the Jackson, Mississippi, Negro
community, the Reverend Robert L. T. Smith and Mr. Aaron Henry, filed
with the FCC a petition to deny the application for license renewal of the
local TV station, WLBT. Their petition, which represented the culmination
of a decade of complaints by Jackson Negroes against WLBT, alleged that
the station systematically excluded Negroes from access to its facilities and
that it had systematically promoted segregationist views and denied presentation of opposing views supported by Negroes.

The Commission, which tended to regard these public intruders as
some sort of unfamiliar pestilence to be scourged from its corridors, refused to accord the petitioners "standing" to participate in the renewal
proceeding as parties. These representatives of the Jackson black community took an appeal to the District of Columbia Court of Appeals and
won. The Court held that local citizens *do* have "standing" as parties before the FCC, remanded the proceeding to the Commission for another
hearing, and retained jurisdiction to finally dispose of the case. The FCC
subsequently held the hearing, admitting the Church as an active party to
the proceeding. It has since granted the station a renewal—over the dis-
senting protests of Commissioner Kenneth A. Cox and myself—and at this
writing the matter is back before the Court for ultimate resolution.

Others have argued that public participation in the license renewal process be made easier. Congressman John Moss says, "It is time to make every single broadcast license renewal application subject to a public proceeding within the city or region where the station is located." Consumers Union has urged that broadcasters be required to carry more meaningful and regular announcements about the public's rights. And Thomas B. Hoving's National Citizens Committee for Broadcasting (609 Fifth Avenue, New York, New York 10017) is showing signs of possessing the capacity and courage to play a very constructive role in this regard.

Agency legal action is not, of course, the only form of popular participation in policy formation. John Banzhaf could have organized mass picketing, protesting the immorality of stations and tobacco manufacturers profiting from the promotion of disease and death. The church could have obtained thousands of signatures on a petition and sent it to the President or to Jackson's Congressman. Either could have conducted a sit-in at the FCC or at station WLBT. (WNDT-TV in New York was seized by twenty hippies during a broadcast-in about a year ago.) The point is not that the activities they chose to pursue were somewhat more gentlemanly. It's that the appropriate legal remedy may be the most efficient and effective path to reform.

Within the past two years a number of other groups have bestirred themselves, by effective legal means, about the broadcasting situation in their communities. Four interesting cases are illustrative. One concerns the renewal application of radio station WXUR in Media, Pennsylvania. Some nineteen local organizations banded together and hired a Washington lawyer to protest WXUR's alleged policy of carrying masses of right-wing political programming unrelieved by programs promoting other viewpoints. They requested, and obtained, a public hearing in their own home town.

On different grounds a group of Los Angeles businessmen petitioned the Commission not to renew the license of TV station KHJ. They charge it has provided inadequate local service to the area. Moreover, these businessmen have asserted their rights under the Communications Act to apply for a license to operate this profitable station themselves.

In Ashtabula, Ohio, a local of the retail Clerks Union petitioned the Commission to deny license renewal to several nearby radio stations which refused to carry the local's paid advertisements urging consumers to boycott a department store with which it had been involved in a labor dispute. It argued that the fairness doctrine required the stations to match the department store's commercials urging people to shop at the store with the union's contrary message.

Another protest was filed from St. Louis by organizations of young blacks who believed three local Negro-oriented ("soul") radio stations were not providing adequate service to the city's Negro population. (A station in Dayton was picketed for similar reasons with signs protesting "Soul Music Is Not Enough.")

On a national level, the American Civil Liberties Union intervened in the FCC's proceeding involving the proposed takeover of ABC by International Telephone & Telegraph Corporation. (The Justice Department ultimately appealed the FCC-approved merger to the U.S. Court of Appeals, and the parties called it off before the Court resolved the matter.)

The AFL-CIO has taken a general interest in the application of the fairness doctrine, especially, of course, when unions are attacked. The Washington-based Institute for American Democracy exists solely to combat hate programming and publishes "How to Combat Air Pollution" and a newsletter (1330 Massachusetts Avenue, Washington, D.C. 20005). John Banzhaf is now supported in his follow-up activities by an organization called Action on Smoking and Health (2238 Fifth Avenue, New York, New York 10037). He has urged a license revocation proceeding against NBC-owned WNBC in New York on the grounds that it has failed to comply with the FCC's cigarette fairness ruling, and intervened in the renewals of several California stations. (In an "unrelated" action the NBC network subsequently volunteered to put on a fixed number of anti-cigarette-smoking commercials during prime-time television programming last fall.) A group of good music lovers in Chicago ("The Citizens Committee to Save WFMT-FM") has made an effort to prevent The Chicago Tribune from acquiring the station.[2] A similar group in Atlanta inundated the FCC with mail protesting the possible loss of broadcast classical music in that city. A new national group, "Television Improvement Society of America" (1500 Massachusetts, Washington D.C. 20005), has been formed to combat violence on television.

The American Civil Liberties Union has recently suggested that, instead of relying on the spontaneous activities of existing organizations or the formation of ad hoc groups, the FCC set up local committees of citizen volunteers to monitor local radio and TV, particularly with respect to the fairness doctrine. Monitoring is one of the most important aspects of effective broadcasting reform. It is an ideal group project for people of all ages, but must be done right to be useful. The United Church of Christ has had the most experience.

[2] Other organizations concern themselves with broadcasting generally. They include the American Council for Better Broadcasts (17 West Main, Madison, Wisconsin 53703) and the National Association for Better Broadcasting (373 North Western Avenue, Los Angeles, California 90004). A number of church groups are involved, such as the Office of Communications of the United Church of Christ (289 Park Avenue, New York, New York 10010), the Television, Radio and Film Commission of the Methodist Church (475 Riverside Drive, New York, New York 10027), and the Broadcasting and Film Commission of the National Council of Churches at the same address. The Columbia Journalism Review (Columbia University, New York, New York 10027) is a quarterly that comments on the performance of both broadcasting and the print media.

Unfortunately there are few presently recognized legal rights or remedies that will affect the quality of programs, protect us from an inundation of commercials, or guarantee the opportunity to express our views or talents over the airwaves. There will be in time—when you, and others like you, finally harness your outrage and your imagination to "the law of effective reform" and pull other newly recognized legal rights into our stable of remedies.

But for now the best defense is still to turn off your set or switch stations. Since the broadcasters are in the audience-delivering business they would undoubtedly respond if enough people refused to watch or listen; but such an effort is admittedly hard, if not impossible, to organize.

On the other hand, it is easy enough to write or phone a local station manager and even to arrange a conference with him. He is not likely to be unresponsive. Similarly, letters to network presidents and to advertisers can be influencial. (If one tenth of one percent of the audience of the average network series show were to request its continuation it probably would not be canceled.) You can also send such general letters to the FCC, which, if you request, will be included in the station's "complaint file" for consideration at license renewal time. However, they will not have maximum impact unless a citizens' group subsequently appears as a party contesting the license renewal.

In fairness to the broadcasters, it should be said that citizens' groups and listeners and viewers are not generally too helpful when it comes to suggesting new program ideas. What many organizations *think* would be a good program often turns out to be a dud. When offered free air time, many organizations do not take it, or do not follow through for a sustained period. (On the other hand, some radio-station managers who have been offered locally produced programs of good quality have turned them down in favor of cheaper and easier disc-jockey or phone-in shows.)

Many communities have the blessing of community-supported noncommercial stations. The Pacifica Foundation operates radio stations WBAI in New York, KPFA in Berkeley, and KPRK in Los Angeles. Seattle has listener-supported KRAB. Public television stations (or "educational television") now exist in about 150 communities (such as Channel 13 in New York and Channel 28 in Los Angeles). Such stations should be especially responsive to listener-viewer commendation, criticism, and contributions, since most are heavily dependent upon audience financial support. If your town doesn't have such a station you might want to investigate starting one. If cable television is to be installed as a profit-making venture in your community (instead of community-owned) you will want to be sure the licensing authority (often the city council) requires it to provide a number of "free" channels for educational programming to schools and community programming to homes.

Television and radio probably have as much effect upon our lives as any other single force. About 95 per cent of American homes have receivers, and the television set is on in the average home from five to six hours a day. This is clearly America's number one consumer product, our most powerful potential force for good—or evil.

Moreover, the whole theoretical foundation of American broadcasting is the tie of a local station to its community and its local service. The station is licensed to serve the needs of the local community. And if it is not doing so we should seriously consider substituting direct satellite-to-home (or cable) broadcasting for a system that gives away 95 percent of the public's most valuable airwaves to the private profit of 7,350 local stations. FCC regulations require the station to survey the community's local needs, and to provide programming to those needs. Station files at the FCC are supposed to be filled with comments from local citizens. The three-year license-renewal process is designed to encourage local participation.

In fact, greater community involvement in stations' affairs ought to be welcomed by the more responsible broadcasters—better local service is usually translated into larger audiences and higher commercial rates and profits.

The philosophy and rhetoric of participatory democracy is on the rise. All that remains is to translate its abundant energy and ideals into effective action. The legal process often offers the easiest route to results. Yet legal rights and powers lie about unknown and unused. Increasing sophistication has been reflected in greater public participation at the FCC. I, for one, welcome it.

Although FCC Commissioner Johnson has told us how the citizen may influence broadcasting, this prescription may not fit other communications media where there is no statutory requirement that the public interest be considered. What, for example, could a reader do if he detected unfairness in the *Reader's Digest,* which does not publish corrections or retractions, or even "Letters to the Editor"? Probably nothing, aside from canceling his subscription, thus depriving the *Digest* of one of its seventeen million subscribers. Against press bias, the individual reader has few weapons although such bias is both widespread and sometimes difficult to detect, as indicated in the following essay by a well-known journalist.

BEHOLD THE GRASS-ROOTS PRESS, ALAS!

Ben H. Bagdikian

For a modest fee, you can put your "message" on the editorial page of hundreds of newspapers—because small-town publishers are surprisingly willing to turn their editorial columns over to the press agents.

The unperishing myth of American journalism is the ideal of the small-town newspaper as the grass-roots opinion-maker of the nation, the last bastion of personal journalism, the final arena where a single human being can mold a community with his convictions and fearless iconoclasm.

Needless to say, there are some small papers like this and they are marvels to behold. But the fact is that most small dailies and weeklies are the backyard of the trade, repositories for any piece of journalistic junk tossed over the fence, run as often by print-shop proprietors as by editors. Mostly they serve as useful bulletin boards of births, deaths, and marriages (providing this news comes in by its own initiative); only in exceptional cases do they raise and resolve important local issues. When it comes to transmitting signals from the outside world, a remarkable number of these papers convey pure—that is, unadulterated—press agentry. Its subject matter, which is printed both as "news" and as editorial comment, ranges from mouthwash to politics—usually right-wing.

Few readers realize that the publicity pipelines supplying the small papers are numerous, gushing, and free. A dozen large syndicates provide such material without charge to local papers, sometimes in printed or mimeographed form but more often in "mats," the pressed cardboard molds into which hot type metal is poured to reproduce pictures and texts cheaply. These syndicates make their money by charging a fee to the propagandists who have something to sell. Some businesses and other organizations by-pass the syndicates and send out their own canned goods to be reproduced as local products.

For the past three years the National Association of Manufacturers has sent out editorials which have been picked up, usually verbatim, by six hundred daily newspapers, most often without attribution to the NAM as source. The AFL-CIO sends out its material, too, but with far less success. In 1962 Medicare was the subject of a syndicated and boilerplate battle, with a volunteer pro-Medicare group sending out through a commercial syndicate (at a cost of about $15,000) canned material, some of it from officials of the Department of Health, Education, and Welfare. In response, the American Medical Association used the usual syndicate channels, plus three articles that it sent to local medical affiliates, which presented them personally to their local papers. The fight still goes on. Within the last few months, anti-Medicare editorials have appeared with miraculous similarity in widely separated places. Last May and June, for example, newspapers in South Carolina, Montana, and Michigan all ran editorials beginning, "Remember the Medicare proposal of the Kennedy Administration? It got nowhere. . . ."

But there is nothing like a political balance in the battle of boilerplate. In 1962 *The American Press,* a trade magazine for small dailies and weeklies, polled a cross section of such papers and found that 84 percent opposed any government-sponsored medical or hospital aid to the aged, were strongly opposed to federal aid to education, and were generally found in the right-wing Republican camp. The vast body of opinion picked up word-for-word by small papers is either strictly commercial or ultra-conservative.

The reader, of course, is almost never told that he is seeing something other than the considered product of his local editor.

Look at the vision of the hard-fighting small-town editor, working late at night, his green eyeshade low, his fingers spasmodically attacking the typewriter, his mind anticipating the angry reaction to his words by people he will have to face in the street, but deciding it is his moral duty to speak his mind. But behold what happens more often. The man is at his desk, all right, but if it is a very small paper, the editor is also the owner, ad salesman, and mailer. And he is not processing issues and words through his mind. He has before him a dummy of Page Two—the girdle ad on the right, the tractor ad on the left, the annual American Legion carnival stepped between them, and nine inches of remaining space reserved for "news." It is not his mind that is creating and discriminating for this space. It is more likely his right hand, fishing through the purple mats and yellow mimeographed canned editorials in his lower drawer, feeling for one exactly nine column-inches long. Depending on the fortuitous length and the luck of his fingers, what will triumph on Page Two the next day may be an article proclaiming the virtues of prune juice for regularity (compliments of the prune industry) or an editorial condemning labor unions (compliments of a conservative lobby). This is not to say that the local editor disagrees with the prune juice or the social doctrine; one must assume that he does not. But the thrifty transmitter of the precast words of a public-relations man in Chicago who happened to plug his product in exactly nine inches somehow seems disappointing as the hero-figure of American journalism.

A FRIENDLY FAMILY BUSINESS

One of the commercial conduits for the canned editorial, but not the largest, is the U.S. Press Association, Inc., which has a cosmic sound enhanced by the parenthetical note next to its address: ("12 mi. from the WHITE HOUSE.") But it is a friendly family business run by a pleasant couple in McLean, Virginia, Mr. and Mrs. Robert Nelson Taylor will take your words and ideas, if they approve of them, and $175 of your money, and send your editorial message, free of charge, to 1,199 weeklies and 150 dailies. The Taylors don't hide from the local editor that he is getting conservative editorials that someone else has paid for. A standing box on top of the weekly batch of editorials says:

This regular, comprehensive service is made possible by responsible American Business Institutions who pay an established fee to present timely business stories of FREE ENTERPRISE to Grass-Roots Americans, "The Most Influential People in the World." Clients do not dictate policy. . . . OUR OPINIONS REMAIN OUR OWN. [The Taylors' devotion to old-fashioned Capitalism includes unashamed deployment of Capital Letters.]

In a brochure inviting clients to buy its service, U.S. Press offers them a measure of freedom of opinion: "EASY TO USE . . . Just give us your story, in conference or by mail or phone. WE DO THE WORK: We write your editorial unless you *want* to. If we write it, or edit your copy, you have final OK."

Among customers listed by the Taylors as having bought or written editorials distributed by U.S. Press since June 1, 1951, are some of the leading corporations in the country, plus such lobbying or special-interest groups as the American Bankers Association, American Cotton Manufacturers Institute, American Legion, American Petroleum Institute, Bookmailer, Bourdon Institute, National Association of Manufacturers, and the Right to Work Committee.

Messages paid for or written by such groups go out under the masthead of U.S.. Press Association, Inc. and typically are picked up by about two hundred papers, each one run as the local paper's own opinion, usually on its editorial page. Mr. Taylor says he never tells the newspaper who paid for the editorial and this makes for an interesting guessing game. One mailing by U.S. Press last year, for example, included an editorial vigorously backing the railroad position in favor of enforced arbitration of its dispute with railroad unions. It called on Congress to make "arbitration compulsory." U.S. Press lists the Association of American Railroads as a paying client. . . .

Naïve or not, the newspaper editor who receives such free editorials would have to be extraordinarily dense not to know that it was paid-for axe-grinding. When U.S. Press, for example, distributed an editorial, as it did, urging the use of reflectorized tape on automobile bumpers as a safety measure, the editor does not have to know that one of U.S. Press's clients is Minnesota Mining and Manufacturing, makers of reflectorized tape, to suspect that someone is making a commercial pitch. While it is not unknown for a newspaper editor to be extraordinarily dense, it is more likely that he recognizes the press agentry but doesn't care because it is a cheap and agreeable way to fill space.

WHAT IT COSTS THE READER

The result is that almost any private citizen or special group can buy his way into the editorial columns of smaller papers with relative ease and low cost. In the process the reader loses his major protector against manipulated news—the professional journalist.

If you were a reader of the Uniontown, Pennsylvania, *Independent* for April 18, 1963, a weekly of about two thousand circulation, you would have seen a column called "About Your Health." It seemed to be a syndicated news feature with a standing logotype of a silhouetted microscope. The author was Dr. R. I. Schattner, whose picture appeared in the text. The subject for the day was "Vacant Smiles," in which Dr. Schattner wrote that 22 million Americans are "without a single natural tooth" and that the major cause of this toothlessness is gum disease and the major cause of that is tartar. "However," the good doctor wrote, "tartar can be coped with. . . . During treatment, Chloraseptic Mouthwash is an excellent topical anesthetic for controlling soreness in these tender gum conditions. This nonprescriptive medication also may be used as an antiseptic to maintain good oral hygiene."

It is no derogation of Chloraseptic Mouthwash (which has received admiring clinical reports) to report that at that time it was owned by Dr. Schattner who had invented, promoted, and was selling it. He is an intelligent, ambitious, and engaging man, a resident of Washington, D.C., who sees the public relations–news syndrome in American newspapering far more clearly than do many practitioners and professors of journalism. His column on "Vacant Smiles" appeared in about two hundred papers, thanks to a strictly cash arrangement. Dr. Schattner told me:

I paid a commercial artist about $25 to draw that microscope logotype and then I paid Derus Media Service in Chicago a little under $300 to distribute the whole thing in mat form to 1,800 weeklies and dailies. We checked placement by using a clipping service: 200 papers picked it up, so it cost me $300. If I had run it as an ad in the same papers I figure it would have cost at least ten times as much. But as a health column or as news, it isn't advertising which would offend some professional codes, and it's much more effective.

Early this year the *Wall Street Journal* reported that Dr. Schattner sold Chloraseptic Mouthwash to Norwich Pharmacal Company for more than $4 million.

Large newspapers are not safe from this flood of unfiltered propaganda. Their own processing of news and editorials is usually more professional, and while the public-relations syndicates get through with successful penetrations from time to time, the mechanical use of canned material tends to be limited in the metropolitan press to special pages like Women, Finance, Travel, and Real Estate. The great, gorgeous photographs of cottage-cheese delight or tuna-fish pizza that are the standardized centerpieces for household pages are provided free by the companies selling the goods in the picture. If it is a color photograph, it is almost a certainty that the food company provided the expensive color separations. The glowing travel articles in some of the greatest papers show up word-for-word—all taken from a publicity release—in still other, otherwise great papers. In such papers, the chief difference from small papers—other than the concentration in special sections—is that the photos and text are engraved and typeset by the local newspaper, rather than being reproduced from mats. Big papers usually have unions which reject the use of mats.

For the earnest, openhearted believer in the editor as the unsleeping guardian of every inch of news and editorial space, it is a shock to look at the scrapbooks of clippings compiled by the public-relations firms. The scrapbooks are important to the process. Some cynics insist that the canned editorials and commercial pluggery have little effect on sales or persuasion and that their chief function is to fill the scrapbooks which the public-relations operators then show the clients as proof that the clients ought to continue.

This explains why most of this press agentry is plainly marked for those who know what to look for. In many photographs and cartoon features there is a symbol printed in a corner. "K," for example, means Central Feature News, which distributes free cartoons and food pictures; is also uses a small "f" for its printed features. "MS" appears on material from Master Syndicate, which has distributed, noncommittally, Medicare, AFL-CIO, and pro-Nixon copy. "Z" is for Editors Syndicate, "G" for Precis, "FM" for Fred Morris Associates, and so forth. The symbol serves as a signal to the commercial clipping services which daily scan every paper in the country and compile the clippings for scrapbooks by which the syndicates and PR men keep score. There are times when an ideological point would be stronger if the lobbying group kept its name out of the canned editorial, but it is often put in nonetheless so that the clipping-service reader can pick up the key words when the time comes to see how well the distribution worked.

It may be that commercial pluggery is relatively ineffective except for convincing the propagandists themselves. But it is hard to dismiss it all. Even if the charge were true, it would put the newspapers in the position of giving away what they ought to sell, advertising space. More important, such irresponsible editing helps destroy in the minds both of the advertisers and the readers the crucial distinction by which the American press lives— the difference between news and advertising.

A PERVERSE RULE

The political effect of canned right-wing messages is not easily measured. For one thing, they appear mostly in rural areas, which tend to be conservative anyway. And, undoubtedly, most editors who put such material in their papers agree with it; perhaps, left to their own devices, they would write the same kind of pieces. But there is a profound difference between the identical NAM editorial appearing in six hundred newspapers and six hundred local editors thinking and writing about what the NAM has to say. The effect of the canned editorial is to make more rigid what is already a limited political and intellectual environment and to inhibit the individualistic responses which defenders of the rural life say they value.

Because rural papers have a disproportionate political impact and because they happen to be the major carriers of canned opinion, we are confronted with a perverse rule: *The smaller the newspaper, the greater its relative influence in national politics.*

There are 435 Congressional districts in the country, and in this year's 88th Congress, 203 of these, 46 percent, were rural districts. Our population is at least 70 percent urban. In many of these rural Congressional districts the leading paper is a small one, in 106 of them the leading paper has less than 10,000 circulation. In twelve of them the only paper is a weekly. To imply that a small circulation automatically means surrender to boilerplate is unfair to a number of small dailies and weeklies which, whatever their politics, are plainly the product of diligent personal editorship, and precisely in those places where this takes courage because the editor does literally have to face his readers on the street. But no one can look at the common run of small papers—and at the collected right-wing opinion which they mechanically reproduce—without being appalled at the standardized puffery that floods the countryside.

The Member of Congress almost never ignores what the small papers in his district say. For one thing, he may be interested in what the editor thinks is important. For another, he wants to know what is going into his constituents' heads. It is irrelevant to the Congressman that the editorial may be a canned one written by a paid propagandist in New York or Chicago or Indianapolis. He knows that, whoever paid for it or wrote it, when it appears in a leading paper in his district it has helped establish the political norm among his constituents.

So behold the small-town editor. He may be a conscientious journalist and community leader who thinks out issues for himself and writes what he thinks. Let the record show, futilely, no doubt, that this writer knows such men exist; some of his best friends are creative and courageous small-town editors. But beware that the grass-roots winnower of great issues may not be the thinking editorial mind, but the circling editorial hand, feeling in the lower drawer for the bit of prefabricated politics and pluggery that happens to fit, in inches and ideology, that sacred interstice for which all newspaperdom is supposed to exist: the space between the ads.

To just whom does the press owe its primary obligation—to its readers or to the advertisers who foot the bill? The "servant of the public" theme receives a great deal of self-congratulatory rhetoric from editors and publishers, and in some instances, is probably justified. In other cases, editors and publisher seem to be quite responsive to the sentiments expressed below.

I do believe that . . . every editor owes his advertisers the courtesy of *primary editorial consideration*. First, I submit that nothing is blinder or more outmoded or more unfair than the sacred cow of *overdone* editorial objectivity. . . . rather than hard-nosed objectivity, an editor owes the advertiser at least a modicum of interest and *favorable prejudice*. If . . . an editor must *choose* between two products for editorial mention, I think the firm who is underwriting the editor's whole editorial project, by putting up the money in the form of advertising, is the firm who should *consciously* be given first consideration.

Advertising man Robert E. Launey in speech to American Business Press (quoted in *Consumer Reports,* March, 1968, p. 120).

Not all newspaper publishers are for sale to the highest bidder. In the example below, a small-town newspaper publisher is willing to defend freedom of the press—meaning equal freedom of all to print and distribute their views, however unpopular or uncouth. Although he faces social ostracism and financial ruin, he persists in his notion that this is what freedom of the press means.

THE OBSTINACY OF BILL SCHANEN

John Pekkanen

William F. Schanen, Jr., looking tanned and fit except for the formidable paunch he feels entitled to at 56, squinted in the bright Wisconsin sun and began his daily amble down Franklin Street, the main stem of his home town. The street slopes through Port Washington's business district —mostly small, privately-owned shops—until it ends abruptly at a narrow inlet of Lake Michigan. Across the inlet is Smith Brothers' Fishery, a legacy of the town's days as a fishing village. The day was pristine—no hint of the musty air that sometimes drifts in from Milwaukee, 25 miles to the south.

Bill Schanen speaks to virtually everyone he meets, always by first name, and the townsmen respond in the easy way one does to someone they've known all their lives. As we walked, Schanen would explain how each person we met was intertwined with his life and the lives of his parents before him. "That woman we just talked to, she was my father's secretary for years. I used to sit on her desk in my diapers." Of a ruddy-faced woman in a flowered dress: "My mother taught her in school. My mother taught here for years. My dad was a lawyer in town for 55 years. Gosh, even the American Legion post here is named after my brother Bob, who was killed in World War II."

For nearly every store we walked past, Schanen had a comment. "Lueptow's, that big furniture store over there, they were our biggest advertiser. They were the first to pull out. Joe Leider runs that drugstore. He and I go way back. Used to go hunting together. He pulled out too. Even the electric company pulled out. Smith Brothers still runs a want ad and Virgil at the gas station puts in ads, but every time he does he gets letters and calls. They're about the only two who have stuck with me."

Schanen's tone betrayed no bitterness though it might well have.

Virtually every store he walked past on Franklin Street had canceled its advertising in Schanen's weekly newspaper, the Ozaukee Country *Press,* and because they did the paper Schanen began in 1940 and nurtured through 30 years is dying. The town is killing it because Schanen also prints *Kaleidoscope.*

Kaleidoscope is an underground newspaper, one of the largest of its kind in the country. Its office is in Milwaukee—the bottom floor of a battered old house. It is run there by a hairy staff that says it is disturbed by the growing rigidity and regimentation of the New Left. The paper reflects this thinking. Mild by comparison to much of the underground press, *Kaleidoscope* carries little nudity but a fair sprinkling of obscenity.

Schanen has nothing whatsoever to do with the content of *Kaleidoscope,* and most people in Port Washington haven't even seen the paper because it isn't distributed in town. But they nonetheless consider it obscene and un-American. So they are boycotting Schanen until he stops printing it. Schanen thinks it would be more un-American not to print it. It is an irreconcilable impasse that will cost him $200,000 in a year, nearly half his gross business.

"*Kaleidoscope* has journalistic merit," Schanen maintains. "I don't agree with a lot of it but what are we supposed to do, get rid of everything we don't agree with? There is an issue here that is much larger than Bill Schanen."

His first indication that the resentment against his printing *Kaleidoscope* was reaching a head came early this year when Lueptow, his biggest advertiser, told him customers were complaining about his advertising in the *Press.* Schanen, perhaps too blithely, ignored Lueptow. But opposition switched and soon came into the open in Port Washington and the surrounding towns. Church groups discussed it. The American Legion and some private groups started to agitate. Schanen held firm. Then in June the dam broke when Benjamin Grob, a wealthy, right-wing industrialist from nearby Grafton, excerpted a *Kaleidoscope* article that suggested indecencies in church and called police inhuman. Grob, an abrupt, sharp-eyed man who has a picture of the late Senator Joseph McCarthy in his factory office, sent the reprint to 500 businesses, groups and individuals. An accompanying letter declared Grob's intention to withdraw advertising from Schanen's papers (besides the *Press,* Schanen publishes *Squire* and *Citizen* which are distributed in nearby towns) and to refuse to do business with anyone who continued to advertise. "Ladies and gentlemen," Grob's letter concluded, "I am looking for company."

That first week, the same week Schanen learned that the *Press* had placed first in general excellence in the 1969 National Newspaper Association contest, 25 advertisers canceled. Soon 25 more followed. They haven't come back. Many stores refused to sell Schanen's weekly papers on their newsstands. As the economic noose tightened, Schanen was publicly called a dope peddler and a smut peddler at a public indignation meeting. The competing paper in Port Washington, the *Pilot,* editorialized on behalf of the boycott and has grown fatter. One day even the FBI came to question Schanen.

"I couldn't believe it. I was stunned. All of these people, my friends, deserting like that. I thought, well, if it comes to that my son Bill and I will run the whole thing ourselves. It hasn't come to that yet. We've cut back on the staff and the size of the newspaper. Some people have helped. A Spanish newspaper in Milwaukee gave us a contract to print their paper because of our stand. A university has asked us to print a book. We probably can keep going with just commercial printing, although I'm not sure of that. We're fighting in the only way we know, keeping it alive. That's why we now call the *Press* 'The Paper That Refuses to Die.' "

Schanen has run into controversy before. He's a liberal Democrat in a conservative, working-class Republican town and over the years he's stepped on many toes. His papers supported water fluoridation, sex education and open housing and have often criticized the local government, sometimes acidly. He also spoke out against the Vietnam war. "That isn't so unusual elsewhere, but around here it's heresy to advocate some of these things. But you know I'm not just someone who pranced into town with some fancy new ideas. I was born here. This is my town."

There is a solidness to Schanen—his deliberate movements and quiet words. He is also an obstinate man—"hardheaded as hell," one friend describes him—who enjoys a fight and is taking some pleasure from this one despite its cost. But as we stopped for a drink at the end of our walk down Franklin Street ("Janeshek's here is a friendly bar. The one over there is hostile to us") I got a glimpse of the frustration and hurt he feels. "I shouldn't have been so shocked by the boycott. Two years ago the high school refused to put a boy's picture in the yearbook because his hair was long. That's the kind of thinking . . .

"I'm not mad at them. Not even Grob. But I can't make any sense of it. Why they all quit. You've talked to them. What do you think they mean by it?"

Trying to explain, I kept remembering what one store owner, a man afraid to have his name mentioned, had told me: "It's damn near unanimous. The people here just don't want any part of that *Kaleidoscope* and what it stands for. They don't want to have it associated with this town in any way." Port Washington abhors the noisy, strident change going on in the world "out there." And because Bill Schanen—even remotely—made them a part of that scene, he is going to have to pay for it.

14 The Personal Pathologies

The term "personal pathologies" refers to a range of social problems in which the common element is use by deviant individuals of certain forms of behavior to escape the demands the culture makes on all members of the society. The commonly acknowledged personal pathologies include alcoholism, drug addiction, gambling, mental illness, and various sexual patterns including prostitution and homosexuality.

This is a very broad range of problems and each one of them provides many complexities, so many that not all of them can be treated systematically in a small book of readings such as this one. We have selected drug addiction and alcoholism for presentation here on the grounds that they are currently very much in the public awareness. Frequent stories in the mass media, concerted police action, and series of court decisions all indicate that the United States is presently very much concerned about the carnage resulting from excessive use of alcohol and about the apparently rapid increase in the use of drugs, particularly marihuana.

Another reason for choosing these two personal pathologies is that these areas are deeply embroiled in controversy. Value conflicts over the true nature and proper approach to drunkenness and drug use grow increasingly bitter. Three very brief excerpts from three very different kinds of publications illustrate the basic positions on drunkenness and alcoholism.

The first excerpt is taken from the booklet *Understanding Alcoholism* printed by the Michigan Department of Public Health Alcoholism Program. It takes the position, unequivocally, that alcoholism is a disease and details what alcoholism is and what it is not.

UNDERSTANDING ALCOHOLISM

William L. Keaton

Consider these in your concept of WHAT ALCOHOLISM IS.

Consider these in your concept of WHAT ALCOHOLISM IS NOT.

1. Alcoholism is a legitimate disease like diabetes, epilepsy, cancer or heart diseases.

1. It is not an illness like a headache, upset stomach or just having had too much to drink.

2. The disease can be divided into four distinct phases: contact, prodromal, acute, and chronic.

2. Alcoholism is not only drinking, getting drunk, getting into fights, causing traffic accidents, getting arrested, cirrhosis of the liver and lack of will power.

3. Alcoholism tends to create and magnify social disorganization, emotional disturbance and physical deterioration.

3. The disease is not caused by social and emotional problems, nor is it caused by bad nerves or personality aberrations.

4. A major symptom of alcoholism is "loss of control" over the amount of alcohol the alcoholic will ingest after any subsequent drinking.

4. The alcoholic does not have to drink all the time. He may abstain from the use of alcohol for weeks, months, years, or the remainder of his life. This "loss of control" is reactivated only when he starts drinking again.

5. The alcoholic may develop a psychological dependence along with a definite physical addiction to alcohol. The physical addiction is the basis for alcoholism.

5. Using alcohol to the extent of creating problems in one or more departments of one's life does not always or necessarily indicate alcoholism.

6. Once the alcoholic becomes sensitive or addicted to alcohol, he remains addicted throughout life.

6. Even though the alcoholic may be able to correct his psychological and emotional dependencies, his physical addiction will not permit him to use alcohol without triggering off the compulsve need for more alcohol.

7. The length of time it may take for the disease to develop varies considerably from person to person. In some it may take only 3 to 5 years of average drinking; however, in others it may take from 20 to 30 years of heavy drinking.

7. The individual who develops alcoholism is not born alcoholic any more than people who develop diabetes are born diabetics. The disease develops as a result of becoming sensitive or addicted to alcohol.

8. Approximately one out of fifteen drinkers develops the disease alcoholism and is referred to as an alcoholic.

8. If the individual does not have the capacity to react abnormally, nor to become addicted to alcohol, he will not develop the disease alcoholism. There are many heavy drinkers who consume as much or more alcohol than alcoholics, yet they never develop the disease alcoholism.

9. A major distinguishing characteristic of the alcoholic is his inability to sober up once he starts drinking. He experiences discomfort and excruciating pain when the alcohol content in his blood falls below the level required to produce the feeling or effect that he strives to maintain.

9. The nonalcoholic may consume large quantities of alcohol and get drunk frequently, yet sobers up whenever he wishes, without the inner demand or need for continued ingestion of alcohol as experienced by the alcoholic.

10. The alcoholic will experience physical and biochemical demands (flare-ups) for alcohol periodically after he stops drinking. Sometimes these flare-ups appear overpowering to him and he starts drinking again despite his determination to remain sober.

10. The alcoholic does not have to have any type of family, job, financial or emotional problem to experience this flare-up or demand for alcohol. Usually the build-up of this demand for alcohol produces tenseness, irritability, and irrational behavior.

11. The first symptom of alcoholism is an increase in the amount of alcohol required to produce the same effect. It may take up to ten to twelve beers, etc. to produce the same effect that five or six beers would formerly produce.

11. Both social and heavy drinkers do not require more alcohol to produce the same effect, even after years of heavy drinking. If they drink more they are doing so in order to achieve greater effect.

12. Denying alcoholism, failing to recognize it, and the lack of acceptance of alcoholism by alcoholics are as much a part of the disease as drinking and getting drunk.

12. Alcoholics give the impression of being super individuals who can "drink or leave it alone," who do not need help, and who resist anyone coming close enough to break down their defenses.

13. Alcohol alone does not cause alcoholism. Only people with the "X-factor" capacity to develop addiction to alcohol become alcoholics.

13. Individuals who do not have this "X-factor" capacity to react abnormally to alcohol do not develop the disease alcoholism regardless of how much and how often they drink.

In sharp contrast to the view just presented is a United States Supreme Court decision as recently as June 1968 that public drunkenness is a crime. The following excerpt, by a staff member of the National Institute of Mental Health, discusses that decision and indicates how several states are moving away from treating drunkenness as a criminal offense and are trying to set up treatment programs for alcoholics.

IT IS A CRIME: NO IT ISN'T

Jack Wiener

National Institute of Mental Health

To a year of bone-jarring surprises, add the Supreme Court decision that chronic alcoholics commit a crime simply by being drunk in public. The court divided 5 to 4 on the decision. (*Leroy Powell v. State of Texas,* No. 405, June 17, 1968.)

Justice Thurgood Marshall's prevailing opinion called attention to the disagreements in medicine about the nature of alcoholism, the uncertainties in treatment, and the current lack of manpower and facilities for treatment. A major argument was that if public drunkenness could be excused because of a person's lack of self-control, then the legal principle could be stretched to excuse more serious crimes like murder. The minority opinion by Justice Abe Fortas said that the criminal penalty was unconstitutional because it was cruel and inhuman punishment.

The Supreme Court decision does not prevent states from treating public drunkenness and chronic alcoholism as a disease. And, early in 1968, two states passed laws which are opposed in spirit to the opinion of

From *American Journal of Orthopsychiatry,* 38 (October 1968) p. 938. © American Orthopsychiatric Association, Inc. Reproduced by permission.

the U.S. Supreme Court. Maryland made it state policy to treat chronic alcoholics as sick people rather than as criminals (see Mental Health Highlights in the July 1968 *American Journal of Orthopsychiatry*). A similar law enacted in Hawaii states, "At present public drunkenness is a criminal offense. In addition to its ineffectiveness, the existing system operates to discriminate against the poor, invites disregard of due process safeguards and ignores the underlying medical, social, and public health problems of drunkenness. It is urgent that a law be enacted immediately to take drunkenness, as an offense in itself, out of the criminal system and to provide for a civil treatment program. . . ."

Moreover, the U.S. Congress changed the law covering Washington, D.C. so that public intoxication is a criminal offense only when it results in substantial danger to the alcoholic, to other persons, or to property. Public intoxication is to be handled as a public health problem and the District of Columbia is required to establish a comprehensive treatment program which includes detoxification, inpatient and outpatient services.

The schism in America over the proper handling of drunkenness and alcoholism runs deep. Those who would punish such behavior emphasize the evil inherent in drinking and the easy extension of non-responsibility to more serious crimes. Those who believe alcoholism is an illness favor, of course, removing the undesirable effects of drinking.

In spite of the apparent reversal indicated by the Supreme Court's 1968 decision, the nation is moving fairly rapidly toward viewing alcoholism as illness. Some groups have moved even further and favor a positive approach to drinking in American society. Our final excerpt on this topic refers to a federally supported interprofessional commission report recommending that youngsters be brought up to accept drinking in their families. Presumably, the best protection against subsequent pathological use of alcohol is learned constructive use.

Drinking in Families Is Advised

A federally financed study on alcoholism and other alcoholism problems says it should be national policy to promote drinking in a family setting to help prevent the development of problem drinkers.

The report titled, "Alcohol Problems—A Report to the Nation," also recommends that the legal age for buying and drinking alcoholic beverages be lowered to 18 throughout the country.

The National Council of Churches has strongly endorsed the proposals which are part of a "total alcohol program" aimed at inducing deliberate "changes in American drinking patterns."

Financed by a $1 million grant from the National Institute of Mental Health, the study was made by a 21-member Cooperative Commission on the Study of Alcoholism over the last five years. . . .

The commission found "a pattern of gregarious social drinking is likely to be more restrained than drinking in exclusively male settings." It also said drinking in a family setting is "likely to be restrained."

It noted the relatively low rate of problem drinking in Italian, Chinese and Jewish families where youngsters generally get their introduction to alcoholic beverages "in the home in a relatively routine and unemotional manner."

"People brought up in totally abstinent traditions who later take up drinking apparently are more likely to become problem drinkers," the commission commented.

Associated Press, October 12, 1967.

Alcoholism is an age-old problem, greater in some societies than in others. It is a major problem in the United States, with possibly six and one-half million alcoholics. The dimensions of alcoholism as an American social problem appear, however, to have been relatively fixed for some time. The number of alcoholics has been increasing roughly in accord with population growth.

Drug addiction, too, is an ancient problem and is much more common in some societies than in others. Historically, drug addiction has been less of a problem in the United States than in much of the Middle-East and the Orient, and more of a problem than in many Western nations, such as England. Unlike alcoholism, however, the dimensions of the drug use problem in the United States have changed within the last decade. The use of marihuana and several hallucinatory drugs has increased markedly, and it has become very difficult even to know what the dimensions of the problem are. The first article in this section presents a comprehensive picture of the drug abuse problem. It makes a number of important points that generally are not understood: (1) there are two quite different patterns of drug use in the United States—a lower-class pattern oriented toward heroin, and a middle-class pattern oriented toward marihuana; (2) contrary to popular belief, the use of heroin may be self-limiting; and (3) the use of marihuana and the hallucinogenic drugs has grown understandably out of the general nature of American culture. Understanding the drug problem requires understanding the larger society.

FACTS AND FANCIES
ABOUT DRUG ADDICTION

Norman E. Zinberg

Assistant Clinical Professor of Psychiatry
Faculty of Medicine, Harvard University

Misunderstanding of the problems of drug abuse in this country is the greatest current obstacle to attempts at their solution. It is my purpose in this essay to sort out what is actually known from what passes as fact; to show something of how these misconceptions have come to be accepted as truths; to point out what we do not know but urgently need to; and, finally, to indicate what lines of investigation seem at the moment to promise the most fruitful results.

How, first, is the problem of drug addiction commonly conceived? In most people's minds, drug addicts are a group of reprobate criminals who "mainline" heroin. This concept is not confined to the general lay public, but pervades even relatively sophisticated discussions of the drug problem. Unhappily, it also dominates professional attitudes toward legislation, law enforcement and clinical treatment. But in its crudity it simply does not correspond with the true picture, even in so far as it is known; and, worse, it subtly undermines attempts to learn more. Given this distortion, the drug problem is rarely looked at for what it is—an endemic disease about which we need more information and less ideology. As a matter of fact, the very notion of the drug problem is wildly misleading. There is more than one drug problem, just as there is more than one kind of drug taker and more than one kind of pernicious drug.

TWO VARIETIES OF DRUG EXPERIENCE

At least two separate types of drug abusers can be clearly distinguished even in our present state of limited knowledge. They differ in

Adapted from *The Public Interest,* 6 (Winter 1967) pp. 75–90. Copyright © National Affairs, 1967.

terms of their places in our society, the kinds of drugs they use, and what they hope to get out of drugs. The first group comes mainly from the lower socio-economic strata of the population; they use drugs to escape from lives that seem unbearable and hopeless. Whatever their individual psychological problems, the general profile of members of this group reflects a direct relationship between social deprivation and specific personality types. I call them *the oblivion-seekers.*

Most public discussion of narcotics "addicts" recognizes only this first group. But there is a second, much larger, group who come from the middle and upper socio-economic strata. They use drugs not to get away from life but to embrace it. Drugs give them a sense of liberation from convention, a feeling that a level of genuine experience which is closed to them by their culture is opened for them by the drug. If they are thought of as presenting a social problem, it is their rebellion, not their addiction, which is viewed with alarm. Because of their class origins and their youth, they are commonly identified not as addicts but simply as participants in the rebellion our culture has come to expect from every rising generation. I call them *the experience-seekers.*

Members of these two groups typically use different drugs—the oblivion-seekers use heroin, the experience-seekers a considerable variety of other drugs. This difference is important, because heroin is illegal in this country for any purpose, medicinal or otherwise, and is reputed among the knowing to have both a greater kick and a greater pull toward dependency than any other drug. Before the typical heroin-taker became addicted, therefore, he probably knew he was committing himself to constant law breaking and to drug dependency. Experience-seekers, who try other dependency-inducing drugs, rarely think of themselves in this way. Indeed, many of them—though they know the drug they are using does often induce dependency—think they are exceptions, and insist that they are not "hooked" long after this is manifestly untrue.

It would not be unreasonable to expect these differences to have been noticed long ago. Yet the situation as it stands now is so muddled that even so elementary a distinction as that which divides the oblivion-seekers from the experience-seekers has not been made by the medical profession. Lacking this or any other meaningful sort of distinction, and in the absence of any accepted clinical procedure, doctors respond to their drug patients emotionally, each according to his own bent. They fill in what they do not know with unexamined notions and feelings. The sentimentalists, the "soft" school, tend to see a curiously attractive innocence in the drug takers. The punishers, the "hard" school, refuse to see drug abuse as a physical and social disease, but insist it is rooted in moral turpitude.

ROMANTIC ILLUSIONS

The "soft" school looks upon the oblivion-seekers as new incarnations of the noble savage. For it, members of the lower classes have a special "earthy" knowledge about Life.

The moral support given to the drug taker by sentimentalists is sufficiently pernicious and persistent to warrant a closer look. In a recent *New Yorker* article, Dr. Marie Nyswander, well known for her work with drug addicts, discussed her sad, tortured charges with a reporter. After describing a young, confirmed opiate dependent who *wanted* to be committed to a state hospital for three years, she was reported as having said: "Man may be able to experience freedom in a degree we can't yet imagine. . . . That's why drug addicts . . . strike me as being among the few comparatively free people I've met. . . . The addict's relationships, except when he's scrounging for drugs, are honest and direct. Deceit is not a basic part of his personality."

Here is a clear instance of the sentimental mystique at work. The nature of the drug addict is assimilated to the supposedly unspoiled nature of the child—he is someone who rejects our hard, competitive adult world and returns to the simple world of children, where truth and beauty are self-evident. He experiences life freely, he is untouched by fraud, oppression, pettiness, and despair. What matter if his arms are somewhat scarred?

In an odd way, it is true that the absence of responsibility for one's self or for the welfare of others does permit an engaging directness and lack of guile. Many oblivion-seekers lie and cheat to get drugs, but they can do so with disarming openness, because like children, they want nothing but the immediate satisfaction of specific, pleasurable desires. The indirection and ambiguity necessary to manage adult responsibilities, the need to slight one wish or responsibility in order to give fuller expression to another, militate against simplicity. Many of those who admire drug users seem unaware that the charm which enchants is nothing more than simple single-mindedness—the conviction that few things other than drugs are worth the complexity and strain of striving for. . . .

"HARDHEADED" ILLUSIONS

The "hard" school, on the other hand, the punishers who see drug abuse almost entirely as crime, find their rationale in the legal history of the drug problem in this country. After many false starts, the medical profession in 1902 did accept as a serious medical problem Dr. Charles

Towns' now classical description of the dependency triad—the compulsive need for the drug, the development of tolerance, and the emergence of a withdrawal syndrome if the drug is withheld. But it was already too late; the lawmakers had taken over. At the turn of the century, before the Flexner Report, there was good reason to mistrust the calibre of doctors produced by our medical schools. Partly for this reason, the 1904 Boylan New York State Law—and the 1914 Harrison Federal Narcotic Act which was patterned on it—gave no discretion to physicians in dispensing drugs to addicts. The Harrison Act, a Federal taxing law, was passed in the same atmosphere which a bit later resulted in the prohibition of alcoholic beverages being written into law. The right of the physician to prescribe narcotics in the course of his professional practice became an issue of law enforcement, and it was on this battleground that the "hard" school was able to win a decisive victory for their punitive point of view. Beginning in 1919, in a series of highly moralistic rulings ("a physician who prescribed narcotics" was stigmatized as intending "to cater to the appetite or satisfy the craving of one addicted to the use of the drug"), the Supreme Court decided that physicians could not prescribe narcotics to habitual users to keep them comfortable even if they were en route to a hospital. In this state of the law, drug abuse could only be seen as a criminal matter. Led by the American Medical Association, the medical profession simply abandoned the field. After the formation of the Federal Bureau of Narcotics in 1930, public discussion of drug abuse was confined to a discussion of criminality. Harry Anslinger, who was head of the Federal Bureau of Narcotics from its inception until four years ago, fabricated reports for public dissemination out of adroit compounds of fact and fiction. As a result, an automatic association between narcotics and criminal activity has been set up in both the public's and the professional's minds. Until recently, this atmosphere made research and experimentation virtually impossible.

Probably no more moralistic government agency than the Federal Bureau of Narcotics has ever existed. Reflecting as it does the nineteenth-century attitude of the temperance societies (i.e., one drink makes a confirmed drunkard) or of the nineteenth-century public attitude toward sex (i.e., one illicit experience makes a prostitute), the Federal Bureau of Narcotics has pointed out over and over again that, after even one single dose of any of the drugs on their list, dreadful moral deterioration sets in. For example, Mr. Anslinger, writing about "a few of many cases which illustrate the homicidal tendencies and the general debasing effects arising from the use of marihuana," cites the case of a cotton-picker, 25 years old, who smoked a "reefer," picked up a 17-month-old baby girl who had been left in her family car, violated and suffocated her. Ignoring the complexity of the motives in so heinous a crime, Anslinger concludes that "the real criminal in this case is marihuana."

The young people who try drugs probably don't read these publications, but their pronouncements do effectively help shape the general public view. By first enormously oversimplifying, and then overstating, their case, government authorities have thus provided young people, who always like to puncture balloons of pompous self-righteousness, with a gratuitous sense of purpose in drug taking.

The punitive rigidity of law enforcement officials changed not at all until the 1962 White House Conference on Narcotic and Drug Abuse; since, they have changed their attitude only minimally. In spite of the enlightened proceedings of this Conference, the old simplistic thinking persists. Recently, when a Justice Department official was asked off the record about his views on the drug problem, he said it was very simple. "Now, about $5,000,000 a year is spent enforcing the Harrison Act; to keep an addict comfortable costs about $25,000 per year, most of which comes from crime. If only 50,000 addicts are involved, by simple arithmetic you arrive at a figure of $125,000,000 yearly that the public, in a sense, pays for the narcotics habit. Put that much money in the hands of the proper (enforcement) agency and we will eliminate the drug traffic." Both his thinking and his arithmetic fail to take into account such obviously germane facts as previous criminality among drug users, the lesson of prohibition, the constantly increasing difficulty any one country has in sealing its borders and acting unilaterally. Most importantly, however, he fails entirely to consider the drug problem as it is related to the experience-seekers. . . .

FACTS AND QUERIES

These, then, are the sort of errors the ideologies of both the "hard" and the "soft" schools have led to. To show fundamentally the substitution of fiction for fact has impeded research, let us look at what seems at first to be a relatively simple question. How many heroin users are there in the United States? Surprisingly, estimates differ widely. If the Federal Bureau of Narcotics' figure of 60,000 is correct, then the number of hardcore drug abusers in this country has hardly changed at all in the last four decades. (Indeed, relative to the rise in population, it has declined.) But the World Health Organization estimates the number of drug dependents as closer to one million!

How can we explain this fantastic disparity? Does the second figure actually include not only heroin users, but other kinds of drug addicts? Does it include persons who have been drug abusers only temporarily? How many times are chronic recidivists counted? The correct figure seems to be difficult to come at, but clearly this is the sort of question that cannot be answered meaningfully without the sort of typological distinctions we have been making.

To ask an even more fundamental question: are we sure that the oblivion-seekers present as dangerous a social problem as they have long been held to do—or is it rather the experience-seekers, hitherto hardly recognized as a problem at all, who present the real threat?

In 1965, John O'Donnell presented a careful analysis of figures about relapse rates. He states that, after a time, many heroin users dose themselves less frequently rather than more, and, further, he suggests that all heroin addiction may be time-limited, since his data point to a precipitous drop-off of drug abuse after the age of 35. This study supports an earlier one by Charles Winick, who concluded from the Federal Bureau of Narcotics' files that "addiction may be a self-limiting process for perhaps two-thirds of the addicts." If this is true, then despite the important social, economic, legal, and criminal problems which the oblivion-seekers present, they may not in fact be the fundamental problem they are thought to be. In the present state of our knowledge, however, we do not know enough, even about the much-studied oblivion-seekers, to answer this question.

Some things about the oblivion-seekers are, of course, well-known. Their personal histories have been shown to follow a distinct pattern: cigarettes at age six or seven, liquor and sex by thirteen, marihuana soon after. Promiscuity and petty thievery merge almost automatically, in late adolescence, into prostitution and organized crime. Drug abusers of this type show a definitely ascending use of drugs, typically moving toward the one with the big kick, "H." But other things we know about this type are puzzling—in particular, the ways in which their pattern differs from that of the nonaddicted delinquent. To begin with, Billy E. Jones finds that the Lexington drug users are surprisingly intelligent: their average verbal IQ is 105. Contrast this with the Gluecks' study of penitentiary prisoners; there, 67 percent have a verbal IQ of less than 90. Nor are the family histories of criminals and addicts identical. Fifty-two percent of addicts come from homes broken by death before age 16. (Indeed, 28 percent of these occurred before age six.) These figures do not refer simply to the loss of fathers, so common to the lower socio-economic class strata; more than 20 percent lost their mothers by age six. So while broken families seem to have something to do with addiction, it is not clear how much they have to do with it.

It also turns out that the drug takers are only or youngest children to a statistically significant degree. Yet birth order has never been proven to be a significant factor among delinquents, alcoholics, or the mentally ill.

But the most striking single correlation to have been established between parental history and drug dependency was parent-child cultural disparity. Among Negroes, for example, Northern-born drug takers had Southern-born parents twice as often as would be expected from the census figures. This statistical incidence is shown to the same degree by children of immigrant parents. By contrast, the incidence of drug dependency in a Northern urban sample who were themselves immigrants or Southern-born Negroes was only 12 percent, which is less than half of the percentage an average projection from census figures would lead one to expect.

Most surprising of all, however, is the fact that 72 percent of the patients studied by Vaillant still lived with their mothers at age 22; indeed, after age 30, 47 percent continued to live with a female relative. Approximately 70 percent were either married or maintained a relatively stable, common-law relationship. These marriages tended to continue in spite of hospitalization. This is holding on to people to a striking extent—an extent markedly greater than similar studies show for alcoholics or other delinquent groups. Glueck's study of criminal delinquents, for instance, shows only 22 percent continuing to live with their family of origin after 30, while about the same proportion maintained some form of married life.

An incidental finding of the same study supports the contention that the drug taker strives for closeness with a maternal figure. When hospitalized or imprisoned, drug takers, like other institutionalized persons, frequently engage in homosexual activity. But in only three percent of the cases studied by Vaillant do the patients report that homosexual activity is a source of significant gratification to them in their outside adult life. This is a surprisingly low figure, particularly in view of the popular notion that drug addiction and homosexuality go together.

DRUGS AND CRIME

One of the most damning arguments used by the punitive school is the relationship of drug-taking to crime. They quote statistics showing that drug takers commit a high percentage of the crimes in the United States and strongly imply that crime results from drug taking. Now, it is true that oblivion-seekers get a lot of the money they need to buy drugs from criminal acts, but nevertheless, drugs do not make criminals. It is the other way around: criminals take drugs. Hill, Gerard, and Kornetsky, among others, indicate that over 70 percent of known drug abusers had criminal records *before* turning to drugs.

What seems to happen is that once a criminal is caught up in drug taking, a vicious circle commences. Drugs are illegal and expensive, large sums of money are needed to maintain a habit, and it takes a lot of time to make sure a connection is available. Moreover, once a habit is established, despite growing tolerance, drugs are debilitating in a way that makes regular work almost impossible. These conditions reinforce previous criminal activities.

This undeniable link between drugs and crime does not, however, invalidate the distinction between the oblivion-seekers and other types of delinquents. The oblivion-seekers' pattern—an intensity of attachment to family of origin and later to a significant female, the preponderance of youngest children, the low rate of psychotic illness, the high rate of intelligence—meaningfully marks addicts off from the others. Certainly, with their high intelligence, the oblivion-seekers know that the drug dependency they court demands antisocial activity of them, and it is inevitably asked how significantly aggression against society is involved as a motive for drug taking. From what we know now, such aggression is not very important. The oblivion-seeker seems, rather, to be a surprisingly dependent person. His drug dependency is a measure of his childishness, immaturity, and inability to cope with adult responsibility. The incidence of schizophrenia, as Vaillant shows, is low; rather, the oblivion-seekers have a high suicide rate. The search for oblivion is above all a flight from the pain of rejection and the fear of loneliness.

This proposition is reinforced by the fact that solitary drug users are an infinitesimal minority. Drug addicts depend on each other; drug taking is a group activity. Drug use spreads by contagion, that is, one drug user encourages, teaches, and recruits so that he can share his activity with others. Once the epidemiology of drug abuse is understood in the context of the character of the oblivion-seekers, the punishers will no longer be able to justify treating the drug abusers as simple moral delinquents. Some steps have already been taken in this direction. For example, the 1962 White House Conference on Narcotic and Drug Abuse specifically labeled as false the widely-held notion that drug abuse in the young was primarily initiated by narcotic salesmen hanging around public schools, coaxing juveniles into trying free shots, and thus working up an insatiable market for their trade.

From all that we know, the basic truth seems to be that drug abuse is simply another way to express fear, deprivation, and aimlessness. For the oblivion-seekers, drug taking in the end is self-defeating; for, in time, drugs reproduce the very situations from which users had hoped to escape. Even at this dead end, however, drug taking is hard to stop. The impulse to escape survives the failure to escape.

THE OTHER KIND OF ADDICT

To turn now to the experience-seekers, the one trait that characterizes them as a group is a terrible fear of lifelessness, of missing something important, of not really living. Beyond this, no such pattern as typifies the oblivion-seekers has as yet been discerned. Here, more than with the oblivion-seekers, the question of what part physiology plays in their drug dependency, and what part psychology, confuses every attempt to analyze experience-seeking addiction. The drugs of choice are often varied; there is no such clear pattern as the oblivion-seekers' relentless preoccupation with heroin. The one characteristic common to them all, one which they share with the oblivion-seekers, is the need for others to share drug taking with them. Indeed, they outdo the heroin takers in their proselytizing efforts.

Because the effects of most of the drugs used by this group vary so widely, all that we know about what individual drug users experience comes from the subjective responses they themselves report. Controlled experiments are simply not feasible; drug users insist that in a clinical setting—such as a hospital or a laboratory—the effect, probably the group effect, is largely cut off, the drug does not convey the real kick. It is hard not to conclude that, at least some of the time, the experience-seekers want so desperately to have drug-induced experiences that they have them psychologically even if not physiologically. What is more, like the Emperor in his new clothes, they want to be sure everyone around them has the same experience, sees the same cloth of gold. If others who have been persuaded to join the group testify that they, too, have had an experience and, more to the point, an "exciting" or "beautiful" experience, the original members of the group feel their drug taking takes on enhanced validity. They can put aside their doubts and fears about drugs at least for a little while. From the point of view of contagion, the desire of the experience-seekers to proselytize presents a real and present danger to our society.

MARIHUANA

Most experience-seekers begin by smoking "pot"; these are the youngsters who stage demonstrations against the classification of marihuana as a narcotic by Federal Drug legislation. They contend that marihuana is probably less and certainly no more harmful than alcohol; they deny that the Federal Bureau of Narcotics' claims that people under the influence of "pot" are socially destructive. Above all, they insist that the notion that "pot" leads inevitably down the road to "H" is nonsense. The delight they take in exploding these official misconceptions, their sense of pursuing an idealistic cause, certainly stimulate their age-specific, culturally-expected rebellion and help to attract adherents.

Although the experience-seekers are probably right in their contention that the above-mentioned ideas about "pot" are silly, they are not as right as they think. Each of the conventional ideas they pooh-pooh deserves more careful investigation. Thus, it is true that, for the great majority of the experience-seekers and for the much greater number of the young who try smoking "pot" once or twice, marihuana has little connection with heroin. Still, one small segment of those who begin with marihuana, and who, in addition, are seriously neurotic, finds the nonconformist support they need in such a drug-experimenting, "pot"-smoking group. Because everyone in adolescence seems in turmoil, these neurotics don't look much different from the rest. But after two or three years pass, the regular bunch—even if they are still a little "beat"—have gone ahead and made necessary life decisions. Yes, they take a year off, but they still manage to be graduated from college or to acquire an interest that leads some-where. The neurotic, however, who may have thought he was just like the rest of the bunch, fails to take these steps when they should be taken. Suddenly he is no longer really part of the bunch. What can he do but reach out for another group who will accept him? This group is likely to be closer to the hard-core drug abusers; it may even be a heroin-taking, oblivion-seeking group where big money is needed to stay "in."

While there are not many who follow this path—indeed, most users of this type seek out a psychiatrist rather than a pusher—they deserve attention because they show dramatically what marihuana can mean to troubled youngsters. Marihuana is a disorganizing agent; it offers no help to people who are already more than suffciently disorganized. Perhaps it is no worse than alcohol—there are 5,000,000 disabled alcoholics in the United States—but that does not mean that we need yet one more rela-tively potent intoxicant to be made readily available to all. Undoubtedly, many people can handle marihuana, use it, and perhaps enjoy it without ill effects. Allentuck and Bowman, Murphy, and the LaGuardia Report, among others, agree that physiological dependency is not induced by mari-huana. But the World Health Organization reports that marihuana-hashish-hemp-bange is the most abused drug in the world. Long-term ex-cessive use results psychologically in a stultifying condition of lethargy, dissociation, and general withdrawal from human contact, a reaction not very different from that of chronic alcoholism. Physiologically, further-more, marihuana can cause hyperglycemia, hyperthermia, and depression of respiration.

The most pernicious property of marihuana is not its potency but its relative weakness. Many experience-seekers want to extend themselves in inner and outer time and space; they strain against personal boundaries, they want all knowledge and feeling to be available to them. It is precisely for this reason that the languid release of the opiate does not interest them. Their intolerance for the strictures of reality, for the limitations imposed by both the outside and the inside worlds, makes the brief and easily ter-minable "high" of marihuana insufficient. Therefore, a sizeable, but cur-rently indeterminable, group of fairly regular "pot" smokers goes on to experiment with the hallucinogens—LSD, mescaline, psylosibin, peyote, dimethyl triptan, or some other variety of the magic mushroom.

THE HALLUCINOGENS

We may really have opened up a Pandora's box with these drugs. For we understand very little about the action of the hallucinogens. A "high" on a 200-microgram dose of LSD usually lasts from 8 to 12 hours, that is, the time during which there is a high degree of concentration in the cerebral system. As soon as almost any other known drug is excreted from the system, so are its effects. But many experiments indicate that this is not true of LSD. A possible return of effect long after no demonstrable blood level remains has been proven to exist. Is this return physiological or psychological? We do not know.

We do, however, know enough to suggest that, for several months after even a single hallucinogenic experience, no one should make an important life decision. Most young people, of course, wrestle with potential changes in their lives all the time. The nature of that struggle often may be characterized as a pull between a more structured or a less structured way of life: serious music or folk music, attending school or taking a year off, and so on. Clearly, each of these ways of life can have validity; that is not the point at issue here. What does concern us is that under drug influence—which means for months after taking the drug—he invariably chooses the looser or less structured alternative; he seems to be deprived of free choice, to be unduly influenced by his drug experience. . . .

Unfortunately, the hue and cry about the hallucinogens has reduced the amount of valid research being done and made it unpopular. Few researchers want to take responsibility for having the drug around or risk its accidental dissemination. We come full circle back to the beginning of the history of narcotic usage. Again, public alarm strengthens the hand of those who see drugs primarily as a problem of law enforcement and punishment and has little patience for essential social and psychological considerations.

ARE WE DRUG HAPPY?

Our discussion of the little understood, indirect, but potent psychological roots of the experience-seekers' drug abuse must not fail to consider the extent to which this country maintains a drug culture. Our culture's rapidly increasing medical dependency on drugs, both for survival and for longevity, makes drug taking a sacred cow indeed. The extent to which we as a nation have become drug eaters was given shocking, but short-lived, publicity during the Kefauver hearings in 1951 and again during the thalidomide scandal. At the 1966 American Medical Association's convention, a great deal of perhaps belated attention was given to this growing phenomenon. Dr. Don Francke sounded the keynote by saying, "The American public is drug happy. Our culture is flooded with remedies of all kinds." In 1963, American consumers spent 4.2 billion dollars on drugs. This figure does *not* include drugs charged to hospital or clinic bills or money spent on drugs by public or government agencies of any kind. . . .

The young drug experimenter is, in fact, imitating his elders when he uses drugs; at the same time, he establishes his independence and rebellion by using those illegal drugs his elders officially decry. To those of his peers whom he wishes to enlist in the drug taking army, he points out the hyperbole of the Federal Bureau of Narcotics and the hypocrisy of his elders as reasons *for* taking drugs. Untenable as this argument is, a lot of college students in the United States have been persuaded by it.

The oblivion-seekers are a relatively clearcut group; they can be studied as a problem. But, in order to study the experience-seekers, we find ourselves studying our society. All too often, they are only exaggerations or caricatures of so much we see everywhere. Indeed, it is the closeness and at the same time the vastness of the problem presented by the experience-seekers that prevents any study of them. We simply do not know what the extent and quality of experience-seeking drug abuse is, nor what are its implications for the future. For instance, we see many users of LSD becoming patients in mental hospitals. Does their number represent only a small proportion of those who take trips, or is there a high ratio between those who take LSD and eventual psychosis?

The medical profession has now, at long last, taken a stand against the crime-oriented Federal Bureau of Narcotics; it is trying to reassert the right it once abdicated, to diagnose and treat drug abusers as sufferers from a disease. But its well-meant effort may be defeated before it begins. In its call for increased research and treatment, organized medicine has placed first importance on sick individual patients, rather than on the broad social problem which drug dependents present to medical practice. The profession may well find itself in a camp as narrow in its own way as that of the Federal Bureau of Narcotics. The emphasis on individual patients limits interest to the oblivion-seekers who, as I have indicated, may be much less of a problem than the experience-seekers. By putting the greatest priority on the search for a nondependency-producing analgesic and on local treatment rather than specialized regional public health hospitals far from their patients' homes, the profession is undoubtedly supporting worthy causes. But it is not facing the enormity of the problem, and it is not searching for truly fresh approaches. Indeed, all too often, it repeats past mistakes. For example, Vaillant shows that involuntary parole is the most effective means of keeping the drug taker abstinent and employed. The experiments with methadone require the patient to report to someone at the hospital who gives him his drug regularly. Consequently, we do not know as yet whether the effective agent is merely the replication of an involuntary parole situation, stringently enforced by methadone's very severe withdrawal reaction. Yet claims for methadone as a cure-all appear constantly in the press, claims that sound very much like those that were made for heroin as a cure for opium addiction in 1898, when heroin was first synthesized.

Obviously, there is no one solution to the drug problem. Before any research effort can begin, there must be a basic shift in public attitudes. Neither hard-school prejudices nor soft-school sentimentalizing can be allowed to continue to distort the public vision. Many approaches and real social flexibility will be necessary to diagnose, prevent, and treat this multi-faceted, economic, psychological, physiological, and social problem. The known possibilities give some sense of the scope that is needed. Some drugs might be legalized; the British system of a license for certain users of certain drugs might be tried; opiate antagonists might be developed; nondoctrinaire, nonritualized, psychiatric approaches might be effective; Synanon-like, cohesive group-living units show some promise; institutional settings could be made available for those who can find tolerable stability only as institutional workers, attendants, or patients. The study of the peculiar nature of this disease, its incidence in groups more than in individuals, its spread by contagion and subsequent infection of those who want warmth, closeness, and social support for some antisocial or dependent propensities, will teach us about a great deal more than just drug taking. But we must begin by knowing that much of what we think we know about this problem is mistaken.

The last article in this chapter offers a more distinctly sociological analysis, focusing not upon drug use as such—the author maintains that we shall have to get used to that—but upon the development of incidents related to drug use on the college campus. Becker presents a more sanguine view than did Zinberg in the preceding article at least partly because he focuses upon the use of marihuana by otherwise normal people and omits consideration of the problems raised by seriously neurotic users.

ENDING CAMPUS DRUG INCIDENTS

Howard S. Becker

Professor of Sociology
Northwestern University

The use of drugs—primarily marihuana and LSD—has become an increasingly important and time-consuming problem on college campuses. Much of the thinking and writing (that done by adults, anyway) focuses on the drug use itself, asking why so many students take drugs and what can be done to prevent them, or lessen the impact of their use of drugs.

But instead of asking why students use drugs, let us ask how a campus comes to have a drug incident—thus suggesting that we *ought* to be concerned with a problem somewhat different from the one we conventionally are.

I propose this, first, because it is very likely impossible, given our resources and our will, to stop students from using drugs. No college administration has the personnel to root out drug use by itself. (It may try, however, to achieve the same end by opening the college to undercover agents of off-campus police forces, or it may—as in the recent action at Stony Brook, Long Island—find off-campus forces invading the campus openly, without asking permission first.)

In addition, we need more knowledge before we can get any firm answer to the question of why students use drugs—and any program designed to eradicate drug use not founded on this knowledge will surely fail. Third, it seems to me that the processes involved in a campus drug incident do not require intensive study, and that we may find a way out of our current difficulties by attacking the problem at this level.

Finally, available evidence and the experience of campus physicians indicate that drugs are a minor health hazard. LSD apparently presents some difficulties, but marihuana (the most widely used psychedelic) has no demonstrable bad effects. Campus psychiatrists know that alcohol presents them with far worse problems. In short, students who think there is no good reason for attempting to restrict student drug use are right.

I thus mean to distinguish campus drug incidents from campus drug use. Students may use drugs without incidents occurring. An incident occurs when students use drugs, the college administration is confronted

From *TRANS-action* (April 1968) pp. 4–5. Copyright © by *TRANS-action* Magazine, New Brunswick, New Jersey, 1968.

with the fact publicly, and it takes some punitive action in consequence. The press, radio, and TV are frequently involved.

What do students and administrators do that produces the typical campus incident? Students contribute to the growing number of incidents in two ways. First, more and more of them use drugs. My guess is that marihuana use is now viewed by many college students in the same way that chastity is said to be viewed by college women. Once students did not recognize any legitimate argument in favor of drug use; they knew that it was, quite simply, "wrong," just as the "nice" college girls knew that "nice girls don't." But college girls now see chastity as a matter for individual decision; they can envision many circumstances in which premarital intercourse is morally acceptable. So each girl must make up her mind for herself; she no longer believes that an absolute moral rule governs such decisions. Similarly with drugs. Students who once thought all drug use immoral now believe that the consequences of use are so negligible that it is a matter for each student to decide.

Further, the greater availability of scientific information convinces students, approaching it as they do in a rational and "scientific" manner, that they have nothing to fear. This, of course, occurs most frequently with respect to marihuana, where the scientific evidence most clearly favors that interpretation.

But increased student drug use alone is not sufficient to create a campus drug incident. For that to happen, students must also be caught, which they are doing more and more frequently. Students get caught in a variety of ways. A number of incidents have been triggered by students who sold marihuana to policemen. Sometimes students smoke the drug so openly as to make detection almost inevitable—the very openness of the act, in fact, makes the police or other officials feel that they are being taunted and thus increases the students' chances of arrest. Sometimes students create a campus incident by giving drugs to other people without their knowledge, possibly as a prank. These people may respond very badly, and official action is provoked by the medical opinion that drug use is thus very dangerous.

What students do to provoke a drug incident, then, is to get caught. And they get caught for two reasons: ignorance and ideology. They are either ignorant of the devices and precautions that might protect them against arrest, or they are willing to risk it on ideological grounds.

Most of the college students who use drugs today have no desire to get caught. On the contrary, they fear arrest and its effect on their lives. They do not want to be kicked out of school, or have police records, or be branded as dope fiends. But they have learned to use drugs in an atmosphere where strict security measures do not seem essential to avoid arrest, and where no one has told them what those measures are.

Drug users of past generations knew that they had to fear the police.

These experienced users were cautious about whom they bought drugs from and whom they sold them to, about where they used drugs and whom they allowed to know, about where they kept their supplies and about the people before whom they would dare to appear "high." These precautions were part of the culture that drug users learned at the same time they learned to use drugs, and the necessity for such precautions and their character were passed on from one user to another. It appears now that a large number of college students have gained access to drugs without acquiring this aspect of the drug-using culture. They know how to get high, but they don't know how to get high without getting caught.

Other students, a smaller number, get caught for ideological reasons. Some believe they have a constitutional right to get high on drugs. (Indeed, constitutional issues have been raised in many cases, some of which will probably find their way to the Supreme Court: These students may be right.) They want to use drugs, feel that they are legally entitled to do so, and wish to provoke a legal confrontation on the question. Or they simply do not wish to bother about being secretive. They may adopt an ideology of psychological freedom, believing that the psychic energy they expend in secretive maneuvers could be spent better in other ways. They recognize that they are taking a chance, but consider the chance worth the price. Either of these ideologies leads students to be quite open about their drug use, perhaps using drugs in public places, or announcing publicly that they use drugs.

In short, whether out of ideology or ignorance, students use drugs with increasing openness and lack of caution. This leads to situations in which they are very likely to get caught and become the objects of publicity. And at this point college administrations complete the process of creating a campus drug incident.

College administrations, as a rule, respond to the pressures of publicity by taking some kind of action. They will very likely not have a reasoned approach to the problem. Confronted with letters and calls from angry and worried parents, with strong pressure from boards of trustees (and, in the case of public institutions, from state legislatures), with continuing newspaper questioning, they act hastily. They may expel the student. They may pass new harsh regulations, or make new interpretations of the broad discretionary powers they already have.

These responses assume that the number of drug users is small; that, once weeded out, they will not be replaced by new users; and that the problem can be dealt with within the confines of the campus proper. But none of these assumptions are correct. The number of users is large and growing; they cannot be weeded out, only driven underground. Since students can always purchase drugs "in town," in nearby cities, or on other campuses, no college can contain the activity on its own. So harsh action by university authorities simply brings even more cases to light and increases the unfavorable publicity—at least until students get the message and become more cautious.

The same considerations apply to the increased surveillance that students are subjected to. Many of the actions students are now caught for might have gone unnoticed, flagrant as they are, if campus officials had not alerted campus police, dormitory counselors, student-health personnel, and others to bring relevant evidence to the attention of the authorities. Some of this increased attention followed FDA Commissioner James L. Goddard's appeal for such cooperation with federal and local law-enforcement officials; some was probably a simple response to massive national publicity. All increases in surveillance, of course, multiply the number of cases that come to public attention as campus drug incidents and thus increase the difficulties the surveillance was supposed to solve.

Administrators take strong actions because they fear there may be some danger to the students involved—and because of the pressure of publicity.

Many deans of students worry about the dangers of drug use. After all, we cannot expect that they will have expert knowledge of drugs. Nor is the most appropriate time for such an educational effort likely to be in the midst of a great public-relations crisis.

In any case, knowledge alone will not solve the problem. Many college administrators know perfectly well that marihuana is a harmless drug. Nevertheless, their public-relations problem persists. We can see how the maintenance of a favorable image lies at the heart of the administrators' concern by comparing the amount of activity against marihuana and LSD use to that against the use of amphetamines, quite widespread on many campuses for years (students use Benzedrine as an aid for staying up and studying at exam time). I do not recall any administration's taking severe action on the use of amphetamines, though I believe that physicians agree that amphetamines are potentially a great deal more dangerous than marihuana. And we can note the same kind of differential response to students' use of alcohol.

Suppose we take as our goal the reduction of the number of campus drug incidents. This might be accomplished by trying to do away with student drug use. But students want to use drugs and can easily do so; few college administrations will decide to use the totalitarian methods that would be required. One might institute a daily search of all student rooms and perhaps, in addition, inaugurate a campus "stop-and-frisk" law. But they are not going to do these things, so student drug use will continue.

We might also educate administrators to take a calmer view of the problem. This, no doubt, would do some good, but even the most knowledgeable administration would not be able to avoid the difficulties of a public-relations crisis.

We might, finally, educate students to take precautions to avoid detection. If an educational program of this kind, perhaps sponsored by the student government, were started on a campus, and if students took their lessons seriously, many fewer might engage in those actions likely to provoke arrest or detection. There would be fewer incidents to make publicity about, fewer incidents for the administration to respond to. The administration no doubt would still be aware that students were using drugs on campus, but it would not be confronted publicly with that use and would not be required to respond.

If students could be so educated, some kind of implicit bargain might be struck between university administrators and student drug users, a bargain not unlike the one that seems to characterize homosexuality on most college campuses. All campuses of any size have a homosexual underground that probably includes both students and faculty members, yet we hear very little about homosexual incidents on campus. Administrations seldom seem to get upset about this problem, seldom take strong punitive measures, and almost never make a big public outcry about it. I suspect that this is because they have, in effect, come to terms with the homosexual community on their campus. They regard it as an evil, no doubt, but not as an evil that can be easily done away with. They worry about the physical and psychological harm the community's existence may cause members and nonmembers. But they know they must live with it, and they do. They take action only when some provocative incident occurs, such as when a student blackmails a faculty member, when minors are involved, or when the matter comes to police attention (as it seldom does). In effect, the homosexual community and the university administration have made a bargain that goes something like this: The homosexuals agree to keep things out of the newspapers and the administration agrees not to look for trouble. An ethic of "live and let live" prevails.

This strikes me as the most likely solution to the problem of campus drug use. Administrators must take a calmer view of drug use, and students must become more cautious. The main obstacles to such a bargain will be nervous administrators afraid to take such a step, and ideological students who wish a confrontation on the issue.

But college administrators have learned to live with sex and drink. They may yet be able to learn to live with drugs as well.

15 Health and Medical Care

The problem of health has many facets. The health level of a people may be affected by their health practices, dietary habits, life styles, exposure to industrial hazards and environmental pollutants, levels of emotional stress, utilization of medical services, and possibly still other factors. By any comparison, the health level of the American people contrasts dismally with that of other advanced nations—sixteenth in general mortality, fifteenth in infant mortality, ninth in life expectancy, for example. And our lag behind other leading nations has been growing in recent decades. Just why this is true has not been definitely established. The low health level of our racial minorities is a contributing factor, yet the mortality statistics for our *white* population still place us behind other leading nations.

There has been relatively little serious comparative study of our dietary habits, life style, etc., as possible explanations. Attention has been focused mainly upon our system of medical care. Alone among advanced nations, we have no system of universal health insurance, state medicine, or—as it is generally termed—"socialized medicine," although we do in fact have a good deal of piecemeal "socialization" of medical care. Some critics maintain that we have no *system* of medical care at all, that we have an inefficient and wasteful hodgepodge of programs and agencies supplementing a basically outmoded form of private practice. A less harshly critical assessment of American medicine is offered in the following essay, written by a prominent medical educator.

PERSONAL HEALTH SERVICES:

Defects, dilemmas, and new directions

Kerr L. White

Department of Medical Care and Hospitals
Johns Hopkins University

The central point I hope to make in this paper is that there is a need to establish traditions, mechanisms, methods, and expectations that facilitate continuing review and innovation with respect to the way in which personal health services are organized and delivered. I doubt if there ever will exist, or if any country or region would want or should ever attempt to develop "permanent" or "final" solutions for these problems. With due respect to the political realities of life, it nevertheless seems desirable to encourage a process of decision making with respect to personal health services that are related more to factual data and the objective evaluation of experience, than it is to colorful assertions or authoritarian exhortations. Whatever solutions are developed for current problems of medical care, they are bound to be inadequate or inappropriate for new and unforseen problems. There is an urgent need to develop confidence in research and evaluation with respect to the organization and delivery of personal health services which is analogous to contemporary competence in biomedical research. The proposal made for a National Center for Health Services Research and Development is an important move toward this goal.

We should be clear about the term personal health services. By personal health services I mean all health services other than environmental health services. Specifically I mean those things done to and for all individuals who request or require health services provided by doctors, nurses, and dentists, and by paramedical, paranursing, and paradental personnel. I do not make a distinction between so-called preventive, diagnostic, therapeutic, and rehabilitative functions. Nor do I find it helpful to separate the physical, emotional, and social components of illness. These are transient divisions of interest, emphasis, organization, taste, and style based more on tradition and arbitrary jurisdictional arrangements than on humanitarian, scientific, or technical constraints. I do not distin-

From the *Bulletin of the New York Academy of Medicine,* Second Series, 44 (April 1968) pp. 446–457. Copyright © 1968 by the New York Academy of Medicine. Reprinted by permission.

guish between the various sites of care at which personal health services may be given, e.g., the solo practitioner's office, the outpatient dispensary, the voluntary, private, or public hospitals and their clinics and wards, the health department clinic, the group practice clinic, the home, the factory, or the school. Nor is the posture of the patient, vertical or horizontal, a factor in the basic definition. Finally, the methods by which the patient's care is financed—whether from public, private, or voluntary sources—and the methods by which the physician's effort is compensated—whether by fee-for-service, capitation, sessional payment, or salary —do not affect this definition.

ALLEGED DEFECTS

There are, I believe, about eight alleged defects in the provisions of personal health services in this country. To support these allegations there is little in the way of objective data; there is, however, a substantial ground swell of social concern, popular journalism, professional discussion, and political action which suggest that they have some basis in reality.

Defect No. 1

Personal health services frequently are not continuously available to all segments of the population except at emergency rooms of hospitals, or through telephone-answering services. General care available at the former, except for immediately life-threatening conditions, frequently is regarded by both the consumers and the profession as inappropriate and inadequate.[1] A telephone-answering service is part of a communication system and not a personal health service.

Persistence of relatively isolated solo practice unassisted by other trained health personnel is an anachronism which is at variance with the objectives of providing continuously available personal health services supervised, if not delivered, by physicians who maintain both their skills and composure.

Defect No. 2

Generalists are decreasing in number and superspecialists are increasing. The rate per 100,000 population for all physicians is said to be too low, and the ratio between the two kinds of physicians inappropriate. The competence of the generalists to manage many problems that require a thorough knowledge of contemporary scientific medicine [2] and the interest of superspecialists in early, nonspecific, and undifferentiated "complaints" on the one hand, and in chronic, terminal medical care on the other, are called into question.[3] The American "specialist" is virtually unknown in other countries; he frequently confuses himself both with the "consultant" and the "generalist." He is perhaps best described as a "consultoid" since he is apt to have the training and aspiration of the former but does the work of the latter.

There is a serious imbalance in the distribution of medical scientists, medical practitioners, and medical administrators. In the long haul, the basic capacity of the health services system to provide "medical cure" will come from the medical scientists. In the long haul, however, everyone is dead and, in the short haul, the capacity of the health services system to provide "medical care" will come from the medical practitioners and medical administrators.

Defect No. 3

Health professionals employ their talents inappropriately, and scarce human resources are wasted.[4] The medical care establishment tends to distribute its skill and knowledge more in accordance with selective individual utilization of services than with the collectively perceived needs and expressed demands of the community.[5] For example, pediatricians are trained to manage complex problems but spend much of their time providing "well-child" care to "private" patients in their offices and "sick-child" care to "public" patients in health department clinics. Responsibility for coordinating the care of patients seen in the latter setting is often the responsibility of the public health nurse; the itinerant or rotating physician advises on medical problems only. The same physician in the former setting may spend his professional time coordinating the care of his patients in the absence of skilled public health nursing services. Nurses could undertake many tasks currently performed by doctors; preliminary history questionnaires and screening tests, clinical triage, instruction, counseling, health education, certain treatments, and domiciliary visiting and care are examples.

Defect No. 4

Communication between different sources and levels of personal health services is inadequate. The recording, storage, retrieval, and transmission of medical information is outmoded compared to developments in other service systems of contemporary society. Information about patients' prior and present health problems and their treatment, or the reasons for referrals or consultations and their outcome, frequently are not transmitted between and within health professions and institutions responsibly, rapidly, and reliably. The technological capacity to accomplish this is available.

Defect No. 5

Inappropriate institutionalization of patients not only increases the cost of the whole health services system but may be harmful and even life-threatening. The former point has been made frequently; it is less widely appreciated that there is a constant and not always trivial risk of experiencing a medication error, an adverse reaction to a diagnostic reagent or drug, or of sustaining an injury in the strange environment of the hospital.[6] There is evidence that patients removed from their natural habitats to nursing homes experience substantially higher age-specific mortality rates than do others who are not so institutionalized.[7] The benefits of appropriate institutionalization must be balanced against the risks of inappropriate institutionalization. Conversely, many generalists in the centers of large cities are said to be without hospital privileges; they must of necessity refer or transfer their patients who need hospitalization.[8]

Defect No. 6

Emphasis on the categorical organization of personal health services, e.g., by diseases (heart disease, cancer, and stroke), by ages (comprehensive child care centers), by geography (neighborhood health centers), by methods of financing (Titles 18 and 19), or by traditional emphasis (public health programs, clinical practice) is inimical to the development of health services organized on the basis of levels of patient care and sophistication of medical knowledge and facilities. Previous experience with regionalization, although not an argument against trying new approaches, suggests that the categorical approach, if not illogical and unworkable, is at least undesirable.[9]

Defect No. 7

The notion that there is only one diagnostic system used in medicine, i.e., the one taught as the conventional wisdom in medical schools, appears to be at variance with the available facts.[10] More is being learned about the epidemiology of "symptoms," "complaints," and "problems" in general populations in the community, as distinct from experience with rare, exotic, complicated, neglected, or serious diseases encountered in university medical centers.[11-14] It is now recognized that although there are many different rare diseases, each occurs infrequently and accounts for only a small part of the morbidity in the community; the common diseases, on the other hand, are relatively few but they occur frequently and account for the bulk of morbidity in the community.[15]

Defect No. 8

There is growing skepticism that academic medicine, community medicine (the new public health), and private medicine (the "organized" profession) always act either alone or collectively in the public interest. This tripartite division of responsibility and accountability can be confusing both to members of the health professions and to the public. There is uncertainty about who is "in charge" of seeing that society has the personal health services it can collectively command from the resources it provides.

CURRENT DILEMMAS

So much for the alleged defects. Now let me try to summarize some of our major current dilemmas. There are, I believe, at least five.

Dilemma No. 1

Will responsible sources of primary medical care be organized and supervised by the medical profession so that care is continuously available, accessible, and responsive to health problems as individual patients and society define them? If the medical profession is not to provide this level of care, who will provide it? The possibilities include chiropractors, pharmacists, nurses, "quacks," neighbors, and relatives. Since the academic machinery for training general practitioners in this country has been dismantled, we need to decide first whether the profession is to be responsible for providing any form of primary medical care and, if so, who will provide this care and how it will be organized. A spate of recent reports that discuss some of the educational problems in training physicians to give primary medical care say little about the problems of organizing this care.[16-19]

Dilemma No. 2

Who is to be responsible for developing the information, providing the leadership, convening the committees, proposing the alternative solutions, implementing programs, and organizing services and evaluating them? If the personal health services of a community are inadequate or inappropriate, with whom do the citizens get in touch?

Broadly speaking it may be said that, at the present time, the medical centers have the "brains" and "information," the hospitals have the "physical facilities" and "administrative capacities," the medical societies have the "medical skills" and "organizational strengths," the welfare departments have documented the "need" and "demand" for services, and the health departments have the "opportunity" and the "mandate." It is far from clear who has the authority, the responsibility, and the political and fiscal muscle to accomplish what needs to be done. The prime contenders would appear to be the president or executive director of the local medical society, the administrator of the "leading" local hospital, the president or executive director of the hospital planning council, the commissioner of welfare, the health officer, the dean of the "leading" local medical school, or the chief officer of some voluntary agency or business enterprise.

The person in charge, in my judgment, should be a physician who combines high intelligence, political sensitivity, concern about and knowledge of the problems, demonstrated executive capacity, and experience or formal training in the administration of health services. To attract a person of the desired caliber from his present position, performance expectations and salaries will necessarily be competitive.

Since the Regional Medical Programs are interpreted as an enticement to the medical schools to become involved in the health problems of the community, it has been concluded by some that the brains and potential leadership in medicine are more likely to be found in medical schools than elsewhere. On the other hand, leaders are in such short supply that the best individuals to assume responsibility for organizing personal health services in each community should be recruited from any source. Certainly the history of persistent lack of interest in problems of medical care on the part of most health departments in the country suggests that few of the leaders for these new responsibilities are likely to be found in them. Hospitals, medical schools, and medical associations are more likely sources.

What agency or institution is to be responsible for organizing, coordinating, monitoring, and evaluating personal health services in the community? The suggestion that the medical school should assume this responsibility through the Regional Medical Programs appears to stem more from the necessity for imbuing their faculties with concern over contemporary health problems in the community than from a conviction that the medical school is the best institution to coordinate the health services of the community. Central involvement is different from primary responsibility. The hospitals have traditionally lacked interest or have not shown concern in vertical patients or potential patients. In one sense, they deal with the failures of the health services system, if I am correct in believing that one of the principal objectives of an effective health services system is to keep people out of hospitals. The medical society is another possibility, but its traditional preoccupations with professional postgraduate training and economic interests to the exclusion of concern with problems relating to the organization of health services tends to eliminate it as the best institution for this purpose. The health departments have the broadest social mandate and the only legal basis for undertaking this function. What they lack is the power, ability, energy, and imagination to undertake it. Power is obtained by appointing a powerful board or commission; the other attributes, by appointing the best available person, and giving him both authority and responsibility.

Dilemma No. 3

In a pluralistic, open society how do we maintain a judicious combination of public, private, and voluntary resources to serve a similar mixture of public and private purposes and interests? Is the revolution of rising expectations with respect to personal health services another example of "redefinition of the unacceptable"? [20] How do we combine the use of both social and private capital with the best features of the entrepreneurial system, and the opportunities, satisfactions, and rewards of individual initiative? How do we motivate and facilitate technically and scientifically autonomous professionals to do their best work? How do we motivate consumers to use services and scarce professional resources effectively? How can we encourage constructive competition designed to increase efficiency, and decrease destructive competition which encourages waste? How do we steer a reasonable course between an inflexible monolithic national health service on the one hand, and the fragmented, uncoordinated, categorical patterns of care which prevail at present? How can we make use of our magnificent opportunities for innovation and experimentation while avoiding the hazards associated with one big experiment? Can we have a national health services policy without having a national health service?

Dilemma No. 4

Do we proceed on the assumption that medical care is a "civic right," an "insured right," or a mixture of "private privilege" and "public charity"? Do we proceed on the assumption that all medical services will shortly be paid for through third parties, partly from social insurance, partly from private insurance, and partly from prepaid comprehensive health programs? Can we agree with William Beveridge that "management of one's income is an essential element in a citizen's freedom?" [21] Granted that things in this world do not necessarily succeed on their merits, can we assume that in an affluent democracy with "free" public education and a high level of employment, the means test, and the equating of "welfare" with charity rather than with "well-being" will not become anachronisms? [22]

Do we proceed on the assumption that whatever the sources of funds which pay for an individual's medical care, there is likely to be increasing insistence that, at the point of receipt of care, the patient will be regarded as a "private" citizen, and that he will present his Medicare or other medical credit card to the physician only for purposes of his identification and the physician's reimbursement? Can we assume that all patients have the right to discuss their personal health problems in private with a physician or nurse, and that distinctions between "private," "service," and "welfare" patients, insofar as receipt of medical care is concerned, will tend to disappear? Distinctions between social, occupational, and economic groupings are likely to remain.

Can we proceed on the assumption that the medical profession collectively is as concerned with those who do not receive adequate medical care as it is with those who do?

Dilemma No. 5

How is the profession to deploy its resources and skills in the face of increasing, effective and informed demand for personal health services on the one hand, and of a relative, if not absolute, stiffening of attitude with respect to the allocation of resources on the other? Six percent of the gross national product is currently devoted to health services; perhaps this allocation will be increased, but it seems probable that pressures to increase efficiency and effectiveness will prevail over those designed to increase resources. For most people, most of the time medical care is neither a luxury nor a necessity; there are many worthwhile things in life on which to spend money other than medical care. How do we encourage in the health services a sense of critical responsibility with respect to the use of scarce resources effectively without applying restrictive measures which might endanger human lives or well-being? How do we translate the human energies and efforts of health professionals into economic units that can be related to measurable benefits and effects? Can we really substitute performance budgets for activity budgets in the health services?

NEW DIRECTIONS

It is easy to describe defects and state dilemmas. The real task of any group attempting to examine public policy with respect to social issues is to advance ideas that meet two conditions. First, the proposals should tend to minimize current defects and encourage early recognition of defects that will inevitably arise in the future. Second, they should provide mechanisms for resolving dilemmas by clarifying issues and encouraging informed discussion and decisions with respect to alternative solutions. The following proposals are advanced as mechanisms for coping with the defects and dilemmas discussed above. I have not included proposals that are now law, such as the Comprehensive Planning and Public Health Service Amendments of 1966 or the recently advocated National Center for Health Services Research.

Proposal No. 1

The president of the United States, the secretary of Health, Education, and Welfare, or the surgeon general of the Public Health Service should have a permanent advisory group whose total effort is devoted to studying and evaluating the current and anticipated problems of health services, considering proposals for their solutions, planning for the prudent use of resources, and recommending policies.

A council of health advisers similar to the Council of Economic Advisers should be established. The members of such a group, including representatives from several relevant professions and disciplines, could serve two- or three-year full-time appointments; they could be on leave of absence from universities, government agencies, and professional and other organizations. Supported by an adequate staff they would provide the basis for informed public discussion of the issues. Their functions would differ entirely from those of itinerant consultants and advisory councils who meet briefly several times a year. This new council would be different from politically motivated commissions designed to provide visibility or instant publicity for some contemplated political activity. Such a council might work toward the development of national health goals and eventually of a national health services policy.

Proposal No. 2

The U.S. Public Health Service should institute a program of awards for career health services administrators. These would be analogous to awards for career investigators and career teachers. The awards, including local matching funds, should be generous and of long duration, if not for life, designed to attract the best possible people to the field of health services administration without regard to previous background, present affiliations, professional degrees in public health, hospital administration, or any other vocational credentials. The awards should be made competitively by a national advisory committee; they might be applied for through the office of the governor of a state or the mayor of a metropolitan district. The object would be to provide sufficient leverage to attract the best possible talent to the top positions of leadership in health departments. Many of these new individuals might replace the present health officers; some would constitute additions to the health departments. Civil Service regulations and salary scales would need to be modified accordingly; obsolete regulations stipulating that health officers should be graduates of schools of public health should be abolished; such requirements are analogous to the notion that all professors should have higher university degrees—some do and some do not.

Proposal No. 3

It is impossible to make decisions without a basic information system. The health services industry in the United States is a 40-billion-dollar industry which spends 0.05 percent of this amount on the evaluation of its own effectiveness and efficiency. I doubt if there is any other enterprise approaching this magnitude that spends so little on evaluating its own activities. In order to do this an information system is essential. Accordingly it is proposed that a system of federal formula grants be developed to encourage state and metropolitan health departments to expand their vital statistics units to health statistics units, similar to the National Center for Health Statistics. Health services utilization studies, operations research, and household surveys, in addition to vital statistics functions, should be undertaken. Health services information systems based on a medical care event record could be instituted. Data on hospital discharges compiled according to the characteristics, diagnosis, and disposal of patients are urgently needed. Similar information for patient-physician transactions, with due regard for the preservation of confidentiality, would do much to provide data on the content of medical practice. With this information the objectives of medical education and of health services could be more clearly stated.

Proposal No. 4

Regionalization should be encouraged in patterns that favor healthy competition, control wasteful duplication, ensure availability of essential services, facilitate innovation, and guarantee minimum standards of performance. Such arrangements would be fostered by judicious combinations of franchising, regulation, competition, and subsidization. The model is the airline system of the United States. Local, regional, and possibly even competing national systems are possible. Health services systems could be owned privately, or by communities, by quasi-public authorities, or by government agencies. Regulations would govern minimum standards of care and franchising would govern competition and availability.

Unusual as this suggestion may seem, it does afford an arrangement for planning and organizing services that avoids the alternatives of a monolithic national health service or a fragmented and uncoordinated series of programs and services.

Each health services system would be expected to contain the elements of a source of primary medical care linked to a source of secondary care at the community hospital, and supported by the full resources of a medical center. Such regionalization would be based on levels of care and sophistication of skills and facilities, not on categorical approaches.

SUMMARY

On the assumption that we are embarked on an era of planning health services as envisaged by the Regional Medical Program and Comprehensive Health Service Planning Act, and that methods for evaluating the demand, organization, and end results of health services will be developed by the new Health Services Research and Development Center, I have advanced four proposals for resolving our dilemmas and decreasing our defects. First, a council of health advisers; second, a fellowship program for attracting outstanding leaders and administrators; third, the development of adequate health services information systems; and, fourth, a system of regionalization based on competition, regulation, franchising, and subsidization. I believe the development of these mechanisms would do much to advance us toward the goals of improved personal health services for all.

REFERENCES

1. K. L. White, "General Practice in the United States," *Journal of Medical Education* 39 (1969) p. 333.
2. O. L. Peterson et al., "Analytical Study of North Carolina General Practice, 1953–4," *Journal of Medical Education* 31 (1956), Part 2.
3. R. A. Aldrich and R. H. Spitz, "Survey of Pediatric Practice in the United

States, 1959," in *Careers in Pediatrics: Report of the Thirty-sixth Ross Conference on Pediatric Research*, R. H. Spitz, ed. (Columbus, Ohio: Ross Laboratories, 1960).

4. College of General Practitioners, *Present State and Future Need*. Reports from General Practice No. 2 (London: The College, 1965).

5. J. M. Last, "Evaluation of Medical Care," *Medical Journal of Australia* 2 (1965) 781.

6. E. M. Schimmel, "Hazards of Hospitalization," *Annals of Internal Medicine* 60 (1964) 100.

7. C. K. Aldrich, "Relocation of the Aged and Disabled: A Mortality Study," *Journal of the American Geriatric Society* 11 (1963) 185.

8. M. Tolchin, "Doctors Training under Study Here," *New York Times*, May 9, 1966.

9. K. Evang, *Health Service, Society and Medicine* (London: Oxford University Press, 1960).

10. College of General Practitioners, *Evidence of The College to the Royal Commission on Medical Education*. Reports from General Practice No. 5 (London: The College, 1966).

11. K. Hodgkin, *Towards Earlier Diagnosis* (London: Livingstone, 1963).

12. D. L. Crombie, "Diagnostic Process," *Journal of the College of General Practitioners* 6 (1963) 579.

13. College of General Practitioners, "Disease Labels: Records and Statistical Unit," *Journal of the College of General Practitioners* 6 (1963) 197.

14. T. J. Scheff, "Decision Rules, Types of Error and Their Consequences." *Behavioral Sciences* 8 (1963) 97.

15. Oxford Regional Hospital Board, Operational Research Unit, *Hospital Out-Patient Services, No. 3* (Oxford: Oxford Regional Hospital Board, 1963).

16. World Health Organization, *Training the Physician for Family Practice*, Technical Report Series, 257 (Geneva: WHO, 1963).

17. National Commission on Community Health Services, *Health is a Community Affair* (Cambridge, Mass.: Harvard University Press, 1966).

18. Citizens Commission on Graduate Medical Education, *The Graduate Education of Physicians* (Chicago: American Medical Association, 1966).

19. Ad Hoc Committee on Education for Family Practice, *Meeting the Challenge of Family Practice* (Chicago: American Medical Association, 1966).

20. G. Vickers, "What Sets the Goals of Public Health?" *Lancet* 1 (1958) 559.

21. W. H. Beveridge, *Social Insurance and Allied Services* (New York: Macmillan, 1942).

22. K. de Schweinitz, *England's Road to Social Security* (Philadelphia: University of Pennsylvania Press, 1943).

23. G. P. Peters, *Cost-Benefit Analysis and Public Expenditure* (London: Institute of Economic Affairs, 1966).

24. W. Gorham, "Allocating Federal Resources among Competing Social Needs," *Health, Education, and Welfare Indicators* (August 1966) p. 1.

25. J. Drewnoski et al., *Cost-Benefit Analysis of Social Projects*, Report of a Meeting of Experts Held in Rennes, France (Geneva: U.N. Research Institute for Social Development, 1966).

26. J. Drewnoski and W. Scott, *The Level of Living Index* (Geneva: U.N. Research Institute for Social Development, 1966).

———————

After years of acrimonious debate over the adequacy of health care for aged citizens, Medicare was enacted in 1966, incorporating some features which have proved to be extremely expensive. This experience raises the question (which most other countries have already answered in the negative) of whether any medical care plan retaining fee-for-service payment to physicians can offer comprehensive care at reasonable cost.

A "GOLD MINE" FOR SOME DOCTORS

Richard D. Lyons

On the eve of Medicare's becoming the law of the land three years ago, 238 physician-politicians of the American Medical Association's policy-making House of Delegates convened at the Palmer House in Chicago. The AMA had lost its 25-year-long fight against the Federal medical payment plan and the speeches and resolutions of the doctors reflected their anger and disappointment. A few called for a boycott of the new program, some castigated the Washington bureaucracy, while others complained about Medicare's methods of payment for professional services.

In the wings a member of the AMA's own staff looked on morosely and said, "The fools. It's a gold mine for most of them and they haven't realized it yet."

His point was that in their bitterness at having a Federal program forced upon them, the doctors had lost sight of some of the facts. Under Medicare they would be getting paid for some professional services that previously had been rendered free to the elderly; that payment of "reasonable and customary fees" for 20 million persons enrolled in Medicare would be guaranteed by the Government; and that many elderly and retired persons who had hesitated to see a doctor because they didn't have the money, now would do so, thus increasing the number of fees.

UNFORESEEN DIVIDENDS

Medicare allowed two methods of payment. The patient could either pay his physician in cash when a bill was presented and then send the receipt to reimbursement offices designated by Medicare, or the doctor sent the bill and the payment was sent directly to him. An important point that was overlooked by doctors when the program went into effect was that in either case a record was kept by the Medicare apparatus.

In the past three years many doctors have found out that the Federal legislation they had fought bitterly for years was indeed yielding professional fees beyond their expectations.

Some doctors were immediately wise enough to sense the financial possibilities of Medicare, such as a general practitioner who was clearing $25,000 a year in his Brooklyn practice. He moved to Miami Beach, started catering to the Medicare generation and his after tax income shot to $75,000 a year. He did complain, however, that the constant round of house calls to the aged was getting him down.

In recent months Federal and state investigators have begun turning up many cases—though still a small minority of the profession—in which doctors and other health care professionals, such as dentists and pharmacists, have been receiving enormous fees from Medicare and another Federal medical payment program called Medicaid which is for the benefit of the poor and the disabled. Medicaid payments are made directly to medical professionals by city or county health or welfare agencies in the 40 states that have programs. The comprehensiveness and administration of the programs vary from state to state.

A Miami osteopath, for example, solved the house call problem by having the patients come to the clinic and hospital he opened. Federal records showed he took in $286,866 in Medicare fees in 18 months.

Last year a spot check of dental work billed to New York State under the Medicaid program showed that 18 percent either had not been performed or was "very poorly" done. Earlier this year, one Harlem dentist was suspended from participation in the Medicaid program after it had been found that he had been taking in $300,000 a year for himself and the nine dentists he had hired to help him.

Last week at Senate Finance Committee hearings Senator Russell B. Long, Democrat of Louisiana, cited examples of a general practitioner who had billed Medicare for $58,000 in 1968 for house calls to 49 patients, and of another GP who had been paid $42,000 by Medicare for administering 8,275 injections to 149 patients in a year.

Senator Long said cases such as these had helped push the voluntary program covering doctors' fees under Medicare to $1-billion a year more than had been originally estimated. The hospital insurance program for the aged under another section of Medicare is costing $3-billion a year more than was foreseen in 1965.

The Senators spilled out reams of statistics: The cost of Medicaid has tripled in four years; cost increases are triple the increased number of Medicaid patients; the average daily cost of hospitalization has risen 25 percent in the past two years, while physicians' fees since Medicare started have risen at a rate that is double the increases of the years before the program started.

Because of the computerized medical records kept by Medicare, Federal overseers are beginning to find out which doctors and which hospitals are charging unexpectedly large fees or treating unusually large numbers of patients. Armed with better records, state and local investigators of the Medicaid program, which is paid for by a blend of Federal, state and city money, also are starting to check into not only the cost of the medical care being paid for but also the quality of the services.

PRESSURES BUILD

Wilbur Cohen, the former Secretary of Health, Education and Welfare who was the architect of Medicare, warned that if doctors don't hold down fees "we are going to see pressures for some kind of control."

Last week these pressures started building. The Internal Revenue Service began checking the tax returns of the medical professionals getting large sums from Medicare, Medicaid, Blue Cross and Blue Shield. A decade ago it was almost impossible to check a doctor's income against his tax return because most payments were made in cash by individuals. Today, however, the check-writing computers of Medicare, Medicaid and other health plans pay most bills—and the machines have long memories.

Some of the doctors who warned of "governmental interference in medicine" three years ago now may have cause for alarm, but for reasons they never anticipated. Doubtful doctors have been told for years that computers were going to revolutionize medical care—soon they are going to know why.

We now have Medicare for the aged and Medicaid for the "poor" of all ages—depending upon how "medically indigent" is defined by the several states. But merely to remove the cost barrier from hospitals and doctors' offices may not be enough. Commercial interests seeking to promote the sale of everything from apples to zircons have long since learned that, if they really wish to increase the use of their product, they had better study seriously the life styles of their prospective patrons. This not very profound discovery has not received wide application in the social organization of health services. Why should it be so much easier for the poor to get to a tavern than to get to a clinic? Possibly because there are people to whom it is highly profitable to get them to a tavern, and few to whom it is highly profitable to get them to a clinic.

In the following essay, a medical sociologist argues that health care for the poor will be ineffective until reorganized to take account of the life styles of the poor.

MEDICAL GHETTOS

Anselm L. Strauss
Professor of Sociology
University of California
Medical Center, Berkeley

In President Johnson's budget message to Congress this year [1967] he proposed a quadrupling of federal spending on health care and medical assistance for the poor to $4.2 billion in fiscal 1968.

The 1968 budget maintains the forward thrust of federal programs designed to improve health care in the nation, to combat poverty, and assist the needy. . . . The rise reflects the federal government's role in bringing quality medical care, particularly to aged and indigent persons.

Three years earlier in a special message to Congress the President had prefaced reintroduction of the medicare bill by saying:

We can—and we must—strive now to assure the availability of and accessibility to the best health care for all Americans, regardless of age or geography or economic status. . . . Nowhere are the needs greater than for the 15 million children of families who live in poverty. Then, after decades of debate and massive professional and political opposition, the medicare program was passed. It promised to lift the poorest of our aged out of the medical ghetto of charity and into private and voluntary hospital care. In addition, legislation for heart disease and cancer centers was quickly enacted. It was

From *TRANS-action,* May 1967, pp. 7ff. Copyright © by *TRANS-action* Magazine, New Brunswick, New Jersey. Reprinted by permission.

said that such facilities would increase life expectancy by five years and bring a 20 percent reduction in heart disease and cancer by 1975.

Is the medical millenium, then, on its way? The President, on the day before sending the 1968 budget to Congress, said: "Medicare is an unqualified success."

"Nevertheless," he added, "there are improvements which can be made and shortcomings which need prompt attention." The message also noted that there might be some obstacles on the highroad to health. The rising cost of medical care, President Johnson stated, "requires an expanded and better organized effort by the federal government in research and studies of the organization and delivery of health care." If the President's proposals are adopted, the states will spend $1.9 billion and the federal government $1 billion in a "Partnership for Health" under the Medicaid program.

Considering the costs to the poor—and to the taxpayers—why don't the disadvantaged get better care? In all the lively debate on that matter, it is striking how little attention is paid to the mismatch between the current organization of American medicine and the life styles of the lower class. The major emphasis is always on how the present systems can be a little better supported or a trifle altered to produce better results.

I contend that the poor will never have anything approaching equal care until our present medical organization undergoes profound reform. Nothing in current legislation or planning will accomplish this. My arguments, in brief, are these:

The emphasis in all current legislation is on extending and improving a basically sound system of medical organization.

This assumes that all those without adequate medical services—especially the poor—can be reached with minor reforms, without radical transformation of the systems of care.

This assumption is false. The reason the medical systems have not reached the poor is because they were never designed to do so. The way the poor think and respond, they way they live and operate, has hardly ever (if ever) been considered in the scheduling, paperwork, organization, and mores of clinics, hospitals, and doctors' offices. The life styles of the poor are different; they must be specifically taken into account. Professionals have not been trained and are not now being trained in the special skills and procedures necessary to do this.

These faults result in a vicious cycle which drives the poor away from the medical care they need.

Major reforms in medical organizations must come, or the current great inequities will continue, and perhaps grow.

I have some recommendations designed specifically to break up that vicious cycle at various points. These recommendations are built directly upon aspects of the life styles of the poor. They do not necessarily require new money or resources, but they do require rearrangement, reorganization, reallocation—the kind of change and reform which are often much harder to attain than new funds or facilities.

HOW TO BE HEALTHY THOUGH POOR

In elaborating these arguments, one point must be nailed down first: *The poor definitely get second-rate medical care.* This is self-evident to anyone who has worked either with them or in public medical facilities; but there is a good deal of folklore to the effect that the very poor share with the very rich the best doctors and services—the poor getting free in the clinics what only the rich can afford to buy.

The documented statistics of the Department of Health, Education, and Welfare tell a very different story. As of 1964, those families with annual incomes under $2,000 average 2.8 visits per person to a physician each year, compared to 3.8 for those above $7,000. (For children during the crucial years under 15, the ration is 1.6 to 5.7. The poor tend to have larger families; needless to add, their child mortality rate is also higher.)

People with higher incomes (and $7,000 per year can hardly be considered wealthy) have a tremendous advantage in the use of medical specialists— 27.5 percent see at least one of them annually, compared to about 13 percent of the poor.

Health insurance is supposed to equalize the burden; but here, too money purchases better care. Hospital or surgical insurance coverage is closely related to family income, ranging from 34 percent among those with family income or less than $2,000 to almost 90 percent for persons in families of $7,000 or more annual income. At the same time, the poor, when hospitalized, are much more apt to have more than one disorder— and more apt to exhaust their coverage before discharge.

Among persons who were hospitalized, insurance paid for some part of the bill for about 40 percent of patients with less than $2,000 family income, for 60 percent of patients with $2,000–$3,999 family income, and for 80 percent of patients with higher incomes. Insurance paid three-fourths or more of the bill for approximately 27 percent, 44 percent, and 61 percent of these respective income groups. Preliminary data from the 1964 survey year showed, for surgery or delivery bills paid by insurance, an even more marked association of insurance with income.

Similar figures can be marshaled for chronic illness, dental care, and days of work lost.

Strangely enough, however, *cash* difference (money actually spent for care) is not nearly so great. The under $2,000 per year group spent $112 per person per year, those families earning about three times as much $4,000–$7,000) paid $119 per person, and those above $7,000, $153. Clearly, the poor not only get poorer health services but less for their money.

As a result, the poor suffer much more chronic illness and many more working days lost—troubles they are peculiarly ill-equipped to endure. Almost 60 percent of the poor have more than one disabling condition compared to about 24 percent of other Americans. Poor men lose 10.2 days of work annually compared to 4.9 for the others. Even medical research seems to favor the affluent—its major triumphs have been over acute, not chronic, disorders.

WHAT'S WRONG WITH MEDICAL ORGANIZATION?

Medical care, as we know it now, is closely linked with the advancing organization, complexity, and maturity of our society and the increasing education, urbanization, and need for care of our people. Among the results: Medicine is increasingly practiced in hospitals in metropolitan areas.

The relatively few dispensaries for the poor of yesteryear have been supplanted by great numbers of outpatient hospital clinics. These clinics and services are still not adequate—which is why the continuing cry for reform is "more and better." But even when medical services *are* readily available to the poor, they are not used as much as they could and should be. The reasons fall into two categories: (1) factors in the present organization of medical care that act as a brake on giving quality care to everyone; (2) the life styles of the poor that present obstacles even when the brakes are released.

The very massiveness of modern medical organization is itself a hindrance to health care for the poor. Large buildings and departments, specialization, division of labor, complexity, and bureaucracy lead to an impersonality and an overpowering and often grim atmosphere of hugeness. The poor, with their meager experience in organizational life, their insecurity in the middle class world, and their dependence on personal contacts, are especially vulnerable to this impersonalization.

Hospitals and clinics are organized for "getting work done" from the staff point of view; only infrequently are they set up to minimize the patient's confusion. He fends for himself and sometimes may even get lost when sent "just down the corridor." Patients are often sent for diagnostic tests from one service to another with no explanations, with inadequate directions, with brusque tones. This may make them exceedingly anxious and affect their symptoms and diagnosis. After sitting for hours in waiting rooms, they become angry to find themselves passed over for latecomers—but nobody explains about emergencies or priorities. They complain they cannot find doctors they really like or trust.

When middle class patients find themselves in similar situations, they can usually work out some methods of "beating the system" or gaining understanding that may raise staff tempers but will lower their own anxieties. The poor do not know how to beat the system. And only very seldom do they have that special agent, the private doctor, to smooth their paths.

Another organizational barrier is the increasing professionalism of health workers. The more training and experience it takes to make the various kinds of doctors, nurses, technicians, and social workers, the more they become oriented around professional standards and approaches, and the more the patient must take their knowledge and abilities on trust. The gaps of communications, understanding, and status grow. To the poor, professional procedures may seem senseless or even dangerous—especially when not explained—and professional manners impersonal or brutal, even when professionals are genuinely anxious to help.

Many patients complain about not getting enough information; but the poor are especially helpless. They don't know the ropes. Fred Davis quotes from a typical poor parent, the mother of a polio-stricken child!

Well they don't tell you anything hardly. They don't seem to want to. I mean you start asking questions and they say, "Well, I only have about three minutes to talk to you." And then the things that you ask, they don't seem to want to answer you. So I don't ask them anything any more. . . .

For contrast, we witnessed an instance of a highly educated woman who found her physician evasive. Suddenly she shot a question: "Come now, Doctor, don't I have the same cancerous condition that killed my sister?" His astonished reaction confirmed her suspicion.

Discrimination also expresses itself in subtle ways. As Frank Riessman and Sylvia Scribner note (for psychiatric care), "Middle class patients are preferred by most treatment agents, and are seen as more treatable. . . . Diagnoses are more hopeful. . . ." Those who understand, follow, respond to, and are grateful for treatment are good patients; and that describes the middle class.

Professional health workers are themselves middle class, represent and defend its values, and show its biases. They assume that the poor (like themselves) have regular meals, lead regular lives, try to support families, keep healthy, plan for the future. They prescribe the same treatment for the same diseases to all, not realizing that their words do not mean the same things to all. (What does "take with each meal" mean to a family that eats irregularly, seldom together, and usually less than three times a day?)

And there is, of course, some open bias. A welfare case worker in a large Midwestern city, trying to discover why her clients did not use a large, nearby municipal clinic more, described what she found:

Aside from the long waits (8 A.M. to about 1 P.M. just to make the appointment), which perhaps are unavoidable, there is the treatment of patients by hospital personnel. This is at the clinic level. People are shouted at, ridiculed, abused, pushed around, called "Niggers," told to stand "with the rest of the herd," and in many instances made to feel terribly inferior if not inadequate. . . . This . . . was indulged in by personnel other than doctors and nurses. . . .

Even when no bias is intended, the hustle, impersonality, and abstraction of the mostly white staff tend to create this feeling among sensitive and insecure people: "And I do think the treatment would have been different if Albert had been white."

The poor especially suffer in that vague area we call "care," which includes nursing, instructions about regimens, and post-hospital treatment generally. What happens to the lower class patient once released? Middle class patients report regularly to their doctors who check on progress and exert some control. But the poor are far more likely to go to the great, busy clinics where they seldom see the same doctor twice. Once out they are usually on their own.

DISTANCE AND DISUSE

Will the poor get better care if "more and better" facilities are made available? I doubt it. The fact is that they underutilize those available now. For instance, some 1963 figures from the Director of the Division of Health Services, Children's Bureau:

In Atlanta, 23 percent of women delivered at the Grady Hospital had had no prenatal care; in Dallas, approximately one-third of low income patients receive no prenatal care; at the Los Angeles County Hospital in 1958, it was 20 percent; at the D.C. General Hospital in Washington, it is 45 percent; and in the Bedford Stuyvesant section of Brooklyn, New York, it is 41 percent with no or little prenatal care.

Distances are also important. Hospitals and clinics are usually far away. The poor tend to organize their lives around their immediate neighborhoods, to shut out the rest of the city. Some can hardly afford bus fare (much less cab fare for emergencies). Other obstacles include unrealistic eligibility rules and the requirement by some hospitals that clinic patients arrange a blood donation to the blood bank as a prerequisite for prenatal care.

Medical organization tends to assume a patient who is educated and well-motivated, who is interested in ensuring a reasonable level of bodily functioning and generally in preserving his own health. But health professionals themselves complain that the poor come to the clinic or hospital with advanced symptoms, that parents don't pay attention to children's symptoms early enough, that they don't follow up treatments or regimens, and delay too long in returning. But is it really the fault of whole sections of the American population if they don't follow what professionals expect of them?

THE CRISIS LIFE OF THE POOR

What are the poor really like? In our country they are distinctive. They live strictly, and wholeheartedly, in the present; their lives are uncertain, dominated by recurring crisis (as S. M. Miller puts it, theirs "is a crisis-life constantly trying to make do with string where rope is needed"). To them a careful concern about health is unreal—they face more pressing troubles daily, just getting by. Bad health is just one more condition they must try to cope—or live—with.

Their households are understaffed. There are no servants, few reliable adults. There is little time or energy to care for the sick. If the mother is ill, who will care for her or take her to the clinic—or care for the children if she goes? It is easier to live with illness than use up your few resources doing something about it.

As Daniel Rosenblatt and Edward Suchman have noted:

The body can be seen as simply another class of objects to be worked out but not repaired. Thus, teeth are left without dental care. . . . Corrective eye examinations, even for those who wear glasses, are often neglected. . . . It is as though . . . blue-collar groups think of the body as having a limited span of utility; to be enjoyed in youth and then to suffer with and to endure stoically with age and decrepitude.

They are characterized by low self-esteem. Lee Rainwater remarks that low income people develop "a sense of being unworthy; they do not uphold the sacredness of their persons in the same way that middle class people do. Their tendency to think of themselves as of little account is . . . readily generalized to their bodies." And this attitude is transferred to their children.

They seek medical treatment only when practically forced to it. As Rosenblatt and Suchman put it: "Symptoms that do not incapacitate are often ignored." In clinics and hospitals they are shy, frustrated, passively submissive, prey to brooding, depressed anxiety. They reply with guarded hostility, evasiveness, and withdrawal. They believe, of their treatment, that "what is free is not much good." As a result, the professionals tend to turn away. Julius Roth describes how the staff in a rehabilitation ward gets discouraged with its apparently unrehabilitatable patients and gives up and concentrates on the few who seem hopeful. The staffs who must deal with the poor in such wards either have rapid turnover or retreat into "enclaves of research, administration, and teaching."

The situation must get worse. More of the poor will come to the hospitals and clinics. Also, with the increasing use of health insurance and programs by unions and employers, more will come as paying patients into the private hospitals, mixing with middle class patients and staff, up-setting routines, perhaps lowering quality—a frightening prospect as many administrators see it. As things are going now, relations between lower income patients and hospital staff must become more frequent, intense, and exacerbated.

It is evident that the vicious cycle that characterizes medical care for the poor must be broken before anything can be accomplished.

In the first part of this cycle, the poor come into the hospitals later than they should, often delaying until their disorders are difficult to re-lieve, until they are actual emergency cases. The experiences they have there encourage them to try to stay out even longer the next time—and to cut the visits necessary for treatment to a minimum.

Second, they require, if anything, even more effective communica-tion and understanding with the professionals than the middle class patient. They don't get it; and the treatment is often undone once they leave.

What to do? The conventional remedies do help some. More money and insurance will tend to bring the poor to medical help sooner; increased staff and facilities can cut down the waits, the rush, the tenseness, and allow for more individual and efficient treatment and diagnosis.

But much more is required. If the cycle is to be *broken,* the follow-ing set of recommendations must be adopted:

Speed up the initial visit. Get them there sooner.
Improve patient experiences.
Improve communication, given and received, about regimens and treatment to be followed.
Work to make it more likely that the patient or his family will follow through at home.
Make it more likely that the patient will return when necessary.
Decrease the time between necessary visits.

This general list is not meant to be the whole formula. Any ex-perienced doctor or nurse, once he recognizes the need, can add to or modify it. An experience of mine illustrates this well. A physician in charge of an adolescent clinic for lower income patients, finding that my ideas fitted into his own daily experience, invited me to address his staff. In discussion afterward good ideas quickly emerged:

Since teen-age acne and late teen-age menstrual pain were frequent complaints and the diagnoses and medications not very complicated, why not let nurses make them? Menstruating girls would be more willing to talk to a woman than a man.

Patients spend many hours sitting around waiting. Why not have nursing assistants, trained by the social worker and doctor and drawn from the patients' social class, interview and visit with them during this period, collecting relevant information?

Note two things about these suggestions: Though they do involve some new duties and some shifting around, they do not call for any appreciable increase of money, personnel, or resources; and such recommendations, once the need is pointed out, can arise from the initiative and experience of the staff themselves.

Here in greater detail are my recommendations:

Speeding Up the Initial Visit

Increased efforts are needed for early detection of disease among the poor. Existing methods should be increased and improved, and others should be added—for instance, mobile detection units of all kinds, public drives with large-scale educational campaigns against common specific disorders, and so on. The poor themselves should help in planning, and their ideas should be welcomed.

The schools could and should become major detection units with large-scale programs of health inspection. The school nurse, left to her own initiative, is not enough. The poor have more children and are less efficient at noting illness; those children do go to school, where they could be examined. Teachers should also be given elementary training and used more effectively in detection.

Train more subprofessionals, drawn from the poor themselves. They can easily learn to recognize the symptoms of the more common disorders and be especially useful in large concentrations, such as housing projects. They can teach the poor to look for health problems in their own families.

Facilitate the Visit

The large central facilities make for greater administrative and medical efficiency. But fewer people will come to them than to smaller neighborhood dispensaries. Imperfect treatment may be better than little or no treatment; and the total effectiveness for the poor may actually be better with many small facilities than the big ones.

Neighborhood centers can not only treat routine cases and act to follow up hospital outpatients, but they can also discover those needing the more difficult procedures and refer them to the large centers—for example, prenatal diagnosis and treatment in the neighborhoods, with high-risk pregnancies sent to the central facilities. (The Children's Bureau has experimented with this type of organization.)

There must be better methods to get the sick to the clinics. As noted, the poor tend to stick to their own neighborhoods and be fearful outside them, to lack bus fare and domestic help. Even when dental or eye defects *are* discovered in schools, often children still do not get treatment. Sub-professionals and volunteers could follow up, provide transportation, bus fare, information, or baby sitting and housecare. Block or church organizations could help. The special drives for particular illnesses could also include transportation. (Recent studies show that different ethnic groups respond differently to different pressures and appeals; subprofessionals from the same groups could, therefore, be especially effective.)

Hours should be made more flexible; there should be more evening and night clinics. Working people work, when they have jobs, and cannot afford to lose jobs in order to sit around waiting to be called at a clinic. In short, clinics should adapt to people, not expect the opposite. (A related benefit: Evening clinics should lift the load on emergency services in municipal hospitals, since the poor often use them just that way.)

Neighborhood pharmacists should be explicitly recognized as part of the medical team, and every effort be made to bring them in. The poor are much more apt to consult their neighborhood pharmacist first—and he could play a real role in minor treatment and in referral. He should be rewarded, and given such training as necessary—perhaps by schools of pharmacy. Other "health healers" might also be encouraged to help get the seriously ill to the clinics and hospitals, instead of being considered rivals or quacks.

Lower income patients who enter treatment early can be *rewarded* for it. This may sound strange, rewarding people for benefiting themselves —but it might bring patients in earlier as well as bring them back, and actually save money for insurance companies and government and public agencies.

Improve Experiences in Medical Facilities

Hospital emergency services must be radically reorganized. Such services are now being used by the poor as clinics and as substitutes for general practitioners. Such use upsets routine and arouses mutual frustrations and resentments. There are good reasons why the poor use emergency services this way, and the services should be reorganized to face the realities of the situation.

Clinics and hospitals could assign *agents* to their lower income patients, who can orient them, allay anxiety, listen to complaints, help them cooperate, and help them negotiate with the staff.

Better accountability and communication should be built into the organization of care. Much important information gets to doctors and nurses only fortuitously, if at all. For instance, nurses' aides often have information about cardiac or terminal patients that doctors and nurses could use; but they do not always volunteer the information nor are they often asked, since they are not considered medically qualified. This is another place where the *agent* might be useful.

It is absolutely necessary that medical personnel lessen their class and professional biases. Antibias training is virtually nonexistent in medical schools or associations. It must be started, especially in the professional schools.

Medical facilities must carefully consider how to allow and improve the lodging of complaints by the poor against medical services. They have few means and little chance now to make their complaints known, and this adds to their resentment, depression, and helplessness. Perhaps the agent can act as a kind of medical *ombudsman;* perhaps unions, or the other health insurance groups, can lodge the complaints; perhaps neighborhood groups can do it. But it must be done.

Improving Communications about Regimens

Treatment and regimens are supposed to continue in the home. Poor patients seldom do them adequately. Hospitals and clinics usually concentrate on diagnosis and treatment and tend to neglect what occurs after. Sometimes there is even confusion about who is supposed to tell the patient about such things as his diet at home, and there is little attempt to see that he does it. Here again, follow-up by subprofessionals might be useful.

Special training given to professionals will enable them to give better instructions to the poor on regimens. They are seldom trained in interviewing or listening—and the poor are usually deficient in pressing their opinions.

Check on Home Regimens

Clinics and hospitals could organize their services to include checking on ex-patients who have no private physicians. We recommend that hospitals and clinics try to bring physicians in poor neighborhoods into some sort of association. Many of these physicians do not have hospital connections, practice old-fashioned or substandard medicine—yet they are in most immediate contact with the poor, especially before hospitalization.

Medical establishments should make special efforts to discover and understand the prevalent life styles of their patients. Since this affects efficiency of treatment, it is an important medical concern.

I strongly recommend greater emphasis on research in medical devices or techniques that are simple to operate and depend as little as possible on patients' judgment and motivation. Present good examples include long-term tranquilizers and the intrauterine birth-control device which requires little of the woman other than her consent. Such developments fit lower class life style much better than those requiring repeated actions, timing, and persistence.

As noted, these recommendations are not basically different from many others—except that they all relate to the idea of the vicious cycle. *A major point of this paper is that equal health care will not come unless all portions of that cycle are attacked simultaneously.*

To assure action sufficiently broad and strong to demolish this cycle, *responsibility must also be broad and strong.*

Medical and professional schools must take vigorous steps to counteract the class bias of their students, to teach them to relate, communicate, and adapt techniques and regimens to the poor, and to learn how to train and instruct subprofessionals.

Specific medical institutions must, in addition to the recommendations above, consider how best to attack *all* segments of the cycle. Partial atacks will not do—medicine has responsibility for the total patient and the total treatment.

Lower class people must themselves be enlisted in the campaign to give them better care. Not to do this would be absolutely foolhardly. The subprofessionals we mention are themselves valuable in large part because they come from the poor, and understand them. Where indigenous organizations exist, they should be used. Where they do not exist, organizations that somehow meet their needs should be aided and encouraged to form.

Finally, governments, at all levels, have an immense responsibility for persuading, inducing, or pressuring medical institutions and personnel toward reforming our system of medical care. If they understand the vicious cycle, their influence will be much greater. This governmental role need not at all interfere with the patient's freedom. Medical influence is shifting rapidly to the elite medical centers; federal and local governments have a responsibility to see that medical influence and care, so much of it financed by public money, accomplishes what it is supposed to.

What of the frequently heard argument that increasing affluence will soon eliminate the need for special programs for the poor?

Most sociologists agree that general affluence may never "trickle down" to the hard-core poverty groups; that only sustained and specialized effort over a long period of time may relieve their poverty.

Increased income does not necessarily change life styles. Some groups deliberately stand outside our mainstream. And there is usually a lag at least of one generation, often more, before life styles respond to changed incomes.

In the long run, no doubt, prosperity for all will minimize the inferiority of medical care for the poor. But in the long run, as the saying goes, we will all be dead. And the disadvantaged sick will probably go first, with much unnecessary suffering.

16 Civil Liberties and Subversion

During periods of rapid social change we find that anxieties and conflicts increase. Formerly quiescent groups become demanding; formerly contented groups feel threatened. Concensus declines and discord grows. Political extremism flourishes as groups become exasperated at the "unreasonableness" of their opponents and despair of winning their goals through rational persuasion. In the name of liberty, extremists proceed to undermine and destroy liberty.

The following survey attempts a current appraisal of extremist movements of both the left and the right. This particular listing will soon be outdated, for extremist movements are notoriously prone to schisms and realignments. Since this survey appeared, Students for a Democratic Society has split into several rival factions, and still other changes will have transpired by the time this book reaches the hands of students. But as long as social change continues, there will continue to be extremist groups to focus and channel the resentments of those whose discontents are intense and whose faith in democratic processes is lacking. And while the *content* of extremism is ever changing, the mental outlook and techniques of the extremist remain constant.

SURVEY OF EXTREMISM

Charles R. Baker

Characteristics

Extremists live in "closed rooms"

They read *their* books, listen to *their* leaders; refuse to consider arguments from the *outside* world.

They take orders gratefully

None of this democracy stuff. Let those up front set the line. They imitate.

From *Homefront,* July–August, 1969, pp. 49–53 (monthly journal of the Institute for American Democracy, 1330 Massachusetts Ave., N.W., Washington, D.C.). Reprinted by permission.

All Evil flows from a "Conspiracy"

They are a part of a group being persecuted by that darned "Conspiracy." It is responsible for everything that goes wrong.

They are "Ideologues"

Your problem had darned well better fit their solution.

They are fighting a "Holy War"

They are so sure they are right that their ends justify their sometimes sinister means.

They rewrite history and news

Everything must fit into their pattern. Outside news media are always corrupt so they develop their own.

They must control or discredit

You can't have "outside" groups producing evidence which refutes the "true" facts: it stimulates "incorrect" attitudes.

They are haters, not lovers

They are not really "for" much of anything, but they "know" where to assign blame, and how to vent their spleen.

They feed on whipping boys

They must have those they feel superior to and can rally against. Racism, however, subtle, and/or character assassination are standard characteristics.

They must change systems

Pragmatic answers to problems are never considered. Out with the old; in with the new.

They work behind camouflage

They set up front groups. They keep their membership rosters secret, and their motives obscured.

Their movement yearns for power

It shows a group-sense of self-interest.

Are these extremists of the far left or far right?
The answer: Both. At both extremes, people act the same. It isn't so much what they believe as how they believe it.

The Institute for American Democracy's third annual survey of Who's Who on the Far Left and Far Right points to the conclusion that extremism is becoming deeply embedded in the fabric of our democracy. Both the Old Right and New Left have shown some growth. The still small but increasingly militant Black Nationalist organizations are becoming more of a factor. What is harder to document, but of greater significance, is that extremism is rotting the cloth. The hard positions of our political extremes are finding increasing acceptance among the hitherto apathetic or uncommitted. The democratic middleground is shrinking. The polarization, noted with anguish in the 1968 Kerner Commission report, is continuing.

Members of the Kerner Commission revisited the same terrain again this year and concluded our "one nation indivisible" is still fragmenting into "two societies, one black, one white, increasingly separate and scarcely less unequal."

Extremist political climate building, a multi-million dollar business on the Right, a lemminglike urge for mindless confrontations on the Left, is having an impact on our national sense of values.

Democracy depends on a rational approach to problem solving. The essential ingredients include an earnest search for truth; a willingness to engage in dialogue; the capacity for compromise and confidence in popular sovereignty. These are not the hallmarks of the decision-making process of our times.

Political Extremism does not grow in a vacuum. It reflects real needs, economic and psychological. We are a nation which has not solved the problem of poverty in the midst of plenty. We have not found the route to peace. We are ill at ease in our relations with the rest of the world. The battle for the allocation of national resource between the military-minded and the social conscious is deep-seated and nobody has a monopoly on the arguments.

The advocates of instant change are riding issues too long neglected. Those idolizing yesterday rightfully conclude that even a slight accommodation may open the door to a dramatic restructuring of our economy. Social progress for the many usually cuts in to the often hard earned preferred position of a few.

As a nation we have not been ignoring the storm warnings, but we haven't developed much know-how for riding out the gales. As Whitney Young and Roy Wilkins and John Gardner have been warning, refusal to pay sufficient heed to those seeking change by reasonable methods plays into the hands of the apostles of discord. Those communities which will not listen to reason cannot ignore a riot.

On the campuses and in the ghettos, the Left seeks to force change through occupation and confrontation. It looks to undermine the Central Authority in order to bring about change. The Right looks to the Central Authority to preserve order. Since no society can endlessly tolerate domestic strife, the Right strikes the more responsive note.

Maintaining Law and Order is relatively easy. Police states of both the left and right are invariably orderly. Dissent seldom gets out of hand in either Russia or Greece. The problem is maintaining order while preserving essential freedoms. If there is any logic to the New Left's violence it is that in triggering repressive measures the latter will ultimately become abhorrent to a great number of poeple who will then join in the effort to change the system.

At the best, this is a cruel longshot. Power comes at the ballot box or at gun point. The revolutionary Left, with all its capacity for creating localized chaos, has little fire power. The zealots it attracts will surely be among the casualties. If the strategy is pressed to the ultimate, democracy itself can be the victim.

What the New Left revolutionaries have done is take issues raised by reformers (the despised of both extremes) and project them on Page One.

The Negroes search for a valid heritage; the need to expand meaningful opportunities for those caught in the poverty cycle; the amount of resource gobbled up by the military are not new issues.

The Left, constantly haranguing against "Dollar Imperialism," sees U.S. corporations and the Central Government as involved in a kind of conspiracy to hold down the have nots at home and abroad. Its efforts to make alliances with the employees of these same corporations, however, have met with no success. Whereas, a generation ago, blue collar workers existed at the poverty line, today the size of their paychecks demonstrates their stake in protecting the basic system.

The issues which raised the New Left above the level of an irritant remain. But the natural interest will be limited chiefly to the areas of poverty and to the intellectual community.

Soaring food prices; Administration efforts to cool off our overheated war-peace-time economy and continued involvement in Vietnam indicate no substantial easing of the pressures is in sight. Only time will tell whether the dissent will be expressed in terms which lead to disaster.

For the Far Right, the New Left is a bonanza. A decade ago, when the Birch Society gave the Right a new impetus, the super "anti-Communists," were hard put to find actual Communists they could point to. Then, as now, the real interest was in rolling back social progress. The "Communists," real and imagined, provided whipping boys to rally against. The real target was the reformers. It still is. Analyze the contents of the Birch Bulletin or a H. L. Hunt broadcast, and you see the real thrust is undermining confidence in churches, schools and other liberalizing influences and in the central government itself.

At the time the Marxists actually begin asserting influence, the Far Right is concentrating its fire on "Marxist-inspired sex education." Here is an issue which attracts some moderates and is extremely useful in forming front groups. The attack is on "liberal" public school education. It ties into the effort to defeat bond issues and capture school boards.

The Far Right aspires to power within the established political channels. Disdaining democracy, it sets about the propaganda campaigns which, in a democracy, can even bring authoritarians into control. The Birch Society is apparently losing ground and some more blatantly racist groups, like Liberty Lobby, are gaining. But regardless of whose star is in the ascendancy, the conditions which make extremist flourish persist.

We Tend to Ignore the fact that several hundred Far Right organizations are carrying on a continuous multi-million dollar campaign to sell their ideology to the American people the same way we sell soap, by repeating claims over and over. Now, like the detergent manufacturers, they have even added sex to the advertising package.

The Far Right deals in prejudice and character assassination, but, for the most part, it stays within the law. While it deals in falsehood and tries to undermine confidence in all institutions Rightests do not yet control—including the central government—there is seldom anything illegal about the efforts to make reform and reformers appear subversive.

When the Far Right claims the Civil Rights movement is "Communist-inspired," it is fighting—not Marxism—but Civil Rights. The charge that the War on Poverty is subversive is not made to combat subversion. The phrase, "Communism equals Socialism equals Liberalism," was not coined to combat communism.

Here is propaganda which, in the absence of countervailing views, takes root.

While we try to make the system work better, extremists on both sides get in the way. On the Left we have those who, in the name of "Social Justice," flaunt the laws and on the other those who, in the name of "law," oppose social justice. Both sides are shouting.

Nationally we seem ready to restore quiet—at almost any price.

The defenders of the democratic middle, by they liberal or conservative, are likely to find the going turbulent. But they may be democracy's salvation.

Like Gaul, The American Far Left is divided into three parts. The Old Left, based on various interpretations of Marxism, is holding its own, but it is not making much noise or growing very much. The New Left, still searching for an ideology, flirts with Marxism but often veers off into anarchism. While it is not growing very much, it is creating such a stir that large numbers of Americans are in terror if it. Both the Old and New Left seek alliances with emerging Black Power groups whose appeal to their converts is not so much ideological as a kind of Negro Nationalism. What these segments have in common is disenchantment with the system; a lack of confidence in democratic procedures and the belief that their ends justify almost any means.

Largest of all is the Communist Party, USA, but its efforts to get an infusion of youth have been pretty well ignored. The Maoist Progressive Labor Party (PLP) came closer, but when PLP tried to take over Students For A Democratic Society (SDS) in mid-1969, that backfired.

An "underground press," featuring SDS and occasionally PLP writers, has about 200 papers issued sporadically and openly sold in most cities. Those carry on a brisk war against the military establishment while providing the "revolutionary" atmosphere.

What money is to the Far Right, membership is to the Far Left. The Communist Party, USA, for example, took in approximately $146,000 in 1966.

TABLE 1. Who's Who on the Far Left

Organization	Ideology	Radio-TV	Estimated Membership	Chief Publication	Estimated Circulation
CPUSA	Soviet		13,000 [1]	Daily World	14,000
				People's World	5,000
WEB DuBois Clubs	Soviet		1,000 [5]	Insurgent	6,000
Progressive Labor	Maoist		1,200 [6]	Pro. Lab. Chal.	8,000
Revolution Act. Mov. (RAM)	Maoist		50 [1]	Black America	Minimal *
Socialist Labor Party	Indp.		2,000	Weekly People	12,000
Socialist Workers Party	Trot.		450	Militant	5,000
Young Socialist Alliance	Trot.		1,000	Young Socialist	
Spartacist League	Trot.		under 100	Spartacist	Minimal *
SNCC	Indp.		470 (est) [3]	SNCC Newsletter	Minimal *
SDS	Indp.		8,000	New Left Notes	7,000 [7]
Weekly Guardian Assoc.	Formerly Soviet		none	Guardian (Nat. Guardian)	27,000
Workers World Party	Maoist		under 300		
Youth Against War and Fascism	Maoist		300 activists (non-membership)	Workers World / The Partisan	2,500 / 1,000
Black Nationalists					
Black Panther Party	Indp.	3 [8]	2,500 [2]	Black Panther	45,000[11]
Black Muslims	Indp.	29 [9] 1 [9]	6,000	Muhammad Speaks	200,000[12]
Deacons for Defense	Indp.		500 [4]	None	———
Repub. of New Africa	Indp.		125 [10]		———

* Not sold regularly on open market
[1] FBI, Appropriations, 1968
[2] New York *Times*, (2/7/68) estimated 7,000 then.
[3] NYT, (10/7/68)
[4] Down from estimated 5,000 reported in *Wall Street Journal*, (7/12/65)
[5] NYT, (3/15/65)
[6] NYT Magazine, (4/25/65)
[7] NYT Magazine, (6/15/69)
[8] One in New York
[9] Muhammad Speaks, (6/13/69)
[10] Wire Service estimates
[11] Press run figures. The Panthers carry on an aggressive subscription solicitation.
[12] According to publications office. Muslims are assigned quotas. Hence full press run is not circulation.

Income appears to be up slightly. SDS' annual dues is $5. SDS relies primarily on chapters financing their own projects. In this year's FBI appropriations statement, Director J. Edgar Hoover reported that one (unnamed) foundation, during a seven-year period "contributed over a quarter of a million dollars . . . to various individuals or groups, most of which have been identified with the communist or New Left movements." That this amount was found noteworthy tells volumes. Lack of sufficient funds probably accounts for the Far Left's inability to reply in kind to Far Right radio. As a propaganda force, the Left relies on people's getting involved in events. It seems eager to get in involved in headline-making situations which, while repelling most Americans, attract dissidents to the movement.

The New Left has shown no significant increase in either membership or fund raising ability in the past year, but it has grown more skilled in engineering confrontations in which larger groups of people are forced to take sides. Having found tinderbox issues in many universities, the New Left, demanding a complete restructuring, is likely to keep on striking matches.

If the Far Right feeds on racism, so do the emerging Black Power extremists. While the organizations attract only a tiny percentage of the Negro population, two of them, at least, operate almost as a state within a state. The relatively new Black Panthers and the much older Black Muslims make and enforce their own rules. Both are demanding reparations for generations of economic depredations. Both want to carve out a section of America as a Black nation as do some even smaller groups. Both are militant, and the Panthers openly urged their members to arm for "defense" against police "aggressions." As the Society breaks down in specific neighborhoods, this takes on many of the aspects of a guerrilla war.

While IAD's annual survey of the Far Right shows the John Birch Society still speaks with the loudest voice in the movement, it does not dominate to the extent it did a year ago. Rivalries and, paradoxically, a measure of success are creating problems.

The Birchers and their ideological allies are still primarily a propaganda force. Some of their positions are becoming standard political fare. Birchers abound in the American Independent Party, but they have to stay on good behavior. The Birchers place ever more stress on front groups like TACT, Support Your Local Police, and the new MOTOREDE. The fronts have been effective, but they, too, put pressure on Belmont to make the JBS look more moderate.

Meanwhile, Liberty Lobby and other groups dominated by that elusive ex-Bircher, Willis Carto, are flaunting a more openly racist line, and getting converts. And the ultra conservative American Security Council in step with other groups associated with Schick's Patrick J. Frawley, are also making a play for broad support. Incredibly, the JBS is in the middle.

While the JBS still fields by far the biggest paid staff, membership (about 65,000) and revenues appear down about 10 percent from a year ago. In contrast, Birchite Billy James Hargis hit the jackpot with the antisex education

TABLE 2. Who's Who on the Far Right

Organization	Chief Publications	Estimated Circulation	Estimated Radio-TV Outlets	Estimated 1968 Income
John Birch Society and Allies	American Opinion	34,098 **	spots only	$3,832,000 a
* Christian Crusade (Hargis)	Christian Crusade	85,513 **	115 b	1,171,000 ***
* (Dean) Manion Forum	Manion Forum News	not avail.	71 rad. 45 TV c	817,600 ***
* Dan Smoot Report	Dan Smoot Report	28,197 **	64 rad. 25 TV d	350,000 ***
* Conservative Society of America (The Courtneys)	Independent American	not avail.	12 d	460,000 e
Liberty Lobby and Allies	Liberty Letter	197,512 **	——	850,000 f
National Youth Alliance (Carto)	The New Right	10,000 g	——	g
Noontide Press (Carto)	American Mercury	6,113 **	——	g
Richard Cotten	Conservative Viewpoint	not avail.	31	106,000 ***
Carl McIntire Complex	Christian Beacon	99,100 **	350 h	2,250,000 ***
Church League of America (Bundy)	News & Views	8,500	30	280,195 i
Life Line (H. L. Hunt-Munn)	Life Lines	7,300 **	562 j	1,205,300 ***
Twin Circle (Fr. Lyons-Frawley)	Twin Circle	45,000 **	20 rad. 2 TV	k
Young Americans for Freedom	New Guard	10,000 **	——	449,173 ***
Christian ACC (Fred Schwarz)	CACC Newsletter	not avail.	——	325,000 ***
Voice of Americanism (McBirnie)	Documentation	not avail.	64 l	——
Bible Institute of the Air (Burpo)	Bible Inst. News	35,000	30 m	461,840 n
America's Future (Scott)	America's Future	7,500	200	200,000 ***
Christian Freedom Foundation (Rev. Howard Kershner)	Christian Economics	not avail.	71 o	——
White Citizens Councils	The Counselor	69,038 **	——	——
Harding College (NEP Program)	Nat'l Program Letter	50,000	——	175,669

The underground Minutemen, with many leaders now behind bars, have a total membership of about 100, with an estimated 500 in fellow-traveling groups. This year, the FBI placed the total membership of the KKK (publication—*Fiery Cross*) at 8,500. The National States Rights Party (publication—*Thunderbolt*) has about 124 members and the National Socialist White People's Party (Nazis), 40.

* Featured at 1966, '67, '68 '69 God and Country Rallies.
** Post Office Reports, 2nd Class mailing statements.
*** IAD staff projection based on 1968 Group Research estimates.
a JBS *Bulletin*, Feb., 1968 placed '67 income at $4,258,000.
b "Partial Listing" in *Christian Crusade*, October, 1967.
c Outlets appear to be about the same as number in late 1966 listing.
d Estimated to be about same as last year.
e 1966—see *Farther Shores of Politics*, p. 198. Separation of Courtneys does not appear to have adversely affected income.
f Projected from LL lobby report filed with Clerk of the House.
g Funds apparently channeled through Wills Carto, who controls circulation lists and direct mail appeals.
h Projected. No listing available.
i Internal Revenue Service Form 990-a return for 1967.
j Listed by *Life Lines*, April, 1969.
k Wholly owned subsidiary of Schick Investment Company.
l Current listing.
m April, 1968 listing.
n Arizona Corp. Commission Report.
o Christian Economics, April 29, 1969.

issue, and his Christian Crusade income appears up by about 10 percent. Hargis is currently wooing the fundamentalist American Council of Christian Churches. While Carl McIntire, who founded the ACCC, still grosses more than Hargis, his troubles are multiplying.

Liberty Lobby's income is up by about a third and its Liberty Letter now has the widest circulation of any Far Right publication. Carto has just gotten control of what is left of the Youth for Wallace organization.

Most of the familiar hucksters of the Far Right line held their ground or showed slight gains in audience and revenues. Some, like aging Howard Kershner, appear to be cutting back, but a good many newcomers are clamoring for a slice of that fat Far Right propaganda market.

Group Research, Inc., estimates that several score Far Right organizations took in and spent at least $50 million last year. The Far Right continues to peddle a blend of supernationalism, racism and authoritarianism. Its zealots want influence, and its leaders still thirst for power.

When enough people believe that public order is collapsing and that their lives and property will not be protected by existing law enforcement agencies, vigilante organizations are likely to appear. The National Commission on the Causes and Prevention of Violence lists some 328 known vigilante organizations in American history, accounting for at least 635 "executions." It may be debated whether vigilante organizations—self-appointed groups of citizens who attempt to enforce upon others some behavior controls which more or less perfectly correspond to "the law"—are an aid or a threat to orderly society. But unquestionably the appearance of vigilante activity is evidence of anxiety, personal insecurity, and dissatisfaction with existing law enforcement. Recently in some areas of the South, Deacons for Defense was organized among Negroes who felt that official law enforcement agencies provided them with no protection and were in fact an actual threat to their safety. Originally composed of "responsible" members of the black community, Deacons for Defense now appears to consist mainly of militant black nationalists. The Black Panthers also has many characteristics of a vigilante organization.

The following journalistic account describes a white vigilante movement in Newark, New Jersey. A prolonged economic decline, a relentless shift in the local black-white population ratio, an increase in black militance, aggressiveness, and (allegedly) crimes against whites, an uneasy feeling among whites that law, order, and decency are slipping from their grasp—all these conspired to give many whites an angry, desperate readiness to "do something." This vigilante movement is one kind of response.

TONY IMPERIALE STANDS VIGILANT
FOR LAW AND ORDER

Paul Goldberger

It was a warm Sunday evening in May, and the crowd, jammed elbow-to-elbow in the tavern parking lot, was wildly enthusiastic. "Give 'em hell, Tony," an old man shouted. "Tell 'em where to go."

Tony began quietly. "I didn't see any flags in the city of Newark lowered to half mast when Gov. Lurleen Wallace died," he said. "Why not, when they could do it for that Martin Luther Coon?" The audience cheered, and Tony gained momentum. "When is it gonna stop?" he cried. "Everybody says, 'Don't bother 'em now. Leave 'em alone, and they'll calm down.' Well, it took riots that burned down half of a town before we learned."

Tony is Anthony Imperiale—5 feet 6¾ inches, a tough-muscled 230 pounds, 39 years old. That evening in Nutley, N.J., five miles north of Newark, he was hailed as a savior by hundreds of white residents who are convinced that the Negro is taking away everything the white man has earned. Tony isn't going to give it up without a fight—and Tony is their man.

Imperiale is the organizer of Newark's North Ward Citizens' Committee, which claims a dues-paying membership of 200 and thousands of enthusiastic followers. In their leader's view, they are "defenders of law and order," banded together in the wake of last summer's Newark riots to stand up to Communist-inspired racial pressures. In the view of Gov. Richard J. Hughes, they are "vigilantes."

They own guns and take karate training from Imperiale, a Black Belt in the art. Ten of their radio-equipped cars patrol the North Ward each weekday night (17 on weekends) to ward off criminals and/or invaders from the adjacent Central Ward, the black ghetto. Chapters in five suburban towns, including Nutley, mount their own patrols. Imperiale used to boast loudly that the committee owned a helicopter and an armored car, and he insisted that members on patrol wear fatigues—but he has of late soft-pedaled these matters.

Last month the windows fronting the committee's cinder-block headquarters on North Seventh Street were shattered by three explosions.

No one was injured in the 1:20 A.M. bombing, but it was a close call. "If a guy hadn't talked me into taking another drink at a bar I was in," Imperiale says, "me and my wife Louise would have been sitting right where that plate-glass window was torn out." He has few doubts about who placed the dynamite, and he has doubled the night patrols. He has also expressed uncertainty about his ability to control committee members: "If this kind of thing happens again, I won't be responsible for what these people here will do."

Tony Imperiale is not alone in America 1968. In Detroit there is Donald Lobsinger, chairman of a 6-year-old organization called Breakthrough. His formula for security: "Study, arm, store provisions and organize." In Warren, Mich., druggist Ronald Portnoy leads a group known as Fight Back. Its literature proclaims: "The only way to stop them is at the city limits." In Oakland, Calif., the leader of the Home Defense Association is Herbert Clark. It has published a manual recommending firearms and ammunition and containing chapters on "Defense of an Individual House" and "Neighborhood Perimeter Defense."

Not many of these men, however, have built up the support or strength of Newark's Imperiale; in fact, there is often an element of bosh about the private vigilance business. Ernest Bradow, for example, a 26-year-old member of the John Birch Society who lives in North Bergen, N.J., created something of a stir in July when he claimed that his group, People's Rights Enforced Against Riots and Murder, had 319 members patrolling 11 towns. Bergen County Prosecutor Guy W. Calissi ordered an investigation that turned up only one member of PRE-ARM. His name was Ernest Bradow.

Imperiale is of another stripe. Last month he sought election to a council that will oversee administration of the Federal Model Cities program in Newark. There were four posts open in each of 13 districts—248 candidates for 52 seats. Imperiale not only won in his district but polled more votes than any other candidate in the city. He called his victory "an affirmation of the people's desire for law and order." Now he is running for the City Council, and his eye is on the office now occupied by Mayor Hugh J. Addonizio.

The Imperiale platform is basically the same cry for law and order that sets crowds cheering wherever he speaks. Some of the planks:

The American people are very guillible. They let the politicians yield to the radical. And the Communists take the radical and exploit him. . . . In the riots, billions of dollars of property was destroyed, and the Constitution of the United States was thrown into the gutter. When is Washington gonna put down their foot and say, "Look, law and order must prevail"?

We look at the policemen—they've been abused, they've been harassed, they've been rubbed under the nose with anything that these radicals wanted to do, and they got away with it. Because the quislings, the politicians with no guts, were selling the decent people out. . . . The first thing I'm gonna do is take politics out of the Police Department. . . . And I intend to fight any group who tries to tie the hands of the police by shouting "police brutality" or this or that. I'm gonna fight you, tooth and nail.

They oughta register Communists, not guns.

Are there no poor whites? But the Negroes get all the antipoverty money. When pools are being built in the Central Ward, don't they think the white kids have got frustration? The whites are the majority. You know how many of them come to me, night after night, because they can't get a job? They've been told, "We have to hire Negroes first." . . .

In the view of Imperiale's constituency, he tells it like it is. The large majority of the ward's 43,000 residents are Italian-American, though there has been something of an influx of Negroes since the 1960 census, when the proportion of Negroes was 17.6 percent. White Protestants have been leaving the area, the Roman Catholic population has increased and some Negro congregations have taken over property formerly owned by white Protestant churches.

It is a shabby neighborhood, once firmly middle class, now in the grip of a slow but insistent deterioration. The percentage of owner-occupied homes has dipped. Many single-family homes have been converted to multiple-occupancy dwellings. There is a crowded, ticky-tacky feeling about it all.

Perhaps the most unhappy facet of the North Ward, however, is a pervasive—and in many ways valid—mental set. The people sense that their backs are to the wall, that conditions are worsening and no help is on the way. There are state and Federal funds being poured into Newark, but they are being spent elsewhere; for bad as the ward's problems may be, they don't compare to the problems of the city's black ghettos.

More than half of Newark's 400,000 residents are Negroes. A third of the city's housing is substandard; unemployment in black areas such as the Central Ward is officially set at 12 percent, unofficially as high as 20 percent; there are 17,000 households "living" on incomes of less than

$3,000 a year. Newark leads all cities of the nation of its size in crime and venereal disease and maternal mortality rates.

When the city celebrated its tricentennial in 1966, it adopted the slogan, "Pride in Newark." But the statistics above don't lend themselves to being pointed to with pride; Tony Imperiale and his followers point to them with fear and anger, and the presence of black faces in their North Ward is a constant reminder that "it could happen here."

It is not, Imperiale insists, that he and the members of the committee are racists. He tells of inviting a Negro neighbor and his family over for a meal. When a Negro woman died in his neighborhood this summer, he took in her 7-year-old boy for several days; the boy still spends as much time with the Imperiales as with his own family, Imperiale says.

But Imperiale is quick to defend whites who attack Negroes entering the ward ("The colored just come looking for trouble"), and he is convinced that the Negro is incapable of dignified living ("Look at this," he says, pointing to a 15-year-old photograph of a North Ward neighborhood. "And look at it now, with garbage on the streets." A committee member adds, "They don't know how to live here; they have no pride." Later, a tour of the neighborhood turns up only a few signs of deterioration. "The garbage man must have just been here," the committee member quickly explains). . . .

In his determination to stand in for Joe in Newark, Imperiale has made a conscious effort to improve his vocabulary and life-style—so that he can better deal with the world outside the North Ward. Thus, when an aide automatically sought to prevent a New York Times reporter from seeing Imperiale because the paper is "a little too far left for us," Imperiale intervened and arranged the interview. His new political career is part of a program to prove that he is a responsible person, that he wishes to operate within the Establishment. ("A Negro lady came to see me just the other day and told me I'm going to get Negro votes. You see, there are conservative and moderate Negroes who want law and order just like us.") The image change is slow in coming, though, and the Imperiale language and syntax still have a way to go.

Any uneasiness Imperiale may reveal in his forays into the outer world vanishes when he makes the rounds of his own small world of the North Ward. His natural life-style blossoms, as it did one warm, humid evening recently during a committee patrol.

Patrols start at headquarters, a one-story building that contains a small office with radio equipment and several telephones. Behind the office is a multipurpose room, once the karate school gymnasium, the walls of which are painted bright orange. A bulletin board is posted with clippings—pro and con—about the organization. Judo posters line one wall, and literature published by black militants is displayed on another.

Street maps abound. A sign beside the door reads: "No profanity. Fine 25 cents."

The office is usually staffed by neighborhood housewives while their husbands patrol the streets and their young children play hide-and-go-seek around the building. They are, respectively, members of the North Ward Women's Auxiliary and the North Ward Junior Auxiliary. The most singular artifact in the office is a telephone directly connected to LeRoi Jones's Spirit House in the Central Ward.

This is Newark's famous "hot line," suggested by Police Director Dominick A. Spina, that is used in the event of threatening racial violence to link Imperiale and Jones—the Black Belt and the black nationalist leader and poet. The two men are on first-name terms. "I don't say I love LeRoi," says Imperiale, "but I respect him. I would meet with the devil himself to hear what he had to say." Jones says, "At least Tony Imperiale is an authentic spokesman for his people."

The hot line has been used several times to head off trouble when rumors of impending race war have filled the North and Central Wards. "There was an incident one night," Imperiale recalls, "when we were supposed to have done something. The hot line rings. It's Kamil Wadu [Jones's Chief of Security]. Immediately through our radios we dispatch one of our cars, check it out and find it's a fallacy. In the meantime Kamil's people are in the area, checking out the same thing. We dispel the rumor together, before all our people take to the street and start something."

Most of the members of the patrol are young, and the cars they drive tend to be old. As dusk falls, the street in front of headquarters comes alive with the roar of faulty mufflers and the impatient engine revving of youth craving excitement. They wear black construction hats decorated with the committee's initials, N.W.C.C., embossed in white. They talk together with a kind of false bravado.

Imperiale gives the word, and the four-man patrols move out. They follow carefully planned routes, studying the scene, looking for signs of trouble. At first, the police used to stop the cars to search them for weapons, and some such searches still occur. "They never find any guns," says Imperiale, "because we never carry any. It would be stupid." The patrol is intended to prevent conflict, he says, not start it.

For Imperiale, a patrol consists of driving from one corner gathering of white youths to another. Invariably he is recognized, and he knows most of the boys by their first names. "Hi ya, Angelo," "Waddaya doin', Stevie?" He urges them to stay cool, stay out of trouble. Older residents often spot his elderly black Cadillac. "Go get 'em, Tony," they shout "They're out to get you." The bombing of committee headquarters is fresh in their minds.

Police calls, monitored at headquarters, are relayed to Imperiale over his car radio. If the call is for a location on his patrol route, he drives over; otherwise, he instructs the headquarters operator to dispatch a nearer car (the patrol assignments are charted on a large map of the city at headquarters).

The crackling of the radio provides a steady punctuation for conversation in the Imperiale Cadillac. He and his followers have absorbed the jargon of radio communications; it pervades their speech. And thus far everything has been 10–4 (O.K.) for the organization—since patrols began, they have never been involved in a blameworthy incident. Actually, though the potential for excitement is most obviously there, the patrols tend to be boring.

Imperiale has time to relax and talk. He notes an unfamiliar Negro face in his ward: "See that guy over there? We don't know who he is, so we keep an eye on him for a while. We'll drive back here later and see if he's still around." (He wasn't.)

The car draws up to the rear of a pizza palace on Bloomfield Avenue; this is where the white youths of the ward hang out, a good spot to keep track of the action. Everybody knows Imperiale (they call him "Big T"), and he seems to know everybody. He favors one boy with a characteristic playful cuff on the cheek (sometimes the cuffs are pretty hard, but no one seems to mind). "Are you O.K.? Did you keep the job I told you about?" To another he says, "Jerk, I saw you and those other bums hotrodding. What did I tell you about that?" They crowd around him in obvious awe and affection, and when Imperiale singles out a boy for attention, the youth revels in the sensation.

At 11 P.M., back on patrol, a police report is relayed about a prowler at a nearby address. The car moves off to the site, within the speed limit. A look around—nothing—the patrol resumes.

Toward midnight, the tour of duty ends. Most of the patrol members drift back home, but a handful return to headquarters. There they sit around with Imperiale, talking things over, working out small improvements in their strategy and logistics. In an emergency, he says, the committee could have 50 patrols on the streets.

Because of such patrols and the other activities of the committee, Imperiale believes, an all-out race war in the city and suburbs can be avoided. "It doesn't necessarily have to come to that," he says. "We're showing the radical blacks that there's whites that will stand up. We're proving that it can be prevented." . . .

There are, however, various groups of citizens with whom Imperiale is not so popular. Clergymen, for example, and not simply because of his tax-exemption position. His followers have been accused of throwing rocks at priests attending a rally, and Imperiale has minced no words in his condemnation of the clergymen who protested a North Ward committee proposal for a police canine corps: "Don't think that because a man wears the cloth of God, he hasn't his hates and prejudices. We knew there was a shortage of policemen and that dogs had proved in other places to be an asset. We didn't make an issue out of it; the clergy did. They came to the City Council and said: 'These dogs will be used against the Negro.' That's a controversy they had no business getting involved in."

City and state officials are not among Imperiale's strongest supporters. Governor Hughes, who sees the committee as analogous to burgeoning Nazi groups in Germany in the nineteen-thirties, has submitted a bill to the New Jersey Legislature making it illegal to belong to any organization "with two or more persons who assemble as a paramilitary or parapolice organization." The bill was passed by the Senate but has been locked up since July in committee in the Assembly. The Governor has also requested Imperiale to disband voluntarily; Imperiale has refused.

Mayor Addonizio, a former Congressman, says Imperiale's group is a "problem." He adds: "Any group that walks around in paramilitary uniforms is undesirable." And he believes that Newark has had a quiet summer this year "in spite of" the North Ward committee which has "acted to further separate the black and white communities." . . .

The Mayor has to date taken no specific action against the committee. Indeed, Donald A. Malafronte, administrative assistant to Addonizio and administrator of the Model Cities program, feels that Imperiale has not had an entirely bad effect on the city. "In some ways he relieves tension among his own people because he tells whites what they want to hear," Malafronte says. "We don't believe Imperiale ever laid a hand on anybody. Like LeRoi Jones, he belongs in Newark, but on the fringes. We want to forge them both together, with Imperiale on one wing and Jones on the other, but none in center stage, because Newark isn't *all* Anthony Imperiale or LeRoi Jones."

Malafronte added, however, that the city is "concerned" about white militancy, and that the North Ward Citizens' Committee is under constant surveillance by the Newark Police Department: "We have the organization so completely penetrated with police that Imperiale can't sit down without our knowing about it." . . .

Recent public disorders have been fully photographed and televised. Many people, deeply shocked and frightened by what they have seen, have begun to wonder if orderly civilized society will be drowned in a rising tide of disorderly protest and violence.

Just how much disorder and violence a social system can tolerate is an unsettled question. If disorderly protest, seizure of buildings, and a shouting down of rational deliberation become the standard response of dissatisfied interest groups, then democratic society becomes impossible and some form of authoritarian rule a certainty. Yet it is possible for a society to continue to function with a good deal of intermittent violence. For example, the campus has been the scene of considerable disorder and some violence in recent years. Higher education has suffered some damage (along with some needed changes) in consequence. A few buildings and some equipment have been damaged or destroyed; academic freedom has suffered some defeats, as when a determined minority forces cancellation of a course of study; shouting has replaced rational deliberation in some instances; a number of classes have been sadly disrupted; at a few colleges the educational process has been brought to a halt for a time. Yet the total financial cost of all campus disorders would finance the Vietnam war for only a few minutes, and most colleges have proceeded with "business as usual" most of the time. The question is, "How much nihilistic irrationality and violent disruption can a university tolerate before it ceases to be an institution of higher learning?"

Neither the campus nor the society has been free from violent protest in the past. The following essay, by a past director of the MIT–Harvard Joint Center for Urban Studies places the question of violence in historical perspective, with an interpretation of current violence and a forecast for the immediate future.

WHY WE ARE HAVING A
WAVE OF VIOLENCE

James Q. Wilson

*Professor of Government
Harvard University*

Whatever the deficiencies with respect to our knowledge of individual forms of violence, at least we know enough to be able to answer the question, "How much of this violence will occur next year, or over the next five years?" The answer, obviously, is "about the same as this year." However, with respect to collective violence—riots, disorderly demonstrations and the like—we cannot even say that. The best we can do—and what, indeed, many commentators are doing—is to predict widespread violence so that if *any* violence occurs the prediction will appear to have been "correct." Logically, of course, it will not be correct: it would be as if a meteorologist were to predict that it will rain every day and then, on the day it does rain, to say he has been proved right.

Most theories of collective violence have as their principal defect that they overpredict the phenomenon. Some say that Negroes riot because their lot is deplorable—they have nothing to lose but their burdens. But the lot of many Negroes has always been deplorable; indeed, by most standards it is much less deplorable today than 20 years ago.

Others modify the theory by introducing the notion of relative deprivation, or the "revolution of rising expectations." But Negroes have experienced such deprivations and such expectations before—during World War I, World War II and the Korean War, when their incomes rose rapidly, migration to the big cities was heavy and an awareness of and contact with the advantages of white society were widespread. There were no major Negro riots then; the only major riots were begun by *whites* and aimed at Negroes (Chicago in 1919, Detroit in 1943). The only major *Negro* riot took place in Harlem in the depths of the Depression (1935), when presumably there was a "revolution of decreasing expectations."

A third theory is that the riots are caused by conspirators who have recently become organized. There may have been one or two riots that were clearly begun by conspiratorial leaders and there probably have been many attempts by such groups to cause riots, but in the major upheavals —Watts, Detroit, Newark—the activities of the conspirators did not begin in earnest until after the riot had begun from apparently spontaneous causes.

The central problem is not to predict violence, but to explain why violence has occurred during the last two or three years *but not before*. Some commentators, of course, argue that there has always been violence in this country—from the Draft Riots in the eighteen-sixties through the labor riots that began with the railroad strikes of 1877 and continued through the nineteen-thirties (15 men were killed in the Little Steel Strikes of 1937)—and that the Negro rioting today is no worse and perhaps no different from earlier forms of violence. It has even been suggested that violence is in some sense a "normal" and perhaps legitimate political strategy for oppressed groups.

Whether the present riots are any worse than earlier disorders is beside the point; whether they are in some sense legitimate is not beside the point but outside the scope of this paper. What can be said is that they are different. The Draft Riots were popular reactions against a certain concrete public policy, the enforcement of which was resisted by Irishmen and others who were not willing to restrict themselves to "going limp." The violence attending the labor disputes (in 1934 alone, nearly 30 people were killed) was in almost every case the result of an effort by a union to persuade management to recognize it. When management responded by calling in the Pinkertons and the scabs, the workers reacted with violent protest.

Labor-management violence was in the nature of an internal war between two organized opponents struggling over a quite tangible stake. With the winning of union recognition, the incidence of such violence dropped off markedly, though isolated cases recur from time to time, especially in the South.[1] Even the anti-Irish riots of the eighteen-forties and fifties were directed at an "enemy" and resulted in the destruction of "enemy" property; in Philadelphia, two Catholic churches and two parochial schools were burned to the ground; in St. Louis 50 Irish homes were wrecked and looted; in New York a mob marched on City Hall to attack anybody who looked Irish.[2]

The Negro riots are not apparently aimed at a specific enemy, they do not arise over a specific *issue* (though they may be precipitated by an "incident") and they do not carry the war to the enemy's territory. While it is true that white-owned business establishments are burned and looted, the amount of property owned or occupied by Negroes that is destroyed is often much greater. The Detroit Fire Department listed 477 buildings destroyed or damaged by fire in the 1967 riot. Of these, 103 were single-family and multifamily homes, 30 were apartment buildings and 38 were stores which contained dwelling units. The vast majority were inhabited by Negroes, and many were owned by Negroes. Only five liquor stores, two loan shops, four jewelry stores and one bank were burned, even though these establishments presumably represent "white business" and may be perceived as "white exploitation." Many other, more obvious symbols of white authority—churches, schools, newspaper circulation offices, police buildings—were scarcely touched. To compare these riots with earlier historical examples is like comparing assault to self-flagellation—such pleasure as the latter confers does not depend on the suffering it causes others.

When people destroy their own communities, even at high risk to themselves (43 persons died in Detroit, most from police and National Guard bullets), it is difficult to assert that the riot was an *instrumental* act—that is, an effort to achieve an objective. (The Draft Riots, the anti-Irish riots, the violence practiced by the Ku Klux Klan and the labor-management violence were all to some degree instrumental acts.) The Negro riots are in fact *expressive* acts—that is, actions which are either intrinsically satisfying ("play") or satisfying because they give expression to a state of mind.

Of course, for many people in all riots—whether instrumental or

---

[1] Philip Taft, "Violence in American Labor Disputes," *Annals,* 364 (March 1966) pp. 127–140.

[2] Arnold Forster, "Violence on the Fanatical Left and Right," *Annals,* op. cit., p. 143.

expressive—there are individual gratifications, such as the opportunity for looting, for settling old scores and the like. But these people operate, so to speak, under the cover of the riot and are not obviously the cause of it. To the extent riots are or can be organized, of course, the need to offer incentives to induce people to participate would make the encouragement of looting a prime objective for a riot leader—not only does it get people out on the street in large numbers and put them in an excited state of mind, it disperses and preoccupies police and military forces. There is little evidence yet, however, that it is the desire for loot that precipitates the riot or even plays a very important part in the early hours.

If we are to construct an explanation for what has occurred—and we may never have a testable explanation, for the requirements of experimental or statistical control necessary to test any riot hypothesis are not likely to exist—we must combine attention to the material conditions in which the Negro lives (which on the whole have been improving but are still poor) with the costs and benefits to him of expressing a desire for autonomy, manhood, self-respect and the capacity for independent action.

On the cost side, we note a significant reduction in the willingness of those who command the police to use them with maximum vigor in suppressing disorder. The attention given of late to real and imagined cases of "police brutality" has obscured the fact, compared to the police response to labor violence even 30 years ago, most big-city police departments, especially in the North, have recently been less inclined, primarily for political reasons, to use instant and massive retaliatory tactics against any incipient disorder. It would appear that this is one reason the majority of serious riots have occurred in the North, not the South—in the latter region, political constraints on the police are less effective.

One need not deny that police-citizen contacts have often been the spark that triggered a riot, or that many departments have neglected or mismanaged their community relations program, to argue that the police, if they wanted to (that is, if they were willing to pay the price in lives and political support), could make the costs of rioting so high that either there would be no riots at all or these would be a massive convulsion equivalent to civil war.

On the benefits side, persons are coming of age who are several generations away from the rural South and who accordingly have lost their fear of white men without yet having had an opportunity to even scores. Young people are always rebellious; when young people grow up and discover that their elders are *also* rebellious, there is perhaps an urge for even more extreme actions. Just as the sons and daughters of New Deal liberals regard their parents as "square" for confining their demands for change to the rules imposed by the existing political system, so also the sons and daughters of Negroes who have demanded integration and equal opportunity may feel that such demands are not enough because they are based on an acceptance of the distribution of power within the existing social order.

Negro (and some white) leaders, aware of the drift toward violent sentiments, have attempted to take advantage of it by using the threat of violence as a way of increasing their bargaining power; the difficulty, of course, is that the responsible leaders have lacked the capacity either to start or stop a riot while the irresponsible ones have simply lacked the power to stop one.

Furthermore, the mass media—especially television—offer an opportunity for immediate expressive gratification that did not exist even 15 years ago. It is interesting to speculate on what the Know-Nothing violence might have been like if every American could watch in his living room the looting of a convent while it was happening and if every would-be looter could be summoned to the scene by immediate radio coverage of the event.

Finally, young people today, white and Negro, have become quite self-conscious, for reasons I obviously do not understand, about the social functions and therapeutic value of violence. A generation that was absorbed by Camus's intricate analysis of how in existential terms one might have justified the effort to assassinate the czar has given way to a generation some members of which are absorbed by Frantz Fanon's argument for violence: Violence, if practiced by the wretched and oppressed, may be intrinsically valuable as an assertion of self and a reversal of a previous act of violence—slavery—by which self has been denied and subjugation institutionalized.[3]

In short, the few things we know about the riots—that they develop out of a seemingly trivial incident, that they are more expressive than instrumental and that they have thus far occurred primarily in Northern cities or in the more "progressive" Southern cities (such as Atlanta or Nashville)—should lead us to be skeptical of arguments that the riots can be explained entirely or primarily on grounds of *material* deprivation, unresponsive local governments, inadequate poverty programs or the like. No doubt these factors play a part. After all, if the class characteristics of Negroes were identical to those of whites (measured by income, education, mobility and level of political organization), it is hard to imagine that there would be any riots, though there still might be a good deal of discontent. If there were no lower class, there would be fewer riots just as there would be fewer murders. But if class is a necessary explanation, it is not a sufficient one. To material (that is to say, to Marxian) explana-

[3] Aristide and Vera Zolberg, "The Americanization of Frantz Fanon," *The Public Interest* (Fall 1967) pp. 49–63.

tions must be added explanations that take into account the role of *ideas* and the role of *force*.

It is hard to discuss such things without being misunderstood. To impute causal power to ideas or to the lack of force seems to imply the desirability of censoring ideas or imposing the most repressive kinds of force. That is not the implication I intend. To try to censor ideas is both wrong and futile; repressive force is neither available nor manageable. The argument here is analytic, not prescriptive, and is designed merely to suggest that we consider the possibility that ideas have consequences.

Theories of social change are often suspect in my eyes because they seem to lead automatically to the policy conclusion favored by their author: It is as if one decided what program one wanted adopted and then decided what "caused" an event in order to justify that remedial program. If one wants a "Marshall Plan" for Negroes, then economic want causes riots; if one wishes the political power of the "Establishment" weakened, then inadequate access and a lack of self-determination are the causes; if one wants Stokely Carmichael and Rap Brown put in jail, then conspirators are the cause. Since almost no one wants (at least publicly) ideas to be controlled, the causal power of ideas is rarely asserted; this theory gets fewer "votes" than it may deserve because it is not in anyone's interest to vote for it.

But if elsewhere ideas are readily conceded to have consequences— "nationalism," "self-determination," "the world community revolution"— might it not be possible that they have consequences here also? Only a fear of being thought illiberal may prevent us from considering that the probability of a riot is increased by demands for "Black Power," by a constant reiteration that white bigotry and racism are at the root of all the problems besetting the Negro, by the reaffirmation of the (untrue) assumption that most Negroes live wretched lives and that matters are going from bad to worse, by constantly predicting apocalyptic violence if "something isn't done" and by "discovering" the nontruth that all Negroes are alike in their hatred of "whitey" and their tacit or open approval of extreme solutions for their plight.[4]

If there is something in the climate of opinion, the mood of a generation or the drift of sentiments that contribute to Negro riots, there is no reason to suppose that only Negroes are affected by these currents. The special and urgent problem of the Negro may lead us to assume, without sufficient reflection, that the Negro case is not only special but unique. But it ought not be taken for granted that 20 million people are affected by ideas that have no effect on the other 180 million living in the same country.

More narrowly, are young Negroes involved in a radical discon-

4 Gary T. Marx, "Protest and Prejudice" (New York, 1967).

534 STUDIES IN THE SOCIOLOGY OF SOCIAL PROBLEMS

tinuity in American history or are they simply at the leading edge of a more general drift toward collective violence? Are we quite confident that there is no connection between Negroes burning down their communities and young whites storming the Pentagon, assaulting Cabinet officers and forcibly occupying university buildings? Or between these acts and the sharp rise in recruitment to the Ku Klux Klan and the emergence of the ominous White Knights and the Minutemen? And if there is a connection, is the entire phenomenon to be put down to "rising expectations" or "unresponsive government"?

I cannot say there is a connection, but I cannot accept without some persuasion the answer that the Negro is wholly a special case. Collective violence was once thought to be an inevitable aspect of the political life of any country, even this one. In 1947, in the second edition of his famous text on political parties, the late V. O. Key Jr. devoted a full chapter to the political role of force. By 1958, when the fourth edition appeared, that chapter had been reduced to a page and a half. And by 1961, when his book on public opinion appeared, there was a chapter on "conflict" but no mention of violent conflict.

Traditionally, one would expect violence whenever there were deep and irreconcilable differences of opinion on fundamental issues in a society where one party had no confidence in the capacity of the other party to govern. (The distrust between the Socialists and Conservatives in prewar Austria was, of course, a classic case; a postwar government was possible only on the basis of a coalition that permitted one party to check the other in the ministries as well as in Parliament—a form of "participatory democracy.") One would also expect violence when, though the nation is not deeply divided, established authority is unwilling to use force to make the costs of violence prohibitively great for any minority unwilling to resign itself to losing in a nonviolent struggle for power.

If the traditional understanding of violence were applied today, one would not expect it to subside once the "demands" of Negroes (or peace marchers, or whatever) were met. One reason is that the demands cannot be met—the competition for leadership among the (largely disorganized) dissident groups will inevitably generate ever more extreme demands faster than less extreme requests are fulfilled.

Another reason is that violent political conflict is only rarely over tangible resources which the government can allocate—it is typically over symbolic values which government either does not control (the sense of equality or human dignity or social acceptance) or does control but cannot redistribute without destroying itself (sending the Irish back to Ireland, abandoning military force as a tool of foreign policy). But primarily violence will not subside because it is the cleavage in opinion which gives rise to it, and concessions sufficient to induce one side to abandon violence (subject to the constraints cited above) might be concessions sufficient to induce the other side to resort to violence.

To cut through the vicious circle, governments historically have increased the application of force to the point that neither side found it rewarding to practice violence, thus inducing both sides to wait for long-term trends to soften or alter the cleavages of opinion. Such increases in force have often required a reduction in the degree to which the use of force was subject to democratic constraints. Parliamentary regimes have been replaced by presidential regimes; presidential regimes have been replaced by dictatorial regimes. Only when it is clear that *neither* side can gain through violent protest does the resort to such forms of protest cease. The case for dealing with the conditions under which Negroes (or poor whites) live is not, therefore, to be made on the ground that such efforts will "stop riots"; it can be made only on the grounds that for other, and essentially moral, reasons changing those conditions is right and necessary

Whether this analysis has any applicability to present-day America is difficult to say. One would first have to estimate the probability of white violence against Negroes (or hawk violence against doves) under various kinds of governmental concessions to Negroes (or doves), and no one is competent to make any confident predictions on these matters. What can be said is that long-term prosperity is no guarantee against political violence of some form. Prosperity cannot by itself eliminate the ideological sources of violence and indeed may weaken the institutional constraints on it so that the effects of the activities of even a few persons with violent intentions may be amplified by an increasingly larger multiplier and thus influence the action of ever larger numbers of persons.

This consequence of prosperity may arise through the dispersal of power and authority that tends to result from the entry of more and more persons into middle-class status and thus into the forms of participation in public life that are reserved for the middle class. Middle-class persons participate in voluntary associations and public affairs more than working-class persons (and certainly more than lower-class persons, who scarcely participate at all). The higher the level of participation, the larger the number and variety of voluntary associations (and social movements) and the more wills which must be concerted in the making of public policy.[5] "Participatory democracy" may be a slogan currently linked with the aspirations of the underprivileged, but in fact participatory democracy has all along been the political style (if not the slogan) on the American middle- and upper-middle class. It will become a more widespread style as more persons enter into these classes.

Additionally, continued prosperity will increasingly free young people

[5] Cf. Edward C. Banfield and James Q. Wilson, "City Politics" (Cambridge, 1963), esp. concluding chapter.

from the pinch of economic necessity (the need to get a job early in life), place more of them in colleges and universities—where, for better or worse, traditional values are questioned—and increase the number (if not the proportion) of those who find various kinds of personal and political non-conformity attractive.

With participation in greater variety and numbers, the possibility of any one or few organizations dominating the expression of some common interest (civil rights, peace, governmental reform) will be lessened and the competition among such groups will increase. The sensitivity of more and more persons to the substance of issues will reduce the capacity of government to act without regard to these views, and the high (but quite selective) visibility given to governmental acts by television will reduce the capacity of government to act at all in ways (e.g., the use of force or a display of indifference) once employed more readily because less visibly.

In short, marches, protests, sit-ins, demonstrations, mass meetings and other forms of direct collective action may become more rather than less common, though it is hard to predict what issues will prove sufficiently salient to generate such activities. How many will be violent no one can say, but it is not unreasonable to assume that if large numbers of people are brought together in public places because of issues about which they feel strongly, a certain though unknown proportion will—either because they seek violence ("confrontation politics") or because they feel provoked by the police or other opponents—take matters into their own hands.

Since people are most likely to feel strongly about symbolic or intangible issues, and since governments can only deal slowly (if at all) with such matters, the probability of at least disorder and possibly violence is likely to increase over time. The civil rights march on Washington in 1963 was orderly and well-led; early peace marches were of the same character. Recent peace marches were less orderly, and it seems unlikely any new civil rights march will be immune from the same forces leading to disorganization, spontaneity and violence.

But even this "prediction" must be hedged with qualifications. Other, as yet unforeseen, changes in sentiment and ideology may occur with the result that such tendencies toward collective assertion and violence may be redirected. Perhaps collective violence will undergo a transformation parallel to that affecting individual violence; just as murder gives way to suicide, child-beating to child "guidance" and rape to seduction and perversion with the middle-classifying of the poor, so also might political violence give way to civility and rhetoric.

The most that can be said for the argument sketched in this article is that one should not assume that these changes in character are themselves sufficient to change the manner in which politics is carried on. Profound institutional and organizational changes are likely to occur also, and these, by making the system more sensitive—even vulnerable—to the diminishing amount of violent instincts among individuals, will produce a net increase in violent *behavior* with no net increase in violent *attitudes*. If that occurs, the existence or threat of lower-class violence, which dominated the politics of the nineteenth century, may be replaced by the threat of middle-class violence during the twenty-first.

17 War in the Twentieth Century

Modern warfare has become unbelievably devastating. World War II, for example, resulted in over nine million military casualties, some twelve million civilian deaths, and involved total economic costs of over one and one-quarter trillion dollars.

Since World War II, beyond the undeclared wars that have cost the United States more than seventy thousand men killed, this country and the Soviet Union have been playing a game of nuclear "chicken." Now the People's Republic of China appears ready to join the game.

Unquestionably the world stands on the threshold of self-destruction. An all-out nuclear war employing hydrogen bombs might kill two billion people. Even if mankind survived, as some military and civilian strategists assure us it would, few argue that life would be worth living.

These are some of the stark facts confronting us as we move toward the three-quarter mark in the twentieth century. Yet, as imminent as the possibility of total destruction is, war may pose an even more insidious threat to the nation. The probability of a nuclear war over the next decade cannot be estimated accurately, but many estimate it at something less than fifty percent. However, there is mounting evidence that preparation for war is steadily undermining the basic values of a democratic society.

The selections in this chapter deal not with war directly but with the impact of war and preparation for war upon the social and economic structure of American society. President Dwight D. Eisenhower, who as Supreme Commander of the allied forces in World War II had every reason to be concerned with the nation's defense, first warned us of the threat posed by the "military-industrial complex" in 1960.

"Arms Dealer Sam" is a condensation of an article that appeared in *Harper's Magazine* in April 1969. Depending upon one's point of view, it is either a tribute to free enterprise or a frightening account of intrigue and deception, aided and abetted at the highest levels of government. The philosophy expressed by Samuel Cummings in the last paragraph of the article is widely shared in the United States and may be more dangerous than all of the nuclear bombs in existence.

ARMS DEALER SAM

George Thayer

Some time in the early 1950's, a sales brochure published by a little-known company called Interarms offered to the American public a handsome and fascinating variety of its wares: armaments. As if aware that such offerings might be of odd interest to the average outdoorsman or homeowner, the brochure-writer permitted himself a certain degree of high spirits. "Why Be Undergunned?" asks one advertisement, announcing the availability of a number of Finnish Lahti 20 mm antitank cannon ("Excellent for defending your driveway"). A Soviet mortar is described as "the ultimate attraction for you smoothbore fanatics," and a bazooka, as the perfect weapon to "get those charging woodchucks."

Interarms, whose proper name is the International Armament Corporation, at present maintains in Alexandria, Virginia, ten large warehouses which may at any one time hold from 500,000 to 600,000 surplus small-caliber weapons, usually up to 20 mm in size—enough, according to Samuel Cummings, Interarms' president, "for about forty infantry divisions." An additional 150,000 to 200,000 weapons of similar type comprise the stock of another large warehouse maintained by the company in Acton, a suburb of London. Indeed, Cummings claims to have more surplus weapons in stock than the military forces of either the United States or Britain currently have in active service.

Interarms of course is not exclusively or even primarily involved in supplying intrepid private individuals with recreational equipment. Since the end of World War II there have in fact been very few independent arms deals in the world in which Samuel Cummings has not been involved. He has managed in the last two decades, for instance, to buy up approximately ninety percent of all the British surplus small arms for sale.

He once paid one million dollars for Spain's entire surplus small arms, and on another occasion sold Austria all the ordnance it needed to equip its border police. He bought 300,000 surplus arms and seventy million rounds of ammunition from Finland; this purchase was so large that it took three years to ship to the United States. He almost bought from Chile the last surviving warship from the Battle of Jutland, but a Japanese group outbid him at the last moment. He helped rearm West Germany by selling it MG-42 machine guns that the Dutch had captured from the Wehrmacht. In one transaction, he bought 600,000 Lee-Enfield rifles, some of them for as little as twenty-eight cents apiece and subsequently sold many of them in the United States for as much as $24.95.

In 1955 he supplied arms to the Costa Rican government of José Figueres. He also sold arms to Nicaragua, which was at the time supporting a group of Costa Rican rebels opposed to the Figueres regime. The following year he bought 2,000 small arms that had been captured by the Israelis from the Egyptians in the Suez campaign. The weapons were predominantly Russian in origin, purchased by the Egyptians from the Czechs, who previously had acquired them from the Soviets. Most of these arms, Cummings told me, "now hang over fireplaces in American homes."

He sold Trujillo twenty-six Vampire jets that had seen service in the Swedish Air Force, and a few years later he sold Venezuela seventy-four F-86 Sabrejets that were Luftwaffe castoffs. For many years he was a major supplier of arms to Batista. Later, he sold Castro a batch of AR-10 rifles—as he did 75,000 Sten guns to Finland, 500,000 FN rifles to Argentina, 2,000 Springfield rifles with extra-long chrome-plated bayonets to Liberia, 50,000 Lee-Enfields to Pakistan's border patrol, and a quantity of the same make of rifle to Kenya to fight the Mau Mau. He has even supplied 144 cavalry lances, complete with pennants, to the Sudan, which maintains one of the few remaining mounted camel cavalry units anywhere in the world.

Walking through the warehouses in Alexandria can be a formidable experience: In crates sometimes piled twenty feet high are rows of Lee-Enfields, German Mausers, Italian Mannlicher-Carcanos, Russian Tokarevs, Finnish Lahtis, and American M-1 carbines. Besides these, there are thousands upon thousands of automatic pistols and revolvers: Lugers, Webley & Scotts, Glisentis, Nagants, Colts, Nambus, Walthers, and Smith & Wessons; and, of course, millions of rounds of ammunition, some of which cannot be obtained anywhere else on the American and British markets. Prior to the passage of the Gun Control Act of 1968, one could at the right time also find grenades, artillery shells, and bazooka rounds; Interarms also stocked a selection of mortars, submachine guns, bazookas, swords, sabers, and bayonets. Occasionally there might also be a lot of used military uniforms. These add something special to the atmosphere, for it was, and is, Cummings' custom to dress his employees in whatever he has in stock: one week they may impersonate the Afrika Korps, the next the British Royal Navy or the Royal Tank Corps. . . .

It is bound to be imagined about any enterprise like Interarms that it is either controlled by, dominated by, or otherwise in the pay of the CIA. Careful research has turned up no evidence of any direct formal connection between the two organizations. There is no doubt, however, that they have often worked closely together; Interarms is much too convenient a potential instrument for the CIA and other government agencies to have overlooked. For one thing, no government bureaucracy could maintain an arms intelligence system in such a high state of alertness as Cummings'; nor as cheaply. For another, a business like Interarms provides the U.S. government a perfect opportunity to buy weapons from unofficial sources. And third, Interarms serves as an ideal buffer between the government and critics of the arms trade.

Although naturally no one in the government would be inclined to talk about it, arms dealers are generally quite certain that the CIA and other agencies of our government maintain stockpiles of foreign weapons in various restricted locations around the country. Such foreign ordnance is tested by our experts, and any technological advances deemed essential to our defense presumably are eventually incorporated into our own weapons system. Despite the fact that it has lately become so fashionable to charge all activities of the CIA and the military to some form of heinous conspiracy, the stocking of foreign weapons is an activity routinely practiced by and taken for granted by all major and many minor powers. In addition to the technological data they yield, these foreign weapons are used in training Special Forces troops, whose job it is to operate behind enemy lines. And, finally, they are used to arm groups friendly to the United States operating clandestinely. . . .

During the early days of the Vietnam war, when the military began arming its helicopters, the government found it necessary to buy from Cummings a substantial number of secondhand AN/M-2's, which are American-made air-cooled .50 caliber wing guns.

According to several sources, in 1960 and early 1961 the CIA bought a large quantity of .30 caliber semiautomatic rifles from Interarms in order to arm the anti-Castro forces for the Bay of Pigs. Interarms has also imported from the Belgian firm of Fabrique Nationale large quantities of 9 mm pistols which do not appear to have been absorbed in the commercial American market; it is said in arms-dealing circles that the CIA bought all of them. Cummings claims he re-exported them to a Latin-American country in return for a batch of old rifles.

From the other side of this close working relationship, Cummings has been selling ammunition that could only come from government sources. For instance, he has sold .30–06 caliber ammunition with a headstamp designation of C/N/40/9. Now, all cartridges, even Communist-made ones, have a code stamped on the base end of their cases indicating the producer and year of manufacture. Queries to the FBI Lab, the National Rifle Association, H. P. White Laboratories in Bel Air, Maryland, the Centre of Forensic Sciences in Ontario, and the Firearms Information Service in Winchester, New Hampshire, asking what arsenal or producer carried the designation C/N, produced a variety of answers. Some said the cartridges were made "overseas" or in Canada or in the

United States. All except H. P. White Labs hinted that they were used by the U.S. government at the Bay of Pigs. The FBI refused to comment. Several weapons experts told me privately that the C/N headstamp mark was simply a phony. Moreover, this ammunition was packed in standard government boxes and crates that carried no markings whatsoever on the side, a highly unusual procedure in a business where everyone normally wants to know exactly what he is getting. Thus it appears that this particular batch was made specifically for the U.S. government and for a specific purpose. At some time, then, it was deemed no longer useful and was sold or traded to Interarms.

Finally there is the matter of Interarms' relationship with a firm called American Firearms and Ammunition Corporation of Long Island City, New York. Little information is available about AFAC, but what there is seems to point to its being a front for government interests: the company has been a very large buyer of equipment from Interarms, particularly in the years from 1960 to 1963; yet nowhere has there been an advertisement by AFAC offering its wares to the public, nor are there any AFAC retail outlets or foreign subsidiaries.

In 1968 three attempts by a credit-rating firm to contact officers at the company's headquarters across the river from Manhattan were unsuccessful, and requests for interviews went unanswered. Two nearby banks could supply no information on the company. Moreover, a telephone call to AFAC at noon one day brought the information via an answering service that all the officers were out for lunch; another at 2:00 P.M., that none had returned, and at 4:00 P.M., that all had gone home. At 10:00 A.M. the next day none had yet arrived for work. And an actual visit to the office—a dingy single room on the top floor with a desk, a telephone, and an empty filing cabinet—was nearly as fruitless. The door was unlocked, no one present, and an accumulation of several days' mail on the floor. (By letter count, over half the correspondence came from the State Department and the Morgan Guaranty Trust Company, two organizations that would not ordinarily conduct business with a firm in such apparent disrepair.) Nevertheless, at one point American Firearms and Ammunition Corporation was such a large buyer of weapons that special prices were quoted to it, known around Interarms as "AFAC units."

In 1962 Interarms and AFAC were mixed up together in a strange episode involving the return to Finland of 32 million rounds of Soviet 7.62 mm and 7.92 mm ammunition—finally reported on in only two local Texas newspapers. It seems that in December 1961, Interarms imported the ammunition through the port of Baltimore and had it shipped to the "American Firearms Corp." of San Antonio for (as one newspaper reported it) "possible sale to sportsmen." No company that meant to sell 32 million rounds of ammunition to sportsmen would be likely to hide its light under a bushel, but as it happens the San Antonio telephone directory carried no listing for such a company in its editions from 1961 through 1967. Moreover, it was stated that the ammunition was also meant to be used for the U.S. Army M-1 and M-14 rifles—an impossible fit, as anyone in the gun business would instantly recognize. Most of the crates had been stamped "Made in Russia 5–4–46," which would indicate that the material was of postwar origin and thus technically ineligible for importation for commercial purposes. U.S. Customs agents were reported to have tested the ammunition and found it in good condition; yet the reason given for returning the material was that it was "defective." Since military standards for ammunition are higher than commercial standards, and since Customs would not ordinarily pass judgment on ammunition imported for military use, it is reasonable to assume that "defective" meant it did not meet U.S. military standards. The material, in other words, had almost certainly been intended for use in Soviet weapons owned by the U.S. government. . . .

Cummings bridles at the idea that he is considered a "merchant of death." "I would call your attention to the fact," he said to commentator David Brinkley in 1962, "that two-thirds of the taxes you and every other American pay go into exactly the same hardware as we deal in. So in a sense we are all in the same business." He feels himself no more responsible for what his customers do with his weapons than distillers for drunks or automobile manufacturers for highway deaths. Nor does he believe that selling to two countries that later go to war with each other is immoral; all large American firms—from Coca-Cola to Standard Oil—he says, sell to both sides, and anyway in actual wartime, the government prohibits him from selling arms to either antagonist.

He is deeply skeptical of the possibility of achieving disarmament and an end to war. Arms, he has said, are the symbol of man's folly throughout the ages. "That's why this is the only business that should last forever." He may be right.

The preceding article was somewhat personal and colloquial; the one that follows examines the pernicious growth of the military-industrial complex comprehensively. It describes the abuses of public trust inherent in the noncompetitive procurement of military hardware, including the virtual guarantee of excessive profits and the tacit sanctioning of unethical bidding practices. It reveals the extent of questionable hiring of military procurement officers by manufacturing companies who have dealt with them directly in their official capacities. Even more frightening is the unauthorized intrusion of the Pentagon into civilian matters that are not properly its concern. The concept of waging "peacefare" suggests that the nightmare of George Orwell's *1984* may already be upon us.

WE MUST GUARD AGAINST UNWARRANTED INFLUENCE BY THE MILITARY-INDUSTRIAL COMPLEX

Richard F. Kaufman

Economist, Joint Economic Subcommittee on Economy in Government

Eight years have gone by since President Eisenhower opened the door on the military-industrial skeleton in the closet. Yet only recently has research started to hang some real meat on his bony, provocative phrase, "military-industrial complex." What is emerging is a real Frankenstein's monster. Not only is there considerable evidence that excessive military spending has contributed to a misallocation of national resources, but the conclusion seems inescapable that society has already suffered irreparable harm from the pressures and distortions thus created.

Military and military-related spending accounts for about 45 percent of all Federal expenditures. In fiscal 1968, the total Federal outlays were $178.9 billion. The Defense Department alone spent $77.4 billion, and such related programs as military assistance to foreign countries, atomic energy and the Selective Service System raised the figure to $80.5 billion. The $4-billion program of the National Aeronautics and Space Administration and other activities intertwined with the military carry the real level of defense spending considerably higher.

To place the defense bill in perspective we should note that 1968 appropriations were less than $500 million for food stamps, school lunches and the special milk program combined. For all federally assisted housing programs, including Model Cities, they were about $2 billion. The poverty program received less than $2 billion. Federal aid to education was allotted about $5.2 billion. The funds spent on these programs and all those categorized as health, education, welfare, housing, agriculture, conservation, labor, commerce, foreign aid, law enforcement, etc.—in short, all civilian programs—amounted to about $82.5 billion, if the space and

The New York Times Magazine, June 22, 1969. © 1969 by The New York Times Company. Reprinted by permission.

veterans' programs are not included, and less than $70 billion if the interest on the national debt is not considered.

The largest single item in the military budget—it accounted for $44 billion in 1968—is procurement, which includes purchasing, renting or leasing supplies and services (and all the machinery for drawing up and administering the contracts under which those purchases and rentals are made). Procurement, in other words, means Government contracts; it is mother's milk to the military-industrial complex.

The Pentagon annually signs agreements with about 22,000 prime contractors; in addition, more than 100,000 subcontractors are involved in defense production. Defense-oriented industry as a whole employs about 4 million men. However, although a large number of contractors do some military business, the largest share of procurement funds is concentrated among a relative handful of major contractors. Last year the 100 largest defense suppliers obtained $26.2 billion in military contracts, 67.4 percent of the money spent through contracts of $10,000 or more.

Similarly, the Atomic Energy Commission's contract awards tend to be concentrated in a select group of major corporations. Of approximately $1.6 billion awarded in contracts last year, all but $104 million went to 36 contractors. As for NASA, procurement plays a larger role in its activities than in those of any other Federal agency. More than 90 percent of its funds are awarded in contracts to industry and educational institutions. Of the $4.1-billion worth of procurement last year, 92 percent of the direct awards to business went to NASA's 100 largest contractors.

In terms of property holdings, the result of almost two centuries of military procurement is a worldwide and practically incalculable empire. An almost arbitrary and greatly underestimated value—$202.5 billion— was placed on military real and personal property at the end of fiscal year 1968. Weapons were valued at $100 billion. Supplies and plant equipment accounted for $55.6 billion. Most of the remainder was in real estate. The Pentagon says the 29 million acres it controls—an area almost the size of New York State—are worth $38.7 billion. (The official Defense Department totals do not include 9.7 million acres, valued at $9 billion, under the control of the Army Civil Works Division or additional property valued at $4.7 billion.) The arbitrariness of those figures is seen in the fact that they represent *acquisition* costs. Some of the military real estate was acquired more than a century ago, and much of it is in major cities and metropolitan areas. The actual value of the real estate must be many times its acquisition cost.

But the important fact about procurement is not the extent of the Pentagon's property holdings; it is that defense contracting has involved the military with many of the largest industrial corporations in America. Some companies do almost all their business with the Government. Into this category fall a number of the large aerospace concerns—such giants as General Dynamics, Lockheed Aircraft, and United Aircraft. For such other companies as General Electric, AT&T and General Motors, Government work amounts to only a small percentage of the total business. But the tendency is for a company to enlarge its share of defense work over the years, at least in dollar value. And whether defense contracts represent 5 percent or 50 percent of a corporation's annual sales, they become a solid part of the business, an advantage to maintain or improve upon. A company may even work harder to increase its military sales than it does to build commercial sales because military work is more profitable, less competitive, more susceptible to control through lobbying in Washington. The industrial giants with assets of more than $1 billion have swarmed around the Pentagon to get their share of the sweets with no less enthusiasm than their smaller brethren.

The enormous attraction of military and military-related contracts for the upper tiers of industry has deepened in the last few years as military procurement has increased sharply. For example, GE's prime-contract awards have gone up from $783 million in 1958 to $1.5 billion in 1968; General Motors went from $281 million in 1958 to $630 million in 1968. While much of this increase can be traced to the Vietnam war boom and many contractors would suffer a loss of business if the war ended, there was steady growth in the defense industry during the fifties and early sixties (in 1964 and 1965, before the Vietnam build-up, there was a decline in prime-contract awards). In the five years from 1958 to 1963—five years of peace—the value of GE's prime contracts increased $217 million and General Motors' rose $163 million. The same trend can be shown for many of the large corporations in the aerospace and other industries.

What seems to be happening is that defense production is gradually spreading throughout industry, although the great bulk of the funds is still spent among relatively few companies. Still, as the defense budget increases the procurement dollars go further. The geographical concentration of defense production in the industrialized, high-income states also suggests that military contracts have come less and less to be restricted to an isolated sector of the economy specializing in guns and ammunition. Military business has become solidly entrenched in industrial America.

Considering the high degree of mismanagement and inefficiency in defense production and the tendency for contractors to want more sales and thereby to support the military in its yearly demands for a larger budget, this is not a healthy situation. The inefficiency of defense production, particularly in the aerospace industry, can hardly be disputed. Richard A. Stubbing, a defense analyst at the Bureau of the Budget, in a study of the performance of complex weapon systems, concluded: "The low overall performance of electronics in major weapon systems developed and produced in the last decade should give pause to even the most outspoken advocates of military-hardware programs." He found that in 13 aircraft and missile programs produced since 1955 at a total cost of $40 billion, fewer than 40 percent of the electronic components performed acceptably; two programs were canceled at a cost to the Government of $2 billion, and two programs costing $10 billion were phased out after three years because of low reliability.

And the defense industry is inefficient as well as unreliable. Albert Shapero, professor of management at the University of Texas, has accused aerospace contractors of habitually overstaffing, overanalyzing and over-managing. A. E. Fitzgerald, a Deputy Assistant Secretary of the Air Force, in testimony before the Joint Economic Subcommittee on Economy in Government, described poor work habits and poor discipline in con-tractors' plants. In the same hearing, a retired Air Force officer, Col. A. W. Buesking, a former director of management systems control in the office of the Assistant Secretary of Defense, summarized a study he had conducted by saying that control systems essential to prevent excessive costs simply did not exist.

In a sense, industry is being seduced into bad habits of production and political allegiance with the lure of easy money. And industry is not the only sector being taken in. Consider conscription (3.6 million men in uniform), the Pentagon's civilian bureaucracy (1.3 million), the work force in defense-oriented industry (4 million), the domestic brain-drain created by the growth in military technology, the heavy emphasis on mili-tary research and development as a percentage (50 percent) of all Ameri-can research, the diversion of universities to serve the military and defense industry. These indicators reveal a steady infiltration of American values by those of the military establishment: production for nonproductive use, compulsory service to the state, preparation for war. In the process, the economy continues to lose many of the attributes of the marketplace. In the defense industry, for all practical purposes, there is no marketplace.

The general rule for Government procurement is that purchases shall be made through written competitive bids obtained by advertising for the items needed. In World War II the competitive-bid requirements were suspended. After the war the Armed Services Procurement Act was passed, restating the general rule but setting out 17 exceptions—circum-stances under which negotiation would be authorized instead of com-petition. The exceptions, which are still in use, are very broad and very vague. If the item is determined to be critical or complex or if delivery is urgent or if few supplies exist and competition is impractical or if emer-gency conditions exist or if security considerations preclude advertising, the Pentagon can negotiate for what it wants.

When President Truman signed this law in 1948 he saw the possi-bilities for abuse and wrote to the heads of the armed services and the National Advisory Committee for Aeronautics. "This bill," he said, "grants unprecedented freedom from specific procurement restrictions during peacetime. . . . There is danger that the natural desire for flexibility and speed in procurement will lead to excessive placement of contracts by negotiation and undue reliance upon large concerns, and this must not occur." Unfortunately, Truman's apprehensions were well justified. Last year about 90 percent of the Pentagon's and 98 percent of NASA's contract awards were negotiated under the "exceptions."

What this means is that there is no longer any objective criterion for measuring the fairness of contract awards. Perhaps more important, control over the costs, quality and time of production, insofar as they resulted from competition, are also lost. Negotiation involves informal discussion between the Pentagon and its contractors over the price and other terms of the contract. It permits subjective decision-making on such important questions as which firms to do business with and what price to accept. The Pentagon can negotiate with a single contractor, a "sole source," or it can ask two or three to submit proposals. If one later complains that he had promised to provide a weapon at a lower price than the contractor who obtained the award, the Pentagon can respond by asserting that the price was not the major factor, that the government simply had more faith in the contractor who won. This, in effect, is how the Army responded to the Maremont Corporation's recent challenge of a contract award to General Motors for the M-16 rifle. The Pentagon, because of its almost unbounded freedom to award contracts, can favor some companies. And over long periods, this practice can lead to a dependence by the government on the technical competency of the suppliers on whom it has come to rely. For example, the Newport News Shipbuilding Company has a virtual monopoly on the construction of large aircraft carriers.

Typically, the Pentagon will invite a few of the large contractors to submit proposals for a contract to perform the research and development on a new weapon system. The one who wins occupies a strategic position. The know-how he gains in his research work gives him an advantage over his rivals for the larger and more profitable part of the program, the production. This is what is meant when it is said that the government is "locked in" with a contractor. Because the contractor knows he will obtain a lock-in if he can do the initial research work, there is a tendency to stretch a few facts during the negotiations.

Contractor performance is measured by three factors: the total cost to the Government of the weapon system, the way in which it functions and the time of delivery. During the contract negotiations over these factors the phenomenon known as the "buy-in" may occur. The contractor, in order to "buy in" to the program, offers more than he can deliver. He may promise to do a job at a lower cost than he knows will be incurred or to meet or exceed performance specifications that he knows are unattainable or to deliver the finished product long before he has reason to believe it will be ready.

Technically, the contractor can be penalized for his failure to fulfill promises made during the negotiations, but the government rarely insists on full performance. The contractor knows this, of course, and he also knows the "get-well" stratagem. That is, he can reasonably expect, on practically all major weapon contracts, that should he get into difficulty with regard to any of the contract conditions, the government will extricate him—get him well.

The contractor can get well in a variety of ways. If his costs run higher than his estimates, the Pentagon can agree to pay them. (Cost increases can be hidden through contract-change notices. On a typical, complex weapon system, the changes from original specifications will number in the thousands; some originate with the Pentagon, some are authorized at the request of the contractor. The opportunities for burying real or phony cost increases are obvious, so much so that in defense circles contract-change notices are sometimes referred to as "contract-nourishment.") The government can also accept a weapon that performs poorly or justify a late delivery. If for some reason it is impossible for the Pentagon to accept a weapon, there is still a way to keep the contractor well. The Pentagon can cancel a weapon program for the "convenience" of the government. A company whose contract is canceled for defaults stands to lose a great deal of money, but cancellation for convenience reduces or eliminates the loss; the government makes reimbursement for costs incurred. An example of this occurred recently in connection with the F-111B, the Navy's fighter-bomber version of the TFX.

Gordon W. Rule, a civilian procurement official who had responsibility for the F-111B, said in testimony before the House Subcommittee on Military Operations that General Dynamics was in default on its contract because the planes were too heavy to meet the height or range requirements. Rule proposed in a memorandum to Deputy Secretary of Defense Paul H. Nitze that the contract be terminated for default. At the same time, Assistant Secretary of the Air Force Robert H. Charles and Roger Lewis, the General Dynamics chairman, proposed that the Navy reimburse the company for all costs and impose no penalty. Nitze's compromise was to make reimbursement of $216.5 million, mostly to General Dynamics, and to impose a small penalty.

In a memo written last year Rule made this comment on the attitude of defense contractors: "No matter how poor the quality, how late the product and how high the cost, they know nothing will happen to them."

There are many other ways to succeed in the defense business without really trying. The Pentagon generously provides capital to its contractors; more than $13 billion worth of government-owned property, including land, buildings and equipment, is in contractors' hands. In addition, the Pentagon will reimburse a supplier during the life of his contract for as much as 90 percent of the costs he reports. These are called "progress" payments, but are unrelated to progress in the sense of contract objectives achieved; they correspond only to the costs incurred. The progress payments are interest-free loans that provide the contractor with working capital in addition to fixed capital. They minimize his investment in the defense business and free his assets for commercial work or for obtaining new defense work.

Investigations by the General Accounting Office have revealed that the government's money and property have been used by contractors for their own purposes. The most recent incident involved Thiokol Chemical Corporation, Aerojet-General (a subsidiary of General Tire & Rubber Company) and Hercules, Inc. From 1964 through 1967 they received a total of $22.4 million to be used for work on the Air Force Minuteman missile program. The government accountants found that the three contractors misused more than $18 million of this money, spending it for research unrelated and inapplicable to Minuteman or any other defense program.

The defense industry is perhaps the most heavily subsidized in the nation's history. Thanks to Pentagon procurement policies, large contractors find their defense business to be their most lucrative. Although no comprehensive study of such profits has been made, the known facts indicate that profits on defense contracts are higher than those on related nondefense business, that they are higher for the defense industry than for manufacturing as a whole and that the differential has been increasing. In a study that compared the five-year period from 1959 through 1963 with the last six months of 1966, the General Accounting Office found a 26 percent increase in the average profit rates negotiated. Admiral Hyman G. Rickover has testified that suppliers of propulsion turbines are insisting on profits of 20 to 25 percent, compared with 10 percent a few years ago, and that profits on shipbuilding contracts have doubled in two years.

The figures cited by Rickover relate to profits as a percentage of costs, a measure that often understates the true profit level. The more accurate measure is return on investment. An example of the difference was demonstrated in a 1962 tax-court case, North American Aviation vs. Renegotiation Board. The contracts provided for 8 percent profits as a percentage of costs; the tax court found that the company had realized profits of 612 percent and 802 percent on its investment in two succeeding years. The reason for the huge return on investment was the Defense Department policy of supplying both fixed and working capital to many of the larger contractors. In some cases the amount of government-owned property exceeds the contractor's investment, which is sometimes minimal. It is no wonder that contractors prefer to talk about profits as a percentage of costs.

Murray Weidenbaum, recently appointed Assistant Secretary of the Navy, found in a study that between 1962 and 1965 a sample of large defense contractors earned 17.5 percent net profit (measured as a return on investment), while companies of similar size doing business in the commercial market earned 10.6 percent. . . .

There is almost no risk in defense contracting except that borne by the government. If a major prime contractor has ever suffered a substantial loss on a defense contract, the Pentagon has failed to disclose his name, although it has been requested to do so by members of Congress. On the other hand, the disputed Cheyenne helicopter and C-5A cargo plane projects could conceivably result in large losses for Lockheed, the contractor in both cases. Lockheed asserts that it might still make a profit on the C-5A (which is being produced in a government-owned plant), and denies that it is at fault in the cancellation of production on the Cheyenne helicopter (on which research work has been resumed). Past experience suggests that one should await the final decision, which may be two years in coming, before making flat statements about profit and loss.

In fairness, it ought to be pointed out that Secretary of Defense Melvin R. Laird has talked about a new get-tough policy with contractors. New procurement techniques that would, for instance, require contractors to meet specific cost benchmarks have been announced; increased prototype development is planned; greater public disclosure of cost overruns and performance or scheduling problems have been promised; the production of the Cheyenne helicopter and the Air Force's Manned Orbiting Laboratory program have been canceled. Whether any of these measures will produce real savings has yet to be determined. The Pentagon is famous for its paper reforms.

The defense industry, in addition to providing high profits at low risk, offers fringe benefits for everyone. One of the important advantages for those in procurement, on either side of the bargaining table, is the opportunity for career advancement. There is a steady march of military and civilian personnel back and forth between the Pentagon and the defense industry. It is not considered unusual for someone like Maj. Gen. Nelson M. Lynde Jr. to retire from the Army after being directly involved in the procurement of the M-16 rifle and go to work five months later for Colt Industries, originally the "sole source" of the M-16; nor is it a matter for comment when Lieut. Gen. Austin Davis retires from the Air Force after playing an important role in procurement for the Minuteman missile program and becomes vice president of North American Rockwell, one of the Minuteman's prime contractors.

This is not to say that the interchange of personnel between the Pentagon and the defense industry is harmful in itself or that it ought to be prohibited. There is a problem in finding qualified people, and one would not want to deprive either the Pentagon or contractors of a source of trained manpower. While it would not be fair to condemn the practice and everyone engaged in it out of hand, there is a serious conflict-of-interest problem.

The conflict-of-interest laws apply primarily to military personnel and are easily evaded. Therefore, the solution to the problem does not seem to lie in expanding the legal restrictions. What might help is the public disclosure of the names of high-ranking Pentagon officials who have moved on to jobs in the defense industry and those who have made the reverse trip. The Subcommittee on Economy in Government has recommended that such a list be compiled. It would facilitate scrutiny of the interchange problem by revealing obvious conflicts of interest that should be investigated.

Individuals in the field of procurement naturally have an interest in the continued growth and importance of their field. The same could be said of people in many other fields. What is disturbing here is the opportunity that many officials have to influence procurement policy while in the Pentagon and then benefit from their actions or those of their former associates when they join the defense industry or, possibly, one of the 16 Federal-contract research centers supported by the Pentagon. . . .

The interchange of personnel, according to testimony by Admiral Rickover, has helped spread a business-oriented philosophy in the Defense Department. One might equally well observe that a military-oriented philosophy has been spread in the defense industry. Several kinds of institutional arrangements in addition to the interchange of personnel help bind military power to industrial wealth. Representatives of industry, in such groups as the Aerospace Industries Association, and of the military, in such organizations as the Air Force Association, agree on the basic issues: a large military budget, a high cost base in defense production, no losses, high profits and Congressional and public compliance. . . .

The danger of the military-industrial complex lies in its scale. Reasonable men will tolerate a war machine as a necessary evil. It is the size of the machine and its claim on national resources and individual lives that is at issue. What is alarming is the growth of the complex.

The great leap of the military budget in the last few years, from about $50 billion to $80 billion, and its earlier growth, beginning with the Korean war, have helped to bring about serious stresses in the economy. Although no one factor can be identified as the sole cause of inflation, it is no accident that the three most recent price surges accompanied sharp increases in military spending, between 1950 and 1953 (the Korean war period), between 1955 and 1957 and since the buildup in Vietnam began. Defense expenditures have contributed substantially to these inflationary trends. The consequent reduced value of savings and fixed-income assets during each of these periods is an indirect cost of defense; the 10 percent tax surcharge made necessary by the Vietnam buildup is a much more direct one.

More ominous than the economic consequences of a bloated defense budget are expanding and sometimes furtive military activities in such areas as foreign affairs, social-science research, domestic riot control and chemical and biological warfare. In hearings last year on Pentagon-sponsored foreign-affairs research, Senator Fulbright quoted from a 1967 report of the Defense Science Board (a scientific counterpart to the business-advisory groups): "The DOD mission now embraces problems and responsibilities which have not previously been assigned to a military establishment. It has been properly stated that the DOD must now wage not only warfare but 'peacefare' as well. Pacification assistance and the battle of ideas are major segments of the DOD responsibility. The social and behavioral sciences constitute the unique resource for support of these new requirements. . . ."

Fulbright's reminder that the military's responsibility is "to prosecute war or to provide military forces which are capable of defending against an external attack" might have sounded like naivete to the Pentagon, but his point is important. Social-science research conducted in foreign countries by foreigners should, if it is to be supported at all, be supported by the State Department, not the Pentagon. Research into socio-cultural patterns or the social organization of groups or processes of change should not be a military responsibility. Yet the Pentagon does support foreign research all over the world, awarding contracts to GE to make projections of "future world environments" and to McDonnell-Douglas to do a study entitled "Pax Americana," later retitled "Projected World Patterns, 1985."

The Army's new domestic "war room" in the basement of the Pentagon is also of doubtful legitimacy. This "operations center" is supposed to help dispatch and coordinate troops for urban riots (maybe that's "pacification assistance"). Even assuming the need for this kind of activity, one can raise the same question that disturbs Senator Fulbright with regard to social-science research: Is this a proper military responsibility?

The most recent example of the Pentagon's "independent thinking," brought to light by the efforts of Congressmen Richard D. McCarthy and Cornelius Gallagher, is the controversial Army plan to transport about 27,000 tons of obsolete poison gas across the country by train to New Jersey to be loaded onto old hulks, towed out to sea and sunk. Both the State Department and the Interior Department have a direct interest in this project, yet the Army did not bother to coordinate its plans with them until long after the plans were formulated.

Such incidents as the construction of the domestic war room and the independent decision to ship poison gas across the country symbolize the drift of power in the executive branch to the Pentagon and show the extent to which military authority has exceeded its traditional limits. Swollen by overgenerous appropriations, the defense budget has become the source of frightening political as well as economic power. Practically freed of the fiscal limitations that restrain other agencies, the Pentagon seems to be able to exercise its will in almost any area it chooses, foreign or domestic, from negotiating a new lease for bases and promising military assistance to Spain (as it was recently alleged to have done) to launching programs of social reform.

The nature of the problem was simply stated recently at a hearing of the House Subcommittee on Military Operations. Testifying was Phillip S. Hughes, deputy director of the Bureau of the Budget. Representative William Moorhead had charged that the bureau was unable to scrutinize Defense Department expenditures to the same extent that it reviews non-defense spending. The budget requests of Government agencies, except the Defense Department, are subjected to an independent analysis and review, which is then submitted to the Budget Director. The director makes his recommendations to the President, subject to challenge by the Cabinet officer concerned. But the Defense Department is treated differently. In the Pentagon, Moorhead said, Budget Bureau analysts must work along-side their Defense counterparts, not independently. The results of this joint review are submitted to the Secretary of Defense, who sends it to the President, subject to challenge by the Budget Director. The result is that the burden of persuading the President to change the budget he receives is shifted from the agency head to the Budget Director in the case of the defense item, but only there. . . .

"The most relevant consideration," Hughes testified, "is, in blunt terms, sheer power—where the muscle is—and this is a very power-conscious town, and the Secretary of Defense, and the defense establishment are a different group to deal with, whether the Congress is dealing with them or whether the Budget Bureau is dealing with them. . . ."

"The military-industrial complex has become a massive, tangled system, half inside, half outside the Government. Like the Gordian knot, it is too intricate to be unraveled. But like the dinosaur, its weakness lies in its great size. If its intricacy rebuffs us, its grossness is vulnerable; it can be reduced by substantially cutting the defense budget.

This is the only viable immediate solution, for innovations in contractual procedures, regulatory statutes such as the Truth-in-Negotiations Act and such watchdog agencies as the General Accounting Office have not been able to cope effectively with the major excesses in military procurement. The Bureau of the Budget has been in a subordinate position, notwithstanding its recent success in challenging the Manned Orbiting Laboratory funds and its claims to more power over the defense budget. The deck is stacked against those who would sit down across the table from the military-industrial complex.

The only way to change the game is to cut the budget.

18 Retrospect and Prospect

Can social problems really be solved? The list of social problems which Professor Hart listed in the first selection of this volume may make one feel pessimistic; most of the ones he listed a half-century ago are still with us.

Perhaps "solutions" are too much to expect. A complete solution to a social problem, even assuming fully adequate knowledge, generally would require such sweeping institutional changes and such costly value sacrifices that the solution would not be tolerated. Restoration of our streams to their pristine sparkle would mean that a lot of taxes and prices would go up and a lot of profits would go down; furthermore, some industries are simply so messy they would have to close entirely and we would have to get along without their goodies. Before long, we may have to choose between smog and cars. We would like complete solutions but we find the cost unbearable, like the fat man who would rather burp contentedly than lose weight.

The following essay suggests that we should not disdain the "halfway measures" which may make a condition more tolerable without fully curing it. In some cases, "superficial" solutions may be an acceptable compromise between an unbearable problem and an unbearably costly solution.

"SHORTCUTS" TO SOCIAL CHANGE?

Amitai Etzioni

Professor of Sociology
Columbia University

In 1965, when New York City was hit by a "crime wave" (which later turned out to be, in part, a consequence of improved record-keeping), the city increased the number of lights in crime-infested streets. Two of my fellow sociologists described the new anticrime measure as a "gimmick"; it was cheap, could be introduced quickly, was likely to produce momentary results, but would actually achieve nothing. "Treating a symptom just

From *The Public Interest,* Summer, 1968, pp. 40–51. Copyright © National Affairs, Inc., 1968. Reprinted by permission.

shifts the expression of the malaise elsewhere," one sociologist reminded the other, reciting a favorite dictum of the field. Criminals were unlikely to be rehabilitated by the additional light; they would simply move to other streets. Or, when policemen are put on the subways, there is a rise in hold-ups in the buses. So goes the argument.

The same position is reiterated whenever a shortcut solution, usually technological in nature, is offered to similar problems which are believed to have deep-seated sociological and psychological roots. Because of a shortage of teachers, television education and teaching machines have been introduced into the schools. But most educators call this a "gimmicky" solution, for machines are "superficial" trainers and not "deep" educators. Or, in the instances of individuals who suffer from alcohol or drug addiction, blocking drugs (which kill the craving) and antagonistic drugs (which spoil the satisfaction) are now used. (Among the best known are, respectively, methadone and antabuse.) But, it is said, the source of the addiction lies deep in the personalities of those afflicted and in the social conditions that encourage such addiction. If a person drinks to overcome his guilt or to escape temporarily the misery of his poverty, what good is antabuse to him? It neither reduces his guilt nor his poverty; the only effect it has is to make him physically ill if he consumes liquor. Dr. Howard A. Rusk, who writes an influential medical column in *The New York Times,* stated recently:

One of the most dangerous errors in medicine is to treat symptoms and not get at the underlying pathology of the disease itself. Aspirin and ice packs may lower the fever but at the same time allow the underlying infection to destroy the vital organs of the body. So it is with social sickness.

Until a few years ago, I shared these views. But I was confronted with the following situation: The resources needed to transform the "basic conditions" in contemporary America are unavailable and unlikely to be available in the near future. So far as dollars and cents are concerned, Mayor John V. Lindsay testified before Congress that he needed $100 billion to rebuild New York's slums; at the present rate, it would take forty years before such an amount would be available to eliminate *all* American slums. And that is housing alone! With regard to all needs, a study by the National Planning Association calculated that if the United States sought, by 1985, to realize the modest goals specified by the Eisenhower Commission on National Goals, it would (assuming even a 4 percent growth rate in GNP) be at least $150 billion a year short.

But even if the economic resources were available, and the political will to use them for social improvement were present, we would still face other severe shortages, principally professional manpower. In the United States in 1966 there were an estimated four to five million alcoholics,

556,000 patients in mental hospitals, and 501,000 outpatients in mental health clinics. To serve them there were about 1,000 psychoanalysts and 7,000 certified psychotherapists. If each therapist could treat fifty patients intensively, a staggering figure by present standards, this would still leave most alcoholic and mental patients without effective treatment. Today most of those in mental hospitals are not treated at all: only 2 percent of the hospital staffs in 1964 were psychiatrists, only 10 percent were professionals of *any* sort; most of the staff are "attendants," more than half of whom have not completed high school and only 8 percent of whom have had any relevant training.

Thus, we must face the fact that either some shortcuts will have to be found or, in all likelihood, most social problems confronting us will not be treated in the foreseeable future. Forced to reconsider the problem, I decided to re-examine the utility of "shortcuts." For example, do criminals really move to other streets when those they frequent are more brightly illuminated? Or do some of them "shift" to lesser crimes than hold-ups? Or stay home? Do shortcuts deflect our attention from "real issues" and eventually boomerang? In my re-examination,[1] I found some facts which surprised at least me.

DECISIONS WITHOUT FACTS

Take, first, the question of crime. It turned out that the sociologist who asserted that, when more guards were put on the subways, criminals shifted to buses, was merely making luncheon conversation; he simply "assumed" this on the a priori proposition that the criminal had to go somewhere. He had neither statistics nor any other kind of information to back up his proposition. I found that the same lack of relevant information held for *all* the situations I examined. One can show this even in such a "heavily researched" area as alcohol addiction.

Alcoholism is very difficult to treat. Most psychoanalysts refuse to treat alcoholics. The rate of remission is notoriously high. Tranquilizers are reported to be effective, but when I asked doctors why they are not used more widely, they suggested that these drugs provided no "basic" treatment and that patients became addicted to tranquilizers instead of alcohol. Searching for the source of this belief, I was directed to a publication of the United States Public Health Service entitled *Alcohol and Alcoholism,* a very competent summary of the knowledge of the field which is heavily laced with references to numerous studies. Here I found the following two statements:

[1] The study is based on work conducted with the help of the Russell Sage Foundation. For additional discussion, see Amitai Etzioni, *The Active Society* (New York: The Free Press, 1968).

[Tranquilizers] are highly effective, but some alcoholics eventually become addicted to the very tranquilizers which helped them break away from their dependency on alcohol.

For most patients . . . [tranquilizers] can produce lasting benefit only as part of a program of psychotherapy.

I wrote to the Public Health Service. Their reply was that

the bases for both of these statements are "social information" rather than substantive research. It is the clinical experience of many physicians (and some therapists) that some alcoholics have a tendency to become dependent on (whatever that means) other substances in addition to alcohol. There is, however, considerable disagreement on the extent to which this is a problem.

Thus, the Public Health Service really does not know if tranquilizers are only a "symptomatic treatment" which results in the shift of the problem from one area to another; it does not know what proportion of alcoholics can be "deeply" helped by these drugs, or even if those who remain addicted to tranquilizers, instead of alcohol, may not be better off than before.

THE CASE OF DRUGS

The same confusion exists about drugs. Until 1925, the regulation of drug addiction in the United States was largely in the hands of the medical profession; then it was declared to be a police matter and turned over to the Federal Bureau of Narcotics. The change drove the addicts underground, pushed up the price of narcotics, and prompted the large number of "secondary crimes" (to finance the habit) which are associated with addiction in this country. Drug users were involved in 22.4 percent of crimes involving property committed in New York City in 1963. While this is less than the more often-cited figures—that addicts are responsible for "half of all crimes"—it is a staggering cost paid for the partial suppression of addiction.

What body of evidence, medical or sociological, led to this rather far-reaching policy change? In fact, the chief reasons had little to do with evidence at all. The central fact was the ambition of the Federal Bureau of Narcotics (formerly the Narcotics Division of the Treasury Department) and of its former head, Harry J. Anslinger. He and his men conducted a systematic and effective campaign—in the courts, Congress, and the press—in favor of the punitive and against the medical approach to addiction because they viewed addicts as criminals.

Or, take the problem of distinctions among drugs. Over the years, many narcotic users, some medical authorities, and several leading social scientists have pointed out that the American drug laws do not distinguish betwen marihuana and heroin. Marihuana apparently has fewer effects than liquor; several experts argue that, unless one is in the proper company and mood, one does not even gain a "high" feeling from it. Alcoholism causes 11,000 deaths in the United States each year, not counting the thousands of fatalities inflicted by drunken drivers; marihuana per se causes none. Marihuana almost surely is less harmful than cigarettes. Some persons have smoked marihuana for years without visible effects. (Fifty-eight-year-old Mrs. Garnett Brennan, an elementary school principal in Nicasio, California, stated that she had smoked marihuana daily since 1949. Her suspension brought her to the attention of national television and press. She showed none of the symptoms widely expected in persons who have been on narcotics for long periods.) Yet the laws against the *possession* (not just the sale) of marihuana and heroin are equally severe —up to a forty-year jail sentence in some states.

Several authorities in the field have called for legalizing the consumption of marihuana. Those who object argue (1) that marihuana's effects are more severe, especially in accumulation, than has been acknowledged by those who favor its legalization, and (2) that the use of marihuana leads to the use of heroin, in a search for higher "highs," or through the mixing of heroin and marihuana by "pushers." Lawmakers, police authorities, opinion-makers, campus deans, and citizens continually make decisions on these matters, yet our information is, at best, quite spotty. Despite police attention to drugs for more than forty years, and the extensive attention focused on drug addiction in recent years, Robert Reinhold reported in *The New York Times,* following about two weeks of experts' testimonies in a 1967 Boston trial of two youths accused of possessing marihuana that

The most striking impression to emerge from the Boston testimony is that there is a paucity of scientific evidence regarding the drug. Witness after witness offered opinion, based on personal observation and anecdotal evidence rather than on scientific experimentation.

On October 17, 1967, James L. Goddard, Commissioner of the United States Food and Drug Administration, stated: "Whether or not marihuana is a more dangerous drug than alcohol is debatable—I don't happen to think it is." He added: "We don't know what its long term effects are." A few days later, citing no more evidence than Dr. Goddard, Sir Harry Greenfield, chairman of the United Nations Permanent Central Narcotics Board, rejected the "tendentious suggestions" that marihuana was not "very dangerous." Nor has research settled the question whether continuous use of heroin is physiologically debilitating, or whether the symptoms usually associated with the use of heroin are actually the effects of withdrawal. And neither do we know whether a user's inability to function in a social setting is a cause or an effect of his use of heroin.

The main point I wish to make, though, concerns not marihuana but "shortcuts." And the common characteristics of this and other such situations is that the decision-makers *and* experts do not have the information needed to provide the answers. We could, as a short cut, reduce much of the drug problem by legalizing marihuana. *That* we do know. The rest is conjecture.

OF TAXIS AND FIRE ALARMS

Many other questions I have examined are in the same condition. Neither the New York City Police Department nor any other city agency knew what had happened to the criminals who were driven off the lighted streets or off the subways. More recently, there was (or was believed to be) a crime wave in the form of holdups of taxi drivers. The police department initiated a new policy which permitted off-duty policemen to "moonlight" as taxi drivers. They were allowed to carry firearms and exercise their regular police prerogatives. This led to a rapid reduction in the number of taxi holdups. Good news—unless, as some claim, these muggers were now driven to robbing old ladies. We know that they are not back on the subways (which is relatively easy to establish). Whether they are operating elsewhere in New York City, in other cities, in other illegitimate pursuits, and whether these are less or more costly to society than mugging, or even if they have switched to *legitimate* undertakings, no one knows. The one thing we do know is that the original "symptom" has been reduced.

False fire alarms plague the cities; there were 37,414 such calls in New York City in 1966. In the summer of 1966 the New York City Fire Department installed a whistle device, which is activated when the glass is broken, to call attention to persons who pull the trigger of an alarm box. This, it was believed, would reduce the number of false alarms. "Gimmick," one may say; the exhibitionists who set the alarms now create some other mischief, such as causing real fires in order to see the fire trucks racing at their say-so. But nobody knows if these were actually exhibitionists and what they now do. Have they turned arsonists—or are they taking more tranquilizers? In this case it is not clear if the "symptom" was handled; in 1967 there were more false alarms than in 1966, but the device was not yet universally introduced and not publicized, so it could not deter.

EMOTIONS AND POLITICS

Although almost everybody wants "facts" on which to make decisions, the obvious point is that facts are frequently less powerful in shaping a decision than the long-held prejudices of a person. Many a decision-maker in effect says, "I don't care what the facts are; I am against 'it' because it is evil." In the case of drugs, the methadone programs are a revealing case in point. There is fairly good evidence that methadone kills the craving for heroin (persons on methadone have shot themselves with as much as sixteen units of heroin without attaining a "high"), removes the physiologically debilitating effects of heroin (if it has any) without introducing such effects of its own, and that this treatment enables those who take methadone to function socially more effectively than when they were on heroin.[2] Methadone thus is a "shortcut" par excellence because while it solves at least part of the problem, addiction, it does not change the personality which craves for an addicting drug (if there is such a personality), nor does it alter the social setting which encourages the craving.

Although each of the preceding statements in favor of shifting patients from heroin to methadone is not unquestionably substantiated, the critics of the program stress something else: the fact that, in the end, the person is still addicted. A person who regularly takes methadone does seem to become addicted to *it;* at least, it is believed that if a heroin addict stops taking methadone, the craving for heroin will reassert itself. Dr. Robert W. Baird, Director of the Haven Clinic for heroin addicts in New York City, has said that using methadone is "like giving the alcoholic in the Bowery bourbon instead of whiskey in an attempt to get him off his alcoholism." Professor Bernard Barber in his recent book, *Drugs and Society,* reports that in the past the United States Public Health Service "has not accepted any treatment of addicts that left the patient dependent on another drug." Methadone is still legally considered a narcotic and Section 151-392, Regulation No. 5 of the Bureau of Narcotics decrees that treatment by the use of such a drug is by definition not a treatment and hence technically illegal.

Now, if the argument that a person addicted to methadone is still not able to function in society, or not as well as a fully rehabilitated person (a position taken by some experts), we then have a question of fact: do they or don't they? But the antagonism to such a resolution will not even permit such a question to be seriously raised. The puritanical tradition is still sufficiently strong in American culture so that the use of any substitute drugs, even if less harmful, is regarded as an indulgence. When the Ameriman Medical Association in November announced the launching of a year-long scientific study of the effects of marihuana to test the question of its harm, AMA president Dr. Rouse Milford added—before the first day of research—"No good can come from its [marihuana's] use. It's an hallucinogenic drug." Many Americans seem to hold that persons who are attracted to a narcotic should view this as a weakness of the flesh which they should fight and overcome. Similarly, the Food and Drug Adminis-

[2] I benefited from a discussion with Dr. Vincent P. Dole and a visit with his patients on methadone at the Rockefeller University.

tration is not particularly friendly to efforts to find "safe" cigarettes, or blocking or antagonistic medication for smokers. It keeps stressing that "Will Power Is the Only Smoking Remedy." Americans, at least when speaking collectively, seem to value a strong person, one able to function without narcotics (however stress-provoking his social environment) and one who seeks a life of achievement and enterprise, not "artistic" existence or nirvana.

Often the underlying prejudice sneaks through when the method of treatment is discussed. When one hears those who prefer the harsh "cold turkey" withdrawal over the painless transition from heroin to methadone, one gains the impression that the heroin users are viewed as sinners, who are to be penalized (or who have to undergo penance) before they are to be considered pure enough to be allowed to return to the flock.

Where there are emotions, politics is not far behind. Politicians have a high sensitivity to voters' sentiments and a low tolerance for risk. If the voters have (or seem to have) puritanical sentiments, a politician prefers "cold turkey" (despite the known fact that 85 to 95 percent of all of those thus treated return to the use of heroin once released from supervision) over "soft belly" methadone (despite the fact that the remission rate is *much* lower).

And there is intraprofessional politics as well. Were the facts cut and dry, few experts would support an ineffectual program or question one which "works." But as the merits of various approaches are almost always contested, battles rage over funds, prestige, and missions, as for example between the Synanon people (who believe in complete rehabilitation via a version of group therapy), the therapeutic professions (psychiatry, psychotherapy) which have little sympathy for "sheer" chemical-medical treatment, and the methadone doctors and their supporters. Similar battles are fought in other fields, for instance between those who would use teaching machines and television to help alleviate the shortage of teachers and those who consider these "gimmicks" and favor high raises in teachers' salaries and improvement in the teachers' working conditions and status to attract more men and women into the field.

"FRACTIONATING" THE PROBLEM

Often a solution to a long-raging controversy over the more effective treatment of a social ill becomes possible once we realize that we have asked the wrong question. Similarly, when we ask whether "shortcuts" really work, we approach the problem in an unproductive way by lumping together too many specific questions.

First, the question must be answered separately from a societal and from a personal vantage point. Some shortcuts "work" for the society, in the limited sense at least that they reduce the societal cost of the problem (not only the dollar and cents cost, but also ancillary social effects), but not the personal costs. For instance, between 1955 and 1965 the number of patients in state mental hospitals declined from 558,922 to 475,761. This decline, however, was not the result of new, therapeutic-oriented, community mental-health centers, but mainly caused by introduction of massive use of tranquilizing drugs, "which do not 'cure' mental illness and often have been called 'chemical straitjackets.' " Tranquilizers obviously do not change personalities or social conditions. Patients, to put it bluntly, are often so drugged that they doze on their couches at home rather than being locked up in a state mental hospital or wandering in the streets. How effective the shift to "pharmaceutical treatment" (as the prescription of sedatives is called) is depends on the perspective: society's costs are much reduced (the cost of maintaining a patient in a state mental hospital is about seven dollars a day; on drugs—an average of fifteen cents). Personal "costs" are reduced to some degree (most persons, it seems, are less abused at home than in state mental hospitals). But, obviously, heavily drugged people are not effective members of society or happy human beings. Still, a device or procedure which offers a reduction of costs on one dimension (societal *or* personal) without *increasing* the costs on others, despite the fact that it does not "solve" the problem, is truly useful—almost by definition.

It may be argued that by taking society "off the hook" we deflect its attention from the deeper causes of the malaise, in this case of mental illness. But this, in turn, may be countered by stating that because those causes lie so deep, and because their removal requires such basic trans-formations, basic remedial action is unlikely to be undertaken. *Often our society seems to be "choosing" not between symptomatic (superficial) treatment and "cause" (full) treatment, but between treatment of symp-toms and no treatment at all.* Hence, in the examination of the values of many shortcuts, the ultimate question must be: is the society ready or able to provide full-scale treatment of the problem at hand? If no funda-mental change is in sight, most people would favor having at least ameliorations and, hence, shortcuts. Moreover, the underlying assumption that amelioration deflects attention may be questioned: studies of radical social change show that it often is preceded by "piecemeal" reforms which, though not originally aimed at the roots of the problem, create a new setting, or spur the mobilization for further action.

Second, shortcuts seem to "work" fully—for sub-populations and for some problems. It is wrong to ask: "Are teaching machines effective sub-stitutes for teachers?" We should ask: "Are there any teaching needs which which machines can effectively serve?" The answer then is quite clear: they seem to function quite well as routine teachers of mechanical skills (typing, driving) and of rudimentary mathematics and language skills. Similarly, machines may be quite effective for those motivated to learn and ineffective for those who need to be motivated. A recent study which compared 400 television lectures with 400 conventional ones at Pennsylvania State University showed the television instruction to be as effective on almost all dimensions studied. It freed teachers for discussion of the television lecture material and for personal tutoring. After all, books are not more personal than television sets.

To put it in more general terms, "gimmicks" may be effective for those in a problem-population whose needs are "shallow," and much less so for those whose problems are deep; and most problem-populations seem to have a significant sub-population whose ills or wants are "shallow." Critics of methadone have argued that it works only for those highly motivated addicts who volunteer to take it. But this is not to be construed as an indictment; while such a treatment may reduce the addiction problem "only" by a third, or a quarter, this constitutes a rather substantial reduction.

The same may be said about procedures for training the hard-core unemployed. These are said to "cream" the population, focusing on those relatively easy to train. Such an approach is damaging only to the extent that the other segments of the unemployed are neglected *because* of such a program and on the assumption that they too can be as readily helped. Otherwise, much can be said in favor of "creaming," if only that it makes most effective use of the resources available.

Debates, indeed fights, among the advocates of various birth-control devices—pharmaceutical means (pills), mechanical devices (especially the IUD), sterilization, and the rhythm method—are often couched in terms of one program against all others, especially when the advocates seek to influence the government of a developing nation on the best means of birth control. The Population Council, at least for a while, was "hot" on the IUD. Some drug manufacturers promote the pill. The Catholic church showed more than a passing interest in a rhythm clock (a device to help the woman tell her more from her less fertile periods). In such battles of the experts and "schools," the merits and demerits of each device are often explored without reference to the persons who will use them. Actually, though, merits and demerits change with the attributes of the "target" sub-population. The rhythm methods may be inadequate for most, but when a sub-population for religious reasons will not use other birth-control devices, some reduction in birth may well be achieved here by the "gimmicky" rhythm clocks. Pills seems to work fine for "Westernized," routine-minding, middle-class women who remember to use them with the necessary regularity. They are much less effective in a population that is less routine in its habits. The IUD may be best where persons who are highly ambivalent about birth control can rely on the loops while forgetting that they are using them.

It is in the nature of shortcuts to be much less expensive in terms of dollars and cents and trained manpower than "deeper" solutions. The HEW cost-benefit analyses reported in *The Public Interest,* No. 8 (Summer 1967) are a case in point. While PPBS is far from a "science of decision-making," it occasionally does provide new insights and raise fresh considerations. If we assume that the following statistics are *roughly* correct, even allowing for a margin of error of 30 to 50 percent, we still see the technological devices are much less expensive—per life saved—than the "deeper," educational, approaches. The problem was the effectiveness of rival programs in the prevention of "motor vehicle injuries." When various programs were compared in terms of their cost-effectiveness, it was found that the use of technical devices was most economical: $87 per death averted by the use of seat belts and $100 per life saved by the use of restraining devices. The cost of motorcyclist helmets was high in comparison—$3,000 per man; but it was low when compared to the "fundamental" approach of driver education. Here, it is reported, $88,000 is required to avert one death. Of course we may ask for both technological devices *and* education; and the benefit of technological devices by themselves may be slowly exhausted. Still, this data would direct us then to search for more and improved mechanical devices (e.g., seat belts which hold the shoulders and not only the abdomen) rather than spending millions, let us say, on "educational" billboards ("Better Late Than Never"). I am willing to predict—a hazardous business for a sociologist—that the smoking problems will be much reduced by a substitute cigarette (not just a tarless but also a "cool" one, as the hot smoke seems to cause some medical problems) rather than by convincing millions to give up this imbedded symbol of sophistication and—for teenagers—protest.

THE POWER OF FORMULAS

Not all shortcuts are technological. There is frequently a social problem which can be treated if social definitions are changed; and this can be achieved in part by new legislation. This may seem the most "gimmicky" of all solutions: call it a different name and the problem will go away. Actually, there is much power—both alienating and healing—in societal name calling, and such redefinitions are not at all easy to come by. After years of debate, study, and "politicking," homosexuality was "redefined" in Britain in 1967; it became less of a problem for society and for the homosexuals after Parliament enacted a law which defined intercourse between consenting adults of the same sex in privacy as legal and, in this sense, socially tolerable. The remaining stigma probably more than suffices to prevent "slippage," i.e., even broader tolerance for other kinds of homosexuality, e.g., those affecting minors.

The extent to which such social definitions of what is legitimate, permissible, or deviant can be more easily altered than personality and social structure is an open question; at best, as a rule, only part of a problem can be thus "treated." This approach is superficial or worse when it defines a social or personal want so as to make it nonexistent (e.g., reducing unemployment by changing the statistical characterization). It is not a "gimmick" in that the problem was created by a social definition—by branding a conduct as undesirable or worse when actually it was one of those "crimes without victims."

GUNS, FOR INSTANCE

There is one area of social conduct where, for reasons which are unclear to me, the blinders fall off, and most social scientists as well as many educated citizens see relationships in their proper dimensions and are willing to accept "shortcuts" for what they are worth. This is the area of violent crime and gun control. Usually, progressive-minded people scoff at gimmicks and favor "basic cures." But it is the conservatives who use the anti-shortcut argument to object to gun control as a means of countering violent crimes. On August 10, 1966, on the tower of the University of Texas, Charles Whitman killed, with his Remington rifle, thirteen people and wounded thirty-one. This provided some new impetus to the demand to curb the traffic in guns. About sixty bills were introduced in Congress folliwing President Kennedy's assassination, but none has passed; it is still possible to order by mail for about $27 the same kind of weapon, telescopic lenses included, which Lee Harvey Oswald used. The National Rifle Association spokesmen typically argue that criminals would simply turn to other tools—knives, rods, or dynamite—if no guns were available.

But actually this is one of the areas where the value of shortcuts is both logically quite clear and empirically demonstrable. Logically, it is a matter of understanding probabilities. While motives and modes of crime vary, most murders are not carried out in cold blood but by highly agitated persons. Out of 9,250 so-called "willful" killings which took place in the United States in 1964, only 1,350 were committed in the course of committing some other crime such as robbery or a sex offense. The others, 80.1 percent, were committed among friends, neighbors, and in one's family, by "normally" law-abiding citizens, in the course of a quarrel or following one. Obviously, if deadly weapons were harder to come by, the chances of these quarrels being "cooled out," or a third party intervening, would have been much higher and most fatalities would have been averted.

Second, the damage caused is much affected by the tool used. While it is correct to assume that a knife may be used where there is no gun, the probability of *multiple* fatalities is much lower. And a policeman can learn to defend himself from most assaults without having to use a firearm. Most policemen who are killed on duty are killed by guns; all but one of the fifty-three killed in the United States in 1965, according to official statistics. Hence if the population is disarmed, the fatalities resulting from arming the police can also be saved. Here, as in considering other devices, one must think in terms of multifactor models and probabilities. No one device, such as a gun-control law, can *solve* the problem. But each additional device may well reduce the probability that a violent act will cause a fatality. This is a "short cut" in the right direction—even if it doesn't lead you all the way home. Not because I don't want to go all the way at once; but because such trips are often not available.

> There are some problems, however, that cannot be cheaply passed over. Beyond all doubt, an ever growing population with an ever rising standard of living is unattainable. We may already have exceeded the population which the earth can support at even its present level of subsistence.
>
> In the following essay, an ecologist discusses some interesting forms of extermination which await *homo sapiens* unless he brings his population growth under control and quits abusing his environment.

CAN THE WORLD BE SAVED?

LaMont C. Cole
Professor of Ecology
Cornell University

My title here is not my first choice. A year or so ago, a physicist discussing some of the same subjects beat me to the use of the title I would have preferred: "Is There Intelligent Life on Earth?" There is evidence that the answer to both questions is in the negative.

In recent years, we have heard much discussion of distinct and nearly independent cultures within our society that fail to communicate with each other—natural scientists and social scientists, for example. The particular

From *The New York Times Magazine*, March 31, 1968, pp. 35ff. Copyright 1968 by The New York Times Company. Reprinted by permission.

failure of communication I am concerned with here is that between ecologists on the one hand and, on the other, those who consider that continuous growth is desirable—growth of population, industry, trade and agriculture. Put another way, it is the dichotomy between the thinkers and the doers—those who insist that man should try to know the consequences of his actions before he takes them versus those who want to get on with the building of dams and canals, the straightening of river channels, the firing of nuclear explosives and the industrialization of backward countries.

The message that the ecologists—the "thinkers," if you will—seek to impart could hardly be more urgent or important. It is that man, in the process of seeking a "better way of life," is destroying the natural environment that is essential to any kind of human life at all; that, during his time on earth, man has made giant strides in the direction of ruining the arable land upon which his food supply depends, fouling the air he must breathe and the water he must drink and upsetting the delicate chemical and climatic balances upon which his very existence depends. And there is all too little indication that man has any intention of mending his ways.

The aspect of this threat to human life that has received the least public attention, but which is, I believe, the most serious is the manner in which we are altering the biological, geological and chemical cycles upon which life depends.

When the world was young, it did not have the gaseous atmosphere that now surrounds our planet. The water that fills the oceans and furnishes our precipitation, and the nitrogen that makes up most of our atmosphere, were contained in the rocks formed in the earth's creation. They escaped by various degassing processes, the most dramatic of which was volcanic action.

The amount of oxygen in the atmosphere was negligible before the origin of living organisms that could carry on photosynthesis of the type characterizing green plants, which during daylight hours take in carbon dioxide and give off oxygen. At first, there was virtually no accumulation of oxygen in the atmosphere. The oxygen produced by marine organisms was used by a combination of natural biogeochemical processes which are still operative today—the liberation of incompletely oxidized iron salts in the weathering of silicate rocks and the decomposition of organic matter. But very gradually, some dead organisms began to pass out of circulation by being deposited in sedimentary rocks where some of them became the raw material for the creation of coal and oil. The oxygen that these well-buried organisms would have used up, had they remained on the surface and been subject to decomposition, was allowed to remain in the atmosphere. And eventually, perhaps not until 400 million years ago, this unused oxygen brought the level of oxygen in the atmosphere to slightly over 20 percent.

This is the same percentage of oxygen in the atmosphere today. Apparently, the combination of green plants and oxygen-using organisms, including animals, became very efficient at taking oxygen from the atmosphere and returning it at equal rates. And this is true in spite of the fact that photosynthesis stops during the hours of darkness and practically stops during winter on land areas in high latitudes. It does continue, however, in low latitudes (although often greatly reduced by seasonal drought) and in the ocean (where marine micro-organisms suspended in water near the surface produce 70 percent or more of the world's photosynthetic oxygen). And we have been fortunate that atmospheric circulation patterns move the air about the globe in such a way that we have not had to be concerned that man would run out of oxygen to breathe at night or in winter. As we shall see, man is today pushing his luck.

Another chemical element essential to life is carbon. Plants use carbon dioxide to build their organic compounds, and animals combine the organic compounds with oxygen to obtain the energy for their activities. And all this is possible only because, millions of years ago, the deposition of organic matter in sedimentary rocks led to the creation of a reservoir of oxygen in the atmosphere.

The carbon-oxygen relationship is essential to photosynthesis and thus to the maintenance of all life. But should this relationship be altered, should the balance between the two be upset, life as we know it would be impossible. Man's actions today are bringing this imbalance upon us.

The carbon dioxide in the atmosphere is created in large measure by combustion. Before the time of man, the combustion in the earth's forests was spontaneous. Early man set forest fires to drive game and burned timber for warmth; he went on to find other uses for combustion and to find new combustible materials. First it was coal for heat and power, then oil and natural gas. The exploitation of these so-called fossil fuels made it possible for more people to exist on earth simultaneously than has ever been possible before. It also brought about our present dilemma: The oceans are the world's great reservoir of carbon, taking carbon dioxide from the atmosphere and precipitating it as limestone; we are now adding carbon dioxide to the atmosphere more rapidly than the oceans can assimilate it.

Industrial facilities, automobiles and private homes are the big consumers of fossil fuels, but to appreciate the magnitude of the problem, consider very briefly a still minor source of atmospheric pollution, the airplane, which may have disproportionate importance because much of the carbon dioxide and water vapor produced by the combustion in its engines are released at high altitudes, where they are only slowly removed from the atmosphere.

When you burn a ton of petroleum hydrocarbon, you obtain as byproducts about one and a third tons of water and about twice this amount of carbon dioxide. A Boeing 707 in flight accomplishes this feat about every 10 minutes. I read in the papers that 10,000 airplanes per week land in New York City alone, not including military aircraft. If we assume very crudely that the 707 is typical of these airplanes, and that its average flight takes four hours, this amounts to an annual release into the atmosphere of about 36 million tons of carbon dioxide. And not all flights have a terminus in New York.

Thus the amount of carbon dioxide put into the atmosphere is rising at an ever-rising rate. At the same time, we are removing vast tracts of land from the cycle of photosynthetic production—in this country alone, nearly a million acres of green plants are paved under each year. The loss of these plants is drastically reducing the rate at which oxygen enters the atmosphere. And we do not even know to what extent we are inhibiting photosynthesis through pollution of fresh-water and marine environments.

The carbon-oxygen balance is tipping. When, and if, we reach the point at which the rate of combustion exceeds the rate of photosynthesis, we shall start running out of oxygen. If this occurred gradually, its effect would be approximately the same as moving everyone to a mountaintop —a change that might help to alleviate the population crisis by raising death rates. However, the late Lloyd Berkner, director of the Graduate Research Center of the Southwest, thought that atmospheric depletion might occur suddenly.

The increase in the proportion of carbon dioxide in the atmosphere will have other effects. Carbon dioxide and water vapor are more transparent to shortwave solar radiation than to the longwave heat radiation from the earth to space. Thus the increased proportion of these substances in the atmosphere tends to bring about a rise in the earth's surface temperature, the so-called greenhouse effect, altering climates in ways that are still highly controversial in the scientific community but that everyone agrees are undesirable.

One school holds that the increase in temperature will melt the icecaps of Greenland and the Antarctic, raising the sea level by as much as 300 feet and thereby obliterating most of the major cities of the world. Another school believes that higher temperatures will bring about an increase in evaporation and with it a sharp rise in precipitation; the additional snow falling upon the icecaps will start the glaciers moving again, and another Ice Age will be upon us.

And these represent only the lesser-known effects of combustion on the world. They do not include the direct hazards from air pollution—on man's lungs, for example, or on vegetation near some kinds of industrial plants. Nor do they include the possibility, suggested by some scientists, that we will put enough smoke particles into the air to block solar radiation, causing a dangerous decrease in the earth's temperature. Just to indicate the complexity and uncertainty of what we are doing to the earth's climates, I should mention that the smoke-caused decrease in temperatures would most likely be offset by the carbon dioxide-caused greenhouse effect.

In any case, if we don't destroy ourselves first, we are eventually going to run out of fossil fuels—a prospect surely not many generations away. Then, presumably, we shall turn to atomic energy (although, like the fossil fuels, it represents a nonrenewable resource; one would think that its present custodians could find better things to do with it than create explosions). And then we will face a different breed of environmental pollution.

I am aware that reactors to produce electricity are already in use or under development, but I am apprehensive of what I know of the present generation of reactors and those proposed for the future.

The uranium fuel used in present reactors has to be reprocessed periodically to keep the chain reaction going. The reprocessing yields long-lived and biologically hazardous isotopes such as ^{90}Strontium and ^{137}Cesium that should be stored where they cannot contaminate the environment for at least 1,000 years; yet a goodly number of the storage tanks employed for this purpose are already leaking. At least these products of reprocessing can be chemically trapped and stored; another product, ^{85}Krypton, cannot be so trapped—it is sent into the atmosphere to add to the radiation exposure of the earth's biota, including man, and I don't think that anyone knows a practicable way to prevent this.

To soothe our concern about the pollution of the environment involved in fission reactors, we are glibly offered the prospect of "clean" fusion bombs and reactors. They do not require reprocessing and thus would not produce the Strontium, Cesium and Krypton isotopes. But to the best of my knowledge, no one knows how this new generation of reactors is to be built. And even if development is successful, fusion reactors will produce new contaminants. One such is tritium (^{3}Hydrogen) which would become a constituent of water—and that water with its long-lived radioactivity would contaminate all environments and living things. The danger of tritium was underlined in an official publication of the Atomic Energy Commission in which it was suggested that for certain mining operations it might be better to use fission (i.e. "dirty") devices rather than fusion (i.e. "clean") devices "to avoid ground water contamination."

A prime example of what irresponsible use of atomic power could bring about is provided by the proposal to use nuclear explosives to dig a sea-level canal across Central America. The argument in its favor is that it is evidently the most economical way to accomplish the task. Yet consider the effects upon our environment. If 170 megatons of nuclear charges will do the job, as has been estimated by the Corps of Engineers which apparently wants to do it, and if the fission explosions take place in average materials of the earth's crust, enough [137] Cesium would be produced to give every person on earth a radioactive dosage 26.5 times the permissible exposure level. Cesium behaves as a gas in such a cratering explosion, and prevailing winds in the region are from east to west, so the Pacific area would presumably be contaminated first. And Cesium moves right up through biological food chains, so we could anticipate its rapid dissemination among living things.

The sea-level canal proposal also poses other dangers, whether or not atomic explosives are used. In that latitude, the Pacific Ocean stands higher than the Atlantic by a disputed amount I believe to average 6 feet. The tides are out of phase on the two sides of the Isthmus of Panama, so the maximum difference in level can be as great as 18 feet; and the Pacific has much colder water than the Atlantic.

Just what would happen to climates or to sea food industries in the Caribbean if a new canal moved a mass of cold Pacific water in there is uncertain; but I have heard suggestions that it might create a new hurricane center, or even bring about diversion of the Gulf Stream with a drastic effect on the climates of all regions bordering the North Atlantic. We know that the sea-level Suez Canal permitted the exchange of many marine species between the Red Sea and the Mditerranean. We know that the Welland Canal let sea lampreys and alewives enter the upper Great Lakes with disastrous effects on fisheries and, more recently, on bathing beaches. We just don't know what disruptions of this sort a sea-level canal in the Isthmus might cause.

So much of the danger to man is summed up in that simple phrase, "We don't know." For example, consider the nitrogen cycle, which provides that element all organisms require for the building of proteins. Nitrogen is released into the atmosphere, along with ammonia, as a gas when plants and animals decay; live plants use both elements to build their proteins, but they cannot use nitrogen in gaseous form—that task is accomplished by certain bacteria and primitive algae in the soil and the roots of some plants. Animals build their proteins from the constituents of plant proteins. As in the case of oxygen, the rates of use and return of nitrogen have reached a balance so that the percentage of nitrogen in the atmosphere remains constant.

If any one of these numerous steps in the nitrogen cycle were to be disrupted, disaster would ensue for life on earth. Depending upon which step broke down, the nitrogen in the atmosphere might disappear, it might be replaced by poisonous ammonia or it might remain unused in the atmosphere because the plants could not absorb it in gaseous form.

Are any of these possibilities at hand? Has man's interference with natural processes begun to have a serious effect on the nitrogen cycle?

The point is, we don't know—and we should, before we do too much more interfering.

We are dumping vast quantities of pollutants into the oceans. According to one estimate by the United States Food and Drug Administration, these include a half-million substances; many are of recent origin, including biologically active materials such as pesticides, radioisotopes and detergents to which the ocean's living forms have never before had to try to adapt. No more than a minute fraction of these substances or the combinations of them have been tested for toxicity to life—to the diatoms, the microscopic marine plants that produce most of the earth's oxygen, or to the bacteria and microorganisms involved in the nitrogen cycle.

If the tanker Torrey Canyon had been carrying a concentrated herbicide instead of petroleum, could photosynthesis in the North Sea have been stopped? Again, we don't know, but Berkner is said to have believed that a very few instances of herbicide pollution, occurring in certain areas of the ocean that are high in photosynthetic activity, might cause the ultimate disaster.

Man has developed ingenious products and devices to bring about short-range benefits. He is constantly devising grandiose schemes to achieve immediate ends—the UNESCO plan of 20 years ago, for example, to "develop" the Amazon basin, which I am happy to say has since been judged impracticable. Surely man's influence on his earth is now so predominant, so all-pervasive, that he must stop trusting to luck that his products and schemes will not upset any of the indispensable biogeo-chemical cycles.

The interference with these delicately balanced cycles is not, however, the only instance of man's misuse of his natural heritage. He has also succeeded in rendering useless huge tracts of the earth's arable land.

We hear a lot today about "underdeveloped" and "developing" nations, but many of them might more accurately be called "overdeveloped." The valleys of the Tigris and Euphrates Rivers, for example, were supporting the Sumerian civilization in 3500 B.C. By the year 2000 B.C., a great irrigation complex based on these rivers had turned the area into the granary of the great Babylonian Empire (Pliny says that the Babylonians harvested two crops of grain each year and grazed sheep on the land between crops). But today less than 20 percent of the land in Iraq is cultivated; more than half of the nation's income is from oil. The landscape is dotted with mounds, the remains of forgotten towns; the ancient irrigation works are filled with silt, the end product of soil erosion, and the ancient seaport of Ur is now 150 miles from the sea, its buildings buried under as much as 35 feet of silt.

The valley of the Nile was another cradle of civilization. Every year the river overflowed its banks at a predictable time, bringing water to the land and depositing a layer of soil rich in mineral nutrients for plants. Crops could be grown for seven months of the year.

Extensive irrigation systems were established in the valley before 2000 B.C. The land was the granary of the Roman Empire, and continued to flourish for another 2,000 years. But in modern times, economic considerations have inspired governments to divert the land from food to cash crops such as cotton in spite of the desperate need for more foodstuffs to feed a growing population. In 1902 a dam was built at Aswan to prevent the spring flood and to make possible year-round irrigation, and since then the soils have deteriorated through salinization and productivity in the valley has decreased.

Salinization is a typical phenomenon of arid regions where evaporation is greater than precipitation. Rainwater soaks into the earth, dissolving salts as it goes; when the sun appears, evaporation at the earth's surface draws this salty water upward by capillary action; and when this water in turn evaporates, it leaves a deposit of salts on the surface. The essential condition for salinization to take place is a new upward movement of water.

Irrigation in arid areas, though it may have short-range benefits, can also be fraught with long-rage dangers. The large quantities of water used in irrigation are added to the water table, raising it to the level of the irrigation ditch bottom—that is to say, the ground below that point is saturated with water. Otherwise, of course, the water in the ditches would soak right down into the earth immediately below, rather than spreading outward to nourish land on either side. But this results in a sideward and then upward movement of the irrigation water toward the surface. And when the salt-laden water reaches the surface and evaporates, salinization occurs. Unless great care is taken, irrigation can thus eventually ruin land —and it has often done so. The new Aswan high dam is designed to bring another million acres of land under irrigation, and it may well prove to be the ultimate disaster for Egypt.

Such sorry stories could be told for country after country. The glories of ancient Mali and Ghana in West Africa were legends in medieval Europe. Ancient Greece had forested hills, ample water and productive soil. In the land that once exported the cedars of Lebanon to Egypt, the erosion-proof old Roman roads now stand several feet above a rock desert. In China and India ancient irrigation systems stand abandoned and filled with silt.

When the British assumed the rule of India two centuries ago, the population was about 60 million. Today it is about 500 million, and most of the nation's land problems have been created in the past century by deforestation and plowing and the resulting erosion and siltation, all stemming from efforts to support this fantastic population growth.

Overdevelopment is not confined to the Old World. Archaeologists have long wondered how the Mayas managed to support what was obviously a high civilization on the now unproductive soils of Guatemala and Yucatán. Evidently they exploited their land as intensively as possible until its fertility was exhausted and their civilization collapsed.

As recently as the present decade, aerial reconnaissance has revealed ancient ridged fields on flood plains, the remnants of a specialized system of agriculture that is believed to have transformed much of South America. This same system of constructing ridges on seasonal swamps—to raise some of the land above the flood level for planting and to capture some of the flood water—has been observed in Tanzania in Africa. The South American ridges occur in areas now considered unfit for agriculture; and though any cause-and-effect relationship between ridges and land ruin has not been established for those areas, it has been demonstrated in Africa where the practice is known to accelerate erosion.

Even our own young country has not been immune to deterioration. We have lost many thousands of acres to erosion and gullying and many thousands more to strip mining. It has been estimated that the agricultural value of Iowa farmland, which is about as good land as we have, is declining by 1 percent per year. In our irrigated lands of the West there is the constant danger of salinization.

We have other kinds of water problems as well. We are pumping water from wells so much faster than it can be replaced that we have drastically lowered water tables; in some coastal regions the water table has dipped below sea level, with the result that salt water is seeping into the water-bearing strata. Meanwhile, an estimated 2,000 irrigation dams in the United States have become useless impoundments of silt, sand and gravel.

So this is the heritage of man's past—an impoverished land, a threat to the biogeochemical cycles. And what are we doing about it?

I don't want to comment on the advertising executive who asserts that billboards are "the art gallery of the public" or on the industry spokesman who says that "the ability of a river to absorb sewage is one of our great natural resources and should be utilized to the utmost." In the face of such self-serving statements, the efforts of those who try to promote conservation on esthetic grounds seem inevitably doomed. It makes one wonder, are we selecting for genotypes who can satisfy all their esthetic needs in our congested cities? Are the Davy Crocketts and Kit Carsons who are born today destined for asylums, jail or suicide?

There have been suggestions made for new ways to supplement the world's food production. We hear talk of farming the ocean bottoms, for example. And there are efforts to use bacteria, fungi or yeasts to convert petroleum directly into food for man. This is superficially attractive because it appears to be more efficient than first feeding the petroleum to a refinery and then the gasoline to tractors and other machines which eventually deliver food to us. But it is a melancholy fact that the metabolism of bacteria, fungi and yeasts does not generate oxygen—as do the old-fashioned green plants.

What alarms me most is that only infrequently, and usually in obscure places, does one come across articles by authors who recognize that no matter what we do, it is impossible to provide enough food for a world population that increases at a compound interest rate of 1.7 percent a year. Thus, there appears to be no way for us to escape our dependence on green plants; and even with them, there is no way for us to survive except to halt population growth completely or even to undergo a period of population decrease if, as I anticipate, definitive studies show our population to be already beyond what the earth can support on a continuous basis. Just as we must control our interference with the chemical cycles that provide the atmosphere with its oxygen, carbon and nitrogen, so must we control our birth rate.

In order to accomplish this end, natural scientists, social scientists and political leaders will have to learn to overcome that failure of communication which I referred to earlier. And all three will have to learn to communicate with the general public. This is a large order, but I have found in recent years that intercommunication is possible between ecologists and social scientists who are concerned with population problems.

For example, as a natural scientist, it would not occur to me that in many cultures it is important to save face and prove virility by producing a child as soon after marriage as possible. In these cultures, population planners must evidently aim at delaying the age of marriage or spreading the production of children after the first. And after it has been pointed out to me, I can easily see that a tradition to produce many children would develop under social conditions where few children survive to reach maturity and families wish to assure they will have descendants.

In a Moslem country like Pakistan, where women will not allow themselves to be examined by a male physician, birth control by such measures as the intrauterine device (IUD) is impracticable, and it is difficult to convey a monthly schedule of pill-taking to the poorly educated. However, just as the reproductive cycles of cattle can be synchronized by hormone treatments so that many cows can undergo simultaneous artificial insemination, so the menstrual cycles of populations of women can be synchronized. Then the instructions for contraception can take such a simple form as: "Take a pill every night the moon shines." But in a country like Puerto Rico the efforts of an aroused clergy to instill guilt feelings about the decision a woman must make each day can render the pill ineffective. Here, the IUD, which requires only one decision, provides an answer.

In any case, there is ample evidence that people the world over want fertility control. Voluntary sterilization is popular in India, Japan and Latin America. In Japan and Western European countries that have made legal abortion available upon request the birth rates have fallen dramatically. With such recent techniques as the pill and the IUD, and the impending availability of antimeiotic drugs which inhibit sperm production in the male, and antiimplantation drugs which can prevent pregnancy when taken as long as three days after exposure, practicable fertility control is at last available.

Kingsley Davis, a population expert at the University of California at Berkeley, has recently expressed skepticism about schemes for family planning on the grounds that they do not actually represent population policy but merely permit couples to determine their family size voluntarily. This is certainly true, but the evidence is overwhelming that a great many of the children born into the world today are unwanted. I think we must start by preventing these unwanted births and then take stock of what additional measures, such as negative dependency allowances, may be called for.

Japan has already shown that a determined people can in one generation bring the problem of excessive population growth under control. The Soviet Union seems finally to have abandoned the dogma that overpopulation problems are byproducts of capitalism and couldn't exist in a socialistic country. So a beginning has been made. It now becomes more urgent that social and natural scientists get together and try to decide what an optimum size for the human population of the earth would be.

I shall try to end on a note of optimism. We have seen the start of efforts at meaningful birth control. A five-year study, known as the International Biological Program, is investigating the effects that man is having on the environment. If the world's best minds can at least come to grips with the population problem and effect its control, and if this can be achieved before some miscalculation, or noncalculation, sends the earth environment into an irreversible decline, then there indeed may be some hope that the world can be saved.

The American tradition of converting the countryside into wasteland and then moving on to fresh spoliation *may* be drawing to a close. As we look around, we can see some striking examples of an awakening concern for our environment, matched by other examples of people for whom nothing in the world is as beautiful as a fast buck!

EMPIRE, COLORADO, AND
DULUTH, MINNESOTA

John Fischer

EMPIRE, COLORADO

A big mining company, American Metals Climax, is behaving in a most peculiar fashion. It is seeking the advice of conservation agencies, both public and private, on ways to carry out its operations with the least possible damage to the environment.

If it had followed the traditional, or nature-be-damned, methods at its Urad project near this town, it would have virtually destroyed two mountain streams, Ruby and Woods creeks. Instead it undertook—at considerable cost—to build two reservoirs and an 11,000-foot underground pipeline to avoid water pollution and maintain the normal flow of the streams. The upper reservoir already has been stocked with trout and opened to fishermen.

A companion project nearby, the Henderson molybdenum mine, is being developed in consultation with the Colorado Open Space Foundation, the Forest Service, the state university's School of Industrial Medicine, and other public-interest groups because, as the company's president put it, "we realize our obligation to protect the environment in which we work." A six-thousand-acre tract of company land has been opened for public recreation.

By way of contrast, at . . .

DULUTH, MINNESOTA

The Reserve Mining Company is dumping thousands of tons of iron-ore waste into Lake Superior every day, in spite of shrieks of protests from conservationists and a somewhat muffled admonition from Washington.

As so often happens, the federal government speaks here with two voices, and the states don't speak at all. The company holds a dumping permit from the Army Corps of Engineers—an outfit which keeps an eye

From "The Easy Chair," *Harper's Magazine,* August 1969, p. 18. Copyright © 1969, by Harper's Magazine, Inc. Reprinted from the August, 1969 issue of Harper's Magazine by permission of the author.

on possible obstructions to navigation, but notoriously doesn't give a hoot about ecology, water pollution, or scenic beauty. A sister agency, the Department of the Interior, produced a report last year recommending that the dumping be stopped; later, apparently as the result of political pressure, it repudiated the report and now merely recommends that the affected states, Minnesota, Wisconsin, and Michigan, should keep the pollution under "continuing surveillance." Maybe they are, but so far they have done nothing else.

Ironically, the "waste" being dumped in the lake contains substantial tonnages of nickel, copper, manganese, zinc, and chrome. At current prices for these metals, they cannot be extracted profitably. But if Reserve Mining piled the stuff on land—as other mining companies operating in the area do—it might profitably rework it in later years, when metal supplies dwindle and prices rise.

Reserve Mining is jointly owned by two steel companies, Republic and Armco—typical members, apparently, of an industry which has never been noted for its foresight, imaginative management, or sensitivity to public opinion.

Will we do what needs to be done if the human race is to survive? Will we reconcile the short-run interests of organized vested interest groups with the long-run needs of humanity? In a final note, a sociologist offers a bitterly sardonic comment on our priorities.

PIGS AND PEOPLE

Donald H. Bouma
Professor of Sociology
Western Michigan University

For at least half a century, state legislatures defeated with dependable regularity all proposals to forbid the feeding of uncooked garbage to pigs. During this period, no fewer than fifteen thousand Americans contracted trichinosis, of whom several hundred died and several thousand carried

Excerpted from "Pigs and People," address delivered by Donald H. Bouma before the National Planning Institute, Cornell University, October 22, 1965. Reprinted by permission of the author.

a permanent impairment to their grave. Suddenly, just a few years ago, state legislatures began falling over themselves in their hurry to pass the same law they had been batting down for decades. Why? A new disease—*vesicular exanthem*—appeared which, like trichinosis, is spread by feeding raw garbage to pigs. But there was one important difference. Whereas trichinosis only killed people, vesicular exanthem killed *pigs*! State legislatures acted promptly. Today nearly every state forbids feeding raw garbage to pigs, thus protecting pigs from vesicular exanthem, and, incidentally, people from trichinosis.

This is no isolated case, for, wherever we look, it seems that our priorities place pigs (or cattle, or fish, or bugs, or birds) above people:

Item: At a recent meeting of the State Penitentiary Board of Arkansas, the question of beating prisoners with a four-foot strap was debated, with a majority favoring its continued use. At the same meeting, the board vetoed a proposal for branding prison farm cattle, calling it "inhumane."

Item: Several decades ago the Federal government began providing *all funds necessary* to stamp out tuberculosis . . . *in cattle*! Today, every cow in the country gets a tuberculosis test every year, but millions of people have never had a tuberculosis test in their lives, and last year tuberculosis killed over 7,000 people in the United States.

Item: A few years ago the Wyoming legislature voted to refuse all help to the state's school system from the funds available under the National Defense Education Act, fearing "federal control." The same session petitioned Congress for federal aid in the control of "noxious weeds."

Item: Michigan has had for years a law to control the overloading of cattle cars. Michigan has no law to control the overloading of school buses.

Item: Michigan's requirements for county agricultural agent have for many years been higher than those for the county juvenile agent who works with dependent and neglected children. For many years, the salary of the lowest paid agricultural agent has been higher than the salary of the highest paid juvenile agent. (Pigs *are* more important than people.)

Item: The Iowa legislature a few years ago turned down a bill setting up a long-range program of higher certification standards for teachers. The same session passed a bill to double the college training required of embalmers.

But, after all, what could one expect? The Society for the Prevention of Cruelty to Animals was organized years before the first Society for the Prevention of Cruelty to Children; for many years the federal government has spent many times as much money on the care and study of migratory birds as on the care and study of migratory workers; and long ago and far away, Jesus was run out of town by the Gadarenes because he cured a man of his "evil spirits," which spirits then entered a herd of swine causing them to dash madly into the sea and drown. For a long, long time, pigs have been more important than people!